Religion and Healing in America

Religion and Healing in America

Edited by Linda L. Barnes
and Susan S. Sered

OXFORD
UNIVERSITY PRESS

2005

OXFORD
UNIVERSITY PRESS

Oxford   New York
Auckland   Bangkok   Buenos Aires   Cape Town   Chennai
Dar es Salaam   Delhi   Hong Kong   Istanbul   Karachi   Kolkata
Kuala Lumpur   Madrid   Melbourne   Mexico City   Mumbai
Nairobi   São Paulo   Shanghai   Taipei   Tokyo   Toronto

Library of Congress Cataloging-in-Publication Data
Religion and healing in America / edited by Linda L. Barnes and
Susan S. Sered.
p.   cm.
Includes bibliographical references and index.
ISBN 0-19-516795-3; ISBN 0-19-516796-1 (pbk)
1. Spiritual healing—United States.   I. Barnes, Linda L.
II. Sered, Susan Starr.
BL65.M4 R436 2004
203'.1'0973–dc22   2003022679

Robert A. Orsi, "The Cult of Saints and the Reimagination of the Space
and Time of Sickness in Twentieth-Century American Catholicism."
Literature & Medicine 8 (1980), 63–77. © The Johns Hopkins
University Press. Reprinted with permission of The Johns Hopkins
University Press.

Karen McCarthy Brown, "Making Wanga: Reality Constructions and the
Magical Manipulation of Power," in *Transparency and Conspiracy:
Ethnographies of Suspicion in the New World Order*, ed. West and
Sanders, 233–257. Copyright 2003, Duke University Press. All
rights reserved. Used by permission of the publisher.

Martin E. Marty, "Religion and Healing: The Four Expectations," *Second
Opinion* 7 (March 1988): 60–80. Used by permission of the
author.

9 8 7 6 5 4 3 2 1

Printed in the United States of America
on acid-free paper

Acknowledgments

This book is a product of the dreams and efforts of both editors. We have chosen to list our names in opposite sequences on the cover and in the introduction to reflect our equal and shared roles throughout this project.

Many people helped bring this book to fruition, but two groups deserve particular thanks. First, we would like to thank the contributors for their enthusiasm and commitment to the project. Second, on behalf of the contributors, we would like to thank all the individuals who kindly agreed to be interviewed and all the communities that graciously allowed our authors to share their rituals, meetings, and other events.

We would like to express our deepest appreciation to Meredith McGuire, whose insight, analysis, collegiality, and vast knowledge of healing in America accompanied this project from beginning to end. This volume received intellectual and financial backing from Harvard University's Center for the Study of World Religions. We particularly would like to thank Lawrence E. Sullivan for his enthusiastic support at every stage of the project. We also would like to thank the Ford Foundation and Boston Medical Center for their financial, institutional, and moral support of the project.

This volume developed out of a conference held in 2001 at the Center for the Study of World Religions and the Boston Medical Center. We would like to thank Jualynne Dodson, Ken Fox, Karen Holliday, Craig Joseph, Sudhir Kakar, Meredith McGuire, Ann Minnick, Richard Shweder, Martha Ward, and Stephen Warner for participating in the conference that inspired this project. Their ideas and contributions are reflected throughout the pages of this volume.

Our deepest thanks to Steve Glazier, David Hufford, and Rosalyn Hackett for discussing the volume as a whole, and the introduction in particular, with us. Barnes is grateful to John B. Carman for his steadfast support over the years of her work in the study of religion and healing, and to Arthur Kleinman for mentoring her work in medical anthropology. Diana Eck and the Pluralism Project at Harvard University served as an ongoing inspiration for this project. We would like to thank our assistants, Justine de Marrais and Susan Lloyd McGarry, for their continued support of our work. Thank you to Cynthia Read and Theo Calderara for their support throughout the process of publishing this volume. And our special thanks to Yishai Sered and Devon Thibeault for sharing our work and our lives.

Contents

Contributors

LINDA L. BARNES directs the Boston Healing Landscape Project, an institute for the study of culturally and religiously based approaches to healing, at Boston University School of Medicine. She chairs the Religions, Medicines, and Healing program unit in the American Academy of Religion and is the author of *Needles, Herbs, Gods, and Ghosts: China, Healing, and the West to 1848* (forthcoming).

MARY FARRELL BEDNAROWSKI is professor of religious studies at United Theological Seminary of the Twin Cities. Her most recent book is *The Religious Imagination of American Women* (1999), and she has a long-standing interest in the subject of healing as a focus for women's theological creativity.

JULIANNE CORDERO is a member of the Barbareño Chumash community in Santa Barbara, California. She has been a practicing herbalist for six years and is involved in the Chumash community's efforts to build and navigate traditional Chumash canoes. She received an M.A. in religious studies at UCSB in June 2003, where she is now pursuing a doctorate.

THOMAS J. CSORDAS is professor of anthropology at University of California, San Diego. He is the author of *The Sacred Self* (1994), *Language, Charisma, and Creativity* (1997), and *Body/Meaning/Healing* (2002).

PRAKASH N. DESAI, M.D., is chief of staff for VA Chicago Health Care System/West Side Division and professor of psychiatry at the

University of Illinois at Chicago. He received in 1987 the Brice Boyer Award (honorable mention) for his paper "Selfhood and Context—Some Indian Solutions." His publications include *Health and Medicine in the Hindu Tradition* (1989).

THOMAS J. DOUGLAS is a Ph.D. candidate at the University of California, Irvine, and a fellow in the Social Science Research Council's Religion and Immigration Program, as well as a grant recipient from the UC Pacific Rim program. He has been conducting research among Cambodian immigrant communities in Long Beach, California; Seattle, Washington; and Vancouver, British Columbia, for several years.

TANYA ERZEN is a Andrew W. Mellon Postdoctoral Fellow in the Department of Religion at Barnard College. She is co-editor of *Zero Tolerance: Quality of Life and the New Police Brutality in New York City* (2001).

GASTÓN ESPINOSA is an Andrew W. Mellon Postdoctoral Faculty Fellow at Northwestern University. He directed the research phase of the Hispanic Churches in American Public Life research project (www.hcapl.org) on U.S. Latino religions and politics, funded by the Pew Charitable Trusts. He is presently writing a critical biography of Francisco Olazábal and two other books on Latino religions, politics, and social activism.

MELISSA FILIPPI-FRANZ is a Ph.D. student at the University of Kansas and researches health and healing in Somali diaspora communities.

KAJA FINKLER is professor of anthropology at the University of North Carolina. Her specialties include medical anthropology; gender, health, and illness; the new genetics; the anthropology of bioethics; and Latin America and Mexico. Her publications include *Experiencing the New Genetics: Family and Kinship on the Medical Frontier* (2000) and *Women in Pain* (2000).

ROBERT FULLER is professor of religious studies at Bradley University. His most recent books include *Spiritual, but Not Religious: Understanding Unchurched American Religion* (Oxford University Press, 2002) and *Religious Revolutionaries: The Rebels Who Reshaped American Religion* (2004).

GROVE HARRIS is the project manager for the Pluralism Project at Harvard University and author of "Paganism" in *On Common Ground: World Religions in America*, edited by Diana Eck (1997).

MARCIA HERMANSEN is professor of Islamic studies at Loyola University Chicago, and works in the areas of Islamic thought, Islam in India and Pakistan, and Muslims in America, among other topics. She has published *The Conclusive Argument from God: A Study of Shah Wali Allah of Delhi* (1996).

CLAUDIA J. HERNÁNDEZ is currently pursuing her Ph.D. in culture and performance with a specialization in folklore in the Department of World Arts and Cultures at UCLA. Her research interests are in Latino traditional medicine and spirituality.

INÉS HERNÁNDEZ-ÁVILA is professor of Chicano studies and of Native American studies at the University of California, Davis, where she also directs the Chicana/Latina Research Center. Her publications include "Mediations of the Spirit: Native American Religious Traditions and the Ethics of Representation," in *Native American Spirituality: A Critical Reader*, edited by Lee Irwin (2000).

JENNIFER L. HOLLIS received her Master of Divinity from Harvard Divinity School, where she was a research assistant at the Religion, Health and Healing Initiative. Her recent publications include the article "Lotus Flowers and Rose Windows: A Season of Visits to Hospital Chapels." She works as a music thanatologist in Chicago.

CLAUDE F. JACOBS is associate professor and director of the Center for the Study of Religion and Society, University of Michigan–Dearborn, and the author, with Andrew Kaslow, of *The Spiritual Churches of New Orleans: Origins, Beliefs, and Rituals of an African American Religion* (1991).

JOHN M. JANZEN teaches anthropology and directs the African Studies Center at the University of Kansas. His recent writing on health, healing, and war trauma in Africa has included *Do I Still Have a Life? Voices from the Aftermath of War in Rwanda and Burundi* (2000) and *The Social Fabric of Health: An Introduction to Medical Anthropology* (2002).

MICHAEL OWEN JONES is professor of folklore and world arts and cultures at UCLA, and director of a project funded by National Center for Complementary and Alternative Medicine to document Latino folk medicine in Los Angeles.

PAMELA E. KLASSEN is associate professor in the Department and Centre for the Study of Religion at the University of Toronto. She is the author of *Blessed Events: Religion and Home Birth in America* (2001) and is currently writing a book on Christianity and healing in twentieth-century North America.

HAROLD G. KOENIG completed his medical school training at the University of California at San Francisco and his geriatric medicine, psychiatry, and biostatistics training at Duke University Medical Center, where he is an associate professor of psychiatry and medicine. Dr. Koenig has more than 200 peer-reviewed articles and book chapters and 24 books in print or preparation.

SOPHON MAM is a Wiccan priest who was ordained at his current church five years ago. He was born in a Thai refugee camp and emigrated to the United States as an infant. He currently resides in Southern California, where he has been involved with various Wiccan groups for more than a decade and teaches classes on witchcraft, magick, and spirituality.

MARTIN E. MARTY is the Fairfax M. Cone Distinguished Service Professor Emeritus at the University of Chicago and has devoted two decades to themes of health and religion as the George B. Caldwell Visiting Scholar in residence at the Park Ridge Center for the Study of Health, Faith, and Ethics.

KAREN McCARTHY BROWN is professor of anthropology of Religion in the Graduate and Theological Schools of Drew University and author of *Mama Lola: A Vodou Priestess in Brooklyn* (1991). She has done extensive fieldwork in Haiti and within the Haitian diaspora community in New York City, as well the Republic of Benin, West Africa.

REV. BOBBIE McKAY, Ph.D., graduated from Garrett Theological Seminary. She received her Ph.D. in counseling psychology from Northwestern University and is a licensed clinical psychologist. Her publications include *The Unabridged Woman* (1979), *What Ever Happened to the Family?* (1991) and, with her husband, Lewis Musil, *Healing the Spirit: Stories of Transformation* (2000).

LARA MEDINA is an assistant professor of religious studies at California State University, Northridge. Her scholarship focuses on U.S. Latino/a gender and religion, ethnicity and religion, and liberation theologies and spirtitualities.

STEPHANIE Y. MITCHEM is director of African American studies and assistant professor of religious studies, University of Detroit, Mercy, and the author of "African American Women, Healing, and Reconciliation," in *Introducing Womanist Theology*, edited by Rosemary Radford Ruether (2002).

LEWIS A. MUSIL, M.A., graduated from the University of Chicago and received an M.F.A. from the Art Institute of Chicago. He has had extensive teaching experience, including at Garrett Theological Seminary, Elmhurst College, and the Goodman Theater School. He was chairman of the Department of Creative Drama in the Evanston Public Schools.

RONALD Y. NAKASONE's Buddhist reflections on aging, cloning, organ transplants, and other dilemmas are summarized in the *Encyclopedia of Ethical, Legal, and Policy Issues in Biotechnology* (2000). At the Graduate Theological Union since 1987, he is associated with the Stanford Geriatric Education Center and Ryukoku University's Center for Humanities, Science, and Religion in Kyoto, Japan.

ADRIEN NGUDIANKAMA, originally from the Congo, now teaches at Bowie State University and does pastoral counseling with Central African refugees in Washington, D.C.

CHARLES NUMRICH is the director of Creative Theatre Unlimited, St. Paul, Minnesota, an organization whose mission is "community building through the arts," and a community-based faculty member for the University of Minnesota's Center for Spirituality and Healing. He is the co-principal investigator and administrator of the research project "Hmong Shamanism in Minnesota and Hmong Health Care Choices."

PAUL DAVID NUMRICH is research associate professor, Loyola University Chicago. He researches religious diversity and new immigrant religions, with special expertise in Buddhism. His publications include the essay "Marriage, Family, and Health in Selected World Religions: Different Perspectives in an Increasingly Pluralist America" and the book *Old Wisdom in the New World* (1996).

ROBERT A. ORSI is Charles Warren Professor of the History of Religion in America at Harvard Divinity School and author of *The Madonna of 115th Street: Faith and Community in Italian Harlem* (2002, 2nd ed.) and *Thank You St. Jude: Women's Devotion to the Patron Saint of Hopeless Causes* (1996).

GREGORY A. PLOTNIKOFF, a physician and theologian, is medical director for the Center for Spirituality and Healing, Academic Health Center, University of Minnesota. His publications include "Should Medicine Reach Out to the Spirit?" in *Postgraduate Medicine* (2000). He is currently a visiting associate professor in the Department of Oriental Medicine at Keio University Medical School, Tokyo, Japan.

PATRICK A. POLK is a visiting assistant professor at the UCLA Department of Arts and Cultures. His research interests include vernacular religion, popular culture, and urban visual traditions, and he is editor of the forthcoming volume *Conjures, Folk Healers, and Hoodoo Doctors.*

REYNA C. RONELLI received a B.A. in anthropology from UCLA.

SUSAN S. SERED is research director of the Religion, Health and Healing Initiative at Harvard University's Center for the Study of World Religions. Her publications include *What Makes Women Sick?: Militarism, Maternity and Modesty in Israeli Society*; *Priestess, Mother, Sacred Sister: Religions Dominated by Women*; and *Women as Ritual Experts: The Religious Lives of Elderly Jewish Women in Jerusalem*.

EDITH TURNER is a faculty member in the Department of Anthropology at the University of Virginia. She is the recipient of honorary doctorates from the College of Wooster and Kenyon College. She specializes in ritual, religion, healing, and aspects of consciousness, including shamanism. She has published widely on these topics and is the editor of the journal *Anthropology and Humanism*.

MICHAEL WINKELMAN is an associate professor in the Department of Anthropology, Arizona State University. He is the author of several books on shamanism, including *Shamanism: The Neural Ecology of Consciousness and Healing* (2000), and was the guest editor of an issue of *Cultural Survival Quarterly* on the topic "Shamanisms and Survival."

CHU YONGYUAN WU, facilitator of the Hmong Circle of Peace in St. Paul, Minnesota, is a conflict resolution and community relations trainer for the Upper Midwest Community Policing Institute.

PHUA XIONG, one of the first Hmong women to graduate from medical school in the United States, is a family medicine physician in private practice in St. Paul, Minnesota, and coeditor of *Hmong Case Book on Cultural and Ethical Challenges in Caring for Hmong Patients* (1998).

DEU YANG is health care manager at UCare Minnesota, an independent nonprofit HMO established in 1984 by the University of Minnesota Medical School's Department of Family Practice. She is a licensed practical nurse and a medical interpreter with broad experience in the Hmong communities in Michigan and Minnesota.

Religion and Healing
in America

Introduction

Susan S. Sered and Linda L. Barnes

Gruesome scenes of a possessed young girl spewing green vomit while a priest wrestles with demons in the horror film the *Exorcist*, together with cynical portrayals of healers as charlatans in comedies like Steve Martin's *Leap of Faith*, have shaped images of religious healing in the United States. Throughout much of the twentieth century, miraculous or nonscientific healing received attention primarily in terms of "exotic," "bogus," or "superstitious" behavior, or when it came into conflict with biomedical practices or government regulatory agencies.

Yet, contrary to predictions that biomedical advances soon would eliminate vestigial needs for religious healers, by the turn of the twenty-first century, spiritual and religious healing actually garnered new popularity, visibility, and legitimacy. Urban and suburban newspapers now openly advertise healing services held at the full range of mainstream churches and synagogues. Cuban *santeros*, Haitian *mambos* and *oungans*, Cambodian Buddhist monks, Chinese herbalist-acupuncturists, and Hmong shamans are increasingly in evidence both inside and outside of particular ethnic enclaves. Hospitals are opening their doors to alternative and complementary healing modalities—many of which include spiritually based therapies. Spiritual counseling and chaplaincy have gained ground as legitimate and desirable psychotherapeutic approaches. Scientists at elite universities are researching the healing power of prayer (Koenig and Cohen 2002). And the American government has made a commitment to fund faith-based organizations that provide health and other social services.

As anthropologists have documented regarding preindustrial societies, religious and medical practices often converge in that both deal with pain and suffering, birth and death, and sexuality, growth, and decay (see, for example, Laderman and Roseman 1996). Thus, one might view the perceived conventional separation of religion and medicine in twentieth-century America as something of a cultural or historical aberration, and the reemergence of religious healing in the twenty-first century as a rather unsurprising re-recognition of the connection between body and spirit, and between individual, community, and cosmos.

This book represents our efforts to bring together, for the first time, a thoroughly multidisciplinary and multicultural discussion of religious healing in the contemporary United States. Chapters in this volume look at religious healing in Native American, European American, African American, Asian American, and Latino/a communities. We have tried to address as wide a range as possible of ethnic and religious groups, acknowledging that our project is necessarily limited by the availability of scholarly work, especially in communities that are relatively new to the United States.[1]

The History and Context of Religious Healing in America

Multiple meanings of religion, spirituality, and healing emerged in a variety of historical and social contexts over the longer course of American medical, religious, and cultural history. In fact, there has never been a time when religious healing in America has not been present *and* pluralistic on multiple levels. In relation to any given historical period, it is important to ask (1) which cultural group or groups were involved, (2) which religious and spiritual orientations informed the particular approach to healing, (3) what kind of healing was sought, (4) how the practice positioned itself in relation to other practices of the time, and (5) what socioeconomic and political variables—including understandings of race and gender—influenced the social climate in which the practice emerged. Particular forms of religious healing rarely have remained in isolated social pockets. To the contrary, interchanges between groups, whether curious, favorable, indifferent, or hostile, spilled over into perceptions of what needed healing, and how that healing ought to be carried out.

Prior to the invasion of European explorers and immigrants, Native American tribes practiced well-established healing traditions that were integral to their respective religious worldviews. Beginning in the sixteenth century, European colonizers—entering the continent first through the Caribbean and later through the Pacific coast—brought with them Chinese and Filipino servants and slaves, along with enslaved Africans. In a relatively short time the three monotheistic traditions of Judaism, Christianity, and Islam, and a variety of African and Asian religions, entered the Americas. Each group brought its own healing traditions, which already represented mixtures of local and cosmopolitan, elite and folk, and indigenous and colonial practices.

The healing systems that European colonizers transplanted to the Americas were far from homogeneous. Galenic medicine, with its humoral paradigm which presupposed the existence of subtle fluids in the body—blood, phlegm, and black and yellow bile—whose state of balance affected a person's health, coexisted with emerging anatomic readings of the body. Both entered the Americas, as did interest in alchemy and other esoteric practices. The books of seventeenth- and eighteenth-century medical writers like Nicolas Culpeper made their way into the English colonies, where they promoted astrologically based understandings of herbal medicine (Culpeper 1651). In Anglo-American colonies, it was not uncommon for Christian ministers such as Cotton Mather and John Wesley to include medicine in their ministry or to write medical manuals (Mather 1713; Wesley 1747). Under the growing influence of the Enlightenment in Europe, the divide between "religion" and "medicine" became increasingly pronounced, with each understood to address different domains of experience and correspond to different objectives. Yet even "regular" medicine—that taught in European medical schools and the American schools modeled after them—varied from region to region as developments in European medical centers filtered into the colonies differently, with London and Edinburgh exercising a greater influence over the British colonies, and Paris over Louisiana.

During the first four decades of the nineteenth century, many "irregular" approaches to healing emerged alongside interests in social reform. The impulse to reform arose out of frustration with perceived deficiencies in contemporary medical practice, particularly with the "regulars" use of heroic interventions such as bloodletting, blistering, and ingesting calomel (a form of mercury). The turn to so-called irregular practices was also a response to the exclusion of women and of Americans of color from the regular medical schools. Many of the reformers in the United States took a strong interest in new theories of healing and medicine, which they did not entirely differentiate from their religious sense of the world and their social visions. Such theories included Sylvester Graham's vegetarianism and other dietary practices, Thomsonian herbalism, hydropathy or water cure, homeopathy, the promotion of exercise and "physical education" for men and women, less restrictive clothing for women, and methods of diagnosis and cure involving the channeling of the spirits of the dead (Rothstein 1972; Risse, Numbers, and Leavett 1977; Rosenberg 1979; Wrobel 1987; Gevitz 1988; Braude 1989; Jacobs and Kaslow 1991).

The religious views of many of the reformers led them to envision a transformative "Christian physiology." How did one cultivate a body fit to actualize the perfectionist Protestant spirit of the day? The reformers identified the individual not only as the locus of change but also as its effective agent. If perfection came about through awareness, then one could hope for change, healing, and even salvation through education. The implicit message of this approach was the concomitant sense of responsibility for transforming oneself. Over time, the overtly religious dimensions faded into the background, and regular doctors incorporated some of the principles of dietary reform and the virtues of exercise into their own ideas of health.

Toward the end of the nineteenth century, one branch of the reform impulse had turned in the direction of institutional medicine and politics, in movements often associated with the Social Gospel, to address social ills such as poverty (Phillips 1996). Another forked off and emerged as the Mind Cure, or New Thought, movement. According to William James, the Mind Cure movement could claim as its forebears such influences as New England Transcendentalism (Emerson in particular), evolutionism, and Hinduism, through the influence of the Vedanta Society (James [1911] 2002). Mind Cure proposed to correct a person's understanding of an illness or problem (the Christian Science approach) or to train a person in the science of autosuggestion (Parker 1973). Both "right belief" and autosuggestion once again located the power—and the responsibility—for healing in the hands of the individual. Many adherents of New Thought or Mind Cure never severed their connections with mainstream religious groups, seeing themselves instead as something of an ecumenical movement that supplemented other affiliations.

Mind Cure did not address the needs of everyone. As the historian William McGloughlin notes:

> Many in the lower middle class and among the rural folk—the less
> well-off and less well-educated—rejected the new light and clung to
> the old. Fundamentalists, Pentecostals, and Holiness people orga-
> nized "prophetic conferences" to discuss the imminent end of the
> world and the Second Coming; they held revivals where the power
> of the Holy Spirit gave them "Baptisms by fire," inner perfection,
> faith to heal illness which "faith-less" doctors could not heal, and the
> ecstacy of communing "in tongues" with the Spirit of God. (1977:
> 153)

Nor did Mind Cure take into account the experience of African Americans, some of whom, excluded from access to biomedical care in mainstream facilities in different parts of the United States, turned to African-descended practices and to small numbers of black doctors (Byrd and Clayton 2000). It was during this time that the Azusa Street Revival gave birth to the Pentecostal church in black communities, which would spread to become a central example of religious healing across the cultural spectrum in the United States, as discussed by Gastón Espinosa in this volume.

Patterns of immigration changed during the nineteenth century, shifting from the groups who had first colonized the Americas to newer groups. Each of them brought culturally and religiously based understandings of illness and healing. Starting in the late 1840s, for example, Chinese immigrants came to dig for gold and to work on the railroads and in other branches of local economies. In the East, the immigrants had once come mostly from Germany and Ireland but now were from eastern and southern Europe. Growing Catholic populations brought with them the saint- and shrine-based healing practices described by Robert Orsi in this volume. By 1890, four out of five New Yorkers were foreign born, and by the first decade of the twentieth century, 70 percent of immigrants in the United States were from Mediterranean or Slavic countries, and/or were Jews in diaspora. These new patterns of immigration led to ugly nativist responses. The evangelist Billy Sunday, for example, talked about "hordes" of foreigners, and it was not uncommon for new groups to be represented as infections or plagues in the larger social body. When confronted by a hostile social climate and by public health officials who stigmatized them, some immigrants viewed their own remedies as preferable to public hospitals—often perceived as the place one went to die.

During these decades of immigration, healing traditions took shape in specific cultural contexts, flowing out of tributaries that traced back to the many countries of origin. Catholic healing practices, for example, reflected both a pan-Catholic understanding of the intercessory healing authority of saints and the particularities of place and ethnic group in the United States. Italian communities in Boston and New York celebrated a variety of festivals of the saints, each one frequently identified as the source of healing for specific afflictions. German immigrants in New Orleans built a shrine to St. Roch in thanks for his having protected them from epidemics. A church was built at Chimayo in New Mexico to mark the finding of a statue of the Santo Niño de Atocha and to help pilgrims find their way to the hole whose dirt had curative properties. The transplanting of religious healing practices also called for accommodation to new factors in American environments. Chinese herbalists, for example—their practices rooted in a religious worldview of *qi*, and yin and yang—had to learn the properties of wild-growing herbs in the Western states. In urban areas, they looked to enter the dominant culture by advertising in city business directories, often marketing themselves as former physicians to the Chinese emperor.

In some cases, European Americans forayed into the healing practices of other cultures. Early nineteenth-century medical textbooks pointed to the medical knowledge of Native Americans and to the need to develop a medicine intrinsic to the natural resources of the United States. A spate of books was published during the first half of the century by European American authors claiming either to *be* "Indian doctors" or to be transmitting the herbal knowledge of particular Indian tribes. Medical journals in Europe and the United States reported on the healing traditions of China and India, sometimes describing both in careful detail, often only to dismiss them due to their basis in nonanatomical paradigms of the body. The same physicians, in some cases, experimented with practices such as acupuncture, clear in the understanding that they were using a Chinese practice and equally convinced that their own anatomic models allowed them to do it better than the Chinese (Barnes, forthcoming).

Each of the trajectories discussed here can be viewed as ongoing streams feeding into a larger river. Few of them died away or remained identical with their earlier forms. Some gave rise to new permutations, as in the case of the Emmanuel Movement—a collaborative venture between Episcopal priests and physicians in Boston—which, in turn, influenced the early version of Alcoholics Anonymous. Over the twentieth century, AA and its core twelve steps contributed not only to spin-off groups that addressed different forms of addiction but also to a notion of spirituality as a generic, universal concept and experience.

During the second half of the twentieth century, several concurrent social movements gave rise to the interest in religious healing that has blossomed in the first years of the twenty-first century. New Age and self-help movements beginning in the 1960s, and holistic and complementary medicine movements that gained ground in the 1970s and 1980s, offered alternative to biomedicine. Awareness of biomedicine's inability to cure the many chronic diseases that plague a rapidly aging American population contributed to the search for other responses and solutions to emotional and corporeal suffering. These social forces have dovetailed with the increasing ordination of women ministers and rabbis—many of whom studied and worked in healing and social work professions during the years when ordination was not open to them. In a variety of ways, these women have brought to their congregations a new sensitivity to human needs.

During the same period, processes of globalization have facilitated the introduction of religious healing systems from outside the United States. Growing immigrant populations, having experienced the intense dislocations of geographic and cultural change, may be particularly attracted to rituals that offer spiritual healing, or they may draw on such rituals to preserve traditions associated with their homelands (Ebaugh and Chafetz 2002). Some of the practices brought into the country also have drawn substantial numbers of Americans looking for new, exotic, holistic, authentic, or more spiritual healing approaches.

Approaching the Study of Religion, Spirituality, and Healing

This complex and fluid social history suggests the difficulties that arise when we try to settle upon a common lexicon for talking about the range of means used to address processes of healing in America. We suspect that some of the language typically used for delineating this field of inquiry excludes particular communities or practices, and highlights or legitimates others.

Definitions

In contemporary America, the word "religion" is variously used in reference to belief in divine beings, adherence to a set of cosmological or ethical tenets, ritual practices such as prayer, institutions that sponsor communal events, and/or the traditions of a community within which one celebrates holidays or life cycle events. Diverse uses of the term "religion" interface in various ways with matters of healing. As institutions claiming a moral mandate to engage in charitable and other good acts, religions have been key actors in the development and support of biomedical facilities in the United States, in the establishment of medical clinics in poor neighborhoods, in training hospital chaplains who work cooperatively with hospital medical staff, and in providing material and spiritual assistance to ill members of their congregations. This model of religious healing generally is accepted and respected in the United States. There has been, and continues to be, a broad public consensus that sees this model as good both for religion and for medicine. Religions also have been active in influencing medical policy, as in the cases of abortion and end-of-life decisions. This sort of religious involvement in health care has been somewhat adversarial, yet it has not challenged the more pervasive expectation that religions legitimately play key roles in relation to the delivery of health care services.

Factors that complicate current American understandings of the convergence of religion with health care include large-scale arrivals in the United States of immigrant groups from non-European and non-Christian countries and a related recognition of multicultural realities. The institutionalized roles of mainstream religions vis-a-vis medical facilities have become only a small piece of a growing religious healing landscape that includes shamans, curanderos, and other non-biomedical healers who typically are not welcomed in biomedical facilities. Another complicating factor is America's ongoing enchantment with a scientific discourse of endorphins, the relaxation response, and the placebo effect—a discourse that secularizes or demystifies traditional religious healing practices. A third factor is the rise of a discourse of spirituality that, sometimes, is seen as distinct from or even antithetical to religion.

The word "spirituality," rarely well-defined in contemporary American usage, typically is invoked to refer to an individualistic, sometimes secular, interior experience that contributes to the well-being of the body, mind, and/or the self. Several of the chapters in this volume document situations in which groups or individuals assert that spirituality is universal and metacultural, and that eclectic and personalized spirituality is a welcome correction both to overly institutionalized structures of organized religion and to an overly mechanical biomedical focus on the physical body (see, for example, chapters by Edith Turner and Michael Winkelman in this volume). Other chapters treat the notion of a universal spirituality as more problematic, arguing that like all human endeavors, spirituality is linked to particular groups, ideologies, and systems of meaning, belief, and practice. For these authors, spiritual experiences are necessarily predicated upon attributing meaning to particular sensations, emotions, or physical signals, and spirituality is no more immune to the machinations of power than is any other arena of human experience (see, for example, chapters by Julianne Cordero and Pamela Klassen).

"Healing" is an equally complex and contested word in the United States today. It can mean the direct, unequivocal, and scientifically measurable cure of physical illnesses. It can mean the alleviation of pain or other symptoms. It also can mean coping, coming to terms with, or learning to live with that which one cannot change (including physical illness and emotional trauma). Healing can mean integration and connection among all the elements of one's being, reestablishment of self-worth, connection with one's tradition, or personal empowerment. Healing can be about repairing one's relationships with friends, relations, ancestors, the community, the world, the Earth, and/or God. It can refer to developing a sense of well-being or wholeness, whether emotional, social, spiritual, physical, or in relation to other aspects of being that are valued by a particular group. Healing can be about purification, repenting from sin, the cleaning up of one's negative karma, entry into a path of purity, abstinence, or more moral daily living, eternal salvation, or submission to God's will.

Mary Bednarowski, in this volume, argues, "Individually and communally, to be healed or to be in the process of healing is to have hope. To offer healing is to offer hope. And hope is the state wherein we know that some kind of response or change or reconciliation or transformation is possible. Whatever the trauma of the present moment or of our circumstances and our histories, there is something more to be said or to be understood, to be experienced or accomplished." In contrast, Kaja Finkler suggests that religious notions of determinism (rather than notions of open possibilities) inform certain kinds of healing, as in the case of the Human Genome Project.

In some of the contexts discussed in this volume, healing is represented as transcending curing. Jennifer Hollis's discussion of the Episcopal Church and Susan Sered's discussion of the Jewish healing movement highlight tensions that exist in both of these settings with regard to curing. Both sets of religious leaders, for quite different reasons and with rather different meanings, repeatedly declare that "we are about healing, not about curing." Although individual Jews and Episcopalians may hope for a cure, their religious leaders locate that hope in a broader framework of meaning that recognizes other nonphysical forms of change as meaningful, or perhaps more meaningful than merely repairing damaged organs. In other situations described in this volume, healing quite clearly is seen as synonymous with curing. Robert Orsi, for example, tells us about Catholic devotees who appeal to saints like Blessed Margaret of Castello, and Gastón Espinosa describes Latino/a congregants who have turned to Pentecostalism to find relief from specific diseases and from the suffering brought on by social ills.

A Methodological Toolbox

Different understandings of the words "religion," "spirituality," and "healing" quite naturally shape how scholars go about studying the meeting points of religion and healing: how they go about selecting phenomena, individuals, groups, or situations to study; how they interpret and analyze their data; and how they evaluate the effectiveness, success, or outcomes of particular healing practices. Acknowledging the rapidly fluctuating valences associated with these and related terms in American society, and recognizing the power of discourse to shape ideas, we have chosen *not* to require that the contributors to this volume adhere to particular linguistic usages. Opting for the sometimes chaotic richness of casting our net too wide rather than for the ethnocentric dangers of adopting a rigid definition of religious healing, we include in this volume chapters that address events, beliefs, and situations described by members of diverse communities, or interpreted by particular scholars, as relevant to the interface of religion and healing.

The authors in this volume represent the cultural and intellectual pluralism of the country, and they bring correspondingly diverse methodological approaches to bear. Kaja Finkler, for example, explores intersections of religion and healing primarily through analysis of textual discourse. Gastón Espinosa, Claude Jacobs, and Robert Orsi bring a historical lens to their studies. Tanya Erzen, Mary Bednarowski, Jennifer Hollis, Lara Medina, Thomas Douglas and Sophon Mam, Patrick Polk, and Susan Sered utilize ethnographic (participant-observation) tools in studying specific communal phenomena. Linda Barnes and Karen McCarthy Brown integrate history, textual discourse, and ethnography. Michael Winkelman uses the tools of neurobiology to illuminate religious healing.

Pamela Klassen, Bobbie McKay and Lewis Musil, Thomas Csordas, John Janzen and his coauthors, and Stephanie Mitchem use interviews or questionnaires to look more closely at life stories of individuals who heal or have been healed. Edith Turner, Grove Harris, Ronald Nakasone, Julianne Cordero, and Inés Hernández-Ávila describe healing events in which they themselves have taken part as full participants, experiencing the transformative power of ritual together with other members of the group. The research team that has tracked Hmong traditions in the Twin Cities for some years includes Phua Xiong and Gregory Plotnikoff, who are physicians, and Deu Yang, who is a nurse: they approach their work on Hmong shamanism from the perspective of biomedical practitioners. At the same time, Xiong, Yang, and Chu Yongyuan Wu are Hmong and write from intimate knowledge of Hmong practices, just as Mitchem writes as both an insider and an outsider to African American women's practices in Detroit.

How It Works

The range of ways in which the chapters in this volume address the meaning of healing complicates the question of how healing works. That is, what kinds of acts, thoughts, or words actually bring about healing and *why* are these acts, thoughts, or words understood and experienced as doing so? We can identify several principal "theories" of how religious healing works that run throughout this volume.[2] First, many of the chapters emphasize the performative nature of healing. In the Haitian case discussed by Karen McCarthy Brown, the act of speaking out loud—of creating reality through words—elicits healing. Thomas Douglas and Sophon Mam, looking at two ritual contexts in the Cambodian-American community, demonstrate how the performance of a healing ritual creates a "special enchantment of experience" that engages the patient in the therapeutic process (cf. Csordas 1996). Similarly, Julianne Cordero's description of the ritual canoe journey of the Chumash community, Lara Medina's account of the Days of the Dead procession in the Latino community, and Jennifer Hollis's observations on the laying on of hands and anointing with oil in Episcopal healing services show how healing is elicited through acts that excite the senses, stir the imagination, and induce sensory attentiveness and engagement. Michael Winkelman takes the power of performance one step further, arguing that the elicitation of altered states of consciousness (in this case, through shamanic drumming) creates healing.

Some of the chapters in this volume emphasize that healing occurs as a result of reinterpreting the causes and meaning of one's suffering. Tanya Erzen, for example, discovers that the evangelical Christian ex-gay movement makes use of a discourse that represents homosexuality as a condition susceptible to change, in place of the discourse, popular in gay activist writings, that describes it as an intrinsic aspect of a person's being. In a somewhat similar vein, John Janzen, Adrien Ngudiankama, and Melissa Filippi-Franz show how telling one's story in a new and powerful theological context can be an interactive process of cognitive restructuring that allows the African immigrant patient-victim to make meaning out of the traumas of the past, and thereby leads to healing. Bobbie McKay and Lewis Musil likewise recount healing experiences of members of the United Church of Christ in which healing is prompted through a new understanding of one's relationship with God, and

Marcia Hermansen gives accounts of healing effected through dreams, dream interpretation, and other techniques of Sufi psychology.

Other chapters focus on healing that grows out of redefining social roles in the family, community, or nation. These case studies correspond to what Richard Shweder and his colleagues (1997) label the "interpersonal tradition" of medicine, that is, healing systems that address illness caused by the ill will of others and that work to restore normal interpersonal relationships. In the Jewish healing settings studied by Susan Sered, healing is a matter of repairing social relations and creating moral unity. Also for Ronald Nakasone, the process of a community coming together to develop a senior citizen housing project that meets the needs of Japanese elders is in and of itself an act of healing— even before the housing center actually opens. In these cases the healing "works" via communal naming and acknowledgment of a problem, the community bearing witness to the suffering experienced by its members, and a public commitment of resources to address the situation.

Several chapters in this volume present healing that is produced through anatomical or physiological manipulation. These case studies involve what Richard Shweder et al. (1997) call the "biological tradition" of medicine, that is, healing systems which emphasize explanatory reference to the fluids, juices, fibers, and organs of the body. Still, as Linda Barnes shows in relation to Chinese medicine, Robert Fuller shows in relation to subtle energy healing, and Kaja Finkler shows in relation to the Human Genome Project, these manipulations are grounded in cosmological and moral paradigms that give particular meanings to the manipulations.

Finally, a few of the chapters focus on healing as a result of purification, confession, atonement, or the (re)dedication to correct behavior. These case studies correspond to what Shweder et al. (1997) call the "moral tradition" of medicine. The most obvious instance in this volume is that of the confessions required in the evangelical ex-gay movement, and the corresponding pledges to abstain from enacting one's same-sex desires. The moral tradition is invoked in more subtle forms in Thomas Douglas and Sophon Mam's chapter, with its account of the young Cambodian man who promises to reform his life in accord with Buddhist and traditional Cambodian visions of personhood.

Patients and Healers

An additional set of considerations lead us to look at questions of agency: at understandings concerning *who* is being healed and *who* is doing the healing. For the substance abuse addicts described by Winkelman, the targeted patient is the individual addict. In contrast, for the Hmong patients described by Xiong et al., healing always involves the network of family relationships within which the "designated patient" is situated. An individual is never ill alone—illness is instead part of a multigenerational family dynamic. The person who manifests the symptoms may not be the one who needs to be healed: the true object of healing may be an ancestor, a spirit, or another family member. In quite a few of our chapters the patient is an entire community that has suffered from racism, sexism, or other forms of systematic violence, or the sick outside world that has inflicted that violence upon community members; sometimes it is both.

A number of our authors describe forms of self-help religious healing. This mode is characterized by the practice of affirmations, visualizations, meditation, personal prayer, dream quests, or personal regimes of spiritual and physical purification. To a certain extent, this is the mode described by Mitchem in her study of African American women in Detroit. Trained by life to rely on their own strengths and capabilities, these women look inside for healing, too. In other cases the healer may be a family member, perhaps a mother or grandmother, who engages in domestically oriented practices aimed at preserving the health of the household. These practices might include tending a household shrine or ancestor altar, providing amulets and other protective objects for the home and family, and offering blessings to children and grandchildren.

Sometimes the healer is a paid practitioner whose expertise may flow from an internal spiritual experience, from apprenticeship, or from formal training. This model is described by Csordas in the context of Navajo healers. Significantly, as both Csordas and Xiong et al. show, the issue of payment (a material matter) for religious healers (who deal with cosmic and spiritual matters) often remains outside of formal structures, governed instead by cultural understandings of reciprocity. Those who are helped are not charged but make their own choice of gifts to the healer. This exchange can sometimes be contentious, particularly if those treated think that a truly spiritual healer should not take money for something given by God or other sacred forces.

Practitioners also may be congregationally or denominationally based healers who treat clients (not always in return for a fee paid directly by the client), freelance religious healers who treat clients drawn from the city population at large, or nurses or other biomedical practitioners who incorporate some sort of spiritual healing modality into their treatment repertoire, as when some doctors elect to pray with their patients (Dossey, 1993). All these possibilities exist within the Jewish healing movement described by Sered.

Several chapters in this volume depict situations in which healing is effected by the group as a whole. We think here of groups of people who gather for the express purpose of healing, for example, in the context of twelve-step programs (such as AA) or yoga groups. Winkelman's description of the healing of substance abuse addicts in the context of shamanic drumming fits this model—the group's communal drumming is what brings about a state of consciousness in which healing can take place. Similarly, Sered describes synagogue-based healing services in which group members and leaders explicitly articulate that the very fact of gathering together, rather than the performance of particular rituals or prayers, has healing power. Sometimes the agent of healing is even larger than a bounded religious group; rather, it is the community as a whole. This model is explored by McCarthy Brown, Cordero, Medina, and Hernández-Ávila.

A question related to "who" is being healed is the question of "what" is being healed. In some cases, the object of healing is (or is perceived as) a clear and contained physical symptom or condition. Erzen, for example, describes Evangelical Christian contexts that propose to cure individuals of the specific "disease" of homosexuality. In other cases, the object of healing is the individual's entire physical and emotional being or the individual's ability to function in daily life, perhaps, as in the case of African immigrants depicted by Janzen et al., in the wake of the traumas of war. Sometimes, what the healing practice sets out to address is a fracture in identity. Many of the Wiccan rituals described by Harris have to do with healing participants from patriarchal structures that have prevented women from developing a true, natural, strong, healthy sense of self. Similarly, in the Jewish healing rituals studied by Sered, healing is construed as the process of leading the individual back to the Jewish sources, texts, community, culture, and roots that will provide him or her with a healthy identity. Several chapters highlight the healing of memory, as Cordero describes in the case of the powerful canoe ritual carried out by the Chumash after a hiatus first of more than a century and then of several decades.

Sites of Healing

The complexities of the religious healing traditions and the contemporary social contexts in which they operate preclude far-reaching conclusions regarding "the meaning" or "the significance" of American religious healing. Within the effervescent diversity of American society, it is possible, however, to identify a range of sites of healing—or, perhaps more accurately, structural categories, helpful for describing the rapidly expanding and constantly shifting geography of contemporary religious healing.

One way of getting at the diversity of religious healing practices in the United States is through mapping the physical sites in which religious healing takes place. McKay and Musil, for example, describe the spiritual healing experiences of members of the United Church of Christ. For the most part, these experiences take place spontaneously at home or in other mundane settings. Douglas and Mam provide vignettes of domestic settings in which a Cambodian monk, on the one hand, and a Cambodian practitioner of Wicca, on the other, carry out their work. Candles, incense, and other sacred object mark the monk's bedroom as sacred space. Klassen describes a house-centered spirituality invoked by women who choose to give birth at home. Yet in their case there is nothing spontaneous about the setting; rather, a home birth is selected for clear religious and ideological reasons. Mama Lola, the Vodou priestess portrayed by McCarthy Brown, also lights candles and makes *wanga* (healing objects) in her own house, but the healing of a Haitian victim of police brutality also spills out into the streets when members of the community make their own *wanga* in the context of a demonstration.

The streets are also the site of healing for the members of the Los Angeles Latina/o community described by Medina. Reviving Days of the Dead celebrations in a community that has experienced intense geographic and cultural rupture, the Artists' Collective mobilizes children and adults in an ambitious program of mask painting, costume construction, and creative revitalization of traditional Day of the Dead rituals, all of which culminates in a massive healing procession through the streets of Los Angeles.

For the Native American Chumash community described by Cordero, the geographic setting for healing is the ocean. As the fulfillment of a collective endeavor to build an oceangoing canoe that could carry members of the community to their sacred island, the arduous journey across the ocean, in itself, contributes to a fundamental act of healing.

Several of the chapters in this volume offer witness to healing taking place in the context of institution building. Nakasone discovered healing in the construction of an old age home responsive to the cultural and spiritual needs of Japanese residents in the Bay area. Bednarowski describes the healing that takes place on a daily basis as members of the Hope Community in Minneapolis transform their neighborhood into a community where all can move about safely, take control of public parks, and negotiate with municipal authorities for better social services.

Other authors look at healing in the geographic context of a practitioner's clinic. Both the New Age healers reviewed by Fuller and some of the practitioners of Chinese traditions described by Barnes perform their work for pay, typically in an office-type setting. And, of course, the biomedical treatments growing out of the Human Genome Project described by Finkler take place in medical clinics and in the context of managed care.

Surprisingly few of our authors depict healing practices located in conventional religious settings such as churches, temples, or shrines. Hollis describes the rise of healing services at Episcopal churches in the Boston area. Despite a fair measure of uneasiness in the Episcopal community regarding practices that might be perceived as bordering on uncontrolled faith healing, a number of Episcopal churches have instituted healing services in which the physical site of the church building is crucial. At these services, priests anoint parishioners with holy oil, lay on hands, and ritually open the (typically quite beautiful) church space to the homeless, those who have been abused, and the sick and suffering. Holding the services inside the church buildings reflects the desire of Episcopal priests to demarginalize the poor and the sick. Situating the services in the church concretizes that desire. Espinosa writes about large-scale healing services at public sites that served at least temporarily as churches and sometimes involved thousands of congregants. Orsi and Polk describe religious healing situated at shrines of saints. In these cases, the devotee establishes a personal relationship with a particular saint whose presence is more fully accessible at the shrines. While healing is not contingent upon coming to the shrines—Orsi describes Italian Catholics who write letters to the shrine instead—the site does serve as the geographic focus of healing activity.

Healing from Structural Violence

Because of their religious valence, the healing practices described throughout this volume link individual experiences to wider cultural, symbolic, social, and cosmic forces. In doing so, these practices underscore the ways in which the effects of these forces are embodied. Many of our authors address contexts in which healing is construed in communities that have suffered collectively from racism, sexism, dislocation, war, or poverty. The economic, political, legal, and religious influences that have buttressed a variety of inequities throughout American history have generated what can be called "structural violence"— that is, social structures and systems that, by their very nature, have perpetrated and perpetuated unequal access to resources and justice for different groups in the United States (Kleinman, Das, and Lock 1997). The result has been the affliction of not only the body personal but also the body social.

Racism constitutes the clearest expression of structural violence in American society. Over the course of American history, racial categories were developed in ways that usually classified non-white groups as "Others." Often, these categories overlapped with non-Christian religious identities. The resulting racial hierarchies were used to justify conquest, conversion, dispossession, and enslavement. The bodies of non-European Americans (and of European-American groups deemed less "white) were often considered less valuable, and were treated as commodities or as sources of cheap labor. They were also regularly deprived of regular medical care, except when related to their ability to work. Even now, study after study shows that when all other factors are controlled for, African Americans are less likely than whites to receive specific medications and procedures (Byrd and Clayton 2000). Non-white bodies have also been more likely to be subjected to display dissection (Blakely and Harrington 1997) and experimentation (Townes 1998). In standard medical settings the effects of racism on people's health frequently are treated as individual conditions. More accurately, they represent individual embodiments of a pervasive social condition. Indeed, the sickening effects of racism are felt on many levels. Mitchem's chapter, for example, argues many health issues experienced by African American women (and, we would add, by other minority communities in the United States) cannot be separated from stresses related to the structural violence of racism.

Almost all the chapters in this volume, in one way or another, talk about illness as a manifestation of social forces, and healing as some way of addressing those forces or their implications. Religious healing often addresses structural violence at a collective level, as a necessary component in the healing of individuals. Such healing sometimes takes the character of resistance, although the form and focus of the resistance vary from group to group. Sered, for example, interprets the Jewish healing movement in terms of resistance to dominant gender hierarchies in Jewish tradition and American medical culture. Espinosa, Cordero, Janzen et al., McCarthy Brown, Bednarowski, Medina, and Nakasone examine how disenfranchised groups come together as communities to defy wrong definitions of who they are and to challenge related social wrongs. As McCarthy Brown's example of competing *wangas* in the case of Abner Louima illustrates, healing can transform affliction by reformulating it and by naming its perpetrators. It is in such contexts that we encounter multiple variations on a phrase used by Medina, *La cultura cura,* or "Culture cures." Healing in these contexts occurs as the action of cultural communities and in the relationship between particular communities and the powerful institutions that shape the spiritual and corporeal experiences of community members.

Bednarowski, as noted earlier, suggests that healing is connected to hope. But "hope" can be defined within quite disparate rubrics, as in Erzen's discussion of New Hope, an evangelical group dedicated to "healing" homosexuality. While we, as the anthology's editors, may not embrace this particular understanding of healing, we have chosen to include in this volume as wide a range as possible of religiously defined approaches to healing in the United States, counterposing examples in order to suggest that not everyone experiences a particular phenomenon in the same way. Thus, Harris's chapter includes a discussion of Wiccan rebuttals to the religious stigmatizing and targeting of homosexuality—including its being treated as a "condition" in need of healing at all.

We do not wish to romanticize religious healing. Meredith McGuire (personal communication, 2002) has noted, for example, that some of the evangelical and Pentecostal churches that practice Headship and submission consider it within the prerogative (or even duty) of the Head to order someone submitted to (usually) him to undergo some "healing" practice, including exorcisms and other self-mortification. Different traditions may assign women the role of keeping the peace of the home—of "healing" a battering partner through prayer—and of continuing to suffer domestic violence in the process. While the intentions of such healing may be benign, the effects may not be. It is not difficult to think of situations in which religious healing emphasizes the acceptance or even the valorization of suffering. In some cases, healing actually reimposes the inequities of structural violence, echoing I. M. Lewis's interpretation (1971) of women's spirit possession and healing cults as opportunities for oppressed groups to blow off just enough steam to allow them to return docilely to their subordinate everyday lives.

The Gendering of Suffering and Healing

Gender-based oppression represents a form of structural violence that tends to elicit particular attention in contexts of religious healing. In American society, women are sick more often than men, visit physicians more often than men, take more medicine than men, and are more likely than men to evaluate their health as poor. While there is some variation based on race and country of origin, statistics generated by the Centers for Disease Control and Prevention consistently show women of all age-groups suffering from a variety of chronic illnesses at rates higher than those for men. Explanations for why women are sicker (especially when, as is the case in the United States, women outlive men) include the double load of paid work and housework; the feminization of poverty; relentless responsibilities of caring for sick children, aging parents, and other family members; cultural expectations that women are weaker than men; increasing medicalization of women's bodies (especially in relation to menstruation, menopause, pregnancy, and childbirth); a tendency to treat women's bodies as "unique" or "exceptional" (in comparison with male bodies, which are treated as normative); repeated traumas of the threat and reality of sexual violence; harmful fashions such as high heels or extreme dieting; and the stress caused by systematic exclusion from the arenas of power where the economic, military, and political decisions that affect everyone's lives are made.

This constellation of social factors impacts upon individual women's bodies. However, medical interventions that focus solely on individual bodies tend to be unsuccessful, inasmuch as they disregard the structural and ideological underpinnings of women's poor health. Thus, not only do women outnumber men in many (and probably most) religious healing contexts in the United States, but the experiences that bring women to religious healing often include multiple sequential or simultaneous chronic illnesses that have not been resolved either through biomedical interventions or through secular complementary or alternative therapies. In such situations, religious healing may offer interpretations of illness that valorize women's experiences, communal settings that provide group validation and support, opportunities for leadership, and the feelings of hope and empowerment that come from opportunities to engage in a variety of healing practices.

In this volume, Sered explores ways in which the American Jewish healing movement reformulates issues related to gender, illness, and the authority to heal, while Harris, as noted earlier, examines the interplay between feminism and healing in the various forms of Wicca. Erzen's chapter discusses conflicting representations of sexual orientation rooted in religious understandings of gender and gender relations. Mitchem's work studies a contemporary interpretion of "Christ the Physician" for African American women. And Csordas provides multiple cases that illustrate how Navajo women take part in religious traditions that allow them different entry points into the practice of healing.

A Typology of Mixtures: Synergy, Syncretism, and Appropriation

None of the authors in this volume depicts a mode of religious healing that is practiced in isolation from a variety of other healing modalities. At this time, we live in the midst of unprecedented degrees of contact and interaction between Native peoples, and earlier and more recent immigrant groups from all parts of the globe. These interactions, both personal and societal, lead to multiple interfaces between *different* systems of healing, as well as to pluralism and diversity *within* cultural groups. The ongoing pluralism of healing modalities is clearly expressed when individuals choose more than one type of healing for a given problem.

One could relate this phenomenon to the American penchant for pragmatism. However, similar utilization of multiple healing modalities is common in other cultures as well. It may be more accurate to speak of people's ability to experience and interpret affliction in more than one way, and to apply multiple strategies to address a problem. Sometimes the plural approach is conceptualized as covering all of one's bases; sometimes the various modalities are understood as treating different aspects of the problem; and sometimes modalities are accessed sequentially—when one healing practice or practitioner fails to resolve the problem, one moves on to the next possible solution. Sometimes the modalities are perceived as being in conflict with one another, and sometimes they are perceived as an integrated whole, as in Desai's example of Indian American physicians who also wear astrologically prescribed gemstones.

Cultural communities often borrow from one another, especially when diverse populations find themselves living in the same neighborhoods and shopping in one another's markets. Sometimes we find dynamic synergies that illustrate the renewal of traditions through the use of modern tools and commodities, as when the Chumash use power saws to cut wood and Kentucky Fried Chicken buckets as measures in the process of making a ritual canoe.

When forms of religious healing come to be used outside of the communities and cultures in which they originated, how do we interpret their significance? Forms of hybridity sometimes have less to do with degrees of assimilation to a dominant culture than with interactions between minority practices. It happens, for example, when Vodou practitioners in New Orleans adopt the Virgin of Guadalupe—the version of the Virgin beloved by many Mexicans and Chicanas/os—as one of the iconic representations of the *lwa*, or intercessory force Erzulie, because Erzulie, too, wears blue and pink. It happens when a Puerto Rican mother in Boston buys a figure of the Buddha in a local botanica while there to purchase herbs and paraphernalia for her Santeria altar, because the Buddha is associated with luck, and religious healing may involve trying to change one's luck.

Another type of mixing occurs when members of one cultural group convert to a religious tradition located in a different cultural community. The new cultural frame infuses the tradition in ways that may make the two difficult to separate. When a European American enters the Gold Mountain Sagely Monastery in San Francisco as a monk or nun, he or she becomes immersed in a Chinese form of Buddhism, with related orientations toward the Medicine Master Buddha. Both Barnes and Numrich examine cases in which a particular tradition includes both ethnic members and new converts. No amount of immersion, however, fully erases one's own cultural formation, and thus new elements become injected into the body of the local tradition.

Following Edward Said's study of Orientalism and Michel Foucault's analyses of how particular power dynamics permeate cultures, it is important to track what happens when members of a dominant culture borrow from the practices of a minority community. Because the former enjoy social privileges and power from which the latter is likely to be excluded, the implications of this sort of borrowing reflect and perhaps perpetuate the status and power imbalances of the wider social structure. This becomes especially critical when the borrowing becomes appropriation—a dynamic that historian David Hufford (personal communication, 2002) characterizes as one of either stigmatizing or stealing. It also is important to understand that even the most benign borrowing takes place within the context of a market economy. We need to ask who is earning profits from books, tapes, workshops, and videos demonstrating or offering instruction in healing practices of various peoples.

Cordero addresses this issue, recounting how it came to be that a traditional canoe crafted by Chumash artisans was claimed by museum officials, who drilled holes in the hull and bolted the canoe to the ceiling of the museum's main auditorium. Barnes similarly notes the problematics of selective appropriation of particular Chinese healing practices by western practitioners. Sered notes the anger that activists in the Jewish healing movement express towards the "Kabbalah Centers" that sell Jewish ritual objects and capitalize on their association with non-Jewish celebrities such as Madonna. And the adoption of shamanic practices by neo-shamanic groups has been hotly contested by indigenous peoples.

The degree of contestation often resides in a history of power disparities. When more powerful groups appropriate—and more particularly make money from—the practices of less powerful groups, reactions often are more negative than when less powerful groups adopt texts or practices of the more powerful (for example, as Sered shows, the adoption of Christian pastoral counseling by Jewish healers has not elicited any negative responses). We would argue that the difference here lies in the tendency for dominant groups to see their own practices as desirable, normative, or universal, and the realistic fear of subordinate groups that their natural and cultural resources will be mined—and possibly distorted in the process—for the profits of others.

As scholars, we must acknowledge the part played by academics in such processes of superscession and dispossession. Native American scholars such as Wendy Rose (1992) and Christopher Jocks (2000) point to anthropologists and historians of religion who claim to know more than the members of a tribe who are the living practitioners of traditions. The cruelest irony may occur when, in a dominant culture that privileges the experiential—so long as it is one's own experience—there is a corresponding devaluation of the experiential and inherited knowledge of other groups. This issue of the experiential raises the question of what functions to legitimize a practice and for whom, and to what extent the dominant discourses of biomedicine, law, and "mainstream" religion shape notions of legitimacy.

Intersections with Dominant Discourses

At the current time, the principal interpretive frame for all healing practices and ideologies in the United States is that of science, particularly when a group wants to assert the legitimacy of its practices. The privileging of science as a language of legitimacy has operated throughout the country's history, and was adopted by groups as diverse as advocates of vegetarianism, Spiritualism, Christian Science, and astrology in the nineteenth century. Although different groups have meant different things by "science," and science's own meanings have changed over time, its stamp retains considerable cultural authority.

The medicine now most widely recognized as "scientific" is biomedicine, the biologically based medicine related to the anatomical understanding of the body. A cultural form in its own right, biomedicine exists in multiple relationships with various aspects of religious healing. Given its influence, some traditions (such as acupuncture) try to appear more "scientific," in terms recognized by biomedicine.

Other intersections with biomedicine exist, not all of them congenial. Engagement in some forms of religious healing may govern patient choices for or against biomedical therapies, the best-known examples being the rejection of blood transfusions by Jehovah's Witnesses and of biomedical interventions by Christian Scientists. What we see in some of these cases is the dominant legal system entering the picture both to challenge and to defend different forms of religious healing. Challenges frequently are brought when pediatricians observe what appears to them to be child neglect or abuse, or the refusal of biomedical therapies that may result in the child's death. Other challenges may arise when the local neighbors of a practice find it objectionable, as in cases that tried to make animal sacrifice in Santeria or the use of peyote by the Native American Church illegal. In some cases, the legal system also engages in the defense of such practices under the heading of religious freedom. The codifying of what is legally allowed and prohibited structures the place of religious healing in the larger culture.

In some instances, the pursuit of religious healing may be related to barriers to access of biomedicine. Economic barriers, language differences, lack of documentation for immigrants, and other factors may function as obstacles to accessing biomedical care. Thus, somewhat ironically, the economic structure of the dominant medical system in the United States may in fact encourage those who lack health insurance to pursue nonbiomedical healing interventions, at the same time as these interventions may be judged as inferior or even illegal by the same medical system.

The authority of biomedicine currently is such that all other nonbiomedical therapies and healing interventions are relegated to the global categories of "alternative" or "complementary" medicine. Both terms articulate a relationship to a dominant system—a practice is used either together with or instead of biomedicine. Yet neither of these two terms says anything about the categories of practice they encompass. Efforts to develop typologies with which to categorize such practices have wrestled—generally without compelling success—with the challenge of imposing order among practices where none had historically existed. For example, do we simply start by clustering every form of herbal practice, regardless of the traditions from which the different herbal therapies derive? If so, what do we do when, in certain traditions, herbs are understood to be fully effective only when infused with specific rituals and/or prayers, while in other traditions such infusions are not part of the picture? Which ends up being more important—the herbs or the rituals? Or is it more likely the case that the two cannot be considered separately? What happens to complementary therapies of this kind, which straddle what might otherwise seem to be "commonsense" categories? We suspect that the religious aspects come to be seen as the trimmings, while substances and procedures that are closer fits for the biomedical paradigm remain the main dish.

These considerations lead us to question the epistemological formulations of how we know what we know, and how we assign legitimacy to different practices. When scientists use biomedical criteria to test the efficacy of religious healing, the forms of efficacy recognized may not be those most valued by the adherents of religious healing. For example, religious explanations of healing that include the transformative experience of the sacred, the restoration of communal networks, understandings of what happens after death, and how one sustains right relationships with the dead may not be registered in the log of scientific outcome measures. Yet in many instances these considerations may be far more salient than more physically quantifiable considerations such as blood pressure or glucose level.

We have chosen to end this book with a chapter by Harold Koenig, one of the foremost medical researchers on the healing power of faith, and with a classic piece on religion and healing written by Martin Marty, an intellectual elder in the field of religious studies.[3] While Koenig addresses the importance of the study of religion to medical religious healing practice, Marty formulates a typology of religious healing that touches on elements, themes, and concepts independent of medical assessments. In very different ways, both Koenig and Marty remind us, again, to think both broadly and in focused ways about how religion addresses matters of suffering, affliction, life, and death.

NOTES

1. We hope that the publication of this volume will spur studies of communities whose healing practices have not received sufficient scholarly attention. For example, we were unable to locate studies of healing among recent Irish immigrants, and among many of the African groups that have come to the United States during the past few decades.

2. In developing this typology we have found quite helpful Richard Sweder's (1997) discussion of the "Big Three" traditions of medicine.

3. Martin Marty, together with Kenneth L. Vaux were leaders in editing and authoring a series of works on religion and healing, published in the 1980s. Ronald L. Numbers and Darrel W. Amundsen ([1986] 1998) and Lawrence E. Sullivan (1989) also edited important anthologies on the topic, aspects of which examined practices in the United States.

REFERENCES

Barnes, Linda L. 2002. Issues of Spirituality and Religion in Health Care. In *Cross-Cultural Medicine*, ed. JudyAnn Bigby, 237–67. Philadelphia, Pa. : American College of Physicians–American Society of Internal Medicine.

———. Forthcoming. *Needles, Herbs, Gods, and Ghosts: China, Healing, and the West to 1848*. Cambridge Mass.: Harvard University Press.

Blakely, Robert L., and Judith M. Harrington, eds. 1997. *Bones in the Basement: Postmortem Racism in Nineteenth-Century Medical Training*. Washington, D.C.: Smithsonian Institution Press.

Braude, Ann. 1989. *Radical Spirits: Spiritualism and Women's Rights in Nineteenth-Century America*. Boston: Beacon Press.

Byrd, W. Michael, and Linda A. Clayton. 2000. *An American Health Dilemma: The Medical History of African Americans and the Problem of Race*. New York: Routledge.

Csordas, Thomas. 1996. Imaginal Performance and Memory in Ritual Healing. In *The Performance of Healing*, ed. Marina Roseman, 91–114. New York: Routledge.

Culpeper, Nicholas. 1651. *Culpeper's Astrologicall Judgment of Diseases*. London: For Nathaniel Brooks.

Dossey, Larry. 1993. *Healing Words: The Power of Prayer and the Practice of Medicine*. New York: HarperPaperbacks.

Ebaugh, Helen Rose, and Janet Saltzman Chafetz, eds. 2002. *Religion across Borders: Transnational Immigrant Networks*. Walnut Creek, Calif.: AltaMira Press.

Gevitz, Norman, ed. 1988. *Other Healers: Unorthodox Medicine in America*. Baltimore: Johns Hopkins University Press.

Glock, Charles Y., and Rodney Stark. 1966. *Christian Beliefs and Anti-Semitism*. New York: Harper and Row.

Jacobs, Claude F., and Andrew W. Kaslow. 1991. *The Spiritual Churches of New Orleans: Origins, Beliefs, and Rituals of an African-American Religion*. Knoxville: University of Tennessee Press.

James, William. [1911] 2002. *The Varieties of Religious Experience: A Study in Human Nature*. Amherst, N.Y.: Prometheus Books.

Jocks, Christopher. 2000. Spirituality for Sale: Sacred Knowledge in the Consumer Age. In *Native American Spirituality: A Critical Reader*, ed. Lee Irwin, 61–77. Lincoln: University of Nebraska Press.

Kinsley, David. 1996. *Health, Healing, and Religion: A Cross-Cultural Perspective*. Englewood Cliffs, N.J.: Prentice-Hall.

Kleinman, Arthur, Veena Das, and Margaret Lock. 1997. *Social Suffering*, Berkeley and Los Angeles: University of California Press.

Koenig, Harold G., and Harvey Jay Cohen, eds. 2002. *The Link between Religion and Health: Psychoneuroimmunology and the Faith Factor*. New York: Oxford University Press.

Laderman, Carol, and Marina Roseman, eds. 1996. *The Performance of Healing*. New York: Routledge.

Lewis, I. M. 1971. *Ecstatic Religion: An Anthropological Study of Spirit Possession and Shamanism*. Harmondsworth, England: Penguin Books.

Mather, Cotton. 1713. *A Letter, About a Good Management Under the Distemper of the Measles, at This Time Spreading in the Country* Boston: s.n.

Matthews, Dale A. 1998. *The Faith Factor: Proof of the Healing Power of Prayer*. New York: Viking.

McCullough, M. E., W. T. Hoyt, David B. Larson, Harold G. Koenig, and C. Thoreson. 2000. Religious Involvement and Mortality: A Meta-analytic Review. *Health Psychology* 19:211–22.

McLoughlin, William G. 1977. *Revivals, Awakenings, and Reform: An Essay on Religion and Social Change in America, 1607–1977*. Chicago: University of Chicago Press.

Numbers, Ronald L., and Darrel W. Amundsen, eds. [1986] 1998. *Caring and Curing: Health and Medicine in the Western Religious Traditions*. Baltimore: Johns Hopkins University Press.

Parker, Gail Thain. 1973. *Mind Cure in New England*, Hanover, N.H.: University Press of New England.

Phillips, Paul T. 1996. *A Kingdom on Earth: Anglo-American Social Christianity, 1880–1940*. University Park: Pennsylvania State University Press.

Risse, Guenter B., Ronald L. Numbers, and Judith Walzer Leavett. 1977. *Medicine without Doctors: Home Health Care in American History*. New York: Science History Publicatiions.

Rose, Wendy. 1992. The Great Pretenders: Further Reflections on Whiteshamanism. In *The State of Native America: Genocide, Colonization, and Resistance*, ed. M. Annette Jaimes, 403–21. Boston: South End Press.

Rosenberg, Charles E. 1979. The Therapeutic Revolution: Medicine, Meaning, and Social Change in Nineteenth-Century America. In *The Therapeutic Revolution: Essays in the Social History of American Medicine*, ed. Morris J. Vogel and Charles E. Rosenberg, 3–25. Philadelphia: University of Pennsylvania Press.

Rothstein, William G. 1972. *American Physicians in the Nineteenth Century: From Sects to Science*. Baltimore: Johns Hopkins University Press.

Shweder, R. A., N. C. Much, M. Mahapatra, and L. T. Park. 1997. The "Big Three" of Morality (Autonomy, Community, Divinity) and the "Big Three" Explanations of Suffering. In *Morality and Health*, ed. A. M. Brandt and P. Rozin, 119–69. New York: Routledge.

Sullivan, Lawrence E., ed. 1989. *Healing and Restoring: Health and Medicine in the World's Religious Traditions*. New York: Macmillan.

Townes, Emilie M. 1998. *Breaking the Fine Rain of Death: African American Health Issues and a Womanist Ethic of Care*. New York: Continuum.

Wesley, John. 1747. *Primitive Physick: or, An Easy and Natural Method of Curing Most Diseases*. London: Thomas Trye.

Wrobel, Arthur, ed. 1987. *Pseudo-Science and Society in Nineteenth-Century America*. Lexington: University Press of Kentucky.

PART I

Sites of Healing

Domestic Spaces, Public Spaces

I

The Cult of the Saints and the Reimagination of the Space and Time of Sickness in Twentieth-Century American Catholicism

Robert A. Orsi

Devotion to the saints has been an essential component of the Catholic experience of sickness and suffering for centuries.[1] Statues of the saints stand on the bedside tables of the sick, and holy images are affixed to the walls above their heads, relics are pinned to their bedclothes by desperate kin, candles are lit for them, and they are bathed in holy water and carried to healing shrines. Despite the familiarity of these practices, however, or perhaps because of it, the role of the popular cult of the saints in mediating the Catholic experiences of sickness has received little careful attention.

What happens when a sick person turns to a beloved holy figure in a moment of fear and pain, and sometimes doubt? What is the meaning of the gestures and rituals performed in the sickroom? How do the devout and their kin understand what they are doing on these occasions? What do these gestures accomplish?

Since the early decades of the twentieth century, suffering American Catholics have left a record of their feelings, hopes, and understanding in letters they have sent to the shrines of various saints in the United States. These letters, sometimes written while the correspondent is sick, sometimes after the crisis is past, recount what the sick person or his or her kin said to the saint, what requests were made, how they were made and when, and the specific uses of various devotional objects associated with the cults (statues, oils, candles, and so on).

The letters do not simply record, however: writing them is the action the devout take to re-create their worlds, which have been unmade by suffering. The devout write to the shrines mainly to request or report assistance from the saints. In constructing narrative accounts of what is happening or what they believe has happened to them, they remake the reality of their experience. They open up the closed space of sickness, connecting it to the spaces and times before, after, and outside it. They impose their own sense of the meaning of the experience on it. They identify the loci of power and authority in the experience—who was truly in charge, who was responsible for what. This reconstruction is the work of theodicy, which on one level is a cognitive task, a way of shaping the understanding in a disorienting time.

But this work always takes place in particular social and political contexts: sick people are already located in other discourses and practices by other authorities, so that on a second level, the work of theodicy is contending with these other powers. All world making is also world claiming. On this level, theodicy making is an oppositional practice in which distressed people draw on the language and gestures of the cult of the saints to construct a world of meaning and practice in opposition to the meaning and practices the dominant cultures—medical, technological, religious—impose on them.

This does not mean, however, that theodicy as the power of world making creates a space of total freedom from other competing and very powerful arrangements and ideologies: in their everyday lives, and even during much of their experience of sickness, the people who turn to the saints accept the legitimacy of these ideologies. Nevertheless, the letters suggest that in the moment of disorientation occasioned by sickness or pain, the symbols and rituals available to the devout in the cult of the saints offer them one way of reimagining their experience. In this way they can reappropriate it.

Almost a hundred years of these letters exist. Therefore, they serve as a running commentary on changes in the experience of sickness in the United States and an ongoing reflection on the changing history of physical and social vulnerability in American society. Doctors and nurses, hospitals and hospital administrators, operating rooms and sickbeds, all appear in these letters, along with explicit, precisely described details of medical procedures.

This aspect of the letters suggests another set of questions about the popular experience of recent medical history. Do the letters offer any indication that people were aware of what critics call the medicalization of American society? If so, did they evolve any strategy of resistance to this process? What do the letters teach us about the relations between doctor and patient in this country? How did people perceive the changing nature and location of medical authority?

The letters referred to in this study were all written to the shrine of Blessed Margaret of Castello, founded in 1980 by the Dominican Fathers in Louisville, Kentucky.[2] Margaret herself was born in 1287 in Umbria, Italy, "a blind . . . crippled . . . hunchback . . . dwarf," as she is described on a poster distributed by the shrine. Rejected by her parents as a child, she lived for a time among the outcasts of Citta de Castello, until her sanctity and spiritual powers were recognized and her reputation began to spread.

After her death in 1320, devotion to Margaret remained primarily local, confined to Citta di Castello and its immediate environs. Then, in the late 1970s, several American Dominicans thought that she would make a good patron saint for handicapped people and antiabortion activists, and they introduced her cult into the United States. This unusual holy figure strongly attracts people, and her devotion began to flourish immediately; Margaret became a popular patron for American Catholics in great physical and emotional need.

Margaret's shrine is typical of such devotions. Her devout write from all over the United States. Internal evidence in the letter suggests that the correspondents are mainly lower-middle-class; they represent all the cultures constituting American Catholicism. As is usual with these devotions, most correspondents are women. The majority of Margaret's devout are over sixty years old. Most of them indicate in their letters their devotions to other holy figures as well. Margaret's cult lies very much at the center of the devotional culture of American Catholicism. A study of these letters therefore illustrates the entire literature.

Space and time are extremely important in the imaginations and narratives of the devout. The time referred to here is, first of all, the whole period of sickness; the devout also specify individual moments within this larger time that were particularly significant to them. Space comprises all the public places that sick people in modern America must go to await and obtain medical treatment or diagnostic tests, as well as spaces of the sick in their homes. Of particular concern is how the devout use the cult of the saints to create, interpret, and inhabit these times and places, and how this reimagination is shaped in and presented by the letters.[3]

Time

The devout consistently privilege certain times: the exact moment in which they discovered the sickness; the various times of medical procedure, particularly those moments when these procedures began working or failing; waiting for the results of tests, especially those for cancer; particular moments in their relationships with doctors—when they must find a new doctor, for example, or go to an unfamiliar specialist, or when they disagree with their doctor about medical care; the time during operations, and, in general moments of high medical intervention; times of sudden change in their conditions; and a particular time experienced as the worst moment of their sickness.

Several characteristics mark these moments apart from any reference to the symbols and myths of the cult of the saints. These are times of extreme uncertainty, when a person's life is suddenly and clearly in suspense. A woman writes to the shrine that she was "OK until Mon. past. At 3 mo. checkup the Doctor found a lump in the other breast. I want to abandon myself to God's loving will for me, Father. I am humanly very frightened" (JB-F-W-65+-Wilkes Barre, Pa.).[4] Another woman writes: "My daughter has gone through three surgerys, and then after a while she contracted lupis. . . . Now [daughter's name] has to go through another test (colin). Please forgive my handwriting and spelling[.] I am very nervous and worried" (LS-F-M?-55+-Chicago, Ill.).

These are also times in which the sick discover they can do nothing for themselves; frequently they also discover their doctors can do little for them; and in these moments their families discover their own helplessness. "Dear Father, I am desperate," another letter begins. "My dear friend has just found out that she has cancer of bone marrow and it is affecting her kidneys and the prognosis is one to three years!" (LV-F-?-?-?). As they describe such moments, finally, the sick identify one time when the pain reached a level they thought they could not endure.

With the discovery of sickness, during the wait for test results, as cancer spreads or blindness deepens, these people discover unavoidably the natural boundaries of their experience; through this, they confront the fragility of what they once thought of as real. They must acknowledge limits in their bodies and their lives. "The essence of pain," philosopher F.J.J. Buytendijk writes, is "a state where man is afflicted in his most intimate unity, his psychophysical nature." "But why," Buytendijk imagines the person in pain asking, "must this wound, this organ, this part of my body give me such acute and continual pain? Why just me? Why at this particular moment? Why at this particular place? Why this abandonment and faintness, this destruction of my freedom, even of thought, sensation, will? Why such helplessness?" (1961: 25–26). The sick must think in new ways about their lives—the plans they must now change, their hopes and fears. In particular they must think about time—the past before sickness, the sick present, and the uncertain future.

Entry into this marked time of sickness is identified carefully and precisely by the devout in their narratives. "In the latter half of November," a man tells a shrine, "my aunt was diagnosed as having breast cancer. A lump was found in the breast and one underneath the arm. Three days after this she had a radical mastectomy" (LU-M-S?-50?-?). Another account, this one by a boy's mother, begins, "About midnight, December 13 Monday, [her son] fell some 80 ft. from a watertower here in White Plains" (Mrs. G-F-M?-40?-New Rochelle, N.Y.). "About a week later," another woman writes, "as I was drying my son's hair (he's nine years old) I came across a lump on his neck" (Mrs. B-F-M-35-Lodi, N.J.). On a December Monday, in the middle of November, "just now," "last Tuesday"—and everything changes forever.

The dreadful clarity with which these moments are recalled emphasizes the way sickness is marked off from the rest of a person's life. In the midst of a mundane domestic chore—symbol of normality and coherence—something else erupts. From that moment, nothing may ever be the same again. The phrase "as I was drying my son's hair" acquires malevolent connotation. The discovery of sickness charges the moment with meaning and threatens to overwhelm it.

But the devout do not stop with this level of meaning or this first interpretive step. The marked moment itself occasions a second move of reinterpretation and reimagination: with the help of the saints the devout will invert the inversion, returning meaning, coherence, and order to the moment. This part of a process the iconoclastic scholar Ivan Illich identifies as the movement from *pain* to *suffering*. Suffering is characterized by its placement within a larger symbolic universe of interpretation (Illich 1976: 144–45). "Drying my son's hair" will acquire yet another significance, marked with reference to a second level of meaning and experience.

Turning to the saints recasts the fundamental meanings of the various times of sickness. "Next Tuesday," a woman writes, she will learn whether the lump on her breast is malignant. "Things look bleak. I need your prayer . . . please—please—keep me in prayer at the shrine" (JB-F-W-65+-Wilkes Barre, Pa.). The woman who discovered the lump on her son's neck prayed to Margaret every night during the long waiting period she had to endure, and she says of this time, "Sick though we were, we held our faith." Another woman, terrified of a scheduled operation, writes, "The doctors would like to operate on me and I'm so scared about this upcoming event which will be by the end of the month. . . . I have prayed fervently for the intercession of Blessed Margaret and had felt better since then. I prayed that I will not undergo such operation anymore, or if it be the will of God let me conform to his holy desires." The devout put themselves into Margaret's hands and thereby change the meaning of time: moments initially marked by fear become occasions for surrender to God's will. They are recast as times under God's loving control.

For the devout, the clearest evidence that this is sacred time is the uncanny fact of the coincident discovery of the saint and the sickness, and they emphasize this in their accounts. Typically the narratives open with a paragraph describing the onset of illness and then abruptly introduce the sudden and unexpected meeting of the sick person (or his or her kin) with the saint: "Recently came across devotion to Margaret of Castello"; "I have heard of Blessed Margaret of Castello just one month ago June 18 and have started to pray to her"; "I went into a church for a very quick visit and picked up a little pamphlet on Blessed Margaret of Castello"; "Just by accident I found Blessed Margaret's pamphlet in the back of the church." These simple details are thought to carry special meaning: the coincidence signals God's presence in the presence of his saint.[5] Now the time is protected and watched over by the sacred; it is not out of control and threatening meaninglessness, but in the control of the source and center of all meaning.

In consequence of the devouts' turn to the saints, powerlessness is recast as dependence on the power and love of God and the saints; fear is transformed into love and trust; and despair is remade into faith. The dates and times of sickness take on new significance. "I was in the hospital for surgery of my left hand," a woman begins her narrative, "and the potassium level was so low that it could delay surgery for the second time. They started to give me potassium orally and intravenously and at 6:00 am the following morning it was enough for surgery it is over now and I came home to recover" (BG-F-?-?-San Diego, Calif.). Six o'clock in the morning is meaningful not because this is when the medical procedure began to work; instead, the medical procedure worked because this was the moment the sacred intervened in the experience of sickness.

The cult of the saints also allows the devout to open up the bounded time of sickness while they are experiencing it. Sick time is closed and limited: this is partially what religious scholar David Bakan means by the "telic decentralization" caused by pain (1968: 49–53). The sick have trouble remembering when they were not sick or imagining when they will not be sick—sickness is a wholly but oddly *present time*. The devotions open a way out of this present by allowing the devout to express confidence in the future actions of the saint. They can anticipate the work of inversion and briefly move into another consciousness of time. A man whose close friend is being operated on for cancer (apparently as the letter is being written) tells the shrine that he is praying to Margaret and is "confident that she will not fail to help." He concludes by promising to "let you know if there is any progress" (QR-M-?-45?-San Francisco, Calif.).

When they turn to the saints in their experience of sick time, the devout always promise something when the sickness is over. (This is why thank-you notices to St. Jude appear in the classified sections of American newspapers.) One man recounts that as he was experiencing the worst moment of a back ailment that threatened to undo his way of life and self-image, he promised to give Margaret $100 if she helped him (?B-M-?-50-Garden City, N.Y.). The contractual element here, the "con artistry" of Catholics in need,[6] is familiar. Less familiar is awareness of what making the contract at just this time does to the experience of the moment. The conditional nature of the promise opens up a point beyond the immediate experience of the sickness to a time when the sickness will be gone and gratitude will be in order.

The devout use novenas to measure the times of their sickness. (A novena, made up of prayers and rituals lasting for nine days, is by definition an experience of time.) Novenas, said over and over, provide an alternative way of experiencing the times of sickness, waiting, and uncertainty. Instead of being marked by fear and dread, these times are now offered to God and the saints, and are thus privileged anew. Furthermore, since novenas are usually said by several people together—in particular, the worried family and friends of the sick person—they allow for mutual support and the public expression of concern and family connectedness at a time in which the bonds between people are most vulnerable. In the shared saying of the novena, the threatened bonds are articulated, affirmed, and sanctified.

But novena time is also extraordinarily powerful time *within which* good things happen. The devout are very clear about this: changes occur while they are saying the novenas. One woman reported the following experience: "I want to say 'Thanks' to Blessed Margaret for a special favor granted. I have been praying to her and made several novenas. It was diagnosed that I had cancer of the liver and since they could not operate I was all set to have a chemotherapy pump inserted in my stomach to the liver. The doctor told me he was going to do an exploratory job first. To my delight he did not have to insert the pump because there was no cancer anywhere. I had finished my last novena two days before the operation. I truly believe it was Blessed Margaret's intercession" (LM-F-M?-60+-New Haven, Conn.). The cancer disappeared during the constant saying of the novena—"within the time of the novena," in the phrase of other correspondents—preceding the operation.

A man already cited, whose aunt had been diagnosed as having breast cancer, added, "Three days after this, she was to receive a liver scan test and bone test to see whether the cancer had spread or not, thus putting her into the terminal stages." The woman's life was suddenly endangered, the ties that bound her to her family threatened. "At this time, I began the novena in honor of Blessed Margaret of Castello. Asking that no cancer be found in those two tests. At the end of the novena, and when we were notified of the test results, no cancer had been detected." This man did something for himself and his aunt: in the saying of the novena, the time of powerlessness becomes the time of power.

Space

The space of sickness, like its time, is constricted and closed. The letters describe the familiar settings of pain and care in United States hospitals (frequently located outside the familiar daily orbits of the sick), the dull waiting rooms of clinics, the various places to which many Americans must go to be certified as eligible for the benefits they need, the room upstairs at home cluttered with medicines and medical paraphernalia, the rooms of medical procedure. The changing science and politics of American medicine in the past century, in the context of broader demographic changes, have shaped the spaces of sickness in the United States. Institutional care replaced home care in this period, largely because American medical personnel committed themselves to a particular understanding of the necessary technology of medical care. This shift also reflects the disruptive mobility of American society. Family members were defined away or defined themselves away as providers of significant care in these medically appropriated spaces. Doctors, hospital administrators, and lawyers determined what could take place in these settings, who could act in them, and what could be done; family members have subsequently been prevented from bathing, feeding, and attending to the bodily needs of the sick. In Illich's terms, "The dominance of industry has disrupted and often dissolved most traditional bonds of solidarity" (1976: 203).

Influenced by those developments in the sociology of medicine and reflecting broader cultural shifts as well, people have become less likely to provide intimate care for their sick relatives and friends, even if they may have wanted to do these things or felt morally obligated to do so. Changes in the ecology of American medicine were not solely determined from above but reflected significant moral changes in the culture at large. Family access to the spaces of sickness was restricted to well-defined times and prohibited at just those times when the presence and touch of a family member were most needed—deep in the night, in the spaces of medical procedure, in the places where the terrifying medical tests are done.

Power and authority in the spaces of sickness were reserved to medical professionals, who made the most fundamental decision regarding a person's daily life and medical care. American doctors in the twentieth century successfully eliminated all competing authority from the spaces of sickness: not only family members but alternative health practitioners were also excluded, and a code of professional ethics developed that prohibited one doctor from criticizing another to the latter's patients. Only one authority existed in the space of sickness. If the patient disagreed, his or her only recourse was to another doctor, bound by this strict code.

In these contexts, devotion to the saints has been essential for the way sick people and their families inhabit and reimagine spaces of sickness. The devout have had access to the various objects made available at the shrines—relics, statues, medals, holy oils and waters, candles, prayer cards, and images of the different saints. Usually when the devout request these objects, they ask for very specific information concerning their proper use. The uses vary: such objects serve the sick and their kin in numerous ways both within institutional settings and at home.

The relics counter the intimate—and, in hospitals, enforced—isolation of sickness. One woman, suffering from an embarrassing and painful case of hemorrhoids that made it difficult for her to leave the house, took to carrying Margaret's relic with her when she went out, and this seemed to help and comfort her: "I don't know if its the [illegible] of the relic or not, but I'm sure

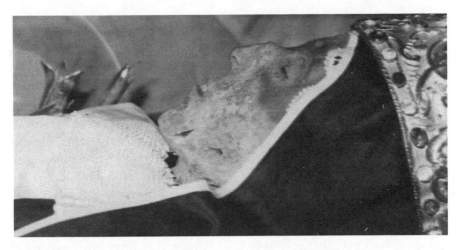

A relic of Blessed Margaret of Castello. Photographer, Sr. Pauline Quinn. Used with permission from the Dominican Fathers, Saint Patrick's Church, Columbus, Ohio, and Rev. A-J. LeCasse, O.P.

Blessed Margaret had a hand in it, at any rate I'm really thankful. (Sometimes I can go out now for about two hours.)" (QR-F-S-60?-Altoona, Pa.). The language used here—that Margaret "had a hand in" the woman's painful, humiliating situation—is significant: the relic represents the touch of the saint; it is the holy come close to the senses of the devout. This woman concludes her letter, "I think I'll be okay." The literal presence of the saint at this woman's side consoled and empowered her, giving her confidence to go out despite her fear of embarrassment.

For the family and friends of sick people, relics and other objects become the items of an intricate system of exchanges. These items reveal and sacralize the bonds of generosity, love, and responsibility that connect family and friends to the sick and the sick to the world. These sacred items also allow the family of the sick to symbolize their continuing presence with the sick person in those times and places when their literal presence is impossible, when their ministrations have been excluded, or when there is nothing else for them to do.

One man went into chemotherapy with a cloth relic given him by his family pinned "over the spot where the radium is aimed" (IR-M-M-60+-Willowdale, Ontario). Here the relic focuses the concern of the absent family and allows them to do something for their sick kin. Another correspondent told the shrine the following story: "A friend of ours who got a stroke was not expected to live, so as I was able to go see him I took the relic of the Cloth [touched to Margaret's body in Umbria] with me and rubbed it on the side that was paralyzed, and today two months later he is starting to walk a little bit" (KF-F-M-50+?-Albuquerque, N. Mex.). People in intensive care, a particularly marked place within the world of sickness, are frequently given relics by family and friends. Relics are also pinned to the clothes of rapidly declining patients.

Relics are not simply tokens of a special love between one person and another; if this were the case, they would not differ from other objects that family and friends give the sick—pictures, flowers, handmade cards, and so on. Although relics resemble these objects, the devout sick and their families evaluate them in another way. The saint whose presence is signaled by the relic is holy and thought to have special powers of healing and protection. This holy friend is also in another place—heaven, a spiritual locus of meaning fulfilled and of triumph over suffering. Relics derive their power from their connection to two places, heaven and earth, and their role in bridging the two. They open from the closed and frightening space of sickness into this other world of coherence and healing. Relics make things happen in the world. Just as novenas do, relics effect changes—they hold some part of inverting the power of the saint. Their use reshapes and transforms the world of sickness.

The devout struggle to remain firm in their belief that what is happening is God's loving will, that their sickness or the sickness of a loved one has—must have—a place in God's plans.[7] The saints—whose clothes, blood, and bones constitute the matter of the relics—have privileged access to God, and the relic makes that privilege available to the sick person. There in the room where chemotherapy is being administered, at a time when the suddenly stricken person might well wonder about the meaning and justice of the world, the relic links the patient to the source of meaning and coherence.

The relics are used in specific ways to restructure the alien space of hospitals. For example, the devout often write that during stays in the hospital, they distributed relics to their doctors, nurses, orderlies, and roommates. In this way the cult makes the unfamiliar, threatening world of the hospital a more recognizable place. Sharing the devotion with one's caretakers, furthermore, is a way of resymbolizing and sacralizing the already marked bonds one must acknowledge in the hospital; the sick will also be visited by unknown specialists, bathed and fed by unknown orderlies, looked at by groups of students, probed by unfamiliar technicians. By scattering relics among these personnel, the sick are drawing the people they must trust into the universe of their moral and religious values, and invoking the healing touch of the saint on those bonds about which they feel so ambivalent.

The relics also serve as concrete points of transformation in the devout's relocation of healing power. They are both symbols and agents of the transformation. This is perhaps the most subversive aspect of Catholic devotion to the saints in the socially constructed world of illness and healing in the United States. As the devout tell the story of their illnesses, it is not their doctors who heal them but the saints who empower and enable doctors to heal. The saints point the devout toward the right specialists and then guide the latter's hands during the operation. The saints instruct doctors when they are baffled and intervene when the doctors have reached the limits of their power and technology.

Medical historian Paul Starr (1982) has emphasized that the image and authority of the American doctor in this century result from both the efforts of the medical profession and the needs of the American people. Devotion to the saints eloquently testifies to what happens when this cherished image fails: the desperate summons of the holy patron just when the doctor's limitations are revealed articulates how high the initial estimate of the doctor was. The saints serve the devout well at this moment of a crisis at least partially of the devout's own making.

The saints also serve the devout well, however, as counters to the authority of the doctor. In place of alternative practitioners exiled by the medical profession, in place of the voices of the sick rendered increasingly less authoritative by developing diagnostic technology, and against the silence surrounding medical decisions stand the powerful figure of the saint, one of the few qualified adversaries of medical authority left in the United States for much of the twentieth century. The devout call on the saints to legitimate their choices in determining their own care. They ask the saints to help them avoid operations, and the saints usually do; as they appear in the letters, the saints seem to mistrust too much medical intervention. One woman writes to the shrine that after a bad fall she "promised Saint Margaret of Castello if she would help me without seeing a doctor I would publish my favor granted in thanksgiving for her help. I am just about 100% back to normal thanks to Saint Margaret of Castello" (Mrs. IJ-F-W?-70+-Louisville, Ky.). This is one of the most common functions of the devotion: to authorize the decision not to go to the doctor. Another woman writes, "I had a cyst on my head which caused me anxiety and fear. I prayed so I wouldn't have to go to the doctor, and it opened and drained and healed" (LF-F-?-?-Chicago, Ill.). Evident here, besides fear of the doctor, is the petitioners' sense that they should be going to the doctor, so to some extent the saint is resolving internal debate.

But the saints are also petitioned when doctors say things their patients do not want to hear, or when their patients dissent from proposed medical procedure. One woman writes, "Twenty years ago the Dr. put on me a leather and steel brace and said I'd be in a wheelchair in a short time—a few years I gradually got rid of the brace myself now eighty years old walk everyplace ride a bike etc." (GR-F-S?-80-Washington, Ind.). Frustrated by what her doctor told her, this woman turned from him and entered another relationship with Margaret Castello, which she found empowering rather than defeating, and which authorized her rejection of her doctor's authority. Another woman "stopped all treatment against Doctor's advice" after she believed herself to have been healed by a visit to a healing shrine (QR-F-?-?-Lakewood, Ohio). She concludes her letter with this rebuke: "The Doctor does not believe in Divine Healing so he is upset because he can't find [cancer] anywhere—pray for his conversion."

Denial of the priority of the doctor's healing powers, often symbolized by the triumphant actions of a relic in a moment of crisis, becomes the pivotal move in what is really a complete reimagination of the meaning of sickness and healing. Again, events have an apparent meaning and motivation—doctors choose and work, technicians study—which are reinterpreted with reference to another level of meaning and motivation. This is the sacral level on which doctors function as the tools of God and the saints. Doctors themselves are said to be "amazed" by the healing power of the relics and the recoveries of their patients, a capitulation of the medical professionals to the cosmology of the devout.

In these ways, doctors' offices, hospitals, clinics, and laboratories are all transformed into the settings of a cosmic drama, in which sacred figures come down from heaven and act on behalf of their supplicant clients. The space of sickness, like its time, becomes the special scene of God's intervention and interaction: this is where God and the saints act. These places have a meaning greater than those who administer them can understand.

Writing to the shrine itself becomes a way of manipulating the space of sickness. Mailing the letter to the faraway place parallels going on pilgrimage: it creates an opening in the bounded world of one's sickness. The discovery of the saint at an especially marked moment of sickness is the simultaneous discovery of another place. Writing the letter is a complex process. It must be divided into a series of moments, all individually important, although connected in the final process: discovering the faraway shrine in a moment of need; thinking about writing; planning the letter; gathering the materials (not a minor feature of the experience for many of the devout, who give evidence of coming rarely to pen and paper); sitting down and writing (which again may involve great struggle: people with dimming eyesight, arthritic hands, back problems, must force themselves through a letter); walking to the mailbox; telling people about the letter; waiting for a reply; and then contemplating the whole sequence all over again if there is to be a second letter. During this process, a certain spatial arrangement occurs: a new place opens up in the person's life, and by the end of the process, the sick have two vantage points from which to view their experience—their immediate surroundings and the shrine.

Some Conclusions

Any notion that the Christian response to pain and suffering is one of passive acceptance clearly must be revised. The idea that sickness is sent by God and so must be submitted to quietly is certainly present among the ideas that make up the cult of the saints, but other ideas exist as well. The sick resist the constriction that can characterize the space and time of sickness, and so they struggle actively against the threat of meaninglessness. They also refuse to inhabit the space and time allotted them by their culture. By turning to the saints they turn away from the way others define the world and reject the experience as others want it experienced. Of course, there are limits here: from the way the devout present themselves in the letters, they are probably not people with the political sophistication to demand changes in the official structuring of sick time and space. But their devotions allow them to resist on an intimate level and to shape at least some part of their experience. "I believe that a man can always make something of what is made of him," Sartre said. "This is the limit I would . . . accord to freedom" (quoted in Hebdige 1979: 167 n. 6). The cult of the saints is a way of being free in this sense.

The devotions constitute one of the oppositional practices by which people live their lives in the highly structured political and technological world of advanced industrial nations. The relationships people form with the saints have been one way that American Catholics, particularly working-class Catholics, have adapted and responded to changes in the science and organization of American medicine and to the imposed orderings of space and time that have characterized that history. Sickness is a historical form, and it would be a mistake to see in the devotions simply human response to the perennial problems of meaning posed by the disorienting onset of illness. The turn to the saints in 1320 and the turn in 1956 or 1981 resemble each other, but no more: modern turnings must be understood on their own grounds.

Finally, the popularity of the devotions encourages us to rethink our understanding of the meaning of religion in advanced technological societies. The very evolution of technology—in the precise ways that it has developed in specific political circumstances, with attendant structures of authority over experience and understanding—creates a whole new set of profound and intractable needs. These are as intimately felt and disturbing as the needs and questions of other societies. Sickness and suffering do not pose general questions of meaning and coherence; they pose specific ones. Standing on the edges with the sick and suffering, watching them cobble together responses to the crises of meaning and experience confronting them, provides a useful place from which to study the inner meanings of contemporary society.

Some Years Later

I wrote this chapter in 1989, and for its republication in this collection I went briefly back into the world of devotion to Blessed Margaret of Castello to see what had become of the cult of this unusual holy figure in the intervening years. Blessed Margaret's devotion continues to enjoy a modest popularity in the United States and in other parts of the Catholic world, with word of her spread abroad by her devout on the Internet. She is not St. Jude, the director of Margaret's shrine in Columbus, Ohio, told me, meaning that this handi-capped holy figure does not capture the widespread devotion—or compel the sizable financial contributions—that the very popular patron saint of hopeless causes does, but, he added, many people in physical and emotional distress pray to her. Blessed Margaret is most widely known today as a patroness of the Catholic antiabortion movement. Her devout say that had she been conceived in the late twentieth century, available technology would have made it possible for little Margaret's parents to have discerned her physical disabilities in utero, and given how bitterly they hated Margaret for her deformities, they surely would have aborted her. "She would have been an abortion" is a common statement about Margaret among her devout. There is a home for "crisis preg-nancies" in Bensalem, Pennsylvania, named for her, and articles recounting her parents' bitter rejection of her and Margaret's sad experience of abandon-ment and her later spiritual renown appear regularly in Catholic antiabortion publications.[8] The message is: See what great things can come of fetuses that are not aborted!!

Blessed Margaret has not been canonized yet, which is a source of great disappointment to her devout, who are convinced that one reason for the church's reluctance to make Margaret a saint, perhaps the main one, is her deformities. This may be: were she canonized, Margaret would be the only officially recognized saint in heaven with congenital disabilities, and this would mean the rupture of the ancient connection between bodily and spiritual soundness so deep in Catholic culture. It is also true, however, that the people campaigning for Margaret are out of step with the shift in recent years in Catholic understanding of the canonization process away from the miraculous as the requisite sign of sanctity (although evidence of a miracle is still required) and toward an emphasis on a holy figure's moral witness. Margaret's followers want to talk about her as a miraculous healing figure.

"I put a miracle through" just recently, the secretary of the national head-quarters of devotion to Blessed Margaret in Louisville told me in September 2002. A woman had contacted the shrine sometime before to report that a particularly severe form of diabetes was threatening to destroy her eyesight. Her family doctor sent her to a specialist, and in the time between making this appointment and going to see the new doctor the woman made a novena to Blessed Margaret. Her eyesight was completely restored during the time of the novena. "She could see when she could not see," the shrine secretary said. The specialist was amazed and agreed that the restoration of the woman's sight "was nothing short of a miracle." All the narrative elements of modern Catholic healing stories are here: the grim and almost hopeless diagnosis, the turn to a new and unfamiliar doctor, the waiting period, the transformation of the waiting period into sacred time as a novena, prayer to the saints, healing, and recognition of the miracle by medical professionals. The shrine secretary for-warded all the records of the case, given her by the woman's doctor, to Rome, but she has not heard back. The director of the shrine to Blessed Margaret in Columbus, Ohio, also told me that he has sent a number of miracle stories to Rome without effect.

Margaret's cause is promoted in the United States at two shrines, both in the care of the Dominican order and located in Dominican parishes. One is in St. Patrick's Church in Columbus, Ohio, the other in St. Louis Bertrand's in Louisville, Kentucky. The Columbus shrine is the oldest: devotion to Blessed Margaret there dates to the 1930s, the actual shrine to her was constructed in the 1950s, and it was renovated in the 1970s. The shrine in Louisville was founded in 1980. (This shrine was moved for the period 1981–86 to Philadelphia when its director was reassigned to a parish there but returned to Louisville when the Dominicans handed the church over to the Philadelphia archdiocese.) Both shrines receive regular correspondence from people seeking healing for themselves or for loved ones from physical distress; despite Margaret's new identity as an antiabortion figure, only very rarely is abortion the subject of a letter. Parents of children "with some kind of deformity" (as the Louisville shrine secretary put it) are among the most regular correspondents to the shrines, especially the mothers and fathers of children with eyesight problems or Down's syndrome. People who are losing their eyesight are the Columbus shrine's main petitioners, particularly those suffering degeneration of their retinas. The hard realities of sickness and physical disability seem to be resisting the politicization of the devotion by some of its promoters. What people want from "little Margaret," as her devout call her, is healing from physical distress, or if not this, then accompaniment in their sufferings. The shrine in Louisville has a mailing list of 1,200, the one in Columbus of about 1,000.

Sometimes bus tours of pilgrims visit the shrines, although the director of the Columbus shrine says this is not common. On June 12, 1999, members of the Mountain (West Virginia) chapter of Handicapped Encounter Christ, a Cursillo-like spiritual renewal and retreat movement for persons with disabilities founded in New York in the 1970s, went as a group to the Columbus shrine. The introduction to the Internet photo gallery of this tour praises Margaret for having "struggled to do God's will while dealing with many serious physical handicaps . . . in a time, 700 years ago, when 'affirmative action' and 'barrier-free design' were unheard of and physical disability was viewed by many as a curse."[9] Devotion to Blessed Margaret gained some national attention when Mary Jane Owen, who would later become executive director of the National Catholic Office for Persons with Disabilities, claimed to have been cured of blindness by the holy figure. Owen's story—brought to my attention by the Columbus shrine director, who considered it as clear an indication of miraculous intervention as Rome could want for Blessed Margaret's cause— has attained the fixed narrative shape of hagiography in its many retellings. Owen says she was arrogant and insensitive before losing her sight, "a person who had actively excluded people with disabilities from the graduate program in which I was involved." Then she went blind. Her eye surgeon proposed surgery to relieve the pain of blisters she suffered from, but he warned that this would not improve her vision. "That would be a miracle," he is said to have told her, "and I'm not about to perform a miracle." Four surgeries—and the intervention of Blessed Margaret—later, and her sight was restored. Owen is surrounded in her office now with images of Blessed Margaret. In a vision Margaret told Owen that "disabled people form a culture," in Owen's words, feeling greater affinity with each other than with people without disabilities.[10]

So the culture of healing shrines endures in contemporary American Catholicism, and people who are sick or their family members continue to bring their prayers and petitions to the saints to this day, they write out their hopes and terrors in letters to the many healing shrines across the American Catholic landscape, and they send in small donations as expressions of gratitude or as a way of bringing the saints into a reciprocal exchange. But there is something subterranean and sad about these shrines—Margaret's in particular but also healing shrines generally—and something almost shameful. Such shrines are very much at the margins of contemporary American Catholic culture. The cult of saints has waned in public importance in American Catholicism and in Catholic theology since the 1960s, but this alone does not account for the strange and disturbing quality attending healing shrines.

Often the shrines are in the care of idiosyncratic clergy or laity, usually the most conservative in their respective parishes, who may be involved as well in a web of marginal Catholic organizations, sometimes with paranoid or retrograde preoccupations—with Marian millennialism, for example, or with the restoration of long out-of-date devotional practice. Other people in their churches are not comfortable with the shrines—you can hear this in the voices of the people who answer parish phones when they are asked about the shrines housed in their churches. There is a clear discomfort and uneasiness about such sites and devotions. It is my impression from having visited shrines around the country that most religious orders would be relieved to be rid of their long-established shrines but cannot be, in part because the shrines are a dependable source of revenue.

Shrine culture in contemporary American Catholicism is shrouded and hidden. Catholics two blocks away from a particular shrine which they may not have had occasion to find out about generally do not know it is there. The shadows enclose even those who participate in shrine culture and even those who preside over it: devout who address their petitions to Margaret in her Columbus shrine, for instance, do not know there is another shrine in Louisville. The occlusion of shrine culture is reproduced on the level of scholarship. Healing shrines are *completely* missing, for example, from the recently published *Encyclopedia of American Catholic History* (Glazier and Shelley 1997); not a single healing shrine or devotion is mentioned, not even the immensely popular devotion to Saint Jude, even though in times of their most intense need, hundreds of thousands of Catholics in this country, across the political and religious spectrum, have recourse to such sites and prayers.

The sick and troubled bring their needs, then, to places that are themselves sick and troubled; the sick who may find themselves socially ostracized in this culture find themselves in their need in places that are likewise ignored. There is a real symmetry between the experience of illness in contemporary American culture and the fate of Catholic healing shrines. Susan Sontag suggests in *Illness as Metaphor,* (1988) moreover, that certain kinds of marked illnesses, those afflicting culturally marked parts of the bodies, for example, or those that do particularly gruesome bodily damage, often attract association with ideas, feelings, apprehensions, and fantasies that are otherwise disallowed in a culture. This seems to be the case with Margaret's appearance on the fringes of the Catholic antiabortion movement. So sick people and their families are compelled by their need to put themselves in relation to places that have become the vectors of strange associations and networks. It is striking that the sick and their families should find solace, recognition, and often enough the strength to take care of themselves with the assistance of displaced holy figures in marginal places. But so they have done in American Catholic history, and so they continue to do.

NOTES

An earlier version of this chapter appeared in *Literature and Medicine* 8 (1989): 63–77 by the Johns Hopkins University Press. Research for this study has been supported by grants from the Fulbright Foundation and Fordham University.

1. The saints are an essential part of what Foucault would call the "ensemble" of the Catholic experience of sickness: the "discourse, institutions, architectural forms, regulatory decisions, laws, administrative measure, scientific statements, philosophical, moral, and philanthropic propositions—in short, the said as much as the unsaid" (1980: 194).

2. In 1985 the shrine of Blessed Margaret of Castello was moved to Holy Name Priory, 701 East Gaul Street, Philadelphia, PA 19125. Excerpts from the letters are reprinted with permission of the shrine clergy.

3. Bibliographic note: Margaret of Castello has a popularly written biography that was based on a serious study of the relevant historical documents by the Dominican priest William R. Bonniwell, O.P. (1979). A critical edition of the earliest vita of the *beata*, with useful commentary and bibliography, is offered by M.-H. Laurent, O.P. (1990). The letters the devout write to shrines are the subject of an interesting discussion in Giovanni Antonio Colangelo (1982). Also valuable for this subject is Serge Bonnet (1976). My understanding of the cognitive functions of symbols owes a great deal to Dan Sperber (1975) and E. E. Evans-Prichard (1956). I also learned from Elaine Scarry (1985).

4. In this chapter, the shrine's correspondents are identified as in the following example:

JB-F-W-65+-Wilkes Barre, Pa.
JB = fictitious initials
F = sex, in this case female; M = male
W = marital status, in this case widow; M = married; S = single
65+ = age, in this case older than 65
Wilkes Barre, PA. = correspondent's location

A question mark alone in any of these categories indicates that internal evidence was not sufficient for any identification; a question mark following other symbols means that internal evidence did not permit a certain identification but that there was enough evidence for a reasonable estimate.

5. For a discussion of Roman Catholic teaching on the saints, see Molinari (1965).

6. This term comes from Antonio Gramsci and is discussed in Marton (1978: 15–47).

7. For the larger Christian context of these ideas, see Bowker (1970).

8. See, for example, Madeline Pecora Nugent, "Blessed Margaret of Castello," on the Web site of Priests for Life, Staten Island, New York, undated, http://priestsforlife.org/testimony/Castello.htm; "Patronness of the Unwanted," *Naples [Florida] ProLife Council Newsletter*, February 2001, http://naplesprolife.org/opage4.htm; "Celebrate Life," on-line newsletter published by the American Life League, Stafford, Virginia, November/December 1992, http://all.org/celebrate_life/cl9211.htm; and the Web site of Our Lady of Loreto Online, http://ourladyofloreto.org/ourorganizations/pavone4.htm.

9. See http://encounter-christ.freeservers.com/margaret.htm; for some brief information about Handicapped Encounter Christ (HEC), see www.campusministry.villanova.edu/hec/hec1.htm.

10. See "Catholic Disabilities Spokeswoman Regains Sight after 30 Years," *Catholic News Service*, December 27, 2001, http://home.attbi.comapridesign/pages/blessed_margaret_story.htm; see also Jennifer C. Vergara, "Congress 2001: The Workshop Experience," *The Tidings*, February 23, 2001, http://www.recongress.org/reviews/tidings2001-2-23f.htm.

REFERENCES

Bakan, David. 1968. *Disease, Pain, and Sacrifice: Toward a Psychology of Suffering*. Chicago: University of Chicago Press, 1968.
Bonnet, Serge. 1976. *Prières secrètes des Français d'aujourd'hui*. Paris: Les editions du Cerf.
Bonniwell, William R., O. P. 1979. *The Life of Blessed Margaret Castello, 1287–1320*. 2nd ed. Madison, Wis.: IDEA.
Bowker, John. 1970. *Problems of Suffering in Religions of the World*. Cambridge: Cambridge University Press.
Buytendijk, F. J. J. 1961. *Pain: Its Modes and Functions*. Trans. Eda O'Shiel. Chicago: University of Chicago Press.
Colangelo, Giovanni Antonio. 1982. Gli emigrati attraverso le lettere ai santuari di Ca-

labria e Basilicata. In *L'Emigrazione Calabrese Dall'UnitN ad Oggi, edited.* Pietro Borzomati Rome.

Evans-Prichard, E. E. 1956. *Nuer Religion.* Repr., Oxford: Oxford University Press, 1977.

Foucault, Michel. 1980. The Confession of the Flesh. In *Power/Knowledge: Selected Interviews and Other Writings, 1972–1977,* ed. Colin Gordon, trans. Colin Gordon et al. New York: Pantheon Books.

Glazier, Michael, and Thomas J. Shelley, eds. 1997. *The Encyclopedia of American Catholic History.* Collegeville, Minn.: Liturgical Press.

Hebdige, Dick. 1979. *Subculture: The Meaning of Style.* New York: Methuen.

Illich, Ivan. 1976. *Medical Nemesis: The Expropriation of Health.* New York: Pantheon Books.

Laurent, M.-H., O. P. 1940. La plus ancienne legende de la B. Marguerite de Cittàdi Castello. *Archivum Fratrum Praedicatorum* pp. 109–31.

Marton, Franco. 1978. La ricerca sulla religiosit popolare oggi in Italia. In *Religiosita popolare e cammino di liberazione,* 15–47 Bologna: Edizioni Dehoniane Bologna.

Molinari, Paul, S. J. 1965. *Saints: Their Place in the Church.* Trans. Dominic Maruca, S. J. New York: Sheed and Ward.

Scarry, Elaine. 1985. *The Body in Pain: The Making and Unmaking of the World.* New York: Oxford University Press.

Sontag, Susan. 1988. *Illness as Metphor,* 2nd ed. New York: Farrar, Straus and Giroux.

Sperber, Dan. 1975. *Rethinking Symbolism.* Trans. Alice L. Morton. Cambridge: Cambridge University Press.

Starr, Paul. 1982. *The Social Transformation of American Medicine.* New York: Basic Books.

2

The "Spiritual Healing Project": A Study of the Meaning of Spiritual Healing in the United Church of Christ

Bobbie McKay and Lewis A. Musil

In 1995, we initiated an inquiry into the meaning of spiritual healing in mainstream religious congregations. The United Church of Christ (UCC) was selected for this study because of its broad socioeconomic, ethnic, and geographic diversity. One hundred churches were invited to participate in the study. Ninety-six churches responded favorably. Five additional churches were invited and agreed to participate to ensure the diversity of the sample.

The United Church of Christ was formed in 1957, joining the Congregational Christian Church and the Evangelical and Reformed Church. Presently there are 1,407,000 members participating in 6,100 churches (Lindner 2002: 359) located primarily on the East and West Coasts and in the Midwest. The denomination is described as "liberal/protestant" (Dudley and Roozen 2001: 5), Christ centered, biblically based, and oriented primarily toward caring and social action (United Church of Christ 2002: 54).[1] The UCC has been supportive of women clergy, has been open and affirming of participation of gays at all levels, and is a leading advocate of civil rights and social change. Currently, two optional healing services are available in the UCC: one for individuals, another for groups. Many UCC churches include lay intercessory prayer groups.

Words and Stories of Spiritual Healing

The sample of 101 individual congregations included more than 2,000 people between the ages of eighteen and eighty-five. Letters were sent to the selected congregations to participate in open, informal, data-gathering sessions on the subject of spiritual healing. The researchers were described as data gatherers, not spiritual healers. Participants, who were self-selected, were not required to have had an experience of spiritual healing to participate. More women than men attended the meetings (approximately 2:1), reflecting the gender distribution in Protestant churches in general (Dudley and Roozen 2001: 12). The group size ranged, on average, from 18 to 20 people.

Participants were asked to consider two questions: (1) What do the words "spiritual healing" mean to you; what do you associate with those words? (2) What stories do you tell about spiritual healing according to your own definition? No instructions were given as to the nature of spiritual healing or regarding the kind, content, or form of the stories sought. Participants were informed they were free to respond or to remain silent.[2]

Within the group meetings, one of every two participants told a story of spiritual healing. A few people reported to us after the meetings that they also had a story but did not choose to tell it to the group: "I don't feel comfortable telling this story in this group"; "My story is between me and God."[3]

The word used most frequently by participants in this study to describe the experience of spiritual healing was "peace." Typically, peace was defined as a transformed state of being, not an emotional response (as in feeling peaceful). The stories offered by participants revealed a core understanding of spiritual healing as an experience of the presence or action of God in one's life which was transforming. This definition was offered by participants representing a variety of gender, ethnic, socioeconomic, geographic, and creedal subgroups (McKay and Musil 2000).

Three Narrative Frameworks

The stories were remarkably consistent in terms of key themes of surrender, surprise, transformation, and peace. We shall return to each of these themes shortly. The plot structure—the narrative framing—of the stories was more variable. Three distinct kinds of stories were shared in the groups: (1) stories of spiritual healing in which no physical disease was present, (2) stories of spiritual healing accompanying the cure of a physical disease, (3) and stories of spiritual healing in which a physical disease was present but not cured.

The largest number of stories involved spiritual healing with no disease present: stories taken from ordinary life, with or without a life stressor. All the stories dealt in some way with the recognition of God's presence or action and a deep sense of healing. For instance, "One time, when I was barreling into church, late as usual, I saw a woman just standing in the doorway. I was feeling pretty down and she seemed sort of anxious. I didn't know her, so I don't know why I did this. But I said, 'Are you OK?' We started to talk and she perked up. I became animated too and soon I was smiling (so was she) and God was present to both of us. She was changed, and so was I! It was that simple." The main elements of this story include the ordinary nature of the occasion (going to church); the unexpected action ("I don't know why I did this"); the awareness of God's presence ("God was present"); and the experience of transformation ("she was changed and so was I!"). The story also expresses the basic simplicity of the experience ("It was that simple").

The following account provides another example:

> When my husband died in his early fifties, I thought I handled it
> OK. But after a while, I wasn't feeling well physically. I went to the
> doctor who said, "There's nothing wrong with you. You're just griev-
> ing." He mumbled something that sounded like I should go home
> and grieve. But I didn't go home. Instead I went to a restaurant
> where my husband and I would go for coffee. When the waitress
> came over, she looked at me and then said, "You're not feeling well
> are you?" I nodded, surprised that she noticed. And then she said,
> "Would you like me to pray for you?" I was really taken aback, but
> figured she meant she would include me in her prayers that night,
> or at church on Sunday. So I said, "Yes." She must have known
> what I was thinking because she said, "No, I mean right here, right
> now." I hesitated, and then I nodded. (I couldn't speak.) She took
> my hands, and in the middle of that crowded restaurant, she prayed
> the most eloquent prayer I had ever heard. I felt a marvelous calm,
> and I felt healed.

This story contrasts two kinds of interactions: the uncaring attitude of the (high-status) doctor and the deeply caring action of the (low-status) waitress. It is a story of the unexpected surprise, common to many of the stories we have heard. It also talks about the willingness of the waitress to bring the gift of God's presence into a situation that might seem inappropriate for such intimacy, and the equally important willingness of the woman telling the story to accept the "gift" being offered. The willingness to give and to receive is a theme in many of the stories of spiritual healing.

The second-largest group in our study included stories of the physical cure of a disease. These accounts are particularly dramatic, generally involving mi-raculous deliverance from disease and death and frequently involve petitionary prayer: "Then I prayed: 'God, there is no way I can convince you to do what I want. But I want him to be well. . . . Please just help me and the children get through this.' He was totally cured."

Several people who had felt alienated from God were able to reconnect to him through the use of prayer in a crisis situation:

> I had several large blood clots which the doctors could not reach and a deep infection in my brain. The doctors suggested further tests . . . but I said, 'I've had enough of that stuff.' They said that I would probably die. Now, I was an agnostic, and that was just the way it was. I called my parents to come to the hospital because I didn't want to die alone. Then I thought, 'If I'm going to die, maybe I ought to pray.' I went into the chapel and in that praying experience, I suddenly felt that my soul was cleansed, that I was going to be OK. At 2:00 A.M., I broke into tears and cried all night. I knew I was being loved . . . but how could God love me.. a sinner? The next day, they did a CT scan. The blood clots were gone, along with the infection. I was healed.

Many of our stories involved the letting go of outcomes and an experience of surrender, as opposed to insisting on physical curing or the granting of one's prayer request:

> Twenty-seven years ago, I was awakened by a voice saying, "After the operation, you will be all right." Seeing as I was not sick, I just forgot all about it. Some years later, I was diagnosed with pancreatic cancer and told that surgery was very risky, the chances for survival almost zero. I desperately tried to control my recovery. But I'd lost forty pounds and was going downhill fast. . . . I prayed with a prayer group. The next day, somehow . . . I don't know how . . . I just let go and said, OK to the surgery. From the moment I surrendered, my life has been a blessing. I survived the operation. I slowly got better. Now every morning, I wake up and say, "thanks" for my new life. The voice was right.

While this is one of the few prophetic stories we collected, it nevertheless embodies themes that are common to many stories of physical cure: the joining of a prayer group and praying for recovery with the group; the giving up of trying to control the disease; the moment of surrender: or saying "yes" to everything, regardless of the outcome; and the common reaction that healing was the benchmark of a transformed life and a new beginning.

The concept of healing taking place, even when there is no curing or when the patient actually dies, may seem paradoxical. But we heard a number of stories in which people described themselves as healed, even though they were not cured of their disease. These stories reflect the stated difference between curing and healing: curing is not necessary to the process of healing.

> In 1991, I was told that I had a terminal illness and was given six to twenty-four months to live. I was a successful, top corporate executive. I cared only for my pleasure and power. But in the face of this disease, and since I have become blind . . . [blindness was a progressive part of his disease] somehow all the women that I meet now are beautiful and all the men are good-looking. . . . I can only tell you how grateful I am for my disease because it has transformed my life.

This story emphasizes the transformational presence or action of God in the life of an individual. The feeling of gratitude for one's illness ("I am grateful for my disease") transcends the disease entity itself and death as well. One person remarked, "Death *is* the great healing":

> My father was a minister and spent a great deal of energy working for the church. Then, he had a heart attack, which left him blind and disabled. He was given six months to live, but lived sixteen years. From this affliction, he made an amazing transition to becoming accepting of his limitations. He assumed a different form of ministry, becoming a spiritual adviser and counselor, and saw this new ministry as the "gift" of his affliction. I was deeply affected by the change in him and decided to go into the ministry myself. We were both healed . . . each in our own way.

This story illustrates the idea of illness as a "gift" rather than a problem and affirms the experience of the healing of others in contact with a patient who is spiritually healed (though not physically cured).

Sometimes prayers for "curing" become the occasion for "healing": "Last August my mother called me and told me my father had stomach cancer. He was on a dozen different prayer chains. After the surgery the report was not good—he was given three to six months to live. But he said to the doctor, 'I guess I'll get to heaven sooner than I expected.' He and all of us had prayed for a cure. But he got a healing instead."

For this participant, unanswered prayer also became an opportunity for a new understanding of spiritual healing: "My son was diagnosed with cancer. I prayed . . . did it all . . . it was no use. He died in seventy-seven days. I said to God, 'I did everything you told me to do. You said you would heal him. But you didn't.' And then I remembered all the trouble he had . . . the hard life he lived, and now he was healed of all of that. This was my introduction to spiritual healing."

Major Narrative Themes

Despite the rather sharp differences in plot or structure of the stories, several core themes echo across all the categories: surrender, acceptance, surprise, transformation, the experience of peace, the experience of God's healing presence and love, the use of prayer in the healing process, and an absence of emphasis on the role of suffering. These themes were often interwoven, creating a powerful portrait of the experience of spiritual healing.

Many stories involved the experience of surrender: the giving up of either the control of a situation or the outcome. For example, one participant explained: "And then I said the hardest words I've ever spoken: OK, God. I give it up. If he lives, you know that's what I want. And if he dies . . . that's all right too. I put it in your hands. And in that moment, *I* was healed."

Many of the stories contained an element of surprise. Surprise, in the context of spiritual healing, represents a paradigm shift: a precursor to the experience of transformation. As one participant recounted "I looked for God in church, and God found me in my house when I was cleaning."

All our stories described an experience of transformation that was a critical part of the participants' spiritual healing. People were not simply "changed." Their lives were transformed and altered. A minister attending a family whose mother was dying related: "The love simply flowed from her and flowed back to her from her family. It was God's love that was flowing between all of us. She was being loved as she died. I still have a total sense of that day, and it transformed my ministry. The memory is as alive today as it was then. I will never forget it."

In all our groups the pervasiveness of the experience of "peace" was a hallmark of spiritual healing. This "peace" represented a change of state, which transcended challenging and even life-threatening situations by making the outcomes irrelevant: "I felt God's arms around me and I knew I would survive, even if the worst happened."

The use of prayer was common in the narratives of our participants. One woman reported that her own petitionary prayer for the cure of her cancer was answered directly: "I was diagnosed with a three-centimeter tumor in my right breast. I asked Jesus to heal me. When they did the surgery, they found that the tumor was gone and clean margins all around the site. I fell in love with God!"

Most of the churches we visited had prayer groups of some kind. These groups were engaged in petitionary prayers for members of the congregation, friends, and family on an ongoing basis. One member of a prayer group reported: "I had cancer of the stomach and was given six months to live. I held hands with my prayer group, and we prayed. That was twenty-five years ago. And I'm still here praying and thanking God for God's miracles in my life and in the lives of others." Many people described the importance of prayer in their individual experiences of spiritual healing.

Many of the stories of healing without cure are stories of people dying. In these accounts, caretakers or family members frequently are involved in the healing process through the catalyst of imminent death and the unique possibilities for relationship it offers. For instance, "My healing was in the form of an understanding between me and a young man of my age who was dying of leukemia. In the course of becoming his doctor, I also became his friend. The last time I saw him before he died, he took my hand and said, 'Thanks for taking care of me.' I helped him, but he uplifted me. For me it was a healing, not a cure."

The Power of Shared Stories

As we listened to the participants share their experiences in the groups, we were struck by how often the telling of the stories was accompanied by tears, not of sadness but of the depth and the remembered reality of the experience: "I'm sorry. . . . I can't tell this story without crying. . . . It changed my life."

Participants told us that while they remembered their stories in vivid detail, they rarely shared them with others. The reasons given for not sharing were the fear of being seen as "crazy" or "too religious." For many of the participants, this was the first time they had shared their story: "I've been a member of this church for thirty-five years, and this is the first time I've had the chance to tell this story"; "I've known you for twenty-five years, and you've never shared this story." This reluctance to share these stories of spiritual healing has been noted in Jodie Shapiro Davie's research on Presbyterian women: "These dramatic stories . . . are rarely shared with anyone, even within the family. . . . There is a discernible pattern of prohibition against openness about personal spirituality. . . . The culture of privacy . . . permits freedom of spirituality, even as it ensures that individual spiritual lives remain hidden" (1995: 129, 135).

Specific behaviors observed during the group sessions included sustained and attentive listening and respectful, intimate silence, with no offerings of advice or explanations concerning the meaning of the stories. Listeners expressed their gratitude for the gifts of words and stories by words of thanks and appreciative statements like "Wow!" or "What a wonderful story!" Nonverbal responses included hugs and/or a supportive hand extended in silent acknowledgment of the importance of the experience for both the teller and the listener. Not infrequently, people in the group responded with tears of their own, an expression of understanding, gratitude, and the depth to which they had been touched.

Insofar as these stories describe experiences of the perceived presence or action of God in one's life, they all are relational, describing the relationship between God and the storyteller and that between the teller and the one who hears, responds, and is touched by the story.

A number of people reported that just being in the group and hearing the stories of others produced a healing for them: "Something is happening here in the group tonight. I almost didn't come. But this experience has turned out to be terribly important to me. . . . There is healing happening right here. I can feel it." Other people indicated they had similar experiences but were unable to identity them as such, due to a lack of vocabulary, venue, or theological grounding. "I've had that experience. I just didn't know what to call it."

Occasionally people experienced a sense of healing while sharing their own stories in the group: "I was so angry when she died . . . so angry with God for not saving her. . . . But here tonight, I'm beginning to see that something happened when she was dying. We became close, intimate in a way we would never have become, when we had all the time in the world. I miss her so. . . . But I'm seeing it differently tonight. . . . I'm not angry. I'm beginning to feel . . . healed."

The group that appeared to have the most difficulty sharing their own stories of spiritual healing were the clergy, as evidenced by their silence in the group meeting or their surprise when they realized how seldom they had shared these experiences: "I am a clergywoman, and this is the first time I have ever told my own story of spiritual healing"; "I was completely out of touch with the experience that led me into the ministry."

With no explicit instruction as to content or form, all the shared stories were stories of critical moments in which God became present in the participants' lives. Participants did not tell "life stories" or "spiritual journeys." Rather, they showed us "snapshots" of God, which had unexpectedly become part of their scrapbooks of life but were strangely nonreligious. By this we mean there were no experiences told from an organized theological point of view or from particular creedal assumptions. Instead, they seemed to reflect the response of ordinary people who were transformed by what they understood to be the presence or action of God in their lives.

The participants described experiences of spiritual healing that were deeply meaningful and profoundly spiritual, unexpected surprises that interrupted ordinary life but were rarely shared before our meeting. There were no formulaic strategies to create these experiences (no ten steps to spiritual healing), nor were there external rules or measurements to determine the validity of one's experiences. People described a direct experience with God that was highly individualized and carried no strings. One was free to respond or not.

The general pattern within the stories therefore included a discovery of the presence or action of God in the middle of ordinary life, the recognition of that discovery, and the decision to accept the transformative possibilities that followed. When one of these stories was retold in our meetings, frequently the person telling it recontacted the experience in a very basic and profound way, as if the spirit and energy of the original experience were still present, even after thirty or forty years of time had passed. Such experiences served to validate the story as well as the extraordinary mystery of the experience.

NOTES

1. The official logo of the UCC is "To Believe Is to Care; to Care Is to Do."

2. A nine-page questionnaire on the nature and impact of the spiritual healing experience, church experience history, and demographic data was completed by approximately 90 percent of the participants and processed by the Center for Learning and Health, Department of Psychiatry and Behavioral Sciences, The Johns Hopkins University School of Medicine.

3. The questionnaires also provided the opportunity for people to write their stories anonymously.

REFERENCES

Davie, Jody Shapiro. 1995. *Women in the Presence: Constructing Community and Seeking Spirituality in Mainstream Protestantism*. Philadelphia: University of Pennsylvania Press.
Dudley Carl S. and David A. Roozen 2001. *Faith Communities Today: A Report on Religion in the U.S. Today*. Hartford, Conn.: Hartford Institute for Religion Research.
Lindner, Eileen W., ed. 2002. *The Yearbook of American and Canadian Churches*. Nashville, Tenn.: Abingdon Press.
McKay, Bobbie, and Lewis Musil. 2000. *Healing the Spirit: Stories of Transformation*. Allen, Tex.: Thomas More Press.
United Church of Christ. 2002. *United Church of Christ Resources*. Cleveland: United Church of Christ.

3

Ritual and Magic: Two Diverse Approaches to Inner Healing in the Cambodian American Community

Thomas J. Douglas and Sophon Mam

Since the arrival of the first Cambodian refugees to the United States in the 1980s, following the Vietnam War, Cambodian immigrants in academic literature have been treated primarily as victims of a massive social disruption who have been largely unable to cope with the aftermath of the killing fields. They have been one of the most highly pathologized of refugee groups in the United States, and are frequently referred to in social science literature as highly likely to suffer from alcoholism, gambling addictions, spousal abuse, and unemployment; are considered at risk for youth violence; and are often diagnosed, almost carte-blanche, as suffering from post-traumatic stress disorder (PTSD). Much of this prior literature has presented Cambodian refugees as an impotent group, persons who are unable or unwilling to respond to their negative situations. What is often missing is a discussion of the refugees' own responses to their circumstances, a presentation of how they are countering some of the negative social forces they have had to face in their daily lives. The following two vignettes present specific ways in which Cambodian refugees are responding to some of the negative social forces of their lives. The two responses presented here are remarkably different, but they reveal an underlying unity. In both cases, there is a purification of the psyche, a cleansing of the old, and a renewal of the spirit. Although these two cases are operating from two decidedly different religious traditions, the goals are the same: the refinement of the soul, the regeneration of the spirit, and the ending of a cycle of suffering.

Vignette 1: A Unique Approach to Inner Healing in the Cambodian American Community

—T.J.D.

One summer afternoon I arrived at the Seattle Cambodian Buddhist temple, or wat, where Saveoun,[1] an athletic, handsome Cambodian man in his early twenties, greeted me in a way that was more friendly than usual. Like nearly all the Cambodians I had met in Seattle, Saveoun had been quite amicable from our first meeting, but today he was especially warm. It took a moment for me to recognize him because his head was freshly shaved, in the style of a Buddhist monk. When I asked him what was up, he told me that his father had recently arrived from Cambodia and that he was visiting with the monks in the *wat* even as we spoke. He then urged me to come inside the wat and meet his father.

We took off our shoes and walked through the sliding glass doors that separated the covered patio from the main shrine area inside the temple. The wat had once been a house, and except for the construction of the Buddhist altar in the front living room, the building still strongly resembled a single-story American home. In fact, from the street it was hard to recognize that this particular home was anything out of the ordinary relative to other west Seattle tract homes, unless one happened to notice the sign on the garage door declaring in both Khmer and English that this building was indeed a wat.

I had expected to see Saveoun's father seated in front of the indoor shrine with some of the monks, since this is where conversations are generally held. However, his father was not there. Instead, Saveoun led me into the bedroom of the temple's head monk, a room into which I had never before been invited.

The bedroom was small, perhaps twelve by ten feet. It had a single window, covered with a rather faded saffron shade. There were a couple of old, weathered wooden dressers and a desk crammed in against three of the walls; a large double closet with doors in need of a new coat of paint took up the fourth wall. A small refrigerator contained the monk's diabetic medications. Books, mostly paperback, were distributed throughout the room, and a number of these books lay on top of the queen-sized bed, which completely dominated the room. Seeing the books piled all over the bed, I thought that they surely must prevent the elderly monk from getting a good night's rest. I chuckled to myself when I noticed that the inexpensive-looking blond headboard was nearly identical to the one my parents had purchased for their own bedroom in the 1960s. The bed itself was covered in a saffron-colored bedspread, which along with the satin pillowcases and even the room's lampshade, more or less matched the robes worn by all the monks. A box of insulin syringes, Kleenex, hand lotion, and Vaseline lay on the floor near the bed. A heavy burgundy curtain could be drawn tight around the perimeter of the bed for complete privacy.

The elderly monk sat on the bed, seated in the traditional Cambodian style with his legs folded under his body, his feet politely pointed away from anyone seated in the room. His brown eyes had a blue tinge, probably caused by mild cataracts. Rugs covered a narrow aisle between the bed and the wall on which sat three Cambodian men, all of whom I supposed to be in their sixties. Saveoun first made the proper acknowledgments to the head monk and then introduced me to the first of the three men seated on the floor. This man was Saveoun's father, recently arrived from Cambodia. The other two men, both of whom I had met in the past, were old friends of his father. All of them received me warmly. Saveoun's father was especially cordial, and after I took a seat on the floor next to him, he squeezed my thigh repeatedly as if we had known each other for years.

Saveoun's father told me, in English, that he was here in Seattle visiting his children and grandchildren on a ninety-day visa (I would later learn that he was also in Seattle for cancer treatment). He told me that he had once been an officer in the Cambodian navy and had traveled extensively in the past. Apparently he had learned English many years earlier during the Lon Nol regime in Cambodia. His English impressed me, especially since I found that most of the senior Cambodian immigrants I had met were far from comfortable speaking the language.

During our conversation an older woman entered the bedroom. She first prostrated herself before the head monk and then sat on the floor with the rest of us. The laymen in the room referred to her respectfully as *Om* (mother). She was not dressed as a nun, so I assumed she was a friend or relative of Saveoun's father.

After a while the "right-hand" monk (the head monk's younger assistant) entered the room and sat on the bed with his mentor. He had brought a bowl of *tek mon* (blessed rosewater) and a wand with long green fibers attached to a wooden handle that is used during Buddhist ceremonies to lightly splash worshipers with the sacred water. The fact that this younger monk had brought this instrument with him made me suddenly realize that what was taking place here was going to be more than a casual conversation among old acquaintances. The monks were preparing for some sort of ritual.

Saveoun, who had left the bedroom shortly after introducing me to his father, returned. I moved over so that he could sit on the floor next to his father. The older woman, who up to this point had been engaged in conversation with the others, excused herself, letting the room revert to a space of men.

I was surprised when Saveoun turned to his father and prostrated himself before him, an act I previously had seen reserved for monks. Although I had been told by one of the monks that Cambodians considered their parents to be "their first gods," I had never seen a son or daughter treat either parent in this manner. Saveoun turned toward his father and lowered his face until it touched the ground three times. I had only seen this kind of respect shown to a monk or to the Buddha.

Saveoun's father began to speak, and his son's eyes became heavy with tears. Saveoun had had a rather tumultuous past, fraught with sexual incontinence, youthful recklessness, and sometimes violence. His father was urging him, in front of the monks, to mend his ways. As his father spoke, Saveoun kept his head bowed and his hands folded together as if in prayer or meditation. What started as barely audible sighs and gasps eventually became a flood of cries and wails as Saveoun openly wept before his father. The two men sitting with Saveoun's father reached over and rubbed Saveoun's back and shoulders as he wept. The two monks, still sitting above us on the bed, looked on but said nothing.

Tears flowed from Saveoun's chin and fell in heavy drops onto the carpets. Clear mucus flowed from his nose and mouth. Tears flowed down his father's cheeks as well, but this did not stop him from speaking to his son. He did, however, offer his son tissues from time to time and occasionally reached over to pat him on the shoulder. The monks looked on and smiled occasionally, though otherwise they appeared to me to be relatively nonchalant about what I considered a highly emotional situation.

Incidentally, it was an August afternoon and quite warm. The door to the bedroom had been shut for privacy, and the air was heavy and thick from the breathing of seven adult men in this tiny space. The small electric fan on the desk did not seem to move the air at all. My heart and head were pounding from both the heat and the emotional tension in the room, and I wondered if I might pass out and ruin the whole event.

Saveoun's father finally stopped speaking, and the five of us seated on the floor directed our attention to the monks. Like his father, the monks spoke to Saveoun about the errors of his past. But their talk was somewhat less serious than the one given by the father, and occasionally a chuckle erupted among the men as something humorous was said. This seemed to put Saveoun at ease, and his tears began to slow and eventually stop altogether. Yet, as the monks spoke, the other Khmer men directed Saveoun to sit with his head lowered in a show of deference. All the men had their heads bowed as the monks spoke, but Saveoun was made by his father to hold his head even lower, relative to the others.

After about twenty minutes, one of the monks took up the wand and the silver bowl of rosewater, and, in unison, the two monks began to chant in ancient Pali. As they chanted, they sprinkled all of us liberally with rosewater from the wand. Eventually the two monks reached a point in the ritual chanting where the other men, including Saveoun, joined in. They all knew the Pali phrases by heart (most Khmer memorize Pali phrases from a young age, though without knowing their literal meanings). After the chanting was over, Saveoun's father spent more time instructing his son on how to live a moral life, how to follow dharma (the path to enlightenment, the basic principles of the Cosmos), how to behave and be a good Khmer man. At one point his father even parodied the way Americans greet each other. He made fun of the way Americans say "Hi" and wave to each other. He laughed and said that this was no good, that this demonstrated a lack of respect and was unacceptable behavior. He told Saveoun that he should greet his fellow Khmer in the traditional Cambodian way, with folded hands and bent head and a proper exchange of greetings. Finally, the event ended, and Saveoun's father asked me to take pictures of him with the monks and his son and various acquaintances to take back to Cambodia. The whole affair had lasted about two hours.

Later that afternoon, Saveoun asked me to give him a ride to the casino where he worked. During the ride over he told me that he wanted to get his American citizenship, he wanted to change jobs and do something his family approves of,[2] he wanted to become settled, to stop playing around, to go to Cambodia and maybe find a wife to bring back to America. He told me that his current girlfriend was not the proper one for marriage, that he should find a more suitable partner.

Returning to the temple a couple of days later, I asked one of the monks about the ritual that Saveoun had gone through. He explained to me that the ceremony is called the *lukh riasey* (from bad to good ceremony). He told me that this ceremony was intended to change Saveoun's luck and to rid his mind of the negative influences that had been holding him back. Saveoun, like some other Cambodian young men, had gone through a period in his life where he had been involved with gangs and gang violence. Other members of the Seattle community had told me Saveoun had sold drugs and even guns in the past. They also told me he had been fired from a previous job for physically assaulting one of his former employers, apparently kicking his boss so severely that he had to be taken to the hospital. Saveoun had tried to mend his ways in the past by serving as a monk in one of the other Khmer wats, but I was told that he had miserably failed in this endeavor and had been forced to quit the temple.

One monk told me that although the *lukh riasey* was designed to change Saveoun's luck, it would do him no good if he did not also dedicate himself to following proper Buddhist dharma. He said that if Saveoun did not initiate a change in his heart, the ritual would do him no good. Saveoun needed to dedicate himself to following the moral path. This particular monk even expressed his doubts, based on his knowledge of Saveoun's past, that the ritual would indeed initiate any positive change.

Saveoun asked me if I could give him a lift over to his relatives' home in Oregon that autumn when I started my drive back to California. He said that he wanted to get away from his life in Seattle. I agreed to pick him up at the temple on my way back home. When the appointed day arrived, however, he told me that he changed his mind and had decided to stay longer in Seattle. He wanted to spend more time with his father, who was undergoing medical treatment.

Like members of the Seattle community, I wondered if Saveoun was really ready to make a change in his life or if he had merely gone through the ritual to please his ailing father. Two months after returning to California, however, I received a phone call from him. He was in San Diego and was serving as a monk in one of the temples there. His father had returned to Cambodia after his treatments, and Saveoun was keeping his promise to live a moral life, the life of a good Khmer man.

Vignette 2: One Cambodian Immigrant's Search for Answers beyond Buddhism

—T.J.D. and S. M.

Like many Cambodian immigrants, Sophon's parents fled Cambodia to Thailand near the end of the Pol Pot holocaust when Vietnam invaded Cambodia. Sophon was born in a Thai refugee camp and emigrated with his parents to Massachusetts as an infant. After about one year, Sophon's family decided to move to the greater Long Beach, California, area. Many other Cambodian immigrants scattered across the United States did the same, and today Long Beach is home to the largest Cambodian community in the nation.

As a child, Sophon went to the local wat regularly and grew up in what he describes as "a normal Buddhist family." Sophon says that from childhood he remembers having a desire to take away pain, perhaps because of the experiences he knew most Khmer immigrants had suffered. When asked as a kindergartner what he wanted to be when he grew up, Sophon, unlike his peers who said that they wanted to be teachers or policemen or astronauts, responded by saying that he "wanted to help people."

Religion and magic have long fascinated Sophon. He recalls that when he was a child, his mother would tell him stories of Cambodian sacred magic, magic that could be used for good or ill. He was keenly interested in the Khmer monkhood and spent two weeks as a child living in the local wat for the purpose of religious education. However, his interests were not limited to Buddhism. Sophon also loved watching the Roman Catholic mass, finding the Latin mass beautiful and breathtaking; at the age of twelve, he had hopes of becoming an altar boy, but this dream was never fulfilled.

At about this time, Sophon's older brother began to get involved in local Cambodian gangs. This was a hard time for Sophon, who had always regarded his big brother with enormous respect. Now his brother was becoming violent and started to shut Sophon out of his life. Sophon felt angry and lost; his world was dramatically changing.

Then Sophon discovered a book on Wiccan beliefs, which he had picked up in a local occult shop. What initially attracted him to Wicca was the idea that it could give him power, especially at a time and age in his life when he felt largely disempowered in a world where gang violence, drugs, and racial tension seemed to rule the day. He now admits that he "got into magick for all the wrong reasons . . . it was about power."[3] He wanted to get back at a world in which he, as well as his friends and family, had suffered. He imagined magick would enable him to get what he wanted in this world or perhaps even allow him to take revenge against those who had wronged him.

At the age of fifteen, after more than a year of reading occult books and trying to practice some magick on his own, Sophon joined his first Wicca order, which he contacted through individuals he met at the occult shop. He was immersed in Wicca theology and learned about basic principles of duality, uniformity, and laws of cycles (what he refers to as cycles of cause and effect). He told me that "the circle is seen as sacred because everything returns to the same starting points." He added, "The universe does not give you what you want, but gives you what you need." He told me that the others in the group taught him that magick was not about using power to seek revenge or to receive personal gains of wealth or prestige. Rather, it was about "basically reclaiming [one's] own personal power."

When Sophon was sixteen, he was ordained as a Wicca priest by this group. However, as a result of internal conflicts, he eventually left this first "church" and joined another group of practitioners. In doing so, he relinquished his claim to a priestly ordination. At the age of twenty he would be ordained again as a priest by his second group. Today he serves as a high priest at a Long Beach Wicca church.

When I asked Sophon to explain what system of magick his church subscribes to, he told me that it is actually an amalgamation of many different systems, all of which he believes lead to the same path. He explained that his group emerged from a magical fraternal order known as Melchizedek, or the Great White Brotherhood, but ties with this organization have been severed. Elements of the Golden Dawn, the Freemasons, the Rosicrucians, Wicca, Druidic practices, the Kabbalah, the cult of Isis, and others have been combined into the system of magick used by his group. Many of these fraternal orders of magick had emerged during the Spiritualist movements of the late 1800s and early 1900s (though some have links that are far older), but most have undergone massive transformations over the past century. This fact is reflected in Sophon's statement that no pagan group practicing today should claim that it derives from any one original or "pure" form; rather, he feels they are all syncretic combinations of earlier religious systems.

Intrigued by the number of different traditions that influence the pagan practices of Sophon's group, I asked him how many ways there are to perform magick. He responded, "How many people are there in the world? We all practice magick at a different level, with differences in skill and power. During any type of religious service, energy is always raised, whether it be a Wiccan ritual or a pastor reading from the Psalms." Sophon went on to explain that magick is everywhere, in the air we breathe, the water we drink, and the people who share the planet with us. Everything is in touch with and touched by the divine.

Sophon further explained that magick offers a perspective that he believes is not found in any dominant religious practice today. He believes that magick opens one's consciousness to new ideas and new perspectives on life and death. Unlike many other religious beliefs, paganism claims that the gods did not intend that we suffer. In other religions, he feels, "suffering is ingrained in our minds. I've suffered because I've sinned. I've suffered because of past evil deeds, things of that sort." In contrast, magick allows one to take responsibility for one's own actions. Having done so, one can make positive changes in one's own life and end any cycles of suffering. Magick teaches the practitioner to "learn to let go, you know, [to stop] harboring intense negative emotions. They learn to let go. It lets them learn to go with the natural flow of things, to stay in balance." Although Sophon did not explicitly say it, the goal of Buddhism, Sophon's natal religion, is very nearly the same. In Cambodian Buddhism, one also seeks to end the cycles of suffering. Traditional Cambodian Buddhists attempt, through chanting and meditation, to free oneself of earthly desires, to purify the soul, to ultimately break out of the cycle of suffering. For Sophon, the cleansing of the soul comes through the performance of ritual spells and prayers to rid people of negative energies and help them achieve balance in their lives.

Sophon teaches regular classes in Long Beach designed to help interested persons learn the proper magickal systems and techniques. He explained to me that spells, on a purely psychological level, help to signify the beginning of change in a person's life. I asked if he believed that spells were merely about psychology, about creating a mental change. He said, "No, spells work at the psychological, spiritual and physical levels. They help to open up the pathways . . . to provide the drive." Spells work at multiple levels, but "whenever someone does a spell, psychologically it tells [that person] that things have been put in motion toward a change."

I asked Sophon if a spell was necessary for a change to occur. He answered, "Yes and no. . . . Everything can be considered magick, the air we breathe down to the emotions we feel for people [even] down to our perspectives, because it is a natural tool." For Sophon, magick is at work all the time, whether or not a spell or ritual is used:

[Magick] is intrinsic. When we fear, we set up our own guards. Physically it may be avoiding eye contact or giving a look. But [fear]

is also happening at the physical, mental, and spiritual levels. At a
spiritual level, the auric field around you changes [when you fear].
Things like the aura will spike. It may seal up close to your own
body in order to protect yourself . . . it may set up your own instinctive barrier. People can pick up on this; they can sense it when they
walk into a room and feel it. When you're happy, your aura spreads
out; it spreads out when you are happy. People pick up on the other
energies around them . . . people will pull their aura back when
things are negative around them. And as the spiritual is attacked, it
will also show itself in the physical.

Sophon stated that negative spiritual energy accumulates and manifests
itself in the mental and physical worlds as well. Various magick rituals can rid
a person of these buildups and help to ease him or her out of negative spiritual,
psychological, and physical energies. Such spiritual cleansings can be done in
many ways, through the use of incense, holy waters, blessed salts, and ritual
baths. Prayers are always involved in these cleansings as well and can be directed to whatever deity the supplicant prefers. For Wiccan practitioners, this
is usually some form of the Lord and the Lady, what Sophon and his followers
consider to be the dual halves of the Almighty, and both members of the divine
couple take on numerous forms.

Sophon has trained approximately eighty students over the past five years,
and I learned that some 20 percent of those, as well as about 30 percent of the
members of his church, are former addicts, recovering from drugs or alcohol
abuse. Traditional twelve-step programs, as well as most religious programs
aimed at helping addicts, had not met their needs. Sophon felt that these mainstream approaches are too focused on notions of guilt. He believed that their
particular approaches to a "higher power" and to divinity are too narrowly
defined, following a Western notion of God as "Father" only—masculine, dominant, sometimes angry and jealous. In contrast, Sophon believes a system of
magick allows for a reclaiming of the self and of one's personal power in the
world. For this same reason, he believed that magick attracts worshipers who
are suffering from HIV, persons who often feel alienated by dominant religious
communities.

As an example of physical, emotional, and spiritual healing, Sophon described to me the experience of one of his students whom he referred to simply
as "D." D had been suffering from chronic diarrhea, fatigue, and other flulike
symptoms for about two years. He had gone to medical doctors for his condition, but they had been unable to determine the nature of his illness. During
this time he was also frequently irritable, experienced problems in his home
situation, and generally felt overwhelmed with the condition of his life. Approximately six months earlier, D approached Sophon with the thought that,
since the doctors could find no cause for his sickness, he might be suffering

from some type of curse. However, Sophon felt strongly that D's illness was not the result of a curse. Without going into detail, Sophon informed me that he and other magick practitioners can determine whether or not a curse has been placed on someone. He believed that the root of D's illness was that he was being bombarded by negative spiritual and emotional energy. D worked with troubled children, and Sophon believed that he was not being properly protected from the negative energy that surrounded him at his work. D was also keeping company with a group of friends who were further exposing him to an almost continuous flow of negative energy. Problems that D was experiencing in his home life exacerbated his condition.

To begin the healing process, Sophon prescribed a systematic healing ritual that would enable D to rid himself of the buildup of years of negative energy. As he described it, "First, I told him to take a ritual bath with blessed salt and lavender oil. Lavender oil is to relax him; blessed salt is used as a cleansing agent. During his bath he was to begin ridding himself of negative energy through meditation and controlled visualization." After the bath, D was instructed to burn frankincense, considered one of the holiest of scents and very cleansing, and a white candle, a symbol of purity. He was to cleanse a ritual space in his home in which he was to cast a circle. He was to call to the four cardinal directions and to the guardians of four elements who reside in them. In the center of this sacred space he was to create an altar consisting of a small table, a black altar cloth, two white candles, and objects representing the four elements: earth, wind, fire, and water. He was also told to place an object representing his own personal deity, the god or goddess of his choice, on the altar. Because he had an affinity for the Wicca female divinity, the Lady, on the altar, he placed a statue of her known as Rosemerta, a Celtic representation. He then stood in the sacred circle and asked for divine protection from the Lady as he visualized the space being filled with white light.

He reenforced the boundaries of protection every morning when he awoke and continued with his prayers and burning of white candles After about a week, the majority of his symptoms had disappeared. Sophon explained that D's "illness" was produced by the negative energies that had dominated his life, attaching themselves to D's body and psyche. The cleansing ritual rid him of these energies, and so he quickly began to recover. Sophon also said that D's experience was intended to be a lesson in patience. Somewhere along the way, Sophon believed that D had lost his ability to be patient with others, enabling the negative energy in his life to attack him. He had to relearn patience in order to overcome the bad influences in his life. Sophon reiterated that the divine universe does not always give you what you want, but it does give you what you need.

Sophon also explained that life is about making active choices. He claimed that we all have control of our destinies, that we are not ruled by fate, and that we get back what we put into life. I found this to be problematic and asked him about those who are suffering from terminal illness. What active choices could they possibly have left? Are they not rather victims of fate? He told me, "If you have a terminal illness, you can't change it, maybe. But you can learn to live with it and to help others along the way. Or you can decide to poison everyone around you. That is an active choice; we all make active choices." I commented that it did not sound like paganism was very different from most mainstream religions, that this talk of "active choice" sounded a lot like Buddhism or Christianity or Islam. He agreed that the Tao, karma, dharma, and the Golden Rule are all about what he called "staying in balance." He went on to claim, "[Magick] is a different path to the same goal."

However, Sophon also felt strongly that paganism, unlike many other religions, provides a strong sense that one is not controlled by fate. He told me, "[Magick] helps people to see they are not mere leaves blown in the wind. It gives them control over their destiny. I don't believe that everything is determined by fate. What would be the point [of living]?"

I asked Sophon if he did not sometimes doubt his Wicca beliefs, if the success stories he and his fellow worshipers had experienced were not just some sort of happy coincidence. Sophon replied honestly, "Yes, of course. Everyone does at least get an inkling of doubt at one point or another. But then I go to a Sabbat, and I see the works of the gods and I believe. It's only human to doubt, but then confirmation in the gods occurs, and my faith is reaffirmed."

Sophon said, "We are all a part of the grand scheme of things, and every little bit of good that we do counts." Yet the good that has emerged from Cambodian American approaches to healing and wellness has been overlooked in the past two decades. Instead, dominant knowledge and power regimes of the United States have repeatedly pathologized the Cambodian immigrant and Cambodian American, while demonstrating little interest in the immigrants' own responses to their perceived sociomedical condition. Yet the unique approaches described in this chapter, coming from Cambodian immigrants and Cambodian Americans themselves, demonstrate the ability of these communities to provide their own meaning, interpretation, and solution to illness, as well as to the larger experience of being human.

NOTES

1. Names have been changed for the sake of anonymity in this ethnographic account.

2. I have met many Cambodian Americans who work at casinos both in the Seattle area and in Southern California. However, it is often regarded as a less than desirable job by the Cambodian immigrant community.

3. The term "magick" is used in this text to denote a religious system and thereby to distinguish this term from connotations with "magic," which is often associated with tricks or hoaxes.

4

Procreating Women and Religion: The Politics of Spirituality, Healing, and Childbirth in America

Pamela Klassen

The contemporary home birth movement is rooted in a countercultural critique of biomedicine that, like many other alternative healing movements in America, draws from religious and spiritual resources. Spanning a continuum from traditionalist Jews and Christians to feminist practitioners of Goddess spirituality, these religious and spiritual resources are quite diverse, especially in light of the fact that only a small minority of childbearing women (approximately 1 percent) plan to give birth at home. Although these women may have very different understandings of the religious significance of childbirth and different theologies of the body, they do share at least one commonality: they are fashioning their religious interpretations of childbirth largely outside of the context of official, religious institutions (see also Sered 1992: 7; 1991).

As Lori Hope Lefkowitz recalled of her experience of giving birth, "Judaism was not officially present at the occasion." In Lefkowitz's rueful words, "I was struck by the irony of Judaism's absence from one of the only occasions that I would dignify with the language of religious experience: 'Awesome,' 'transformative,' 'at once terrible and wonderful,' and 'miraculous'" (1994: 5). Lefkowitz's distinction between official Judaism and her own religious experience resonates with a contrast drawn by many women I met in the context of my research on home birth in North America. For these women, both the process and the aftermath of childbirth provoked a desire to make or find religious meaning in the act—meanings that were rarely made explicit by official or formal religious institutions. Located within an arena of domestic piety, the religious interpretations of child-birth developed by these women reflect a form of religious practice that one might easily place within the generously broad and implicitly feminist category of "women's spirituality." Ironically, the eclectic religious innovation in which the home birth movement participates could also be seen, in some cases, in a particularly antifeminist light. For some women, home birth is a breeding ground for a new conservatism, or what marketing gurus have enthusiastically called "new traditionalism" (Leslie 1997: 310). By this, they mean the embrace once again of home and family as the proper spheres for a woman to develop her "true" identity. In this guise, home birth becomes another site for the policing of boundaries of gender, religious orthodoxy, and political identities.

The tension between the traditionalist and feminist dimensions of the home birth movement (both of which claim the expansive and universalizing discourse of spirituality as one of their sources of authority) is my focus in this chapter. I approach this nexus in three ways, radiating from the intimately descriptive to the wide-angled theoretical. First, I show how home birth assumes religious dimensions by telling some of the stories of the women I met in the course of my work. Second, I show some of the ways this traditionalist-feminist tension has been exacerbated and productively alleviated within the home birth movement. Third, I set my research within the context of women's spirituality as a scholarly category, suggesting that both terms in this phrase need to undergo some scrutiny. Throughout, my analysis demonstrates one example of how religiously inspired critiques of biomedicine can create unexpected allies across both political and religious spectra.

These alliances can only be understood within the context of North American conditions of maternity care. Home-birthing women are creating innovative traditions of religious experience and narrative that value childbirth as more than a medical event. Working against the twentieth-century medicalization of childbirth that saw the act of giving birth shift from a social and physical event attended by women to a medical event attended and pathologized largely by men, these women claim childbirth as a normal, natural state of health (Leavitt 1986; Wertz and Wertz [1977] 1989). They do so within a North American context where women, especially those who are middle-class, have the privilege to critique biomedicine knowing that they can turn to it if necessary. They act, therefore, within what I have called "postbiomedical bodies," as women who make religious and political critiques of biomedicine but knowingly depend on it as part of their contingency plans for birth (Klassen 2001).

Stories of Home Birth

The home birth movement is an alternative health *movement* only in a fairly fluid sense, as a collection of childbearing women, birth activists, midwives (whose legality varies by state), and doctors work to increase options for childbirth in North America (Rooks 1997). Home birth attracts women from a wide range of religious traditions, some of whom are formally affiliated with churches or synagogues, others who draw from more eclectic sources. The forty-five women I interviewed included Pentecostals, traditional and not so traditional Catholics, Orthodox Jews, Old Order Amish, United Methodists, Presbyterians, Reconstructionist Jews, and varieties of spiritual feminists (and more).[1] Although not all these women considered the choice to give birth at home to stem directly from their religious tradition, they almost always considered their births to be religious or, more frequently, spiritual experiences. The answer to my question, "Was giving birth a religious or spiritual experience for you?" elicited a similar refrain from many women: "Religious, no, spiritual, yes." Although using both terms—"religion" and "spirituality"—in my question may have set up this dichotomous answer in the minds of some women, I did not want to use only one of the terms in case the one I chose had little meaning for the woman. For many women, as I came to find out, the distinction between religion and spirituality was one that they had already drawn in their own lives.[2]

The lines the women drew between religion and spirituality became less clear, however, once they began to describe their births. For the most part, those women involved in formal religious institutions, such as church and synagogue communities, found that these institutions and their leaders were not actively concerned with the process of birth and did not specifically guide their choices about particular ways to birth. On a more personal level, however, women felt traditional religious considerations—in terms of domestic ritual or devotional traditions, or a relationship to God/Goddess—to be important to their choices. This disjuncture between institutional and experiential dimensions of religion is in part what shaped women's understandings of their births as spiritual, a word to which I will return later in my discussion.

One woman who most dramatically showed the transformation that giving birth may effect in a woman's religious life was Debra Lensky, a Jewish woman in her early forties with six children.[3] Debra's story straddled the feminist and traditionalist dimensions of the home birth movement and, as a result, was especially interesting for me. I was put in touch with Debra through her direct-entry midwives, who, given the laws in their state, were not practicing legally.[4] Debra, who grew up a "secular Jew," recalled grappling repeatedly with what she called the "woman issue"—since childhood she had a strong sense that her family and culture valued boys more than girls. When she decided to forgo her career as an accountant after her first child was born, she found herself asking, "Who am I? What am I? Do I have to be home in order to take care of babies? And that's my value? That's my *whole* value? Nobody cares about me doing this kind of thing." She recounted that only when she had her first home birth, after a cesarean and a vaginal birth after cesarean (VBAC) in the hospital, did her anguish begin to abate.

With her third birth Debra feared she was carrying a girl, when she wanted another boy. Given her conflicted attitude toward being a woman, Debra said, "the thought of carrying a girl inside of me was very, very strange. I couldn't eat, I just could not take care of myself." She did give birth to a daughter and remembered feeling shocked, with a "sense that something major was going to happen in my life, you know, an awareness of something. . . . That was like the finishing touches of really coming to grips with being a woman." According to Debra, this change came through her participation in the alternative childbirth movement, when she became interested in home birth. Later, in the course of her work as a childbirth instructor, Debra went to an Orthodox Jewish community to train some women as childbirth educators and was moved to question her own Jewish identification. Her dedication to reforming childbirth, which at first was rooted in trust in "nature" learned in her birth classes, became rooted in trust in God, as she became an Orthodox Jew.

Giving birth to a girl at home and becoming aware of the power of childbirth were catalysts in Debra's and her husband's transition to Orthodox Judaism, in Debra's view. As she explained:

> The transition had to do with . . . coming to an understanding of
> who I am and what I am, and that first part of it was recognizing
> the woman inside of me. And I remember one day saying to myself,
> "Ha! Now you understand that you're a woman and you're delighted
> and you appreciate what it is to be a woman. Now you need to find
> out what it's like to be a Jew, that you're truly a Jew and that you
> need to understand that and start living that also." And so it's really,
> for me, it was through childbirth that I was able to take those steps
> and become myself first as a woman, and then my connection to
> God. And my connection to God, as I was given it in this world at
> this time in this life, was that I was born a Jew, so I had to find my
> connection through Judaism. . . . That's how it was, so it was a road,
> it was a real road, but the basis of that road was trust in the design.
> And the basis came from childbirth, and the basis is childbirth.

According to Debra, the design she trusted in was that of God. She came to terms with being a woman by finding divine justification for the differential treatment of women—not by challenging it but by reinterpreting and embracing it (see also Davidman 1991: 133, 195).

Procreative Tensions

Home birth, as a countercultural movement, has attracted passionate proponents from a diversity of religious and political identities. This includes
women like Debra, who have become more orthodox in the process, and other
women who have taken the reverse path and have left traditional religions to
find more experimental women-centered spiritualities. For example, Tessa Wel-
land, a mother of four, described her home births not as religious but as "rooted
in spirituality." She did, however, think that her Catholic background, especially
her experiences at youth retreats while an "active Catholic" in high school,
shaped her birth choices:

> I think that [retreats] afforded me the opportunity to really become
> in touch with who I was spiritually. And probably to Catholicism's
> dismay, I realized that I wasn't necessarily a Catholic. But I defi-
> nitely think that that experience made me attuned to that kind of en-
> ergy—to have the time to reflect and really think about spiritualism,
> and to sort of study religion, and what it meant in the world, what it
> meant historically, how it affects people's lives. All of those things
> were helpful in sorting out who I was spiritually. And helped me to
> come to those kinds of decisions that were important to me, like
> birthing my children.

In a common New Age adaptation of the language of physics, Tessa thought
of spirituality as "energy" (Hess 1993). In contrast, she defined religion as a
"social construct." In her eyes, "religion is an expression of spirituality. Spirituality is universal. Like you could recognize spirituality manifested in Judaism
or Catholicism, born-again Christians, Jehovah's Witnesses." After "church-
shopping . . . everywhere but in a synagogue," Tessa said that she and her family have found their religious community within domestic rituals—including
those surrounding childbirth—shared with their extended family.

The cultures home-birthing women are countering, then, are not necessarily the same. Yet in the context of childbirth, their diversity is managed in
the service of what is perceived as the greater good: working for alternatives
to the medical model of childbirth. Two assertions act as currents carrying
along the movement and mediating its diversity: (1) Given a healthy pregnancy,
most women share a common ability to give birth with little interference, and
(2) birth is imbued with spirituality, in that it connects a woman to powerful
forces both within and without herself. Both of these currents are constructed
as having something universal about them. The latter current especially makes
the home birth movement part of a discourse of spirituality that runs through
a broad spectrum of religious diversity in North America. This discourse of

spirituality, rooted in venerating nature (in a selection of its many guises), affirming selected "universal truths," and trusting in a power external to the human will (in most cases, God), was common to most of the women, as well as to much of the home birth literature.

Within this spirituality-in-common, however, lie sharp differences of gender politics. Approaches to mothering and employment, relations of authority between men and women, opinions about abortion and birth control, and openness to homosexuality and divorce are all issues that evoked divided and often impassioned, *religiously* informed opinions among these women. In the face of this difference, the currents of birth as a spiritual event and women as natural birthers do not always flow together harmoniously.

Mediating the procreative tensions becomes an exercise in what one might call, after Gayatri Spivak, a sort of double "strategic essentialism" (1993: 3). That is, in coming together through a conviction that women are essentially capable of giving birth with little interference, home-birthing women also strive to draw upon an essentialized spirituality that crosses boundaries of place, politics, and religious tradition. The commonality is strained, however, once the strategy dissolves, leaving only essentialism. The procreative tensions bubbling beneath the home birth movement are exacerbated when certain specific issues come to the fore, such as regulating sexuality and upholding specific religious doctrines. Those same tensions are alleviated when the focus becomes the threat of the medical model of birth to women's power to give birth, and when spirituality is used as a relatively vague term capable of encompassing a diversity of childbirth experiences.

I turn to Debra once more to show how this spirituality-in-common can both work and be strained. In Debra's present interpretation as an Orthodox woman, God not only designed women's bodies in an act of omnipotent creation but also more specifically intervened in her life to lead her to Orthodox Judaism through childbirth activism. Before she became Orthodox, Debra worked with two other women in her childbirth activism, one a Christian and the other more eclectically spiritual, with her own "spiritual leader." Debra felt that her work with these two women did not come about by coincidence:

> And very honestly it felt very much very designed, very destined that
> three major religions were coming together to work on childbirth
> and awaken women. And the three of us were very much aware,
> very much aware of what we were doing when we worked individu-
> ally with individual women and as an organization working for the
> world. We felt a very strong sense of mission that we needed to
> bring women back to the realization of who they were and what they
> were. Not again telling them that you *have* to have children, not
> again saying to them you *must* birth at home or at a hospital center
> or anywhere, none of that. But just that they be reconnected to their

design, that they honor themselves and they feel their own strength and their own power in a positive way.

These three women were not official representatives of their respective religions, but nevertheless Debra saw their collaboration as a legitimate and important act of interreligious cooperation. Her perspective begs the question of just how official religion is constituted, and how the boundaries of institutional religion are drawn. For Debra, partaking in childbirth activism as a Jew made her work Jewish work despite that fact that no Jewish organization was sponsoring her. The boundaries of what is or is not religious grow fuzzy, as people constitute their actions in the home or in the community as actions fostered by their religious traditions.

Not only did Debra's Judaism support her childbirth activism, but conversely, her experience of childbirth also shaped her Judaism. The childbirth-provoked sense of women's power that Debra described had a profound effect on her Jewish identity. She asserted that her family joined an Orthodox community at her instigation, because of the "strength that I gained through childbirth." In a metaphor I have heard repeated by Mennonite women and Jewish women alike, Debra asserted, "They say that the man is the head of the household, and that's true, he is. He should be the head. He's the king. He makes the ultimate decisions, right? But the woman's the neck, and the way she turns the head, that's how he goes." The power behind the throne, in Debra's opinion, is rooted in women's awareness and insight, based on the capabilities embedded in their bodies.

Although Debra is still somewhat involved in childbirth activism, the breadth of her ties to that community has lessened as she develops relationships in her Orthodox Jewish community. In some ways her empowering experience of activism, in which she wanted women to "reconnect" to their power without necessarily feeling they had to give birth, is at odds with the very pronatalist environment of Orthodox Judaism (Davidman 1991). The power Debra felt called to evoke in all women became transmuted in the course of her religious transformation, becoming power less broadly accessible, instead achieved mainly through birth and mothering.

Power rooted in procreation was central to the way many women used the notion of spirituality to describe the significance of childbirth. For most of these women, Christians, Jews, spiritual feminists, New Agers, and even some self-described "nonreligious" women, spirituality was an evocative and useful term to describe their births, generally meaning a personal and embodied connection with a supernatural power that had universal applicability. The relationship between birth and spirituality was in many ways premised on the proclaimed universality of both. As one feminist woman put it (as she perched at the interstices of recalling memories of a Catholic childhood, being marriage to a Jewish man, and having an adolescent daughter seeking her Jewish roots),

"Women are born to birth. It's just a faith, that's a matter of faith." This spiritualizing of home birth, however, was rooted in particular models of embodied and spiritual power that were professed to be universal but were not all shared.

Given these differences, some women were more hesitant to give spirituality such wide applicability. For example, Brenda Matthews, a Pentecostal woman, said she only selectively used one of the long-standing, germinal works in the home birth movement entitled *Spiritual Midwifery* (Gaskin 1990). In reading this book, Brenda said, she wanted "birth fact" and nothing else. She stated, "Spiritually I am very tuned in to [i.e., suspicious of] things that are not from Jesus, and I am very cautious with something called 'spiritual,' because I'm not sure what spirit they are tuning into. I want God's spirit." However, despite her wry assertion that "I don't open myself up to the cosmos," in the case of birth Brenda did extend the scope of the spiritual, saying, "Every birth is a spiritual experience." For her, childbirth trumped theological differences, if only briefly—Brenda limited that universality again in describing her own first birth. She recounted: "I had a divine birth, because Jesus actually brought that baby out without me doing anything." Other women, including another Pentecostal and a traditional Catholic, were careful to distinguish the spirituality of their births from new age versions of spirituality but still happily and liberally made use of the term "spiritual" to describe their experiences.

The procreative tensions that I found among the women I interviewed can also be located in the wider home birth movement. First, I offer an example that parallels Debra's story of "three major religions coming together," in which difference was submerged in common purpose. In Ohio, where direct-entry midwifery was investigated recently by a legislative study council, several hundred people came forth to give testimonies to the benefits of home birth. These people included conservative Christians (fathers and mothers), mainstream Christians, "secular" folk, and Old Order Amish (who particularly impressed the legislators, given their usual reluctance to involve themselves in affairs of state). Although the council could not reach a consensus (the two doctors dissented), when it released its report in January 1998, the majority decision recommended decriminalizing home birth, developing a registration system for midwives, and offering more public education about childbirth options (Thomas 1998).

At times, however, the essentialism overwhelms the strategy, as when the Midwives Alliance of North America (MANA) has repeatedly tried to find ways to be supportive of feminist lesbian midwives among their membership without alienating the conservative, and vocal, Christian midwives among the group. This delicate balancing act continues to threaten the unity of MANA, and conservative Christian midwives have stymied attempts to develop ethical codes overtly supportive of lesbian midwives (MANA 1992). The tensions in this community of midwives point to what Gayatri Spivak acknowledges as the hazards of any recourse to essentialism. In embarking on strategic essentialism, she writes, one must be aware of "the dangerousness of something one cannot not use" (1993: 5). In fighting for childbirth reform, women cannot not use—they cannot deny—the abilities of their bodies as women. But in calling forth the category of woman to unify their efforts, the differences in what it can mean to be a woman will never be masked entirely.

Women's Spirituality

This brings me to question two of the terms in the double strategic essentialism I have laid out: women and spirituality. What is spirituality? And what does it become, once modified by women, as in "women's spirituality"? Several scholars have embarked on a discussion of the term "spirituality" in the last several years, prompted by the growing popular use of the term. In Margaret Chatterjee's words, contemporary spirituality is marked by a "desire to avoid the reified concept of religion per se, a stress on ambience rather than on belief, and a wish to point up the experiential" (1997: 29; see also Roof 1993). Given this kind of definition, spirituality is protean, and this flexibility is the source of both its potential and its downfall, depending on one's perspective.

As Jung Ha Kim points out, "spirituality" has its critics from both the Left and the Right. Those on the Left may consider that "given the reality of deeply privatized spiritual experimentation in the United States, a resort to spirituality may mean resort to a 'false consciousness' that ignores and disguises the systemic causes for social and religious problems as matters of individual mentality and perception." Similarly, spirituality as a "post-Christian" or, I would add, a "post-Jewish" phenomenon may raise suspicion from those on the Right and provoke a defense of "orthodoxies in the name of world religions and their historical establishments" (Kim 1996: 59). Although Kim draws an important connection here in showing how the Left and Right may share a negative reaction to the flexibility of spirituality, her analysis also reveals a certain blind spot in much research on contemporary American spirituality. In many cases, scholars ignore instances where the "ambient" exploration of spiritual seekers is not limited to those experimenting with religious innovation but also includes practitioners of "traditional" religions.

For example, in drawing what he seems to think is a commonsense link, Peter Van Ness offers proof that spirituality in North America has distanced itself from traditional religion: "A large number of Americans apparently believe that the sacred can be experienced without allegiance to a central tenet of biblical religion; in fact, [in a *Newsweek* survey] 26 percent of the persons polled said that they obtained a 'sense of the sacred during sex'" (1996: 1). Why experiencing the sacred during sex should be added proof of a lack of allegiance to the tenets of biblical religion is not immediately clear to me, and is most likely a particularly Christian assumption, given traditions within Judaism that have celebrated the holiness of marital sexuality, at least within proper ritual conditions. If we were to transfer this example to self-consciously Jewish and Christian home-birthing women who experienced the "sacred" (and sometimes even sexual pleasure) during childbirth, the link would be equally obscure (see Moran 1981).

Van Ness's slippage in thinking of embodied or even sensual spirituality as necessarily "untraditional" points to a difficulty in the ways the term "spirituality" is used. Embodied spirituality is not necessarily beyond religious traditions—it may be, but it may also involve a (critical) reinterpretation of religious tradition within both orthodox and experimental communities. Turning to the body as a spiritual resource can result in both "gender radicalism" (Ortner 1996: 184) and the intensification of gendered norms within a religious tradition—rarely does it leave gender, and the power relations that shape it, untouched.

Accepting that twentieth-century North American spirituality is protean does not entail thinking of it as unconstructed—as somehow just "in the air." Instead, I share and reformulate Talal Asad's question in his critique of the scholarly construction of religion as a category: "How does power create religion?" (1993: 45). For Asad the concept of religion is the product of "historically distinctive disciplines and forces" that themselves have defined and produced religion in opposition to other spheres such as the state, law, and science (54). The scholar of religion, then, needs to be self-conscious of the baggage carried within the term itself and unpack the "heterogeneous elements" it conveys. Those elements, Asad suggests, can be found by paying specific attention to "the occurrence of events (utterances, practices, dispositions) and the authorizing processes that give those events meaning and embody that meaning in concrete institutions" (43).

That many of the women in my study preferred the term "spirituality" to "religion" in the case of childbirth, and in many cases derided religion as superficial (even when they claimed religious affiliations themselves), does not mean I will do the same. Instead, I want to subject "spirituality" to the same question: How does power create the complex of relations and dispositions that these women call spirituality? Although in many instances an explicitly extra-institutional phenomenon, spirituality is no less "created" than religion. In the case of home birth, women shape spirituality in reaction to a range of institutions in addition to religious ones, including those of medicine and publishing. A woman interprets her spirituality, within a social context reticulated by her religious and ethnic traditions, her life history, and her experiences (or lack thereof) of sexism, racism, and economic oppression. Choices rooted in "spirituality," then, while often understood as grounding themselves in the depths of one's being or in the mystery of the cosmos (Van Ness 1996: 5), are also grounded in much more material concerns.

One reason I see for these women's preference for spirituality, beyond a wider cultural language in which spirituality reigns as more authentic than supposedly reified religion, is that Christian and Jewish traditions, in different ways, have not valued childbirth as a religious experience from the perspective of a birthing woman. While the birth of Jesus and the birth of Jews are important to Christianity and Judaism, respectively, the labor of childbirth has not been accorded religious significance as an act that profoundly transforms the birthing woman. Historically, these religions have even considered childbirth to be polluting. When traditional religions do attend to birth, they quickly move from the messy experience or supplant the physical altogether with a metaphoric, theological, purified "new" birth of some kind (see Jay 1992: 147). These women's choice of spirituality is a rejection of the authorizing processes that have deemed religion as the realm in which one truly meets God but have abandoned childbirth to superstition or, more recently, medicine (see Hammer 1994: 182).[5]

Since religious traditions and contemporary clergy, generally speaking, have not been concerned with the transformative possibilities of birth for a woman, women have turned elsewhere to find ways to make sense of childbirth religiously. They draw from a range of sources—not all of which are explicitly religious—to create religion or spirituality in the context of their births. As Susan Sered has suggested in the context of her research on childbirth in Israeli hospitals, a deeply rooted conceptual conflict keeps women from naming what they consider to be a spiritual experience as "really" religious. Sered writes: "Women whose religious lives are constructed within the context of a male-oriented culture that neither celebrates nor sacralizes women's bodies and concerns, may lack the language (both verbal and ritual) to express that feeling" (1991: 15; See also Sered 1994: 111). In Sered's study, when the foreign territory of the hospital was added to the silences of religious traditions regarding female experience, even women who wanted birth to be a religious experience were stymied (cf. Sandhaas 1992: 8–9; Caldecott 1987; Beecher 1982).

Home-birthing women create spirituality, then, in reference to religious traditions that they perceive to be ignorant of the diversity of ways in which sacredness can be encountered. Valued by devout Jews and Christians, as well as by those seeking more eclectic sources of the sacred, a North American sense of spirituality is formed in a society that esteems individual conviction of the divine and is fearful of "dead ritual" but that also desires communal expression. In the case of home birth, women use declarations of the spirituality of childbirth to support their challenge to the medicalization of childbirth, and in some cases to the state sanction of that medicalization. In so doing, they assert that naming a bodily act as spiritual creates its power, not only for its potential transformation of a woman's identity but also for her relationship to her community and the state.

The flexibility of the spirituality shared by a diversity of home-birthing women is perhaps not surprising given Catherine Albanese's argument that

the left and right ends of the contemporary "American religious spectrum"—
what she calls "New Agers" and "fundamentalists"—are characterized by a
particular convergence of "mystical/metaphysical qualit[ies]" (1988: 347). In
her analysis, a focus on healing, a "non-elite, do-it-yourself . . . spiritual de-
mocracy," "ongoing revelation," and personal transformation that leads to the
transformation of society are commonly held goals for both fundamentalists
and New Agers (349–50; Roof 1993). Home birth is another environment in
which these goals converge. Women stress holistic views of the body that allow
for both self-sufficiency and supernatural influence in birthing, and they consider birth to be a time of personal revelation that holds within it the possibility
to change the world by birthing a new generation in a gentler way. As Olivia,
a self-identified secular Jew with New Age interests, put it, "If more people
give birth naturally then the whole of humanity can elevate themselves."
Women's choice to do so—whether they are traditionally religious or experi-
mentally so—is often a theological action in the face of both ignorance and
trivializing of women's experiences.

But, to return to my notion of the strategic essentialisms that bind diverse
women into a loose affiliation in support of home birth, what are "women's"
experiences? Similar to my assertion that spirituality is differentially constructed, so is the category of woman. As feminist theorists have shown,
woman is not a stable category. They argue that women are differentially constructed through discourse and representation shaped by class, race, and sexual
orientation, among other influences, and that in some cases women have a lot
more in common with men than with other women (e.g., Butler 1993; Hurtado
1989; Riley 1988; Spelman 1988). Certainly, in the case of my study, that these
women were predominantly (but not all) white, middle-class, and from Jewish
or Christian backgrounds profoundly shaped their understanding of the significance of childbirth and, for that matter, of having children. At the same
time, other feminists have insisted that while gender is constructed in many
ways, there is something to the material physicality of being female that shapes
women's lives regardless of their historical or social conditions (Kahn 1995:
381; Spretnak 1991: 126, 134).

The first view, put in a colloquial fashion by Sherry Ortner, reads this way:
"Personally, I thought the whole point of feminism was to bring about a situation in which women were not seen as a natural class of being, defined primarily by their bodies" (1996: 137). Robbie Kahn phrases the second view more
conditionally: "Although I do not believe that there are innate differences between the sexes, the activities of pregnancy, birth, and lactation must be considered an exception since only the woman can do them and the instructive
possibilities of these experiences may change women in ways not accessible
to men" (Kahn 1995: 381). The political repercussions of these two arguments
are obviously intense, and the discussion has become more complex than assenting to or refuting simple equations of "biology is destiny." Biology matters

when nine months of a woman's life are given to nurturing a child in her womb, twelve, twenty-four, or thirty-six hours are given to birthing her, and the next twenty years are given to nursing, cleaning, feeding, and loving that child, with the help of others. Biology also matters if a woman wants to give birth and cannot, or if she can and chooses not to. How much it matters, and in what ways for which people, are questions that will always be culturally negotiated.

But how do those scholars attending to women's spirituality grapple with these dilemmas of essentialism? Many of the scholars who specifically treat women's spirituality do so from a theological perspective of some kind— whether that of Christianity, Judaism, or feminist spirituality (Levitt 1996; Purvis 1989; Raphael 1996; Schneiders 1986). As such, their concerns often concentrate on ideals and activism: how to change the inequities women face in traditional religions, or how to create altogether new women-centered religious traditions. The same splits found in feminist theory can be found among these scholars. For example, British scholar Ursula King warns against romanticizing birth and biology in a Western context where women exercise significant control over their fertility. Furthermore, she insists that "women's experience, like all human experience, must ultimately be body-transcendent rather than exclusively body-dependent" (1993: 77). In King's understanding, women's spirituality must be concerned with "autonomy, freedom, and transcendence" (1993: 78). On the other hand, American scholar Kathryn Rabuzzi has devoted much of her energies to exploring childbirth as the "deeply spiritual gynocentric experience it potentially is" (1994: ix). She insists on the transformative capacities of childbirth, and the difference that biology can make, without insisting that all women must be mothers.

In contrast to the more prescriptive endeavors of the theologically inclined, works by historians and anthropologists of religion concerned with women's religious lives more generally have tried to trace the commonalities between women of very different religious and political identities (Ginsburg 1989; Griffith 1997). For example, Marie Griffith, in her study of the evangelical women's prayer group Women's Aglow, argued that despite the vitriolic rhetoric that passes between feminists and conservative Christian women, these two female cultures are "overlapping" in some important respects. Most important for my consideration of home birth, she writes: "One shared premise is that the social and cultural tasks, traits, and affinities traditionally coded as 'female' or 'feminine' ought to be accorded greater respect and value than they have been" (1997: 208).

That a revaluing of women's ability to give birth has come from both traditionalist and feminist women should perhaps give us pause in the way we use those altogether inadequate and polarizing labels of conservative/liberal or traditionalist/feminist. What may seem like a strange confluence of religious values and political dispositions is in fact a characteristic of women's spirituality as an observed phenomenon, which the starkly gendered character of birth brings into sharp relief. Women's religious lives in a diversity of settings seem consistently woven through with the concerns of generativity, relationship, and healing, with maternity as a very common symbolic resource (e.g., Brown 1991; Sered 1994). Perhaps these strange confluences, or what in the home birth movement become strange alliances, only seem odd when viewed from the symbolic and material terrain of androcentric institutions. What is strange is itself constructed within a particular grid of power. Representatives of Christianity, Judaism, and the American Medical Association have all, in their own ways, downplayed or subverted the potential symbolic power within maternity.

Closing Thoughts

The religious innovation within the home birth movement can be situated in multiple ways. Some women within traditional religious institutions, like Debra, innovate while continuing to feel deeply orthodox. Others develop "personal spiritualities" (Davie 1995: 4) that they do not share with their wider institutions—effecting what one research team called "defections in place" (Winter, Lummis, and Stokes 1994). Still others, like Tessa, abjure the institution altogether. But all the women with whom I spoke felt that in giving birth at home they were participating in a wider movement that had societal consequences. As such, the spirituality that these women evoked should not be disdained as narcissistic, feminized "sheilaism" (Bellah et al. 1985: 221) that begins and ends with the woman as individual. Although the actions prompted by the religiosity of birth may not be social in the same way as going to church or working in a soup kitchen, women see the birthing, mothering, and activism emerging from their childbirth choices as directly improving the lives of women, babies, and families. Home birth often creates new social networks, as women consider others who have given birth at home to be sympathetic and like-minded people, and they join groups like Citizens for Midwifery or La Leche League (see Ward 2000).

Interpreting these women's religious lives with equanimity, however, should not lead to a romanticization of birth, spirituality, or women. All members of this trio are socially located in particular histories—none of them come to us in a natural form lying beneath layers of artifice, be it medical, religious, or gendered. Instead, in choosing to birth at home and interpret their actions through religious lenses, these women are creating religion in ways that are transforming their personal identities, the birth process in the contemporary United States, and, in some cases, their religious traditions. That they do so as postbiomedical bodies, with the privileged knowledge that a cesarean section could save them and their babies if absolutely necessary, demonstrates that even the most trenchant American critiques of biomedicine accept some of its benefits. This fact does not reduce the power of their critical stance, nor does it make their experience less profound. It does show, however, that the entwining of spirituality and healing in a context of class privilege is often an embrace of God's will or cosmic fate tacitly supported by a simultaneous underlying faith in biomedicine as well.

NOTES

1. I interviewed forty-five women in two northeastern states and participated in home birth–related activities (such as midwife visits, workshops, and a birth) over the course of two years. Two of the forty-five women were African American, one was Hispanic, and the rest were Euro-American. Several women held advanced degrees, and most had at least some college education. The women and their husbands spanned a range of occupations and incomes, but for the most part they were middle-class. More than three-quarters of the women cared for their children at home, and about a third of these women also worked part-time at jobs that ranged from assisting in their husband's chiropractic office to being veterinarians. Six women had full-time employment, all in professional occupations such as teaching, nursing, ministry, or chiropractic. Traditional Catholics are those who critique the reforms of Vatican II, especially in terms of liturgical change (Weaver and Appleby 1995).

2. For a nursing-based study focused on Mormon and Orthodox Jewish women's understanding of childbirth as a spiritual experience, but one not concerned with the distinction between spirituality and religion, see Callister, Semenic, and Foster 1999.

3. All names describing the women in the study are pseudonyms.

4. A direct-entry midwife differs from a certified nurse-midwife in that she does not have a nursing degree but has taken a midwifery course and is more likely to have been trained by apprenticeship (Rooks 1997).

5. While some women in my study spoke of their ministers (particularly female ones) as supportive of their home birth, most said their clergy had nothing to do with the birth. Within Judaism two radically different approaches to childbirth are found in the work of Tikva Frymer-Kensky (1995), a Reconstructionist Rabbi, and that of Finkelstein and Finkelstein (1993), who, from an Orthodox perspective, compiled a "halachic guide" to childbirth that warns against home birth.

REFERENCES

Albanese, Catherine L. 1988. Religion and the American Experience: A Century After. *Church History* 57:337–351.

Asad, Talal. 1993. *Genealogies of Religion: Discipline and Reasons of Power in Christianity and Islam.* Baltimore: Johns Hopkins University Press.

Beecher, Maureen Ursenbach. 1982. Birthing. In *Mormon Women Speak,* ed. May Lythgoe Bradford, 45–55. Salt Lake City: Olympus.

Bellah, Robert N., Richard Madsen, William M. Sullivan, Ann Swidler, and Steven M. Tipton. 1985. *Habits of the Heart: Individualism and Commitment in American Life.* New York: Harper and Row.

Brown, Karen McCarthy. 1991. *Mama Lola: A Vodou Priestess in Brooklyn.* Berkeley and Los Angeles: University of California Press.

Butler, Judith. 1993. *Bodies That Matter.* New York: Routledge.

Caldecott, Leonie. 1987. Inner Anatomy of a Birth. In *Sex and God: Some Varieties of Women's Religious Experience,* ed. Linda Hurcombe, 147–60. New York: Routledge and Kegan Paul.

Callister, Lynn Clark, Sonia Semenic, and Joyce Cameron Foster. 1999. Cultural and Spiritual Meanings of Childbirth. *Journal of Holistic Nursing* 17:280–95.

Chatterjee, Margaret. 1997. The Smorgasbord Syndrome: Availability Reexamined. In *Modern Spiritualities: An Inquiry,* ed. Laurence Brown, Bernard C. Farr, and R. Joseph Hoffman, 17–30. Oxford: Prometheus.

Davidman, Lynn. 1991. *Tradition in a Rootless World: Women Turn to Orthodox Judaism.* Berkeley and Los Angeles: University of California Press.

Davie, Jody Shapiro. 1995. *Women in the Presence: Constructing Community and Seeking Spirituality in Mainline Protestantism.* Philadelphia: University of Pennsylvania Press.

Finkelstein, Baruch, and Michal Finkelstein. 1993. *B'Sha'ah Tovah: The Jewish Woman's Clinical and Halachic Guide to Pregnancy and Childbirth.* Jerusalem and New York: Feldheim Publishers.

Frymer-Kensky, Tikva. 1995. *Motherprayer: The Pregnant Woman's Spiritual Companion.* New York: Riverhead Books.

Gaskin, Ina May. 1990. *Spiritual Midwifery.* 3rd ed. Summerton, Tenn.: Book Publishing Company.

Ginsburg, Faye. 1989. *Contested Lives: The Abortion Debate in an American Community.* Berkeley and Los Angeles: University of California Press.

Griffith, R. Marie. 1997. *God's Daughters: Evangelical Women and the Power of Submission.* Berkeley and Los Angeles: University of California Press.

Hammer, Margaret L. 1994. *Giving Birth: Reclaiming Biblical Metaphor for Pastoral Practice.* Louisville, Ky.: Westminster/John Knox Press.

Hess, David J. 1993. *Science in the New Age: The Paranormal, Its Defenders and Debunkers, and American Culture.* Madison: University of Wisconsin Press.

Hurtado, Aida. 1989. Relating to Privilege: Seduction and Rejection in the Subordination of White Women and Women of Color. *Signs* 14: 833–55.

Jay, Nancy. 1992. *Throughout Your Generations Forever: Sacrifice, Religion, and Paternity.* Chicago: University of Chicago Press.

Kahn, Robbie Pfeufer. 1995. *Bearing Meaning: The Language of Birth.* Urbana: University of Illinois Press.

Kim, Jung Ha. 1996. Sources outside of Europe. In *Spirituality and the Secular Quest,* ed. Peter Van Ness, 53–74. New York: Crossroad.

King, Ursula. 1993. *Women and Spirituality: Voices of Protest and Promise.* 2nd ed. University Park: Pennsylvania State University Press.

Klassen, Pamela E. 2001. *Blessed Events: Religion and Home Birth in America.* Princeton, N.J.: Princeton University Press.

Leavitt, Judith Walzer. 1986. *Brought to Bed: Childbearing in America, 1750–1950*. New York: Oxford University Press.

Lefkowitz, Lori Hope. 1994. Sacred Screaming: Childbirth in Judaism. In *Lifecycles: Jewish Women on Life Passages and Personal Milestones*, ed. Debra Orenstein, 5. Woodstock, Vt.: Jewish Lights Publishing.

Leslie, D. A. 1997. Femininity, Post-Fordism, and the "New Traditionalism." In *Space, Gender, Knowledge: Feminist Readings*, ed. Linda McDowell and Joanne P. Sharp, 300–318. London: Arnold.

Levitt, Laura. 1996. Feminist Spirituality. In *Spirituality and the Secular Quest*, ed. Peter Van Ness, 305–34. New York: Crossroad.

Midwives Alliance of North America (MANA). 1992. Statement of Core Values and Ethics. *MANA News* 10 (4): 10–12.

Moran, Marilyn. 1981. *Birth and the Dialogue of Love*. Leawood, Kans.: New Nativity Press.

Ortner, Sherry. 1996. *Making Gender: The Politics and Erotics of Culture*. Boston: Beacon Press.

Purvis, Sally B. 1989. Christian Feminist Spirituality. In *Christian Spirituality: Post-Reformation and Modern*, ed. Louis Dupre and Don E. Saliers, 500–19. New York: Crossroad.

Rabuzzi, Kathryn Allen. 1994. *Mother with Child: Transformations through Childbirth*. Bloomington: Indiana University Press.

Raphael, Melissa. 1996. *Thealogy and Embodiment: The Post-patriarchal Reconstruction of Female Sacrality*. Sheffield, England: Sheffield Academic Press.

Riley, Denise. 1988. *"Am I that name?": Feminism and the Category of "Women" in History*. Minneapolis: University of Minnesota Press.

Roof, Wade Clark. 1993. *A Generation of Seekers: The Spiritual Journeys of the Baby Boom Generation*. San Francisco: HarperSanFrancisco.

Rooks, Judith Pence. 1997. *Midwifery and Childbirth in America*. Philadelphia: Temple University Press.

Sandhaas, Kari. 1992. Birth, Choice, and the Abuse of the Sacred: A Personal Story of Resistance. *Daughters of Sarah* 18 (4): 8–11.

Schneiders, Sandra M. 1986. *The Effects of Women's Experience on Their Spirituality. Women's Spirituality: Resources for Christian Development*, ed. Joann Wolski Conn, 31–48. New York: Paulist Press.

Sered, Susan Starr. 1991. Childbirth as a Religious Experience? Voices from an Israeli Hospital. *Journal for the Feminist Study of Religion* 7 (2): 7–18.

———. 1992. *Women as Ritual Experts: The Religious Lives of Elderly Jewish Women in Jerusalem*. Oxford: Oxford University Press.

———. 1994. *Priestess, Mother, Sacred Sister: Religions Dominated by Women*. New York: Oxford University Press.

Spelman, Elizabeth V. 1988. *Inessential Woman: Problems of Exclusion in Feminist Thought*. Boston: Beacon Press.

Spivak, Gayatri Chakravorty. 1993. *Outside in the Teaching Machine*. New York: Routledge.

Spretnak, Charlene. 1991. *States of Grace: The Recovery of Meaning in the Postmodern Age*. New York: HarperCollins.

Thomas, Jan. 1998. Politics and Pregnancy: The Contested Terrain of Childbirth in Ohio. Paper presented at the annual meeting of the American Sociological Association, San Francisco.

Van Ness, Peter H. 1996. Introduction: Spirituality and the Secular Quest." In *Spirituality and the Secular Quest,* ed. Peter Van Ness, 1–22. New York: Crossroad.

Ward, Jule DeJager. 2000. *La Leche League: At the Crossroads of Medicine, Feminism, and Religion.* Chapel Hill: University of North Carolina Press.

Weaver, Mary Jo, and R. Scott Appleby. 1995. *Being Right: Conservative Catholics in America.* Bloomington: Indiana University Press.

Wertz, Richard W., and Dorothy C. Wertz [1977] 1989. *Lying-In: A History of Childbirth in America.* Expanded edition. New Haven, Conn.: Yale University Press.

Winter, Miriam Therese, Adair Lummis, and Allison Stokes. 1994. *Defecting in Place: Women Claiming Responsibility for Their Own Spiritual Lives.* New York: Crossroad.

5

Healing into Wholeness in the Episcopal Church

Jennifer L. Hollis

St. Stephen's Episcopal Church in Boston's South End is a working-class congregation in a sea of recent gentrification. It began as a mission church for English mill workers and servants of members of Trinity Episcopal Church in Copley Square. During the 1960s, the Puerto Rican community joined African Americans who had been living in the neighborhood for forty years. In the 1970s, St. Stephen's worked with members of the community to develop the Emergency Tenant Corporation, helping to create a nearby tenant-run community development called Villa Victoria. As a result of its work in community organizing, some families that were drawn to St. Stephen's at that time are now in their third and fourth generation of membership. On an average Sunday, sixty to eighty people attend services, and even more attend large events.

In September 2000, I moved to Boston's South End before beginning Harvard Divinity School. I discovered St. Stephen's while walking around my new neighborhood one Sunday morning, and the congregation surrounded me with an immediate welcome. The day I began my fieldwork, St. Stephen's held a Public Service of Healing, the formal healing service of the Episcopal Church. It includes a responsive prayer, called a litany of healing. Laying on of hands and anointing with blessed oil allow participants to receive individual attention for their concerns during the service, which also includes a celebration of the Eucharist. Instructions for a Public Service of Healing are found in *The Book of Occasional Services*. The service has been adapted from the Book of Common Prayer from the rite for anointing and laying on of hands.

On the night of the healing service at St. Stephen's, I found myself in the pews with, it seemed, the entire congregation. A diverse group of more than forty people gathered on this Wednesday evening. The service was conducted in both English and Spanish. St. Stephen's uses a bilingual text, and the participants respond in the language of their choice. The sermon is also read in both languages.

The Public Service of Healing follows the basic structure of a Eucharistic celebration and includes hymns, readings from the New and Old Testaments of the Christian Bible, intercessory prayers, and a sermon. As we approached the time for laying on of hands and anointing, the vicar, the Reverend Timothy Crellin, explained that he would like to invite members of the congregation to the front of the church. There, he and the assistant minister would speak quietly to individuals about their concerns, then offer laying on of hands and prayer. Several people stood up and proceeded to the front of the church. They did not seem to pick one minister or the other; when it was their turn, they simply moved to whoever was available. They whispered their concerns to the minister. When they were done speaking, the minister touched them on the head, the shoulder, or the arm, and prayed softly and extemporaneously over them. They then remained at the front of the church, standing to one side.

I moved to the front of the church. When my turn came, I mentioned a few things that were on my mind. Crellin nodded and rested his hands on my arms, and quietly prayed that I find support in the community and through my family. His tone was gentle, and I found it comforting to listen to the prayer. When I moved away, I noticed several people crying. Some were held by those around them while others stood weeping quietly. The service ended in prayer, and people turned to leave.

About a week later, I spoke to Crellin, who explained that when he arrived at St. Stephen's the previous year, the Sunday morning service was two hours long and included healing prayer. He decided to make healing the focus of a separate service three times a year. At the end of our discussion, I asked if he knew of any other Episcopal healing services. The only one he knew about was at Trinity Episcopal Church in Copley Square, and he suggested that I attend that church's weekly service. Disappointed that my fieldwork would be so short-lived, I decided to attend the service he mentioned.

"Oh Lord, Holy God, Giver of Health and Salvation":
Healing Services in the Episcopal Church

I need not have wasted any time being disappointed. Healing services like this one are alive and active in the Episcopal Church in the Boston and Cambridge area. Healing services were reintroduced to Episcopal congregations during the AIDS/HIV crisis of the 1970s and 1980s. During the years before drug therapies provided for long-term survival, these services focused on offering community support and healing rather than prayers that focused on an instant cure (Privitera 2002). Healing services have continued into the present day in many varied forms.

I discovered a diverse range of healing services within the Episcopal Church, from services of healing that occur once per year to charismatic healing teams that offer healing prayer several times each week. The nineteen healing services I attended varied in form. Some offered laying on of hands as part of a traditional Sunday worship service, and others created a separate service with a focus on healing. Seven churches I attended offer healing once per week, while five offer healing monthly. Two churches I visited offer annual healing services with a particular focus, one for survivors of abuse and one for those who have experienced "loss of life in the womb." Some congregations offer training or small conferences on healing, which I also attended, speaking to Episcopal priests and laypeople about their healing ministries. As I gathered this information, I became more and more interested in the ways in which the people I interviewed defined "healing" and "curing" and what they believed could result from sacraments, services, and prayer. This question arose as a theme throughout my interviews and is one I will develop in this chapter.

This research builds upon Meredith McGuire's pioneering 1988 study of suburban healing movements in America. McGuire found that Episcopalians tended to work in specialized prayer ministry teams, laying hands on individuals and providing personal support to them. This was true in many congregations I visited. She also found that some Episcopalians, whom she called neo-pentecostals, used blessed substances to promote healing (McGuire 1988: 65). Episcopalians in her study were more likely to see "positive aspects of suffering and pain" (45), which was reflected in the theme I heard that illness can bring a person into closer relationship to God and other people. Contemporary Episcopal churches in the Boston area seem to hold similar values for healing as those of McGuire's consultants in New Jersey.

There are also several differences between McGuire's work and mine. Whereas her study focused on suburban churches, my fieldwork was conducted primarily in the urban areas of Boston and Cambridge. McGuire's study of Christian groups included pentecostal and neo-pentecostal groups, as well as "healing cults" in mainline churches. My fieldwork focused primarily on healing teams and services in mainline churches. In the nearly twenty years since McGuire's study, healing, alternative medicine, and spirituality have become more widely accepted in mainstream media and culture. This seems to be reflected in the healing ministries of mainline churches, which have begun to incorporate healing services and ministries into their worship life.

The sacrament of anointing with oil, laying on of hands, and prayer are the primary ritual elements of a healing service. Anointing in the contemporary Episcopal Church has its roots in the New Testament of the Christian Bible and, later, in the development of the sacraments in the Catholic Church. The Gospel of Mark (6:13) mentions that the early disciples of Jesus "anointed many sick people with oil and cured them." Liturgical texts indicate that early Christian healing was associated with oil. In the year 215, Hippolytus of Rome wrote *The Apostolic Tradition*, which contains a prayer to bless oil. After the service that Hippolytus describes, attendants took home the oil to be used as medicine (Martos 1982: 372).

People who received reconciliation while dying were also anointed with oil. The sacrament eventually came to be associated with penance and the end of life. By the twelfth century, the prayers for physical healing in this sacrament were replaced with prayers related to forgiveness and salvation. Anointing with oil was made the final action of the rite for the dying person, after reconciliation and communion. During the Middle Ages, anointing came to be called *extrema unctio*, last anointing (Martos 1982: 376–79).

The English Church, from which the Episcopal Church in America is derived, classified unction as a sacrament but later moved it out of the rituals of the church. In 1563, it was listed as one of the five sacraments of the Church, and the Book of Common Prayer contained a rite for extreme unction until 1552. The rite was then left out of new editions of the prayer book until the American Prayer Book of 1928. Anointing was fully reintroduced into recent editions of the prayer book, but the emphasis was on physical rather than spiritual healing (Martos 1982: 385).

Two holy oils are used today in the Episcopal Church. Chrism is used for baptism and the oil of the sick is used for anointing the sick. Both the holy oil and the chrism are blessed for the year during Holy Week, the week that precedes Easter in the Church calendar. I attended this service in April 2001 at the Cathedral Church of St. Paul, the center of mission for the diocese in eastern Massachusetts. The service was led by bishops of the diocese, who bless the oils. There were fourteen leaders of worship, including eight clergy. The majority of those attending the service, about seventy-five people in all, were clergy. The service included readings from the Old and New Testaments and a meditation on these readings. The sung music for the service was made up of simple, repetitive chant with English text. The bishop blessed the oil of the sick with the following prayer:

> O, Lord, Holy God, giver of health and salvation: Send your Holy Spirit to sanctify this oil, that, as your holy apostles anointed many that were sick and healed them, so may those who in faith and repentance receive this holy oil be made well; through Jesus Christ our Lord, who lives and reigns with you and the Holy Spirit, one God, for ever and ever. *Amen*

The bishop blesses the chrism with the following prayer:

Eternal God, whose blessed Son was anointed by the Holy Spirit to
be the Savior and servant of all: We pray you to consecrate this oil
that those who are sealed with it may share in the royal priesthood
of Jesus Christ; who lives and reigns with you and the Holy Spirit,
for ever and ever. *Amen*

The bishop blesses the mingling of the oil and chrism with this prayer:

And so, Father, by the power of your love, make this mixture of oil
and balsam a sign and source of your blessing, that all who will be
anointed with it may be filled with the gifts of your Holy Spirit, be
inwardly transformed and come to share in eternal salvation. *Amen*

The service ended in a celebration of Holy Communion. The clergy in attendance lined up to take small bottles of the blessed oil back to their congregations. Anointing for the rest of the year in Episcopal churches in eastern Massachusetts will be done with the oil blessed at this service.

The contemporary Episcopal Church offers a wide spectrum of anointing
practices. For example, at the Church of the Advent, a large, urban church with
an Anglo-Catholic, high liturgical style, anointing is offered once per month.
Following the Sunday service, several people gather and kneel in a small side
chapel. A priest makes the sign of the cross on the forehead of those who
kneel, without speaking to anyone individually. Following the anointing, a
blessing is offered.

In contrast, at the Church of Our Savior, a small church in Arlington with
a commitment to multiculturalism and social justice, members anoint one
another. During the 10:00 A.M. service on the last Sunday of the month, a
small bowl of holy oil is passed, and each person anoints the person next to
or behind him or her. Congregants are welcome to pass the oil if they do not
wish to participate. Each person anoints another by making a sign of the cross
on his or her forehead, while standing in silence or saying a short blessing
such as "The Lord bless you and keep you."

The structure of the healing service as a whole also varies widely. It can
follow the formal structure of the Public Service of Healing or can incorporate
prayers, songs, and ritual. For example, at Episcopal Divinity School I attended
a weekly healing circle in its kiva chapel, a name that refers to sacred spaces
in the American Southwest.[1] Native American cultures are reflected in the
design of the chapel, which includes an icon depicting Mary and Jesus as a
Native American mother and child. During this service, a small group of students and community members gathered to sing, pray, and lay hands on each
other, using A Service of Prayer for Healing adapted from the Iona Community
in Scotland. The Iona Community is an ecumenical Christian community with
a commitment to social justice and ecumenical renewal of the church. The
service differs from the Public Service of Healing in its use of chant, silence,

and spontaneous prayer. During this service, instead of an ordained priest, a lay leader led songs and prayers, and the participants laid hands on one another while offering prayers.

Ecclesia Ministries, which reaches out to people who are homeless in Boston, offers ecumenical worship services called "common cathedral" outdoors on Boston Common. Led by the Reverend Deborah W. Little, Ecclesia Ministries is an "ecumenical community devoted to mutual learning, reconciliation, and healing."[2] They also hold a weekly Eucharist celebration and healing service at the Cathedral Church of St. Paul. The service includes singing, a reading, a sermon, and a celebration of the Eucharist. During the sermon, Little invites participants to offer their own reflections. No prayer book is used. Little anoints participants with a brief prayer. The tone of this service is more informal than the Public Service of Healing, with participants taking an active role in the service. There is less of a clear line between the participants and the leader.

In addition to separate services that are identified as "healing services," several elements of the Church's Sunday worship service, while not explicitly identified as healing, also offer similar support and care. The Reverend Linda Privitera, rector of Church of Our Saviour in Arlington, suggests that intercessory prayer is one way in which congregants support one another. Intercessory prayer occurs during every Eucharistic celebration. The list of those in need of prayer may include people who are sick, people who have died, or those who are celebrating birthdays or anniversaries; prayers also may address local and global concerns, and personal concerns of the congregation. The prayers are read out loud by an intercessor, and the congregation responds antiphonally. Intercessory prayers may also be offered outside of regular worship. In some congregations, a prayer chain is formed when a member has an emergency. The nature of the emergency and the request for prayer travel through the prayer chain by telephone or e-mail, with the understanding that intercessory prayer will be offered.

The Confession of Sin during the Eucharist service can also be considered a healing element. In this prayer, congregants confess their sins collectively, and are then assured of forgiveness by the celebrant. Individuals may also speak with a priest about their sins and receive reconciliation outside a service. Privitera notes that forgiveness and reconciliation are extremely important parts of the Episcopal Church's work of healing.

"God's Love Conveyed through Touch": Healing Prayer and the Distinction between Healing and Curing

I discovered during my interviews that Episcopalians distinguish between healing and curing. While no simple definitions were offered, the general tenor of remarks suggests that they see "curing" as end of disease or illness and "healing" as an experience of transformation, peace, or improved relationships with other people or God.

The word "healing" is the universal term used in the Episcopal Church. Healing services, healing teams, and a healing ministry are all ways in which congregations described what they offer to those who suffer. Many priests defined healing as a movement toward wholeness. Several suggested that illness can contribute to growth in sick individuals and in those around them. The Reverend Jon Strand, of St. Paul's in Natick, told me that illness can bring a person into closer companionship with God. It is a chance to "claim belovedness by God" because illness forces people to ask if God really cares about them. Healing prayer can be part of transforming a person's relationship with God, as it is "God's love conveyed through touch."

The Reverend Martha Giltinan, of Christ Church of Hamilton and Wenham, explained that healing happens not only for the person who is ill but also in the person's family and community. An experience of illness can help build relationships. Giltinan made a clear distinction between healing and curing, saying that God always heals but does not always cure.

The Episcopal Church has not limited its healing ministry to physical illness. On October 29, 2000, I attended a service at the Cathedral Church of St. Paul called A Healing Service for Those Who Are Affected by Abuse.[3] The service followed the format of a celebration of the Eucharist, with prayers, readings, a sermon, and Holy Communion. The readings had been chosen for the theme of the service and included a story of rape from 2 Samuel, a poem called "The True Love" by David Whyte, and a story from the Gospel of Matthew. Following the homily, a bishop of the church knelt in the center of the room and recited a "confession of sin," which asked for forgiveness on behalf of the Church from people who had suffered abuse. It asked forgiveness for not listening to survivors' stories, for blaming them and asking them to be silent. The prayer closed with the following apology:

I confess, to God and to you, that very often we were the people
who initially abused you, took advantage of you, broke your trust. I
know that in doing this we jeopardized your relationship with God,
made this relationship more difficult for you. I am immensely grateful that somehow you have not completely given up on your faith
and on the church. On behalf of the church I ask God's forgiveness
and your forgiveness. For all this, and much, much more that you
have endured, I am sorry. I am very sorry.

The confession was followed by a communal prayer for healing: "Through the love of God made known in Jesus Christ may God's grace flow through our lives, restoring wholeness to our relationships with God and others. Amen."

This service also included laying on of hands and prayer for healing, during which the rest of the participants sang.

Other Episcopalians I spoke to discussed the possibility of curing, or the end of illness, as a result of prayer. During one of my interviews, an Episcopal priest shared a story about a woman in her congregation who had an illness. Without the knowledge of this woman, the priest and a friend decided to offer long periods of prayer for her over several days. The priest called the woman's family to plan a visit to her in the hospital. She was told that the woman's upcoming surgery had been canceled; her illness had disappeared. The priest believed this woman had experienced a miracle as a result of healing prayer and wanted to celebrate within the congregation. The woman, however, did not believe she had been cured through prayer and did not want to discuss or celebrate the incident.

The healing team with whom I spoke at Christ Church of Hamilton and Wenham, a congregation that is part of the Charismatic Renewal, also discussed both healing and curing. I interviewed the team during January 2001, when a healer was in residence at the church, attending services and working with the healing team. She and the rest of the team had been meeting with people individually for healing prayer. They describe their work as "intuitive, cooperative" rather than the work of willpower. They understand that healing is not magic but a confirmation for the sick person and the healer that the living God is within that person. This healer emphasized that healing is a process. She has seen some people heal in a dramatic way, but generally, God focuses on one area of a person's life, then another, then another. She said, "To grow up in Christ is life-long."

When I spoke with the Reverend Jurgen Liias, the rector of the church, he explained to me that the Charismatic Renewal within the Episcopal Church began in the 1970s–1980s and attempts to bring healing into the mainstream. It is an offshoot of the Pentecostal church, a massive Christian movement attempting to rediscover the charisms of the Holy Spirit. Meredith McGuire, in her study of healing in suburban America, notes that charismatic movements in the Catholic, Episcopal, and other mainline churches since the 1970s have contributed "relatively widespread" Pentecostal-style healing among middle-class persons in these American churches (1988: p. 19).

I attended three different services at Christ Church and spoke to Liias and the church's healing team. Christ Church holds weekly healing services on Wednesday mornings, where a team of lay ministers, as well as a priest, offer laying on of hands and healing prayer. They offer the same in a side chapel during the Sunday morning services. The healing teams pray in a way that I had not seen in other churches: one person on the team prays for the person coming for healing. The second person prays for the other member of the team.

"We Do Not Need to Be Timid in Telling Our
Stories of Healing"

Two of the people I interviewed hold more public positions in the work of the Episcopal Church. Both insist that they do not do the work of healing, God does. Both emphasize the mystery of how healing can and does happen and suggest that people should have an expectation of healing. Finally, both resolve the tension between healing and curing in different ways.

Nigel Mumford, author of *Hand to Hand: From Combat to Healing* (2000) and the director of the Oratory of the Little Way in Gaylordsville, Connecticut, states that whenever people pray, something happens. One does not have to make a distinction between healing and curing because God will always respond to prayer. A former member of Her Majesty's Royal Marine Commandos, Mumford came to his ministry of healing while running a frame shop in Connecticut. After prayer healed his sister Julie of dystonia, a neurological condition, Mumford began to think about the nature of prayer and healing. One day a woman he knew named Betty came into the shop and complained of a headache. Mumford suddenly found himself drawn to place his hands on her head. As he recalls, "I think I must have given a lot of subconscious thought to prayer since Julie's healing because I simply found myself praying silently, asking God to take the headache away. As soon as my hands touched her head, she looked at me in astonishment and said the pain had gone. I shared her amazement and felt another, equally powerful emotion—fear. I knew that in this moment my life had changed. God had taken over and I had no idea where he was about to lead me" (Mumford, 2000: p. 26). Following this incident, Mumford began to see people in his frame shop who were interested in healing. Eventually, a friend offered to share office space with him, and he turned to healing work full-time. In 1995, he sold his framing business and now works as a lay minister of healing. He was installed by his bishop for this healing ministry.

Mumford offers training to congregations that wish to create a ministry of healing. I heard him speak at two such trainings during my fieldwork and interviewed him in March 2003. He was the homilist and a workshop leader for the Leadership Development Institute of the Episcopal Diocese of Massachusetts: "Encouraging the Healing Ministry in Congregations," in February 2001. He gave the homily during the first part of the day, led a workshop, and offered healing prayer during the final Eucharist service. The second time I heard him speak was at St. Paul's Episcopal Church in Natick in February 2002.

During the latter daylong training, Mumford outlined his theology of healing, which contained the idea that when one prays, something always happens.

I had heard this statement made by others with healing ministries. Healing is guaranteed, whereas curing is not. Mumford emphasized this, saying this should be one thing that participants in this daylong training should take away. The theme is repeated early on in his book: "Not everyone who asks for prayer is cured, but everyone is healed in some form or another. I firmly believe that something always happens when we pray for each other. It may not be in the form of immediate physical or emotional healing (although it often is) but a door is always opened. . . . Sometimes healing comes in a most unexpected area and not necessarily in the way we want, but prayer is always answered" (Mumford 2000: 36).

Mumford also spoke of the difference between physical healing and emotional healing. While he states clearly in his book that he always advocates for biomedical care, he also suggests that some physical ailments are manifestations of emotional or spiritual crises. For example, Mumford writes of working with a man who had experienced childhood sexual abuse and who in adulthood had leg pain and a limp. Once this man and Mumford completed their healing prayer about his abuse, the pain disappeared and the man was able to walk without a limp (Mumford 2000: 101).

During our interview, Mumford explained the process that he goes through when meeting with people for healing. The person wanting healing prayer contacts the Oratory of the Little Way by phone or e-mail to make an appointment. A prayer team meets with the person to take a history, and then Mumford sees him or her, with members of the prayer team. They go into the chapel at the Oratory, and "if the Spirit moves," they may have more conversation about what is happening in the person's life. Mumford thinks of this as peeling the layers of an artichoke, rather than an onion, to get down to the heart.

Mumford always explains ahead of time what will happen during healing prayer and asks permission to lay hands on people and anoint them. The primary question he asks is, "How may I pray for you?" He thinks of himself as a "prayer partner" for the people who come to him and encourages them to bring other people to pray with them as well.

A leader in the Boston area Episcopal Church is the Right Reverend Steven Charleston, President and Dean of Episcopal Divinity School. Bishop Charleston has served as the chaplain of Trinity College in Hartford, Connecticut, and as the Episcopal Bishop of Alaska. During our interview in April 2003, Bishop Charleston resolved the tension between healing and curing by defining healing as "the physical, mental, and emotional embodiment of the peace of Christ." Curing occurs when a physical condition is altered. This peace might impact the body, but it does not have to. This peace is experienced when one who needs healing is no longer afraid. He noted that peace is not the absence of conflict. Life is changing and fragile. Bishop Charleston emphasized that the healer is not the agent. Rather, the healer releases what is already within the person being healed. When a person offers healing prayer for someone, he or she reconnects that human being to whatever Christ has already given them. Bishop Charleston stated that we are "always well."

At a daylong conference in February 2001 at Episcopal Divinity School entitled "Partners in Healing: Spiritual and Medical Perspectives on Health and Illness in Communities of Faith," Bishop Charleston offered an opening meditation on healing. During this meditation he encouraged participants to speak about healing, saying, "We do not need to be timid in telling our stories of healing." In telling his own stories of healing, Bishop Charleston weaves issues of social location into his discussion.

During an interview in April 2003, Bishop Charleston listed three ways that social location impacts healing in Episcopal churches in the Boston and Cambridge area. First, affluent people are less likely to recognize their need for healing. When people have fewer resources and are suffering, they are more likely to answer yes to the question, "Do you need healing?" Second, those in affluent contexts compartmentalize and say that only doctors can heal, whereas less affluent people find healing in many different ways, such as going to herbalists. Third, the expectation of healing differs according to social location. White suburban churches have a low expectation of healing, so they might not see healing when it happens. Bishop Charleston also stresses the importance of dialogue across diverse social locations. He suggests that more affluent groups that import healing modalities of other cultures should participate in that dialogue by offering justice and economic redistribution, such as access to health care.

When Bishop Charleston first arrived at Episcopal Divinity School, there was no liturgical healing. He created a healing prayer circle that now meets every week; the group does laying on of hands for those who wish to participate. During a talk at Harvard Divinity School in February 2002, he noted that he believes that healing and curing do happen. "[I] have seen miraculous healings occur and am absolutely convinced that spiritual healing can and does occur. . . . You happen to be the agent of it in that moment, that any human being is capable of that. And in fact all of us are much more capable of it than we're ever willing to entertain."

Conclusion

The healing services of the Episcopal Church offer several appealing elements to those who attend. First, the service builds a community around those who are ill and allows them to speak publicly about their illness. In an American culture where illness is often taken care of within a small circle of family and friends, healing services welcome individuals into a broader church community. A church that offers a healing service acknowledges the private illnesses of its members and makes explicit the church's ability to hear and respond to them. Being acknowledged by the larger community seems to be an essential element of "healing into wholeness."

One of the ways that the Church creates a community of "wholeness" is with a broad definition of healing. The majority of the healing services I attended emphasized that healing can be emotional, spiritual, or physical but is not limited to the body. This definition is so broad that anyone can participate in a healing service. Participants discover through healing services that they do not suffer alone and that other participants, priests and lay leaders, as well as God, are invested in their return to health and wholeness. The services offer a theology that health is the will of God for all people.

Finally, healing services offer participants beauty and a sensorial experience of readings, music, touch, and the scent of holy oil or incense. Healing services often include special hymns, chants, or songs. Readings may focus on healing themes, such as the cures that Jesus performed in the Gospels. Services may also include readings that are not scriptural, such as a poem. Perhaps most important, healing services offer physical touch to participants, through the laying on of hands. This touch varies from a light touch to a close embrace during healing prayer. This prayer and anointing may follow a brief formula or may be a long, spontaneous prayer that lasts several minutes. In an American context, well known for its lack of physical closeness between strangers, individuals who are sick may not be offered pleasant physical touch for long stretches of time. A healing service allows them to be touched in a supportive and loving way that does not require reciprocation. This physical contact is another way of welcoming them into the church community.

Episcopalian theology puts its faith in the will of God, which cannot be fully known by humans. It defines healing in a broad way, relating to all elements of the human experience, with its goal being a return to "wholeness." This wholeness is loosely defined and seems to relate primarily to a rebuilding of relationships, both with God and with one's community. Biomedicine can be criticized for looking too closely at the part of the body that is ill or broken without relating it to the whole life of the individual. Healing ministries attempt to take this larger view and consider the illness within the context of the individual's church community, family, and personal life story. Healing ministries in the Episcopal Church then focus on this broader context, knowing it is impossible to predict when and if suffering will end.

NOTES

1. This information is taken from www.episdivschool.edu/worship/1worship.htm.

2. This quotation is taken from www.ecclesia-ministries.org/aboutcgi.

3. I would like to note that this service preceded the allegations of clergy sexual abuse in the Catholic Archdiocese of Boston. These allegations were reported more than a year later, in January 2002.

REFERENCES

Charleston, Stephen. 2001. Partners in Healing. Opening meditation presented as part of the conference "Partners in Healing: Spiritual and Medical Perspectives on Health and Illness in Communities of Faith," Episcopal Divinity School, Cambridge, Mass.

————. 2002. Ambivalent Healers: The Suburban Suspicion of Healing. Talk given at brown bag lunch and discussion group at Harvard Divinity School, Cambridge, Mass.

————. 2003. Interview by author. April. Cambridge, Mass.

Church Hymnal Corporation. 1988. A Public Service of Healing. In *The Book of Occasional Services*. New York: The Church Hymnal Corporation.

Crellin, Timothy. 2000. Interview by author. September 13. Boston, Mass.

Episcopal Divinity School. N.d. Seminary as a Place of Worship: The Episcopal Divinity School. Electronic document. http://www.episdivschool.edu/worship/1worship.htm. Accessed July 2, 2002.

Giltinan, Martha. 2001. Interview by author. January 24. South Hamilton, Mass.

Iona Community. N.d. About the Community. Electronic document. http://www.iona.org.uk/. Accessed July 2, 2002.

Liias, Jurgen. 2001. Interview by author. January 24. South Hamilton, Mass.

McGuire, Meredith B. 1988. *Ritual Healing in Suburban America*. New Brunswick N.J.: Rutgers University Press.

Martos, Joseph. 1982. *Doors to the Sacred: A Historical Introduction to Sacraments in the Catholic Church*. New York: Image Books.

Mumford, Nigel. 2000. *Hand to Hand: From Combat to Healing*. New York: Church Publications.

————. 2003. Interview by author. March 2. Walpole, Mass.

Privitera, Linda. 2002. Interview by author. October 22. Cambridge, Mass.

Smith, David H. 1986. *Health and Medicine in the Anglican Tradition: Conscience, Community and Compromise*. New York, Crossroad.

Strand, Jon. 2000. Phone interview by author. November 30. Boston.

6

Miraculous Migrants to the City of Angels: Perceptions of El Santo Niño de Atocha and San Simón as Sources of Help and Healing

Patrick A. Polk, Michael Owen Jones,
Claudia J. Hernández, and Reyna C. Ronelli

The problem is not whether Latinos suffer. That is terribly and cru-
elly evident! The problem is how they explain their suffering, know
it as suffering, and make at least some sense of it.

—*Espín 1997: 167*

I am here to see El Niño de Atocha. He is my protector and my
children's protector. He is everything to me. Without him we are
nothing.

—*Female interviewee, Our Lady Queen of Angels,*
Los Angeles

The religious diversity of Los Angeles is nothing short of astonishing. As in many other megacities in the United States, the sacred
landscape of the City of Angels is composed of innumerable cathe-
drals, mosques, synagogues, storefront churches, temples, and
shrines dedicated to nearly every form of religion imaginable. Indeed, it has been estimated that more than 600 distinct faith communities have established religious centers in the city (Orr 1998).
Besides providing immigrants and native-born residents with opportunities to maintain the sacred traditions of their ancestors or perhaps

to choose new ones, this multiplicity of faiths also plays a significant role in the emergence of residential patterns, the establishment of educational institutions, the support of political and social movements, and the operation of health care facilities.

The therapeutic aspects of religiosity in Los Angeles are especially remarkable. Ecclesiasts of all sorts whose pastoral missions directly or indirectly involve health care operate hospitals, hospices, and clinics providing mainstream biomedical techniques. Juxtaposed, but not necessarily at odds, with these resources are countless ethnomedical practitioners (channelers, shamans, spiritual advisers, etc.) who offer alternative or "folk" therapeutic modalities that are based, at least in part, on systems of religious belief. Reflecting the city's demographics, a large number of these healers are Latino immigrants, as are most of their clients. According to the 2000 U.S. Census, more than 4 million Latinos reside in the county of Los Angeles. Of these, almost 2 million were born in Mexico or Central American countries. In the city of Los Angeles itself, Latinos number 1,719,073, thus constituting nearly 47 percent of the total populace. Consequently, health care seekers can find numerous *curanderos* (folk healers), *espiritistas* (spiritists), *parteras* (midwives), *santeros* (practitioners of Afro-Cuban religion), *sobadors* (massage therapists and/or bonesetters), and *yerberos* (herbalists). Many of these have established *botánicas* (religious supply stores), *centros esprituales* (spiritual centers), and clinics through which they offer traditional therapies to the general public.

In this chapter we examine some of the ways that the veneration of a pair of miraculous spirits—El Santo Niño de Atocha and San Simón—is incorporated into Latino vernacular religion and healing traditions in Los Angeles and related to social, familial, and somatic dimensions of migrants' experiences. Following Primiano (1995), we understand vernacular religion to be spirituality "as it is lived: as human beings encounter, understand, interpret, and practice it." By describing aspects of the intersection of Latino popular religiosity and healing, we seek to gain insights into the processes by which, beliefs are manifested, reinforced, and perpetuated. More directly, we wish to show where, how, and why specific individuals turn to El Santo Niño de Atocha and San Simón to find health in times of illness, solace in moments of misery, and salvation in the face of despair.

Blessed by the Holy Child

> I'm not very religious, but when I have time I pray wherever I can. When I have time, I come here to pray. That's life.
>
> —*Female interviewee, Our Lady Queen of Angels,*
> *Los Angeles*

At the north end of Founder's Square in the historic Olvera Street section of downtown Los Angeles stands Our Lady Queen of Angels Catholic Church (Nuestra Señora de Los Angeles). Popularly referred to as "La Placita," it was founded in 1781 and is a Catholic landmark because of its status as the oldest and largest congregation in the Archdiocese of Los Angeles.[1] As testimony to the church's importance within the Latino community, thousands of infants or toddlers are baptized there each month. Further evincing this vibrant cultural connection, the church maintains two elaborate outdoor shrines: one dedicated to the Virgin of Guadalupe, the divine patroness of Mexico; and one for El Santo Niño de Atocha, the patron of children, pilgrims, and those unjustly accused of crimes (Thompson 1994; Lopez de Lara 1990).

Viewed as a true incarnation of the Christ Child, El Santo Niño de Atocha is immensely popular in Spain, Latin America, and increasingly, the United States. In Los Angeles, murals and yard shrines dedicated to him are commonplace. He is usually depicted as an angelic adolescent with curly locks of

El Santo Niño de Atocha. Popular print sold in public markets.

hair and dressed in pilgrim's garb. Candles and chromolithographs bearing his image appear on public and private altars throughout the region as well as at accident sites, murder scenes, and protest marches. La Placita's grotto-like *santuario* for El Niño features a waterfall that spills over a wall of ornamental rocks accentuated with faux cacti (*nopales*). Poised near the top of the shrine is a glass-enclosed statue of the Christ Child. A pool that collects at the base of the cascade sparkles with light reflected off coins that have been tossed into the basin by the faithful. Although the icon itself is surprisingly diminutive, little more than one foot in height, its position within the ritual architecture of La Placita is formidable. Nearly all who attend mass in the church or line up outside the tiny baptismal rooms must pass by El Niño's shrine. Many take the time to offer a prayer or some other sacramental devotion.

Popular tradition holds that the cult of El Santo Niño first arose in medieval Spain and was subsequently transplanted to the Americas by missionaries and settlers (Thompson 1994; Kay 1987). According to legend, he initially appeared when an army of Moors captured the Spanish village of Atocha and held its adult inhabitants hostage. The families of the starving captives prayed for divine intercession, and shortly thereafter an unknown child dressed in pilgrim's garb and bearing a basket of bread and a gourd of water appeared at the city's gates. Allowed into Atocha, the mysterious youth nourished the imprisoned citizens with helpings of food and drink that did not diminish, regardless of how much was given out. It was soon decided that such providential assistance, meted out in the guise of a child, could only have been the work of Jesus Christ, the Son of God himself (Thompson 1994; Lopez de Lara 1990).

In the Americas, two sanctuaries are particularly renowned for public devotions to El Santo Niño de Atocha: one at Plateros near the town of Fesnillo in the Mexican state of Zacatecas and the other in the United States at Chimayo in northern New Mexico. Both have been significant pilgrimage sites since at least the nineteenth century.[2] At Plateros, the earliest recorded miracle attributed to the Holy Child occurred in 1829 when he interceded on behalf of an imprisoned woman. In the years that have followed, he has been credited with assisting countless devotees, and it is estimated that 2 million pilgrims now journey to Plateros annually. One early visitor to the shrine in Plateros was Señor Blas Severiano Medina, who in 1856 was cured of rheumatism and subsequently made the pilgrimage as an act of appreciation. Upon returning to his home in Chimayo, New Mexico, Medina erected a chapel to house an image of El Niño. Tales of miraculous cures and interdictions soon spread. Today, especially during the Holy Week, thousands of adherents make the trek to this shrine as well (Thompson 1994; Lopez de Lara 1990; Kay 1987).

For nine days in 1998, the sacred icon of El Niño de Atocha belonging to the Church of Nuestra Señora de Atocha in Plateros was brought to Los Angeles and ensconced in the courtyard of La Placita. Church officials estimate that from July 18 to 27 approximately 100,000 devotees made the pilgrimage to see him. On each of the nine days, many of the sermons, proclamations, and public events that took place were dedicated to the physical and spiritual welfare of children. Highlighting this overarching emphasis, one cleric declared that this representation of Christ as an infant is also the image of all children who are "despised, mistreated, defamed, offended, violated, forgotten and in lesser cases treated with indifference" (Trujillo 1998). The lasting impact of El Niño's visit is best attested to by the fact that within two months the administrators of La Placita had erected a permanent shrine to him and opened it to the public with great fanfare, including Aztec dancers and mariachis.

Since its installation, the *santuario* has become a locus of vernacular rites and devotional practices. Either kneeling or standing erect, the faithful dutifully recite prayers before the image of El Niño. Usually they do so with quiet reverence, but occasionally they sound out the words loudly and passionately. Bouquets of colorful, sweet-smelling flowers—roses, geraniums, and marigolds—are set on the ground in front of the grotto. Many individuals light glass-encased candles (*velas*) and place them on special shelves. Some even bring embroidered garments intended for use in dressing the statue. Most notably, though, visitors have left thousands of votive offerings pinned, taped, or otherwise affixed to a large message board located to the right of the Holy Child's statue. Along with numerous small pewter ex-votos (*milagros*), most cast in the shape of pilgrims or afflicted body parts, one finds scores of photographs, prayer cards, and handwritten notes and letters.[3] Material dialogues projected onto the object of faith by adherents, these items broadcast shared concerns to the wider community of believers and, in many cases, provide evidence of answered prayers.

The predicaments regularly referenced by offerings include freedom from incarceration, safe journeys, and assistance with immigration procedures. Exemplifying this last category is a seventeen-year-old female who was born in Zacatecas, Mexico, but has lived in Los Angeles most of her life. She came to offer prayers of thanks to El Niño. She said, "I had an appointment for citizenship, and I asked him for everything to go OK and it did. It's like a miracle." In him she found not only a divine protector but also a compatriot with a common history of immigration. Like her, she noted, he too came to Los Angeles from Zacatecas. Another worshiper claimed that this incarnation of the Christ Child actually originated in his own hometown in the Mexican state of Jalisco. "Just like the Virgin of Guadalupe is from the Basilica [in Mexico City]," he proudly announced, "El Niño is from Huescalapa." Still others maintained that different Mexican cities and even Cuatepeque, El Salvador, represent El Niño's earlier place of residence or at least his most important sanctuary. Pivotal here is the popular understanding of the Christ Child as a fellow traveler or *compañero* on the roads that lead migrants from their birthplaces to distant, unfamiliar terrains north of the border. He comes from their place of origin, walks with them, and shares their experiences. For this reason, he is thought to be more apt to help devotees transcend the difficulties of the journey.

Although the Holy Child is petitioned for numerous reasons, the vast majority of the objects left at the shrine relate to issues of physical and mental health. References to cancer, work-related injuries, surgical procedures, and birth defects appear frequently. One letter reads, "Dear Santo Niño de Atocha, I write you this note as a petition and plea to you. Please do me the favor of helping me, so that tomorrow, my right shoulder operation goes well. I know that you are going to help me." Another states in part, "Santo Niño de Atocha, please watch over my uncle Panchito and cure him of his cancer. Only you can help him." Both agonizing and inspiring, most of the items concern children. Baby pictures, sonograms, swaddling clothes, clippings of hair, and even tiny hospital bracelets are prominent. Out of the more than 150 photographs observed during one visit, nearly two-thirds showed infants, adolescents, or expectant mothers. A slip of paper placed next to a picture of a young girl reads, "Dear Niño, Please heal Hannah. Give her a quick recovery. We leave her in your precious hands." The Holy Child of Atocha may or may not be able to intercede on every petitioner's behalf, but it is certainly thought to be a possibility given his reputation for performing miracles.

Some of the cases put before El Niño deal with more complicated social aspects of child welfare. Coming directly to the shrine from a meeting with Child Protective Services, a young woman whose infant had been removed from her custody affixed a blue baby cap in the hope that Santo Niño would straighten out the situation. Not far from the little hat, someone else had placed a miniature pair of tennis shoes. Written on one of them were the words "My husband and I are not able to have children. If you would like to give your child up for adoption so that he/she will have a better life call [telephone number]." Although we do not know how often such requests are made, they do frame a burgeoning dilemma. Latino children constituted 31 percent of children in foster care in California in 1998, and they currently represent the fastest growing ethnic group in the child welfare system (Quintanilla and Mroz 2002; U.S. Department of Health and Human Services 2000). At the same time, Latinos are underrepresented among foster and adoptive parents. Barriers to formal adoption include mistrust of government agencies, eligibility requirements that often eliminate potential minority adoptive parents, and lack of culturally and linguistically responsive recruitment strategies (Bausch and Serpe 1999; Quintanilla and Mroz 2002). Thus, the Holy Child of Atocha is turned to for help in bringing children out of state custody, as well as utilized as an adjunct to informal processes of adoption.

The apparent desperation of petitioners and the anxious wait for divine power to manifest are especially compelling. Miguel, a Mexican national who migrated to Los Angeles from Puebla in the early 1990s, visits the *santuario*

Petitions to El Santo Niño de Atocha. Used with permission from Patrick A. Polk.

on a regular basis. "Twice a week," he said, "I come to see El Niño de Atocha, to talk with him and pray." During these conversations he asks the Holy Child to guarantee the health of his children, parents, and brothers as well as his own. On the occasion of our meeting, Miguel was waiting for his girlfriend to arrive with their infant child, who was suffering from a glandular problem. Although Miguel had left offerings at the shrine just the day before, he confided that the baby was "not doing too good." Asked if this second visit was a plea for help, Miguel responded, "Exactly." He then added, "My girlfriend is bringing something for him as well, like this here [points to a *milagro*], or like some little booties." When his girlfriend arrived, the baby carefully wrapped in a blanket, she and Miguel pinned to the bulletin board a handwritten note asking for divine intercession. They then affixed a tiny pair of shoes, an act that references both the age of the sick infant and the popular belief that because El Niño travels far and wide to assist petitioners, he constantly requires new shoes to replace those he wears out. After reciting silent prayers and lighting several *velas*, the hopeful parents tenderly dabbed a little holy water on the baby's forehead and left.

Reassuringly, many of the votive messages left at the sanctuary articulate feelings of appreciation to the divinity for having helped when called upon. The missive attached to one infant's photograph simply declares, "Thank you Santo Niñito de Atocha for the life of this marvelous being." In response to a successful medical procedure, another grateful family wrote of their child, "His kidney operation on the twentieth of June 2001 went well, and we offered you a promise of letting his hair grow without cutting it for two years. We are keeping the promise like you kept yours." One woman we interviewed visits El Niño as often as she can, usually once or twice a month. Explaining the reason for this, she exclaimed:

> I have a daughter who is a miracle. A number of doctors had told me that I needed to abort her. Well, I actually didn't know that it was going to be a girl yet, but the doctors told me that I was going to have a dangerous pregnancy and that it was going to be too risky for the baby and I. They told me that I should think about the children I already had. But we don't believe in abortions or things like that, so what I did is I offered my baby to El Niño de Atocha. And there is my little girl now. She is a miracle.

The thankful mother claims that she did not grow up as an active devotee but only began to venerate the Holy Child upon her marriage. She noted, "I was very devoted to the Virgin of Guadalupe. But the more I would hear about him, the more he caught my attention. He was in my subconscious." When advised by doctors that she should abort the fetus, she and her husband turned to El Niño. "My husband said, 'God sent this baby to us, and God will have the last word.' And I was of the same opinion. God knows why he does things, and I put my baby in the hands of El Santo Niño de Atocha."

Some petitioners have been adherents since childhood; others became so later in life. Some assert deep and unconditional belief in El Niño; others profess less resolute degrees of commitment. They may come to offer prayers regularly, occasionally, or only in times of dire need. Asked if El Niño was especially important to him, one young man replied, "Well, definitely I'm not a devotee of anybody. It's just that when I'm not feeling well, I come and talk out my problems and that gives me a feeling of relief. It's not so much that I have a lot of faith in him. I simply talk and de-stress. It's an outlet." If nothing else, El Niño de Atocha acts as someone with whom this recent immigrant can vocalize and vent the tribulations of daily life. Such interludes with the Holy Child also serve as an antidote to alienation. Touching on this aspect of popular religiosity, the young man commented, "When I was living in Mexico, I could visit other family members and I could escape my reality. But here where do you go? You can't go to your neighbor's house. They are only going to put up with you for half an hour before they start wondering when you are going to leave [laughs]. It's very difficult to not feel alone here."

The existence of a sanctuary specifically dedicated to El Niño and the countless visible testimonies to his active presence provide, at the very least, a sense of closeness to his power. Accordingly, a woman whose son has an inoperable tumor and who has made pilgrimages to several shrines for St. Jude in search of divine assistance came to the *santuario* to leave a prayer card and *milagro* for El Niño. She stated, "We were in Los Angeles, so we came here." Likewise, another adherent, a woman who currently resides in Los Angeles, stated that she used to undertake the pilgrimage to Plateros in honor of the Holy Child. Now she comes to Our Lady Queen of Angels. When asked why, she responded, "The priest said that if you owe a promise, you can pay it here." Indeed, from the point of view of the faithful, the sanctuary and icon are palpable manifestations of El Niño's spiritual essence. The clerics at La Placita did not just bring an image of the Holy Child closer to the residents of Los Angeles; El Santo Niño de Atocha, himself, was brought nearer to them.

Hermano San Simón

> What I believe is all about San Simón. God first, and then San Simón. Yes, I believe. Because without God and San Simón, I would not be what I am. I cure many people that can't be cured. Not even by doctors. What I can do is put faith in God and in San Simón and plants.
>
> —*Curandero from Guatemala*

San Simón, a Guatemalan folk saint, is fast becoming one of the most familiar of the multitude of immigrant gods, spirits, and saints whose icons and representations are used to mark sacred space in Los Angeles. Nearly a dozen botánicas bear his name, and another refers to Maximón, by which he is also known.[4] This is not surprising, given that Los Angeles is second only to the capital city of Guatemala as the largest urban concentration of Guatemalan citizens. Accordingly, the walls and display windows of botánicas that cater to Guatemalans and other recent immigrants from Central America often feature murals fashioned in San Simón's likeness. Inside, they invariably have small altars dedicated to the saint, who typically is shown as a light-complexioned adult seated in a chair with a cane or staff in his right hand. He normally wears a wide-brimmed, black hat and a white shirt, black suit, shoes or boots, and red tie. He generally has a cigarette or cigar in his mouth or one of his hands.

Although the Vatican does not recognize him, San Simón is nonetheless greatly revered. Offerings consist of cigarettes, liquor, money, tamales, and fruit accompanied by prayers and candles intended to safeguard or enrich the petitioner. A red candle stands for love, green symbolizes prosperity, white guards children, yellow protects adults, pink secures health, blue brings work and luck, and sky blue assures money and happiness (Tedlock 1993: 219). A person may also exhort Brother Simón to cause harm to enemies; one sometimes sees black candles in front of altars, often with a name scratched on the surface. As Schwartz observes (1983: 153), "One may petition him for things one would not ask of other saints, for example, sexual success, revenge on enemies, overlooking of debts and so on." Prayers to San Simón possess a tone of familiarity; "he is called 'brother,' spoken to in diminutives, and addressed in informal (the Spanish 'tu' form) verbs" (Schwartz 1983: 153; see also Glittenberg 1994: 169).

Nobody knows exactly where, when, how, or why veneration of San Simón began. Effigies appear in numerous shrines, or, *santuarios*, throughout Guatemala. Famous sites include Zunil in the western department (region) of Quetzaltenango, Santiago Atitlán in Solalá, and San Andrés Itzapa in Petén. The figure's appearance and name differ from one place to another. Visitors to Santiago Atitlán report that he is called Maximón and describe him as sporting multicolored scarves attached to the brim of a large black hat and "colorful Mayan pants and two-tone leather shoes" (Bronstein 2001). Castañeda-Medinilla (1979: 131–35) includes photos of the saint dressed as a policeman (San Andrés Itzapa), a man of means in fashionable black suit and hat (Cuilco), a worker in straw hat, dark shirt and pants, and heavy shoes (Zunil), and with a wadded-up native cloth as his body (San Jorge La Laguna). Because San Simón and St. Jude Thaddeus have the same birthdate (October 28), some people suggest that they are brothers (or the same person). Others refer to the folk saint as San Simón, Maximón, Jude, Judas Iscariot, or Judas Simón (Schwartz 1983). "The confusion of personalities appears to hinge a good deal on the name Simon," Mendelson writes, "an interesting fact given the present-day etymology of Maximon as *Mam-shimon* [from the Mayan deity Mam] and frequent mention of Judas as Simon Judas." Mendelson refers to Simon Peter as well as Judas, son of Simon, as possible sources of appellations (see also Cook 2000; Christenson 2001; Tedlock 1993).

Regardless of his varied names and dress, and his likely syncretic origins in Maya, Catholic, and local traditions, most commentators seem to agree that San Simón qua Hermano Simón appeared in Guatemala in the twentieth century (e.g., Mendelson 1959; Schwartz 1983). A story told about the saint's or-

igins by a botánica owner calling himself Hermano (Brother) Carlos coincides
with this assumption:

> He came from Italy and when he arrived, he chose a place where
> the poor lived and this place was called Zunil. They say he came es-
> pecially to Guatemala on a small airplane. He became very famous
> because he would give out medicine, money, vaccines and he would
> protect people. . . . And everyone liked him, but those people who
> envied him wanted to kill him. They would say that he was not a
> doctor but a witch. . . . They didn't let him work and prohibited him
> to give anything to people. . . . Since they wanted to kill him, the In-
> dians would protect him.

With the help of some Maya, the Italian doctor traveled towards Guatemala
City to escape those who would persecute him. While on his journey he stopped
at an isolated house on a mountain path in the place that would later become
San Andrés Iztapa. Here a mysterious old man greeted him and offered him
coffee. After drinking from the cup, the Italian was transformed into San Simón. "Now," claims Carlos, "this saint is very miraculous in Guatemala. Whatever you ask him, he will grant it."

A spiritist (*espiritista*) and folk healer (*curandero*) from Zamayac Sochilte-
peques in Guatemala, Hermano Carlos established his botánica in Los Angeles
in 1994. He treats a wide variety of ailments with herbs and rituals, counsels
people who have personal problems, provides *limpias* (spiritual cleansings),
and performs *trabajos*, or "works" (the removal or casting of spells). Born in
1959, he became aware of San Simón at the age of six when he began working
at a *barrotería*, a store that sells food and liquor. The owner believed in this
saint, so Carlos helped build an altar in the store, and every Tuesday and Friday
the two of them would put an image of San Simón outside to attract customers.
By the age of eight Carlos knew he had special powers, including clairvoyance.
He arrived in Los Angeles on February 25, 1988, a migration fraught with life-
threatening situations and whose success he ascribes to the divine intercession
of God and San Simón. Upon reaching Los Angeles, Carlos worked at a variety
of jobs including cleaning homes, construction, and tree trimming. One day
a neighbor in his apartment building told him, "I'm bringing you something."
He gave him a small statue of San Simón. "He picked it up from the street
and brought it to me as if someone would have told him, 'Take it to Carlos.'
And that's how I have it. Ever since I was in Guatemala I knew about him, but
here in the U.S. is where I got this statue."

Devoted to the saint, Carlos uses half the space in his botánica as a *templo*
for San Simón. Approximately twelve feet wide by thirty feet long, the temple
contains at one end a nearly life-size representation of San Simón inside a
glass case illuminated with fluorescent lights. Satin cloth adorns the back,

Hermano (Brother) Carlos. Used with permission from Patrick A. Polk.

behind the straight-back chair serving as the saint's throne. Fresh flowers in vases stand on either side. A large bouquet rests in his lap. The encased figure reposes on a raised platform flanked by smaller statues of this saint, along with the Virgin Mary, Jesus Christ, and other holy personages, as well as offerings of food, drink, and cigarettes to San Simón. A table in front of the shrine holds dozens of lighted glass candles, or *velas*. Supplicants have placed more burning candles on the floor under and around the table. In a corner at the opposite end of the room stand crutches left by individuals who have miraculously regained the functioning of their lower limbs. Another, smaller figure of San Simón sits on a table nearby with his mouth open to receive liquor that drains through a tube into a vodka bottle, transforming it into a curative bath. Three fire extinguishers hang on the walls. The air is heavy with fragrances, the temperature ten to fifteen degrees hotter than outside.

Hermano Carlos told us proudly that his altar replicates the one in San Andrés Itzapa. Like the grotto at La Placita in Los Angeles that reproduces sanctuaries for El Santo Niño de Atocha in Mexico and New Mexico, Hermano Carlos's temple dedicated to San Simón imitates the shrine in his natal country. This *curandero* has brought more than a temple to Los Angeles, however; he has transported the folk saint, as well as other spirits from San Andrés Itzapa who were family members and noted healers. Among them are uncles and aunts whom he refers to as "Brother Rodolfo, Brother Francisco García, Brother Fidelino Figueroa, and Sister Catalina," along with Brother Ronaldo, his mother, whose name was Rosa Figueroa, and his grandmother, Francisca Orizaba. "It's with them that I work. If I ask them to cure someone, I can cure them." When asked if they are the ones who always help him, he answered, "Yes. I am working with them and always with San Simón from San Andrés Itzapa and Zunil. I ask them to help me and to give me clairvoyance so I can say things."

Hermano Carlos maintains that his temple and, more specifically, the large effigy of San Simón are community resources. Individuals bring bouquets of flowers to place in the lap of the saint, and they even dress him. Cigarettes are lit, puffed on twice, and then placed in the mouth of one or another of the smaller replicas flanking the large statue. Some people bring liquor, take a shot, and leave the rest for the saint. They ask for his help and offer the toast "Cheers, San Simón." Believers often whisper their requests in his right ear, a mode of pleading that is thought to be especially efficacious. Some write letters that they place in the hand of the large figure, or they bring photographs of those who have mistreated them, petitioning San Simón for protection or retribution. They put the photos under San Simón's left foot, said to be the one that he uses to dominate.

In association with the local Brotherhood of San Simón (Cofradía de San Simón), a lay association to which he belongs, Hermano Carlos plays host to a festival annually on a Sunday in late October, on or near the feast day of San Simón (October 28). Mostly attended by Central Americans, the festivities include a procession during which worshipers "walk" the saint through the streets near the botánica-temple. Participants take turns hoisting a platform bearing a statue of the saint onto their shoulders while swinging back and forth to the music of a marimba band. The parade ends at a tented parking lot behind the botánica where the congregants welcome San Simón with his favorite song, "El Rey de Mil Coronas" (The King of a Thousand Crowns). Later, people perform traditional dances, a group of women in native costume enact a story through dance of how one was healed with herbs, and food, beer, and soft drinks abound. Throughout the event many visit the temple, light candles, and pray to San Simón.

Questions begging answers, if we are to understand the reasons for the adoration of San Simón and the popularity of this folk saint, are, first, how has he assisted people, and second, why do they think they *need* his help? At a festival on October 22, 2000, several people who entered the temple talked about what San Simón has done for them. One woman from Guatemala said, "For me, San Simón is the best. He is great, and he has given me all I've asked him for. He is lovely, he is powerful, and that's why I *love* San Simón. *¡Que viva San Simón!* [Long live St. Simon!]." When did you first hear about him? "Four years ago I started believing in San Simón. I didn't believe in him before, but now I love him, and que viva San Simón!" What miracles has he performed for you? "I'm not living with my husband now. He took my two girls with him to Mexico, and I asked San Simón to bring them back to me, and he did. That's why I love San Simón." She said that she visits the saint at this temple "when I need him to help me with something, and I bring him some flowers." She was dressing him this day, replacing his shoes with a pair of light blue ostrich boots. "They're not very expensive, but for me they don't cost anything if they are for someone as wonderful as he is, and he's worthy of something even more expensive."

Another woman who also emigrated from Guatemala said, "The first time I heard about San Simón was when a friend of mine who's very devoted to him told me that he had done many miracles, so that's when I started believing in him." On this feast day she brought flowers for the altar. Asked why she was devoted to him, she replied, "The first great thing he did for me was to help me pass the citizenship test, when I didn't know how to speak a bit of English. There was also another time when I crossed the border through Tijuana with two kids [her niece and nephew]. They didn't do anything to me. They just arrested me and took one of the kids with them and I had prayed to him so much that nothing really happened. I could have lost my green card."

A man from El Salvador who is now an American citizen said that he first learned of San Simón the previous year and visits him often in the temple: "I have an allergy on my head. And I started coming here, and they [botánica staff] gave me medicine, and they made me pray for him so that he would cure me. And through his power and the will of God, I feel better now. And I also want to add that he has granted me everything that I've asked him for. And I have kept my faith toward him. I put all my problems in the hands of his spirit, and I'm always able to solve them."

San Simón has helped these three people deal with troubling familial and somatic problems (gaining custody of one's children, reducing the suffering from a chronic ailment), as well as the kinds of tribulations that befall many immigrants (crossing the border without incident, passing the test to become a U.S. citizen).

For Hermano Carlos, who established the temple, San Simón "gives me strength and ideas," helping him assist others who are ill or suffer other problems. "What most people come to see me about is when they're dealing with stress [*estres*]," as well as functional complaints such as headache, body aches, arthritis, colds, coughs, impotence, and "love problems" (*problemas de amor*). In addition, "There are people from our countries [in Central America] who believe they do not have good luck in life or cannot have children, so I give them something. Or people affected by witchcraft . . . , I can take that away. . . . I get a lot of cases having to do with people getting treated very badly by their bosses at work, or that of people being humiliated and treated badly by workers that have been at the workplace longer. Also, I get a lot of people that are unemployed. These people have a lot of faith in God, San Simón and me, and they come to me." They "light a candle or something, and they calm down. Sometimes they get treated bad at work and they can't complain or fight back so they come here and San Simón listens to them."

Conclusion: Place, Faith, and Healing

> When we leave this world, that is the only thing we will leave our
> children: our culture and faith. That stays. And in a moment of
> need, the person goes back to that place.
>   —*Female interviewee, Our Lady Queen of Angels*

Vernacular devotions to El Santo Niño de Atocha and San Simón arise and are maintained because they address fundamental human concerns in effective and meaningful ways. Among other things, they provide adherents with evidence of the divine manifested in everyday life; they enable practitioners to develop personal, often liberating, relationships with sacred powers; they help individuals and groups (families, neighbors, parishioners, etc.) to better deal with their immediate emotional and physical needs; and they encapsulate key notions of cultural, ethnic, and regional or national identity (Lippy 1994; Orsi 1997). Additionally, scholars of Latino popular religiosity have emphasized the role of such devotions in the maintenance of cultural values and familial relationships across generations, as a resource for interpreting and explaining suffering and death, as a basis for crafting responses to oppression and social inequity, and as a means of making sense out of cultural displacement and transnational migration by filtering the experience of border crossing through the prism of mythology and hagiography (Espín 2002; Goizueta 2002).

As we have seen, devotees interact with El Niño de Atocha and San Simón in much the same way as they would with friends, loved ones, and family members. They speak with them in loving tones, dress them in handsome outfits, celebrate their birthdays, offer them their favorite foods, and present them with special gifts. And, as is the case with human relationships, believers sometimes complain to them, chastise them for inattention, and may even question their commitment to the faithful. In short, the sacred is made *familiar* through the experiences of human life. Artifacts such as paintings, chromolithographs, statues, and votive objects give a visual presence to divine beings, while rites, rituals, and processions bring mind and movement into communion with them. Stories, tales, and personal experience narratives serve as verbal testimonies to the effectiveness of faith. The specific ways in which the sacred is envisioned, enacted, and recounted, of course, depend very much on the day-to-day contexts in which adherents live, work, and pray.

In our exploration of vernacular religious traditions among Latinos in Los Angeles, we see that immigrants have replicated spiritual sites associated with their homelands as a means of becoming more at home in this city. Beyond acting as mere replicas, however, these nascent shrines are invested with new uses and meanings evolving out of the realities of resettlement in Los Angeles. Drawing on faith traditions and reacting to lived experience in Los Angeles, individuals turn to El Santo Niño de Atocha and San Simón when anxious and under stress and when seeking answers to problems that do not admit ready solutions, such as making ends meet, migrating to and living in an unfamiliar place, finding a soul mate, holding a family together, treating chronic illness, or protecting oneself in a dangerous environment. More often than not, the exact nature of an adherent's trouble is clear-cut, whether cancer, loneliness, fear, unemployment, domestic violence, or immigration status. Sadly, though, understanding the immediate source of a problem does not mean that it is easily remedied or rectified. Thus, for those faced with seemingly insurmountable difficulties, a cause for hope can be found in the grace and guidance of supernatural entities. Whether migrant, immigrant, or lifelong resident, many devotees regularly confront structural inequities that render them impoverished, unprotected, or otherwise in of need social and spiritual assistance. Altars, shrines, and sacred sites make the divine knowable and accessible in time of need, which all too often, and for all too many Angelenos, is every day. The simple truth of this—whether or not one is a believer—can be seen in the fact that the Holy Child of Atocha never lacks tiny shoes for his weary feet, and the stern-faced saint from Guatemala always has an ample supply of coffee, cigars, and alcohol to enliven his spirit. Thank you, Santo Niño! *¡Que viva San Simón!*

NOTES

The research on which this chapter is based was funded in part by a grant from the Harvard Pluralism Project. The project was also supported by Grant No. 5 R21-AT00202 from the National Center for Complementary and Alternative Medicine (NCCAM). The chapter's contents are solely the responsibility of the authors and do not necessarily represent the official views of NCCAM or the National Institutes of Health. We wish to thank Jules Hart and West Barbar for assistance in interviewing and videotaping at the San Simón temple during the festival on October 22, 2000.

    1. On September 2, 2002, the Cathedral of Our Lady of the Angels was dedi-

cated in downtown Los Angeles, not far from La Placita. It remains to be seen how this church site, one widely described by clergy as the new "spiritual home" of Los Angeles's growing Catholic population, will affect utilization of the Church of Nuestra Señora de Los Angeles.

2. Unlike other Mexican and Central American popular devotions such as those for the Virgin of Guadalupe, the literature on the cult of El Niño de Atocha does not suggest much connection to indigenous pre-Christian traditions. Fuller study, of course, may reveal historical continuities that have been overlooked.

3. All of these are periodically removed and stored by church officials. Occasionally, special items are sent to the shrine for El Santo Niño in Plateros, Mexico.

4. Although botánicas are most frequently associated with the practice of Afro-Cuban religion, in Los Angeles the majority of these shops seem to be run by Mexicans, Mexican Americans, and Central Americans (Jones and Polk 2001; León 2002).

REFERENCES

Bausch, R. S., and R. T. Serpe. 1999. Recruiting Mexican-American Adoptive Parents. *Child Welfare* 78: 693–716.
Bronstein, Hugh. 2001. Guatemala's Protestants Collide with Mayan Beliefs. http://www.imadr.org/project/guatemala/news2.html.
Castañeda-Medinilla, José. 1979. Maximón, un caso de magia imitativa. *Guatemala Indígena* 14: 131–42.
Christenson, Allen J. 2001. *Art and Society in a Highland Maya Community: The Altarpiece of Santiago Atitlán.* Austin: University of Texas Press.
Cook, Garrett W. 2001. *Renewing the Maya World: Expressive Culture in a Highland Town.* Austin: University of Texas Press.
Espín, Orlando O. 1997. *The Faith of the People: Theological Reflections on Popular Catholicism.* Maryknoll, N.Y.: Orbis Books.
———. 2002. Mexican Religious Practices, Popular Catholicism, and the Development of Doctrine. In *Horizons of the Sacred: Mexican Traditions in U.S. Catholicism,* ed. Timothy Matovina and Gary Riebe-Estrella, 139–52. Ithaca, N.Y.: Cornell University Press.
Glittenberg, Jody. 1994. *To the Mountain and Back: The Mysteries of Guatemalan Highland Family Life.* Prospect Heights, Ill.: Waveland Press.
Goizueta, Roberto S. 2002. The Symbolic World of Mexican American Religion. In *Horizons of the Sacred: Mexican Traditions in U.S. Catholicism,* ed. Timothy Matovina and Gary Riebe-Estrella, 119–38. Ithaca, N.Y.: Cornell University Press.
Isasi-Díaz, Ada María. 1993. *En la Lucha/In the Struggle: A Hispanic Women's Liberation Theology.* Minneapolis: Fortress Press.
Jones, Michael Owen, and Patrick A. Polk, with Ysamure Flores Peña and Roberta J. Evanchuck. 2001. Invisible Hospitals: Botánicas in Ethnic Health Care. In *Healing Logics: Culture and Medicine in Modern Health Belief Systems,* ed. Erika Brady, 39–87. Logan, Utah: Utah State University Press.
Kay, Elizabeth. 1987. *Chimayo Valley Traditions.* Santa Fe, N.M.: Ancient City Press.
León, Luis D. 2002. Soy una Curandera y Soy una Católica: The Poetics of a Mexican

Healing Tradition. In *Horizons of the Sacred: Mexican Traditions in U.S. Catholicism*, ed. Timothy Matovina and Gary Riebe-Estrella, 95–118. Ithaca, N.Y.: Cornell University Press.

Lippy, Charles H. 1994. *Being Religious, American Style: A History of Popular Religion in the United States*. Westport, Conn.: Greenwood Press.

López de Lara, J. Jesús. 1990. *El Niño de Santa María de Atocha*. Plateros, Zacatecas, Mexico: Santuario de Plateros.

Mendelson, E. Michael. 1959. Maximon: An Iconographical Introduction. *Man* 59: 57–60.

Ochoa, Pilar Sanchiz. 1993. Sincretismos de ida y vuelta: El culto de San Simón en Guatemala. *Mesoamérica* 26: 253–66.

Orr, John. 1998. *Los Angeles: A Civic Profile 1998*. Los Angeles: University of Southern California, Center for Religion and Civic Culture.

Orsi, Robert. 1997. Everyday Miracles: The Study of Lived Religion. In *Lived Religion in America: Toward a History of Practice*, ed. David D. Hall, 3–21. Princeton, N.J.: Princeton University Press.

Pieper, Jim. 2002. *Maximon/San Simon, Rey Pascual, Judas, Lucifer, and Others*. Los Angeles: Pieper and Associates.

Primiano, Leonard Norman. 1995. Vernacular Religion and the Search for Method in Religious Life. *Western Folklore* 54: 37–56.

Quintanilla, Maria L., and Carol Mroz. 2002. Remove Barriers and Latino Families Will Adopt. *Newsletter of North American Council on Adoptable Children (NACAC)*. http://www.nacac.org/newsletters/familieschildrenofcolor/latino.html.

Schwartz, Norman Boris. 1983. San Simón: Ambiguity and Identity in Petén, Guatemala. *Sociologus* 33: 152–73.

Sexton, James D., and Ignacio Bizarro Ujpán. 1999. *Heart of Heaven, Heart of Earth and Other Mayan Folktales*. Washington, D.C.: Smithsonian Institution Press.

Tedlock, Dennis. 1993. *Breath on the Mirror: Mythic Voices and Visions of the Living Maya*. San Francisco: HarperSanFrancisco.

Thompson, John. 1994. Santo Niño de Atocha. *Journal of the Southwest* 36(1): 1–18.

Trujillo, Emma. 1998. La esperanza de la humanidad está en la niñez. *La Cruz de California*. September. http://www.lacruzdecal.com/ed/articles/1998/0998et.htm.

U.S. Department of Health and Human Services. 2000. Child Welfare Outcomes 1998: Annual Report. Washington D.C.: U.S. Department of Health and Human Services.

PART II

Healing from Structural Violence

La Cultura Cura

7

"God Made a Miracle in My Life": Latino Pentecostal Healing in the Borderlands

Gastón Espinosa

Despite the centrality of healing and sporadic references to "Spanish faith healers" in works by American religion scholars such as Robert Orsi (1985), we know almost nothing about who these healers are, what they want to accomplish, when they began, where they conduct their services, and why they attract the allegiances of the masses. This chapter will explore some of these dimensions through moments in the life and ministry of one of the most famous Pentecostal healing evangelists, Francisco Olazábal (1886–1937). The Latino Pentecostal and Charismatic movement that he helped propagate has grown from one Mexican participant at the Azusa Street Revival in 1906 to more than 9 million Latino practitioners in 2002 (Espinosa 2003).[1]

The key to Olazábal's ministry and those of other Latino Pentecostal faith-healing evangelists lie in their emphasis on the holistic relationship between body, mind, and spirit, and their conviction that sickness, disease, and illness are the result of supernatural forces. For many Pentecostals and Latin Americans, there are no such things as "bad accidents" or "good luck"; everything is shaped by the supernatural world, for good or ill. This conviction is prevalent throughout popular Catholicism, *curanderismo* or folk healing, Spiritualism, Spiritism, and some other Latino metaphysical traditions. These cultural and religious factors, along with the practical difficulties of finding, understanding, and paying for modern medical services in a foreign country, have made visiting healers in the United States all the more appealing, particularly among immigrants. Furthermore, Latino healers have tended to focus on healing not only the body, but also the mind and spirit. The decision to visit a Latino healer is not simply an act of superstition, desperation, or ignorance; rather, it can also be interpreted as resistance against and rejection of certain aspects of Anglo-American society, epistemology, and biomedicine's rationalistic mind-body dichotomy. However, it should be stressed that many Latino Pentecostal practitioners and evangelists claiming to have the gift of healing encourage people to see doctors and use modern medicine.

Mexicans, Healing, and the Azusa Street Revival

Latino participation at the Azusa Street Revival was neither fleeting nor insignificant. Latinos aided William J. Seymour (1870–1922), the revival's leader, in evangelistic work in the Mexican Plaza District in Los Angeles and throughout the migrant farm labor camps in California. Latino accounts of healing were not unique. Almost all of the extant reports about Latino participation in the revival involve healing. The famous Mexican American evangelist A. C. Valdez reported how his father was miraculously healed at the Azusa Street Revival. The first edition of the Azusa Street Mission newspaper, the *Apostolic Faith,* carried a story about a Mexican Indian who prayed for a young white girl to be healed. A Pisgah mission leader in California wrote that the movement was spreading among Mexicans because of their "immemorial traditions and belief in divine healing" (Espinosa 1999b).

Why was there such a strong interest in healing among Latinos in the early Pentecostal movement? History and socioeconomic conditions. After the Spanish conquest of Mexico and the Caribbean, these two traditions combined and blended into a number of new hybrid *nepantla*[2] religious healing traditions, the most famous of which is *curanderismo,* or folk healing, and *brujería,* or sorcery. In the mid–nineteenth century, a number of new Spiritism, Spiritualism, Theosophy, and related metaphysical traditions sprang up throughout Mexico, Puerto Rico, and Latin America, complementing and sometimes competing with *curanderismo.* Although these traditions differed in history, theology, and aesthetics, they all shared an assumption that the spirit world was responsible for most sickness, disease, and healing. They also believed that many supernaturally induced illnesses could be cured only by supernatural forces (see Kiev 1968; Madsen and Madsen 1972; Macklin 1979; Hess 1991; Trotter and Chavira 1997).

By the time Latinos began attending the Azusa Street Revival in 1906, healing, the miraculous, and the supernatural were in the marrow of Latino culture and worldviews, especially among Mexican Indians, campesinos, and middle-class *mestizos,* those likely to emigrate to the United States. Pentecostalism provided a new combinative religious *via media* that resonated with

Latino popular Catholicism, metaphysical traditions, and mainline Protestant-ism. At the same time, it offered its own uniquely U.S. Latino reinterpretation and reimagination of American Pentecostalism—one focused on healing, empowerment, and cultural liberation.

Latino socioeconomic conditions also help explain the early attraction and growth of Pentecostalism. During this period Latinos were relegated to some of the most physically demanding and injury-prone work in U.S. factories, mines, agriculture, railroads, ditch digging, and construction. Without medical insurance, workers' compensation, social security, or aid to dependent families, most injuries spelled financial disaster. A 1920 study found that while Mexicans made up at least one-twentieth (probably an underestimate) of the Los Angeles population, they made up one-fourth of all the poverty cases handled by the Los Angeles County Charities. The top two contributors to poverty were "acute illness" and "chronic physical disability." That is, acute illnesses and chronic physical disabilities left fully one-third of all Mexicans poverty-stricken (Oxnam 1920; Espinosa 1999b). In light of this fact, it is not difficult to see, the economic reasons for seeking healing and restoration are clear.

Birth of Charisma: Olazábal, Catholicism, Methodism, and the Assemblies of God

Francisco Olazábal was born into a traditional Catholic family in El Verano, Sinaloa, Mexico, on October 12, 1886. In the world in which he grew up, popular Mexican Catholicism taught that sickness and disease were caused not by chance or microbes but by evil spirits and spells cast by witches (brujas), spiritualists, and angry village saints. It was a world in which the supernatural was alive, and divine healing was an accepted part of everyday life (Cano 1938; Domínguez 1990; Frank Olazábal 1998). Yet Olazábal's spiritual world took a dramatic turn away from popular Mexican Catholicism when, around 1898, his mother, Refugio, converted to Evangelical Protestantism and became a lay Methodist evangelist. She took Francisco on her evangelistic journeys through-out the rugged Sierra Madres of north central Mexico. Although Olazábal went through a rebellious phase around 1903, turning away from his mother's evan-gelistic ministry after he went through a rebellious streak and traveling north to visit his relatives in San Francisco, California, around 1904 he rededicated his life to Jesus Christ through the evangelistic work of George Montgomery, a member of the Christian and Missionary Alliance. After his rededication, he then returned to Mexico (Cano 1938; Domínguez 1990; Frank Olazábal 1998).

From 1908 to 1910, Olazábal attended the Wesleyan School of Theology in San Luis Potosí, Mexico. As the fires of the Mexican Revolution (1910–20) engulfed the nation, thousands of Mexicans fled across the U.S. border, in-

Francisco Olazábal, ca. 1920s. Used with permission from Gastón Espinosa and Francisco Olazábal Jr.

cluding Olazábal, who assumed the pastorate of a small Mexican Methodist church in El Paso, Texas, in 1911 (Tomlinson 1939; Domínguez 1990). During his time in the United States he kept up regular correspondence with his childhood sweetheart, Macrina Orozco, the daughter of a family of prominent Protestant ministers in Mexico, and married her in 1914. After returning to California, he took up the Methodist ministry and was ordained in 1916 (Domínguez 1990).

Arriving in San Francisco, Olazábal ran into George and Carrie Montgomery. To his surprise, they had become Pentecostals, a group he had often criticized from the pulpit. However, through them, he became persuaded that the baptism with the Holy Spirit was, after all, a second definite experience and a necessary part of the Christian life, although he was still reluctant to affirm a belief in miracles and divine healing. His skepticism was tested when Macrina sought relief from a painful medical condition. He turned to the Montgomerys, who asked if they could anoint her with oil and pray that God would miraculously heal her. With few options left open to him,

Olazábal and Macrina reluctantly accepted the invitation. Shortly there after they prayed, Macrina claimed finally to have found relief and healing. As an eyewitness to the event, and confronted by his own wife's testimony, Olazábal reportedly asked God to give him faith not only to believe but also to pray for the sick.

Olazábal realized the political reality that his newfound belief in divine healing, speaking in tongues, and the gifts of the Holy Spirit placed him at odds with most of the Methodist Church, which not more than twenty years earlier had expelled the Holiness people from its ranks. He decided to leave the denomination in order to preach the "full gospel." Shocked to hear that one of their most promising young evangelists had defected to the Pentecostals, and convinced that his ministry would fail, the Methodists neither accepted his resignation nor handed over his credentials. They said the door would always remain open, and many whispered that he would soon be back before the year was out. Such predictions, however, were premature. (Tomlinson 1939; Domínguez 1990; Espinosa 1999b).

Because the Montgomerys had extensive ties with the Assemblies of God, Olazábal decided to receive ordination from the couple in 1917. Armed with his new Pentecostal conviction that evangelism and healing went hand in hand, he accepted an invitation from Alice E. Luce in 1918 to conduct a series of revivals at her Mexican mission in Los Angeles. He conducted services for several weeks and Luce claimed that many people were saved, baptized with the Holy Spirit and healed (Luce 1918; Francisco Olazábal 1921; De León 1979). Although Luce invited Olazábal to stay longer, he decided to start Assemblies of God work in the key border city of El Paso, Texas—the primary port of entry for Mexicans arriving in the United States and the main railroad hub connecting the U.S.-built railways in Mexico with their counterparts in the United States.

Independent and Indigenous Latino Pentecostal Healing Movement

By 1921 Olazábal had acquired a reputation as a person who prayed for the sick, along with his renown as a charismatic personality, leadership skills, and rhetorical gifts (Olazábal 1921; De León 1979). However, it was not long before Olazábal ran into conflict with H. C. Ball and Alice E. Luce, which erupted in 1922 when Ball stood up at the Victoria, Texas, convention to postpone the creating a new Mexican District and the election of a leader until next year. Olazábal and many of his Mexican associates considered this a vote of no confidence and a power move to thwart their freedom and desire to elect a Mexican to the leadership of the new district. Recognizing the racialized politics he now faced, and with nine cents in his pocket, he resigned from the

Assemblies of God in December 1922. When later asked why he resigned, he answered, "The gringos have control" (Ball 1933; Tomlinson 1939; De León 1979; Espinosa 1999b).

On March 14, 1923, the Interdenominational Mexican Council of Christian Churches (Pentecostal) was legally incorporated in the state of Texas; a Mexican American Pentecostal denomination was born. Despite the hardships it faced, by 1924 it had churches in California, Texas, Arizona, New Mexico, Kansas, Illinois, Michigan, Ohio, Indiana, and Mexico (Guillén 1991). Only then did Olazábal's evangelistic healing ministry begin to take on national proportions, reignited by the alleged healing of the twelve-year-old deaf-mute daughter of Guadalupe Gómez. Olazábal had never before performed what was, in the minds of his followers, such a "great" and obvious "miracle."

Empowered by a newfound confidence in God's ability to heal, throughout the 1920s Olazábal crisscrossed the Southwest, preaching and praying for thousands of Mexicans in migrant farm labor camps, factories, and inner-city barrios. In 1927, the glamorous Aimee Semple McPherson heard from Mexican American parishioners about his healing crusades in Los Angeles and Watts. After attending one of his services, she dubbed him the "Mexican Billy Sunday," a clear compliment, as Billy Sunday was the most famous and successful evangelist of the day. She invited Olazábal and his two Mexican congregations to her 5,000-seat Angelus Temple in Los Angeles for joint services (Anon. 1927; J. T. A. 1927).

After a number of positive encounters, McPherson asked Olazábal and the council to merge with her Foursquare Gospel denomination. Olazábal said the decision to merge had to be decided by council, which soundly defeated the proposal, not wanting to submit to Anglo control or to replace one set of Anglo leaders with another. McPherson was indignant at the rejection of what she considered a very generous offer to a Mexican denomination made up of migrant farm laborers, maids, ditch diggers, and the like. The working relationship between her and Olazábal came to an end.

Nevertheless, the symbolic impact of Olazábal's preaching onstage with McPherson in Angelus Temple, one of the largest churches in the United States at that time, cannot be overstated. In a day when Mexicans were considered cheap labor and cultural "outsiders," McPherson's recognition convinced many of Olazábal's followers that he was indeed "anointed of God." McPherson's success no doubt also helped convince him (if his mother's lay ministry had not) that women were as capable as men of preaching, teaching, and pastoring churches. However, his experience with McPherson may have also prompted him to restrict the role that he allowed women to play in his movement. Although he licensed them to preach, teach, evangelize, pray for the sick, and pastor (in some cases, quite large) churches, he would not ordain them and did not allow them to perform baptisms, funerals, weddings, or the sacraments if a male minister was present. Whether this decision was for theological, legal, and/or practical cultural reasons is uncertain. Still, he and McPherson shared the same conviction that healing served as a natural handmaiden to evangelism.

Word of Olazábal's evangelistic healing services spread to the Midwest and East Coast. In 1929 a Pentecostal minister invited Olazábal to Chicago to conduct an evangelistic-healing campaign. At first he rebuffed the request, thinking there were no Mexicans in that city. After assurances that a small but growing population of Mexicans worked in various industries and factories, however, he accepted and was surprised to find thousands of them when he arrived that year. The campaign started off slowly until reports circulated that an Italian mobster had been healed of a gang-related injury. Mexicans and a scattered number of Italians began to pour into Olazábal's services until he was forced to move to the Palace Opera House. Three thousand people attended his standing-room-only services for weeks (Anon. 1929, 1930; Tomlinson 1939).

In the summer of 1931 Olazábal traveled to Spanish Harlem in New York City for what would become the most important chapter in the birth of his transnational ministry. Despite the humidity and summer heat, thousands attended his healing services at the gigantic Calvary Baptist Church in Brooklyn. These services blazed with power and emotion. Despite the grinding poverty the Great Depression was wreaking on the Latin American community outside of the church, inside people sought spiritual relief for their aching bodies and souls. Every night, Olazábal walked onto center stage, led the congregation in rousing singing, preached a twenty-five minute evangelistic sermon, and then lifted his hands in the air and asked those in the balcony to come down to the altar of the church, repent of their sins, and convert. Thousands answered his call. After the "altar call" Olazábal began what many, perhaps most, of the people had come for—divine healing by El Azteca, or the mighty Aztec, as his followers called him (Tomlinson 1939).

Both Olazábal and his followers claimed that scores of people were healed of blindness, tuberculosis, deformity, tumors, heart conditions, rheumatism, deafness, and many other physical ailments and diseases during this 1931 campaign. As at the Azusa Street Revival twenty-five years earlier, people threw the "relics" of their former lives—rosaries, amulets, canes, and crutches—into a large pile onstage as a symbol of God's power to transform their weary spirits and broken bodies. The campaign converted thousands to the Pentecostal movement and prompted Olazábal to organize a mother church, Bethel Temple, in New York City. The church, an enormous former synagogue, had grown from a handful of members in August 1931 to more than 1,500 members by 1932, making it one of the largest churches in the city. Most of his parishioners were former Catholics, Spiritists, Spiritualists, folk healers, agnostics, socialists, and Puerto Rican cultural nationalists. By 1932, many claimed that every Spanish-speaking country in Latin America was represented in his congrega-

Watts revival in California, ca. 1927–28. Used with permission from Gastón Espinosa and Francisco Olazábal Jr.

tion. For such reasons, he decided to change the council's name to the Latin American Council of Christian Churches (Tomlinson 1939; Frank Olazábal 1998) to reflect his growing transnational ministry and vision.

The healing of María Teresa Sapia seized the attention of the press in the 1930s. Famous in Puerto Rico for her ties with the underworld there, and a staunch cultural nationalist who called for the country's independence, she was a notorious gambler, gun woman, and rumrunner during Prohibition. Castigation by some as one of the "worst" women in Puerto Rico was the least of her problems: asthma and other ailments had wasted her body to a scant seventy-five pounds. She turned to Olazábal for healing and redemption. At one of his services, she claimed she was dramatically healed and converted. Immediately she gave up her former lifestyle and began to assist Olazábal at his crusades, becoming a key staff member (Frank Olazábal 1987; Tomlinson 1939).

Thousands of other women joined the Pentecostal movement because it afforded them the opportunity to preach and teach (Espinosa 2002b). No doubt partly due to the tireless work of women, Olazábal's healing services spread rapidly not only through Depression-era Spanish Harlem but also through New York's Italian and Anglo-American boroughs. Growing numbers of Italians and Anglos began attending regularly. The number of non–Spanish speakers at Olazábal's services was so large that he began holding English-language services on Monday night and Italian-language services on Thursday evenings and Sunday mornings. He also regularly ministered in black Pentecostal churches in Harlem and throughout New York City. His ministry now crossed linguistic and racial boundaries in a day when the Ku Klux Klan, white supremacism, and racial segregation shaped the racial and social imagination of a large segments of Anglo-American society (Anon. 1932).

Although Olazábal's preaching style was casual, he required that a person

who came forward for prayer have attended previous services and thus have heard (and hopefully received) the Christian message, as Olazábal understood it. To come forward for prayer, persons seeking help had to show the usher their tickets, hole punched on a previous night. After waiting in a long line leading up to the stage, when they reached Olazábal he would ask if they believed in Jesus Christ and the power of God to heal. He said that if they did, he would *agree with them in prayer* for God to heal their ailment. He was clear that he himself had no healing power and that he was only agreeing in faith that the same God who raised Jesus from the dead could also heal them. As a testimony to God's healing power, he often instructed the person claiming to be healed to place crutches, hernia belts, slings, glasses, wine bottles, or anything else for which they sought healing onstage or on the rope or pole that surrounded the inside of the stage. He then encouraged them to give a public testimony of the healing, visit a doctor to confirm it, and then write up a short testimony to be published in his *Christian Messenger*. Olazábal disliked being called a "faith healer," "divine healer," or anything else suggesting that he himself had the power to heal, insisting instead that only God had that power. Nor did he claim that everyone he prayed for was healed; rather, he and his son believed the number to be only about 80 percent (Olazábal Jr. 1987).

Olazábal and His Critics

Olazábal attracted more than the faithful masses. He also attracted criticism. When prominent Anglo Pentecostal leaders like Robert A. Brown and J. R. Kline asked J. R. Flower and H. C. Ball[3] about Olazábal, they were told that he had vilified the Assemblies of God and "done a great injustice to the work of the Lord." Ball claimed that Olazábal's evangelistic work "soon goes to pieces" when his campaigns are over. A few Mexican pastors left the council and accused Olazábal of being too heavy-handed. Others accused him of authoritarianism and favoritism. Still others complained that he was too lenient with pastors who had fallen "into sin" or had compromised their Christian testimony (Brown 1931; Ball 1931; Flower 1931, 1933; Kline 1933).

Many of the complaints were justified. Despite the large crowds at the campaign, the churches Olazábal organized afterward were often considerably smaller. His ministry style could be authoritarian at times, especially by today's standards. Sometimes he assigned ministers to a part of the country where they did not want to serve. He also publicly criticized a church congregation that did not financially support its minister. In a day when divorce was grounds for immediate dismissal from the ministry, Olazábal made exceptions, allowing some divorced people to continue their ministry if it was their spouse who had committed adultery and/or abandoned the family (Frank Olazábal 1998).

Olazábal also faced criticism for not healing all for whom he prayed. He responded by stating that it was God's prerogative to heal, and that he himself was nothing more than a vessel through which God manifested his healing power. A critical reading of the testimonies published in the *Christian Messenger*, a magazine he founded in 1923 and coedited, reveals that a majority of those who claimed healing were women. Furthermore, most "healings" were for minor ailments, although a number of people did claim to be healed of more serious conditions like tuberculosis, cancer, tumors, blindness, deafness, and terminal diseases. Most doctors would probably categorize many of the reported "healings" as examples of the power of positive suggestion. The Latino community's long tradition of folk healing and most people's inability to afford a doctor during the Depression no doubt also help explain some of these outcomes (Domínguez 1990).

Then there was Olazábal's commitment to speaking in tongues. Following a successful mission to Puerto Rico in 1936, Olazábal stood at the height of his popularity. Letters were arriving from all over the United States, Latin America, and Europe, asking him to conduct evangelistic-healing campaigns. Although Pentecostal in creed, ritual, and practice, Olazábal recognized that his interdenominational evangelistic-healing message transcended denominational borders and boundaries. Rather than push his brand of Christianity on people, he simply invited them to receive the baptism of the Holy Spirit and spiritual gifts when ready. While he often said privately that speaking in tongues was the key to his healing ministry, publicly he stated that he was not Pentecostal—at least not the stereotypical kind; he was simply "a Christian."

It was, however, his speaking in tongues that led to denunciations from religious leaders of other denominations. The famous Presbyterian foreign mission leader Robert E. Speer, for example, withdrew his support for Olazábal's Puerto Rico Para Cristo campaign in 1936 after he found out that Olazábal spoke in tongues. Later that year, Father Lourdes F. Costa publicly criticized Olazábal in the El Paso newspaper *El Continental* after hearing about his enormous campaign taking place at the Liberty Hall City Auditorium. Thousands of Catholics attended Olazábal's services, where many were converted and reportedly healed. Costa challenged Olazábal to heal him of his deafness in one ear or pack up and leave El Paso. Eyewitnesses also claim the Catholic leaders sent spies into Olazábal's meeting, where they stood in line to have themselves prayed for so they could call him a "fake." Some later converted. Olazábal defended his practice both in his services and in writing. He charged Costa with using refined sarcasm to unfairly mock and attack his campaign and dignity without provocation. He said that if people left the Catholic Church it was not because of his evangelistic-healing services, which people attended voluntarily, but because the Catholic Church lacked real transformative power. He ended his letter by stating that he would be happy to pray for Costa but that Costa would have to wait in line like any other person seeking healing. Costa never accepted Olazábal's offer (Sepúlveda 1936a, 1936b; Costa 1936a, 1936b; Francisco Olazábal 1936; Tomlinson 1939).

Healing Southern White Bodies: Mexicans and Southern Pentecostalism

Olazábal realized that if he were ever to have an international and multiracial ministry he needed major financial support and the freedom to travel unrestrained by the cares of administering the council. Energized from the crusade in El Paso, he attended the 1936 annual assembly of the Church of God in Cleveland, Tennessee. On September 10, before an audience of 6,000 white southerners, the somewhat reluctant Olazábal placed his hand on a Bible and swore allegiance to the Church of God. When asked if he was a healer, Olazábal replied, "The only thing I know is I am a believer in Jesus . . . [and] that he is the same yesterday, today, and forever" (Hedrick 1936: 1, 7). The response of the southern white crowd was overwhelmingly positive. Despite his Spanish accent, or perhaps because of it, thousands of white southerners streamed forward to be healed by the tall Mexican evangelist. Such was his impact there that hundreds of letters continued to pour into the Church of God headquarters for the next two years requesting that Olazábal pray for the writers (Tomlinson 1939). Triumphant in the eyes of his followers, Olazábal returned to New York City. He had entered the Anglo-American world and had taken center stage. Reignited by these campaigns, Olazábal confidently led 2,000 Latinos in a planned march down New York's Fifth Avenue. Standing six abreast, shouting, "praising God," and singing, they waved colorful banners much as Pentecostal and evangelical Christians do today in the International

March for Jesus. They gathered at the plaza at the end of Fifth Avenue and 110th Street for a rally. The parade was a powerful symbol that Olazábal and the Latino Pentecostal movement were here to stay (Tomlinson 1936).

"A Great Oak Has Fallen upon the Mountain": The Death of Charisma

"Rev. F. Olazábal . . . Dies of Injuries Suffered in Auto Accident," read the *New York Times* obituary on June 12, 1937. Near Alice Springs, Texas, on the way to an ordination service in Mexico, Olazábal's car had skidded off the slippery blacktop surface and turned over on June 1. Critically injured, he was taken to a hospital, where he appeared to recover. Then, on June 9, 1937, he died of internal hemorrhaging. He seemed to know that death was imminent and reportedly dictated a message to his followers, admonishing them to continue the work he had started and to keep the Holy Spirit at the center of their ministry.

In the minds of his followers, a giant of the faith had fallen. In a scene reminiscent of funeral services for presidents and other national figures, his body was placed in a $2,000 vapor-filled casket and publicly displayed for three days in his great temple in the heart of Spanish Harlem. Some estimate that no fewer than 50,000 Puerto Ricans, Anglo-Americans, and blacks paid their last respects. Olazábal's body was then taken to and put on display in his main churches in Chicago and El Paso before being laid to rest in Evergreen Cemetery, not far from the grave of William J. Seymour (Evans 1937; Tomlinson 1939; Domínguez 1990; Espinosa 1999b).

The Legacy of Francisco Olazábal

Francisco Olazábal's story is important to the study of religious healing in America for at least eight reasons. First, it reveals the profound interest in healing, the miraculous, and the supernatural in Latino communities. Health and healing are directly tied not only to physical well-being but also to economic and mental stability, opportunity, and hope. Healing has provided Latinos with a mechanism to take control of their lives, affirm their culture and traditions, and criticize Anglo-American life, health, and society.

Second, the story challenges the stereotype that Latino healing has taken place almost exclusively in popular Catholicism and metaphysical traditions. Rather, a long and vibrant indigenous Pentecostal healing tradition stretches back almost 100 years in the United States.

Third, it reveals that Pentecostal success has been due in large part to the religion's strong emphasis on healing, the miraculous, and the supernatural. In many respects, Pentecostalism has functioned as a religious *via media* that simultaneously drew on and yet was distinct from popular Catholicism, metaphysical traditions, and mainline Protestantism. Pentecostalism has provided Latinos a third way to find healing and come into contact with the miraculous and the supernatural. Olazábal functioned as a Protestant version of Catholic folk healers like El Niño Fidencio, Don Pedrito Jaramillo, and María Teresa Urrea. His healing ministry tapped into the tremendous emphasis on supernatural healing in Latino spirituality already in place in Latino Catholic culture and religiosity.

Fourth, Olazábal's story challenges the conventional image of the healer as a loner or solitary magician working outside of existing organizations and structures. Although Olazábal did break away from Anglo-American control, he formed his own religious organization. He worked almost daily with people and spent considerable time on the road with his evangelistic-healing team, planning his next campaigns and deciding who would shepherd the flocks of converts they produced. While other healers focused their ministries on the individual, Olazábal sought to create a movement that could transform the religious aspirations and theological orientation of his people.

Fifth, Olazábal left a strong imprint on the Latino Pentecostal and Protestant movement by contributing to the birth and/or development of more than fourteen independent denominations and Spanish districts within existing Anglo-American denominations. Although his movement fragmented after he died, this invariably helped to spread his evangelistic-healing message and method throughout the United States, Mexico, Puerto Rico, and Latin America. His ministry also helped shape and in some cases give birth to other Pentecostal evangelistic-healing ministries like those of Rev. A. C. Valdez (who often visited Olazábal's services and his home), Rev. Carlos Sepúlveda, Rev. David Ruesga, Rev. Matilde Vargas, Rev. Leoncia Rosado Rosseau, and Rev. Aurora Chávez in the United States, Mexico, and Puerto Rico (Villaronga 1934; Duryee 1936; Cano 1938; Domínguez 1990; Espinosa, 2002b).

Sixth, Olazábal's story demonstrates that the Latino Pentecostal healing tradition began earlier and was larger, more widespread, and more indigenous, independent, diverse, and transnational than previously believed. In fact, strong evidence suggests that healing plays an even greater role among independent and indigenous Pentecostal traditions than among those still affiliated with and/or controlled by Anglo-American or black Pentecostal denominations.

Seventh, Olazábal's story reminds us that healing transcends the border and that healing in America needs to be reconceptualized to take into consideration not only the geopolitical borders of the dominant Euro-American culture but also the transnational Latino experience.

Finally, we continue to see the importance of Olazábal's story about the miraculous, healing, and the supernatural in thousands of storefront churches in inner-city barrios and *colonias*. If the demographic shifts presently under way in the United States continue, stories of people like Francisco Olazábal may become an even greater part of the fabric and narrative of North American religions and healing in the twenty-first century.

NOTES

Portions of this chapter have been previously published in the articles noted in the bibliography for the *Journal of the American Academy of Religion* (Espinosa 1999a) and for the University of Arkansas Press (Espinosa 2004). The author wishes to thank Catherine Albanese, Mario T. García, Sarah Cline, Colin Calloway, John Watanabe, Robert Gundry, Rick Pointer, Mike McClymond, Grant Wacker, James Goff, Linda Barnes and Susan Sered for their critical feedback on early drafts of this chapter. This work will serve as the basis for a critical biography I am writing on Francisco Olazábal for Oxford University Press.

1. See Espinosa 2003: 14–16. The findings in this study are based on one of the largest national Hispanic-framed random sample telephone surveys of U.S. Latino religions and politics in U.S. history.

2. *Nepantla* is an Aztec Nahuatl term that means to be "in the middle" or "in between."

3. Ball was the overseer of the Mexican District of the Assemblies of God and J. R. Flower was the General Council of the Assemblies of God Missionary-Secretary Treasurer in 1922 at the AG headquarters in Springfield, Missouri. Olazábal received modest funding from the AG as a "home missionary"—or someone who served as a missionary to a "foreign" group in the United States.

REFERENCES

A., J.T. 1927. Un Servicio Evangelio Para Los Mexicanos. *El Mensajero Cristiano*, November, 7–8.

Anon. 1927. La Hermana McPherson en la Carpa de Watts y el Hno. Francisco Olazábal en "Angelus Temple" de Los Angeles. *El Mensajero Cristiano*, October, 6–8.

———. 1929. Primera Sesion De La Iglesia Interdenominacional de Chicago. *El Mensajero Cristiano*, September, 8–9.

———. 1930. Testimonios de Sanidad Divina. *El Mensajero Cristiano*, September, 12–16.

———. 1932. Cuatro Meses con el Rev. Francisco Olazábal en la Ciudad de Nueva York. *El Mensajero Cristiano*, January, 11–12.

Ball, H. C. 1931. Letter to J. R. Evans. October 14.

———. 1933. Letter to Pastor J. R. Kline, 7 February, 1–2.

Brown, Robert A. 1931. Letter to H. C. Ball. October 13.

Cano, Juárez. 1938. El Rev. Francisco Olazábal: Datos Biográficos. *El Mesanjero Cristiano*, June, 6–8, 12–13.

Costa, Father Lourdes F. 1936a. Letter to Francisco Olazábal. June 9.

————. 1936b. Letter to Francisco Olazábal. June 11.

De León, Victor. 1979. The Silent Pentecostals. Taylors, S. C.: Faith Printing Company.

Domínguez, Roberto. 1990. Pioneros de Pentecostés: Norteamerica y Las Antillas. Vol. 1. 3rd ed. Barcelona: Editorial Clie.

Duryee, Spencer. 1936. The Great Aztec. Christian Herald. August, 6.

Espinosa, Gastón. 1999a. El Azteca: Francisco Olazábal and Latino Pentecosatal Charisma, Power and Faith-Healing in the Borderlands. Journal of the American Academy of Religion. 67(3): 597–616.

————. 1999b. Borderland Religion Los Angeles and the Origins of the Latino Pentecostal Movement in the U.S., Mexico and Puerto Rico, 1900–1945. Ph.D.diss., University of California, Santa Barbara.

————. 2002a. Francisco Olazábal: Charisma, Power and Faith Healing in the Borderlands. In Portraits of a Generation: Early Pentecostal Leaders, ed. James R. Goff Jr. and Grant Wacker, 178–197, 400–404. Fayetteville: University of Arkansas Press.

————. 2002b. "Your Daughters Shall Prophesy": A History of Women in Ministry in the Latino Pentecostal Movement in the United States. In Women and Twentieth-Century Protestantism, ed. Margaret Lamberts Bendroth and Virginia Lieson Brereton, 25–48. Urbana: University of Illinois Press.

————. 2004. Francisco Olazábal and Latino Pentecostal Revivalism in the North American Borderlands. In Embodying the Spirit: New Perspectives on North American Revivalism, ed. Michael McClymond. Baltimore: Johns Hopkins University Press.

Espinosa, Gastón, with Virgilio Elizondo and Jesse Miranda. 2003. Hispanic Churches in American Public Life: Summary of Findings. Notre Dame, Ind.: Institute for Latino Studies at the University of Notre Dame.

Evans, A. D. 1937. Brother Olazábal Killed in Auto Accident. White Wing Messenger, June 19, 1.

Flower, J. R. 1931. Letter to H. C. Ball. October 21.

————. 1933. Letter to J. R. Kline. February 7.

Guillén, Miguel. 1991. La Historia del Concilio Latino Americano de Iglesias Cristianas. Brownsville, Texas: Latin American Council of Christian Churches.

Hedrick, Travis. 1936. Hundreds Seek Faith Healing. Chattanooga Times, September 12, 1, 7.

Hess, David J. 1991. Spirits and Scientists: Ideology, Spiritism and Brazilian Culture. University Park: Pennsylvania State University Press.

Kiev, Ari. 1968. Curanderismo: Mexican American Folk Psychiatry. New York: Free Press.

Kline, J. R. 1933. Letter to J. R. Evans. February 4.

Luce, Alice E. 1918. Mexican Work in California. The Weekly Evangel. April 18, 11.

Macklin, June. 1979. Curanderismo and Espiritismo: Complementary Approaches to Traditional Health Services. In The Chicano Experience, ed. Stanley A. West and June Macklin, 207–226. Boulder, Colo.: Westview Press.

Madsen, William, and Claudia Madsen. 1972. A Guide to Mexican Witchcraft. Mexico City: Minutiea Mexicana.

Olazábal, Francisco. 1921. God Is Blessing on the Mexican Border. *Weekly Evangel*, October 1, 10

————. 1936. Letter to Father Lourdes F. Costa. July 13.

Olazábal, Frank, Jr. 1987. *Revive Us Again!* Los Angeles: The Christian Academic Foundation.

————. 1998. Latino Pentecostal Oral History Project. Telephone interview. May. Hanover, N.H.

Orsi, Robert A. 1985. *The Madonna of 115th Street: Faith and Community in Italian Harlem, 1880–1950*. New Haven, Conn.: Yale University Press.

Oxnam, G. Bromley. 1920. *The Mexican in Los Angeles: Los Angeles City Survey. Los Angeles: InterChurch World Movement of North America*.

Sepúlveda, Carlos. 1936a. La Campaña Olazábal en el Paso, Texas. *El Mensajero Cristiano*. August, 6–7.

————. 1936b. Glorióso Servicio De Despedida. *El Mensajero Cristiano*. August.

Tomlinson, Homer A. 1936. Big Parade of 2,000 Lead Down Fifth Avenue New York City. *White Wing Messenger*, November 7, 1, 4.

————. 1939. *Miracles of Healing in the Ministry of Rev. Francisco Olazábal*. New York: Homer Tomlinson.

Trotter, Robert, and Juan Antonio Chavira. 1997. *Curanderismo: Mexican American Folk Healing*. 2nd ed. Athens: University of Georgia Press.

Villaronga, Luís. 1934. ¿Quién es Olazábal? *El Mundo*, May 5, 31.

8

The Gathering of Traditions: The Reciprocal Alliance of History, Ecology, Health, and Community among the Contemporary Chumash

Julianne Cordero

Ya 'iyitak husiwon kakunupmawa
Let us listen to the ancient song of the mystery behind the sun
Kihu sak'ni'tox lokoi xutash
So that you will pay attention to the voice of the earth
Ka' lo'kal'ixipsh 'iti 'ishup
That which there is of creatures in this land
Hu'am susamha sip' entes
That all we creatures of the earth may feel the powers of the sun,
the spirit of this land
                    —The late Chumash elder Maria Solares
                              (Walker and Hudson 1993: 63)

Today, one of the most pernicious stumbling blocks on the path to greater individual and community health in Chumash country is an assumption held by many that (largely non-Indian) social scientists have the final say in what is "the correct interpretation" of the Californio and Chumash past,[1] languages, and arts and the communities' present sense of identity as mixed-heritage Indian people. This belief is a mirror of the intricate crisis faced by a world dominated by colonialist social policies of Western consumer economies. In providing each other with a place to stand and speak, and in helping each other out in times of need, all people, including the many bands of the Chumash people, must give themselves permission to act like family, to trust, forgive, make real and lasting amends, to accept who we are at this moment in history, and to know that who we presently are will change yet again.

Old stories can help us make new decisions about our place in the world. Couched in the ancient Chumash idea that telling stories "breathes out" the power of the sun, this chapter begins the process of using transformative tools of thought toward the healing of both Native and non-Native peoples in the Chumash homeland. In this chapter I critique previous historical analyses of written data on local Santa Barbara history and identify those that have silenced the voices of nonacademic Native and non-Native community members or deemed them unreliable and subjective, and thereby denied their "authenticity" in creating a healthy community based on local philosophies and practices.

I begin with an attempt to blur the lines between "us" and "them," between "subjective" and "objective." In that initial section I describe lessons learned from indigenous "texts," such as plants and translations of particular Barbareño Chumash verb forms, including the action words most closely approximating words for "health" and "power." In the second section I sketch a decolonized methodology for gathering human traditions.[2] In the third section I compare the lessons learned from nonwritten "texts" with practices used by three scholars in their interpretations of Chumash history and identity. I do this in order to delineate the harm done to communities whose living cultural practices cannot be explained using reductionist methods. In the final section I describe a living practice that transcends previous attempts by anthropologists and others to naysay contemporary Californio/Chumash cultural constructions of tradition, spirituality, and ethnic heritage. The exemplar I have chosen for the chapter's final section lies at the very heart of the coastal Chumash culture and spirit: the Chumash oceangoing canoe, called a *tomol*.

Thinking with Our Hands: A Barbareño Chumash Binding of Mind and Heart

In entering the seemingly endless chicken-or-egg, universalist-or-relativist, objective-or-subjective debate that rages within scholarly formations and deconstructions of social scientific theory and method, we would do well to heed the words of Albert Einstein when he said, "The significant problems we face cannot be solved by the same level of thinking that created them." In attempting to work within a simultaneous understanding of the pros and cons of both sides of this debate while also learning from philosophical traditions that are not informed by this paradigm, I bring to this writing a model that considers the set of Barbareño Chumash words beginning with the prefix *us*- (which varies with the form *ush-*), which has the meaning "with the hand." It is what is called an instrumental prefix and will form the central paradigmatic instrument of my attempt here at a reciprocal ethnological theory.

The Barbareño Chumash verb, *Us'ismon*, "to gather, collect, or join together," shares the instrumental prefix *ush-*, with verbs that mean "to gather plants," "to tie or bind together (to be strong)," and "to paddle a canoe." These four words are here unpacked in consonance with the four sections of my analysis.

The co-opting of Native American place-names, Indian role playing, and the construction of an imaginary past as the romantic backdrop to both of those activities has caused everyday Native people either to appear as characters in a fictional vision of "how it was" or to vanish altogether in mainstream thought.[3] Anthropologist and ethnobotanist Janice Timbrook points to how "many non-Indians seem to think that, having 'lost' their 'original' culture, the Chumash today are somehow less pure, less valid, less important than their ancestors" (quoted in Walker and Hudson 1993: xii). As Philip Deloria asserts, "Here, then, lies a critical dilemma of American identity: in order to complete their rite of passage, Americans had to replace either the interior or the exterior Indian Other. . . . there was, quite simply, no way to conceive an American identity without Indians. At the same time, there was no way to make a complete identity while they remained" (1998: 37).

The strands interweaving the histories of living indigenous people and the people who have recently rooted themselves in Native lands tell a powerful story. The warp of this history is the dispossession of the Chumash people and the illegal acquisition of their enormous wealth and homeland. The richly patterned weft is the contemporary Native and non-Native population's genuine quest for healing and sanity in a world driven insane by greed, violence, and domination.

Despite the damage wrought by the spiritual and academic commodification of culture, and by the practice that Indigenous scholar Wendy Rose terms "whiteshamanism" (1992: 403–21), many Native American communities recognize the need for reconciliation between all people of colonized and colonizing nations if we are to work toward the compassionate healing of our diverse, yet innately permeable and reciprocal, worlds. Non-Native social scientists can and do gain acceptance in Native communities, provided the relationship is mutually beneficial. It is imperative to this nonoppositional line of inquiry to refrain from labeling the Anglo-Protestant Enlightenment paradigm the "Other," thereby shifting the assignation of inferior morality. I have no wish to discredit groundbreaking work done by scholars—Native and non-Native alike—whose operational paradigms emerged from the North American European diaspora, as this would engage in what I consider to be a nonproductive dialectical process. As a mixed-heritage child of the colonial collision in North America, I must recognize my status as both indigene and a member of the American consumer culture. I know that many share this paradoxical location in our rapidly changing world.

Ushpak: (to pick up small things, to gather plants): Toward an understanding of reciprocal ethnological theory and method

Occupying North America for thousands of generations, Native American peoples can speak meaningfully and eloquently of their histories here. Those meanings have been, for the most part, lost on audiences unfamiliar with Native American oral traditions. The intellectual traditions of North American indigenous peoples are held in trust not only by highly trained ritual specialists, storytellers, singers, and craftspeople but also by ordinary people who have engaged in the deliberate analysis of traditional philosophies and cultural norms in an effort to "decolonize" minds and life practices. Since I am an herbalist, most of my work revolves around the practices of gathering and using plants in this area.

Chumash ancestors referred to air as "the breath of the sun," and this is, according to what little science knows about transpiration and photosynthesis, true. All our theoretical posturing aside, we breathe, speak, exhale, are fertilized, and reproduce by and through mechanisms developed by plants, and "we creatures of this earth" are the source of their fertile continuity. Their continuity, unlike that of a transcendent God, is ultimately dependent on the mortality of living creatures. The plants themselves embody this paradoxical power, power as a verb, power as a motion through matter and time. The Chumash verb for "power," *atiswin*, "to heal," "to dream," and "to poison," is wielded through a networked intent toward this profane illumination. Two of the strongest local herbs, tobacco and datura, are healers, dreamers, and poisoners. To call this an anthropomorphic view of tobacco and datura would be absurdly inverted, since those plants have given us their sense of power, strong healing, fertile dreaming, decomposing poison, all of which we embody whether or not we name this profanely illuminated process.

Since scholarly power has touched with its hands and been touched by living, dynamic beings, our discussions of it must be couched in a discussion of all of life. When an individual has power *in mutual, reciprocal correspondence with* another being, all elements of this relationship have the power to support—or to poison to death—the entire ontological context in which one exists. As with any medicine, the difference between cure and poison lies in the skilled administration of the medicine in proper dosage.

The most profound concept I have been exposed to on community plant-gathering trips has to do with practices of reciprocity with the land: ongoing, sustainable exchange with a flourishing ecosystem. This idea that a plant community can flourish after repeated visits from a community of human beings is, for the most part, alien to members of global market-driven consumer cultures. But this idea is more than a sociological trope; in a sense, hunter-gatherer peoples have conducted exhaustive trials for millennia and see no need to further complicate this line of practiced "inquiry." I like to think of a sharp cutting tool placed at just the right angle above the growth nodes of a woody perennial plant as an indigenous Occam's razor, demonstrating over time and through endless repetition that the simplest bodies of practical evidence supporting a theory are often the correct ones. Through selective pruning, careful soil aeration, precise, controlled burning, and a detailed knowledge of each plant's sensitivity, growth cycles, and multisituated role in the overall habitat, and by repeatedly and reverentially returning to those places over the seasons, years, and generations, people practice the art of reciprocal flourishing in their homelands. In these ways gathering traditions are actions that encourage health in both human and nonhuman communities.

The word for "health"—as translated from the nearly lost language of the Barbareño Chumash of Santa Barbara, California—is a verb. The verb root *shumawish* means to be healthy, or, more literally, to deal well with situations (Whistler 1980: 30). "Health" as an action verb is the trope on which turn consciously undertaken interactions between beings and landscapes. It is therefore, for humans, a profoundly and pragmatically spiritual activity in nature. The action of health requires us to overcome our ignorance about how our embodied activities can contribute either to an individual and systemic picture of health or to functional, organic, psychological, cultural, and environmental disease. In everyday terms, this means people know about or personally care for the actual places where their food and medicine grow by repeatedly visiting those places, observing seasonal changes for each layer of the bioregion, creating informative mythology about those places that are passed on collectively, and learning the techniques for gathering the innumerable, constantly changing materials—techniques that cause the flourishing of those places, flourishing that is returned through our physical, emotional, intellectual, and spiritual health. In this context, theories *about* health share reciprocal standing with the practices that *perform* health.

When an individual or community has power *in mutual, reciprocal correspondence with* another individual or community, all elements of this relationship have the power to support—or to poison to death—the entire ontological context in which one exists. The word for power, like the word for health, is a verb with "chemically active" constituents, which can be wielded to cause both flourishing and death, sometimes simultaneously.

From this perspective, ordinary people act in their everyday lives as mediums to power, power that many Indigenous languages define differently than the word is defined and acted upon in English. The preceding concepts of flourishing within an ecosystem are often refuted by scholars who present evidence of Native Americans' "destruction" of the land by overhunting, intensive farming, and controlled burning. It is folly to assume any species could live in a place and not have some impact on the land, positive or negative. To "flourish" does not mean to avoid the consequences of mistakes, to not feel pain or death, or to not inflict or suffer violence in some way. The Chumash people, like many other Native North American peoples, have long used "powerful," "healthy" tools in our striving to attain equilibrium in our home communities. The languages, practices, and teachings of those traditions reflect that imperfect, human struggle for survival, health, and balance.

Us'ismon (to gather or join together): An old methodology revisited

All gatherers wish for the highest quality materials available. The gatherer of material or cultural resources must return and cultivate the area for a long while—sometimes several years—before the materials reach their highest quality. First and foremost, the gatherer must obtain permission to gather, whether through birthright or through local systems regarding traditional and legal protocols. Ideally, the healthiest areas are identified and observed for some time, checking for animal habitat, signs of stress, proximity to potential chemical pollution, and countless other factors. The gatherer then addresses him- or herself to the stand of plants, leaving offerings of prayer, sometimes a pinch of tobacco or another sacred substance, and often songs of healing and respect. The gathering of these materials is performed with knowledge and skills handed down for generations: pruning the white sage just there and there to stimulate growth, digging bulbs correctly to encourage flourishing and increase, burning deer grass and hazel at just the right time of year to ensure the sprouting of straight, strong, and perfectly clear shoots. The gatherer must stay home to keep abreast of seasonal changes and must return for the entirety of his or her life to continue the mutual flourishing of the human and plant communities. The gatherer must also pass along his or her knowledge and experience to future generations. Finally, the gatherer must accept that, sometimes for reasons unfathomable, the rules for gathering in that area and the resources available can change at any time.

In this fluid, reciprocal relationship, the plants use human beings for their success in the world as surely as they take advantage of other creatures and the wind for pollination and seed distribution. If a gatherer focuses only on what is easily taken from the fringes, or gathers in such a way as to weaken the overall health of the area, the area simply will not produce the quality material desired or, worse, will stop providing for the gatherer at all. On this point, the reciprocal view differs radically from the concept of stewardship. "Stewardship" implies that one species—humans—are the caretakers. When the interspecies relationship is reciprocal, the whole is dependent for its health upon the whole. Conversely, the whole may also be poisoned by elements or practices that affect the whole.

If present and future generations of ethnographers—both Native and non-Native—wish to gather the highest quality ethnographic and historical materials available, they may wish to demonstrate their learned wisdom and innate intuition by following a similar gathering protocol. It is also well to be mindful that the most critical "rule" in the gathering of traditions is the last one: that the rules constantly change. What remains constant in nearly every context is that our continued health and flourishing are dependent upon this exchange being of sustained, mutual benefit to all parties involved.

Kiysa'ushq'ak (*Ush*: with the hand. *K'al*: to tie or to bind.
Emphatic form: *Ushq'al*: to be really strong): We (three or more) bound together will be really strong

Santa Barbara is a place where California history was made, and is being made, will always be made by interactions of diverse peoples. In the rich, local historical narratives I have heard over time, however, the dominant version of the story of Santa Barbara has rung hollow in my ears. That version goes something like this: the Spanish came in 1769, missionized all local indigenous people by taking over trade routes and creating dependence on Spanish agriculture. The padres, assisted by the Presidio soldiers, banned the languages and traditional ceremonies; tens of thousands of people died of foreign diseases and were utterly disenfranchised. Chumash men and women staged a rebellion in 1824 and were crushed. Then, in 1849, the state was flooded with murderous gold seekers during the gold rush, and the wholesale, U.S. government–sponsored slaughter of California Indians began in earnest. Presently, the oft-told tale goes, California Indians are still around in small numbers and retain vestiges of traditional heritage and knowledge, which they learned mostly from anthropologists. From old Spanish days to Anglo-America, California Indian bodies, culture, religion, and political sovereignty in California were, it is said, annihilated.

While this version of Barbareño Chumash and Californio ethnohistory once fit my sense of indignation and loss over the injuries suffered by California Indian nations, my primary objection now is rooted in my Californio/Chumash family's observations that *both* the family members who work to retain and recontextualize ancient Chumash philosophies *and* the members who observe the ancient and changing traditions of Christianity, Buddhism, Islam, or one of the many other religious traditions to be found in Southern California today, and who live more mainstream lifestyles are representative of old traditions and philosophies and have demonstrated skilled, conscious adaptation to contemporary, multisituated lifestyles. There is therefore no sensible way to calibrate the constantly changing, interdigitated situations of these families into sociological binaries that aim to determine who is more "genuine," "traditional," or "real," and who is not.

The silencing of local peoples in the telling of our past roars loudest in recent theoretical misinterpretations of indigenous agency by anthropologists, archaeologists, and ethnohistorians who continue to publish positivist, binary models for indigenous identity. Their models have for years violently polarized local mixed-heritage, indigenous families. Only in recent years have members of these interrelated Californio and Chumash communities entered the academy in sufficient numbers to muster a focused critique of these interpretations of our culture and religion. Here my critique is also couched in a proactive response to the social scientists who have gathered and interpreted these traditions. I hope that this response may lead to a "decolonized" methodology that is mutually beneficial to all parties involved. These scholars may then find themselves invited away from the social margins of "pedigrees" and "certified degrees of Indian blood" and into the flourishing circle of local community in a way that is life-changing, meaningful, and that may also beneficially and rigorously augment the theories and practicum of their fields.

This is the story of the *Helek* and its family. In 1975, during the establishment of the Brown Power and Native Pride movements, members of the Californio/Chumash community built the *Helek* (the Barbareño Chumash word for peregrine falcon, the guardian bird of ocean canoe voyages). The *Helek* was the first seaworthy Chumash *tomol* (plank canoe) to be built in nearly 100 years. Using directions given by Chumash elder Kitsepawit to John P. Harrington— an ethnographer and linguist who recorded what now comprises the main body of written material about ancient Chumash traditions—and guided by master boatbuilder Peter Howorth, the modern-day Brotherhood of the Tomol performed one of the more eloquent expressions of the Native Pride movement, the building and paddling of the *Helek*. The late Travis Hudson, who worked through the anthropology department of the Santa Barbara Museum of Natural History, directed this project. It was a time remembered by local families as a flowering of an indigenous maritime tradition too long buried by oppression and despair. The canoe-building tradition was to be buried once more before the decade ended, however. The ownership of the *Helek* was contested through what many residents of Santa Barbara consider to be a professionally unethical accusation leveled by a local anthropologist: that the members of the Brotherhood of the Tomol and their families were not *actually* Chumash.

Using death, marriage, and baptismal registers kept by the Franciscan padres of the Santa Barbara Mission, census records, transcribed interviews, diaries, and newspapers, the ethnohistoric interpretation of Chumash social, religious, and cultural life performed by John R. Johnson (1988)—then a graduate student in physical anthropology at the University of California at Santa Barbara—produced a textually based interpretation of mission life in the

1800s. Johnson's project, carried out with all the rigor and "objectivity" appropriate to his training in physical anthropology, was intended to document the "most likely descendants" of traditional Chumash village sites slated for development projects on National Park Service lands within Chumash territory. Johnson's text-based methodology continues to negate local Barbareño Chumash families' assertion that *they* hold the knowledge of who is blood and adopted kin and who is not. His gathering of these textual materials therefore excluded the vast majority of the families in the area of Chumash heritage and ancestry. This methodology is, I believe, akin to studying plants in a herbarium in order to discern patterns in a living ecosystem—very valuable in terms of precision of information and ease of access to dead materials but wholly inadequate in terms of comprehending fluid, dynamic adaptation and change in a functioning plant community.

Johnson, in his current capacity as curator of anthropology at the Santa Barbara Museum of Natural History, created an official-looking "Pedigree of Indian Blood" form. This form does very little besides document a few Chumash individuals' connection to another set of forms, the mission registers and U.S. Census records. Some members of the Brotherhood of the Tomol either did not appear to share this documented proof of connection to the mission registers, or the Chumash ancestry of those family names that did appear in the Franciscan records was represented as ambiguous. Consequently, the *Helek*, which had been all but promised to the Chumash people after being paddled by the brotherhood along a traditional trade route between Santa Rosa Island and Santa Cruz Island, was instead claimed by museum officials, who drilled holes in the canoe's hull and bolted it to the ceiling of the museum's main auditorium. The brotherhood's historic paddle through one of the most treacherous ocean passages on the west coast was to locate itself in the community's memory as a story fraught both with triumph and with wrongs that have yet to be righted.

Johnson's textual reconstruction of Chumash history and genealogy and his position of scientific certainty are part of a legacy of cultural negation and damage carried on through the use of an anthropological method not designed to deal with the fluid nature of intermarriage and multicultural identity. When I was an undergraduate in Washington State, I traveled to Santa Barbara and conducted several interviews with Johnson. I was so convinced by his passionate assertion that there were several hundred confused people running around pretending to be Chumash that I wrote a paper and published a newspaper article expressing my outrage. I did not then have the level of intimate contact with my extended family that I do today, and I did not know the more complex dynamics of the situation. Only after living back home in Santa Barbara for several years and hearing many different "species" of this story, and only after four years of graduate work learning current ethnological and ethnohistoric theory and method, and only when I worked with respect alongside the people in my family as we gathered traditional materials did I begin to realize how uncertain are such positions of scientific certainty. Not only are a series of flawed texts inadequate to infallibly identify an entire people, but Johnson's data disputing the indigenous identity of local Chumash people are used by landowners and developers challenged by those same local people. Californio and Chumash definitions of family, personhood, and lineage—each of which can include canoes, and even baskets, in this context—are fluid elements within an entirely different ontology than those ascribed to and for us by Johnson and a few of his colleagues. The communities' joining together of these elements goes beyond bloodlines, *and* it stays within the particular boundaries determined by the communities themselves.

Ushtap (*Ush*: with the hand. *Tap*: To go, enter; or visit. To enter the ocean with our hands): An oceangoing canoe journey and gathering of community healing

Today there is but one canoe owned by the Chumash people. This canoe tells a story of healing and reciprocity between one of the most resource-rich and contested bioregions in the world, a people struggling to maintain cultural identity in the face of past and recent cultural genocide, and members of the dominant society who are seeking a better, more sustainable way to be in the world. The resurgence of Chumash maritime culture and philosophies of healing is bringing about an exchange of healing ideas that require all beings to practice living in a manner that strives for equilibrium. Chumash scholar Dennis Kelley claims the traditional Chumash *tomol* as a primary symbol and literal vehicle for a life lived in balance (2001a). Here, I tell part of the story of the Chumash *tomol* '*Elye'wun* and her people.

The Crossing

The first man in this world said that all the world is a canoe, for we are all one, and that which we finish now is a canoe. When the first canoe was finished, the first man who made it called the others to pay close attention to his canoemaking. Later this maker and his contemporaries died. The next generation remembered how the first man had made a canoe so they too made one. There was always a little difference in their work, so their canoe was a little different from the first one. This generation died and another followed. They always did as the first man in making their canoes, and so it continued.
                                                    —Kitsepawit (Hudson, Timbrook, and
                                                                          Rempe 1978: 143)

A small but significant part of a larger movement among indigenous "Canoe Nations," the alliance of Chumash communities has, against all odds, brought back a once-dying tradition. Inspired by the spiritual, intellectual, and physical health demonstrated by Northwest Coast Nations, the First Nations of Canada, and the Pacific Island Nations of Hawai'i and New Zealand—especially among the youth and elders of those nations—members of what became the nonprofit group called the Chumash Maritime Association rallied other Californio/Chumash community members to accomplish that which many local families had desired since the degradation of the *Helek* in the 1970s.

In 1996, representatives from each of the Chumash tribal territories—Malibu, Ventura, Santa Barbara, Santa Ynez, Santa Maria, San Luis Obispo, and Inland Chumash people now living mainly in Bakersfield—came together to bring about this reconnection of a maritime people with the sea. Our numbers included a Huichol man and a Filipino man who are beloved relatives by marriage, several mixed-heritage Californio/Chumash community members, and others who often lent a hand during complicated steps. Boatbuilder Peter Howorth, the same man who assisted the modern-day Brotherhood of the Tomol in building the *Helek*, guided us through every step. The eight apprentices used power tools and commercially available materials to facilitate the learning process. During each step, we constantly discussed which traditional tools and materials would be used for our next canoe, as well as how those materials could be acquired sustainably by coming generations.

The Chumash Maritime Association's use of power tools was somewhat controversial, mostly among non-Indian anthropologists and archaeologists who felt that we had lost "traditional" knowledge. Chumash scholar Dennis Kelley argued that our use of these tools "provide[s] the form, not for assimilation, but for . . . providing ways to enact important cultural constructs, providing contemporary American Indians with strategies for maintaining cultural continuity" (2001b: 10). While we held in our minds and hearts the importance of interacting with our local sphere of natural materials for building our next canoe, our employment of power tools, milled lumber, nylon cordage, shipbuilder's epoxy, and some rather unorthodox measuring tools (a Kentucky Fried Chicken bucket) reflected Kitsepawit's observation that succeeding generations' canoes were "a little different from the first one." We knew the time to build the canoes had come, and, with our adopted tools at hand, "so it continued."

The builders began each day of work with prayers for balance, goodwill, and the support of the larger local and indigenous community. Strict rules of conduct were adhered to during the entire process. It was imperative that builders take care of themselves by not abusing drugs or alcohol, and that respect for each other was demonstrated at all times. No fighting or abusive comments about others were allowed. The canoe builders took care of themselves and each other.

Over breakfast at Denny's, the building crew discovered that nearly all of us had thought about, dreamed, or otherwise pondered the name "Swordfish" for the nearly finished *tomol*. Unanimously, and with little fuss or ceremony, we named the canoe *'Elye'wun*, the Barbareño Chumash word for swordfish.

The *'Elye'wun*'s first ceremonial launch took place on Thanksgiving weekend in 1997, attended by more than a hundred Native American and Chumash community members. It was a time of great pride in who we are, who we will become, and what we are gaining the strength to do together as a community.

In the years between 1997 and 2001, the Chumash Maritime Association worked alongside several community and governmental organizations to bring our vision to fruition: a permanent place to build our canoes using traditional and modern techniques and materials, a program through which we can come together as a people to mentor Chumash young people, and an avenue through which to educate the public regarding our maritime activities—past and present. As we worked with the people of the local environmental nonprofit organization, Community Environmental Council, to accomplish the first two goals, the Chumash Maritime Association became partners in the brand-new Watershed Education Center, located at Arroyo Burro Beach in Santa Barbara. As we continued our six-year partnership with the fledgling Santa Barbara Maritime Museum to accomplish our mutual goal of educating the public, all eyes were on one goal that would weave everything together. We looked to the ancestral Island home of the Chumash people, Santa Cruz Island, known to the Chumash as Limuw.

As we prepared for the first paddle from the Chumash mainland to Limuw in more than 150 years, we realized how many aspects of our maritime traditions are actually taught to us by the *tomol 'Elye'wun*. The members of the paddling crew, which grew larger with each passing month, were taught to condition their bodies and minds through attention to nutrition, exercise, and the mental balance necessary to "enter the ocean with their hands" safely as part of a team on the open sea. As part of a tradition now in deep practice throughout Indian Country, the members of the Chumash Maritime Association learned to work in strong alliance with our primary supporters, both moral and financial, in organizing a gathering of Chumash people, an event that would take place on the island of Limuw on the second weekend of September 2001. Funded by the Channel Islands National Marine Sanctuary and by the Seventh Generation Fund, organizers spent ten months working as a team to make our collective dream a reality.

There is perhaps no healing skill learned by contemporary urban Indian people as complex and necessary as organizing a cultural gathering of this magnitude. As moderns accustomed to e-mail and cell phone communication, we were confronted with the reality that these tools were limited in this context. If we were to perform our duties "in a good way," as this critical sense of "old-school" courtesy is rather cryptically referred to throughout Indian Country, we would need to put aside our high-tech tools and set out, with offerings in hand, to talk about our plans to the heads of each family *personally*. This invitation protocol was not a set of rules our parents or grandparents handed down to us. As far as anyone knew, there had never been a return of 150-plus Californio, Chumash, and Native American people to Limuw, many of them elders, camping together for days to witness the first *tomol* crossing since the mission period. Miss Manners, we joked, could not help us with this one. Our decision to issue the invitations personally was common sense at work in a land where people still know each other. There was no book to refer to, no paper to quote from, no archaeological evidence to guide us, no anthropologist who could offer expert advice, solicited or otherwise, on how to invite Chumash families from violently divided communities to a historic gathering during which their relatives would quite literally risk their lives for love of their ancient traditions. But the *tomol* spoke to each one of us of a time when people's intimacy with each other, with the land, with the ocean, and with the ancestors was all there was in the world. That was all we had. It was more than enough.

After ten months of excruciatingly difficult and complex organization, the white sage was carefully gathered and tied into gift bundles, and the invitations were made. Interorganizational alliances were initiated and strengthened, travel arrangements negotiated and paid for. The Park Service campground at Limuw was generously donated, and we were given excellent deals on the "luxury" tent accommodations for the elders, thanks to the support of sporting goods stores in Santa Barbara. Safety issues were addressed, the crew training was stepped up, and RSVPs poured in.

The gifts from the larger community just kept coming. Ed Cassano, director of the Santa Barbara Maritime Museum, arranged for the museum's boat, the *Just Love*, to accompany the canoe as a support vessel across the channel. In an uncanny coincidence, the *Just Love* had been the support vessel for the *Helek* when the Brotherhood of the Tomol paddled it between the islands in 1976. Cassano was also responsible, in his previous job as the manager of the Channel Islands National Marine Sanctuary, for securing the grant that paid for the building of the *'Elye'wun*. He worked tirelessly with the Chumash Maritime Association to bring about this canoe renaissance.

Our gracious and talented cook—who wishes to remain unnamed for reasons of privacy and modesty—committed her tremendous skill and experience. The food was hunted, gathered, purchased, and packed in coolers, and our relatives' pickup trucks stood at the ready to take us to the harbor. At the last minute, word ran through the community that an amazing gift was being sent to the people. Dear friends, respected leaders of the Nisqually Indian Nation of Washington State, had caught, packed on ice, and shipped to Santa Barbara more than 150 pounds of king salmon to be enjoyed at the feast the night of the crossing. It was a gift, the Nisqually elders said, from a Canoe Nation that understood the importance of what we were doing.

The advance setup crew of twelve people were taken to Limuw by two boats: the *Xantu*, captained by Matt Kelly of the Channel Islands National Marine Sanctuary, who would also pilot the *Xantu* as a support boat for the *tomol* crew the following day; and the *Lady Raquel*, captained by Nick Tonkin, the husband of one of my mother's coworkers. Before the long weekend was over, "Captain Nick" would make the one-hour crossing between Santa Barbara and Limuw ten times. With the boats loaded down with crew and all the gear for the encampment—kitchen tents, stoves, tables for workshops, countless coolers, and the mountain of gear that would create a veritable "Kamp Komfort" for the elders—the trip took two hours. On all the trips, scores of dolphins came and rode the bow waves of both boats, energetically escorting us home.

At 3:00 A.M. on September 8, 2001, the crews of the *Just Love* and the *'Elye'wun* left the Channel Islands Harbor in Oxnard. Twenty-seven miles across the dark and windy channel, at the site of the Chumash village Swaxil, many of the waiting families had roused themselves from their tents and were assembled on the dark beach, singing songs of protection and healing, praying for the safety of their loved ones about to face the waters that had taken so many of our ancestors before us, some of them recently. When the families greeted the pale light of dawn, we prepared for a day like no other.

The paddlers, too, threw themselves into their day with energy and prayer. Michael Cruz, a member of the *tomol* crew, had this to say about his experience during the crossing: "I can remember when it was my turn to paddle, around 6:00 A.M., I climbed into *'Elye'wun* and the sun was coming up—you know, the beautiful oranges and pinks—and all the people on the *Just Love* were singing the sunrise song. I could see my sister singing to me, and the islands so close in the fog. It was just so beautiful, I cried; but it was a good cry because I knew that we had connection to everything and that we were going home" (2001: 14). Michael Cruz and his sister Eilene, for whom this trip to Limuw was their first, were two Chumash young people who had no confusion about their role in bringing the *tomol* back home to its people. Along with twenty-one other Chumash, Californio, Pacific Islander, and Native American crew members, they took turns paddling for nearly twelve hours over seas that were difficult even for powerboats.

Elders, young adults, teenagers, and small children set up chairs, towels, and mats on which to spend the day on the beach, waiting under gray skies for news of the *'Elye'wun* and its crew. Several of the men applied their barbecue skills to roasting rabbit, quail, and the Nisqually Nation's gift of fresh salmon over open fires fueled with chopped wood from downed trees, courtesy of the strong backs and chainsaws of the Park Service staff. The smell of the roasting meat warmed the beach. No matter what the outcome, we would all eat well, including the park rangers, who, to their extreme delight, were all invited to the feast.

Relying on the Park Service radios for news from the *Just Love*, we anx-

The Chumash *tomol* traveling to Santa Cruz Island. Used with permission from Frank Magellanes and Althea Edwards.

iously prepared for any emergency, having received reports that the *'Elye'wun* had sustained a huge crack and was taking on water almost faster than the crew could bail. Within a few miles of the village, the crew was not certain they would make it to land without the assistance of the support boats. The *tomol* captain, Perry Cabugos, after consulting with the entire crew, made the call to heave some of the ballast overboard and to relieve the heaviest crew member of his post. This left four crew members in the *tomol*. The other nineteen watched from the deck of the *Just Love*, most of them having already put in their time paddling across the rough channel. "Every paddle is a prayer," crew members were told numerous times throughout their training. On this day, those prayers performed the crossing. Each stroke of the paddles was heartfelt and profound.

On the beach at Swaxil, Michael Sanchez, the teenage boy who sat for hours at the top of the hill as the official lookout, came running breathlessly into the village. "The *tomol* is here! They're just around the corner!" It was his first glimpse of any *tomol*, a moment full of pride for a young Chumash man. The people jumped to their feet and, while assisting the elders to stand and watch, prepared to land the *'Elye'wun* and its exhausted crew on the rocky beach. The landing crew stood at surf's edge, while the ceremonial leaders conferred with each other on how best to proceed. Here we faced another of those powerful, potentially make-or-break cultural moments for which nothing the books had reported, nothing the anthropologists had constructed, nothing at all in written or living memory had prepared us. Our beloved family leaders once again followed the commonsense instincts of protocol—their practiced ability to do things respectfully, "in a good way." When the *'Elye'wun* and its four crew members appeared around the rocky bend of the island, everyone fell to pieces and wept and laughed and hugged each other and wept some more. The eldest among us were solemn, some trying to hide the tears streaming down their faces under their sunglasses, others openly weeping.

We had always heard that our ancestors ceremonially wept whenever a *tomol* would depart or land. We had not planned or prepared to enact such a ritual. But now, as we watched while the four paddlers, our brothers, husbands, fathers, uncles, cousins, and friends, lifted their eleven-foot redwood paddles

The arrival of the *tomol* at Santa Cruz Island. Used with permission from Frank Magellanes and Althea Edwards.

straight to the sky in a salute to the village assembled there, we understood the full emotional impact behind our ancestors' ritual expression. Truly, the *tomol* and its crew were as beautiful "as a flower on the water," as Kitsepawit said to us through the pen of J. P. Harrington. Kitsepawit was there at Swaxil that day, weeping with us. They all were.

Home at last, the people did what came naturally to all people on such an occasion: we ate until we nearly burst, we danced, we sang, we told wild tales under the stars, and we remembered. Home at last, our ancestors dreamed of us dreaming of them.

Epilogue

Chumash and Californio families are, by allying ourselves with the larger community, working within an ancient model of gathering power and performing health. We have for generations prayed for, and now receive, our *'atiswin*: power to begin healing and supporting each other, power to recover from centuries-old collective trauma, power to flourish, and power to protect and encourage the flourishing of our homelands. My cousin and colleague Dennis Kelley, an Obispeño Chumash scholar of religious studies, approaches his deconstruction of positivist archaeological method with rigor tempered with his well-known sense of humor. He asks, "How can we discern anything but the most rudimentary aspects of human dwelling patterns, diet, and social structure via exhumation? . . . I often wish I could travel ahead several centuries and listen as a future archaeologist tries to explain an unearthed Thighmaster®. No doubt it would have *some* religious significance" (2001b: 10). Another cousin, Rosemary Castillo, is poised to obtain a master's degree in education and is committed to bringing to local elementary schools an innovative, decolonized methodology for teaching world history. Michael Cruz, a Chumash graduate student in archaeology at the University of Oregon, is working to improve upon the method of "discernment via exhumation" in his studies of geophysical readings of Chumash sites, a precise, highly accurate method that requires no digging. Deana Dartt, another Californio/Chumash archaeology graduate student at the University of Oregon, brings to her studies powerful arguments regarding archaeological representation of ancient cultures and its effect on contemporary indigenous peoples. All four are actively "decolonizing" culturally interpretive methodologies.

Using the best tools of our traditions, using our hands, using cues from our languages that bind together minds and emotions, Native American scholars, community members, and our allies will gather what we can use from our scholarly and ecological contexts, which in turn may find us useful. Whether we prune, weed, or perform a methodical, controlled burn, we will leave these fields healthier than we found them.

NOTES

This paper is dedicated to Cresensio Lopez, *tomolero*, artist, uncle, and friend.

1. The word "Chumash" is a term delineating observed socio-cultural, linguistic, economic ties between autonomous village areas from San Luis Obispo to Malibu, California. Barbareño Chumash is the name used here for the language traditionally spoken in the Santa Barbara/Goleta area. All Chumash terms used in this paper are Barbareño terms.

The communities who call themselves "Californio," have been residents of California since before the Treaty of Guadalupe Hidalgo in 1848, which defined the terms of the annexation of Northern Mexican territories to the United States. These "Old California" families recognize themselves as descending from a mixed Indigenous, Mexican, and Spanish heritage.

2. References in this chapter to a "decolonized" methodology for performing academic research are informed by the work of Maori scholar Linda Tuhiwai Smith (1999).

3. See Philip Deloria's treatise on the complexities of Anglo-American role playing in *Playing Indian* (1998). See also Grounds 2001.

REFERENCES

Blackburn, Thomas C. 1975. *December's Child: A Book of Chumash Oral Narratives.* Berkeley and Los Angeles: University of California Press.
Cruz, Michael. 2001. In Their Own Voices. *News From Native California* 15:14.
Deloria, Philip. 1998. *Playing Indian.* New Haven, Conn.: Yale University Press.
Grounds, Richard A. Tallahasee, Osceola, and the Hermeneutics of American Place-Names. *Journal of the American Academy of Religion* 69: 287–322.
Haley, Brian D. and Wilcoxon, Larry R. 1997. Anthropology and the Making of Chumash Tradition. *Current Anthropology* 18: 761–94.
Hudson, Travis, and Ernest Underhay. 1978. *Crystals in the Sky: An Intellectual Odyssey Involving Chumash Astronomy, Cosmology,and Rock Art.* Santa Barbara, Calif.: Ballena Press/Santa Barbara Museum of Natural History.
Hudson, Travis, Janice Timbrook, and Melissa Rempe. 1978. *Tomol: Chumash Watercraft as Described in the Ethnographic Notes of John P. Harrington.* Santa Barbara, Calif.: Ballena Press/Santa Barbara Museum of Natural History.
Hurtado, Albert L. 1988. *Indian Survival on the California Frontier.* New Haven, Conn.: Yale University Press.
Johnson, John. 1988. Chumash Social Organization: An Ethnohistoric Perspective. Ph.D. diss., University of California, Santa Barbara.
———. 1994. Missionization among the Coastal Chumash of Central California: A Study of Risk Minimization Strategies. *American Anthropologist* 96: 263–99.
———.1988. Mission Registers as Anthropological Questionaires: Understanding Limitations of the Data. *American Indian Culture and Research Journal* 12(2): 9–30.
Kelley, Dennis. 2001a. Chumash Religious Identity and the Tomol. Lecture, March 7.

————. 2001. Our Ancestors Paddle with Us: Tradition and Construction within Native American Religious Practice. Paper presented at the annual meeting of the American Academy of Religion, Denver, Colorado.

Mithun, Marianne. 1999. *The Languages of Native North America.* New York: Cambridge University Press.

Nabokov, Peter. 1996. Native Views of History. In *The Cambridge History of the Native Peoples of the Americas: North America.* Vol. 1. Edited by Bruce G. Trigger and Wilcomb E. Washburn. Cambridge: Cambridge University Press.

Rose, Wendy. 1992. The Great Pretenders: Further Reflections on Whiteshamanism. In *The State of NativeAmerica: Genocide, Colonization, and Resistance,* ed. M. Annette Jaimes, (ed), 403–421. Boston: South End Press.

Simpson, Lesley B. 1962. *The Letters of José Señán, O.F.M: Mission San Buenaventura, 1796–1823.* Ventura, Calif.: Ventura County Historical Society.

Smith, Linda Tuhiwai. 1999. *Decolonizing Methodologies: Research and Indigenous Peoples.* London: Zed Books.

Timbrook, Janice. 1993. Introduction. In *Chumash Healing: Changing Health and Medical Practice in an American Indian Society,* ed. Philip Walker and Travis Hudson, ix–xii. Banning, Calif.: Malki Museum Press.

Walker, Philip L., and Travis Hudson, eds. 1993. *Chumash Healing: Changing Health and Medical Practice in an American Indian Society.* Banning, Calif.: Malki Museum Press.

Whistler, Kenneth W. 1980. *An Interim Barbareño Dictionary.* Washington, D.C.: National Anthropological Archives, Smithsonian Institution.

9

Religious Healing among War-Traumatized African Immigrants

John M. Janzen, Adrien Ngudiankama, and Melissa Filippi-Franz

This chapter explores religious healing among recent Somali and Great Lakes/Congolese African refugees and immigrants in the United States.[1] As part of the more than 600,000 African-born U.S. residents (American Public Health Association 2000, citing the U.S. Census), they come from all over the continent: Sudan, where thousands have fled civil war and the repressive regime; Somalia, following civil war and the collapse of the state; Nigeria, because of ethnic violence and government repression; Rwanda and Burundi, following ethnic cleansing and genocide; Congo/Zaire, in the shadow of government repression, economic hardship, and civil war. Increasingly familiar in these groups are the stories of hardship and persecution, flight, and arrival in the United States, the quest for a means of livelihood, and the struggle to become established in a new home (Holtzman 2000). For many there is the gnawing question of return, although this rarely happens (Janzen 2004).

Traumas and the resulting memory constructions in immigrants should concern scholars, practitioners, and policy makers alike, for they affect the manner in which these new residents and citizens relate to their nations of origin and to their newly adopted home. The thesis of this chapter is that unresolved traumas and lingering memories of conflict not only threaten to exacerbate the cycles of violence within the immigrants' societies of origin but also have the potential to afflict the American social fabric. Constructive resolution, or healing, of such traumas lessens the potential of chronic contin-uing conflict.

A growing body of research in anthropology and related disciplines has laid out the parameters of war trauma and healing in home societies (e.g., Daniel in Sri Lanka [1996]; Kleinman in China [1995]; Janzen in Rwanda and Burundi [1999; Janzen and Janzen 2000]). Research on the circumstances of unresolved trauma and trauma memory among Africans in exile or in a newly adopted country is beginning to appear (Malkki 1995a and b; Gozdziak and Shandy 2002), but more research is needed, especially for the United States (Ngudiankama 2001b). Refugee and immigrant communities that have been in the United States for decades offer guidance for new research.

For the Hmong, who left Southeast Asia in the 1970s following the Viet-nam War, the manifestations of traumas of war, attack, loss of next of kin, flight, and the refugee experience included "fright," "soul loss," and fear of persecution at hands of old enemies and rivals (Capps 1994). In the Kansas City Hmong community that had converted to Christianity in Laos, the traumas of war, flight, and loss were addressed with intense prayer and fellowship gath-erings. Hmong-specific syndromes such as "fright" and "soul loss" were han-dled with traditional treatments and the maintenance of strong clan ties, com-bined with "making it" in American society. Elsewhere, in larger Hmong communities, lingering trauma and the challenges of a new land were ad-dressed with shamanism, spirit rituals, and avoidance of old rivalries. For Viet-namese Americans, in one study, signs and symptoms of the traumas of the war are "nightmares," "recurring same bad dreams," "headaches," and "anxiety attacks" associated with physical reminders of the original traumatic experi-ences (Choby 2000). Growing up in America did not fully resolve these trau-matic flashbacks, which in fact worsened in adulthood. Recurrent traumatic associations were greatly relieved through the disciplined practice of martial arts and the creation of community around this practice (Choby 2000).

Lines of Inquiry of Religious Healing among African Immigrants

The Somali and Great Lakes/Congolese vignettes to follow represent a range of religious responses to trauma experience and memory that can serve as a basis for further research and action. We suggest four lines of inquiry. The first—a basically ethnographic task—is to identify how traumatic experi-ences of war, loss, displacement, and disorientation are dealt with in a new land. The people described here display signs and symptoms of recurrent nightmares, fears, sense of isolation, sexual impotence, and feelings of guilt and despondence. Some of these individuals were brought to clinics by coun-selors or family members. Others, perhaps the majority, are never seen by professional therapists. Family and community members act as therapists. The role of congregations—mosques and healing churches—will be especially scrutinized in this chapter, on the hunch that families often are too traumatized or internally conflicted to heal themselves. In Gozdziak and Shandy's study of religion and spirituality in situations of forced migration (2002), religion plays a significant role in helping adherents deal with the transition of migration if the religious fabric is not destroyed by the conflict that drives them from home. Ngudiankama's (2001a) work with Congolese refugees in London and Washington, D.C., recognizes the embracing and discerning community as an important resource for healing.

A second line of inquiry explores what happens when the syndromes of trauma are not or cannot be handled within the tradition-appropriate means in family or community. Several cases illustrate this dilemma. What are the consequences of sufferers' avoidance, denial, repression, or lingering trauma that are too painful to confront? By selecting the road of least resistance, or by default, such individuals may come to believe that their best option is to move on in life in the new society. "Simply becoming American" is tempting for some. The complex emotions surrounding unresolved trauma may, however, with reinforcement from others in the community, fuel the recourse to vengeance against antagonists, either directly or indirectly through financial and political support of ongoing conflict in the former home. Recognition of this dynamic process on the part of community members and health officials, and figuring out how to avert it, can be an important contribution to the welfare of new immigrants to the United States.

A third line of inquiry explores involvement in a religious congregation as a way of coming to terms with war trauma, painful memories, and attendant symptoms. Either Islam (in the case of the Somalis) or Christianity (in the case of the Great Lakes/Congolese individuals), with strong themes from Central African traditional religion, provides the themes and forms of this orientation. Also at issue is the embrace of new religious community and identity in the quest for trauma healing.

A fourth line of inquiry is seen in the return to earlier identity and healing following a period of attempted forgetting, without success. Our cases are too recent for this to have occurred. Evidence over the long term from victims of the Russian Revolution, the Russian Gulag, and the Holocaust of World War II, as well as from the previously mentioned case of Vietnamese in America, suggests that painful memories usually cannot be repressed indefinitely.

The Somali War Experience

The war of the 1980s that drove so many Somalis into refugee camps and later into resettlement elsewhere in Africa, Europe, and North America, has its origins in the complicated alliances of the Cold War, on the one hand, and in the segmentary character of Somali society, on the other. Located strategically in the Horn of Africa, within aircraft striking distance of the oil fields of the Arabian Peninsula, Somalia and Ethiopia became entangled in shifting alliances with the United States and the Soviet Union. At the end of the Cold War, however, the patron powers allowed President Siad Barre to be forced out by opposition clan leaders who promptly began to fight among themselves for control of the capital, Mogadishu. Thousands were killed, and millions fled to refugee camps in neighboring countries and on to Europe, North America, Australia, and elsewhere. Somali writer Nuruddin Farah, now residing in South Africa, and "Mohammed," a former Somali merchant and now a hotel clerk in Kansas City, provide the narrative themes of the traumatic flight and the conditions that prevailed in refugee camps and new homes for up to 2 million Somalis: the recollection of trauma; what has happened to their society; how they have changed from what they were before they fled; how they have reconstructed their families and their communities; how they have shaped a memory of their experiences of trauma, flight, and becoming refugees; and how they are rebuilding their lives in a new home—themes that are profound and ultimate, and therefore framed in religious terms.

Why Did We Flee?

Among Somalis in exile, discussion of "why we fled" allows them to ask what the experience was all about. Behind the question is the awful ill that needs healing and resolution. In Farah's narrative, his sister suggests that it was not because of clan conflict or because they were members of a particular clan that they fled but because of the despair they faced. "It wasn't who one was, or what clan one was born in that mattered, it was the nadir of helplessness. That made us up and go" (2000: 3). Flight was the only way they could face their life. This statement upsets the father because it reminds him of something deeper, more dreadful, than despair. "We fled," he counters, "because we met the beasts in us, face to face" (3).

Mohammed, for a long time, could not speak of the situation from which he fled because it was too awful. When he finally spoke of this, in a highly agitated tone, the horror was transparent. "My father was killed by a Hawiye [clan member]. Two of my brothers were killed. You understand? Because we were aligned with the Marahan [clan]. That's the way they judged us" (Filippi-Franz 2002: 43). His closest kin were killed in the brutality of clan alliances and oppositions gone awry, in the midst of the Somali war. He describes the moment Siad Barr fled the capital city and his forces were shelling the city against the clan militias. Because clans were present not in territorially segmented areas of Mogadishu but intermixed through the city, "bombs were falling everywhere. . . . People were moving off, everybody was dying. There was miscommunication everywhere. Let's get out, Let's get out. I had to move" (45). An additional reason for Mohammed's flight is similar to that of Farah's father. Mohammed relates an encounter with a righteous and religious man who refused to trade in arms for loot because of his faith in Allah. When Mohammed's own store was being looted before his eyes, this man upheld faith in Allah. Mohammed in effect says he fled for fear of losing his faith, of being drawn into the trade in arms to kill others to defend his property, what Farah's father called "the beasts in us" (44).

Wounded Relationships, Scarred Perceptions of Others

For Somalis who experienced the horrors of this war, the wounds remain in the form of suspicion of those against whom one was aligned, either those who were in actual incidents of fighting or looting and defense or in a categorical clan identity sense. Mohammed relates, "If I see somebody with dark glasses, or somebody with a queer walk, it creates in me a kind of fear." Other Somalis tell him, he says, that "when they see someone in the street they start trembling, their heartbeat increases, and there is fear of people because [they] do not know. . . . You may find a kind of deceit [sic] that he or she avoids to go to the doctor because the translator is Somali . . . the patient has a feeling that the translator will expose the secrets of a neighbor" (52–53). A pervasive suspicion continues to fill the lives of Somalis in their new settings. This, among other matters, led one person in a Kansas City immigrant service agency to suggest that the Somalis were the most difficult of all the immigrants with whom they worked; they had the greatest problems to overcome. Another aspect of this suspicion among Somalis is the conviction that their society has become pathological, pervaded by a kind of virulent clanism. Farah's sister tries to say that Somali clans include both the bad and the good, as "a spectrum of rainbow colors" (2002: 3). Nevertheless, she identifies the stereotypical Somalis, the pastoralist clans, as "aggressive bellicose beasts, forever at each other's throats, beasts who remain mistrustful of one another's intentions" (3–4). Likewise, Mohammed speaks of clan society as a poison, a cancer, that destroys individuals. Both Farah and Mohammed understand that this negative character of Somali clan structure emerged in the context of the collapse of the Somali postcolonial state. Yet for Mohammed this awful aspect of Somali society, clanism or tribalism, is essentialized into something that he cannot separate from Somali identity. Farah, on the other hand, is better able to speak of this aspect of Somali society and experience objectively, although it frightened him to hear the "tempestuous outpourings of strong sentiments and emotions expressed in intense clan terms . . . such venom in their recollection." He was shocked by what he heard but understood it to be an expression of the severity and the depth of the hurt, which now ran "in their blood" (5).

Old Selves and New Selves

Both sources describe the jarring contrast between their new reality and what they were formerly. Farah wonders "what [his family's] old selves would say to their new selves." Mohammed could not forget the former good life of the urban merchant, with shop, car, and good ties across clans. Farah's father reminded him and his sister that formerly, when the country functioned, property meant something, being educated, being neighborly, being responsible to the community, life itself, had meaning and value. Now all these had no meaning, no value (2000: 4).

These former values might or might not be redeemable, although they continued as memories and dreams of a distant future. Farah, more than Mohammed, speaks of the practical acts of rebuilding selves, families, and society. Farah says that, as always, it is the women who do the nurturing, the caregiving, the small acts of daily life that keep individuals going: "mending the broken, healing the wounded, taking care of the elderly and the sick, martyrly women, forever prepared to sacrifice their lives for the general good of the entire community" (2000: 5). For Mohammed, only in the mosque could he find respite from the division and misunderstanding of society and his own suspicion: "In the mosque we listen to what the imam says. [He] speaks not of tribalism, he's telling us about a chapter or verse [in the Koran]" (Filippi-Franz 2002: 74).

Damaged Memories

Both sources portray memory as the ultimate and most dangerous wound inflicted by the Somali war. Farah speaks of "damaged memory" brought along by escapees in Mombasa's refugee camp. He describes this aspect of the long-term consequences of war trauma, the one that is most difficult to speak and write about, as follows: "I sensed that, buried among the ashen memories which they had brought along, there were incommunicable worries. There were areas of their lives that I had no access to; because I was not there when the horror came to visit their homes" (2000: 5). For Mohammed, who tries to communicate his pain, fear, and worry, the pathology of clanism, the false and virulent turn of his society, is foremost in his mind. It is a kind of false memory, too, one that constructs a negative stereotype on all that he associates with his personal trauma.

The Great Lakes/Congo War Experience

These case studies of African immigrants to the United States from the Great Lakes/Congo region all fled the 1997–99 fighting that occurred initially in eastern Congo and then moved westward as the Rwandan conflict metamorphosed into or was echoed as a Congolese conflict. At first the Tutsi-controlled and Tutsi-identified governments of Uganda, Rwanda, and Burundi allied with the Congolese opposition, which in 1996–7 coalesced into the Democratic Alliance for the Liberation of Congo/Zaire (ADFLC), with Joseph Kabila Sr. as its nominal leader. On the other side of the conflict were Mobutu's Zairean government and the Hutu-controlled and Hutu-identified Rwandan government in exile. By 1998 these alliances flip-flopped, as Kabila expelled Tutsi fighters and embraced the exiled Hutu. The various paths that brought the Great Lakes/Congolese individuals to Washington, D.C., reflect the backlash of these shifting alliances.

These immigrants come mainly from eastern Congo and Uganda and speak Swahili, French, Lingala, and English. They are mostly in their twenties, and in conversations with Ngudiankama, who is in his thirties, they frequently used the words *vieux* or *mukubua* ("elder" in French and Swahili, respectively), which Congolese popular culture imposes when addressing one's seniors. As a group, they appear astonishingly healthy and elegant. They reflect a dimension of Congolese popular culture known as "religion Kitendi," whose motto since the late seventies remains "Well Shaved, Well Combed, and Well Perfumed." Musician Jules Shungu Wembadio, alias Papa Wemba, whose impact on Congolese youth for the last twenty years is second to none, remains its highest priest. Yet the Kongo proverb "Nzo kualeka ko, kuzebi bitatikanga mo ko" (meaning literally "The house in which you have never slept, you will never know what afflicts it") is apt among them.

Conversations with these young men and women reveal that beneath this surface of elegance they are other persons, persons with stories about broken lives, torture, and pathological experiences. Fear, anxiety, introversion, migraine headaches, insomnia, nightmares, anger, hatred, palpitations, stress, anorexia, and sexual impotence are among the main symptoms of trauma discerned among them. In brief, they are traumatized people who since their exile in the United States regularly visit therapeutic centers for victims of torture. In addition to their regular visits to clinical or therapeutic centers, they have become part of African immigrant churches that actively respond to their trauma.

All the individuals reported here were Christians in Africa. But their ready involvement in the African healing churches of Washington, D.C., is a tribute to the way that these churches, following the strong trend of independent Christian healing churches of Central Africa, have promoted African healing traditions that include laying on of hands, anointment, confessions and forgiveness, dancing and singing, exorcism, and inspiration or possession by the Holy Spirit within small independent fellowships with dynamic pastors who bring together many traditions from Christian Africa that defy easy classification (Bediako 1995; Parrat 1995).

Shabani: Rape and Killing of a Loved Family Member

Shabani, about twenty-five years old when he fled Congo in the late 1990s, is from Goma, North Kivu, where he worked as an electrician. Politically, he joined the ADFLC, the party that dethroned Mobutu. He became the party spokesman in his *quartier*. When the tide turned, and the ADFLC and the Rwandan government had a falling out, and a new war began, Shabani was arrested and beaten. Released after four weeks, he was told that his wife had been so violently raped that she had died. As the war continued, in his own words, "watu wa Kagame" (people of Kagame, Rwandan Patriotic Front soldiers) destroyed his house and raped his sister. He fled to Kenya, from where he traveled to the United States. On his arrival in the United States, Shabani suffered constant headache (*kichua kinaniuma kila wakati*) and insomnia, which no painkiller and no counseling could help. He constantly spoke of his life before the war and his hatred of the Tutsi. As he put it, "Mukubwa, Nina chukia nchi ya Kagame, Nina chukia nchi ya Rwanda" (Big brother, I hate the people of Kagame, I hate people from Rwanda).

Once every two weeks, Shabani visited a counseling center, where experts on trauma listened to his stories. He told Ngudiankama, a pastoral counselor, of the powerlessness he experienced in the dialogues with these trained psychologists. In fact, "the more he talked with them about what happened, the more he became angry, the more he suffered bouts of insomnia." In a second session, Ngudiankama mentioned Christian spiritual themes and asked Shabani whether he has ever visited a church or participated in pastoral counseling since he arrived in the United States. Then, in July 2001, Ngudiankama introduced him to an African immigrant Christian community while he continued to visit him. In mid-2003, Shabani continued working at menial jobs in Washington, D.C., attending an African immigrant Christian church, and otherwise was less troubled by his earlier symptoms.

Kalayi and Marthe: Their Children Were Executed before Their Very Eyes

Kalayi and Marthe are from the Lokele ethnic group of northeastern Congo. Both worked as teachers in Kisangani. Married for six years, the couple had two children. When Ugandan and Rwandan forces invaded Kisangani in 1998 in pursuit of Rwandan militia and the old army regulars, he was among those arrested. Their two children were executed in their presence and they were told, "This is your reward for having joined Kabila's party." In Kalayi's words, "From that day, we are not the same people anymore. We look at each other as strangers. My wife has become as my daughter, I cannot even approach her [sexually]. Whenever I try, I feel powerless. This is our life."

Symptoms of trauma in this couple in addition to sexual impotency included constant nausea, anger, and hatred. Marthe developed a serious inability to speak that made life more difficult for the couple. The complexity of this case led to urgent pastoral interventions by Ngudiankama, who asked them to pray with him. Having introduced them to some African immigrant pastors in mid-2001, Ngudiankama continued to visit them and assess their progress. By 2003 both Kalayi and Marthe were working and attending classes to further their education in the United States.

The therapeutic dimension of African immigrant churches in the histories of traumatized people like Kalayi and Marthe can be discerned from the first contacts. A new language and a sense of restoration characterize these moments whose hallmark is personal commitment to church activities and healing from one's psychosomatic diseases. "God has healed us," stated Kalayi and Marthe seven months after the first meeting with Ngudiankama. This is the language of forgiveness and of the possibility of new beginning. Stories of anorexia, sexual impotence, guilt, anger, and hatred gave way to talk about sharing meals, expecting a child, smiling, and joining church committees.

Mbolekisha and Julienne: Relationships with Those Who Persecuted You

Mbolekisha is from Idiofa, Bandundu, in southwestern Congo. He had a store in Kisangani, where he had lived with his family for seven years. A Ugandan general who accused him of being from Kabila's ethnic group took his business away from him. "Thank God," said Mbolekisha,

> for all this happened at the time that my wife and three children were on holiday in Nairobi, where my sister has been living for the last four years. I joined them in Nairobi, where we had no choice but to go into exile. For four months I could not sleep, nor could I speak about what had happened to me. I hated life, I hated Kabila, I hated everybody from Rwanda and Uganda. Insomnia has invaded us, and for more than a year no one in our family was able to really sleep or laugh. What was terrible for us where we lived in Washington, D.C., was that our neighbors were from Uganda. Can you imagine?

Mbolekisha and his family were approached by the same Ugandan neighbors, whom they discovered to be refugees, too. They spoke about their mutual experiences and finally became good friends. The Mbolekishas were invited to join their Ugandan friends' church, which, in the words of Julienne, Mbolekisha's wife, "helped us more than any other thing. In this church we were healed from our pains." In 2003 they continued with this group. Economically, they were just surviving by working at odd jobs.

This case illustrates the theme of forgiveness in religious trauma healing. Songs, testimonies, and prayers of healing are characterized within African immigrant churches by a focus on the theme of God as healer, forgiver, and restorer. The gathered congregation becomes the arena of stories about people's afflictions and testimonies about being healed from trauma symptoms through prayers and forgiveness. Testimonies often lead other afflicted people to stand up and in tears ask for prayers. Testimonies are given in a liturgical manner in songs that reiterate the healing power of Christ. The church is thus a place of musical therapy for trauma. In many observed cases, the person who was afflicted starts or ends his or her testimony by singing and stating, as did Mbolekisha and Julienne, "I am healed, I have forgiven and I am forgiven."

Mbeya and Palata: Awful Memories

Mbeya and Palata are from Bunia, South Kivu. He worked as an agronomist and also taught in a secondary school. His wife, Mbeya, worked as an accountant in a clinic. The following is his story:

> When the war of liberation of Congo, 1997, started in Bunia, for two weeks, I was unable to see my family, for I could not go out of my office. The third week, I could not bear it anymore and managed to get out and walk home. On my way, I smelled what cannot be smelled. Everywhere one saw dead bodies. I got home; there I saw nobody. I did not know what to do, for the clinic where my wife worked had become the base for Kagame's forces. Big brother [*mukubwa*], when you hear that millions of people have died since this war started, this includes our children. Life has never been the same again for us.

As Palata continued to talk, his wife suddenly stood up. Palata added, "Mukubwa, it is always like that with my wife. Her actions have changed ever since. It is now six months since we have been visiting doctors and psychologists, but there is no change. I decided to not bother any longer." The couple lived far from an area where they could find an African immigrant church. In his third visit, Ngudiankama asked a pastor to accompany him. The couple joined his church. By early 2003, they had, however, moved to North Carolina, where they joined relatives.

This case reflects the importance of home visits in the healing churches, in which those like Meya and Palata, afflicted by traumatizing experiences and memories, are subjected to therapeutic discipline consisting of long hours of pastoral dialogue in which they narrate their personal experiences. Prayers, fasting, and exorcism are centrally featured in these home sessions, with the pastor and the pastoral team constituting the main therapy managing group.

Rituals such as laying on of hands and encircling the afflicted as signs of protection are common.

Often embedded with African Christian metaphors and legends, sermons, and exhortations are special therapeutic tools in the history of healing trauma among African immigrants. The whole pastoral activity within African immigrant churches is a healing performance, similar to African independent and charismatic churches (Devisch 1996). The liturgical events incarnate a healing dimension whose ultimate act is the pastoral kerygma and prayer. The sermon and exhortation speak of the word of God and prayers as the real remedy. Stressing forgiveness, repentance, and newness in Christ, the pastor is seen as the healer, the psychologist who is able to effectively address the spiritual and physical ailments of the afflicted.

Pastors who lead these African immigrant churches have little or no formal training. They are from Pentecostal or charismatic backgrounds where hierarchies of spirits, radical repentance, and complete obedience to the Scriptures are held and evoked as the basis for their calling and ministry. Their pastoral counseling sessions are either collective or individual. Their appeal to traumatized immigrants includes the open-ended nature of the time commitment to the sufferer, use of African symbolic languages of touch, dance, gesture, and voice, the use of Scripture in exorcism, and extensive application of fasting and praying.

Lines of Inquiry Revisited

The Somali and Great Lakes/Congolese vignettes reveal patterns suggested by the four lines of inquiry at the beginning of this chapter. Following the first line of inquiry, there is abundant evidence of the continuity of instituted social forms and procedures for the treatment of war trauma by family, kin group, and community. Farah, for example, writes about his family and the way they sort through their memories of loss and flight as evidence of trauma healing without specialists. McMichael's work (2002) with Somali women in Melbourne demonstrates the healing and coping strength of informal Islamic routines and rituals they had known at home. Ngudiankama's study of Congolese refugees in London and Washington, D.C., identifies the significance of the embracing and discerning kin and non-kin community as an important resource for healing—as divination within kin and community therapy management.

To follow the second line of inquiry, there is the strong sense that some of the new immigrant families and communities are so shattered that they cannot be reconstituted sufficiently to play a healing role. Nurrudin Farah's account (2000) of Somali migrants in Italy, Britain, Switzerland, and Sweden depicts many households in which the men are pathetic wounded souls routinely derided by their mothers, wives, and sisters for doing nothing, while the women take on menial jobs to support their families. While most Somalis continue to consider themselves Muslims, the congregation, or religious leadership, seems to have a minimal role in offering a community within which healing might take place. In this context the fear and horror of what happened in the war continue to be remembered, along with unrealistic dreams of a romanticized Somalia that perhaps never existed and cannot in any case be reconstituted. Mohammed in Kansas City, although he says he finds release from thoughts of clan conflict in the mosque, actively seeks to deny his Somali clan-based society. Farah depicts a kind of national paralysis among the exiles, especially the men, no doubt related to the continuing conflicts in Somalia.

Farah articulates the extent and nature of this trauma by Somalis as ever deepening layers of despair: "The Islamic clergy have failed as much as every other segment of Somali society, and must share in the blame" (2000: 128). The "descent into savagery" in Mogadishu left him "more or less bereft of the notion of sin, as if the distinction between evil and good were no longer obvious." "For a Somali, this has been a decade of self-doubt . . . of doors opening and letting in a history marked by the extent of its maledictions" (130). Instead of answers, he finds only more questions. "Is this why, in such trying times as these, my vision filters through a placenta of eternal destruction?" (130).

The young Congolese refugees of Washington, D.C., as a group seem better able than their Somali counterparts to reconstitute their religious institutions or to join new religious communities. Despite the deep wounds of war trauma, loss of loved ones, and the tearing asunder of flight, as describe by Ngudiankama, these individuals seem to respond quickly to the healing churches and such examples as neighbors discovering each other and reconciling quickly. The manner in which Congolese and at least some Great Lakes individuals participate in the intense rituals and gatherings of the healing churches suggests that they are on familiar ground, culturally and socially speaking. The healing churches reproduce a familiar African framework, a powerful institutional resource that has not been shattered, within which to reconstitute their wholeness.

These actions stand in sharp contrast to those of the Somali men who remain withdrawn and fearfully suspicious of each other. The Somalis by and large face an exploded society, where trust in their very world was shattered. It would be tempting to conclude that the Somalis represent a greater danger than the Great Lakes/Congolese for continued cycles of revenge and conflict. But we must be careful with this scale of generalization, for the intensities of trauma and the contingencies of resolution vary greatly and are open to endless and serendipitous possibilities (Janzen 1999).

NOTE

1. The sources for this chapter are mainly the firsthand experience of the authors. Janzen participated in relief work in the Great Lakes region in 1994–95 (Janzen 1999, 2000). Since then he has served as expert witness in the defense of Central Africans facing deportation. Ngudiankama personally experienced traumatic flight from his home in Central Africa, then conducted theological studies at King's College, London, and received his Ph.D. from the Institute of Education, University of London. He does pastoral counseling with African immigrants at La Philadelphia Mission Baptist Church and with other religious congregations in Washington, D.C., and teaches social science courses at Bowie State University, Maryland. Melissa Filippi-Franz wrote her M.A. thesis on Somalis of Kansas City (2001) and continues her graduate study on refugees in the Horn of Africa.

REFERENCES

American Public Health Association. 2000. http://www.apha.org/ppp/red/afrgeodis .htm.
Anderson, Allan. 1997. Pluriformity and Contextuality in African Initiated Churches. http://www.artsweb.bham.ac.uk.
Apraku, Kofi. 1991. *African Emigres in the United States.* New York: Praeger.
Arthur, John. 2000. *Invisible Sojourners: African Immigrant Diaspora in the United States.* Westport, Conn.: Praeger.
Bediako, K. 1995. *Christianity in Africa: The Renewal of Non-Western Religion.* Edinburgh: Edinburgh University Press.
Capps, Lisa. 1994. Change and Continuity in the Medical Culture of the Hmong in Kansas City. *Medical Anthropology Quarterly,* n.s., 8: 161–77.
Choby, Alexandra. 2000. Trauma Memory and Healing in Vietnamese-Americans. M.A. thesis, University of Kansas.
Daniel, E. Valentine. 1996. *Charred Lullabies: Chapters in an Anthropography of Violence.* Princeton, N.J.: Princeton University Press.
Devisch, René. 1996. "Pillaging Jesus": Healing Churches and the Villagisation of Kinshasa. *Africa* 66: 555–86.
Farah, Nurrudin. 2000. *Yesterday, Tomorrow: Voices from the Somali Diaspora.* London: Cassell.
Filippi-Franz, Melissa. 2002. War Trauma among Somali in Kansas City. M.A. thesis, University of Kansas.
Gozdziak, Elzbieta M., and Dianna J. Shandy, eds. 2002. Editorial Introduction: Religion and Spirituality in Forced Migration. Special issue. *Journal of Refugee Studies* 15(2): 129–35.
Holtzman, Jon D. 2000. *Nuer Journeys, Nuer Lives: Sudanese Refugees in Minnesota.* Needham Heights, Mass.: Allyn and Bacon.
Janzen, John M. 1999. Text and Context in the Anthropology of War Trauma: The African Great Lakes Region 1993–95. *Suomen Antropologi* 24(4): 37–57.
———. 2002. *The Fabric of Health: An Introduction to Medical Anthropology.* New York: McGraw-Hill Higher Education.

————. 2004. Illusions of Home in the Story of a Rwandan Refugee's Return. In *Coming Home: Toward an Ethnography of Return,* ed. Ellen Oxfeld and Lynellyn Long. Philadelphia: University of Pennsylvania Press.

Janzen, John M., and Reinhild Kauenhoven Janzen. 2000. *Do I Still Have a Life? Voices from the Aftermath of War in Rwanda and Burundi.* Lawrence, Kans.: Publications in Anthropology 20. Department of Anthropology, University of Kansas.

Kleinman, Arthur. 1995. *Writing at the Margin.* Berkeley and Los Angeles: University of California Press.

Malkki, Liisa. 1995a. *Purity and Exile: Violence, Memory and National Cosmology among Hutu Refugees in Tanzania.* Chicago: University of Chicago Press.

————. 1995b. Refugees and Exile: From "Refugee Studies" to the National Order of Things. *Annual Review of Anthropology* 24: 495–523.

McMichael, Celia. 2002. "Everywhere Is Allah's Place": Islam and the Everyday Life of Somali Women in Melbourne, Australia. *Journal of Refugee Studies* 15: 171–88.

Ngudiankama, Adrien. 2001a. Concepts of Health and Therapeutic Options among Congolese Refugees in London: Implications for Education. Ph.D. diss., University of London, Institute of Education.

————. 2001b. Refugee Studies: The Nature of Scholarship. Unpublished paper, African Studies Resource Center, University of Kansas.

Parrat, J. 1995. *Reinventing Christianity: African Theology Today.* Grand Rapids, Mich.: Eerdmans.

10

Making *Wanga*: Reality Constructions and the Magical Manipulation of Power

Karen McCarthy Brown

In August 1997, Abner Louima, a thirty-two-year-old Haitian immigrant living in Brooklyn and working as a security guard, got in trouble with the New York City police. The encounter sparked what is now an infamous case of police brutality. Analyzing the media coverage of the incident and comparing it to the coverage of a more recent case of police violence in New York reveal an elaborate dance of secrecy and transparency, a contredanse, if you will, in which secrecy demands transparency and transparency provokes new forms of secrecy, in spite of itself and at times in the name of justice. So it goes. When raw power and the most fundamental kinds of racism are involved, as they are in the Louima case, both victims and perpetrators are at times compelled to hide the truth and to keep secrets while simultaneously making claims on some of the most rudimentary of institutions created to enhance transparency, the news media and the judicial courts.

The night Louima was arrested, Phantoms, his favorite band, was playing at the Club Rendez-Vous in Brooklyn. Around four o'clock in the morning the almost entirely Haitian crowd spilled out onto the street. As I later heard the story, two women started exchanging ritual insults about each other's clothing. Bystanders playfully urged them on; the shouting increased, and someone called the police. A Haitian friend who had been there assured me that, before the police arrived, no one in the crowd had crossed the line between play and violence. The police cars arrived with lights flashing and sirens screaming. Officers yelling and brandishing nightsticks pushed their way into the crowd. Before Abner Louima knew what was happening, he was facedown on the ground with his hands cuffed behind his back.

Then, according to witnesses, he was thrown roughly into the back of a police car. By Louima's account, the four policemen involved in the arrest stopped twice to beat him en route to the seventieth Precinct stationhouse; they used fists, clubs, and even a police radio. Once there, Officer Justin A. Volpe rammed the wooden handle of what appeared to be a toilet plunger into Abner Louima's rectum, yanked it out, and, rudely pushing it at his mouth, told him, "Now you are going to taste your own shit."[1] Louima was then placed in a holding cell, where he sat bleeding for a long time, perhaps hours, before being taken to a hospital. Louima's rectum was perforated and his bladder torn. His injuries required a two-month stay in the hospital and three surgeries, including an initial colostomy that later was reversed. He is now in better health than his doctors had predicted.

Eventually it was revealed that Officer Volpe had mistaken Louima for someone else in the crowd who had taken a punch at him. At the time of Volpe's trial, David Barstow reported in the New York Times, May 21, 1999, that when a nurse at the hospital where Louima was originally taken referred to him as the man who had beaten up a police officer, Louima replied, "Lady, do you think I'm stupid? I'm a black man. Do you think I would beat a police officer in New York City?" From the beginning, the press was suspicious of Louima's accounts of what happened to him. The jury in the initial trial also did not appear to trust him. It dismissed all charges related to the arrest and to the beatings administered on the way to the police station, events for which he was the only prosecution witness. At times, during the two trials that have so far been occasioned by this incident, Abner Louima was treated as if he were the one accused of a crime.

Mama Lola Reconfigures Louima's Reality

In 1997, shortly after he was released from the hospital, Abner Louima was introduced to Mama Lola, a respected Haitian Vodou priestess and healer living in Brooklyn. She is also my main teacher in the arts of Vodou and my friend. These days Louima occasionally visits Mama Lola at her home, and that is how I came to know him. When Mama Lola first mentioned him to me, she said simply, "He' a very quiet, respectable man. His family always in church." Then she mused on what happened to him: "Maybe they think he some bum in the street. Like he don't have no family . . . no one to help him." If that is what the police thought, they were mistaken because a significant proportion of the

Haitian immigrant community in New York City, along with many non-Haitians, stepped forward to protest what had been done to him.

In April 1999, I interviewed Lola about Louima's situation. It was a strange conversation. At the time, Lola was caught between powerfully conflicting desires. She wanted to discuss Louima with me because we were working on a book on healing, and she considered Louima one of her most interesting and important cases, yet the trial of his attackers was just about to begin, and she did not want to say anything that might compromise that process.

Mama Lola chose to deal with her ambivalence by telling me and my tape recorder substantially different stories. With the tape rolling, she spoke with all the caution of a public figure facing the press, yet at the same time, she signaled further, secret meanings to me. For example, she would occasionally pull down her right eyelid with a finger to signal that I should not take something she said too seriously; if I asked a sensitive question, she would silently draw her thumb and forefinger across her lips as if closing a zipper. Once she shut off the tape recorder and whispered to me even though no one was in the room except the two of us. I have repeated here only the taped version of the interview. For the purposes of this chapter, the contorted progress of the conversation and its modes of secrecy production are far more important than any of the particular topics discussed.

When I asked Mama Lola if she was "doing some work" for Louima, a tactful reference to Vodou healing practices, at first she evaded the question:

ML   Oh, we pray. We do prayer! I always pray for him a lot.

KB   Right.

ML   I . . . uh . . . do something . . . but I don't think he know if I do it or not. . . . I go downstairs to my altar, I pray to the spirits, and do some work with coconut. I use coconut water for clarity. I take the coconut water, and I put some good-luck powder. I take lots of *veven* leaves . . . High John the Conqueror root too. . . . I add olive oil and I make a lamp for him . . . for three days.

KB   So, the lamp has to burn for three days, huh?

ML   Yes. After three days, I put the coconut [shell, with ingredients] in the sea to sail it away. . . . I go to Coney Island to do that.

KB   Why did you have to take it to the sea?

ML   To wash all the bad in him, all the bad thing people talking about him. You know, to clear him . . . to clear him . . . in front of everybody.

KB   Don't you also take it to the sea because you can get closer to the spirits there?

ML   Yes, my ancestors, that's right. His ancestors too. . . . The pigeon was after that. I do it in my house . . . in the basement. I talk to the pigeon, and then I put Abner' name inside the pigeon's mouth, and I let it fly away.

KB   You talked to the pigeon first, like you told it what needs to happen?

ML   Exactly. Exactly. Then I sent it away.

KB   But when you're with Louima, you just pray?

ML   He don't ask me, don't pay me to do nothing. . . .

KB   He's afraid if somebody thought he was doing Vodou, it would hurt his case?

ML   Oh, that's the truth! They will think maybe he come to me to do something. . . .

KB   Something evil?

ML   Exactly, yup!

KB   Is his name on your altar now? [I knew she did that for her clients.]

ML   No, I don't put his name on the altar. I don't want nobody to come in to my altar to see his name there.

KB   But otherwise you would have put it there?

ML   Yes.

KB   Did you put anything else of his on the altar?

ML   His name. I put it um . . . um . . . behind the statue, but nobody don't see it.

KB   Lola, it's so sad. . . . You're helping him . . . and you have to be so secretive. . . .

ML   You know, people take everything in the wrong way. And they just blah, blah, blah, blah the mouth. So, in this world you have to be careful.

Mama Lola set out to change Louima's "luck" through the manufacture of two types of *wanga* (charms) drawn from her repertoire of ritual healing practices, one based on a coconut and the other a pigeon (see Brown 1995). Her intention was to bring about a situation in which Abner Louima and the things that motivated him would be more transparent to those who were judging him every day in the media and on the streets. For her to do this, it was necessary to keep some things secret.

Secrecy and Discretion in the Lives of Haitian Immigrants

If Louima did "serve the spirits," the most common expression for what outsiders call "practicing Vodou," he would have denied it if asked about it by journalists pursuing the police brutality case. Thanks to the advice of his community, practically every time Louima was in front of television cameras he was accompanied by a Protestant minister said to be his uncle. This was a politically astute move if not an absolutely honest one. For Haitians, conversion to Protestantism automatically entails a total rejection of the Vodou spirits. Thus, while the minister's presence communicated many things, chief among them was that Abner Louima is not into Vodou.

Furthermore, even if Louima were not the central character in a major news story, he probably would ask Lola to keep any spiritual work she did for him secret. Healing work almost always deals with personal problems, and so it follows that the most respected healers are those who know how to be discreet. For political, social, and religious reasons, secrecy is an important virtue in the lives of Haitians living in Haiti, a crowded country with scarce resources. In somewhat different ways, secrecy is important in the diaspora communities as well. In general, poor immigrants from Haiti dislike giving out information about themselves. Officially, there are around 250,000 Haitians living in New York City itself, a significant underestimation, since many Haitians living in the city are undocumented and resist being counted. Yet even those who have their papers try to avoid bureaucratic accountability. They routinely have the telephone bill in one name and the mortgage in another. They frequently give misleading information about age, family, and work history. This reflects a deep lack of trust in bureaucracy of any kind, but it also is influenced by everyday social relations. Since so much of what it can mean to be a Haitian (poverty, illiteracy, blackness, Vodou) provokes prejudicial treatment in New York City, immigrants keep their heads down and school their children in secretiveness as a survival strategy in urban America. This old pattern is currently shifting. What happened to Abner Louima and the community response it evoked have contributed to a new assertiveness among Haitians, a new willingness to take a public stand on issues that affect their lives.

The Haitian Community Acts against Police Brutality

Historically, Haitians in the United States have avoided political activity. This attitude began to change when Jean-Bertrand Aristide, a populist candidate for president of Haiti, won the election in 1990. Much of his campaign was financed by expatriates. Aristide's victory galvanized members of the diaspora community, increasing their pride and making them bolder participants in U.S. and Haitian politics. Even though the United States was complicit in the 1991 coup, afterward, Aristide set up his government in exile in Washington, D.C. Then the Haitian political presence in New York City took on a new character as angry crowds demonstrated on several occasions. The demonstration for Louima in 1997 was in this tradition, but it also marked a new stage in the growing involvement of Haitians in local politics. Many protest signs blamed Mayor Rudolph Giuliani for what happened to Abner Louima. When Louima was first interviewed by the police, he said Officer Volpe, while attacking him, bragged, "It's not Dinkins time anymore. This is Giuliani time now." (David Dinkins, an African American preceded Giuliani in the mayor's office.) Louima later retracted this testimony. A Haitian community leader had told him to say it so what happened to Louima would get the attention of the media and not be quickly forgotten as other cases of police brutality against Haitians have been.

The crowd that marched from Grand Army Plaza in Brooklyn to City Hall in Manhattan to protest the brutalization of Abner Louima at the hands of the New York Police Department (NYPD) made up one of the largest Haitian demonstrations ever held in New York City. There were many reasons for the size of this August 1997 event. Al Sharpton, a well-known African American minister and activist, stepped in to help organize the march for Louima, while at the same time a half dozen other Caribbean communities in New York chose to stand in solidarity with Haitians on the issue of police violence. Yet I doubt that either of these circumstances was as responsible for the protest's size and energy as the basic affront to human worth and dignity that the Louima case represented. Haitians were simply fed up. This time the New York City police had gone too far.

Mustering early at the Manhattan end of the Brooklyn Bridge, the police were out in force on the day of the demonstration, and they were nervous. Hours before the protest was scheduled to begin, more than 100 officers, men and women, gathered in lower Manhattan. A dozen police cars were parked in formation at the end of the bridge, a roadblock ready to be deployed if things got out of hand. Helmets, shields, and batons were in evidence everywhere. Metal gates cordoned off areas for the police along the edges of the demonstration route.

As soon as the crowd appeared over the crest of the Brooklyn Bridge, it was clear that the Haitian demonstrators and the NYPD had quite different scenarios in mind. This was not a crowd bent on violence. Colorfully dressed, carrying a wide variety of protest signs, accompanied by energetic dancers and drummers, singing songs and shouting slogans, the protesters articulated a virtual directory of strategies for handling fear and outrage. In order to contain the awful power of the Louima event and turn it toward something more constructive, the Haitian community was calling on every meaning-making system it had access to, traditional or newly acquired.

Some of the protest rhetoric focused on psychological explanations; "Justin A. Volpe is a sexual sadist," one sign declared. Others protesters turned to the authority of the Christian religion, terrain Haitian Americans share with most other Americans.[2] A huge placard, dense with earnest longhand script, argued for the connection of this terrible event to the Second Coming of the Messiah. In addition, rhetorics of justice and human rights were peppered throughout the signs carried by the protesters. Marking it a truly Haitian event were two people in costume, both possessed by Vodou spirits. One had Papa Gede, the spirit of sex, death, and humor, and another had the peasant farmer Azaka, a character valued for his plain speech and blunt truth telling. The first was dressed in black, and his face was covered in white powder. The second wore the embroidered blue denim outfit that in Vodou temples has become emblematic of Haitians from the countryside.

Many homemade placards castigated the current political climate in the city, a problem for which they laid the blame squarely at Mayor Giuliani's feet. Because of his "get tough on crime" policies, many people, not only Haitians, hold the mayor responsible for a general increase in racial discrimination in New York City and specifically for an increase in police harassment of blacks and Hispanics. The mayor was depicted on one sign with his head in a toilet bowl. Other signs showed Giuliani, not Louima, as the one whose pants got pulled down. This was not a crowd that was going to gloss over the details of the attack on Louima or turn away from its shaming aspects. At short intervals along the route of the march, a theater group reenacted the brutalization of Abner Louima, albeit in a somewhat abstract way.

Several Haitian marchers had drawn caricatures of the offending police officers on their placards; many other demonstrators carried toilet plungers, which they used in creative ways to comment on the frightening events in the Seventieth Precinct. A couple of men in the crowd fixed the rubber cup of the plunger to the top of their heads. Other Haitian men communicated more directly and attached it to their crotches. Three men carried a coffin with a toilet plunger handle emerging from its lid, positioned like the erection of a corpse, a further signal of the presence of the randy Vodou death spirit, Gede. Dozens of people in the crowd painted their plunger handles red, and sign after sign depicted toilet plungers with blood dripping from the stem.

Late in the afternoon, the crowd gathered near City Hall to listen to speeches about police violence. On the stage were the Reverend Al Sharpton and several leaders of the Haitian community, including the Reverend Philius H. Nicolas, Louima's putative uncle and pastor of the Evangelical Crusade Church in Flatbush, Brooklyn. When one of the speakers made an especially powerful point, a sea of toilet plungers bobbed enthusiastically over the heads of the crowd. A marcher told me it was impossible to buy a toilet plunger in Brooklyn that day. He reported that all the hardware stores were sold out before the march began. The *New York Times*, which otherwise covered the demonstration in detail, made no mention of toilet plungers.

I remember thinking at the time that there was something very *wanga*-like about the way the Haitian protesters used the toilet plungers. One of the most important things this demonstration accomplished was changing the emotional valence of an instrument of torture. Prior to the march, the toilet plunger was a sign of shame and pain, but on that hot August day, Haitian immigrants took what they feared most, brought it out into the light of public scrutiny, and turned it into an instrument of resistance. What initially appeared to be mere play with the plungers was actually what Vodou practitioners call "working the *wanga*." It is true that, as a rule, the making of Vodou charms is a private matter, yet in some circumstances, it is the public exposure of such a secret thing that gives it real clout. For example, I once heard a story of a shop owner in Port-au-Prince, Haiti, who was trying to ruin the business of a competitor by telling false stories about her. A trail of yellow powder across the doorway of the gossip not only served as a serious warning but also moved that person's offense into the realm of the larger community's responsibility.

Black Magic and the Making of *Wanga*

Issues of secrecy, especially the malevolent kind, are overdetermined in relation to anything that has to do with Haiti, a country and culture that, in the eyes of white America, is virtually synonymous with black magic. Haitians have absorbed the colonial language about magic. These days they refer to both "white magic" and "black magic" in their traditional African-based religion, Vodou.[3] In spite of this superficial rhetoric, Haitian Vodou actually tends to avoid the good-evil dichotomy. Vodou priests and priestesses make *wanga* to help clients with love, health, money, and, not infrequently, legal problems, and giving such help is often morally complex. Helping one person may mean limiting or controlling another. Those who specialize in the Vodou arts of healing are as likely as not to refer to all dimensions of these practices as *maji* (magic). Because this is such a deeply rooted part of the culture, it is understandable that the larger Haitian community turned to a kind of *maji* to deal with the trauma of the Louima incident.

Wanga, such as Mama Lola made for Abner Louima, are simultaneously representations of troubled relationships and the means for solving the problems they represent. The High John the Conqueror root in Lola's coconut *wanga*, for example, points both to the fact that Louima is under attack and to the resources he has to fight that battle. The coconut "water," a clear, sweet liquid, prefigures the power of the ancestors and spirits to improve the vision of those having trouble seeing Abner Louima clearly and to sweeten their attitudes toward him. Ideally, the person with the problem should "work the

wanga," that is, maintain a prescribed regimen of ritual practices such as praying and lighting candles before the *wanga,* but I have seen Lola take over this
responsibility for clients other than Louima when they could not conveniently
keep a *wanga* in their own home. This was the case, for example, with a *wanga*
Lola made for a woman whose husband was unfaithful. Lola made a soft,
pliable little doll, complete with male genitalia, out of an article of the husband's clothing and then, using heavy wire and a padlock, bound the doll into
a small wooden chair. For months it was Mama Lola who kept an oil lamp
burning next to the bound figure of the woman's husband. Here, also, the
wanga describes both the problem and the solution. Lola predicted that sooner
or later the wandering husband would "bow his head" before his wife just as
Santa Clara bowed her head in the image of the saint that, as a finishing touch,
Lola placed on the wall directly in front of the male doll. Bringing an imagined
change into reality is what working a *wanga* is all about. The making of *wanga*
and related diaspora practices are venerable, old traditions. I will never forget
the emotional impact of an eighteenth-century *wanga* I saw in the Port-au-
Prince ethnographic museum on one of my first trips to Haiti. It was composed
of an old pitted glass bottle and a short section of slave chains. *Wanga* can be
traced to ritual practices found throughout West and Central Africa. Among
other sources, Haitian Vodou *wanga* have roots in Dahomean *bocio* (Blier 1995)
and Kongo *minkisi* (MacGaffey 1993). Bocio and minkisi are wanga-like creations—charms used to heal, protect, or otherwise remedy undesirable social
situations.

In all cases the practices associated with *wanga* are used to manipulate
power by changing human relationships. When looked at in this way, it is clear
that the power of the *wanga* is largely discursive; it is the power to rewrite the
existential narrative at issue. The *wanga* Mama Lola made for Abner Louima
are not, therefore, all that different from newspaper accounts of Louima's experience with the police, or from arguments made by defense and prosecuting
attorneys in the courtrooms where the crimes committed against Louima were
adjudicated. All, including Mama Lola's *wanga,* are competing narratives empowered by their various abilities to convince key audiences (including spiritual
ones) of their points of view and therefore shift problematic situations. This
process is complex because each new narrative is unavoidably launched into a
sea of old ideologies, automatic associations, and rigid interpretations. Some
people have to work against this situation; others profit from it. While some
masters of narrative must anticipate and guard against possible points of deliberate misunderstanding, *meconnaissance* (perhaps by keeping certain things
secret), others work at making a narrative say things indirectly, things that
otherwise would be unspeakable in this particular place and time. The discussion now turns to what I will call "word *wanga,*" and thus to the many ways in
which the person and the experience of Abner Louima were reconfigured in
the press and in the courtroom. Following the path of the African *wanga* has

led to the magical practices of largely white, bureaucratic institutions in the United States.

The Media Construct Abner Louima and Amadou Diallo

On February 4, 1999, eighteen months after Louima's encounter with the officers of the Seventieth Precinct, Amadou Diallo, a West African immigrant who worked as a sidewalk merchant in New York City, was fired upon forty-one times at close range, late at night, while standing in the entryway to his Bronx apartment. He was unarmed. All shots came from four NYPD officers, members of an elite anticrime unit that traveled in plain clothes. According to a *New York Times* editorial of February 12, 1999, the macho slogan of this unit is "We Own the Night." Nineteen bullets entered the body of Diallo, who died shortly thereafter.

Approximately two months after Amadou Diallo's death, in a guest editorial in the *New York Times*, April 19, 1999, titled "For Most Brutality Isn't the Issue," New York City police commissioner Howard Safir called the shooting of Diallo "a tragedy" that "only the judicial system can produce answers for." He added that, even though he did hear complaints about the police, "the complaints . . . are not of officers being brutal, but of officers being brusque." He concluded with the announcement of a police "civility campaign." "We are giving officers tips on how to be more polite," Safir wrote. He made no mention of Abner Louima. Nevertheless, the two cases were immediately linked by the media and by the general public.

The Louima and Diallo cases both involved police violence against recent immigrants to the United States; both victims were black. Given these similarities, it was initially puzzling that the two cases received significantly different treatment from the public and the media. The Diallo case was in the news continuously beginning the day he was killed. There were dozens of events protesting the shooting of Diallo: a memorial, demonstrations before and after the memorial, vigils, religious services, and concerts. These events attracted people from across New York's social, racial, and ethnic spectrum. There were several demonstrations for Abner Louima, one of them sizable, yet Haitian immigrants made up the great majority at all events. Also, in contrast with Diallo, Abner Louima disappeared from the newspapers and the evening television news rather quickly. His case actually got more coverage later, during the second trial, for obstruction of justice. By then, the offense against Louima had become so involved with other incidents of police violence, including Diallo's death, that jury verdicts often seemed to be responding more to the larger context of police brutality in New York City than to the specific events the jury members were asked to judge.

A U.S. film crew followed Diallo's mother at the height of her grief back to Africa, to Guinea, where she took her son's body for a traditional funeral and burial. Long segments of this footage were broadcast on the evening news on several U.S. channels. Since her first visit, occasioned by her son's death, Kadiatou Diallo has become something of a public figure in the United States, speaking out repeatedly against police violence and for gun control. An "interfaith prayer and community healing" service was held for Diallo, a Muslim, at the Brooklyn Academy of Music. At the service, according to David M. Haiszenhorn, in a *New York Times* article of March 15, 1999, titled "Mayor Expresses Regret over Police Shooting of Immigrant," Mayor Giuliani referred to Diallo's death as the "loss of an innocent person." He also called the event "a terrible rending tragedy." I do not recall anyone in the media characterizing Louima as an "innocent" person. However, a *New York Times* story on the Web, June 8, 1999, reported that one of the attorneys defending the police officers did refer to him as "a 'professional victim' looking for big money damages from the city." Furthermore, the newspapers I read never mentioned the names of Louima's parents, his children, or the place where he was born in Haiti. On the contrary, parts of Louima's identity—his Haitianness in general and especially his religion—had to be muted and handled with discretion. In spite of the fact that the great majority of people in Haiti serve the Vodou spirits in one way or another, any possible Vodou connection to Abner Louima had to be thoroughly hidden so that, in a context of prejudice, he could remain a credible witness against his attackers.

Mayor Giuliani and Commissioner Safir honored Diallo by going to his memorial service at the impressive Islamic Cultural Center of New York on East Ninety-sixth street in Manhattan. That event and the one at the Brooklyn Academy of Music became occasions on which multicultural and religiously pluralistic New York City was put on display, but Abner Louima's case represented nothing about the city that the larger public wanted to honor.

The cases of Abner Louima and Amadou Diallo differed in other ways. Diallo came from Africa, and in death he conveniently went back there, sounding an end note for the whole affair. Louima survived the sadistic sexual attack against him and thus must continue to be dealt with, like all the other impoverished people from his country who will not stop knocking at the back door of the United States. Furthermore, Louima has a personal damage suit pending against the NYPD.

Deeper and more trenchant reasons for the different media treatment of Louima and Diallo have to do with the hypersexualized black body. Viewing blacks in this way is a historically deep habit of mind for Euro-Americans. Reason might never have been crowned in the aftermath of the French Revolution if Africans, and a few others, had not long been designated to carry the burden of sexuality, with its inherent irrationality and potential for untidiness and loss of control. Partly because Louima was already in place to carry the burden, Diallo escape being branded in this way. His sexuality simply got erased by the media. It was never an issue. Diallo's body-under-attack was configured as a clean, fully clothed body. Visually it was at times represented by an anonymous two-dimensional outline of a human body crosshatched by nineteen bullet trajectories. The more common visual icon of the violence unleashed against Diallo, however, was a photograph of the empty, bullet-pocked entryway to his Bronx building. Diallo, doubly contained (both safely buried and on the other side of the ocean), is gone from this picture, and thus he could be reconfigured as deemed necessary by the media. Thus, Diallo approached the type of pure victim that motivates politics on both the Left and the Right in America.

Partly because of the comparison with the murdered Diallo, Louima, who is alive, has not been allowed to be an innocent victim. What is more, his body-under-attack was highly problematic; it had trousers pulled down around the ankles. The media's visual icon of the violence against Louima, like Diallo's vestibule, was empty of a human presence. In this case, however, the iconic photograph did not show a neutral, public space but an empty precinct bathroom. This scene-of-the-crime photo, printed in newspapers and shown on television several times during the early coverage of the attack on Louima, functioned as a highly suggestive erasure, daring the reader to imagine what happened there. The hypersexual, penetrable, and penetrating, black (read colonized) body, made excitingly vulnerable and accessible through extremes of social power and physical control, is positioned at the center of Abner Louima's story of torture, as it was at the center of slavery.

In another, related dimension of media word magic, homosexuality can be detected as a partially submerged theme in the narrative of Louima's torture. A *Washington Post* article of May 28, 1999, repeatedly refers to Louima having been "sodomized," a word whose common usage neatly erases the violence from the incident and accentuates the fact that it occurred between two men. During the two years following Louima's torture by the police, the verb "to sodomize" appeared in several articles such as the one just cited, yet more recently members of the press (including more than one writing for New York's *Haitian Times*)[4] have almost unanimously fallen into this extended, half-conscious fantasy that Abner Louima is gay. "To sodomize" is now, across the board, the verb of choice in the frequent articles on police brutality that mention Louima's case. In such word *wanga*, some degree of unconsciousness (a form of keeping secrets from oneself) on the part of the writer is essential. Were the language more transparent to its meaning, its foolishness and lack of integrity would also be more apparent.

A more straightforward charge of homosexuality was at issue in the first trial of Abner Louima's attackers. In his opening statements, Marvyn Kornberg, Justin Volpe's attorney, suggested that Louima might have sustained his injuries prior to arrest, from consensual gay sex in the bathroom of the Club Rendez-Vous. In the weeks of testimony, this stunningly irrational argument did not made it back into the courtroom. Nevertheless, the damage had been done. Kornberg's underlying point, coyly signaled to the jury, was that if Louima had sex with men, then what happened to him, grotesque as it was, was in some way his own fault. Robert Volpe, Justin Volpe's father, spun his own tale about how Louima shared the blame with his son.[5]

Abner Louima's moral stature was attacked in other ways as well. For example, he was called a liar because of discrepancies between his description of the attack when he was first interviewed in the hospital and his current version of it. According to Joseph P. Fried, in a May 17, 1999, *New York Times* article on the Web, one issue was his comment about it being "Giuliani time"; another concerned his body posture at the time of the attack. Was he crouched down and bending over, as he now claims, or was he pinned down on the floor, as he said when first questioned? It is not difficult to see how Louima might have initially hedged his story, feeling his manhood at stake in these postural differences. Either way, such goings-on do not produce good victims. Sexual tension lies just below the surface in practically everything written about Louima's story, and it is fed by secrecy, silence, and erasure. The biggest erasure was what I kept expecting to see in print, but never did: "Justin Volpe raped Abner Louima."

Reconfigurations from the Judge's Bench and Jury Box

The trial of May and June 1999 led to acquittals for all officers involved on charges related to the immediate circumstances of Abner Louima's arrest and to the beatings he received on the way to the police station. This is significant because these are the dimensions of the crime against Louima that connect with patterns of police violence widely experienced in the Haitian (and other) immigrant communities. The Louima case, like Diallo's, involved racial profiling (suspecting people of color for no reason other than their color) and street justice (precipitous and unjustified use of force by police on the streets). When these dimensions of the Louima case are taken away, the whole affair shrinks to a weird event that happened in a precinct bathroom, a onetime thing to be dealt with and quickly forgotten. In the first trial Justin Volpe, who did the deed, got thirty years; Charles Schwarz, who assisted, received the same sentence. Even though neither Volpe nor Schwarz pleaded insanity, as a result of the way the jury sorted out the evidence and decided whose claims were credible and whose were not, these two men were transformed from rogue cops who were part of a larger pattern of behavior in the police force to idiosyncratic sick individuals. Due to the individualism on which the U.S. justice system is founded, making sense of institutionalized violence is not something it does well.

In February 2000, Amadou Diallo's attackers were on trial for murder. By this time, the case had become *the* police brutality case, the lightning rod for a city's fear and suspicion of its police force. Around the same time, three of the four former police officers who attacked Louima went on trial again, this time for conspiracy to impede a police investigation. In Diallo's trial, it was also the way the event was reconfigured—what evidence was admissible, what was not, and how the defense and prosecution shaped their cases—that determined the outcome. During the trial the defense repeatedly discredited witnesses who were not present for the entire event because they did not have the context to interpret what they saw and heard. There were, however, no witnesses who were present the whole time except the officers themselves. The case against the men who shot Amadou Diallo thus came to rest entirely on the state of mind of the four defendants. It all came down to whether the officers believed Diallo had a gun and continued to believe he had a gun and was dangerous for the entire time it took them to fire forty-one bullets. It was no surprise that all four testified in the affirmative on that point, and no surprise that all were acquitted. After the verdict, groups of young men stood a silent and angry vigil in Diallo's Bronx neighborhood, holding up their black wallets. It was a black wallet Diallo had in his hand, not a gun.

A leaflet, written in Haitian Creole and circulated in Brooklyn shortly after the Diallo verdicts, announced a protest demonstration and encouraged people to come: "Pote tanbou! Pote plonje twalet!" (Bring drums! Bring toilet plungers!). The tie between the Louima and Diallo cases lived on among the people. I am convinced that it was the offense caused by the acquittals in the Diallo case that ricocheted into the second Louima trial courtroom, producing unexpected guilty verdicts there. Three officers involved in the Louima arrest, Charles Schwarz, Thomas Bruder, and Thomas Wiese, were indicted on charges of conspiracy to obstruct justice. Volpe confessed and plea-bargained halfway through the first trial, so he was out of the picture by the time of the second trial, even though he was worse than any of the other officers when it came to impeding the internal police investigation. For example, he never provided the name of the other man who was in the bathroom with him when he assaulted Louima. In the second round of verdicts, Schwarz got another fifteen years and eight months, and Bruder and Wiese each ended up with a sentence of five years in jail. Again, police officers received what were probably well-deserved sentences, but at the same time, a larger, structural source of police brutality, in this case the undercover police units who claim to "own the night," sidestepped accountability. As the Haitian proverb says, "Konplo pi fo passe wanga" (conspiracies are stronger than magic).

Racism in the Shadow of the Fetish

It seems that whenever Haitians are in the news, a reference to Vodou cannot be far behind. In a June 20, 2000, *Village Voice* article titled "Police Brutality and Voodoo Justice," Peter Noel, a black journalist whose byline appears frequently in the that publication, wrote that "the father of Justin Volpe, the white cop who was accused of sodomizing Louima . . . told friends he was warned by Haitian spiritual healers that Louima is a wicked voodoo high priest bent on deadly revenge." In the same article, Noel also reported that a cop improbably named Ridgway de Szigethy, who spends his time investigating occult organizations, told Noel that to protect his son during the first trial Robert Volpe carried "a little purple crystal . . . and a little vial of holy water." By virtually equating crystals and holy water with Vodou *wanga*, Noel exhibits a democratic disdain for all religions, but as a result he misses the depth and significance of the racism in Robert Volpe's attempt to condemn Abner Louima through references to the African-based religion of his homeland. This is an old ploy and one with a long, continuous history. This maneuver is in fact a cornerstone in the historic and current structure of European and American racism. A look at the history of the term "fetish," a word that is in most cases interchangeable with *wanga*, will give a glimpse into the depth and complexity of the racist tropes peppered throughout the coverage of Louima's encounter with the officers of New York's Seventieth Precinct.

More than 400 years ago, Europeans chose the term "fetish" to stand for powerful material objects used in traditional African religious settings. Chief among these objects were charms related to what would later become Vodou *wanga*. Not long after, the term "fetishism" or "fetish religion" began to be routinely applied to all aspects of all indigenous African religions. To this day the Vodun (Fon spirits or deities found in the Republic of Benin, formerly Dahomey) are called *fetiches* and their priests, *feticheurs*, another instance of a colonized people swallowing colonial rhetoric. Diviners throughout Benin are called *charlatans*, yet another remnant of the French presence in the former Dahomey.

According to William Pietz, who has written an important series of articles on the history of the concept of fetishism, "The fetish, as an idea and a problem, and as a novel object not proper to any prior discrete society, originated in the cross-cultural spaces of the coast of West Africa during the sixteenth and seventeenth centuries" (1985:5). Fetish theory, Pietz says "was fully established in European intellectual discourse by 1800" (1987: 25). The term subsequently became an unusually influential one in a wide range of intellectual, political, and economic interactions between Europe and Africa. For a remarkably long time, fetish theory has provided the most pervasive and broadly influential rationale for racism, colonialism, and general Western cultural chauvinism.

Newton and Locke, figures of the seventeenth and early eighteenth centuries, both had in their libraries copies of the book that introduced "fetish religion" to the European world, Wilem's Bosman's 1702 publication, *A New and Accurate Account of the Coast of Guinea* (Pietz 1988). According to the theory of fetishism, "consecrated at the end of the eighteenth century by no less than G.W.F. Hegel in *The Philosophy of History*, Africans were incapable of abstract and generalizing thought; instead their ideas and actions were governed by impulse," and as a consequence, it was commonly assumed that "anything upon which an African's eye happened to fall might be taken up by him and made into a 'fetish,' absurdly endowed with imaginary powers" (MacGaffey 1993: 32). In the nineteenth century, the concept of fetishism became theoretically indispensable to three of the founders of social science: Comte, Marx, and Freud. It is my purpose here to demonstrate that this intellectual arrangement has, from the beginning, been devastating for black people, and that at the beginning of the twenty-first century, the fetish trope still covertly and overtly shapes the images Euro-Americans hold of Africans and African Americans in cosmopolitan New York City.

A "theoretically suggestive" term (Pietz 1985), the word "fetish" provided the rubric under which all of Africa came to play the Other to Enlightenment rationalism. Most important was the role the European idea of the fetish played in crystallizing the notion that so-called primitive thinking was characterized by a false theory of causality, a mistaken belief that material objects could be manipulated in such a way as to change the conditions of a person's life (Pietz 1988). When the presumed immorality of the *feticheur* was added to this mix, the fetish became the perfect foil for making the (illogical) connection so crucial to the Enlightenment, the connection between reason and righteousness. When seen from this perspective, it appears the humble, antiaesthetic fetish was nothing less than a midwife to the Enlightenment.

Two things are thus important to remember from this short history of the fetish/*wanga*: first, the act of almost unbelievable meconnaissance that led Europeans to characterize all African religions, each one different from the other and each a rich moral universe, as nothing but instrumental magic carried out by bumbling sacerdotes paradoxically characterized as both childlike and evil; second the equally inappropriate characterization of African religion as bad science, that is, as primitive thinking or mistaken reasoning.

The European indictment of the African fetish was not merely a matter of slander. The configuration of African religion as fetishism had very tangible political and religious effects. This was the story in Haiti, for example, from the beginning of the eighteenth century until long after the end of European domination. In the early eighteenth century, Haitian slaves found making the benign protective charms called *gad-ko*, (bodyguards), which usually consist of herbal mixtures put under the skin or small cloth bags pinned inside clothing, were tortured brutally as sorcerers who gained power by deception." Even after the Haitian slave revolution (1791–1804), what Anna Wexler (forthcoming) calls "the long shadow of the fetish" did not lift. President Jean-Pierre Boyer Of Haiti, 100 in his 1835 Penal Code, outlined punishments for all religious practitioners who "nourish in the hearts of people the spirit of fetishism," that is to say, all "makers of wangas, caprelatas, vaudoux, donpedre, macandale and other sorceries" (Metraux 1972: 270). In 1935, President Sténio Vincent "single[d] out for persecution priests and others who make and possess *wanga* and exploit the public by making them believe that it is possible to change life situations by 'occult' methods" (Hurbon 1988).

It is sobering to realize how important maneuvers such as the misrecognition of African religion and its equation with bad science are to the representation of the African-based religion practiced in Haiti and by Haitians in diaspora today. A small example: the *New York Times* currently refuses to spell "voodoo" with a capital *V* (spelling it "Vodou," as Haitians prefer, is out of the question) even though it capitalizes the names of other religions, including other African-based Caribbean religions.⁶ This commitment to a deeply compromised form of the term keeps it handy for use in put-down phrases such as "voodoo economics."⁷

A more complex and weighty example is to be found in the language of Stephen Worth, a lawyer from the Patrolmen's Benevolent Association (PBA). On the same day jury selection was completed for the Louima case, May 3, 1999, the official coroner's report on Diallo was finally released—three long months after the shooting. An earlier autopsy, requested by lawyers engaged by the Diallo family, concluded that the police continued to shoot after Amadou Diallo was already down and immobilized. The coroner's report confused this issue by initially making no judgments about which shots came first or how fast they were fired.⁸ Kevin Flynn, in an article in the *New York Times*, May 4, 1999, reported that Stephen Worth, attorney for one of the men charged with second-degree murder in the death of Amadou Diallo and at the same time attorney for one of the officers accused of beating Louima, celebrated the second coroner's report, crowing that it "puts the lie to the Dream Team's voodoo autopsy and shows it for the pseudoscience that it is." Thus Worth called on one of the oldest and most enduring "voodoo" tropes, its equation with bad science, and in so doing managed simultaneously to compromise the authority of scientific evidence in the Diallo case and, in his other case, to cast doubt on the credibility and morality of both the lawyers and the main witness, Abner Louima. Worth sent a potent racist message that demeaned the lawyers working for Louima and the Diallo family (initially Johnnie L. Cochran's infamous Dream Team served as counsel for both) by making an invisible reference to the O. J. Simpson murder case while simultaneously linking the lawyers to a religion whose name is synonymous with "black magic" and as a result with Haiti, Abner Louima's country.

Conclusion

Our language and the habits of our bodies and minds carry our history. Such habits as race prejudice, sexual fundamentalism, and even habitual disdain for all things Haitian are prominent in the U.S. *habitus* (Bourdieu 1977, 1990). The latter prejudice is pervasive among Euro-Americans9 and has endured since blacks and mulattoes in Haiti had the temerity to win their freedom and dignity by fighting for them, and had the further rudeness to do so during a period when the United States and many European countries were still holding slaves. Such habits of heart and mind exercise a downward pull on transparent civic values such as those represented by a free press, trial by jury, and police accountability. In the events surrounding Abner Louima, the strategies of transparency set in place actually spawned elaborate strategies of secrecy, and vice versa.

In theory, secrecy and transparency are opposing power dynamics, yet in the Abner Louima case, they appear to have worked together, evoking one another in a paradoxical dance of increasing complexity. Major players in this drama, convinced of the importance of their ultimate goals (or at least equipped with those goals as rationalizing devices), competed for the control of institutions of transparency, such as the press, the judicial system, and police review processes. In the name of keeping peace, Commissioner Howard Safir painted a ridiculously mild, even insulting, picture of the problems between police and civilians in New York City. Police Benevolent Association lawyers Kornberg and Worth, in the name of providing their clients with the best defense possible, began to mount that defense in the press through innuendo, secrecy, and erasure. The news media, in the name of covering the news, repeated what Kornberg and Worth said and eventually laid the Louima case to rest in order to focus on Arnadou Diallo's death. In the name of revealing all the dirty secrets, Peter Noel reported that Robert Volpe carries a bottle of holy water and uses it to make crosses on his own forehead to protect against Louima's Vodou powers.

The way that race interacted with these complex impulses was especially visible in the repeated connection of the Louima and Diallo cases, a linkage that remained in the minds of Haitians and other immigrants even as the second eclipsed the first in the news. The dense, racially charged images that public personalities and journalists called up so effortlessly in commentary on the cases are representations constructed "in the shadow of the fetish." Like the charms Mama Lola made to help Louima, they are *wanga*.

Like *wanga*, these representations of Louima—spoken out but also present in the silences within the words of police, lawyers, and journalists—characterized complex relational situations with the intention of influencing them. The police commissioner, the press, and lawyers involved in the Louima case deployed their own word *wanga*. The Haitian community, in turn, responded to the affront to Louima, and to decades of mistreatment at the hands of New York City officials, by putting their universe of explanations on display, including their much maligned religion, Vodou. More to the point, they put their fear-charged, blood-soaked toilet plunger *wanga*, an externalization of their most intimate and most horrific relational nightmares, on public display. They literally thrust their plungers in the face of the NYPD. This process of exposing *wanga* power in public worked to some extent, like sprinkling yellow powder across the threshold of a troublemaker. It brought Abner Louima's experience to public attention. It threw down the gauntlet in a challenge to the city government to do something about police brutality, while simultaneously tempering the fear of the Haitian community and increasing its political capital. It also contributed to a lengthy legal process that finally got jail sentences for the four men directly involved in the arrest and brutalization of Abner Louima.

In the year 2000, a focus on *wanga* and *wanga*-like constructions does a surprisingly good job of revealing the everyday workings of power on all levels of society in New York, an ethnically diverse city with a heritage of racism. One of the most interesting aspects of this comparison is the similarity between the workings of Mama Lola's *wanga* and workings of what I have called the word *wanga* of politicians, journalists, and lawyers. All are narrative reconfigurations, and all are constructed to control those key narratives. It is ironic that the homely African *wanga*, the very objects used by Europeans at the dawn of the Enlightenment to draw absolute boundaries between themselves and primitive others, should reveal themselves as close cousins of Euro-American "charms" and other "magical" maneuvers.

To some extent, the Haitian community won the battle only to lose the war. The police conspiracy of silence and especially Volpe's withholding of crucial testimony, the evidentiary rulings of the courts, the unconscious racism and homophobia of the press, the ancient racist tropes buried deeply in the speech of just about everybody who got near the case proved more powerful than what either Mama Lola or the Dream Team could do to bring justice not only to Abner Louima but also to the larger Haitian community that experiences continuous police harassment. Institutionalized patterns of abuse, including what could be called racial profiling and street justice, were identified in the 1994 Mollen Commission report on corruption in the NYPD, but nothing was done to address these problems at that time, and nothing has yet been done to address them. While convictions in the Diarlo case would at least have raised these issues of institutionalized racism, the convictions of the four men who brutalized Louima were never seen as relevant to such concerns.

Brian Stevens, writing for *Haitian Times* (July 19–25, 2000), acknowledged that Volpe and his new lawyer had already been to court seeking to cut Volpe's sentence in half. So far such efforts have not succeeded. Abner Louima turned down more than one offer to settle his civil suit because it involved no promises for reforms in New York police practices. In the summer of 2001, Louima finally accepted an offer for $7.125 million from the city and $1.625 million from the PBA. Although the PBA payment involved no admission of guilt, it was the first time a police union anywhere in the country had been forced to pay in a police violence incident. Yet Louima still got no official promises for police reform. He had to settle for informal promises that had more to do with public relations than with a commitment to change oppressive police practices.

On February 28, 2002, a federal appeals court threw out the obstruction of justice convictions for Schwarz, Bruder, and Wiese because of a technicality. In addition, Schwarz's conviction for aiding Volpe in the attack on Louima was set aside because of another technicality, a conflict of interest on the part of his attorney, Stephen Worth. From the moment Schwarz was freed on $1 million bail, the district attorney made it clear he would be indicted and tried again on these charges.

During the 1999 trials of the cases concerning Louima and Diallo, a large percentage of New Yorkers was deeply concerned about police violence. It was a high-priority issue, but the atmosphere had changed drastically by the time Schwarz's convictions were set aside. Jeffrey Toobin, writing for the *New Yorker* (June 10, 2002, 34–39), described the *Times* coverage of Schwarz's return to the Staten Island home of his mother as "a dewy portrait." He also noted that the three leading New York tabloids—*New York News, Newsday,* and *New York Post*—were also Schwarz boosters. "Free," trumpeted *New York News,* while *Newsday* and *New York Post* cried out, "He's Home" and "He's Out." The events of September 11, 2001, caused this dramatic change. Because of 9/11, every policeman, including former officer Charles Schwarz, automatically became a hero, a person larger than life, someone no true patriot would even consider criticizing. In July 2002, Schwarz's third trial ended in a single perjury conviction with a possible five-year sentence, while the jury was unable to reach verdicts on any of the charges that concerned Schwarz's participation in torturing Louima. There may well be another trial, whether or not justice is served by it.

After the attack on the World Trade Center, the United States plunged with astonishing speed into a period of feverish patriotism. The words "At War" appeared in the *New York Times* headline of September 12, 2001. What transparency there had been in the U.S. media and the criminal court system is rapidly being crowded out by yet another word *wanga,* the War on Terror. On a daily basis, irrational acts of war are being simultaneously revealed and concealed, justified and obscured in the U.S. media and, at times, in its courts of law.

NOTES

1. It was later revealed that the instrument Volpe used to torture Abner Louima was actually the broken-off handle of a broomstick. The toilet plunger, nevertheless, continued to be mentioned in newspapers, and its image became the icon of the protest movement that developed out of this case of police brutality.

2. Most of those who serve the Vodou spirits also consider themselves to be good Catholics.

3. The most basic difference between white and black magic, as the terms are used in Haitian Vodou, is that the first is practiced for the good of the family or a larger community, whereas the second is about the pursuit of selfish and/or individualistic goals.

4. The *Haitian Times,* an English-language newspaper started by former *New York Times* reporter Gary-Pierre Pierre, routinely refers to the "sodomizing" of Abner Louima.

5. David Barstow, in *New York Times* Web article of June 2, 1999, reported that Robert Volpe claimed his son's trial was a "modern day lynching." Barstow quoted the senior Volpe as saying, "This was not an unprovoked situation There was no innocence on the street that night." Barstow continued: "He said his son took Louima to the bathroom that night because he wanted to hit him, to continue the fight. After assaulting him with the stick, Officer Volpe, his father said, yelled, 'Look what you made me do' at Louima."

6. The oddness of this practice was apparent in a January 10, 2000, *New York Times* article, "Catholics Battle Brazilian Faith in 'Black Rome,' " in which the following sentence appeared: "Like Santeria in the Spanish-speaking Caribbean or voodoo in Haiti, Candomble merges the identities of African deities and Roman Catholic saints." An example of the usefulness of the generic "voodoo" comes from the June 15, 2000, edition of the *New York Review of Books,* which carried a full back-page ad for Robert Park's book, *Voodoo Science: The Road from Foolishness and Fraud,* published by Oxford University Press. A blurb from Richard Dawkins promises that "Park does more than debunk, he crucifies. And the result is huge fun . . . Not only will you enjoy reading it. You'll never again waste time or your money on astrologers, 'quantum healers,' homeopaths, spoon benders, perpetual motion merchants or alien abduction fantasists."

7. The low-budget film *Voodoo* released in the 1990s is a textbook example of the first part of the operation by which Europeans positioned Africans in relation to themselves, the one whereby all Africa-related religion becomes fetishism. Oddly enough, there are no black characters in this film, and an atmosphere of fear and dread is created entirely with drumming and quick glimpses of dolls, lighted candles, bits of raffia, and knotted pieces of rope—all the materials of wanga making. That is the only way in which anything connected to Vodou appears in the film that bears its name.

8. A fuller report from the Coroner's Office issued at a later date agreed with the first autopsy report that Diallo was fired on after he had been knocked down by police bullets.

9. According to Roosevelt Joseph, writing for the *Haitian Times* (22–28 March 2000), Dorismond, a twenty-six-year-old security guard, was shot to death by a mem-

ber of NYPD's Gang Investigation Division. Dorismond, the son of a popular Haitian musician, had just left a midtown cocktail lounge when he was approached by an undercover policeman participating in a marijuana sweep. It was a "buy-and-bust" operation. The plainclothes officer asked Dorismond if he had drugs to sell. Dorismond said no, but the assumptions behind the approach angered him. There was a struggle, and the undercover agent's gun went off. Patrick Dorismond died from a single shot. He had no gun. Neither Police Commissioner Safir nor Mayor Giuliani went to his funeral. Quite the contrary, they went on the attack instead. Giuliani commented that Dorismond was "no altar boy" and instructed Safir to release his criminal record. Dorismond had two juvenile indictments for disorderly conduct. He did not go to jail for either. Both were resolved through plea-bargaining.

REFERENCES

Blier, Suzanne Preston. 1995. *African Vodun: Art, Psychology and Power*. Chicago: University of Chicago Press.

Bourdieu, Pierre. 1977. *Outline of a Theory of Practice*. New York: Cambridge University Press.

———. 1990. *The Theory of Practice*. Stanford, Calif.: Stanford University Press.

Brown, Karen McCarthy. 1987. The Power to Heal: Reflections on Women, Religion, and Medicine. In *Shaping New Vision: Gender and Values in American Culture*, ed. Clarissa Atkinson, Constance Buchanan, and Margaret Miles, 123–42. Ann Arbor, Mich.: UMI Research Press.

———. 1991. *Mama Lola: A Vodou Priestess in Brooklyn*. Berkeley and Los Angeles: University of California Press.

———. 1995. Serving the Spirits: The Ritual Economy of Haitian Vodou. In *Sacred Arts of Haitian Vodou*, ed. Donald J. Cosentino, 205–23. Los Angeles: UCLA Fowler Museum of Cultural History.

———. 1998. The Moral Force Field of Haitian Vodou. In *In Face of the Facts: Moral Inquiry in American Scholarship*, ed. Richard Wightman Fox and Robert B. Westbrook. New York: Woodrow Wilson Center Press and Cambridge University Press.

Hurbon, Laënnec. 1988. *Le Barbare Imaginaire*. Revised edition. Port-au-Prince, Haiti: Henri DeschampsMacGaffey, Wyatt. 1993. The Eyes of Understanding: Kongo Minkisi. In *Astonishment and Power*. Washington, D.C.: National Museum of African Art, Smithsonian Institution Press.

Metraux, Alfred. 1972. *Voodoo in Haiti*. New York: Schocken Books.

Moreau de Saint-Mery, M.E.L. 1797. *Description topographique, physique, civil, politique, et historique de la partie francais de I 'isle de Saint-Domingue*. 3 vols. Philadelphia.

Pietz, William. 1985. The Problem of the Fetish I. *Res: Anthropology and Aesthetics* 9:5–17.

———. 1987. The Problem of the Fetish II: The Origin of the Fetish. *Res: Anthropology and Aesthetics* 13:23–45.

———. 1988. The Problem of the Fetish IIIa: Bosman's Guinea and the Enlightenment Theory of Fetishism. *Res: Anthropology and Aesthetics* 16:105–23.

Wexler, Anna. 2001. Fictional Oungan: In the Long Shadow of the Fetish. *Research in African Literature* 32(1): 83–97.

II

"Our Work Is Change for the Sake of Justice": Hope Community, Minneapolis, Minnesota

Mary Farrell Bednarowski

Several years ago I was working at articulating a definition of healing that had both sufficient content and enough versatility to fit the multiple interpretations of healing I was encountering in many women's theological writings. It was St. Joseph's Hope Community in Minneapolis, an enterprise that began as a homeless women's shelter, that helped generate the definition I eventually came up with: that, individually and communally, to be healed is to have hope. To offer healing is to offer hope. And hope is that state wherein we know that some kind of response or change or reconciliation or transformation is possible. Whatever the trauma of the present moment or of our circumstances and our histories, there is something more to be said or to be understood, to be experienced or to be accomplished.

I have been aware of the Hope Community for many years, almost since its beginnings, and have had some modest connections with it. It was not until I received an opportunity to participate in the Center for the Study of World Religion's conference on healing in the urban setting that I began to think about Hope as a compelling example of some of the new forms that healing is taking in cities—healing, particularly, of neighborhoods whose earlier capacity to sustain a good, if not affluent, life for its residents has declined to a state that is not only lacking in basic necessities but dangerous. My particular interest in Hope emerges from my work in the theological creativity of American women—creativity that takes shape not only in words but also in new visions and actions for social transformation (1999, esp. chap. 6). I am particularly interested in how "healing" is becoming a major category of interpretation for women of many different traditions and how it is likely to be defined as an everyday part of life, not a onetime, dramatic occurrence. It is understood, further, as a reciprocal, relational process that does not make distinctions between those offering and those experiencing healing. They are in it together.

A close look at Hope motivates not only the construction of some new understandings of healing but a better knowledge of the cultural realities within which it dwells and to which it responds. This is a landscape that is urban, religiously and racially diverse, and mostly poor. It is also filled with energy and possibility for new creative configurations among people in American urban society who might otherwise never have encountered each other. Hope's ongoing efforts at self-understanding and of action based on its best wisdom about its circumstances likewise offer insights into the kinds of reciprocal illumination that religion and culture offer each other.

Material for this chapter comes from two major sources: conversations with Hope staff members and the community newsletter, which has had several different incarnations over its twenty-five-year history. Conversations with staff members both preceded and followed my presentation of this material during the conference in September 2001. My revisions for purposes of publication reflect some of their responses, particularly their concern that I did not pick up adequately on the extent to which Hope works to offer its members a sense of power over their own lives and the skills to take that power to the public arena. It is a goal, staff members say, that is complicated and that they continue to work at articulating. "Power to shape the direction of their own communities belongs to the members," one staff member told me. This is the stuff of hope, it seems to me, and, therefore, as I understand it, of healing.

When I first asked Mary Vincent, one of the staff members at Hope and a Sister of St. Joseph of Carondelet, how she thought the community would feel if, for this conference, I presented Hope as a compelling example of a healing community, she said, "We would really hate that." Her worry was that I wanted to describe Hope as a community of healers and healees, what staff member and community organizer Mary Keefe calls "that soft, icky kind of healing." When I explained that I understand Hope as a community that works to generate a powerful sense of possibility and power for those who live in its inner-city neighborhood, that its work depends on the reciprocal energy of all who are involved, Mary said, "Give it a try."

In that attempt, I would like to focus on four aspects of Hope: a description and brief history; two instances of "healing realizations" that have radically changed the direction of the community since 1977; some strategies the com-

munity has put in place in response to those realizations; and several concluding thoughts about where Hope fits in the dynamic and always-changing relationship between religion and culture. Overall, one of the main points of
interest in the story of Hope as a generator of healing in the inner city is its
constant attention to matters of self-understanding, public identity, and motivation. The community's essential strength is its capacity for candid self-
critique that does not deteriorate into paralyzing self-denigration. Staff and
neighbors alike are always willing to reassess and go in new directions. They
are funny and wise and relentless. "The fun starts after you hear 'no,'" says
Deanna Foster, the executive director of Hope.

The "big red house" at 2101 Portland Avenue South was opened in 1977
by the Sisters of St. Joseph of Carondelet as a temporary shelter for homeless
women and children. For many years it was called St. Joseph's House and then
St. Joe's Hope to include the expanding enterprise of the community into the
rehabilitation of other homes on the block. Hope is in the Phillips neighborhood, generally thought to be among the most economically challenged in the
city: full of violence, guns, crack houses, diverse groups at war with each other,
and very little in the way of cultural or social amenities.

The people of the neighborhood are well aware of popular opinion about
them, including the fact that some organizations offer "crack tours" of their
blocks. "We are known as the land of 10,000 social services," said one resident.
"Eventually," says Jeri Schultz, a community organizer who has conducted "listening sessions" among residents, "someone makes the comment that these
are just perceptions of people who don't know that there is a whole different
reality." Those who actually live there see "a neighborhood with a rich history
and beautiful historical homes . . . people who watch out for each other and
accompany each other. . . . The PEOPLE are the strength here. . . . There's so
much diversity" (2000: 2). Asking people in the community what they think
will make it a place where people want to live and asking them to take responsibility for bringing their visions to reality have been the foundation of Hope's
neighborhood-healing mission since the early 1990s, to be "a catalyst for
change, growth, and safety in our neighborhood," as the new mission statement declares.

When St. Joseph's House opened in 1977, the founders felt they were on
the cutting edge in terms of providing shelter for homeless women and their
children. There were almost no such facilities in the metropolitan area. At that
time the neighborhood, though old—with many houses dating from the end
of the nineteenth century—was reasonably stable, and many residents owned
their own homes. Deanna Foster describes it as "'the inner city of the seventies—poverty and daily challenges co-existed with self-respect and hope."
Twelve years later it was obvious that the neighborhood surrounding the big
red house was falling down and falling apart. "We were under siege," says

A winding sidewalk dubbed "the yellow brick road" welcomes children and families living at Hope Community and their guests. Used with permission from Hope Community.

Foster, "in the most profound sense" (1997b: 4). It became obvious that the shelter was no longer a safe place physically, and the despair that permeated the neighborhood began to seep through its windows and doors.

It took a little longer for the Hope community to acknowledge that the shelter was not only unsafe; the way it worked was perpetuating dependence and hopelessness. St. Joseph's House could alleviate homelessness for thirty days, the maximum stay. Residents then went from St. Joseph's House to another shelter for a brief stay or to a temporary rental unit, after which they were homeless again. The social structures that caused the homelessness were still in place. Deanna Foster sums up the increasingly frustrating and heartbreaking story of the shelter with a story about one woman, Kitty McCann, who had spent time at the shelter but was alienated from the community when she died. Foster came to suspect a fundamental dishonesty in her friendship with Kitty: "She loved to talk about her commitment to being homeless and the freedom it gave her, and I pretended to believe her." Foster wondered whether "Kitty's efforts to keep her dignity drove her away from the 'helping hands' that reached out to her. What if we had reached out to her with the expectations of her responsibility to the community? Would she have been drawn into life instead of death?" (1996: 3). It was Kitty's death that made clear to her, Foster says, that the shelter was nurturing "defeat and hopelessness" rather than change, growth, and healing. That clarification was community-wide, in fact. It led Hope to expand its efforts in affordable housing and revitalization of the neighborhood and in 1996 to change the way the big red house functioned: from a thirty-day shelter to a residence that houses women for as long as six months and requires that they work or go to school, contribute to the operation of the household, and set aside money each month that is saved for them as a nest egg upon their departure.

Foster articulates what I think of as the primary healing or hope-producing insight that has led Hope to its present mission in Phillips: "We seek to change prevailing policy and risk believing that a strong, safe community can be achieved by building what we want rather than destroying what we fear" (1997a: 11). Pat Mullen, the chair of the Hope board, amplifies this by saying that when the board discusses whether a new project fits into Hope's mission, "We try to look for its potential to release the energy and ideas of the people we live and work among. The test is: Does the project bring hope?" (1998).

There are several ways to illustrate what the Hope community thinks of as "projects that bring hope," and therefore healing, to Phillips. One is to point out some of its most visible efforts at revitalizing the community, among them increasing the amount of affordable housing, restoring a neighborhood park, and participating in the Forward on Franklin project, collaboration with fifty other groups to make nearby Franklin Avenue once again a commercially thriving neighborhood Main Street. The Children's Village, another collaborative plan in Phillips, is conceived of as an actual neighborhood and a model for what a community should be if it is to help children prosper. African American and Somali women's dialogues in Hope's "power spaces" are only one example of Hope's efforts to heal conflict-ridden relationships in the neighborhood.

A second example involves Hope's efforts to build community by making connections with and beyond Phillips through its supporters. Their very variety is instructive about the process of healing both social and religious divisions. Hope has built successful relationships with over more than thirty foundations and there are at least 1,000 individual donors, some of whom have contributed for more than twenty years. Some of them have obvious connections to Hope: retired nuns, relatives and friends of staff members, former shelter and neighborhood residents, priests, Catholic and Protestant congregations. But some of the money, including government grants, comes from unlikely places that indicate the widening circle of Hope's supporters. A prominent Twin Cities Jewish family foundation began its ongoing support by contributing money to rehabilitate a duplex that replaced a crack house, and several wealthy, somewhat conservative Catholic families make contributions as well, evidence that the appeal of Hope's work cuts across liberal-conservative boundaries. Some contributions are "in kind." Virginia Rickeman (2000), minister of outreach at Plymouth Congregation at Church in Minneapolis, spent a month of her sabbatical working on the flower gardens that are so important to the neighborhood. There is, in fact, a lot of attention paid at Hope to the healing power of beauty for its own sake. For several years there were Christmas gifts from the

Honeybelles, a women's group at Honeywell, where Hope members were protesting every Wednesday against the building of cluster bombs. There are often
letters in the newsletter from people who are not wealthy but are devoted to
Hope's causes: "This may be the last from our old railroad friend. I have cancer
of liver and pancreas. No need to acknowledge. I know you are as happy to get
this [contribution] as I am sending it. Bob" (Community Correspondence
1996).

A third way to understand Hope as a healing rather than a fixing community is to pay careful attention to what its spokespersons have to say about
what is going on there. Hope works constantly to be clearer about what motivates its efforts and the principles on which it bases its understanding of
community. "Our goal," they say, "is change for the sake of justice." The fruits
of their labors are not the primary end of their efforts; they are a by-product
of it. "Hope is about connections, relationships, self-reliance, community." If
there is anything community members are vehement about it is the need to
demonstrate to the people of the neighborhood that they have the wherewithal,
the power, to participate in the public arena—that they, themselves, can make
changes in their lives and in their neighborhood. What stands in the way, Mary
Keefe repeated in our several conversations, is what she calls the "social service
culture" that she sees as "diagnosing" people as needy and that insists that
"these people" are not ready to think about power. Keefe herself says, "I believe
in people."

Pat Mullen (2000) speaks of Hope's core values, like building a diverse
community and holding all members within it accountable for the common
good. These values motivate the responses to a variety of questions people ask
about Hope: "Why are our apartments so nice [a policeman once asked a staff
member why Hope was building such a beautiful house in *this* neighborhood]?
Why are we planting flowers? Why have we stopped providing all the food for
neighborhood gatherings and started having potlucks instead? Why do we
make an effort to rent to people from many cultures and backgrounds? Why
isn't it enough to fix up houses and rent them cheaply to poor people? Why
do we have several staff who spend significant time asking others for their
ideas instead of presuming to have the answers? Why is peacemaking a theme
of our newsletters?" Through these efforts to empower people to take responsibility for their lives and their neighborhood, residents begin to experience
the hope that transformation is both possible and sustainable. "It's good for
the soul," says Hope neighbor Mercedes Seigana, an Ojibwa from the Red
Lake Nation, "to go and talk to your neighbors and see how they're doing, let
them know you're behind the community" ("Living in the Heart of the City"
2000).

There are poignant reminders, of course, that utopia has not yet been
achieved, among them the fears of neighborhood residents that this is all a

matter of power but the kind of power they do not yet have and may never have. Mary Keefe describes their anxieties this way: "When things change, it won't be for us. It will be for people who have money and we will be gone" (2001). Issues related to historic racial tensions in American culture also continue to produce conflicts among various groups that are part of the Hope neighborhood, but Keefe sees these tensions as inevitable in the kind of work Hope does. She has come to believe they are not all negative. As people work out the tensions together, they begin to realize their strengths. Rebecca Rojas and Mary Vincent report that Somali native Ardo Abdulkadir, a resident of one of Hope's housing units, sees Hope as providing opportunities "for people to gather around, as a group, and share their ideas . . . so people who are needy can think of themselves as people who are rich" (1999: 9). Some staff members laughingly call Hope "the country club of the inner city" because so many connections are made there.

Where does the neighborhood-healing mission of Hope fit in terms of the interplay between religion and culture in America? Efforts to interpret Hope as a "religious" community are intriguingly complicated. "Remember," the staff tell me, "we're spiritual, not religious." "OK, OK," I say, wanting very much to honor their self-description. But, as my friends at Hope know from our conversations, I see Hope as a community that draws inspiration from at least four aspects of American Catholicism, among them the Catholic heritage of social justice, sometimes manifested in radical ways; a traditional Catholic piety that is recognizable if you know what to look for but that has been transformed by its encounter with the postmodern realities of twenty-first-century, pluralistic, urban life; the history of Catholic women's communities; and more than a dash of what theologian David Tracy and priest-sociologist-novelist Andrew Greeley refer to as "the Catholic imagination": an orientation toward the world that both theologically and aesthetically emphasizes divine presence over divine absence and community over individualism (Greeley 2000).

In addition to their loyalty to causes of social justice, many of the early and continuing supporters of Hope were shaped by the traditional piety of pre–Vatican II Catholicism. That is certainly the case with Char Madigan, whose "Inpulse" columns in the newsletter make references to saints and holy days and devotions. This is her language, her native tongue, and it comes from the tradition that formed her and that she loves, no matter how many quarrels she has with the hierarchy over issues of sexuality and women's roles. She is also the spokesperson for the community who says, "We are Christian, Jewish, Buddhist, Muslim, etcelera." Hope's religious worldview, as I understand it, combines Catholic piety and devotionalism with an openness to the truth and wisdom of other religious traditions and with postmodern insights into the nature of power. What might seem to the outsider to be a startling juxtaposition of irreconcilable elements makes powerful sense in the context of Hope. There is a statue of St. Joseph buried in the backyard, and there are sophisticated articles in the newsletter about how to make radical changes in the social structure.

I also see Hope as a women's community. It does not exclude men; many men are involved. But it was initiated by women to meet women's needs, and it continues to be inspired and sustained by women. And while only two of the staff members are now Sisters of St. Joseph of Carondelet, the historical and contemporary experiences of women's religious communities are a very real part of Hope's heritage. Hope falls easily, in my opinion, into a broader lineage of American women's healing movements, in great part because it offers a compelling example of women's theological creativity acted upon: a reinterpretation, a reimagining, of a religious tradition that demands new ways of being Catholic and thus new ways of acting in the world. Historically, women's healing movements have pointed to the need for a change of con- sciousness about the nature of reality in order to make something new of one's circumstances.

Hope's insistence that we have to change the way we see reality in order to bring about healing in the world is familiar to those who have studied women's healing movements. But Hope wants to change more than conscious- ness. The community wants to change not just public perception of what con-

Char Madigan, one of the founders of Hope Community, visits with neighbors in the living room of the Red House. Used with permission from Hope Community.

stitutes a "good" neighborhood but public funding policies for housing and development that try to prevent "too many poor people from living in one place." In their efforts to bring about healing in the Hope neighborhood, members of the community envision not only alternative theological realities but alternative social realities as well.

There are by now numerous agencies and efforts in the Twin Cities working to provide affordable housing and to revitalize inner-city neighborhoods so that residents may live human and fruitful lives. Many of them are sponsored by churches or religious agencies. Hope is certainly one among many of these groups, but it is distinguished by its insistence that it would not consider itself successful even it if made possible housing, food, jobs, and self-respect for every person in the area. Hope wants, above all, to bring about the "kin-dom" of God on its block and in its neighborhood, to heal the traumas and divisions that cause so much suffering by offering hope in the urban core. It wants to do all these things for the sake of justice. In a sidebar of a recent issue of the newsletter 2002, an artist identified only as "Whitefeather" includes with her two drawings her conviction that helps to convey the ethos of healing hope that pervades the community: "I cheer for the underlying spirits who haunt us, heal us, who fill us with hope. I cheer for the dreamers, for without dreams there is no hope."

REFERENCES

Anniversary Edition. 1997. *St. Joseph's HOPE Community News* 11:2.
Bednarowski, Mary Farrell. 1999. *The Religious Imagination of American Women.* Bloomington: Indiana University Press.
Community Correspondence. 1996. *St. Joseph's HOPE Community News.* 10:1, 13.
Eyes Open on a World: The Challenges of Change A Collaboration by the Sisters of St. Joseph of Carondelet St. Paul Province. 2001. St. Cloud, Minn.: North Star Press.
Foster, Deanna. 1996. What Do You Expect? *St. Joseph's HOPE Community News* 10(1): 3–4.
———. 1997. This Holy Place. *St. Joseph's HOPE Community News* 11(1): 10–11.
———. 1997b. Turning the Tide on Desolation: A Window of Hope on Oakland Avenue. *St. Joseph's HOPE Community News* 11(6): 4–6.
Greeley, Andrew. 2000. *The Catholic Imagination.* Berkeley and Los Angeles: University of California Press.
HOPE Community. 2000. Annual Report 15:2, 7.
Keefe, Mary. 2001. *Essentials. A Journal of HOPE Community* 15:4, 1.
Living in the Heart of the City. 2001. *A Journal of HOPE Community* 15:2.
Madigan, Char. 1998. Inpulse. *St. Joseph's HOPE Community News* 12:2.
Mullen, Pat. 1998. From the Chair of the Board! *Hope Community News* 12:6, cover page.
———. 2000. From the Chair of the Board! *Hope Community News* 14:7, cover page.

Rickeman, Virginia. 2000. *A Journal of HOPE Community News* 14:6, 10.

Rojas, Rebecca, and Mary Vincent. 1999. Community Life. *HOPE Community Annual Report 1998* 13:2, 9.

Schultz, Jeri. 2000. An Experience of Community: A Listening Session. *A Journal of HOPE Community* (6): 2–3.

Segana, Mercedes Candace. 2000. How I Found Hope and How Hope Found Me. *HOPE Community News* 14(4): 4–5.

12

Communing with the Dead: Spiritual and Cultural Healing in Chicano/a Communities

Lara Medina

Remembering and honoring the dead during the Chicano tradition of Días de los Muertos, or Days of the Dead, is a spiritual and cultural practice responding to a complex historical process of colonization, including displacement from land, language, religion, and identity. These elaborate public rituals rooted in indigenous Mesoamerican and Mexican Catholic beliefs in communing with the dead have proliferated in the last three decades due to the efforts of Chicana/o artists, teachers, students, and cultural workers. As ancient Mesoamerican indigenous populations cyclically asked the hearts of their dead ones to return from the sacred mountains so that new life and new harvest might continue, so too Chicanas/os are replenished with new life and new hope when they invite their dead to return.[1] The reinvention of traditional ways to express contemporary concerns renews and recenters a people hungry for spiritual nourishment in their ongoing struggle for justice and healing. In Spanish, the verb *curar* (to heal) refers to a holistic sense of healing. The physical, mental, emotional, and spiritual aspects of a person must be attended to if he or she is to be fully healed. The popular saying "la cultura cura," or culture heals, is often used to refer to the significance of Days of the Dead for Chicanos, a tradition that holds the healing power and memories of the ancestors.

This chapter explores Días de los Muertos as celebrated in the heart of East Los Angeles during 1998 at the internationally recognized Chicano/a community art center, Self Help Graphics (SHG). As a case study of how one Chicano community annually celebrates, it offers insight into the process that numerous Chicano communities engage in as they honor their dead. The healing aspects of the tradition receive emphasis, as does its political significance for a population committed to the task of self-determination. In ritual and artistic expressions of Chicano/a spirituality, the political cannot be separated from the spiritual. In light of the history of colonization and the ongoing marginalization of Chicano and Latino communities, the public expression of honoring the dead contests Western dichotomies between the living and the dead, between the spiritual and the physical. For a historically subordinated population, publicly remembering their ancestors takes on political meaning as the genealogy being honored is indigenous and of mixed blood, a genealogy not intended to survive in the Western world. Claiming public space, including streets and parks, to honor these "others" is "an ultimate act of resistance against cultural domination" (Mesa-Bains 1988: 9). And "others" themselves parading en masse refute daily efforts to dismiss their very presence in an increasingly segregated society. I argue that for Chicanos/as, a key to healing from the trauma of spiritual and physical colonization is the claiming of ancestral indigenous epistemology that values interdependency between the living and the dead, between living communities and ancient ones.

Días de los Muertos at SHG

Self Help Graphics, the first and primary Chicano/a community arts center and gallery in Los Angeles, has played an instrumental role in reintroducing Days of the Dead to "Angeleños" and the larger U.S. population. Begun in the early 1970s with the instrumental support of Karen Bocallero, O.S.F., SHG has enabled Chicana/o artists to exhibit and further develop their work. Since then it has emerged as the leading visual arts organization producing and exhibiting Chicana/o art and culture in the country. SHG began celebrating Días de los Muertos as a communal public ritual in 1972. While many Chicano families have honored their dead for generations, ritual practices were of a more private nature, with home altars and family visits to cemeteries. According to art historian Sybil Venegas, "Sister Karen credits Mexican artists Carlos Bueno and Antonio Ibañez with suggesting that El Día de los Muertos be celebrated as a collective, public art project aimed at cultural reclamation, self determination and definition" (1995: 18). Community trauma experienced at the Chicano Moratorium in 1970 in East Los Angeles when police killed three Chicanos in a peaceful anti–Vietnam War protest could also be addressed in the ritual. The first celebration was on a small scale, involving primarily artists and including a procession from the local cemetery, the building of an *ofrenda* (an altar for the dead), and the sharing of food among the participants. By

1976, community members expanded the number of participants to several thousand. "Several years later, SHG was host to the largest and most widely attended annual day of the dead celebration in California, if not the U.S. The festivities included a cemetery mass, a street parade, altar and art exhibits" (Venegas 1990: 1). Catholic clergymen, Gary Riebe-Estrella and Juan Romero presided at several of the liturgical celebrations until the archdiocese notified Sister Karen that Catholic liturgies in a secular cemetery could not be approved. The archdiocesan action and a growing integration of indigenous beliefs and practices in the lives of the artists created a separation between the Catholic Church and the art-centered ritual celebration. SHG continued to sponsor Los Angeles's largest Días de los Muertos celebration independent of church involvement.

Honoring the Dead in East Los Angeles

The several hundred people gathering on a sunny November 1, 1998, morning at the intersection of "Five Corners" attest to a journalist's claim that "Los Angeles must be the United States' Day of the Dead capital" (Anon. 1998). Many are in full *calavera*, or skeleton attire, the predominant icon for Días de los Muertos. Adults and children enthusiastically line up to have their faces painted to represent the skeleton within. Others mingle with anticipation as they wait for the mile-long procession to begin. Many carry bouquets of bright orange *cempoaxóchitl*, or marigolds, the traditional flowers for the *ofrendas*; the bright color and pungent smell will attract the spirits of the dead. Others attentively watch a *teatro* performance on the north side of the small plaza, portraying a son speaking with the spirit of his dead mother. Words of forgiveness help reconcile a lifetime plagued by drugs and violence. The beat of the Aztec drums notifies the crowd that the procession is about to begin. *Danzantes*, or Aztec dancers, wearing feathered headdresses and beaded ceremonial clothing offer prayers of thanksgiving to the four cardinal directions with the scent of *copal* (holy incense) floating to the heavens. Their prayers also invoke the presence of the ancestors from all directions of the universe. Individuals, couples, and families quickly maneuver into line to begin the short trek down Cesar Chavez Avenue. Banners publicize the political sentiments: "*Cuantas más masacres?*" refers to the recent killing of forty Zapatistas in Actael, Mexico, and "*Vivan los muertos*" stresses the enduring presence of the dead. An oversized papier-mâché *calavera* on a flatbed truck brings up the end of the parade. The living proceed to honor their dead. Death does not have the last word, here in East Los Angeles.

Preparations actually began four months earlier. Between September and October a total of fourteen art workshops were offered free to the public, with Chicano/a artists teaching mask making, altar making, *calavera* crafts, and

Impersonating Mictecacihuatl, goddess of Mictlan, place of the dead. Olvera Street, Los Angeles, 1998. Used with permission from Lara Medina.

mural painting, all in honor of the dead. The creations would be used in the public ritual.

By noon on the day of the celebration, the facilities at SHG are clearly marked as sacred space. Led by Mexica *danzantes*, the procession of living *calaveras* finds its way to the parking lot decorated with oversized papier-mâché masks, large, richly painted canvas murals, and a centrally located pyramid-shaped structure. The all-female *danzante* troupe blesses the event with *copal* and drumbeats as they circle the pyramid. The procession of 400 begins to disperse and join the others waiting in anticipation. A float depicting Quetzal-coatl, the feathered serpent deity, maneuvers to the middle of the lot as the six-foot *calavera* on the flatbed truck parks close to the fence. Children's masks, *papel picado*, or intrically cut tissue paper, and two long *tlatzotzompantli*, or skull racks, decorate the chain-link fence enclosing the parking lot. The *tlat-zotzompantli* resembles the one found in the Templo Mayor in Mexico City. But these skulls, with sunglasses and teeth bared in smiles, reveal their Southern Californian roots as they purview the festivities under way. The opening prayer offered by En Lak Ech (You Are My Other I), a group of Chicana poets, emphasizes the spiritual significance of the day ahead:

> We would like to offer you all, in a good way, in a humble way,
>   a prayer song.
> We would like to honor all those who have passed on, all our
>   ancestors, our grandmothers, and our grandfathers.
> We want to pray for those who are yet to come and those that
>   are here present with us today.
> We, En Lak Ech *mujeres*, pray to the women and *mujeres* who
>   have died through violence or through life and struggle. We
>   offer this prayer for you.

The day's schedule includes twenty-seven performances offering more prayer, music, *teatro*, poetry, comedy, and dance. The music reflects the diversity of the crowd: mariachi, Chicano rap, blues, Mexican, rock, salsa, and reggae. Groups with names like Quetzal, Aztlán Underground, and Quinto Sol reflect the Los Angeles music scene incorporating an indigenous consciousness. The program for the day announces what can be expected:

> Culture is not static. And in the hands of artists, it is volatile and
> exciting. The traditions of Mexico are honored and respected, and
> then added to, modified to accommodate the North American expe-
> rience of La Raza. As is Day of the Dead, a custom both secular and
> religious, sacred and sacrosanct, Christian and pre-Columbian, the
> modern celebrations are old and new, maintaining the most popular
> customs and prompting the next edge of invention. Day of the Dead
> has become a paradigm for how local artists contribute to the quality
> of life in their community, and it has become the ideal vehicle for
> sharing culture with the larger realm of society.

As the performances get under way, it is evident that political concerns will be heard throughout the day as community members gather to remember and renew themselves for ongoing social struggles. Social criticism informs many of the musical compositions. The lead singer of Aztlán Underground responds to the power of the system toward Chicanos/as:

> So they can see a strong brown man, a strong brown women
> And feel proud of who they are.
> So we can finally stand up
> and take the foot of the oppressor out of this land.

Themes of the *actos* reflect an indigenous consciousness: Acto 1, *Nezahualcoyotl*; Acto 2, *La Carpa Tezcatlipoca*; Acto 3, *Luchando con la Vida*; Acto 4, twenty-five years of *Chicanahuatl* fashion; and Acto 5, poem to *Miquitztli*. One performance group, Indians Teaching Spaniards (ITS), speaks to "taking back the streets of Los Angeles" not just one day a year in a procession for the dead but for all the living in Los Angeles. Throughout the day, people sit, stand, dance, and mingle with family and friends as they soak in the richness of these cultural and political expressions.

The gallery space on the first floor of SHG is packed with people viewing the "room altars." These sacred spaces reflect intimate, lifelike scenes from the homes of those remembered. One of the altar makers dedicates a sewing room to her mother. A black Singer sewing machine, a full-length mirror, and a dress form create the center of this *ofrenda*. An ironing board draped with clothes provides a sense of the activity that once filled the sewing room. Flowers, crochet needles, sewing boxes, crocheted dolls, and bolts of fabric fill this woman's room: a creative sanctuary away from the problems of everyday life or perhaps the workplace of an efficient seamstress. Another room altar displays a 1940s kitchen, one familiar to many Chicanos who grew up with a grandmother who healed others through her cooking. A "dining room altar" adjoining the kitchen displays a buffet table filled with photographs, flowers, and food offerings. This "altar within an altar" emphasizes how the *ofrenda* tradition held a central place in this family space. A "backyard porch altar" includes potted plants and a swinging chair where the artist's *abuelos*, or grandparents, used to sit. Their shrine to Guadalupe calls to mind the home religious practices embedded in Chicano Catholic culture.

Near the entrance to the second floor, another altar is dedicated to migrant farmworkers. Its five levels are filled with a dozen small black-and-red United Farm Worker (UFW) flags and plenty of orange marigolds. Black-and-white photos of farmworkers fill three of the levels. At the top of the altar is a photograph of Cesar Chavez and Senator Robert F. Kennedy after Chavez's 1968 fast. A Guadalupe image is placed in the center of the altar with a crucifix nailed to the wall above. Red and black *papel picado* outline the altar. Another altar sponsored by the Wall, an organization for gay Latinos, honors those who have died of AIDS. Photographs, a statue of Guadalupe, teddy bears, and burning sage bless their presence. Space is reserved for people to add names or prayers for others remembered. By the end of the evening, many names on green and white sheets of paper decorate the wall. Pamphlets on AIDS prevention and services for gay Latinos in Los Angeles are freely distributed as part of this *ofrenda*.

From noon until ten in the evening, several thousand people participate in the day's activities. No alcohol is served at the event, but an espresso stand provides coffee. The aroma of Mexican food fills the air. Vending booths sell

An *ofrenda* created by a third-generation *altarista*, or altarmaker, Ofelia Esparza. Los Angeles, 1998. Used with permission from Lara Medina.

Días de los Muertos iconography. Participants line up to get their faces painted *calavera* style. Guitarists roam the area singing *"La Llorona"* (The Weeping Woman), and others serenade the dead. In the far corner of the parking lot stands a fifteen-foot mosaic statue of Our Lady of Guadalupe. Neighborhood women clean and maintain the shrine on a regular basis. Many folks who come to SHG identify her as Tonantzin, the Nahua mother goddess. This permanent shrine at SHG blesses the crowd and the celebration.

Approximately one half of the forty participants interviewed identified as Catholic, and the other half no longer associate with organized religion, or, as one woman shared, "I follow Indigena ways, that makes me balanced." All recognized the importance of the day as they offered their respect for the dead. As one informant explained, "Días de los Muertos has become a significant spiritual celebration for Chicanos. Without that sense of who we are, and who our ancestors are, we become a lost culture. Many segments of our society are lost because they don't know their ancestry and they don't understand death." Despite diverse religious affiliations, the sense of a communal identity pervades the celebration. With a shared purpose of remembering and renewing, many participants acknowledge the value of passing on traditions, and affirming cultural, spiritual, and political values. As one stated, "I love how families with their children are here, teaching them the traditions, and how to honor their elders. Unless we teach them, they won't know." Knowing that the tradition aids their resistance to marginalization adds to the importance of the celebration. Another participant emphasized, "All we get from the media is that we [Chicanos] are worthless; our children need to know their traditions so that they will know right from wrong when they hear stereotypes."

The rituals of making and exhibiting art, constructing *ofrendas*, parading in *calavera*, and performing from the heart, sanctify what is important here in East Los Angeles. As one participant remarked, "Remembering and honoring is praying." Through Días de los Muertos, Chicanos and Chicanas find healing, strength, and renewal in their struggle to survive and prosper as a people.

Discussion

Días de los Muertos does not replicate Western patterns of exclusion. The rite, with its color, humor, and friendly spirit, invites all people to approach death and the "other" without fear. The silence of death and the pain of exclusion are healed in the festivity of this public mourning ritual. As Father Grey Baumann of Mission Dolores reflects, "In Anglo culture an altar for the dead seems bizarre because we divorce ourselves from the fact that we die. . . . We try to put it off in the corner and only face it when we have to. The Latino culture is not afraid of death. . . . When you age, you don't have to be ashamed."[2]

Although the majority of Chicanas/os have been Christianized, there is a concerted effort by many to reinstate and identify with indigenous ancestral knowledge. Estrangement from Roman Catholicism is due in large part to a historical attempt to assimilate Chicanos into a "universal" Euro-american Catholicism, compounded by the absence of native-born Chicano clergy, and the limitations placed on the authority of women in the ecclesiastical structure. Many Chicanos, however, who have left the institutional church continue to identify with symbols that represent the faith, courage, and survival of their Catholic parents and grandparents. Días de los Muertos reflects these allegiances as participants consciously construct a symbol and ritual system that contains significant elements of indigenous spirituality alongside the elements found meaningful in Mexican Catholicism. Icons of saints, Madonnas, Guadalupe, and the sacred hearts of Jesus and Mary, among many others, continue to assert a strong presence in visual expressions of Chicana/o consciousness and spirituality. Catholic icons share physical space with indigenous elements such as earth, water, fire, herbs, symbols of duality, and images of non-Christian deities, such as Coatlicue, the Nahua Mother Earth Goddess, on many of the *ofrendas*.

This coexistence of Catholic and Mesoamerican symbols reflects an aspect of *nepantla* spirituality, a spirituality at the biological and cultural crossroads where diverse elements converge, at times in great tension and at other times in cohesion. *Nepantla* is not syncretism in its limited meaning but an example of transculturation, or a continuous encounter of two or more divergent worldviews. The use of *nepantla*, a Nahuatl term meaning "in the middle," was recorded by Friar Bernardino de Sahagún in the sixteenth century. Dominican friar Diego Durán had reprimanded an indigenous elder for his behavior, which appeared to the friar to be in discord with Christian and Nahua customs and morals. The elder responded, " 'Father, don't be afraid, for we are still *'nepantla'*—in other words, 'in the middle,' or as he later added, 'we are neutral' " (León-Portilla 1990: 10). The elder's presumed indecisiveness, interpreted as the "trauma of nepantlism," resulted from forced cultural change, producing a psychological and spiritual condition filled with ambiguity, confusion, and conflict. The indigenous or non-Western self is forced to deny its essential being and become like the conqueror.

The state of *nepantla*, however, can become a site of transformative struggle and creativity, a state of inherent being and meaning making (Anzaldua 1987; Pérez 1998). Once the tensions of *nepantla* are understood and transformed, and the indigenous self is reclaimed and continuously healed, *nepantla* becomes a psychological, spiritual, and political space that Chicanas/os can appropriate or recast as a site of power. Rather then being limited by confusion or ambiguity, Chicanas/os act as subjects or agents in deciding how diverse religious, cultural, and political systems can or cannot work together. Just as the indigenous elder could have very well been maneuvering the fissures, boundaries, and borders of his new world, Chicanas/os can consciously make choices about what aspects of diverse worldviews nurture the complexity of their spiritual and biological *mestizaje* (cultural/racial mixture), and what for them enables communication with transcendent powers. As a professor of religious studies and Chicana/o studies, I have witnessed Days of the Dead as one of the central expressions of *nepantla* spirituality in the pathway to healing.

Días de los Muertos provides opportunities for healing, for renewing and enlarging a group identity. In a society that ignores Chicanas/os as historical actors, the mere act of remembering one's ancestors carries subversive elements. For Chicanos/as, who are consistently portrayed as "aliens" to the dominant Euro-American culture, continuity with ancestral ways heals the wounds incurred by ongoing attempts to silence indigenous and mestizo peoples. Remembering the dead who struggled to ensure life would continue for their descendants strengthens communal identity. In the process, a community of individuals heals itself. As Chicanas/os revisit and consciously select an indigenous heritage that supposedly was obliterated through colonial pursuits, they make a political decision as well as a spiritual decision. As government and corporate actions show, it is still not advantageous to be indigenous or Mexican. Legislation opposing Latino immigration, affirmative action, and bilingual education reflects mainstream sentiments toward these populations. And amid the deeper political meaning lies a rich spirituality "respecting those who have gone before and celebrating our ability to communicate with them."[3] The poem "Miquiztli" by Olga García concludes as follows:

> Us Mexicans,
> We love our dead,
> Love 'em like we do chile,
> Like we do guitar wailing
> *Corridos* on drunken nights,
> Like we do loud *abuelas*
> Smoking on blue porches . . .
>
> We love our dead
> like fire
> like memory
> like the bouncing reflection of all of us here,
> now,
> *con caras pintadas,*
> *bocas sonriendo,*[4]
> dancing in front of this smoking mirror,
> waiting for it
> to break.

NOTES

1. See Alfredo López Austin, *Tamoanchan, Tlalocan: Places of Mist* (Niwot: University Press of Colorado, 1997).

2. Father Gregory Baumann of Mission Dolores Parish, interview with author, November 1998.

3. Pastor Mike Kennedy, Dolores Mission Parish, interview with author, January 1999.

4. Translated as "with painted faces, smiling mouths." Poem read at SHG, November 1, 1998.

REFERENCES

Anon. Celebrate Día de los Muertos All Month Long. *BOCA* 1(3): 6.
Anzaldua, Gloria. 1987. *Borderlands La Frontera: The New Mestiza.* San Francisco: spinsters/aunt lute.

Durán, Diego. 1969. *Historia de las Indias de Nueva España e Islas de la Tierra Firme.* Vol. 1. Mexico, City: Porrúa.

León-Portilla, Miguel. 1990. *Endangered Cultures.* Dallas: Southern Methodist University Press.

Mesa-Baines, Amalia. 1984. Altarmakers: The Historic Mediators. In *Offerings: The Altar Show,* 5–7. Venice, Calif.: Social and Public Arts Resource Center.

———, ed. 1988. *Ceremony of Memory.* Santa Fe, N.M.: Center for Contemporary Arts of Santa Fe.

Pérez, Laura. 1998. Spirit Glyphs: Reimagining Art and Artist in the Work of Chicana *Tlamatinime. Modern Fiction Studies* 44: 36–76.

Sahagún, Fray Bernardino de. 1969. *Historia general de las cosas de la Nueva España.* Vol. 2. Mexico, City: Porrúa.

Venegas, Sybil. 1990. The Day of the Dead in Los Angeles. *Report.* Los Angeles Photography Center.

———. 1995. Day of the Dead in Aztlán: Chicano Variations on the Theme of Life, Death and Self-Preservation. M.A. thesis, University of California, Los Angeles.

13

Spirituality and Aging in the San Francisco Japanese Community

Ronald Y. Nakasone

Religious diversity and cultural diffusion are ever-present and pressing realities in health care facilities, often appearing in the smallest details. The staff of Chaparral House, a skilled nursing facility in Berkeley, California, noted an attitudinal change in an elderly Japanese resident when she was given a pair of chopsticks to take her meals. Residents and their families welcome such attentiveness to their cultural and spiritual needs, especially at times of critical decision making and at the end of life. Although Japanese and Japanese Americans[1] believe in and rely on the efficacy of modern medical practices and pharmacology, their cultural traditions are important resources for health maintenance, healing, aging, dying, death, and grieving. They, consciously and unconsciously, creatively engage both worlds.

In an attempt to reconcile its traditional culture with its modern American experience, the Japanese American community of San Francisco initiated a unique experiment in community-based education for elder care as part of the newly built Kokoro Assisted Living Facility. In envisioning a seamless blend of modern medicine and spirituality in caring for Japanese American elders in a multicultural and multifaith setting, the Japanese America Religious Federation of San Francisco (JARF) commissioned the design and implementation of "Spirituality and Aging in the Japanese Experience."[2] The year-long, six-unit graduate course would serve as a blueprint for a comprehensive and continuous in-service training strategy for the health care team that plans to include the elder residents, their families, volunteers, seminarians, community leaders, clergy, and others in need of or wanting information and training in geriatrics. It was offered through the Graduate Theological Union (GTU) in Berkeley, California, in partnership with Sanford Geriatric Education Center (SGEC) in Palo Alto, California.

This chapter describes the context, conceptual framework, implementation, and outcomes of "Spirituality and Aging in the Japanese Experience." The course syllabus is appended. It begins with a brief history of JARF and its role in responding to the housing needs of the Japanese community.

Context

JARF's interfaith consortium of eleven Buddhist-, Christian-, and Shinto-based congregations is an outgrowth of the Shūkyōka konwakai (Gathering of Religious Persons) that coordinated the temporary housing needs of newly released Japanese nationals and Japanese American internees. As a result of Executive Order 9099, the U.S War Department had removed approximately 112,000 persons of Japanese ancestry, who were living primarily on the West Coast of the continental United States, to thirteen concentration camps. Though the Shūkyōka konwakai closed its last hostel in 1954, the changing housing needs prompted the creation of the Japanese American Religious Federation, Inc., a nonprofit entity, in 1968. Four years later, JARF incorporated the Japanese American Religious Federation Housing, Inc. (JARF Housing) to build and manage Nihonmachi Terrace, a 245-unit low-income and affordable housing complex primarily for seniors with a $6,100,400 loan from the Department of Housing and Urban Development (HUD). While Nihonmachi Terrace has been operating successfully, it is unable to serve elders who no longer meet its respective ambulatory requirements. Responding to this need, JARF and JARF Housing incorporated the Japanese American Religious Federation Assisted Living Facility, Inc. (JALFI), in 1997, to build Kokoro Assisted Living, Inc. The leadership capitalized on the long-ingrained virtue of filial respect, embraced by all Japanese spiritual traditions, to galvanize community support. The JALFI mission statement reads as follows: "JALFI seeks to fulfill the desire of its community for seniors to live in dignity and comfort within the Japanese community of the San Francisco Bay Area. It will provide for the physical, social and spiritual care of seniors under the supervision of a culturally sensitive, qualified and licensed service."

As part of this vision of providing culturally sensitive care, the clerical and lay leadership of the respective JARF congregations insisted that the spiritual and cultural components be integral parts of the design of the facility, staff training, services, and administrative policy, not an afterthought. Their insistence is based on anecdotal evidence and is supported by recent systematic research (Smedley, Stith, and Nelson 2002; Ellor, McFadden, and Sapp 1999).

From left to right: Rev. Gary Barbaree of the Pine United Methodist Church; Rev. Ronald Y. Nakasone (Pure Land Buddhist cleric) of the Japanese Religious Federation of San Francisco; Honorable Shirley Dean, mayor of Berkeley; Revs. Sumiyo and Katsumi of Tenrikyo Church. Back: Jim Johnson of Chaparral House. Used with permission from Chaparral House.

To this end, JARF solicited the expertise of the faculties of the SGEC and the GTU to develop and implement "Spirituality and Aging in the Japanese Experience."

The Course

The course was listed in the GTU's 1999–2000 catalog of offerings as follows: "Spirituality and Aging in the Japanese Experience, an interdisciplinary, multi-faith and cross-cultural exploration of the spiritual/cultural needs of older persons, which integrates medical/scientific and spiritual and cultural understanding of aging within a living community." The yearlong, two-semester course consisted of six daylong weekend modules. Offered on Friday and Saturday, one weekend a month, the course was divided into two tracks: (1) medical perspectives on health and aging and (2) religious perspectives on health and spirituality. The former familiarized the student with the physical, medical, ethical, and legal issues, focusing on culturally appropriate geriatric care, assessment, health care interventions, access, and utilization. The second section explored Japanese Buddhist, Christian, Confucian, and Shinto reflections on aging and the human spirit and discussed the Japanese and Japanese American notions of self, family, community, health, dying, and death. Rituals and ceremonies were also part of the instruction. The course set aside the last hour of both days for instruction and practice of calligraphy, massage, tea ceremony, storytelling, folk songs, and hand dance, all of which provided a window into Japanese life.

Continuing education in nursing and social work was offered through Stanford University. Nursing home administrator continuing education credits were also available.

While Marita Grudzen, assistant director of the SGEC, and I were the primary instructors, where and when possible, we enlisted the expertise of instructors who worked and lived in the community. This pedagogical strategy was based on the assumption that the people who were known and loved by the community would be the best teachers. Moreover, since elder care is a community effort, it was important to utilize the wisdom embedded in organizations and individuals committed to providing geriatric care. Additionally, the course would end, and the instructors would leave, but the community organizations and individuals would continue their work with the elderly.

Pedagogical Framework and Implementation

"Spirituality" and "aging" were understood to be aspects of a living, organic, and ever-changing reality that engages health care, social services, and cultural and spiritual traditions in concrete and pressing ways. "Spirituality and aging" is an age-specific experience. For the purposes of the course, the "aging experience" signified individuals sixty-five and older. "Spirituality" referred to experiences that touch and emerge from the deepest core of our humanity, where a person is open to the transcendent and/or immanent. Additionally, we understood "spiritual experience" to be inseparable from the story—history and cultural background, and current context—of the elder person. Thus, the course applied narrative whenever possible on the principle that "we are the stories we tell." Buddhist, Confucian, Shinto, and folk beliefs, as well as the massive displacement of the population during World War II, are part of the Japanese American experience.

Gwen Yeo of the SGEC introduced the course with a historical overview of cohort experiences that impacted the Japanese elders' health and well-being. This cohort experience was recounted by five elders who had been displaced from their homes during World War II. They were invited to address the questions, "To what do you attribute your health and longevity?" and "What is the role of spirituality in your life?" Their cohort experiences were instructive and inspiring, setting the tone for subsequent modules. All the elders, two Christians, two Buddhists, and one from the Konkōkyō, credited their respective faith traditions with giving them the courage to live through their concentration camp experiences and the indignities of racial prejudice.

Eighty-three-year-old Mary Misaki recounted the Buddhist lessons of gratitude that enabled her to endure the loss of her home and livelihood. She drew strength from the images of the Amida Buddha that internees whittled from wood scraps in the interment camp.[3] A native of Florin, California, a farming community approximately ten miles south of Sacramento, and eight months pregnant with her first child at the time, Mrs. Misaki exhibited no bitterness. "We were all together; the accommodations were not the best, but we had a roof over our heads. The food was not great, but we were fed." As with most Japanese American elders, Mrs. Misaki's American experience has not been with rarefied systems of thought but with concrete encounters with governmental and societal discrimination. Her Japanese American story threads its way through oppression, incarceration, injustice, and also with attempts to reconcile traditional culture with modernity.

Cognizant of the plurality of faith traditions and diversity of cultures, the course provided instruction on the different faiths and rituals that are especially urgent during a resident's later and last stages of life and in helping families cope with grief and mourning. To this end, during Module 3, "Rituals and Ceremonies," a Buddhist, Christian, and Konkōkyō cleric each gave a minisermon on "The Story of a Pheasant," a popular folktale. This edifying tale weaves beliefs of transmigration, karmic retribution and reward, and filial piety. We devoted our subsequent session to the relation between mortuary and memorial rites and filial piety.

In short, a one-eyed pheasant fleeing from the local magistrate's hunting party takes refuge in a farmhouse. Believing the pheasant to be the incarnation of her father-in-law, the farmer's wife hides the bird in a large, empty rice pot and rescues it. When the farmer returns from laboring in the fields, the wife relates the incident and shows him the pheasant. Like his father, the pheasant was also blind in the right eye, and with its good eye it scrutinizes the son in the manner the father often did. The son is convinced that the pheasant is indeed his father. "Poor Father must have thought to himself, 'Now that I am a bird, better to give my body to my children for food than to let the hunters have it.'" Thereupon the farmer snatches the pheasant from his wife and wrings its neck. Outraged and terrified, the woman immediately flees and reports the incident to the magistrate. The woman is appropriately rewarded by the authorities, but the farmer is banished from the village (Hearn 1958: 33–36).

As a Buddhist cleric, I understood the tale as a lesson in karmic responsibility. Clearly, the son deserved to be run out of town for his outrageous behavior. For her righteousness the wife reaped an appropriate reward. The law of karmic retribution simply states: one reaps what one sows. Ted Thompson, an Episcopalian priest, spoke of the father's sacrifice for his son as a lesson of love and divine grace, reminding Christians of the need to be open to the unusual ways grace manifests itself. The story is illustrative of humanity's breaking its covenant with God and expulsion from the kingdom of heaven. The Reverend Masato Kawahatsu, noting that Konkōkyō believe that Tenchi Kane no Kami is present in all things and all beings, faults the son for failing to understand *aiyo-kakeyo*.[4] Unaware of this truth, the son unhesitatingly dispatches his father-pheasant, causing distress to himself, his wife, and Kami, who agonizes over human suffering.

In the discussion that followed, it was interesting to note that regardless of their faith the Japanese American participants recoiled at the son's lack of gratitude and reverence toward his father. The father gave abundantly of himself. In addition to being the son's progenitor, the father provided for, protected, and no doubt found a suitable wife for his son. The son did not respond with gratitude and affection but wrung his father's neck to satisfy his own hunger—a most unfilial act. Such disrespect is a violation of the most fundamental relationship between parent and child.

Filial piety, a fundamental tenet in Confucian thinking, pervades Japanese and other East Asian cultures that have come under the influence of Chinese civilization. We spent the remainder of the session discussing *hsiao*, or filiality, a notion that explains much of Japanese social behavior and the importance of the long, complex memorial cycle. In short, the ancient Chinese believed that the feelings nurtured between parent and child are fundamental. The responsibilities and obligations engendered from this most intimate relationship provided and continue to provide East Asians with the inspiration for much of their thought, the basis for their societies and governments, and their ideas of the afterlife.

Filial piety places certain obligations and responsibilities on both parent and child. Parents normally love, provide for, and protect their children without any expectation of being repaid. Nurtured and cared for, children respond with feelings of gratitude, respect, reverence, and affection; later they come to understand that their very existence is owed to their parents and a long line of ancestors. A filial child observes regular memorial rites and makes suitable sacrificial offerings to mourn and remember his or her deceased ancestors. The parent-child relationship is nonegalitarian, and the indebtedness and responsibility associated with this relationship are asymmetrical. It is not a debt that the child incurs voluntarily, and it is a debt that the child can never fully repay (McLaren 1990).

We devoted the rest of the afternoon to mortuary practices. While the historical rationale for the death and memorial rituals interested the participants, Christians learned that their practice of *ohanaryō* (monetary offering for the purchase of flowers for the deceased) was adapted from the Buddhist practice of *okōden* (monetary offering for the purchase of incense for the deceased) and memorial observances. Such monetary offerings from those who had any relation to the deceased are so deeply embedded in Japanese culture that many Christian churches serving Japanese and Japanese Americans have retained this practice. For the Shinto devotee the monetary offering is called *tamagu-shiryo* (monetary offering for purchasing a sprig of the sacred *Cleyera orchnacca* for the deceased).

As part of Track B, Module 4, the section on "Folk Practices, Alternative Beliefs, and Other Coping Therapies," continued the discussion on filiality initiated in Module 3. Buddhists have ritualized the mourning process with a long, complex memorial cycle, which is a synthesis of Indian Buddhist notions of karma, Chinese Confucian thinking on filial piety, and Japanese Shinto ideas of personhood. This memorial ritual cycle, which begins immediately after death and continues for thirty-three or more years, has been modified by the Japanese American Buddhist experience. Traditionally, after the funeral rites the family observes a memorial service every seventh day until the forty-ninth day; subsequently, the hundredth day, the first year, and the third, seventh, thirteenth, seventeenth, twenty-fifth, thirty-third, and forty-ninth years call for special observances. The first seven memorial services are of Indian origin. The hundredth-day and the the first-year and third-year services are of Chinese Confucian origins. To these ten memorial observances the Japanese added the services in the seventh, thirteenth, seventeenth, twenty-fifth, thirty-third, and forty-ninth years. The memorial cycle crystallizes the dynamic and evolving roles of an individual in life and in death, highlighting the importance of family lineage and cohesion, the reciprocity between the living and dead, and the nature of our memories.[5]

Venues

Again, based on the assumption that elder care is a community-wide concern, classes were held on-site. Nihonmachi Terrace in San Francisco's Japantown was our principal instruction site. In addition to being owned by JARF Housing, the site was ideal for a number of reasons. Instruction on-site brought together theoretical training and practical realities. It impressed upon the seminarians the daily reality of elder care and the community's need for more information on geriatrics. Moreover, the centralized location allowed for richer instruction. Thus, for example, our lesson on Buddhism was given at the San Francisco Buddhist Church, two blocks away. The lesson on Japanese tea ceremony was held at the Nichibei Kai's tearoom; it was given by the chief instructor, Mrs. Kikuyo Sekino, who at eighty-eight years is a master of her art and a model elder. The inclusion of Mrs. Sekino and other elders meshed well with Japanese educational pedagogy of mentoring. Our primary mentors were the elders themselves, who provided inspiration and insight in the best ways everyone could partner in providing optimum care. In this way the course highlighted the importance of elders as active participants in their care (Korsch 1984).

The on-site instruction aimed to engage community leaders. Our module "Caregiving and Caring" included a visit to Kimochi Home, a twenty-bed board and care facility owned and operated by Kimochi Senior Services, Inc., two doors away. Alternating instruction sites also engaged community members, who came to see the program as beneficial to their future needs. Instruction was coupled with advocacy. Senior residents at Nihonmachi Terrace provided lunch at nominal cost and donated their profits to the Kokoro building fund. The course evolved into a community event. The last module was held in Berkeley at the Chaparral House (figure 13.1).

Assessment

"Spirituality and Aging in the Japanese Experience," a community-based educational experiment with on-site instruction and the inclusion of medical and religious experts, community leaders, and elders, attempted to replicate the multidisciplinary team approach to elder care currently being advocated (Klein 1996: 57; Smedley, Stith, and Nelson 2002). In addition to receiving the most up-to-date medical information and cultural and historical instruction, the class benefited from the wisdom of the community, especially the elders, who related their life stories and the importance of their faith and culture as they approach the end of life. The student participants also shared their expertise. Notably, the staff of Chaparral House, a skilled nursing facility in Berkeley provided their expertise with Track A, Module 5, "Health Care Services," and Track B Module 6, "Community Resources." The involvement of the community galvanized widespread support. Those who met every week to plan the classes sensed the emergence of a revitalized community core, which was one of the tacit goals of the Kokoro project.

The success of the course was due in part to the student demographics, instructors, and instruction venues. Each module averaged twenty-five participants, which included seminarians, health care professionals, JARF clergy and lay leaders, potential community volunteers, concerned families, and seniors themselves. During the fall 1999 semester, six seminarians from the GTU enrolled in the class for academic credit. Six health care professionals enrolled for continuing education units in nursing and nursing home administration. In the spring 2000 semester, seven seminarians and five health care professions enrolled. Various individuals from the community, JARF clergy and lay leaders, and seniors who resided in Nihonmachi Terrace often drifted in to attend specific modules. At times, there were more than thirty participants. We evolved into a knowledge-sharing community. Carolyn Fee, a nutritionist with the SGEC who provided a scientific breakdown of the Japanese diet, learned the practical ways in which food was prepared at the senior lunch program run by Kimochi Senior Services.

It is difficult to evaluate the outcome of the course, since it was designed to be an integral part of Kokoro Assisted Living's in-service training for staff and other professionals, families, and volunteers who will be part of the care team. The facility began operations in October 2003. However, a review of the course evaluation sheets has been overwhelmingly positive. The success of the course is reflected in anecdotal evidence from former students, who report that they have been sensitized to the needs of peoples of other ethnic and spiritual traditions. Health care professionals and social service professionals who received continuing education units were able to maintain their licenses.

Conclusion

The San Francisco Japanese community has embarked on a unique experiment in elder care. In addition to honoring spiritual and cultural diversity and incorporating up-to-date medical and scientific information, the community is attempting to engage the wisdom and experience that is readily available in organizations and individuals committed to providing geriatric care. The care of elders is a community-wide effort, which all spiritual traditions embrace. "Spirituality and Aging in the Japanese Experience" attempted to crystallize this vision.

APPENDIX: SYLLABUS MOVEMENT AND COURSE MODULES (ABBREVIATED)

Track A: Medical and Scientific (Fridays)
Module 1   Aging in America
   Aging in America
   Ethnogeriatric
Module 2   Health Care
   Diseases of the older adult
   Health promotion and disease prevention
Module 3   Caregiving and Caring
   Physical needs and aids
   Drugs and other therapies
Module 4   Elder Concerns
   Illness and disability
   Dying, death, and bereavement

Module 5   Health Care Services
  Health Care Services
  Aging and spirituality: Insights and clinical applications
Module 6   Older Persons and the Law
  Public policies, professional practices, and polity
  Ethics

Track B: Religious and Cultural (Saturdays)
Module 1   Theory: Context/Spiritual
  Cross-cultural communications
  Spirituality and faith
Module 2   Practical: Folk Beliefs/Cultural Context
  Images of aging
  Expectations of the elderly
Module 3   Family
  Family dynamics
  Rituals and ceremonials
Module 4   Therapies
  Counseling
  Folk practices, alternative beliefs, and other coping therapies
Module 5   Family and Community
  Role of family and community
  Family and minister on the health care team
Module 6   Community Resources
  Model programs and future projects

NOTES

1. Within the Japanese community there is a distinction between Japanese whose primary language is Japanese and those whose primary language is English.

2. The founding congregations were Buddhist Church of San Francisco, Christ Episcopal Church, Gedatsu Buddhist Church of America, Japanese Church of Christ (Christ United Presbyterian Church), Konkōkyō Church of San Francisco (Shinto lineage), Nichiren Buddhist Church of America, Pine United Methodist Church, St. Francis Xavier Catholic Church (St. Benedict–St. Francis Xavier Catholic Church), San Francisco Independent Church, Seventh-Day Adventist Japanese Church, and Sōtō Zen Mission—Sōkōji Temple of San Francisco. Three of the founding congregations have either left San Francisco or disbanded. These are the Gedatsu Buddhist Church, the Seventh-Day Adventist Church, and the San Francisco Independent Church. They have been replaced by Hokkeshū Honnōji Buddhist Temple, Risshō Kōsei Kai Buddhist Church, and Tenrikyō—America West.

3. Amida (Amitābha, Amitāyu) Buddha, the Buddha of Infinite Light and Life, is the principal focus of devotion for the Jōdo and Jōdoshin sects. Mrs. Misaki is a Jōdoshin devotee. Shinran (1173–1262), the founder of the Jōdoshin, scandalized the Buddhist world when he proposed that birth in the Pure Land (Nirvana or Enlightenment) was possible through *shinjin*, or true faith. Heretofore, Buddhism emphasized

the necessity of discipline and morality to purify the mind. Shinran based his theology on the larger *Sukhāvativy ūha sūtra,* in which Amida Buddha has already established the Pure Land for all beings, especially for the most evil. All that is required from the Jōdoshin devotee is to believe wholeheartedly and surrender his or her will to the Buddha's compassionate embrace. Shinran's teaching had great appeal, especially to the farmers and other poor working folk who had neither the time nor the resources to commit endless years to meditation exercises.

4. Konkōkyō was established by Ikigami Konkō-Daijin in 1859. Konkōkyō, "Teaching of the Golden Light," has often been associated with Shintoism because it has incorporated many Shinto features. The Konkō faith believes that the universe is the Grand Shrine of the Tenchi Kane no Kami, the Principle Parent of the universe. Human beings owe their existence and being to the infinite benevolence of the great universe. Since the divine is present in all things, daily life is the setting for spiritual training. By earnestly practicing a life of sincere faith based on the principle of *aiyokakeyo* (mutuality between Tenchi no Kami and human beings), the devotees are able to realize a good life for themselves and their families, which in turn will lead to happiness and world peace wherein both the Kami and human beings will receive mutual fulfillment.

5. Before the introduction of Buddhism and Chinese thought, the Japanese believed that with the end of a physical life a person must begin to cultivate his or her spiritual life. The living assisted the deceased toward ancestorhood through the efficacy of memorial observances, which in turn provided the ancestral spirit the power to protect the family's health and ensure its prosperity (Namihira 1997: 64–65). Local custom designates different years for the *toikiri,* the last service. On the island of Okinawa the thirty-third year memorial service is the last service dedicated specifically to the memory of an individual unless the person is especially noted. The final service marks the complete transition of the individual to an ancestral spirit, or *kami.* After the completion of the service, the individual is honored as an ancestor with all other more distant and even nameless ancestors (Heishiki 1994: 27–31). Other locales may observe the forty-ninth-year memorial service.

While the long memorial cycle ritualistically marks the transformation of a person's identity from a physical being to a *kami* or ancestorhood, it in fact reveals something of the nature of our memories. As years pass, our recollections of the deceased become less and less distinct, and he or she gradually loses his or her individuality. This dimming of memory is seen in the infrequency of families observing the more remote memorial services. Except when a death has occurred at a very young age, after three decades, very often few persons will have any direct memory of the deceased.

REFERENCES

Drummond, Donald C. 1998. The Creation of JALFI: A Senior Assisted Living Project in the Japanese American Community. Unpublished study submitted to the University of San Francisco's Executive Certificate Program for Non-Profit Management.

Ellor, James, Susan McFadden, and Stephen Sapp. 1999. *Aging and Spirituality: The First Decade.* San Francisco: American Society on Aging.

Hearn, Lafcadio. 1958. *Kōtō.* Tokyo: Dai'ichi gakushūsha.

Heishiki Yoshiharu. 1994. Okinawa no ihai saishi. In *Tootoomee to sōsensūhai, higashi ajia ni okeru ihai saishi no hikaku* [Memorial tablets and ancestral veneration: A comparative (study) of memorial tablet rituals in East Asia], ed. Okinawa kokusai daigaku nantō bunka kenkyushō. Naha, Okinawa: Okinawa taimuzu sha.

Home Care Guide Committee. 1994. *Home Care: A Help Guide for Japanese American Seniors and Their Families.* San Francisco: Japanese American Skilled Nursing Home Project.

JALFI Services Committee. 1998. *The JALFI Survey of Assisted Living for Japanese American Seniors in the San Francisco-Bay Area.* San Francisco: American Religious Federation Assisted Living Facility, Inc.

Japanese American Religious Federation Assisted Living Facility, Inc. 1998. *Japanese American Religious Federation Assisted Living Facility, Inc. By-laws.* San Francisco: American Religious Federation Assisted Living Facility, Inc.

Klein, Susan M., ed. 1996. *A National Agenda for Geriatric Education: White Papers.* Vol. 1. Washington, D.C.: Bureau of Health Professions, Health Resources and Services Administration.

Korsch, B. M. 1984. What Do Patients and Parents Want to Know? What Do They Need to Know? *Pediatrics,* 74: 352–66.

McLaren, Ronald. 1990. *Kawaiso,* Justice and Reciprocity: Themes in Japanese and Western ethics. In *Aesthetic and Ethical Values in Japanese Culture,* ed. Jackson H. Bailey, 5–21. Richmond, Ind.: Earlham College.

Murase, Kenji. 1992. *An Executive Summary, Long-Term Health Care Needs of Japanese Americans in the San Francisco Bay Area: A Community Survey.* San Francisco: Japanese American Skilled Nursing Home Project.

Nakasone, Ronald Y. 2000. Buddhist Issues in End-of-Life Decision Making. In *Cultural Issues in End-of-Life Decision Making,* ed. Kathryn L. Braun, James H. Pietsch, and Patricia L. Blanchette, 213–28. Thousand Oaks, Calif.: Sage.

Namihira, Emiko. 1997. Japanese Concepts and Attitude toward Human Remains. In *Japanese and Western Bioethics: Studies in Moral Diversity,* ed. Kazumasa Hoshino, 61–69. Dordrecht: Kluwer Academic Publishers.

Smedley, Brian D., Adrienne Y. Stith, and Alan R. Nelson, eds. 2002. *Unequal Treatment: Confronting Racial and Ethnic Disparities in Healthcare.* Washington, D.C.: National Academy Press.

PART III

Gendering of Suffering and Healing

14

Healing as Resistance: Reflections upon New Forms of American Jewish Healing

Susan S. Sered

Curing is a simple biological fact. Healing is more wide, it overlays above the cure/not cure distinction.
> Rabbi Eric Weiss, Bay Area Jewish Healing Center

Throughout the twentieth century, Jews had been in the vanguard of Americans utilizing conventional biomedicine and biomedically trained physicians; for example, American Jews were among the first to adopt the practice of regular physician visits for healthy babies. Jewish immigrants quickly targeted medical school as the best possible path to success in their adopted country; "my son the doctor" became the symbol of triumph for Jewish families. As Neil Cowan and Ruth Schwartz Cowan have shown, "In the space of one generation the physician replaced the rabbi as the Jewish cultural hero" (1989: 110).

Jewish culture has a long, rich, and venerable corpus of healing traditions, including, for example, the wearing of various protective amulets, consulting rabbis and holy men in order to receive their blessing and their instructions regarding the ritual actions necessary to alleviate illness and other misfortune, and pilgrimage to tombs of saints associated with healing (see Sered 1992; Lesses 1998). These sorts of traditional practices, commonplace among Jews in North Africa and Asia as well as in Eastern Europe and Israel, did not survive in the United States except among small groups of Hasidic Jews living in a few tightly knit communities. Observers of Jewish life in the United States throughout most of the twentieth century would surely have had to search far and wide to find public instances of Jewish ritual healing or even to find significant interest among Jews in religious responses to illness. In American Jewish culture the way to deal with illness was to seek the "best" internist, specialist, surgeon, or psychiatrist, a networking task made possible through the extensive presence of Jews in the medical profession. For several generations of American Jews, the title "the big man," or even better, "the big man in New York," meant one thing—the chief of staff, and the words "good man" (as in the phrase "I'll send you to a good man") had nothing to do with moral worth but rather was understood by all to mean a physician, and preferably a specialist.

This chapter explores the still evolving, loosely structured Jewish healing movement that has taken American Jewry somewhat by surprise as it has developed and spread during the last two decades of the twentieth century and the first years of the twenty-first.[1]

American Jewish Healing

Initiated in the 1980s, most likely synchronously by several small groups of feminists, rabbis and rabbinical students on the East and West Coasts, the Jewish healing movement is more a convergence of projects and programs developed by individuals around the country than a centralized or ritually or theologically unified association or organization. There is, however, a great deal of communication among Jewish healing activists both in the context of regional and national conferences and via the many and varied publications put out by individuals and groups (see, for example, Freeman and Abrams 1995; Weintraub 1994; Friedman 2001). A newsletter called *The Outstretched Arm*, published by the National Center for Jewish Healing (in New York), has a distribution list of 10,000 names. Many branches of Jewish Family Services, a nationwide social services organization, recently have taken on commitments to support Jewish healing activities in the local communities it serves. There now are more than thirty communities nationwide with local healing centers in various stages of development.[2]

Contemporary American Jewish healing events include community-sponsored rituals and support services for the elderly and the chronically ill; private healing offered by individual practitioners boasting a wide variety of techniques and training; synagogue-based healing services led by rabbis, cantors, and laypeople; and small-group healing rituals carried out regularly or intermittently in response to the needs of friends or community members. Healing services vary greatly from community to community, and there is no standard liturgy used by all groups, yet some of the following elements do tend to be found at many of the services: communal singing, an opportunity for participants to speak, silent prayer or meditation, some sort of teaching based on Jewish sources, guided visualizations, physical contact among participants (holding hands in a circle, hugging one another before or after the service), and recitation of Hebrew or English prayers. Healing services take place in Reform, Reconstructionist, and Conservative synagogues. Community chaplains and programs organized by Jewish Family Services serve all Jews: unaffiliated, liberal, and orthodox. Orthodox synagogues would be unlikely to hold innovative healing services but might well organize study sessions on healing and committees to extend help to ill community members.

In this chapter I seek to contextualize this movement both in terms of American medicine and in terms of Judaism. This exercise is particularly important because the Jewish healing movement, for the most part, does not challenge the hegemony of either mainstream medical or Jewish institutions. Physicians, psychotherapists, massage therapists, acupuncturists, cantors, and rabbis are among the supporters of the Jewish healing movement, often serving on boards of various Jewish healing organizations.[3]

Unlike religious healing in more traditional cultures, late twentieth-century and early twenty-first-century American religious healing tends to be one of an array of healing options voluntarily engaged in by individuals struggling with illness and is rarely seen as the primary or most authoritative of those options.[4] Contemporary American religious healers are, implicitly or explicitly, in dialogue with nonreligious healing systems, as well as in dialogue across faith traditions. Within the marketplace of contemporary America health care, individuals pick and choose, try out and abandon a variety of methods, and contribute to the cross-fertilization of diverse healing approaches. This sort of marketplace culture limits the possibility that religious healing will present itself, or be experienced by practitioners, clients, or congregation members, as hegemonic.

Knowing that patrons of Jewish healing utilize at least one and more likely several other healing systems and that one of those systems—biomedicine—has a uniquely powerful position in the healing marketplace demands that Jewish healing develop a self-definition that sets it off from the other therapeutic options available in the United States. To draw out the healing map in very broad strokes, it tends to be the case that Jewish healing patrons turn to mainstream medical care, often at the hands of noted specialists in state-of-the-art hospital departments, for cure and medical treatment; to psychotherapy to help cope with the distress of illness; to a variety of complementary and alternative therapies that offer alleviation of symptoms and a personal touch often absent from mainstream medical treatment; and to Jewish healing to ask about the meaning of illness, to learn what their tradition has to offer those who are ill, to reconnect to their roots, and to explore the possibility of attaining spiritual health even while the body hurts or fails. The order in which I have listed these healing modalities reflects the typical order in which they are pursued by patrons of Jewish healing.[5] The first step in the usual healing

trajectory is to consult physicians in hope of cure; the second step is psychotherapy and various types of integrative and mind-body therapies for help with
coping, stress reduction, and symptomatic relief. Finally, religious healing is
turned to either in hope of miracles or in hope of reaching a deeper moral or
spiritual understanding of suffering.

American Jewish healing is not intended to be a "stand-alone" healing
system: Jewish healers do not urge clients or congregation members to dis-
continue mainstream or holistic treatments. Significantly, the oldest and still
premier Jewish healing service in the Boston area is held at a synagogue located
in the heart of the medical district that includes Beth Israel Deaconess Hospital, Brigham and Women's Hospital, Children's Hospital, and other internationally known medical facilities. Rather, Jewish healing concentrates on
developing Jewish identity as an alternative to "sick role" identity, on constructing ties to the Jewish community as an alternative to the social isolation often
brought about by long-term illness, on offering "Jewish time" (holidays, Shab-
bat) as an alternative to the hospital- or medication-driven calendar that tends
to dominate the lives of those who are ill, and on lauding spirituality as an
alternative to the painful corporeality experienced by many who live with illness. As Rabbi Dayle Freedman, who has worked extensively with Jewish elderly in her role as chaplain of the Philadelphia Geriatric Center explains,
"Jewish life has the capacity to touch the hearts of broken people and to create
a subversive culture of respect and dignity. I help people live in Jewish time,
and not just institutional [hospital] time."

Healing, Not Curing

"It isn't always possible to cure, but it's always possible to heal."

"This is about healing, not about curing. If you want to be
cured, go see a doctor."

Central to the American Jewish healing movement is the distinction between healing and curing. While this distinction does not exist in Hebrew (the
word *r'fuah* encompasses both), it lies at the ritual and ideological heart of
contemporary American Jewish healing.[6] The sentiments, and even the
phrases, expressed in the epigraphs to this section are heard often at Jewish
healing events. Rabbi Nancy Flam, one of the pioneers of American Jewish
healing, explains the meaning of healing:

[In a traditional prayer we had the words] *r'fuat hanefesh urfuat
haguf* [healing/curing of the soul and healing/curing of the body]. So
we said that the Rabbis must have recognized different dimensions,

not only curing the body but healing the *nefesh*, the whole person, the displaced role in the family, disorientation in terms of self, being shaken up, the relationship with God, financial burdens. Healing is a sense of wholeness, perspective, reintegration, and not the removal of the tumor or clearing of infection. We always made this distinction, sort of as a disclaimer, but also to address the dimension of the person that was suffering and not just the disease.

Rabbi Simkha Weintraub of the National Center for Jewish Healing shares similar reflections: "[Healing is] reaffirming that a person is more than a physiological entity. Reassertion of emotional, psychological, religious, cultural, social dimensions of being human. Attending to the whole person. So many people are cured but not healed."

The Jewish healing movement has emerged during a period in which the power of conventional biomedicine is being challenged from many directions. First and foremost, a gradual and growing awareness of the failure of biomedicine to cure many of the chronic diseases of the late twentieth century has contributed to the search for other sorts of responses and solutions for individuals living with pain, depression, chronic fatigue, limited physical mobility, and so on. Jewish healing services, like a wide range of other religious and holistic healing venues, tend to be populated by people suffering from chronic rather than acute illnesses. Those who attend Jewish healing events describe themselves as living long-term with cancer, infertility, AIDS, or diabetes or as serving as the primary caregiver of a family member suffering from mental illness, Alzheimer's, or other degenerative diseases.

At the same time, emerging recognition of the importance of palliative and end-of-life care, especially in the hospice movement, has opened the door to notions of medical care that go beyond the emphasis on curing that has characterized most of twentieth-century American medicine. This shift in focus has had a profound influence on the Jewish healing movement. The development of this movement has come also in the wake of self-help groups and organized patients' rights groups, such as AIDS and breast cancer support and activist groups that have demanded that health care institutions provide information to patients, guarantee informed consent, and include patients in an active way in decision-making processes. Indeed, several of the founders and leaders of the Jewish healing movement made their way to Jewish healing via AIDS activism.

The Jewish healing movement is part of a cultural milieu in which alternative medicine of myriad types has been proliferating both in terms of quantity and in terms of variety. The movement quite consciously situates itself in the sphere of holistic, mind-body, and alternative medicine. Most obvious, the paraphernalia and vocabulary of the holistic health movement are part and parcel of Jewish healing: words such as "energy" and practices such as guided visualizations are commonplace in Jewish healing settings. The emphasis on spirituality and healing of the whole person does not, for the most part, preclude attention to the body. Rabbi Miriam Klotz, healing coordinator at the Kimmel-Spiller Jewish Healing Center of Jewish Family Services of Delaware, emphasizes the "integrity of physical healing and Jewish spirituality. . . . Even before entering rabbinical school, I became a yoga teacher and therapist and massage therapist. I entered the Reconstructionist Rabbinical College with the intention of combining those parts of myself within a Jewish rubric. I wanted to bring those things to Judaism. I was working as a healer already."

While the Jewish healing movement does not pose overt institutional challenges to conventional biomedicine (for example, participants are not encouraged to avoid or terminate standard medical treatment) the insistence that their concern is with "healing" rather than "curing" often is presented in a manner that diminishes the value of cure. Curing—the domain of physicians—is reduced to mere mechanical or chemical manipulations of the finite physical body. Healing, in contrast, has to do with the whole person, the infinite divine, and the enduring community.

It is telling that the severe chronic illness of Debbie Friedman, the premier songwriter of Jewish healing songs, is popularly attributed to iatrogenic causes (this was pointed out to me, often in whispers, by dozens of informants). I was repeatedly told by those who love her music that physicians had given her medicine that made her sick, and that out of her suffering and illness she wrote the healing songs that so many American Jews have found to be exceptionally potent. As healer and songwriter Hanna Tiferet Siegel relates, "Debbie Friedman was very ill for a long time. In a wheelchair. She really suffered. What came out after was powerful healing music. That is her album [*Renewal of Spirit*]. She is definitely divinely inspired. She doesn't read music." Statements like these contrast the natural wisdom ("She doesn't read music") of Jewish healing with the inability of educated physicians to cure her suffering. Debbie herself concurs that her illness was caused by medicine: "It is probably a genetic predisposition that was triggered by some medication I was given." The trajectory she traces goes like this: "medicine, I became toxic, misdiagnosed, mismanaged, more medicine. They said I was depressed and doubled the dose of Prozac." Echoing the sense of marginality experienced by many American women vis-à-vis the medical establishment, Debbie draws attention to the connection between gender hierarchy and the failures of biomedicine. Frankly asserting that her chronic illness was caused, or at least exacerbated, by male physicians, Debbie notes, "Doctors would have taken my symptoms seriously if I had been a man."

The often repeated phrase "It is not always possible to cure, but healing is always possible" seems to me to represent a significant ideological challenge to scientific medicine of the late twentieth century, which posits that cure *is* always possible—provided that science has sufficient resources and time at its disposal. The cracking of the human genome, following upon a century of medical successes in surgical procedures, organ transplants, immunization programs, and fighting infection, holds out the promise that cure for all disease is just around the corner. The paradigm of late twentieth-century biomedicine has been one in which death is equated with failure (one of many reasons that physicians are obligated to perform heroic measures to "save" dying people).

This paradigm is vigorously rejected by many Jewish healing activists. In the words of Hanna Tiferet Siegel, "Healing ultimately is about how we face death. How do we approach our lives knowing that we will eventually die. How do we face tragedies, face letting go [of people who die]." Similar thoughts were expressed by Chaya Sarah Sadeh, a healer and teacher who trained as a nurse in the 1960s: "Curing—that is what doctors talk about, maintaining life—that the person lives at all costs. The medical model is compartmentalized. Healing—a true healing may be death. True healing to me is holistic, integrated. A doctor would cut out a tumor. I help the client understand it and know how it got there and what the lesson is and embrace it. All the people I work with want to know that. To create a unity out of a duality."

For American Jewish healers, death is not an enemy to be overcome. In the words of healer Matia Angelou, "Death is the ultimate healing, if you can do it right and be conscious." As Rabbi Eliot Baskin, the Jewish community chaplain of Denver, explains, when he works with people close to death, "The point is r'fuah shlema [full healing], not cure. Healing. If someone is at peace they can die with a sense of completeness and closure rather than anger. I help people let go and die. Get people to hold hands around the bedside. . . . Aggressive comfort measures instead of aggressive health care measures."

Deconstructing "Health"

On a larger scale, I would argue that the Jewish healing approach to the body deconstructs one of the most profound premises of American culture— the promise that unlimited scientific and medical progress will ultimately lead to the conquest of disease, decay, and death (cf. Callahan 1998). Mainstream American culture, or at least the American culture portrayed in the popular media, seems to equate health with success. Perhaps a legacy of the Protestant ethic, middle-class Americans seem to believe that good health is a real possibility for most people and that illness is some sort of personal failure. Individuals diagnosed with cancer are likely to be suspected of in some way having failed to "take care" of themselves. The American cancer industry, utilizing doublespeak jargon in which cancer screening is called "secondary prevention," has contributed to the belief that if one is "good enough," comes for regular mammograms, and lives a "healthy lifestyle," illness can be averted.

The message is that illness not only *can* be averted but *should* be, and that if one becomes ill, it may well be because of improper behavior or, at the very least, failure of will.

In fact, as Amanda Porterfield has argued, in contemporary American culture

> wellness itself has taken on spiritual dimensions. Aerobics, dance, hiking, football, horseback riding, massage, and cooking have all been associated with spiritual experience at least partly because of their connection to health, wellness, and life itself. In American culture especially, the scientific and technical aspects of these activities are an important part of their appeal. The focus on effective techniques for attaining both spiritual and physical well-being reflected a general American tendency to see things in practical terms and to expect beneficial results from investments of time and energy. (2001: 195; see also Whorton 1988)

Jewish healing, like many other forms of contemporary American religious healing, challenges that stance by presenting illness both as an opportunity for spiritual growth and as a normal part of life rather than as a failure of will. The refusal of the Jewish healing movement to work on "curing," I would argue, constitutes resistance to mainstream American beliefs in the ultimate perfectibility of the body.[7] Jewish healing activists challenge the kinds of "blaming the victim" ideologies omnipresent within both conventional and alternative medicine. Rachel Cowan, one of the pioneers and greatest supporters of American Jewish healing, sadly describes the hospital experience of her husband, Paul, during his illness and eventual death from leukemia: "It was like 'What did you do wrong that you ended up here?' "

Resistance to popular notions of blaming those who are ill for having somehow failed to "take care of themselves" is clarified by Matia Angelou: "I don't believe that people bring on their own illness. We've almost gotten to the point of saying that 'if you have any problems in your life you caused them.' I don't believe that. Life happens, we live in fragile physical bodies. We take care of them the best way we know how. For whatever stresses, environmental, accidental reasons—I don't believe we make decisions to put ourselves in that place to cause it [illness]. I do believe that once it happens we have a choice about how we will relate to it, learn from it."

Malka Young, the director of an innovative interfaith healing project in Framingham, Massachusetts, questions conventional notions of illness and health as discrete, even opposed, states: "I found a lump in my breast six weeks after a mammogram in which the radiologist told me 'You don't have breast cancer.' This was inappropriate. He should have said he doesn't see breast cancer." Young's critique is threefold: technology has its limits, medical professionals are not omniscient, and anyone can appear "healthy"—even to sophisticated imaging equipment—yet still be "sick." Despite a rocky personal history of multiple chronic and acute illnesses, the high level of creativity, activity, and vibrancy that Young brings to her work further subverts the "sick"-versus-"well" dichotomy.

Billion-dollar cosmetics industries, the burgeoning profession of personal trainers, and of course the ever-increasing use of cosmetic surgery all proclaim that if one tries hard enough, one can achieve corporeal perfection. The Jewish healing movement, while not condemning or overtly opposing these practices, offers an alternative to a mainstream cultural ethos that defines illness, disfigurement, old age, and being "fat" as personal failures that need to be cured— for a fee—at the hands of experts. Moreover, and I see this point as especially significant, Jewish healing has little or no paraphernalia associated with it— patrons are not asked to purchase any equipment, and healers do not need to assemble esoteric or expensive ritual objects. In this way as well, the Jewish healing movement resists the consumer-driven corporeal ethos of American culture.

While women significantly outnumber men as both healers and participants in healing events, a significant number of gay men have made crucial contributions to the movement's rise. The prominence of women and gay men in American Jewish healing reflects the ambivalent relationships that both populations have had with both biomedicine and traditional Judaism. Female bodies and gay male bodies share the honor of having been perceived both by medicine and by religion as in need of cure. Over the course of the twentieth century, the medical establishment has removed women's wombs as a "cure" for hysteria, performed a variety of harsh "procedures" to "cure" homosexuality, defined homosexuality as an illness to be "cured" by psychotherapy, and produced drugs to "cure" such female "syndromes" as PMS and menopause. The idea that illness is caused by "improper" gendered behavior continues to resonate in American culture. For example, articles regularly appear in the press "blaming" the rise in infertility on women "choosing" to have careers, and HIV/AIDS has been interpreted by many, especially on the Christian right, as God's punishment for "rampant" homosexuality. Traditional Judaism has similarly labeled homosexuality as a sin and thus in need of cure, or even better, punishment, and women's normal bodily experience of menstruation has been defined by Jewish law and custom as polluting to the community and in need of ritual cure via separation and then immersion in the ritual bath. Small wonder, I should think, that the Jewish healing movement reiterates that it is "not about curing."

In short, while the Jewish healing movement does not overtly challenge the practices of conventional biomedicine, it does subvert the paradigms on which the system of biomedicine rests. I shall now suggest that the Jewish healing movement has adopted a similar approach to "conventional" Judaism.

Healing and Tradition

Leaders of the Jewish healing movement stress the Jewishness of what they do. Penina Adelman, a writer and social worker who has developed rituals and programs for the mentally ill, explains, "Torah and tradition have so much to offer those who are hurting and want to be part of the community. . . . I use Jewish study and celebrate holidays as part of this job [at the Jewish Healing Connections in Newton, Massachusetts]." Jewish healing services always incorporate at least some Hebrew, even when few participants understand what the Hebrew words mean. The phrases "our tradition" and "our Jewish tradition" are reiterated in a variety of contexts. Patrons of Jewish healing events are told "Our tradition has a lot to offer people struggling with illness" and "Our tradition is rich in healing resources." The authenticity of American Jewish healing is reinforced by healer-songwriter Hanna Tiferet Siegel, who explains that she finds Jewish ideas and phrases that she had never been taught "coming through" (spiritually) in the songs she writes.

Robert Orsi has described the proliferation of new religions in the United States as "wildly creative and innovative, where there seems to be no end to the fecundity of religious imaginings" (1997: 11). Amanda Porterfield has similarly described the "personalized forms of spirituality that incorporate elements from various traditions and into which new elements can be added at will" that have proliferated in the United States since the 1960s (2001: 12). Yet I would argue neither that the American Jewish healing movement is "wildly creative" nor that new elements are "added at will." Rather, the movement's leaders are committed to a process of careful and conscious syncretism in which elements gleaned from New Age spirituality, gospel singing, Buddhist meditation, Christian pastoral counseling and spiritual direction, and more generally the full repertoire of American religious practice and thought are translated into ritual idioms that "feel" authentically Jewish.

Rabbi Nancy Flam explained to me, "If I went too far over the edge, chanting 'om'—red flags would come up. But usually it's sort of *parve* [neutral; literally neither meat nor milk] enough and syntonic with secular norms of self-help groups, and so on. Nothing huge comes up to challenge it. It has to do with connection to the past. It's got some Hebrew. It feels comfortable. . . . And the need is so great. You've provided a venue, and it's good enough because the need is so great." Flam describes the conscious syncretism of American Jewish healing: "We saw people we knew going to Buddhist retreats and Christian devotional literature. [And so we said,] Why not Jewish resources? On complete faith [knowing nothing] we postulated that the wisdom is there [in Jewish sources]. We need to translate it and make up what doesn't exist. . . . We developed our approach very intuitively. We looked for texts that support what we knew about healing. . . . I had done the clinical pastoral education course [a Christian-oriented course]. For me, sitting with suffering felt comfortable, familiar."

As Rabbi Amy Eilberg puts it, "We creatively adopt things from within the tradition. . . . This is hybrid work. . . . I use traditional resources sometimes in a traditional way and sometimes in a less traditional way. I encourage people in gratitude practice. Mantra work. Jewish music."

The ritual form that has been most developed within the Jewish healing movement is singing. The songs heard at healing rituals include both traditional liturgical phrases, often put to new music, and healing songs written during the past decade that incorporate words, phrases, or images from traditional Jewish culture. A song that has become synonymous with Jewish healing is Debbie Friedman's "MiSheBerach":

> Mi-sheberach avotaynu, mikor habracha l'emotaynu[8]
> May the Source of Strength who blessed the ones before us;
> Help us find the courage to make our lives a blessing and let us say,
> Amen.
> Mi-sheberach emotaynu, Mikor habracha l'avotaynu
> Bless those in need of healing with r'fuah sh'layma
> the renewal of body, the renewal of spirit, and let us say, Amen. And
> let
> us say, Amen.

Sung to a moving melody, the song radiates inspiration and pathos. Several people whom I interviewed told me that this song helped them "get through chemotherapy" or other difficult illness episodes. In the words of one woman, "I have had mystical experiences listening to Debbie Friedman. Like gospel music. Our life experiences." I shall return to the theological imagery of this song later on, but here it interests me to reflect upon how some of the movement leaders with whom I have spoken explain the popularity of Debbie Friedman's songs: "There is a little Hebrew in them, which gives a sense of authenticity."[9]

Healing and Community

Despite energetic framing of American Jewish healing in terms of tradition and authenticity, the basic paradigms of contemporary American Jewish healing differ as radically from the traditional Jewish healing of Eastern Europe, Asia, North Africa, and Israel as they do from mainstream American biomedical culture. While there certainly have been variations through the ages and across disparate Jewish societies, it seems to be the case that in traditional Jewish cultures illness typically has been interpreted as punishment for sin, a conceptualization found in biblical texts and further elaborated in midrashic

(exegetical) and folk stories. Healing generally has been cure and miracle oriented, felt to be an ancient tradition, and oriented toward the written Hebrew
text (even if the person being healed could not read or understand it). Traditional Jewish healing contexts have tended to be socially and theologically hierarchical, practiced in a dyadic framework between the healer and the patient
or in a family framework, and linked to the charisma of particular healers.
Most traditional Jewish healers (at least those utilizing Jewish texts and liturgical formulas rather than nonliterary substances such as foods or minerals)
have been men. Cults of holy men were more developed among Jews of North
Africa and Hasidic Jews in Eastern Europe than among non-Hasidic Eastern
European Jews (*misnagdim*), yet the underlying conceptualization of connections between sin and illness and good behavior (*mitzvot*) and healing have
been widespread throughout the Jewish world.

The traditional Jewish prototype of intercessory prayer is laid out in a biblical passage (Numbers 12: 1–15) in which Aharon asks Moses to pray to God on
Miriam's behalf after she has been afflicted with leprosy as a punishment for
inappropriate words or acts. This paradigm continues to be well known to Middle Eastern and Hasidic Jews who ask a variety of rabbis and holy men—alive
or dead—for their blessings. Moses' cry, "Heal her now, O God, I pray thee,"
has remained the conventional liturgical formulaic healing prayer. Interestingly, this healing plea is one of the few utterances in Jewish culture in which
the feminine form ("heal her") is used generically (the masculine is often interpreted as a "generic masculine," but the feminine almost never is).

In contrast, the contemporary American Jewish healing movement declares that the individual is not to blame for illness. Quite the opposite: American Jewish healers explain that illness often causes the soul to become damaged, rather than a damaged soul leading to illness as in the traditional model.
Illness, in the American version, leads to social isolation, loneliness, depression, and loss of hope. Whereas in the biblical text exclusion from the community is a typical punishment for misbehavior and the prescribed response
to the illness of leprosy (as in the case of the Miriam narrative just mentioned),
in the American Jewish healing movement exclusion from the community is
what healing sets out to overcome. A key goal of the movement is to break up
the illness–exclusion–loneliness trajectory by strengthening the bonds between
those who are ill and the wider Jewish community. Unlike traditional Jewish
healing, American Jewish healing is not cure or miracle oriented, makes little
use of esoteric texts and great use of communal singing, and is understood to
be innovative. Above all, contemporary American Jewish healing is communal
rather than dyadic and highly egalitarian in the sense that the healers and
patrons together form a community of sufferers.

Penina Adelman, who has created rituals and support groups for mentally
ill Jews, explains, "Mentally ill people feel disenfranchised from the Jewish
community. . . . They practice [doing Jewish rituals] in our group, and then they

feel confident to participate in the community. It is also spiritual." She goes on to clarify that her work is really about healing the individual vis-à-vis the community. "My goal is not to heal them of their mental illness but to help them be part of the Jewish community." The implication is that the illness is on both sides: the Jewish community "disenfranchises and doesn't understand or care about these people, and these people feel cut off from the community. Both sides are in need of healing."

Rachel Cowan recalls the importance of connection during the final illness of her husband, Paul: "Being part of the synagogue was very important. A counselor told him Judaism makes you cling to your life and body too much, and he should be macrobiotic. Paul thought the opposite, and people in the congregation cooked for him every day. That's what he wanted. The room was full of cards. He received love and was valued by the shul [synagogue]."

Rabbi Simkha Weintraub expressed a similar sentiment: "Home-cooked food for people with cancer. This is the way to get to sick people—not support groups." Again, in his words, the implication is that true healing necessarily involves the community providing care and services for ill members, a model very different from the Miriam-Moses scenario, and even different from the secular support group scenario in which those who are ill form a closed group in which only they support one another.

The impact of this community-oriented approach has reached Jewish congregations around the country via a highly significant innovation over the past fifteen years or so in the format of the conventional synagogue prayer for healing of the sick. Until recently, at most American synagogues the traditional Hebrew "MiSheBerach" prayer was recited during the Torah service. Typically, the rabbi would quietly whisper the names of individuals on whose behalf he had been asked to pray. Now it has become the norm at many synagogues around the country for members to stand up and say aloud the names of ill friends, neighbors, and relatives. The public recitation of the names of those who are sick reflects a new approach in which illness is not a stigma, and in which the community at large is expected to reach out to those who are ill.

The interpretation of healing as community connection (in contrast to illness, which is isolating, and curing and magic, which are dyadic) seems to me to be the most pervasive and spiritually and morally powerful aspect of American Jewish healing. Marjorie Sokoll, director of Jewish Healing Connections of the Jewish Family and Children's Service in Newton, Massachusetts, explains: "The essence is connection. People going through times of trouble—not to feel alone. The essence is feeling connected." Rabbi Simkha Weintraub describes how he evaluates the success of a healing group: "If someone reports that they feel less isolated after a support group, or felt able to ask their own rabbi to work with them like I do. Empower people to ask their own rabbi to pray for them. Reconnection to the organized Jewish community."

Carol Hausman, a psychotherapist and the coordinator of the Washington

Jewish Healing Network, expands on this idea: "Compassion and helping others is a tool of healing. *Hesed* [loving-kindness]. That's why groups are healing. These are not regular support groups. We rarely talk about the illness. People don't even say in introduction why they came. Rather, we talk about ways to heal. We learn that helping others is healing. [In one group there was] a bereaved father whose son committed suicide on a Tuesday. He now volunteers at the Hebrew Old Age Home every Tuesday. Other people in the group learned about this and started doing similar kinds of things."

Rabbi Rafael Goldstein of the Jewish Healing Center of San Diego has organized volunteers to visit sick members of the community. As he explains, "I do this job because of community. People who have community will live better as long as they live. What we learned from AIDS is to rally people around ill people and in so doing generate healing."

Rabbi Eliot Baskin of Denver trains volunteers to assist in visiting the sick. His teaching includes instruction in carrying out rituals and in active listening: "My goal is creating a healing community that includes volunteers, networks, healing services, pastoral counseling. . . . Denver is beautiful because of the mountains, but there is a sense of rootedless-ness, an immigrant community, and it can be lonely and isolating. The tradition of the Marlboro man. We need to build a sense of community. . . . People here are very spiritual but not religious. But when the poop hits the fan, you need other people."

Songwriter Debbie Friedman understands the power of music to create community:

> Music is what does it—it resonates for people. Music has never
> been just about fun. [The music is so important in healing services
> because] the objective is to be part of a community, to create a sense
> of community and support. . . . This is about people in their chal-
> lenges—physical, spiritual, emotional. When you are in that space
> [of suffering], there is a sense of isolation. No one understands.
> Your pain is extraordinary. You feel that no one else can understand
> your pain, it is only yours. At the healing service people stand to-
> gether. It's almost like *bikur holim* [visiting the sick]. They say that if
> you visit the sick you take away one-sixtieth of their pain. Like in
> food one-sixtieth.[10] That is what it is like at the service.

Referring to the public singing of her version of the "MiSheBerach" prayer that has now become common in American synagogues, Friedman comments, "I started singing it, and it picked up. It is a step away from the self. It is sung not just for oneself. Knowing you can give someone a blessing is empowering and makes life meaningful. It is not enough to focus on the self. We have to know that our actions contribute to the healing or destruction of the world. Our actions have powerful impacts. We might feel like we're nothing, dirt and ashes. And that is the problem. There is clearly a ripple affect."

Healing, Not Superstition

> We're not into magic and superstition. This is about healing—
> wholeness [shlemut]. . . . The stuff in Israel with holy men and tombs
> is curing. Superstition. American healing is in the sense of creating
> wholeness—shlemut, which allows you to realize that you are more
> than your illness.
>
> —Rabbi Moshe Waldoks, Temple Beth Zion,
> Brookline, Massachusetts

I have already pointed out that the words "We are not about curing, we are about healing" is something of a motto among Jewish healing activists. In addition to the follow-up sentence mentioned earlier ("If you are looking to be cured, go see a doctor"), the curing-healing motto is often followed by "We're not about miracles here" or "We're not into superstition." These last two declarations are meant to distinguish American Jewish healing from traditional Jewish healing practices and from Christianity, which assumedly are "about miracles" and "into superstition." Rabbi Nancy Flam explains in an interview: "We don't do these services so that people will be cured and throw away their crutches. One always hopes for people to get better physically, but the truth for all of us is that we will get sick and die. These services are to strengthen the spirit and the bonds of community, to provide hopefully an environment where God can be felt" (Vara 1997).

Movement founder, pastoral counselor, and healing activist Rabbi Amy Eilberg frames the healing-curing issue in terms of emphasizing r'fuat hanefesh (healing the spirit) rather than r'fuat haguf (healing the body). She offers three reasons for this emphasis:

> One, it is important to us not to encourage or be associated with be-
> lief in magic or superstition. Two, we want to be humble in this
> work, acknowledging that we cannot possibly know what practices
> or experiences will affect healing. We shy away from claims about
> the possibility of physical cure because we want to be sure to re-
> member that God is the Healer, and the ways of God's healing are
> far more mysterious than we can know or predict. Three, we em-
> phasize r'fuat hanefesh because we want to encourage people to ap-
> preciate the many spiritual possibilities that reside within experi-
> ences of illness and suffering. I believe that sometimes spiritual
> well-being does affect the course of a disease process, but we can
> never predict when or how. We want to encourage people to culti-
> vate spiritual growth and wellness and possibility for its own sake,
> in the midst of the challenges of life.

Objecting to the whole traditional package of "magical" acts and divine retribution for ritual infringements, Debbie Friedman relates, "When I got sick, I was told to check my *mezuzot*." (These are the small boxes containing certain biblical verses that Jews traditionally have put on their doorposts. A common explanation given by traditional rabbis and holy men for illness or misfortune is that the verses inside the *mezuzah* are damaged.) "I didn't do it," Debbie explains. "I didn't like the whole idea."

Founders and leaders of the Jewish healing movement are concerned with showing the wider Jewish community that they are not too "far out." As Rabbi Amy Eilberg explains:

> We have been very sensitive to the possibility that the mainstream Jewish community would see our work as too funky, marginal, inaccessible. The group of us [founders] are basically mainstream people. We wanted very much for the mainstream Jewish community to get the message that what we are doing is Jewishly authentic and accessible to all kinds of Jews—not just those with active spiritual lives. We were aware that wonderful healing work was being done in the Renewal community, for example, at Elat Chayyim [a Jewish retreat center] and Renewal Kallot. But we wanted to make sure that more conventional Jews didn't think that Jewish healing was only for Jews who like a countercultural, progressive style.

When I ask for an example of what would be considered "too funky," she mentions amulets or "certain approaches to chanting that cross the boundary into magical faith healing." Overly "funky," then, includes both New Age novelties and old-fashioned superstition.

While kabbalistic notions often are incorporated into Jewish healing writings and liturgy, many Jewish healing activists express suspicion of the kabbalah centers (such as the one in Los Angeles run by the charismatic Rabbi Philip Berg). Rabbi Moshe Waldoks of Temple Beth Zion in Brookline, Massachusetts, says "the kabbalistic centers that Madonna and Roseanne have gone to, non-Jews go to this, where they get a red thread [to be worn as an amulet] and are told that holding the Zohar[11] even if you don't read it has magical power. This is very different from the healing of healing services. At the kabbalistic centers of this sort people pay $1,000 for red thread or the Zohar. It is a rip-off."

My sense is that the critique is not of ritual objects per se but of commercialism, exploitation, and the notion that if one purchases an object or recites a formula, God will be induced to produce a cure. In fact, a number of Jewish healers encourage clients and practitioners to create their own ritual art. One of the greatest proponents of material creativity is Rabbi Rayzel Raphael, whose house is filled with a blessing quilt, tambourines (associated with the biblical Miriam), *hamsa* (the traditional "hand of Fatima" amulet), ritual cups, moon symbols, candles, goddess and angel statues, healing bowls, ritual jewelry, and even a ritual tissue box used during emotionally laden moments.

For American Jewish healers and healing activists the issue is not whether material objects are intrinsically powerful but rather how those objects fit into social and theological arrangements. Rabbi Rafael Goldstein of San Diego told me, "I give people thread from Kever Rachel [the tomb of the biblical matriarch Rachel]. One woman said that the link connected her to women in Israel praying for her." This model, it seems to me, differs radically from the more conventional Jewish understanding of selected holy individuals who possess unique abilities to imbue physical objects with curative powers. Rabbi Goldstein neither sells the thread nor suggests that it is imbued with magical powers.

What is encapsulated by the words "superstition" and "magic" for American Jewish healing activists is the entire dyadic, gendered model of healing that has in fact been mainstream in most traditional Jewish cultures. American Jewish healing challenges that model through an emphasis on community. The miracles and superstitions disdained by the contemporary American Jewish healing movement are part of a hierarchical theology in which God stands outside of human experience and chooses to grant or not to grant healing dispensations, often via selected holy men and rabbis. The theological vision of the Jewish healing movement, in contrast, is radically egalitarian. In the words of Rabbi Amy Eilberg, "In my work I am increasingly drawing on spiritual direction, the holiness of human encounters, and the attempt to recognize divine—in some sense, whatever that means as the person understands it—presence in life, in circumstances, in others, in oneself. This increasingly informs the way I listen. I have become less of a teacher and mentor, and more a sort of guide. The two of us sitting and listening together for God's voice in her [the client's] story, her life, pain, relationships."

American Jewish healing is egalitarian in both a social and a theological sense. Leaders and healers do not have special healing powers, nor, for the most part, does God.[12] In the ritual and rhetoric of the Jewish healing movement, divinity tends to be highly immanent, present in the room rather than up in heaven.[13] The traditional Jewish conceptualization of divine immanence—the Shekhina, or the Indwelling of God—is frequently called upon in healing services. "Shekhina," a grammatically feminine word in Hebrew, traditionally has been imaged in Jewish mystical texts as the feminine divine manifestation. This mystical imagery has been expanded and revitalized by Jewish feminists over the past several decades. Hanna Tiferet Siegel elucidates, "Shekhina, for women she is an affirmation of how we do spirit. It makes a crack in the wall, stronghold, of how things are done Jewishly. Arouse the flowers to come out and grow in the hard places. Nature is more powerful than constructs or formulations human beings created to make sense out of life. Shekhina moves through us, pulses through us, allows us to know God." To my mind, theological emphasis on the feminine Shekhina in a healing movement founded by and led by far more women than men constitutes an important layer of resistance to traditional Jewish notions of healing.

Two of the most powerful healing services that I have been privileged to attend invoked the Shekhina's presence through communal singing. In one service, held at a large suburban synagogue in White Plains, New York, Debbie Friedman led the congregation of about 200 people ranging in age from their midtwenties to late seventies in a song drawn from the traditional Jewish prayer recited before going to sleep. In this prayer, the angels Michael, Uriel, Raphael, and Gavriel are imaged as standing guard while one sleeps, each positioned in front of, behind, to the right, or to the left of the sleeper, and the Shekhina is imaged as "on my head." In Friedman's English translation of the prayer, the last line is simply "All around us Shekhina." Inviting the congregation to stand up and sing with her, she repeats this line over and over again as the divine presence becomes palpable in the room.

In a quite different sort of service held in center city Philadelphia, Rabbi Rayzel Raphael encouraged her somewhat ragtag congregation consisting primarily of Jews too poor, too marginal, too old, or too ill to have joined the Jewish exodus to the more prosperous suburbs to stand up and sing and dance to a rock and roll Shekhina song. "Ha-le-lu-ha! Its coming time, we've seen the signs. Coming times we seen the signs, Shekhinah glory will surely shine!"

Healing and Gender

Dissolving the traditional Jewish association between illness and femaleness (as mythically presented in the Miriam story) is as important as the dissolution of the traditional association between divinity and maleness. I see it as especially significant that in Rayzel Raphael's version of the traditional liturgical formula "Please God heal her," she replaces "her" with "him" in half of the iterations: "*Ana El Na R'fa Na Lah;* Ana El Na R'fa Na *Lo.* Let's send our love to those who need it so; *Ken Y'hi Ratzon.*"[14] This sort of gender symmetry is common in American Jewish healing music; for example, in Debbie Friedman's "MiSheBerach," cited earlier, "Our Mothers" and "Our Fathers" switch in order in the two verses, replacing the sole "our fathers" of the traditional liturgical text.

Many healers and movement activists grew into Jewish healing through their involvement in women's Rosh Hodesh (New Moon) groups.[15] Hanna Tiferet Siegel explains, "Women by our nature created ritual. [We] weren't educated necessarily. [We] just had the desire to find [our] voices, and have a good time and connect. We went through a lot of passages together. One woman had breast cancer. So we did rituals. . . . Rosh Hodesh became the model for healing rituals.... [In our Rosh Hodesh group] we took chances. We learned how to pray, use the elements—earth, fire, our breaths. We saw a transformation come out."

The ordination of women rabbis has been instrumental to the development of the Jewish healing movement. (This development parallels the ordination of women in Protestant denominations and the rise of women lay leaders in the Catholic Church.) In fact, the Jewish healing movement may well constitute the most profound and important theological and ritual change in American Judaism brought about by the first generation of women rabbis and religious leaders.

The prominent role of women leaders in the Jewish healing movement is a radical change vis-à-vis traditional Judaism, yet it is wholly congruent with the nature of American women's religious activism. Women have been active in American religion not only as participants but also as leaders and founders (such as Mary Baker Eddy). The well-documented feminization of American religion in the nineteenth century was followed in the twentieth century by demands for the ordination of women in many denominations and by the rise of the contemporary feminist spirituality and Goddess movement. Aspects of American life that have encouraged women's religious leadership include the breakdown of the centralized religious institutions found in Europe; the disassociation of religion from the state; the prominence of nuclear rather than extended family arrangements; the rise of capitalism, which associated men with the material world and women with domesticity, morality, and spirituality; and the spirit of entrepreneurism, which has allowed individuals of vision to create new structure.

Matia Angelou observes, "As women became rabbis, the interest in spirituality and healing increased." Rabbi Amy Eilberg explains, "The leadership of women is new in Jewish communities. Women rabbis were, and still are to a significant extent, outsiders and marginal." This was part of the reason that women rabbis were interested in healing—they themselves were marginal in the Jewish community. Rabbi Dayle Freedman agrees: "At the beginning there was no obvious network [for me]. The [male] Reform rabbis were invalidating. I became involved with the Women's Rabbinical Network and an interdenominational spirituality and aging group."

I would estimate that men constitute a bit under a quarter of Jewish healing participants and leaders. One pioneer remembers, "In the beginning, potential [financial] supporters would say 'this is all women.'" One of her colleagues further explained, "[Two other founders] and I went to see an important (male) rabbi. He put our efforts down. It turned out he had had affairs with four congregants!"

In contrast to the poor interpersonal relationships said to be plaguing the male rabbinical establishment, the women involved in the Jewish healing movement stress the importance of human interactions. Rabbi Amy Eilberg suggests that "women as a generalization are enculturated to take issues of relationship seriously. This is a relationship issue, and a caregiving issue." Rabbi Nancy Flam concurs: "Mostly women come to the services, like in all self-help activities." Quite a few of the movement's founders and activists had been trained as social workers before entering rabbinical school. These women brought to the rabbinate a skill set and interpersonal approach quite different from the traditional hierarchical rabbinical model.

Conclusion

American Jewish healing openly discards the gendered cultural weight of the saints, sages, rabbis, rebbes, and holy men of traditional Jewish societies. Rejecting the culture of "cure," contemporary American Jewish healing has developed a theological vision in which illness is a manifestation of the community's failure to respect all its members rather than an individual's failure to behave according to social or religious norms, and an existential vision in which the perfectibility of the body is irrelevant, and therefore no one can be judged by how well he or she measures up to society's standards. That the movement has managed to develop its vision without overtly challenging either conventional biomedicine or traditional Judaism (as we have seen, Jewish healing patrons rely heavily upon physicians, and Jewish healing rituals are replete with phrases and stories drawn from traditional Jewish texts) is one of the movement's greatest accomplishments.

NOTES

The research on which this chapter is based was supported by the generous assistance of the Lucius N. Littauer Foundation. Many Jewish healing activists kindly shared their time and experiences with me as I carried out my research. I especially wish to thank Marjorie Sokoll, Rabbi Amy Eilberg, and Linda Barnes for their close reading of this chapter. The opinions and interpretations and any factual errors are mine alone.

1. My comments are based on observations of Jewish healing services and interviews with Jewish healing leaders, founders, and practitioners in New York, Boston, San Diego, Denver, Washington, D.C., and San Francisco during 1999–2001 and on the many books and essays written by leaders of the Jewish healing movement.

2. I would like to thank Susie Kessler of the National Center for Jewish Healing for providing this information.

3. I find it intriguing that a fairly large number of the women healers and healing activists are married to physicians.

4. This is not true across the board; for Christian Scientists and some other small groups, religious healing is the sole or the dominant healing option.

5. This is not always the trajectory of help-seeking. Those who have used alternative or complementary medicine in the past may be more likely to seek it out more quickly the next time around; those who pray regularly throughout their lives may turn to healing prayers more quickly. Linda Barnes points out that Jews have played a large role in the alternative medicine movement.

6. This is true of many of the liberal American Protestant denominations as well. See, for example, Hollis 2001.

7. This stance is congruent with a significant trend in the religious thinking of American women to conceptualize healing not as the achievement of perfection but rather as "the generation of hope: to be healed is to have sufficient hope to proceed, whatever that might mean in particular circumstances" (Bednarowski 1999: 152). Mary Farrell Bednarowski has identified five themes that pervade the religious writings of American woman across a variety of religious communities: an ongoing, creative ambivalence toward their religious communities, a theological emphasis on immanence, regard for the ordinary as revelatory of the sacred, a view of ultimate reality as relational, and an interpretation of healing as a primary rather than a secondary function of religion (1999: 1).

8. The two Hebrew lines translate: The One Who Blessed Our Fathers, Source of Blessing for our mothers. . . . The One Who Blessed Our Mothers, Source of Blessing for Our Fathers.

9. Hebrew language and writing are considered to have curative powers in traditional Jewish cultures as well. Hebrew incantations and amulets were common among Jews of Europe and North Africa and continue to be widely used in Israel.

10. This is a reference to one of the laws of kosher food.

11. The foundational book of Jewish mysticism, its language and cosmology are extraordinarily difficult even for those highly educated in Jewish sources.

12. Similar to the approach of twelve-step programs, Jewish healing generally encourages individuals to develop their own conceptualization of and relationship with God, however one chooses to define God. There is a great deal of theological diversity both among leaders and practitioners, and among participants and clients.

13. The trend toward immanence in theological thinking, according to Robert Wuthnow, characterizes small groups of various sorts in the United States today. In these groups "God is now less of an external authority and more of an internal presence. The sacred becomes personal but, in the process, also becomes more manageable, more serviceable in meeting individual needs" (1994: 3–4). See also Porterfield 2001: 18ff. and Albanese (1999: 352ff.) on the rise of religious relativism in the United States.

14 "Please God heal her; please God heal him. . . . May it be Your will."

15 While the festival of the New Moon is an ancient holiday mentioned repeatedly in the Bible, it had become of minor calendrical importance during the past centuries for Jews in most parts of the world. Traditionally associated with women more than men, Rosh Hodesh was an obvious and fruitful choice for Jewish feminists to adopt and expand. Around the United States today there are hundreds of Rosh Hodesh groups, some associated with synagogues, in which women of various streams of Judaism meet monthly to talk, study, and engage in creative ritual.

REFERENCES

Albanese, Catherine. 1999. *America, Religions, and Religion*. Belmont, Calif.: Wadsworth Publishing Co.

Bednarowski, Mary Farrell. 1999. *The Religious Imagination of American Women*. Bloomington: Indiana University Press.

Callahan, Daniel. 1998. *False Hopes: Why America's Quest for Perfect Health Is a Recipe for Failure*. New York: Simon and Schuster.

Cowan, Neil M., and Ruth Schwarz Cowan 1989. *Our Parents' Lives: The Americanization of Eastern European Jews*. New York: Basic Books.

Freeman, David L., and Judith Z. Abrams, eds. 1995. *Illness and Health in the Jewish Tradition: Writings from the Bible to Today*. Philadelphia: Jewish Publication Society.

Friedman, Dayle A., ed. 2001. *Jewish Pastoral Care: A Practical Handbook from Traditional and Contemporary Souces.*, Woodstock Vt.: Jewish Lights Publishing.

Hollis, Jennifer L. 2001. God Always Heals but Does Not Always Cure: The Search for Healing in the Episcopal Church. In *Religious Healing in Boston: First Findings*, ed. Susan Sered and Linda Barnes, 15–18. Cambridge Mass.: Center for the Study of World Religions, Harvard University.

Lesses, Rebecca. 1998. *Ritual Practices to Gain Power: Angels, Incantations, and Revelation in Early Jewish Mysticism*. Harrisburg Pa.: Trinity Press.

Orsi, Robert. 1997. Everyday Miracles: The Study of Lived Religion. In *Lived Religion in America: Toward a History of Practice*, ed. David D. Hall, 3–21. Princeton, N.J.: Princeton University Press.

Porterfield, Amanda. 2001. *The Transformation of American Religion: The Story of a Late Twentieth-Century Awakening*. New York: Oxford University Press.

Sered, Susan. 1992. *Women as Ritual Experts: The Religious Lives of Elderly Jewish Women in Jerusalem*. New York: Oxford University Press.

Vara, Richard. 1997. *Houston Chronicle*, Novmber 22.

Weintraub, Simkha Y., ed. 1994. *Healing of Soul, Healing of Body: Spiritual Leaders Unfold the Strength and Solace in Psalms*. Woodstock Vt.: Jewish Lights Publishing.

Whorton, James C. 1988. Patient, Heal Thyself: Popular Health Reform Movements as Unorthodox Medicine. In *Other Healers: Unorthodox Medicine in America*, ed. Norman Gevitz, 52–81. Baltimore: Johns Hopkins University Press.

Wuthnow, Robert. 1994. *Sharing the Journey: Support Groups and America's New Quest for Community*. New York: Free Press.

15

Healing in Feminist Wicca

Grove Harris

The contemporary religion of Witchcraft features a lively and dynamic ritual repertoire centered on nature. Participants in Witchcraft rituals acknowledge the turning wheel of the seasons of the year and the seasons of their own lives. Contemporary Witchcraft encompasses numerous formal and informal groups. One of the best known, the Reclaiming Tradition, is a U.S.-based international tradition focusing on the Goddess in Her multiple forms. This tradition includes both women and men, connects spirituality and politics, and focuses on healing the culture and the earth. Reclaiming holds annual camps across the country where Witches come together for training and for collective ritual.[1] Witches have often had to be secretive, and gatherings such as these camps have provided an important way of coming together openly. Healing is often a focus of the camp's large rituals, as well as being the focus of much ritual activity outside of the camp setting.

Healing in feminist Witchcraft takes many forms and occurs in many settings. Gatherings range in size from small covens to large groups of many hundreds. Techniques may include bodywork such as massage, spells such as herbal charms, chanting, dancing, trance work, and energetic healing through connecting to others and to the earth's forces.

Healing rituals and techniques may be applied to varied ills, ranging from physical conditions such as cancer or arthritis to heartache, childhood trauma, sexual abuse, and low self-esteem. Healing is associated with becoming whole, healthy, and in balance. The role of the healer is "to reconnect the individual with her own spiritual forces, to restore balance" (Jade 1991: 153). Healing can be applied to the immediate community, to larger political contexts, and to the land. Healing through Witchcraft addresses emotional pain and psychic repair, as well as specific bodily illnesses. Healing often addresses wounds incurred from the dominant patriarchal culture. In feminist Witchcraft, "Ritual is a way of becoming 'unpossessed' from patriarchy" (Greenwood 2000: 145). Susan Sered (2000) argues that patriarchy literally makes women (and men) sick. Additionally, she suggests that "the might of patriarchy is that it embeds its conceptualizations in the very bodies of the men and women whose lives it governs." (157). Releasing these embedded conceptualizations requires healing practices beyond those generally offered by Western medicine.

Connection

Many Witches see healing as creating connections (Crowley 2000: 160) and connections as healing. Healing connections can occur between people, with trees, and in relationship with the earth. Sarah Pike's research highlights the importance for Witches of healing through relationships.[2] Healing requires intimate connection with one's community, with the natural world, and with the sacred. According to Pike, "Religious belief and practice in the late twentieth century must focus on healing ourselves, our communities, and the planet. And this healing . . . must take place through relationships—with deities, the land, and each other. What 'relationship' means in this case is not simply a conversation between self and other, but an intimate connection with the natural world, with a goddess or god, and with one's community" (2001: xxi–xxii). These new or renewed connections can be seen as the beginning of new social formations representing a healing and potential reshaping of patriarchy into less isolated and individualistic social forms. The theme of connection as healing runs through two settings to be explored, a large annual Reclaiming Witch Camp and a smaller, private circle, which is a common and frequent type of gathering for Reclaiming Witches.

Healing Ritual at Witch Camp

At sunset, more than a hundred people form a large circle on the hillside meadow overlooking a lake and surrounded by mountains. Drummers move close to a large fire in the center, and those who wish to receive healing cluster around the drummers and the fire. This Reclaiming Witch Camp community will dance and chant to generate energy for healing: for those in the center, for those dancing, for loved ones at a distance, and for the earth. Some participants think the ritual follows an ancient pattern, others believe that current community leaders created the form, and some see that both may be true.

Around the outskirts of the circle, participants prepare healing stations as alternatives to the central space. In the Reclaiming Tradition, the four directions and the center are associated with elements that are held sacred. The East corresponds to the element of Air; at this station incense is often used for purification, bells or rattles may be used to cleanse with sound vibrations, and aura cleansing may be offered to clear and smooth the energy field that surrounds the body. In the South, the Fire station is a place to get warm, with blankets available. In the West, the element of Water is honored, and offerings include water to drink and comforts related to emotional healing. In the North, the Earth station may have food, such as apples and nuts, as well as a quiet place to rest.

A simple circle dance is performed either in one large ring or two smaller concentric rings around a central fire and healing space. People find partners so that they will have assistance in receiving and using the focused attention and force that is available in the center. This partnership is especially important for those who are physically ill, with limited resources to manage the intensity of the energy unaided.

I have researched, participated in, and observed Witchcraft in the United States since 1993 in a variety of settings, including many in the Greater Boston area, and mostly focusing on Reclaiming and feminist Goddess spirituality. Research methods include a survey, participant observation, and interviews. In 1998, I sent out a survey about healing and community to all the participants of the prior summer's camp. I wanted to know what people experienced and thought about that year's large healing ritual, as well as information about the Witches' community inside and outside of the camp setting. I asked open-ended questions about the experience and meaning of healing and of community. To get quantitative data on the same topics, I offered statements for disagreement or agreement.[3] I received 63 responses to the 110 surveys I sent out. Respondents were predominantly white women, ranging in age from twenty-seven to eighty-one, mostly middle-aged, and mostly college educated. In this chapter I offer preliminary excerpts from the qualitative results, as well as selected quantitative findings.[4] I also offer information from participant observation at subsequent healing rituals at this camp.

Healing and Connection

Ritual participants reported feeling that healing energy was available in all areas of the ceremonial circle, including the outer rings of dancers, as well as the center of the circle. Within the context of this Reclaiming healing ritual, healing was offered for a wide range of healing needs, from serious physical illness to emotional heartache. Some of the gay men at camp have used the opportunity to heal from relationship difficulties, as have many of the lesbians and heterosexuals. In 2002, at least one woman did extensive psychic and emotional healing of wounds incurred from being raped.

In Witchcraft, healing is not an individual's isolated private task; it is assisted by and typically requires connection with others. The survey results reported that some of the kinds of healing from the ritual in August 1997 were temporary cancer remission, clarity about where one fits in and what one stands for, and renewed energy. Participants also reported emotional opening, opening to feel the good earth and life force, healing from disconnection, and the experience of being held through intense crying release.[5]

Connection was mentioned multiple times, including connection to all parts of self and to others. One respondent wrote that "connecting with others is a way of healing the separateness our society calls for." Connection may take many forms. It can happen through communal dancing or chanting, through shared ritual experience, or through profound experience of self in relation to nature. It may involve reconnecting with others from earlier parts of one's life. For example, a Witch Camper who is a veteran of the Vietnam War was moved to return to Vietnam as part of his healing path to reconnect peacefully with the people against whom he had previously waged war. The welcome he received was deeply healing for him.

Connection also can be crucial for healing even when there is no prior history among the people involved. In Jone Salomenson's study of the Reclaiming community in California, she cites a healer who was able to heal a stranger from great pain and breathing difficulty: "The skills we are talking about are real. It is not a metaphor; we can heal. . . . it was the knowledge of the elements, the knowledge of the way to work psychically, which is connecting instead of separating" (2002: 258–60). Within the Reclaiming community, healing depends on connection.

For some, the healing offered by this circle was inseparable from that of the entire week retreat. Close to half reported personal healing during or after the ritual. Some did not perceive healing for themselves, but most perceived others as receiving healing and the community as receiving healing. Witch campers agree that doing healing ritual together is a way to build their community. Healing both requires and enhances community. This connectedness is enhanced by shared experiences in group ritual such as chanting.

Chanting in Witch Camp

Chants can carry powerful healing messages. Chanting is one means of challenging and changing damaging internalized cultural messages and moving toward wholeness and balance. For example, this chant has been used at the Witch Camp:

> My body is a living temple of love.
> My body is a living temple of love.
> My body is the body of the Goddess.
> My body is the body of the Goddess.
> Oh oh oh I am what I am.
> Oh oh oh I am what I am.[6]

When sung in large group ritual, this chant affirms celebration of the profound respect for the human body and sexual expression. The chant avows the sacredness of the body, the necessity for self-acceptance, and the variety of individual physical expressions of divinity. The process of singing it and hearing it sung encourages exploration and release of internal obstacles to this fully embodied sacred humanity and this positive vision of sacred sexuality. Sexuality is fully integrated with love and sacredness, without other prohibitions. Intentional repetition, particularly within a ritual setting, allows the song to penetrate deeply and provides a new framework for viewing the body.

Those who chant together can share a sense of affirmation and participation in community that honors the female, as well as the male, body. Individuals can mirror and affirm each other in this process of chanting and benefit from the collective singing that is more tonally complex than that of a solitary voice. Chanting can also be used by a solitary practitioner to continue to release internal constructs and affirm an alternative reality. The transformative powers of chanting may be subtle; however, they may also be powerful.

Earth Healing

Chanting is one means of directing healing energy toward the environment. In a spiritual practice that sees human life as participating in and sustained by the larger ecological system, the focus of healing may well be some specific location or aspect of the earth. As part of the annual camp ritual, a direct connection is made between the personal healing of individuals and healing the earth. The following chant is frequently used:

> Every step I take is a healing step.
> Every step I take is a sacred step.
> Healing, healing, healing my body.
> Healing, healing, healing the land.[7]

The chant constructs parallels between healing the body and healing the land. Healing is seen as relational, as taking place through connectedness with the land. The earth both needs and offers healing (Crowley 2000: 161).

Political Healing

The Reclaiming Tradition, in service to the stated goal of unifying spirit
and politics, includes political aspects of healing rituals, particularly concerning
the environment.[8] In 1997, ritual participants were invited to cut a lock of their
hair for a magical spell to protect the threatened redwood forests in California.
The hair was woven into a collective braid that was brought to the trees, carrying the intention of protection. This ritual linked the opportunity for personal
healing with the opportunity to care for the earth. In 2002, an additional Earth
healing station where people could make commitments to take action in their
local communities was part of the healing ritual. This activist component is
typical of Reclaiming rituals and can be seen as efforts toward healing the
larger society.

Healing in a Women's Circle

Although Witch Camp meets just for a short time every summer, throughout the year camp participants may gather in smaller groups on a more regular
basis. Most of the campers do healing rituals at other times, and many are part
of ongoing small circles that meet frequently.[9] These circles are an important
site of healing.

At a typical small circle in Massachusetts, eight women gathered together,
bringing sacred objects for the altar, wearing festive ritual clothes and other
adornment, and offering foods to share. We met in a living room, and each
time two different women led the ceremony. For three years in the 1980s this
particular circle met twice a month, at every full moon and on most new
moons, as well as on the eight annual solar holidays. At the time, the participants were in our middle to late twenties, mostly lesbian and bisexual, living
in the liberal environment of Cambridge and looking for spiritual help. We
first met one another at a weekend retreat led by the feminist Witch Starhawk,
a cofounder of Reclaiming, and were encouraged by her to continue meeting
on our own. Another women's circle nurtured us for a while, until we established our own. Guests were occasionally invited, most notably the male partner of one of the women.

This women's circle provided a regular time and place for creative rituals,
which were initiated, designed, and led by members of the group. In this small
egalitarian circle, the setting itself offered healing to participants through connection with others as well as through specific healing work. Healing was a
major focus of the circle; we were working to reclaim our lives. This healing
spiritual community supported members who were recovering from addictions
to drugs and alcohol.[10] Members of the group had suffered many forms of

Flower altar representing the navel of the Earth. Used with permission from Sharon Bauer.

sexual violence, including incest, harassment, sexual attacks, and homophobia. Low self-esteem had serious repercussions for circle members. One woman was directly repudiating her religious upbringing; incest perpetrated by her parents, who were stalwart members of their Protestant church, led her to see the church as complicit in the abuse. In the company of another circle member, she burned her baptismal certificate as part of her healing process. For her, the circle functioned as an alternative spiritual community that could witness, support, and participate in her healing from horrible abuse. Another woman used the circle context to support her in recovering from cancer of the throat that she intuited was directly related to childhood abuse and the ensuing enforced silences she had suffered.

At one gathering, the circle worked together to produce healing charms. Inspired by years of witnessing the psychic pain of lesbian friends in the aftermath of holiday visits to families that did not accept their sexuality, the small herb-filled cloth bundles were designed to provide protection from homophobia. The intention was to offer safety for lesbians from external homophobic family settings and also from their own internalized homophobia. The healing charms were intended to act as a preventative, to assist women in retaining their sense of self-respect. They were distributed to friends and graduate school classmates before the winter break.

Naming homophobia as a problem and taking action against it with herbal charms proclaims that fear will no longer be accepted as a form of social control. When a survivor of abuse no longer has to keep silent or blame herself, her energy is freed up. For the circle's members, breaking the silence around abuse served to demystify the abuse; learning that the abuses happened to virtually every woman in the group furthered that demystification. Delegitimating former beliefs of worthlessness was part of the process of healing and reestablishing self-esteem.

The acts of reaching out and establishing this small women's moon circle for ourselves indicated that the positive deconstruction had already begun. When women come together and affirm values that go against the dominant culture, they are affirming an alternative discourse. Women gathering in exclusive settings are making a statement about their needs and where they get them met. We supported each other through the deconstructive work that was essential to healing from damage done by patriarchal society. Lesley Northup (1997: 91) goes further to suggest that the act of women gathering to worship together is inherently, although possibly only subliminally, a disruptive political statement that is critical of religious institutions and social structures. Connecting with like-minded women in this circle offered companions on a healing journey.

Celebration as Healing

Some of the power of healing in Goddess spirituality ritual lies in experiencing transcendence of the prevalent dualistic constructs of mind-body, spiritual-physical, and work-play. Sometimes healing toward wholeness can be exquisitely celebratory and playful. Celebration, creativity, play, encouragement, taking on leadership, and direct contact with the divine through numerous senses are all part of this healing path. The safety and creativity of the ritual form offer healing. Being "between the worlds" in a spiritual circle offers a container and a spiritual contact that can be profoundly comforting and allow room for connecting with a childlike inner self in playful exploration.

At one of the Cambridge circles, I recall a ritual where the text called for round bread, which we translated into bagels for our ritual purposes. Upon arriving at the home where we would hold the ritual, we found that we could string up the bagels and use pushpins to dangle them from the ceiling. Later in the ritual, we spontaneously stood and started eating the bagels without the use of our hands. The effect was similar to bobbing for apples, but with a vertical stance and air rather than water as the medium. The freedom to reinterpret and re-create in ritual can lead to awareness of a world full of new possibilitites. This joyous engagement can spill over beyond the ritual time and space; it can begin as easily and playfully as bobbing for bagels or chanting a new tune.

Chanting in the Small Women's Circle

Most circle meetings included chanting. One ritual included immersion in herbal baths to the accompaniment of chanting, naming many parts of the body with the repeated refrain: "It's great to have a body; I have a great body." This simple chant was spontaneously created by the participants. Like the chant from the camp setting, this chant affirms the body. It speaks to a childlike aspect of the self and celebrates the body. With playful intentional repetition in a sacred circle, it functions to repattern "embedded conceptualizations" by affirming all parts of the female body. Chanting is used to disrupt a dominant cultural teaching that the body is less than sacred, less than spiritual. The chant offers a new discourse that honors and heals the body.

A final Reclaiming chant reiterates the theme of connection in healing; it affirms the connections among the group and with the earth and challenges participants to take up the fullness of their role as healers:

> We are alive, as the earth is alive.
> We have the power to create our freedom.
> If we have courage we can be healers;
> Like the sun we shall rise.
> If we have courage we can be healers;
> Like the moon we shall rise.[11]

NOTES

1 In 1997, campers self-identified as Witches, Pagans, Wiccans, Goddess worshipers, ecofeminists, Neo-Pagans, Unitarian Universalists, Buddhists, Jews, Quakers, and a Catholic and Protestant. For this chapter I subsume these internal diversities into the term "Witch."

2. Technically her research is on Neopagans, which is a related tradition that includes Witches. Her research settings were more loosely organized festivals rather than a Reclaiming Witch Camp.

3. I used a Likert scale variant. The survey questionaire was constructed in consultation with members of the group under study. Face validity was provided by outside review, and content validity was further assessed by consultation. A pilot group of nine responded to the questionaire and/or offered critical comments.

4. In further analysis my intention is to compile a full record of the variety of healing experiences and to use Strauss's grounded theory and let the data generate qualities of community.

5. Some participants reported no healing from the ritual.

6. Written by Michael Stillwater.

7. Written by Donald Engstrom.

8. See http://www.reclaiming.org.

9. These circles may be called covens if all the members are Witches. A circle may include members who simply consider themselves spiritual seekers. Survey data showed that among Witch Campers, the average coven size was eight to nine members, with an average duration of 4.6 years.

10. Many of the members were also in twelve-step programs, and that recovery was enhanced by participation in this circle. In her article entitled "Thriving, Not Simply Surviving: Goddess Spirituality and Women's Recovery from Alcoholism," Tanice Foltz answers the question " 'What does Goddess spirituality provide for recovering alcoholic women that is missing from AA?' Three overlapping themes emerged from the data: a holistic approach, a healing spiritual community, and women's celebration" (2000: 127).

11. Written by Rose May Dance and Starhawk; adapted by Shawna Carol.

REFERENCES

Berger, Helen. 1999. *A Community of Witches: Contemporary Neo-Paganism and Witchcraft in the United States.* Columbia: University of South Carolina Press.

Bowie, Fiona. 1998. Trespassing on Sacred Domains: A Feminist Anthropological Approach to Theology and Religious Studies. *Journal of Feminist Studies in Religion* 14: 40–62.

Crowley, Vivianne. 2000. Healing in Wicca. In *Daughters of the Goddess: Studies of Healing, Identity, and Empowerment,* ed. Wendy Griffin. Walnut Creek, Calif.: AltaMira Press.

Foltz, Tanice. 2000. Thriving, Not Simply Surviving. In *Daughters of the Goddess: Studies of Healing, Identity, and Empowerment,* ed. Wendy Griffin, pp. 119–35. Walnut Creek, Calif.: AltaMira Press.

———. 2001. Women's Spirituality Research: Doing Feminism. In *Feminist Narratives and the Sociology of Religion,* ed. Nancy Nason-Clark, and Mary J. Neitz, 89–98. Walnut Creek, Calif.: AltaMira Press.

Glendinning, Chellis. 1982. The Healing Powers of Women. In *The Politics of Women's Spirituality,* ed. Charlene Spretnak, 280–93. Garden City, N.Y.: Anchor Books.

Greenwood, Susan. 2000. Feminist Witchcraft: A Transformatory Politics. In *Daughters of the Goddess: Studies of Healing, Identity, and Empowerment,* ed. Wendy Griffin, 136–50. Walnut Creek, Calif.: AltaMira Press.

Griffin, Wendy. ed. 2000. *Daughters of the Goddess: Studies of Healing, Identity, and Empowerment.* Walnut Creek, Calif.: AltaMira Press.

Harris, Grove. 1997. Paganism. In *On Common Ground: World Religions in America,* ed. Diana L. Eck. New York: Columbia University Press.

———. 1999. Our Many Names: Pagan, Witch, Wiccan . . . Reflections on Religious Identity. *Reclaiming Quarterly,* no. 76: pp. 5, 52–53.

Jade. 1991. *To Know.* Oak Park, Ill.: Delphi Press.

Lincoln, Bruce. 1989. *Discourse and the Construction of Society.* New York: Oxford University Press.

Neitz, Mary Jo. 2001. Queering the Dragonfest: Changing Sexualitites in a Post-patriarchal Religion. In *Feminist Narratives and the Sociology of Religion*, ed. Nancy Nason-Clark, and Mary Jo Neitz, 29–51. Walnut Creek, Calif.: AltaMira Press.

Northup, Lesley A. 1997. *Ritualizing Women*. Cleveland: Pilgrim Press.

Pike, Sarah M. 2001. *Earthly Bodies, Magical Selves: Contemporary Pagans and the Search for Community*. Berkeley and Los Angeles: University of California Press.

Pluralism Project. 2002. Statistics by Tradition. http://www.pluralism.org/resources/statistics/tradition.php. Accessed September 1, 2002.

Reclaiming. 2003. Reclaiming Homepage. http://www.reclaiming.org Accessed September 1, 2002.

Ristock, Janice L., and Joan Pennell. 1996. *Community Research as Empowerment: Feminist Links, Postmodern Interruptions*. Toronto: Oxford University Press.

Salomonsen, Jone. 2002. *Enchanted Feminism: The Reclaiming Witches of San Francisco*. New York: Routledge.

Sered, Susan. 2000. *What Makes Women Sick*. Hanover, N.H.: University Press of New England.

Starhawk. 1993. *The Fifth Sacred Thing*. New York: Bantam Books.

———. 1999. *The Spiral Dance*. San Francisco: HarperSanFrancisco.

———. 2002. *Webs of Power: Notes from the Global Uprising*. Gabriola Island, B.C.: New Society Publishers.

16

Sexual Healing: Self-Help and Therapeutic Christianity in the Ex-Gay Movement

Tanya Erzen

> Spoken in time, to the proper party, and by the person who was both the bearer and the one responsible for it, the truth healed.
> (Foucault *The History of Sexuality*, Vol. 1, 1978)

New Hope Night

New Hope Night is one of the most dramatic events of the year for the ex-gay men who have come to heal their homosexuality at New Hope Ministries. It is the first time they testify about their personal struggles with homosexuality in front of the other members at Church of the Open Door, the ex-gay-affiliated church. Hidden behind a Safeway grocery store in a small northern California town, Open Door has a stage with a single podium but no pulpit, sacraments, or images. An antiquated disco ball slowly revolves above the smattering of fifty people in attendance. The congregation is composed of mainly middle-aged men and women, former ex-gays and long-term members with their teenage children. The pastor, Mike Riley, stands at the podium speaking into a makeshift public address system with the Open Door band: his son on electric guitar, a keyboardist, drummer, and three singers set up alongside him. "God is good, amen, amen, God is good," he tells the men from New Hope. "What I most appreciate is the courage and vulnerability in your lives, to be as transparent as you."

The New Hope men have been preparing for this night for

months by memorizing long biblical passages from Romans. Abruptly, one at a time, they rise from their seats and begin reciting scripture as they stride toward the front of the church. Some have memorized longer passages and pronounce their verses in booming voices, and others speak timidly. One proclaims, "For a sin shall not have dominion over you." When they all reach the front, they intone in unison, "For the wages of sin are death and the gift of God through eternal life." The band launches into a song: "I will never be the same again, I will never return, I have closed the door." Each man approaches the microphone. Doug tells the congregation, "Thank you to a bunch of prayer warriors in Spokane who never gave up on me," referring to his Pentecostal parents who prayed regularly for him during the years he lived in San Diego as a gay man.

Mitch, a house leader at New Hope, gives a testimony. He relates how he was forced to resign as a youth pastor when his church discovered he was a homosexual. Two years earlier, he had arrived at New Hope with piles of gay pornography on the backseat of his car after driving across country, stopping in rest areas, and cruising for sex. When he sheepishly mentioned his stash to the ministry, Anita Worthen, the wife of the New Hope director, marched out to his car with gloves and a garbage bag to dispose of the contraband. Now he tells the congregation that the temptation to look at pornography lingers, but he is well on his way to recovery. Within two weeks he will leave the ministry after he admits to having gay pornography in his bedroom, but at the moment there is no reason to doubt the veracity of his testimony.

Afterward, the congregation stands and claps. Pastor Mike asks the people to gather around the men fanned out on either side of him and pray for them. "We encourage you to adopt some of these men into your lives this year. You are a big part of what happens in their lives. Come now, Holy Spirit, come, come, come Lord, come. Come out of your seats and pray for these men." The congregants pour down the aisles and lay their hands on each man, kneeling and standing around them until the New Hope men are no longer visible in the crush. The service functions as an introduction of the ex-gay men to the church and symbolizes the fusion of two parts of their lives that had previously been separate—conservative religion and sexuality. As one man explained, "New Hope night is like a giant therapy session."

The ex-gay movement, of which New Hope Ministries is a part, is a product of the confluence of religion and therapeutic culture. It draws heavily from the self-help and recovery movements' notion of twelve steps to conceptualize healing homosexuality. In their rhetoric and practices, men and women at New Hope have replaced the concept of sexual orientation change with the idea that homosexuality can be healed through religious belief and therapeutic means. As part of the twelve-step model, the ex-gay movement focuses on sexual addictions that stem from homosexuality. Lingering "problems" of same-sex behavior and attraction become part of a therapeutic language of addiction. Personal testimony is central to healing sexual addictions, and people are urged to constantly confess sexual lapses to one another in small accountability groups and more public forums. At New Hope, testimony blurs the distinction between the public and private, religious and therapeutic, making sexuality and sexual addiction part of a public discourse of confession and public intimacy.

New Hope?

New Hope is directed by Frank Worthen, a former gay man. Frank founded the first ex-gay ministry in 1973, and New Hope is one of three residential ex-gay programs in the United States.[1] Located in a Marin County suburb ten miles north of San Francisco, the ministry sits off a suburban main road that is discreetly lined with alcohol and drug treatment centers. There are no signs outside the ministry, a low-slung, stucco building almost completely obscured by flowering vines. Across the street is an apartment complex where twenty men live during their year in the residential program. From 1999 to 2001, there were fifteen men in the residential program. They are predominantly white, from working-class and middle-class families, raised primarily in rural areas or small towns of the United States. A similar program for women flourished in the 1980s but was eliminated due to a lack of space and leadership. Instead, New Hope currently sponsors Grace, a weekly ex-gay women's support group led by a woman who had spent years at New Hope and eventually married a man from Open Door church. With the help of a board of directors and house leaders who have successfully completed the program, Frank oversees New Hope, teaches classes to the men, and serves as a pastor at Open Door. His wife of eighteen years, Anita, spearheads a ministry for parents of gay children from the same office. After two decades of marriage, Anita and Frank are paragons for other Christian men and women who pray that they will be healed enough to get married.

New Hope is part of the Christian ex-gay movement, which sponsors hundreds of ministries in the United States and abroad where men and women attend therapy sessions, Bible studies, twelve-step-style meetings, and regular church services as part of their "journey out of homosexuality."[2] The wider ex-gay movement consists of a network of organizations with overlapping but not necessarily coordinated agendas, including psychoanalytic organizations and independent therapists throughout the world. It has also expanded beyond Christian ministries and now includes Jewish and Catholic groups, Homosexuals Anonymous, Sexaholics Anonymous, Parents and Friends of Ex-Gays (PFOX), and the National Association for the Research and Treatment of Homosexuality (NARTH). New Hope is funded entirely from donations and the money that men pay to enter the program; like Exodus International, it is registered as a nonprofit organization. To come to the program, an applicant must be willing to pay $1,200 upfront for a security deposit, program books, and the first month's rent. The monthly fee is $850 to cover the cost of a shared bedroom, ten meals a week, and all utilities, phone calls, and household necessities. The program does not have the financial resources to provide scholarships. To prove that they can afford the program, applicants must disclose their financial information and credit history.

Almost all the people who decide to come to New Hope were raised within conservative Christian traditions, and many experience a profound conflict between their religious and sexual identities. They are Christians from Nazarene, Presbyterian, Catholic, Assemblies of God, Baptist, Pentecostal, and Lutheran backgrounds. Unable to reconcile their sexuality with their religious beliefs, and suffering from guilt, shame, and what they call a sense of distance from God, these men and women are drawn to ex-gay ministries because they hope that as their religious identities strengthen, their sexual conflicts will diminish. Many arrive with distressing tales of anonymous sex, pornography, sexual addiction, and suicide attempts. While the majority never participated in a gay community, others have given up long-term relationships and active political and social lives.

Healing for ex-gays involves an identity transformation in which an individual is born again and becomes a new creation in Christ. They gain a specific identity—ex-gay—which aids them in reconciling the opposing frameworks of homosexuality and conservative Christianity. The new identity comes about as a result of conversion. As they spend time at the ministry and with God, they also believe that their homosexuality will change. Despite disparate backgrounds, many ex-gays describe a crisis point in their lives when they were no longer able to conceal their sexual identities and live as Christians. Most reached a point at which the conflict became unbearable, and this crisis led to the onset of spiritual conversion.

What does it mean to become healed from homosexuality and gain a new ex-gay identity? Based on eighteen months of fieldwork at New Hope Ministries, I examined this and other questions. I conducted two- to three-hour interviews with forty-five men and women, with follow-up interviews when it was possible. I chose New Hope as the research site because of Frank's position as the founder of the movement and the fact that it is the oldest and most established residential program. Aside from men currently enrolled in the program, I met and interviewed many ex-gay and ex-ex-gay men and women living in the surrounding area who had completed the program, left to live as gay men and lesbians, or married. After a few months, Frank granted me permission to peruse his carefully cataloged archive of articles, letters, and pictures from the early 1970s, and I spent part of my days reading and copying these files. At night, before I drove back to San Francisco, I would often eat dinner with the entire house of men and listen to their praise and worship sessions. I met others through church on Sundays and group outings on weekends.

Evangelical Healing and the Rise of Twelve-Step Recovery

The ex-gay movement emerged during a period when the concept of self-help was gaining greater popularity and currency in American culture. Ellen Herman writes that after 1945 the social influence of white male psychological experts began to wane as psychological authority shifted from the domain of academic institutions and became more of a worldview and factor in everyday life (Herman 1995). Therapy was no longer a stigmatized activity that took place in mental institutions. By 1970, approximately 20,000 psychiatrists were ministering to 1 million people on a purely outpatient basis (Herman 1995: 262–63). The self-help recovery movement also gained prominence as a result of "modern, anti-authoritarian developments in psychology (and popular psychology) since Freud" (Simonds 1992: 52). The shift toward using therapy for exploring personality rather than as a prelude to mental institutionalization was implicated in wider cultural trends, including feminism and gay liberation, that counseled self-actualization, as necessary for human evolution and social change. The trend toward therapy, self-actualization and self-help also overlapped and intersected with evangelical and charismatic theology. In these religious traditions, any person who believes he or she possess a gift of prophecy can speak the word of God. There is a focus on personal freedom, self-fulfillment, self-worth and growth, and adherents are urged to discover their own inherent abilities and spiritual gifts.

As ideas about healing and recovery gained prominence in the 1970s, the concepts of self-help became interwoven with religious precepts. "By the 1960s and 1970s, most evangelical spokespersons embraced modern psychology with great enthusiasm and only minor reservations. By then, the evangelical subculture was less a bulwark against than a variant of the therapeutic culture" (Simonds 1992: 138). The confluence of the religious and therapeutic accounts for the emergence of the ex-gay movement. Like evangelical Christianity, self-help is the ideology that salvation occurs through personal effort, sanctioned by the idea of grace. The ex-gay therapeutic worldview considered homosexuality as not simply a sin but a sickness or addiction that could be healed through personal effort in conjunction with a relationship with God. This overlapped with the increasing popularity of twelve-step programs during the same period. The idea that a person can save him- or herself through close adherence to a twelve-step program intersects with born-again Christian notions of the creation of a new self through religious conversion. The ex-gay movement reinte-

grated evangelicalism and recovery, combining religious and twelve-step therapeutic principles.

Alcoholics Anonymous (AA), the forerunner of most twelve-step groups,
materialized out of an evangelical tradition of the 1920s and 1930s known as
the Oxford Group, "a nondenominational, theologically conservative, evangel-
ically styled attempt to recapture the spirit and the impetus of what its members
understood to be primitive Christianity" (Kurtz 1988: 9). The Oxford Group
operated according to six basic assumptions, five of which became the foundation for AA's Twelve Steps: men are sinners, men can be changed, confession
is a prerequisite to change, the changed soul has direct access to God, and
those who have been changed must change others (Kurtz 1988: 23). AA had
been in existence for thirty-five years in 1970 and possessed a growing membership base. However, its concept of the Twelve Steps did not gain pervasive
acceptance within the medical community and American culture until the pop-
ularization of therapy and the focus on self-betterment in the 1970s. By the
1990s, the influence of the twelve-step model was ubiquitous, extending from
the corporate retreat to the Overeaters Anonymous meeting.

In the Twelve Steps, "sin" is specified as being "powerless over alcohol"
and having "character defects." In place of the Bible, AA's primary text is the
Big Book. Confession becomes "a moral inventory" that is admitted to oneself,
God, and another human being, but the basic assumptions of the Oxford
Group remain intact. Just as an Oxford Group member experienced a spiritual
conversion in stages or steps, an AA member recovers from alcoholism by
following the Twelve Steps one by one, achieving a spiritual awakening as a
by-product. The fellowship (the meetings themselves and the interactions
within the group) and the program are based on the premise that recovery
from alcoholism requires a spiritual transformation, one that can be achieved
through the Twelve Steps. The language of the Twelve Steps both obscures and
magnifies AA's evangelical origins. Alcoholics are not required to submit to
Jesus, but they must turn their will and their lives "over to the care of God as
we understood him" (Kurtz 1988: 13). Although the evangelical concept of God
becomes a universal higher power, in both movements recovery is dependent
on submission to a higher authority. The twelve-step program emerged as the
answer to alcoholism, drug addiction, overeating, gambling, and a variety of
other addictions and "diseases." As practices once billed as bad habits and
dilemmas became redefined as addictions, therapeutic syndromes like co-
dependency gained currency in American culture.

Ex-Gay Sexual Healing

New Hope Ministry has adopted ideas about sexual addiction and elements
of the twelve-step process for its residential program. During the week at the

ministry, twenty to thirty men live together communally, dividing their time between jobs, nightly prayer, accountability groups, group outings, and classes on topics such as masculinity, anger management, and dating. They even have "straight men" meetings with men from Open Door church at which they ask questions about being heterosexual. The first step toward "coming out of homosexuality" is to admit to yourself and to God, "I have a problem" in the same way that AA's first step is to admit, "We are powerless over alcohol" (Alcoholics Anonymous 1955: 59). Other steps include "We came to perceive that we had accepted a lie about ourselves, an illusion that had trapped us in a false identity" and "We learned to claim our true reality that as mankind, we are part of God's heterosexual creation, and that God calls us to rediscover that identity in Him through Jesus Christ" (New Hope 1996: 3). All ex-gay ministries have three crucial components: healing, teaching, and discipleship. New Hope believes that people need healing in the areas of "sexual and relational brokenness." Healing from addiction involves recognizing the following:

- God's powerful love for us and how Jesus is central to our hope for wholeness
- The depth of our brokenness and our profound need for him
- The power of the cross to restore our souls, sexuality, and relationships

New Hope leaders emphasize that although they believe in the process of recovery as central to healing from homosexuality, their Christian identities come first. Frank tells the men, "Although today it is popular to identify yourself by your problem, this is not healthy or the way God intended us to identify ourselves. Our identity is Christian, this, in itself is a full and complete identity; nothing more needs to be added" (New Hope 1996: 21). The program acknowledges that the ex-gays are Christians with addictions, and that any form of lust is a sin. However, the leaders stress taking on a Christian identity rather than an identity as an addict. They do not want the person and the problem to be synonymous. "We can admit to an unmanageable problem (Step One of AA) without having to take on the sinful identity" (New Hope 1996: 21). Men at New Hope avoid the terms "gay" or "homosexual" because it is imperative to treat homosexuality as a condition that can be healed. They make a distinction between the binding nature of an identity versus an addiction that can be healed. Rather than explaining, "I am Frank, and I am a homosexual," the men in the program state, "I am Frank, and I am dealing with homosexual tendencies," or "I struggle with homosexuality." All sinful sexual behaviors and feelings are contained within their new identity—ex-gay. They are neither homosexual nor heterosexual, but still Christian. Instead of a person who has used pornography, they are Christians and recovering porn addicts. Instead of a homosexual, they are ex-gays or strugglers. The concept of being "ex-gay" alters the regulatory behavior and norms of their identity: it is expected that a man will fall (succumb to same-sex desire) and be saved (return to ex-gay ministry).

Ex-gay Christians become conversant in a therapeutic language that is specific to the ex-gay movement, reinventing the language of sin and pathology. The term "sexual brokenness" describes their current state of homosexuality or addiction. "Brokenness" is the term that ex-gays use to describe the addictions in their lives. New Hope's program manual reads, "Christ's capacity to touch and restore us at deep levels of shame and brokenness extends to all of us, regardless of the specifics of our issue." "Sexual sobriety" illuminates the process of recovery. Having sex outside of heterosexual marriage is "acting out." When a man or woman has a same-sex experience or looks at pornography, he or she has had a "sexual fall." An attraction between two people is an "emotional dependency." The estrangement from their parents that many people describe is called "defensive detachment." When they leave the program unhealed, they have gone back to the "lifestyle," thus distinguishing between being gay (a temporary lifestyle choice) and being homosexual (a changeable condition that results from "gender deficits" in childhood).

In their daily classes, the men at New Hope utilize a four-part workbook entitled *Steps Out* that devotes eight weeks to the question of sexual addiction. The workbook covers everything from finding a job to Christian beliefs to theories about homosexual development. In addition, the men consistently practice journaling, a technique borrowed from the recovery movement that enables them to record their feelings on a daily basis as a way to hear God speak to them. At the first class, men are given a scenario of two options for a Saturday and asked to pick one. The first option involves going to a local men's room where they know a man will be there to service anyone sexually. The book asks: Will you be there at three o'clock? The second option involves going to the beach with an old friend who happens to be visiting that day. The book asks: Will you choose to go to the beach? The lesson explains that those who choose the beach option are less addicted than those who forsake their friend to have anonymous sex. After a lengthy discussion of these choices, men spend time sharing with each other and are permitted fifteen minutes to write in their diary page at the end of the lesson. At the next lesson, they discuss characteristics of addiction like obsession, anger, denial, boredom, paranoia, and self-degradation. Together they answer the questions, "Do you feel trapped by your addiction?" and "Are you in denial?"

Self-sufficiency is a sin in the ex-gay model of addiction and healing. Frank teaches that we are not the masters of our fate and that we must acknowledge our dependence on God. The men at New Hope call the inability to rely on God the "Sinatra syndrome." Rather than looking to Jesus for healing, many men who are addicted to homosexuality insist on "doing it my way." Without turning to Jesus, any person struggling will always revert to his or her prior behaviors. "Freedom comes through surrendering to Jesus. If addiction stops us from facing the truth in our lives, then it can only be Jesus who knows the way out," according to Hank, a New Hope house leader who completed the program several years ago. The reliance on Jesus offers ex-gays not only the promise of salvation but also the assurance that they need not push themselves too hard or fret unduly about their failures. Within the sexual addiction model, Jesus welcomes and forgives any individual no matter how much their life is in shambles.

The Enemy's Tool? Battling Addictions

New Hope Ministries believes that addictions are a form of idol worship and that Satan has a direct interest in feeding addictions (New Hope 1996: 22). Addiction is surrendering to anything other than Jesus, and Satan is the enemy who lures one from God and closer to harmful behaviors. "Satan will reach us one way or another with a distortion of God's plan," according to Frank. "Many of our initial childhood sexual fantasies may have come directly from the evil one." The New Hope program teaches that compulsive addictions and behaviors are useful to Satan and that a man's urge to masturbate is often instigated by satanic suggestion. Mitch often described his gay pornography addiction as satanic.

Many ex-gays speak of their homosexuality as part of a wider problem of sexual addiction that includes pornography, masturbation, and any form of sex that occurs outside of marriage. New Hope focuses on these problems, but the main issue is homosexuality, from which other addictions may stem. The New Hope workbook explains, "Homosexuality in itself may be a type of addiction, but usually homosexuality is broken down into a series of supporting addictions." These addictions, including compulsive masturbation or "body-watching," "feed into" the main problem of homosexuality. Despite his fervent belief that God would cure him, Hank argues, "Yes, I would say I was addicted in the sense that my behavior was uncontrollable in that it dominated me." However, by defining the behaviors of homosexuality as addictions, the program can treat men while acknowledging that healing is a long process.

Critics of the ex-gay movement insist that no one changes his or her sexual orientation, and the New Hope men would have readily agreed that healing is a recovery process, a conversion, and a gradual transformation. Even Frank acknowledges that full heterosexuality is not the ultimate goal. The men in the New Hope Program believe that a new "identity in Christ" emerges and that accountable community living provides the religious support to keep men and women from returning to homosexual behaviors. Most acknowledge that their desires do not change even after many years, and the common sentiment among the men at New Hope was that healing is a process that is uncertain, fraught with relapses and some kinds of successes. More often, religious identities change rather than sexual feelings or behavior. Bob Davies, the president of Exodus for twenty-two years, explained, "We know behind closed doors that change is possible, but change is rarely complete. I know many men who are totally transformed compared to twenty years ago, but that doesn't mean that they never have a thought or a memory or a temptation or a struggle. It means that the struggle has diminished significantly. It means that for all of us, redemption is still incomplete."

For many, years after doing a program, healing remains simply a leap of faith or a belief that they are doing what God wants for them. The idea that healing may occur in unexpected forms is borne out by the experiences of ex-ex-gay men and women at the ministry. Some men and women are unable to live with the idea of denying sexual feelings, and some of these people who left the program moved on to form their own ex-ex-gay community. They believed not only that their sexual feelings did not change but that they finally came to accept themselves as gay because of the program. Most felt it was a necessary step in figuring out their sexual identities. If these men had residual anger, it was aimed at the ministry's contention that by choosing to live as gay men they could no longer have a relationship with God, and the fact that New Hope often disassociates itself from men who have left the program. One man completed three years of the program before realizing he was still gay. Over the holidays, he sent Frank a letter explaining that he could not understand how he could be separate from God because he had accepted his homosexuality: "The message I felt I received from the program when I was there was that if I ever chose to become gay, I would then become cut off from my relationship with God. I have since found that to be untrue. Indeed my relationship with God is burning bright to this very day! I am a gay man, which is clear from the feelings inside me. How do you explain that?" Other men who had accepted a gay identity often still struggled to reconcile this with their religious beliefs.

For people who had been gay for years and lived out the fantasies and relationships they had wanted but still found they were not happy, New Hope's methods of recovery, occasional sexual falls, and healing seemed to be more successful. Frank writes, "The strange truth about change is that often those who have been the most involved, the most addicted, those who may have cross-dressed or undergone a sex-change operation are the most motivated." They seem able to emerge from the program and still lead celibate lives because they have already had same-sex experiences. Most of the ex-ex-gay men never had same-sex experiences before entering the program, and when they leave the repression and prohibitions of New Hope are counteracted by extreme promiscuity.

New Hope utilizes a variety of techniques to regulate the men in the program to control potentially addictive behaviors. Accountability to the group and each other is crucial. The men meet all together at least twice a week, as well as in smaller groups to dutifully relate any feelings of lust or sexual temptation they might have experienced. Every week they fill out an accountability report that they submit to their house leader, and any improprieties are brought up for group discussion. The sheet is an elaborate two-page questionnaire that asks everything from "Have you had a quiet time with God in prayer and Bible reading each day?" to "Have you looked at someone in a sexual way (cruise) or gone anywhere hoping to meet someone?" The questions begin on a more general level: "At any time did you compromise your integrity?" "Have you taken time to show compassion for others in need, or demonstrated a servant's heart?"

However, three-fourths of the questionnaire is devoted to any possible behaviors related to same-sex attraction or the potential for sexual falls. The questions include "Have you had sex with anyone?" "Have you looked at any personal ads, answered a personal ad, or placed a personal ad for yourself?" "Have you looked at, or do you have any pornography, fitness/muscle magazines?" "Have you gone into a video store alone or looked at the adult video section?" and "Have you masturbated, and is it compulsive?" Other questions ask about phone sex, entering public bathrooms without an "accountability partner," going to the beach alone, listening to music that is a reminder of the past, leaving work early, using the Internet, opening a private voice mail account, and contact with friends "in the gay lifestyle." The sheet anticipates any possible form of behavioral transgression an ex-gay man might engage in and even presents ex-gays with ideas they may not have considered. At the end of this barrage of questions the sheet asks, "Is there anything else that has happened since your last accountability sheet that you should confess?"

The men at New Hope believe that absolute truthfulness in their answers is the key to healing. Curtis, a twenty one year old from Canada, explains, "I'm very honest, because if I'm lying about these things, I'm wasting my time and money here. If I'm going to come here, I might as well do it all the way." Although designed to stem addictive behaviors and give men structure, the accountability sheets and confessional structure also may incite the possibility of transgressive behavior on the part of the men. The explicitly detailed prohibitions actually grant off-limit behavior more power precisely because it is prohibited.

Darren, an ex-gay who is now a father with several children, admitted that he still has to keep certain forms of sexual addiction at bay. He married a woman from Open Door church and talks openly about the fact that gay pornography is still a difficult area for him. After his wife "nailed him on it," he joined a support group at Open Door for men struggling with pornography. He participated for a year and a half in a weekly accountability group and felt what he calls "the compulsion" gradually diminish. However, he conceded, "I still have to watch where my eyes go." Darren attributes his healing to God and to his support group: "I believe that I'm sitting in God's hands. I could never have the strength to stop pornography. I've just been held." Despite his assurance that God had been aiding his battle, he still had incidents every few months that he revealed to his wife. When she presented the ultimatum that he would have to leave her rather than continue with his addiction, he decided to take more drastic measures. He visited every video store in his town and nearby towns with a letter he composed himself. It said, "My name is Darren _____, and my wife is Miranda _____. Here's our phone number. If you see me in here renting pornography please call my wife." As Darren recalls, "It was like cutting off my own arm. That nixed it. I walked out of there and knew I could never go back." While many ex-gays continue to struggle with sexual addictions and assert that it is God who changes their lives, at times the more direct threat of personal abandonment rather than God's disapproval provides the impetus to regulate their behavior.

The model of sexual addiction at New Hope and other ex-gay ministries still tends to focus primarily on lust and sexual purity as a problem for men. Frank admits that when he began New Hope in the 1970s, he knew absolutely nothing about women. The first women's program began in 1979, and Frank characterized it as "a total disaster." A married couple with two kids directed the program. The wife, who had been an ex-gay for several years, fell in love with another woman in the program and divorced her husband. It was not until Frank married Anita in 1985 that New Hope initiated another program for women. Frank admits, "I couldn't handle it. I had no idea what their issues were."

As a result of the early years, New Hope's program and its models of change still cater primarily to men. The accountability sheets, straight men nights, and ideas about addiction presume that men are sexual and women experience little or no sexual attraction or lust for one another. The program asserts that lesbianism consists of primarily emotional relationships, whereas gay men are sexual predators who cannot control their desire. The problems of pornography, masturbation, and lust are gendered as male. Frank explained that the reason there are so few lesbians in the ex-gay movement is because homosexuality is not a sexual issue with women as it is with men. This is reiterated throughout ex-gay literature and conference speeches. At New Hope's annual conference, Starla Allen, an ex-gay therapist and former lesbian, elaborated on her point that lesbianism is a problem of emotional dependence on another woman. In describing her previous lesbian relationship she told the audience, "Sex was the last thing I wanted. Mine was mostly emotionally dependent. That was what broke up most of the relationships—emotional dependency."

Although women have sexual falls, people like Frank either disregard them or view them as too rare to warrant extensive prohibition. Starla Allen uses the term "monster enmeshment" to describe the idea that all women's friendships were potentially codependent. Allen also claimed that women have "anger issues" and come into lesbianism as they get involved with feminist organizations. The ex-gay model in which all lesbians are asexual reinforces certain Christian ideas about gender roles and female asexuality. A nonsexual ex-gay woman will ultimately become an appropriate Christian wife in a marriage in which sexuality is designed simply for the purposes of procreation. The notion that women are nonsexual is also essential in the Christian narrative that women domesticate men. According to this model, a sexually promiscuous ex-gay man needs an asexual female partner to control his sinful and addictive behavior.

A Culture of Public Intimacy

As part of their intimacy with God, ex-gays are also encouraged to testify about their sexual transgressions in twelve-step-style meetings. Recovering from homosexual addiction requires individual motivation and self-discipline, but at New Hope the group is also extremely important. Little of a personal nature is felt to be off-limits for discussion, and whatever remains hidden is a potential source of shame. Private confession or prayer is encouraged but not considered to have as much efficacy as a public confession. New Hope expects ex-gays to speak publicly about the most private and harrowing aspects of their lives in small groups, in published materials, and in front of churches and large audiences. According to Andy Comiskey, creator of another ex-gay program called Living Waters, "The only bridge that can connect the two parts of the struggler—pious Christian and detached addict—is confession to other people who mediate the reality of Christ's grace and truth."[3]

By testifying about their past experiences, ex-gays attempt to convince others that sexual conversion is necessary to retain a relationship with God. Ex-gay men and women express how God has come into their lives, how they have become convinced of his presence, and how he has helped them transform their sexuality. By giving witness to the changes in their lives, they attempt to convince others that their only option is to disavow their sin of homosexual behavior and/or attraction. The point of testifying is to instill in the listener the sense that his or her life is empty, and that only God can fill and change it. As Mitch's story demonstrates, each testimony progresses to a crisis point that results in a born-again experience and the discovery of the relationship with God and finishes with participation in the ex-gay ministry and the path to conversion. The most celebrated cases end with marriage or children.

New Hope has an entire wall in its office with different shelves for every type of testimony: homosexuality, lesbianism, masturbation, pornography, transgender identities, parents, and materials for teenagers. Every month, the Exodus newsletter presents a testimony or story on the front cover. Most of them feature a ministry leader who has been out of the lifestyle for several years. The headline in March 2001 was "From Prostitute to Pastor: Mike Haley Was Once Addicted to Homosexuality. Today He Is a Fulfilled Husband and Father. How Does He Explain the Change?" Mike completed the New Hope program in the early 1990s and now works for Focus on the Family, one of the largest Christian public policy and media organizations dedicated to the perservation of the family and the eradication of homosexuality.[4] His testimony contains a brief description of his life as a gay prostitute, his sexual relationships with other men, his experience of being saved by another ex-gay, and his eventual marriage to a woman. Other testimonies have a similar narrative structure but are geared to other issues. Barbara Swallow, a former lesbian gives a testimony called "All Things Made New." The byline reads, "After being molested, I decided it wasn't safe being a girl. So I began to construct a new Barbara who wasn't female at all." There are other testimonies by wives of men who are struggling, daughters of lesbians, and parents of gay children.

As Mike Haley's and Barbara Swallow's testimonies demonstrate, to a certain extent, ex-gays lay claim to victimhood as a primary source of identity. Doug says he becomes weary of everyone in the program proclaiming their brokenness: "We all have brokenness, but if you keep on using that as a crutch, then you're never going to move on. I think that's one of the big problems we have here. We get into this brokenness contest. I'm like, let's move on people." The discourse of victimhood tends to imbue the trivial with grave import so that every event from having a sexual fall to having a bad day at work is validated as equally terrible. The emphasis on group sharing often leads to what one man called "group hysteria." In many of the group meetings, one or two people begin crying, and then suddenly everybody is weeping.

The New Hope culture enables a candid discussion of sexuality that would not occur at other churches or in other religious settings. Since most of the men testify about same-sex feelings, looking at gay pornography, and having anonymous sex, the ministry frequently deals with sex on an explicit level. Self-disclosure opens the way to healing because it creates shared, honest, and mutual vulnerability. Many men feel that the secrecy about their homosexuality and sexual addictions had been the most destructive force in their lives. Curtis explains, "You see, the thing for me and for most of us is this secrecy, where it's all secret and you can never share. The aim is to bring our diseased attitudes and misdeeds to the light of others and God to be done with them. When it comes from such an attitude, sharing becomes a liberating and life-giving experience."

The idea that someone would not confess is inconceivable. When I asked what would have happened if Mitch had not confessed his pornography addiction, Curtis remarked that he had not even considered the possibility. Addiction and recovery from homosexuality mirror the Christian ideas of sin and redemption. As with the idea of a sexual fall, the ex-gay movement believes that no matter how many sex acts a person has committed, there is still the possibility of healing. Grace and forgiveness are extended to all people as long as they vow to stay with the ministry and maintain their trust in God. The individual who experiences a sexual fall can still become a new creation in Christ.

The ex-gay worldview is structured by unwavering faith in the fact that God has a plan for each of them, and that becoming heterosexual is the only path that enables them to remain close to God. Healing their same-sex desires is a religious process, bolstered by the twelve-step elements of the ministry. Although their feelings may not change, and their sexual falls continue, they feel transformed religiously.

New Hope is part of a wider public culture of intimacy in which ex-gay confessions of traumatized identity become part of a public testimonial discourse of conversion. Bringing the intimate into public prominence is the vehicle for self-help and healing. Although the ex-gay movement views confessions as central to healing, this relentless focus on personal testimony also fosters myopia. In many cases, ex-gays are too caught up in their own healing to envision their relationship to a wider politics. Yet their narratives of healing have become part of a wider political antigay discourse promulgated by organizations like Focus on the Family. Based on the testimonies of ex-gay men and women, Focus on the Family promotes wider antigay activism cloaked in the rhetoric of choice, healing, and compassion.

New Hope and the ex-gay movement have created a religious culture of therapy for troubled individuals in an increasingly fragmented world through an emphasis on self-help and healing. For ex-gay men and women, to believe that God would create a person to be gay and then condemn homosexual behavior is incompatible with their theological view that heterosexuality means a closer personal relationship with God. It is a far more hopeful mode of thinking to believe that homosexuality is a learned behavior or condition caused by arrested development that can be cured through therapy, religious faith, community, and accountability.

NOTES

1. Formerly known as Love in Action, New Hope changed its name in 1996. In 1994, Love in Action moved to Memphis, Tennessee, where it still runs a residential program for men and women. The other residential program is Freedom at Last in Wichita, Kansas. Most ex-gay ministries are support groups that meet on a weekly basis.

2. Exodus includes more than 100 local ministries in the United States and Canada. It is also linked with other Exodus world regions outside of North America, totaling more than 135 ministries in seventeen countries.

3. Exodus International Conference, July 26–28, 2000. Point Loma Nazarene University.

4. Focus on the Family, founded by James Dobson in 1977, is a conservative Christian conglomerate with daily radio broadcasts and more than sixteen publications geared toward youth, parents, teachers, physicians, and church leaders. It also overseas missionary organizations and other media ventures. Dobson sends a monthly letter to everyone on his mailing list in which he outlines his thoughts on

current political controversies. According to Focus, Dobson's syndicated radio broadcast is heard on more than 3,000 radio facilities in North America and in nine languages on approximately 2,300 facilities in over ninety-eight other countries. By the mid-1990s, Focus had an annual budget of more than $100 million. See Sara Diamond, *Not by Politics Alone: The Enduring Influence of the Christian Right* (New York: Guilford Press, 1998), 30–36. For more information see the Focus on the Family Web site at www.family.org.

REFERENCES

Alcoholics Anonymous. 1955. *Alcoholics Anonymous*. New York: Alcoholics Anonymous World Services Inc.

Berlant, Lauren. 1997. *The Queen of America Goes to Washington City: Essays on Sex and Citizenship*. Durham, N.C.: Duke University Press.

Christianity Today. 2002. Ex-Gay Sheds the Mocking Quotes: An Interview with Bob Davies. *Christianity Today*, January 7:4

Foucault, Michel. 1978. *The History of Sexuality Vol. I, An Introduction*. New York: Pantheon.

Griffith, Marie. 2000. *God's Daughters: Evangelical Women and the Power of Submission*. Berkeley: University of California Press.

Herman, Ellen. 1995. *The Romance of American Psychology: Political Culture in the Age of Experts*. Berkeley: University of California Press.

Kaminer, Wendy. 1992. *I'm Dysfunctional, You're Dysfunctional: The Recovery Movement and Other Self-Help Fashions*. Reading, Mass.: Addison-Wesley.

Kurtz, Ernest. 1988. *AA: The Story*. New York: Harper and Row.

Miller, Donald E. 1997. *Reinventing American Protestantism: Christianity in the New Millennium*. Berkeley: University of California Press.

Simonds, Wendy. 1992. *Women and Self-Help Culture: Reading Between the Lines*. New Brunswick, N.J.: Rutgers University Press.

Swallow, Barbara. 2000. *Free Indeed: One Woman's Victory Over Lesbianism*. Seattle, Wash.: Exodus International North America.

Worthen, Frank. 1996. *Steps Out Program manual*. New Hope Ministries.

17

"Jesus Is My Doctor": Healing and Religion in African American Women's Lives

Stephanie Y. Mitchem

"Jesus is my doctor," a claim made by many black women, raises a rich mélange of culturally resonant issues. Faith is articulated as an active, powerful, protective, creative partnership with a God who loves completely and without reservation. Lived in the body, community, and world, African American women's faith often extends to hope for the healing of all people as a natural corollary of envisioning a new, more perfect world. Faith in "Doctor" Jesus is neither superstitious nor contradictory when grounded in such social and ideological understandings.

This chapter offers a brief exploration of black women's beliefs in faith healing. While faith healing is widespread, public, and perhaps almost ubiquitous in black communities, little systematic research has delved into its forms and meanings. Thus, this chapter is neither definitive nor exhaustive but rather a preliminary effort to scratch the surface of the epistemological frameworks through which African American women understand faith and healing. Over the past few years (1996–2003), I have interviewed black women, mostly in the Detroit area, about their understandings of faith, health, healing, and spirituality. These interviews, informed by historic and contemporary contexts of African Americans, yield a rich tapestry of which "Jesus is my doctor" constitutes a principal thread.

I approach this work from my stance as an African American womanist theologian. Womanist theology, which has been developing since the 1980s, draws from black women's life experiences and everyday religious understandings as primary sources. For African

American women, healing, health, and spirituality come together to provide an important text within black experiences. Multiple strands of meaning, related to layers of self, communities, and wider society, are thrown into sharp relief when these issues are explored. Against the backdrop of racist tendencies to stereotype or essentialize black women, this study deconstructs existing myths about black women and emphasizes that black women in the United States experience and interpret healing in diverse and meaningful ways.

The first two sections of this chapter provide a brief sketch of the contexts that are created by interactions between white-dominated American society and black women. The first considers some of the basic issues when gender and health cross in black women's lives; the second is found in the crossings of medicine with the lives of African American women. The next section turns to the story of one woman—Valeria. The final section will widen the lens from Valeria and consider accounts from members of the grassroots Detroit Metropolitan Black Women's Health Project.

Gender, Black Women, and Health

American society has exhibited a doublethink mentality about black women (Roberts 1997). On the one hand, black women are rendered invisible or with broom in hand. On the other hand, Oprah's chat and Della Reese's angel present national images of black women that would seem positive. Yet the question must be raised: Do these images reinforce other stereotypes, particularly that of the mammy? Other stereotypes of black women such as the sex-mad jezebel and the castrating sapphire continue to throw boundaries around the lives of black women (Collins 1991: 67–89). These images constitute separate spaces for American black girls' growth into women that requires learning to balance the conflicting, destructive messages from society. Socialization becomes a process of countersocialization. Gender construction, for black women, is hazardous duty. As bell has hooks stated, "Stress is a hidden killer underlying all the major health problems black women face" (1993: 53).

In spite of, or because of, these separate spaces, black women have been able to retain some gender role understandings and views of self that do not correspond to those of Western white cultures. Despite their reduction to feel-good-be-happy stereotypical symbols serving America, Oprah and Della Reese also represent a healing strand that black women themselves have woven into their gender identities. Sociohistorical factors created the climate in which black women's continued strength for the benefit of others became an expectation. African American women's activism for community survival of black people and their assistance in maintaining families are such aspects of the strength and endurance tied into their gender identities. African American women often tie their very sense of themselves to their continued strength, taking as a given that their social roles must include working on behalf of their communities with little regard for their own needs. The image of making a way out of no way, of doing what has to be done, is based on the very bodies of black women.

Community survival is an integral value underlying black women's health understandings. African American women seldom have had the luxury of being taken care of by others and seldom have had the economic option of being stay-at-home mothers who hire "a girl" to help. Therefore, the idea of what a woman *ought* to be is shaped differently in most black communities than the well-promoted ideal image of women in middle-class white communities. Some of these gender concepts are woven through black women's understandings of faith healing.

Medicine and Black Women

The history of the development of Western medicine provides an important context for understanding black women and faith healing. I am grateful to Dr. Sharon Oliver, a physician in the Detroit area, for pointing to these dimensions. She contends that most medical doctors are unaware of the social and racialized history of Western medicine; it is not part of their training. As a black woman, Dr. Oliver was liberated from the confines of Western medicine during her residency, as she witnessed how black and poor people were treated in hospital systems. Her experiences are reflected in the ways black women participate as professionals in health care, which becomes another gulf between black cultural perspectives and Western medical practice.

American women were systematically excluded from medical professions as these developed in the eighteenth through the twentieth century. Women's folk-based healing activities were generally and systematically eliminated with the establishment of professional medicine, consequently establishing the male figure as the normative healer. However, gender and race combined in different and more intense levels during this same development, strengthening the divisions between who legitimately had access to "professional" health care while furthering black people's suspicions of those same professionals. Until legal segregation ended in 1954, black people had a checkered history of access to regular professional health care. While black men and women in small numbers found their way into the medical profession, significant gaps in community access were established.

Because enslaved Africans were not viewed as human, they were not expected to receive the same health care as white people (Savitt 1978; Smith 1995). Health care became a site of struggle for black people to maintain positive views of their own bodies in the face of negative views of European American society. White Europeans also compared black women with white women unfavorably, viewing them with disdain. In general, black women were rendered socially invisible except for their productive and reproductive labors for the benefit of white American society. This marginalization of black women, however, has created locations where the women have been able to re-create themselves, to employ moral agency, and to affect their communities, even in health care.

The historical exclusion of African Americans from Western medicine combined with African American popular culture to create a fertile ground for connecting faith and healing. A rich body of folk cures and home remedies are part of the culturally accumulated knowledge of black people throughout the diaspora. As Fayth M. Parks states, "The practice of folk healing is grounded in African traditions. It is a process that acknowledges mind, body, spirit connections to healing both physical illness and psychological distress. Folk healing provides coping strategies . . . embedded in the fabric of black life" (2001: 661).

Concepts from black folk traditions continue to be transmitted, with differences in regions, familial structures, and so on. How not to stunt the growth of a boy child; cures for acne or morning sickness or headaches or nosebleeds; predicting the sex of the child of a pregnant woman; birth control: each of these becomes part of the knowledge base on which black women and men, consciously or not, draw in daily living. The relationships between body and soul, individuals and communities, and human life with the greater universe are sketched out and given meaning in these understandings. For instance, in this African American meaning framework, both the individual human body and the body of the community are considered locations requiring healing. The power to bring about healing resides in the members of the community. Wisdom from elders and unnamed sources became a foundation for this thinking.

Historically, within African American cultures, a healer could be female or male. The power to heal was seen as a charism, a spiritual gift, and gender was not a determinant of who received the gift. From the granny midwives to the folk-doctoring root women to spiritual healers, women have been an integral part of black communities' experiences of healing. Black women, in their own homes or through kinship networks, were and often still are the first dispensers of extant folk cures. Historically, with good reason, the white medical establishment was often perceived as the last line of defense against illness, especially when contrasted with healers who were known to be trusted parts of the communities of black people. Today, advertisements for spiritual healers or root workers—Madame C or Sister Rosa—are still found in black newspapers throughout the United States.

That these healing traditions continue to have some life in black American communities, often without a specific one-to-one correspondence in any African culture, gives credence to the theories of Sidney Mintz and Richard Price (1976), who conceptualize how African American cultures developed. They posit that African "cognitive orientations" constituted part of the mentalities of the enslaved. Perhaps as remnants of African orientations, the interconnections between physical, mental, spiritual, and emotional life are deeply felt. Within such orientations, the testimony of cures is part of the religious expression of black people.

One study of black, rural women in a North Carolina community construed folk concepts of disease and healing as barriers to diagnosis and treatment of breast cancer. When asked about their attitudes toward cancer testing, the women in the study said that they saw cancer as a disease that, once activated, needed care "not to stir it up." They viewed cancer testing as "looking for trouble," and they viewed cancer as a disease in need of a spiritual remedy. As one woman stated, "The only one powerful enough to overcome it is the Lord. You just have to trust in Jesus to do battle for you and save you from the horrible affliction." Another woman told of her response to the diagnosis of cancer: "So I just decided then and there that I wouldn't worry any more. That I would give it to God, and that I would never speak of it again, I trusted God to heal me and I believe he has. That's all I need to know" (Davis-Penn 1996: 150–51). The study would seem to indicate mere ignorance on the part of these women. However, an alternative reading points to a different epistemological framework that informs their pronouncements.

At the heart of this discussion is a chasm between the understandings of black folk methods and the world of professional medicine that cannot be addressed simply as allopathic versus holistic or scientific versus superstitious. Karen McCarthy Brown correctly contrasts Haitian Vodou with Western medicine and refers to this gulf as a clash of root metaphors. Western medicine locates disease primarily in the physical. In this view, healing is a commodity, to be controlled by the powerful, appropriately trained person. "Seeing healing power as property, subject to all the dynamics of a capitalist system, is one of the most significant root metaphors of Western medicine and one of the most damaging to women" (1987: 123–24).

Religion, Black Women, and Healing

Valeria is a middle-aged African American woman who believes in and has experienced faith healing. Valeria lives in the suburbs and works in a management position with the state of Michigan. She is nearing retirement and is thinking about starting her own business. In our conversations, Valeria related two personal faith-healing experiences. In one, she was diagnosed with a type of hepatitis. Following the test, she went to her church in Detroit, where there were ministers of healing on that particular Sunday. At one point, those with blood diseases were invited to come forward to be prayed over. She did, and at her next blood test, there was no sign of the blood disorder. Valeria experienced another healing through her church's ministries that ended her chronic back pain. To this day, she follows a morning regimen of prayer and anointing herself with special oil. Valeria's faith-based healings represent a common theme in the experiences of black women in the United States.

Valeria is a member of a nondenominational, black, Christian church— Great Faith Ministries International. This Detroit-based church is now housed in an old movie theater and its adjoining buildings in a poor part of the city. The church services are broadcast in Detroit, but other markets have also picked up its energetic events. I have attended the church services several times with Valeria and learned much each time. (The church also has an extensive bookstore.) Valeria and her church's members understand God as active in their everyday lives. Even her membership in that church is seen by Valeria as part of God's plan. She stated, "I stay [at this church] because God hasn't told me I need to go anywhere else. And I really feel that you have to be grounded in the word of God and not be moved by anything that comes down the pike. And also I believe that God's power is demonstrated there."

Charism is important in determining members' roles. Identification of those Spirit-granted gifts becomes the way those in ministry are selected. Believing that one is called and gifted to do something, for God's glory, is a key to discernment. The bishop, blessed by God to lead the community, has the healing gift. The bishop blessed the oil with which Valeria anoints herself. I asked her to tell me about the theological grounds for understanding the gift of healing. Valeria directed me to a book by Dr. Charles Dixon, who defined the healing gift as one that comes from God. As such, "[Healing] is not a Midas touch. That is, there is no such thing as a gift that makes it possible for one to heal others automatically, as though one were a healing machine. Faith is always to be reckoned with. . . . The gift of healing is the God-given ability to impart the healing virtue of Jesus Christ to others. . . . To heal the sick signifies: to restore to health; to cure; to make sound; [and] to reconcile" (1997: 133, 141–42).

This faith-centered life involves healing on more levels than just a single person's physical body. For instance, prayer and action are intertwined with a holistic sense of what needs to be healed, including economic troubles. Valeria explained how she prays for things to be birthed into the natural:

> I [might] pray for natural finances. Like, we have a project at our
> church, and we're going to be breaking ground sometime next
> month. There's a certain amount of money that we need, and so
> there have been different things that have been put in place that we
> can do that we can birth this money in. So we go to 6:00 A.M.
> prayer to birth in that money. We've been praying for a while. We've
> been praying to have that money secured. Each month, when it's
> time to pay that bill due to [the bank], that is there.

Explorations into faith and healing reveal the continued existence of black popular religion and, by extension, suggest that there are core "ordinary theologies" embedded within African American communities. African American women express black cultural understandings in the retention of an embodied spirituality, that is, a connected body-spirit view of self that yields culturally informed religious understandings. Valeria's understanding of illness demonstrates these connections: "Illness to me is when you don't have a spirit of forgiveness and you don't have joy. You know, just to see the sun outside, I was joyous. I was excited. I felt like I had some pep, some energy."

Faith lies at the core of the ordinary theologies of African American women such as Valerie. Faith, for many black women, becomes a self-defining center that resists socially constructed stereotypes. God is known as one who can make a way out of no way. Therefore, taking a problem in life to God is seen as an active step toward its resolution. As such, faith becomes a tool of resistance, rejecting limits and dehumanization. Faith offers the believer self-empowerment through God's power. Believing is an activity that taps power. "God is able" is both a statement of faith and a battle cry. Thus the development of black women's faith is not merely a response to social conditions or a form of denial. Faith can provide the alternative space in which black women become self-empowered. Faith in this framework has the cultural groundings of the black community and black women's networks, but it involves a lifelong process of spiritual maturation.

Karen Baker-Fletcher, a womanist theologian, writes of faith and body-soul connections in black women's religious thought: "God is present in our everyday lives, and infinite possibilities for healing and wholeness are in our midst. . . . It is in our human bodies, souls, and minds in our everyday lives that we experience and reason about the sacred. Such everyday experience of and thought about the sacred enables humankind with powers of sustenance to practice survival, healing, and liberation in the midst of oppression" (1997: 127).

The grounds for black women's acceptance of faith healing cannot be dismissed as simply a response to economic stress. That Valeria, who is in a management position, is not in an economically depressed situation to which she responds by believing in faith healing highlights the complexities in this study. The key, Valeria stressed, is belief: "You gotta *believe* to be healed. You must have faith."

Detroit Metropolitan Black Women's Health Project:
Another Voice

Valeria's words resonate with the community-based efforts of the Detroit Metropolitan Black Women's Health Project (DMBWHP). While DMBWHP members' ideas sometimes lack the explicit theological language of Valeria's, the black cultural and communal connections come through clearly.

The Detroit project is a chapter of the national project. Both operate primarily as informal support networks among black women, aiming for wellness. The organization's definition of health states this perspective clearly. Wellness is "not merely the absence of illness, but the active promotion of emotional, mental, and physical wellness of this and future generations. Such wellness is impossible without individual and group empowerment. Such personal and collective empowerment is essential to the redefining and reinterpretation of who Black women are, were and can become" (National Black Women's Health Project, Mission Statement).

The project sponsors community events, and members meet regularly to discuss health issues. Small self-help groups are the primary work of the project. These groups, which meet in homes or community centers, focus on what they perceive as one of the most health-threatening problems affecting black women: the lack of self-care. This form of activism reflects Parks's fourth category of faith healing, through a process of self-awareness. The project's self-help meetings become a focused time in which participants speak strictly about their own health—their needs and concerns, not those of their children, spouse, or coworkers. This feeling is stated eloquently in the book *Body and Soul: The Black Women's Guide to Physical Health and Emotional Well-Being*, referred to as "the bible" among Project members. "Talking about our health issues in groups provides a framework for understanding why Black women have poorer health status than other women. As we talk about lifestyles and confront the realities of being both Black and female in America, we bring personal awareness to impersonal statistical data" (Villarosa 1994: 386).

The Detroit project members, whom I interviewed over a two-year period as part of my larger research on black women and healing, directly linked ideas of healing with spirituality. Mattie is one of the members who reflected upon the dynamics of faith in relation to healing from her own experience with cancer treatment:

> Healing to me is something come by the grace of God. . . . Because it depends on how you want to be healed. See, you don't really have to be, say, cancerous to want to be healed. So healing to me comes by the grace of God. . . . You got to get it for yourself, you got to believe God is able. . . . See the doctor told me I wouldn't be able to do this [she raised her left arm over her head, the side where the cancer was found]. . . . The doctor said, "You'll never be able to get your arm over your head." And I looked at her and told her, "You ain't no God." . . . I get up in the morning and I say, "Lord, I want to thank you for getting me through the night. Put your shield around me. Lord, I want to thank you." Mattie's everyday theology is revealed

through her belief in human limitations compared with God's power, as well as her prayerful relationship with God.

P Jazz is a member of the project who has a doctorate in nursing. Drawing from her experiences as a health care worker and a black woman, P Jazz defined healing and dying:

> I could be in disequilibrium—say my blood sugars are up, I've got high blood pressure, and I get treated. The medicine could make the blood sugar go down, blood pressure go down, and everything starts coming normal—and I may not have any healing occur. I think healing occurs when there's something more that happens. . . . I kind of integrate within my being. . . . My viewpoint is that [healing] doesn't just occur unless your inner being is receptive, you know, that you can take it to a different level. You can understand what's going on, and if you need to release, release. But something occurs in addition to the medication,'cause I don't think that medication heals. I think that's just one small piece of helping us move on that continuum, but the healing aspect is greater. So when I see repeaters, there's no healing there. Even when symptoms reoccur, the people that have had some healing experience it differently. . . . They've got tumors, but they've been healed. They feel they are at a point where healing has occurred. They die peaceful. It's a different level, I think, in terms of the healing. We don't begin to really touch that a lot in health, in Western medicine.

Quincy, another member of the DMBWHP, discussed barriers to belief in faith healing:

> If you don't have the faith of a mustard seed, you don't understand healing. 'Cause we are so technologically educated, and we've always got a reason. My husband says that all the time: "There's a reason for everything." There's not a reason for everything! My husband stopped saying that, I took him to a healing service. He saw a lady get up out of her wheelchair, who we know, who we *know*, has been in this wheelchair since a kid. It changed his whole attitude. . . . 'Cause when you talk about a mustard seed, do you know how little a mustard seed is? 'Cause when you have that much faith without a doubt, that's not very much.

REFERENCES

Baker-Fletcher, Karen. 1997. The Strength of My Life. In *Embracing the Spirit: Womanist Perspectives on Hope, Salvation and Transformation*, ed. Emilie M. Townes, 122–39. Maryknoll, N.Y.: Orbis Books.

Brown, Karen McCarthy. 1987. The Power to Heal: Reflections on Women, Religion, and Medicine. In *Shaping New Vision: Gender and Values in American Culture*, ed. Clarissa W. Atkinson, Constance Hall Buchanan, and Margaret R. Miles, 123–42. Ann Arbor, Mich.: UMI Research Press.

Collins, Patricia Hill. 1991. *Black Feminist Thought: Knowledge, Consciousness, and the Politics of Empowerment*. New York: Routledge.

Davis-Penn, Dolores. 1996. Rural Black Women s Knowledge, Attitudes, and Practices toward Breast Cancer: A Silent Epidemic. In *African-American Women's Health and Social Issues*, ed. Catherine Fisher Collins, 150–51. Westport, Conn.: Auburn House.

Dixon, Charles. 1997. *Life in the Spirit: Understanding the Gifts and Operations of the Holy Spirit*. Bogota, N.J.: End Time Wave Publications.

Gilkes, Cheryl Townsend. 2002. A Conscious Connection to All That Is: The Color Purple as Subversive and Critical Ethnography. In *Personal Knowledge and Beyond: Reshaping the Ethnography of Religion*, ed. J. V. Spickard, J. S. Landres, and M. B. McGuire, 175–91. New York: New York University Press.

hooks, bell. 1993. *Sisters of the Yam: Black Women and Self-Recovery*. Boston: South End Press.

Mintz, Sidney W., and Richard Price. 1976. *The Birth of African American Culture: An Anthropological Perspective*. Boston: Beacon Press.

Orfield, Myron. 1999. *Detroit Metropolitics: A Regional Agenda for Community and Stability*. Report to the Archdiocese of Detroit. Detroit, Michigan.

Parks, Fayth M. 2001. When Mighty Waters Rise: African American Folk Healing and the Bible. In *African Americans and the Bible: Sacred Texts and Social Textures*, ed. Vincent L. Wimbush, 661–70. New York: Continuum.

Price, Betty J. 1997. *Through the Fire and through the Water: My Triumph over Cancer*. Los Angeles: Faith One Publications.

Roberts, Dorothy. 1997. *Killing the Black Body: Race, Reproduction, and the Meaning of Liberty*. New York: Vintage Books.

Savitt, Todd L. 1978. *Medicine and Slavery: The Diseases and Health Care of Blacks in Antebellum Virginia*. Urbana: University of Illinois Press.

Smith, Susan L. 1995. *Sick and Tired of Being Sick and Tired: Black Women's Health Activism in America, 1890–1950*. Philadelphia: University of Pennsylvania Press.

Villarosa, Linda, ed. 1994. *Body and Soul: The Black Women's Guide to Physical Health and Emotional Well-Being*. New York: HarperCollins.

18

Gender and Healing in Navajo Society

Thomas J. Csordas

The Navajo are among the three largest indigenous tribes in North America (the Cherokee and Lakota, or Sioux, are the others) and as a people possess a land and natural resource base larger than that of any other tribe. Ritual healing, in the context of either traditional Navajo ceremonies, Native American Church (NAC) peyote prayer meetings, or Pentecostal Christian revivalism, is a prominent feature of contemporary Navajo life for both men and women (Csordas 2000).[1] Navajo women have been recognized as having relatively high status and considerable social power in relation to men (Kluckhohn and Leighton 1962), yet they are only infrequently encountered among ceremonial practitioners of the prestigious chantways. This chapter is a step toward understanding the motivation and experience of those Navajo women who do become healers.

Navajo society was traditionally both matrilineal and matrilocal, with women able to own property and exercise significant authority within the family. Navajos express a strong spiritual connection to Mother Earth. In contemporary society women are often the stable centers of extended families. The Navajo word *shimı*, or mother, has powerful associations of warmth and nurturance that encompass the senses of one's birth mother, Changing Woman, and Mother Earth. Men may also be strong presences in families, and there is a clear articulation of the importance of Father Sky as a complement to Mother Earth, but men are relatively more likely to be absent from the home for extended periods to engage in wage work or to be indisposed because of alcohol abuse. With relatively little stigma attached to divorce, serial monogamy is not uncommon. Domestic violence, especially associated with alcohol abuse, is widely reported, and father-daughter incest (especially by stepfathers) is a long-standing concern.

It is perhaps not surprising that the relatively high status of women can coexist with domestic violence and tension between the genders, or that with respect to the place in society of women the ideal and real are in some ways inconsistent. In myth the Navajo are said to have originated from Asdzaan Nadleehi, or Changing Woman, who remains highly venerated today. At the same time, gender relations are underpinned by a mythic charter contained in the widely known story of the "separation of the sexes." The story is of a time when men and women tried to prove they could live without one another by segregating themselves on opposite sides of a river, with abominable consequences, including the begetting of monstrous offspring as a result of some of the practices resorted to during the ultimately unsuccessful experiment. It is possible that some male ceremonial prerogative is rooted in the claim that it was women who begat the monsters and who relented first in asking the men to return.

In practical terms, with the noted exceptions of expertise in herbalism and ritual diagnosis, ceremonial knowledge and practice are largely male prerogatives. Though women are not expressly excluded, they are often considered out of place when inquiring about such matters, and medicine women often begin their careers as apprentices to an immediate male relative, particularly when there is no male apprentice on the horizon. Yet it remains important to acknowledge and examine the role and experience of women ceremonial practitioners in contemporary Navajo society. Indeed, such an undertaking offers a highly specific view of gender among Navajos: women are unique among healers because they are women; and they are unique among other women because they are healers. In this respect our principle is that a general cultural situation can well be understood by a close look at exceptional cases within that situation.

The impressive but inconsistent Navajo Ceremonial Practitioners' Directory, dating from 1981, which includes herbalists, Traditional chanters, and Native American Church ceremonialists but not Navajo Christian healers, allows us to add a degree of specificity.[2] Frisbie and Tso's (1993) summary of the directory shows that 21.5 percent of Navajo ceremonialists were women. Among those whose primary specialization was divination, 68 percent were women, and among those whose primary specialization was herbalism, 66 percent were women. On the other hand, among Blessingway chanters, only 6 percent were women, and among Native American Church healers, only 8.5 percent were women.

The data presented by Frisbie and Tso also allow for a regional breakdown within Navajoland of the proportion of women with different types of ceremonial knowledge (table 18.1). Uniformly across the geographic regions of the reservation, the representation of women declines as the level of ritual special-

TABLE 18.1. Proportions of Women Navajo Ceremonialists

Agency/Region	Women Hand-Tremblers (%)	Women Blessingway Chanters (%)	Women Major Ceremonial Chanters (%)
Chinle	34	1.4	2
Fort Defiance	57	6.0	2
Shiprock	43	6.5	1
Tuba City	37	0.0	1

Source: Frisbie and Tso 1993

ization and prestige increases. Handtrembling (*nidilniihi*) is perhaps the most frequently sought form of Navajo diagnosis or divination, but while diagnosticians are gatekeepers who direct patients toward major healing ceremonies, they generally carry less prestige than chanters. Blessingway is the central and most frequently performed of Navajo ceremonies, but it is also the one that chanters often begin with before moving on to more specialized and advanced rituals. Regionally, among chanters women are represented in the highest proportion in the eastern area of the reservation (Crownpoint), which is regarded as relatively more acculturated, or at least much more thoroughly exposed to influences from the dominant Anglo-American culture. By the same token, the lowest proportion of women chanters is reported in the western region (Tuba City), which is typically regarded as most "traditional" in orientation.

Frisbie (1992: 496) reports being told by one of its administrators that the Rough Rock Demonstration School's Mental Health Training Program for Medicine Men and Women, funded by the National Institute of Mental Health from 1969 to 1983, had "14 or 15" women among its 104 graduates during this period. Our own work beginning a decade later, in 1993, was conducted among Christians and Native American Church practitioners, as well as among adherents to Navajo Traditional religion. Although healers were recruited primarily from the personal networks of Navajo members of our project staff, the reservation-wide character of the work and the use of four separate ethnographic teams that tended to cancel one another's recruitment biases lend credence to the suggestion that this group of healers is to at least some degree representative. Indeed, the overall proportions of women healers across all three religious categories corresponds closely to those cited by Frisbie as having completed the Traditional training at Rough Rock: during the period since 1993, we worked with a total of 112 healers (38 from the NAC, 39 Traditionalists, and 36 from various forms of Christianity), 15 of whom were women. Women accounted for 5 percent of NAC healers, 12 percent of Traditional Navajo healers (including both Blessingway chanters and chanters of other ceremonies but excluding diagnosticians numbering 5 of the total, with 3 of these 5 being women), and 16 percent of Navajo Christian healers.

TABLE 18.2. Marital Status of Male and Female Navajo Healer

Healers-Gender	Single/ Separated/ Widowed/ Divorced N (%)	Married/ live with partner N (%)	Total N (%)
Male	15 (16.7)	75 (83.3)	90 (100)
Female	7 (46.7)	8 (53.3)	15 (100)
Total	22 (21)	83 (79)	105 (100)
Pearson Chi-Square	value = 6.987 df = 1		Asymp. Sig. (2-sided) = .008
Fisher's Exact Test	Exact Sig. (2-sided) = .015		Exact Sig. (1-sided) =.015

Source: Navajo Healing Project

In this preliminary discussion, I will present brief sketches of three women (one representing each religious healing tradition) from among the fifteen with whom my research team worked. I make no claim that their experience is typical, but rather that their experience is likely to be distinct from that of their male counterparts in a variety of ways. To begin, we can note a prominent difference in marital status (table 18.2). Whereas 83.3 percent of the males were married or living with a partner, only 53.3 percent of female healers were married; 20 percent were single, 13.3 percent widowed, and another 13.3 percent divorced. This is significant even given the small number of people involved. It is a social fact that appears to be in accord with the observation that, for women, marriage and its responsibilities are perceived to be in conflict with the demands of being a healer. Stated otherwise, the cultural expectation is that women should be married instead of becoming healers, and to a certain extent the choice of being a healer is a choice to remain unmarried. For men, in contrast, being married is a sign of the stability and maturity expected of a healer, and the role of healer's wife is often one not only of active support but also of considerable influence both ceremonially and socially.

What a Women's Libber He Made Out of Me

The Traditional Navajo chanter, to whom I will refer as Desbah, is unique among women healers in her relative youthfulness: whereas eleven of the fifteen women we encountered were over the age of fifty, she was in her early forties. Despite her age, she was, she averred, one of only two women on the Navajo reservation capable of performing a ceremony in its full nine-night version (many Navajo healing rituals are performed in one-, two-, or five-night versions, which lack the elaboration of many ceremonial details). She is among five of the seven Traditional women healers we interviewed who is unmarried (in her case never married) because she "didn't like to be controlled" and "wanted more independence," though she has had boyfriends. Yet in an interesting affirmation of the traditional pattern, not only did she inherit her practice from a great uncle, but that uncle's wife remains as her principal assistant. In other words, the elder woman continues in her accustomed role of "medicine man's wife," though her husband's place in the practice has been taken by her younger kinswoman. Desbah is relatively well educated, having completed slightly more than two years of college and having experience as a mental health consultant. Moreover, her interviews were more extensive, articulate, and reflective than those of any other healer, male or female, with whom we worked. She clearly understood the experiential focus of our work, commenting that our interest in healing was not so much in the details of how she performed her ceremonies but in "things like states of mind."

Desbah was born the middle child of eleven siblings, at least two of whom attended college before her. She is comfortably bilingual in Navajo and English. She attended a Catholic high school until her junior year, when her parents were divorced and she transferred to a public school on the reservation where there was no tuition. Following graduation she earned an associate's degree in college, then worked in several tribal government jobs. Desbah was raised in the Traditional Navajo religion, saying of the elders, "I always thought that they had some kind of power. They had a way to, even by just speaking a word of advice or something, to heal or correct something." She remembered her mother relying on a medicine man, and being healed of a bad headache by a medicine man when she was quite young. She began attending Traditional ceremonies regularly in her early twenties because "it appealed to me . . . made sense to me, so I would follow different medicine men. They would be doing it and I would be there. And then slowly I got drawn into it. . . . And it never dawned on me that I was going to sing [or] do actual ceremonies. It just happened." During this time she was part of a group of ceremonial dancers when a significant event occurred: "We did our part of the ceremony, and somewhere along the way, I felt overwhelmed with what was going on. And it affected me in a way where I felt like I was depressed. And there was a longing in my thinking, a certain longing in my life that I wasn't quite able to grasp. . . . And pretty soon it started bothering me to a point where I was not really able to sleep and not really able to eat. So there's a certain breakdown, emotionally."

A Traditional diagnostician told her that the spirit of the ceremony had affected her in a way that indicated a potential calling to become a healer, for after expelling the spirit he said, "You might think about learning it in a little more depth, maybe. There's really no harm in knowing some of these things, because it will eventually make you a little wiser, and eventually make you think a little deeper and make you think a little more about a lot of the things that are going to be taking place in this world, in your life. So, it will add more meaning to your life." She discovered that this healer, whom she had barely known, was her uncle. As they continued their conversations, he told her, "This ceremony itself has all the luxuries that you are probably wanting throughout your lifetime—what you are going to accomplish, and what you're going to have to live comfortably. It has all the luxuries, plus knowledge and some little bit of wisdom. And you get to travel all over the reservation, too." In this way he attempted to persuade her that the ceremony was a self-sufficient way of life—a philosophy, a spirituality, and a way of making a comfortable living.

During a second period of depression, she was again diagnosed by a hand-trembler who told her that "Lightningway was bothering me." She returned to her uncle for assistance and asked him to administer some peyote to her during the ceremony. This is unusual, since many Navajos say the two forms of religion should not be directly mixed, but her uncle was among those who accepted peyote when it first came to Navajoland in the 1930s. Her visionary experience included a moment in which the Navajo deities appeared and identified themselves to her and told her they were placing her on a particular path. She felt that this was a critical crossroad in her life and that "my being alive, my existing today, depended on that very decision I made that day." Her uncle encouraged her, saying, "Quit your job, get rid of your vehicles. This ceremony has everything. There is not anything that you would want that's not in there. All you have to do is ask." From that point she had a strong thirst for knowledge, for stability, and for a clear state of mind. Although she had wanted to go back to school for further education, she realized she had no need for it.

Initially her relatives were skeptical, wondering why with a good education and a good job she would want to start all over with a new career as healer. Eventually, she reports, her siblings came to treat her with respect and seek her advice, recognizing her status as a "medicine lady." When we asked if she felt that people act differently toward her than toward others, she responded affirmatively, attributing the difference to her role as a medicine person who was younger than most—not to her gender. Her sense of calling is strong, and she reports being able to see and hear things others can not, to have revelatory dreams about her patients, and to be able to tell if someone is ill or distressed. "It's a gift," she says, "not something that was handed down through teaching. I think I was selected for the gift."

Desbah made the following response to the question of why there are so few female chanters:

> Maybe because they're not as determined as I am. It's harder for a
> female person to get the corporate jobs, or a real high-range job,
> maybe their colleagues are male, and maybe [the idea that] it's a
> man's world kind of rubbed off on them. And while they were grow-
> ing up, maybe they were taught the only way a female should make

a good life is to find a good man, and find a good home and maybe
stay home. And have kids, you know. . . . So far, I haven't seen a
place where a male medicine man would come up to me and say,
"What you're doing is wrong; you shouldn't be doing it because
you're a woman." I haven't seen that. Because most of the people
that do come and help me [i.e., assist in her ceremonies] are medicine men anyway, and I guess they are in position where they say,
"It's real easy for her to learn, and now we're wondering why our
kids can't learn."

These men, well respected themselves, ask her to perform ceremonies on their
children to instill in them a sense "somewhere in the back of their mind, that
this ceremony is a way of life that's for real and for keeps." In addition to being
regarded as a good example for young people, she acknowledges not only that
many men do not have the knowledge that she does but that her mentor himself is regarded as a kind of "chief"—and hence an influential senior male
sponsor for her. Nevertheless, this mentor himself is not exactly an enlightened
feminist. As Desbah says, "He has a theory that since time began, back in the
old days, he said the woman's role is just like from here on, he said the woman
only meets the man's equal from the hip on down. That means you're always
the underdog. [But I say] the hell with it [laughs]. I think that's one of the main
reasons why I became a medicine lady—to kick around his theory. See what a
womens' libber he made out of me! [laughs]."

In her practice Desbah recognizes men and women as fundamentally the
same in that they are human, but different with respect to gender. In our
interviews, this observation leads not to the discussion of psychological differences between men and women but to that of sexual appropriateness: "Now if
I was doing a ceremony and a man was physically handicapped and he couldn't
pull down his pants, and say he lost his pants, I wouldn't be the one standing
there laughing. Because I would be the one that would have to understand and
say, 'Cover it up.' Maybe the peer group would be laughing. And the same with
a lady." She mentions instances she has heard of in which a male medicine
person has "decided to carry on, maybe makes passes at the patient, and then,
you know, touches her in a way that wasn't called for." Such an action is a
serious violation that requires correction through performance of a major ceremony for the patient, and Desbah reports having had to deal with three such
cases in her role as healer. The healer must also atone ceremonially for such
a mistake, whether it was made through negligence, ignorance, or intent to
harm the patient. Otherwise the consequences of divine retribution may be
severe: "If you've done something wrong like that, then you better pretty well
answer to the Beings for it. If you don't—we've lost a lot of medicine men
before they reached old age."

God Does Favor Men

Nora, our Christian healer, is in her midfifties, with five grown children. Two grandchildren live with her and her husband, to whom she has been married for more than thirty years. She is a full-time teacher studying part-time for a doctoral degree and is fluently bilingual in Navajo and English. Nora and her husband are also skilled and highly successful silversmiths, making jewelry in the distinctive Navajo style. She was raised in the Traditional religion; indeed, her grandfather was a distinguished chanter and her father a Bless-ingway singer. Her mother died when she was two years old, and by tradition she and her baby brother went to live at her grandmother's home, where she was physically and psychologically abused. This included being called such insulting names as "devil's daughter," "cruelty's daughter" and "coyote's daughter," and being told she "killed her mother" by constant crying, which in Navajo thought can bring witchcraft on the family. By age six she was able to return to live with her father, but by the time she was seventeen he, too, had died. Then she felt truly abandoned: "And then from there, I'm DANG! I just went crazy. [loud banging on table; interviewer laughs] I said, 'Okay, guys.' I said to my mother, 'You left me when I was a baby.' My dad, 'You left me just when I needed you the most. So what? I'll do anything I want to.' But fortu-nately, I never did anything so bad that . . . [laughter] I never smoked, I never drank." Though her early education was (not atypically) marked by several episodes of running away from school, by her early teens she settled in and completed an education that led her ultimately to a teaching job that she had held for twenty-six years at the time of her participation in our study. She was deeply respected and sought out for advice and was addressed as *shimı* (mother) by students and colleagues alike. Nora is thus a mature person with a long and stable marriage, and a long and stable job, highly skilled in the respected craft of silversmithing, and not only a successful teacher but an innovator in Navajo language curriculum development—and a prominent member of her Pentecostal church.

Nora was converted to Christianity through the process of healing. When her beloved husband contracted cancer, he underwent two major surgeries and was in the hospital for chemotherapy four days of every week. She says:

We were just living like that, and we began to sink. When you're sick, you'll do anything, you'll go anywhere to get healed, and that's how we happened to go into church. But we didn't stay in church the first time we went in. We ran out three times. The fourth time, we stayed [note that the number four is often sacred in American Indian myth and ritual], . . . and I think it was the word of God that got to me. [But] I said, "Wait a minute. Before I really take hold of it,

I want to settle it with you." I said [to God], "I want my husband back. I want my husband healed. Make yourself real to me. I will walk, I will talk, I will live the very essence of what you're telling me. That God is God." I guess I let my faith loose. And I gave my mind, my whole being to God, and I came out a different person. And my husband was healed instantly. . . . They named the cancer by name, and they commanded the cancer to leave his victim now because he is the property of God.. I didn't see the cancer leave, but I felt it. Because my husband and I, we have been so close. . . . They were praying for my husband, and I knew. I knew that I knew— they call it the touch of God. And I thought, understood it, that touch of God, because I felt it myself. And I said, "God, is this what it is to be one in a husband and a wife?" I said, "You touch him, and you touch me, too. Let it be that way, when you touch him in any way. Anything that touches him, it touches me." And that's why I believe in prayer so much. . . . I pray for people that have marriage problems. I pray for people that have other ailments, illness, name it. And I do believe it very much.

This event had occurred twenty-two years earlier, and Nora and her husband had remained loyal members and leaders in the church ever since, attending services typically three times per week. Prominent in this narrative are several distinctively Christian themes: Nora's assertiveness in making deals with God, the personal basis for her willingness to embrace healing prayer, and her conception of a certain kind of gender ideal embodied in the relation between man and wife.

Nora noted that much of her healing prayer has to do with troubled marriages:

Most of the time, the problem is there because we really believe as Christians that the husband is anointed by God to take care of his family. He has to make a choice, and this is really biblical. If I get ahead of my husband, and start making a big decision on my own, I'm going to get in trouble. I may not see it, but it's going to manifest itself down the road somewhere. I'm not going to be happy with my husband. He's not going to be happy with me until I come back and respect my husband as a man of the family. He rules his house. . . . And the Bible calls the wife a worthy woman. You have to be worthy of your husband and your children. In other words, your husband is going to call you a blessed woman. A blessed mother of my children. And the children are going to call you a blessed mother. That is happening in most every [home], even in Christian homes.

The concern with marital relations is not distinct to Christian healing; what is distinct is the overtone of Christian patriarchalism in her words. When we asked Nora about the meaning for her of the important Navajo word *shimı*, she said, "I think a [real] mother is a mother that makes a stand by her family . . . a mother is somebody that stays home for her kids." Yet Nora also told a story in which she exhorted the mother of a sick child to pray for healing with the words "You are the mother, you are the key." I regard this latter statement as a clue, subject to further research, that despite the overall tone of conservative Christianity projected by Nora and other Navajo Christian healers, the traditional notion of maternal prominence remains subtly in the background.

Man also has greater spiritual power than woman. Nora attested to this in referring to a male healer in her congregation who is "more powerful. Because, it could be that he's a man. And God does favor men. Well, not only does he favor, but he's just anointed them as the head of the family." The same male healer affirmed this notion, mentioning that Nora requested prayers for a health problem of her own based on her knowledge of "the power and prayer of a man, of a male—the male is very powerful, and God has planned it this way, also. So she recognized her position that way, and my position as a male . . . [his prayer had effect] by recognizing my authority, as a man, and then the faith that I have, with her faith, what we believe we share, and putting all that together." In recognizing a hierarchy of spiritual power in the congregation, Nora interestingly invoked the analogy of the pastor as being like a medicine man in "holding more power than anybody else that we know of within the church structures." She then immediately shifted to a more conveniently gendered analogy to conventional medicine, saying that the hierarchy included the equivalents of nurse's aides, nurses, doctors, and beyond that a head doctor equivalent to the pastor. In elaborating this analogy she variously referred to herself as a nurse's aide, a registered nurse, and a surgical nurse assistant to the head doctor, but though she was willing to promote herself with the female side of the hierarchy, she deferred to the males as invariably more powerful spiritual equivalents of doctors.

She Told Me That I Should Take Over the Fireplace

In the Native American Church, a person who runs peyote prayer meetings and heals or "doctors" others is called a road man because he leads others on the spiritual path of life called the peyote road. Effie is a rare example of a road woman. Sixty-seven years old when she began participation in our project, she had been married for forty-four years. Unlike Desbah and Nora, she has had only a few years of formal schooling and speaks Navajo almost exclusively. She has part-time employment providing home day care for senior citizens, but much of her time is spent in her healing practice.

Effie's family became involved with the NAC when she was fifteen years old, in the early years of peyote's presence in Navajoland. Her mother became seriously ill. As she recounts, "My mother participated in Navajo Traditional ceremonies several times and had gotten worse. She did not want to go to Traditional ceremony and the hospital. So she decided to take peyote because she heard about its healing power. She wanted to overdose on peyote to really feel the effect. So she sent my father up to Towaoc for peyote buttons. Whatever she got she took it all—about a hundred or more pieces of peyote. She got well from that." Effie said that at the time, her mother did not care whether she lived or died. Some people had told her that the peyote could cure her and some that it would kill her, and she was apparently aware that such an incredibly large dose would be either deadly or miraculous in its effect. Not knowing how to prepare the medicine, she got a pot of water and cooked all of it, including the bag it was in. According to Effie,

> When my mother was passed out on peyote, she had a dream. She
> saw in her vision the cause of her illness. There was a blockage in
> her digestive system. An angel being also came to visit with her and
> told her that it was not time to pass on. The being went into all
> types of commotion afterward. She kinda got down and started cry-
> ing. Afterward she felt light and well. I guess you know when you
> are going to die from your sickness. Your body feels like dead
> weight, and you are very tired out. This was what she felt. She was
> at the verge of dying. She could not breathe. So overnight the Lord
> had given her renewed strength and breathed a breath of life back
> into her. That is how she got well.

From this time on, Effie's family was devoted to peyote, rejecting Traditional ceremonies. Unlike many adherents of the NAC, she expresses a degree of hostility toward Traditional practices. She teaches that her method of healing can be successfully substituted for Traditional ceremonies even when the cause of illness is one of those typically recognized in Traditional religion, such as exposure to lightning or violation or injury of an animal. In contrast, along with her NAC involvement, she claims membership in the Christian Reformed Church and expresses affinity with many Christian ideas. Indeed, her ceremonial hogan is decorated with several portraits of Jesus.

Following her mother's cure, Effie's father himself became a renowned road man, developing a distinctive form of the peyote meeting based on the use of water. When Effie was twenty-three, she had an experience of sudden trembling in her body, beginning from her feet and moving through her body and hands. Her father identified this as a calling to become a Traditional diagnostician or handtrembler, though a peyote meeting is not the most typical setting for the onset of this Traditional form of giftedness. Effie did develop this capacity and uses it to diagnose and treat patients to this day, but true to her unique attitude toward Traditional practices, she does not attribute her diagnostic insights to inspiration by Gila monster spirits, but to angels from God understood in a Christian sense.

Prior to his death, Effie's father indicated that she should prepare to become his successor as leader of peyote meetings. As Effie recalls,

> He said to keep practicing it, and he told me that I had a lot of potential to carry this practice on, since I already knew the handtrembling. He told me that the peyote will give you the wisdom and advice on how to run the meeting and that my mother, who knows about NAC meetings, will instruct on the finer points of doing things in the meetings. [He said,] "She already knows and has observed how I ran the meeting, so it will take another thirty years, maybe." So he gave the fireplace to her [i.e., passed on his practice, including knowledge of and responsibility for the fireplace or altar constructed during prayer meetings], but he always just told me that I had the most potential to take care of the fireplace. So it was at that time in my life that this fireplace was already prepared for me and given to me. The same fireplace as taught to Arthur Wilson, a Cheyenne, who gave it to my father. He had instructed me, but I did not really understand everything, and I depended on my mother, but she passed away. We were just out in the open then. So Emily [a kinswoman who later became her first patient] said that I should take over the fireplace. So that was given to me and voted on [by the congregation]. So I told them that "you're asking me to conduct the meeting and take over the fireplace," and I told them, "Okay. You guys have to help me and correct my mistakes and do not look at me. You are sending me into this business of running the meeting and I will need your support. Although I got reassurance back then, here to this day, it is only my children and I that are involved in the NAC practice.

In Effie's story we see a kind of female line of succession, in that her mother's self-medication was the beginning of the family's involvement with peyote, her mother was the caretaker of the family fireplace following her father's death, and Emily was the person who sanctioned Effie's taking over the fireplace after her mother. That devotion to the peyote fireplace as a kind of family cult is not unusual; what is more worthy of note is that Effie's practice as a road woman whose following is largely composed of an extended family is supplemented by a more traditionally female practice as a handtrembler (i.e., Traditional ceremonial diagnostician or diviner) whose clientele appears to be drawn from a broader base. Those who come for handtrembling may or may not pursue treatment in a full-scale peyote prayer meeting; meanwhile, within her peyote meetings Effie often makes use of her handtrembling ability to help individual participants.

Conclusion

Arguably, the three women I have discussed are remarkable. To the extent that this is so, their stories must in some ways be read as exemplary rather than as representative; but perhaps, given their relatively small numbers in comparison to their male counterparts, all Navajo women healers are best regarded as exemplary rather than representative. At the same time, we must understand that each of these women represents a particular spiritual healing tradition, either Traditional Navajo, Native American Church, or Christian. Although these modes of ritual healing are inextricably intertwined in Navajo social life, each has distinct features, and in the stories of these healers are hints that there are modes of gender enactment distinctive to each of the healing traditions. Thus Desbah, the Traditional healer, insofar as she adopts the stance of the chanter of a major ceremony with a broad public reputation, exhibits a personal style that is in some respects masculinized, having taken over her mentor's practice and maintaining his elderly wife as a primary assistant. Nora, the Christian healer, has adopted the stance of a devout advocate within her congregation, a stance that might be characterized as militantly submissive insofar as she defers to male authority without abdicating the role of strong and competent Navajo woman. Effie, the Native American Church healer, adopts the stance of the wise, nurturant bosom of the family, playing the dominant maternal role of the Navajo woman whose followers are primarily members of a tight, extended family network.

Finally, for contemporary Navajos the issue of gender per se—that is, of women in relation to men—is in some sense subordinate to the pivotal issues of the healer's identity as a Navajo and in relation to biomedical professionals of the dominant society.[3] Desbah touched on this issue in expressing her desire to be recognized for her knowledge as an indigenous doctor with an honorary degree from a mainstream institution of higher learning. Nora, despite her Christian commitment, touched on it in describing her Traditional grandfather as a "big-time medicine man. . . . If he lived today, he would have several titles, for sure M.D., a neurosurgeon because he had to deal with the brain, a psychologist or psychiatrist because he talked right along his ceremony, he had to counsel people." Effie, in the context of noting that it was inappropriate for a Navajo healer to set a fee but that the more a patient chose to pay, the more effective the prayer would be, remarked on the inequity between the pay that physicians receive and what religious healers receive: "Your surgery over there probably cost you thousands of dollars, that's what it cost, the doctor's bills, too. On this side, when you wanted help with the Handtrembling Way, you paid me forty dollars." Closely related to the issue of identity, the equation is that therapeutic efficacy is in part based on respect, and that respect is in part expressed by money. In the domain of healing, as a woman, as a Navajo, as a person who by the standards of the dominant society is of an impoverished class, the common denominator in the healing equation is expressed by one central idea: respect.

NOTES

This work is part of the Navajo Healing Project (NHP), funded by National Institute of Mental Health grant MH50394. The project was carried out under Navajo Nation Cultural Resources Investigation Permit C9708-E, and this chapter was approved by the Navajo Nation Research Review Board in its meeting of March 2003. Special thanks are due to Janis Jenkins and to members of the NHP staff, including Derek Milne, Wilson Howard, Nancy Maryboy, David Begay, Jerrold Levy, and Mitzie Begay.

1. Traditional Navajo religion is composed primarily of major ceremonial events that may last as many as nine days and nights, and a variety of procedures for ritual diagnosis or divination. The rituals address the *Diiyin Din4*, or Holy People, who have strong correspondences with forces of nature. The Native American Church entered Navajo society in the 1930s under the influence of Plains Indians, among whom it originated. It is based on direect contact with the divine stimulated by sacramental ingestion of the hallucinogenic peyote cactus during prayer meetings that last from dusk to dawn of one night, and that are characterized by inspired prayers and songs performed to the accompaniment of drums and rattles. Christianity gained its foothold in Navajoland with the influence of Franciscan missionaries around the turn of the twentieth century. It was followed by various mainstream Protestant denominations, and then, beginning around the 1950s, by various strands of Pentecostalism, which account for much of the contemporary Navajo Christian healing activity.

2. For example, spouses with ceremonial knowledge, most often the wives of male ceremonialists, may or may not have separate entries (Frisbie and Tso 1993: 57).

3. On the relation between Navajo ritual healing and identity politics, see chapter 5 in Csordas 2002.

REFERENCES

Csordas, Thomas J. 2002. *Body/Meaning/Healing*. New York: Palgrave.
———, ed. 2000. Ritual Healing in Navajo Society. Special issue, *Medical Anthropology Quarterly*, 14, no. 4.
Frisbie, Charlotte. 1992. Temporal Change in Navajo Religion 1868–1990. *Journal of the Southwest* 34: 457–514.
Frisbie, Charlotte, and Eddie Tso. 1993. The Navajo Ceremonial Practitioners' Registry. *Journal of the Southwest* 35: 53–92.
Kluckhohn, Clyde, and Dorothea Leighton. 1962. *The Navaho*. Garden City, N.Y.: Doubleday.

PART IV

Synergy, Syncretism, and Appropriation

19

Multiple Meanings of Chinese Healing in the United States

Linda L. Barnes

Following a front-page story in the *New York Times* in 1972 by James Reston about his experiences with acupuncture in a Chinese hospital, virtually every article on complementary and alternative medicine (CAM) in United States media has featured this modality as CAM's poster child, with the patient presented as a wide-eyed face bristling with needles. To a lesser degree, Chinese herbs have made the news as well. Both acupuncture and herbs are configured under the heading of Chinese medicine. But if we cast a wider net, we draw in a good deal more—not only needles and herbs but also practices like *taijiquan* and *qigong*, relationships with the dead in the form of gods, ghosts, ancestors, medicinal understandings of food, and all manner of divination. Many of these practices entered the United States through immigration begun in the mid–nineteenth century and, more recently, resulting from Lyndon Johnson's rescission of the Oriental Exclusion Act in 1965.[1]

Such traditions and practices have never constituted a uniform system. Upon their arrival, they have generated further complex systems. This phenomenon raises the question of why some forms of healing appear to transcend cultural boundaries. What is it about some traditions that makes them more transferable than others? Who are the stakeholders, and what is at stake for each of them? In this chapter, I suggest four interpretive frameworks with which to address these questions. The first involves constructions of *race* in the United States, in which understandings of Chineseness have emerged within overarching categories of blackness and whiteness.

This approach treats "race in the United States as a fundamental *organizing principle* of social relationships." Over time, the Chinese have found themselves inserted into this "continous process of formation and superseding of unstable equilibria"—the country's changing but persisting system of racial meanings (Omi and Winant 1986: 78–79). Each of the other three frameworks must be set within this larger process.

The second framework points to ways that Chinese healing practices in the United States interface with issues of *religious identity and expression* for Chinese American practitioners. The third addresses tensions between *conversion and appropriation*, particularly as both pertain to European American practitioners. The fourth involves a different aspect of acculturation, the phenomenon of *medicalization*. Finally, these four frameworks are reviewed in relation to broader issues of cross-cultural transmission in the context of globalization.

A Racialized Framework

Through the centuries of European reports about peoples in other parts of the world, the governing descriptive polarity was that of blackness and whiteness. Over time, each group new to Europeans found itself involuntarily positioned within the polarity through the imposition of racial meaning. Up through the middle of the eighteenth century, the Jesuits repeatedly described the Chinese as "white," or as "very much like us," emphasizing the sophistication of Chinese civilization. Over time, "whiteness" emerged as an exclusionary category, concealing the degree to which the racializing of the Chinese coincided with the erasing of other white ethnic identities. Toward the end of the eighteenth century, with the typologies of Karl Linnaeus and the taxonomy of German anatomist and naturalist Johann Friedrich Blumenbach (1752–1840) in the third edition of his *De Generis Humani Varietate Nativa* (On the Natural Variety of Mankind), "Asians" routinely became described as "yellow." The tension generated by such efforts to stabilize categories of race—an inherently unstable undertaking—has been exacerbated through the living presence and witness of Chinese individuals, imagined and real.

In the United States, dominant cultural orientations constituted the Chinese as not-white, within the rubric of the three legal categories of "white," "Negro," and "Indian." Reflecting the confusion inherent in these categories, in 1854, in *People v. Hall*, the California Supreme Court determined that the Chinese were equivalent to Indians and therefore had no recourse to the political rights afforded to whites. Such positioning has also intersected with formulations of class—most recently, for example, in such contrasting categories as "the so-called Hong Kong money elite" and Cambodian immigrants positioned "as black Asians in sharp contrast to the model-minority image of Chinese, Koreans, and Vietnamese (including Sino-Vietnamese), who are celebrated for their 'Confucian values' and family businesses" (Ong 1996: 742–44).

The earliest instances of Chinese healing in the Americas date back at least to the early seventeenth century, when Spanish colonizers brought Chinese servants and slaves to Mexico and what would eventually become California (see Dubs and Smith 1942). Textual and archaeological evidence shows that when immigration increased following the gold rush of 1849, Chinese immigrants brought their systems of healing everywhere they settled. Yet as Chinese healing practices have come into the United States, the dynamics I have described guaranteed their being located along Eurocentric polarities structured by race. Perceptions of different practices and practitioners ever since have been informed by these variables, whether consciously or not. Each of the phenomena described in the following sections must therefore be understood as occurring within pervasive organizing principles and processes of racial formation.

Chinese American Practitioners and Matters of Religious Identity

The American counterculture of the 1970s romanticized images of barefoot doctors in the People's Republic of China (PRC). Chinese practitioners already in the United States were sought out and in some cases recruited from countries with Chinese populations. These teachers offered classes in acupuncture, often in the model of lineage systems. As schools of acupuncture gradually emerged in the United States, they recruited teachers trained in the PRC, some of whom left China—often for political reasons—to work as cultural transmitters. They brought with them the residue of a history of interaction between Chinese and Western understandings of religion.

Early Western observers of China started with the premise that Christianity was the one true religion, and they assessed other traditions accordingly. Did the other tradition have a deity, a founder, a scripture based on revelation, an inducted body of religious authorities, and some collective body analogous to the church? When other traditions could not exhibit precise correspondences, at worst they were represented as heathenish idolaters; at best, they were seen as dim reflections anticipating God's truer revelation in the form of Christianity.

Early Jesuits in China—most notably Matteo Ricci—wrote to their superiors in Rome that the Confucian tradition was not a religion but a philosophy. By presenting the tradition in this light, the Jesuits hoped to avoid butting heads with Chinese literati and government officials over the practice of ancestor veneration, thereby finessing the conversion process. I have met Chinese practitioners in Boston who still say that the Confucian tradition—the teaching

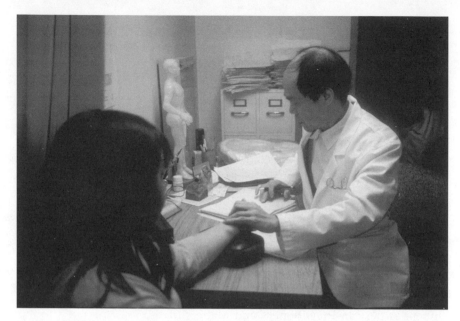

Pulse reading from Dr. Wong Kwok Lap. Used with permission from Linda L. Barnes.

of the scholars, of those knowledgeable in the things of heaven, earth, and man—is not a religion but a philosophy. During the eighteenth and nineteenth centuries, Christian observers regularly represented Daoism as a degenerate version of an older, more Epicurean philosophy. They dismissed both Buddhism and the traditions of local gods as having misled and corrupted the populace.

Ironically, the PRC government effected a far more crippling influence, in condemning religion as a whole, including such practices as shamanism (see Jia 1997). Even so, the transmission of the Confucian, Daoist, and Buddhist traditions persisted. Chinese practitioners in the United States, like herbalist-acupuncturist Lu Weidong, remember absorbing older teachings while growing up in China under the PRC:

> I was not exactly *taught* the older philosophies of China. Still, we
> learned these things anyway. It's very funny that, during the Cul-
> tural Revolution, they would give out older philosophical articles for
> us to criticize. So people had to read them and repeat them, in order
> to criticize them. We became very interested. . . . This, of course,
> was not the government's intention, but it happened anyway. . . .
> Also, almost everyone still could get it from their family. In my fam-
> ily that happened, because my mother read a lot of books, and she
> talked to me about them. My father, too. When we were young we

had to write calligraphy every day as part of our homework, and to
memorize famous old poems, so we learned the spirit of these
things. . . .

These older philosophies are not like something you *get*. It's just
a whole body. You live in that kind of society, and you get it from the
society—from your relatives, your friends. It fills your whole life.
Like here, although here it happens differently.[2]

Acupuncturist-herbalist Zhang Yao, who received her medical training in
mainland China, spoke of how the very practice of acupuncture "gives you a
hollow feeling—maybe I should say a feeling of being open to receive a lot of
things, instead of being closed and refusing a lot." For other practitioners,
certain tenets of a tradition like the Confucian are so deeply embedded in what
they identify as qualities of being human that they do not explicitly identify
them either with Confucianism or with religion, unless pressed. For example,
Ch'ing-ling K'ung—also from mainland China—described qualities that matter deeply to her:

One evening I was eating dinner with my father. Some patient's
husband came to my house and said, "Doctor, please, can you come
to my house?" I said, "Can you wait a minute, please? I'm eating."
My father said, "The patient is important. You should go." After
that, I didn't care if it was raining or snowing, I didn't care what
kind of weather it was. In China, I would go. . . . My father didn't
believe in any religion. He taught me to have a warm heart, to be
honest. This was most important. A lot of people follow a religion
but only talk in the mouth. But their heart is a block. You should have
a warm heart and should be doing. For myself, I believe in *de*.

The term *de* refers to moral character, virtue, or excellence. When asked if it
was not a central tenet within the Confucian tradition, she said, "Yes, that is a
Confucian value." Then, drawing herself up with quiet pride, she added, "I am
seventy-second generation Confucius. In everything he taught us, like in
Mengzi [Mencius], is the heart." This statement is resonant with Zhang Yao's
description of becoming "hollow" "open"—receptive—in order to be more responsive within one's relationship with a patient. It resonates as well with the
Confucian tradition of cultivating one's human-heartedness, as opposed to becoming numb—or, in the words of Ching-ling Kung, having a block for a heart.
Becoming a doctor in this context is, for some people, infused with religious
dimensions, even when—due to what they associate with "religion"—they do
not explicitly identify it as such.

Different Chinese American practitioners go about it differently.
Acupuncturist-herbalist Mai Ruixiong, a traditional Chinese medicine doctor
from China now based in Newton, Massachusetts, practices *taiji quan* each

morning as often as he can. He says it helps him to cultivate openness and keep his balance during the day, and to bring patients into a balanced state. In so doing, he keeps faith with generations who have used this physical discipline to cultivate their awareness of *qi*, as attested by the bamboo slips from the Mawangdui Western Han dynasty tombs, painted with figures engaged in such movements.

Although Dr. Mai claims not to identify with a particular religious tradition, a figurine of Guanyin, the Buddhist bodhisattva of mercy, presides over the doorway into his treatment rooms. He talks about how his mother, a Buddhist, goes to the Guanyin temple in Quincy, Massachusetts, and points to a postcard from another temple in New York. Such temples, which now punctuate the American religious landscape, are frequently sites of petitions for health and healing. In San Francisco, for example, the Gold Mountain Sagely Monastery celebrates a monthly cycle of sutra recitation to the Medicine Master Buddha, the version of the Buddha who offers the great healing of enlightenment and inspires the Chinese Buddhist practice of medicine.

Popular Chinese religious life flows into other practices related to healing, often associated with the preservation of life, the pursuit of protective forces, and the repelling of afflicting influences. Larger herbal stores in American Chinatowns sell figurines not only of Guanyin, the Buddha, and various bodhisattvas but also of entities embodying longevity—carp, tortoises, the old

Weighing out the ingredients for a Chinese herbal prescription. Used with permission from Linda L. Barnes.

man with a peach. Multiple sizes of the red-faced, spear-brandishing General Guangong converge at the end of one shelf—the divinized patron of acupuncturists, businesses, policemen, firemen, and gamblers. Many herbal medicine shops hang a large red altar to the general in a prominent location, changing the offerings of oranges, apples, and incense each morning. Some shelves in the herbal stores hold small, six-sided *fengshui* (wind and water) convex mirrors, surrounded by the hexagrams of the *Yijing* (The Classic of Changes). One of the historically most important roles of the *fengshui* practitioner has been to plot the correct positioning of graves, to ensure the quiet rest of the dead. Here the mirrors function to deflect harmful influence known as *sha*, produced by inauspicious alignments of forces resulting from interacting configurations of the ground, angles of buildings, and positioning of objects.

Herbal stores, curio shops, and food markets may also sell bamboo cups containing thin bamboo slips marked with numbers, accompanied by booklets that explain the divination corresponding to each number. Many queries involve matters of health and healing. Other shelves contain cellophane-wrapped packets of spirit money for the dead, who, if untended, become afflicting ghosts.[3] Near the money are packages of what, at first, look like Christmas wrapping paper but on closer inspection prove to be red paper stamped with pictures of cars, watches, microwaves, and other riches, designed for burning at grave sites to furnish the dead with the comforts of the living. (A burned stretch of grass in a Chinese section of a local Boston cemetery points to the vitality of this tradition.) Still, *taiji* teacher Yon Lee laments that young people no longer visit the Lee family's lineage hall in Boston and that, at family funerals, he and his family members no longer know all the necessary elements to the rituals. Like Chinese herbs grown in American soil, the rites are perceived to be weakened by their distance in time and space from China.[4]

Chinese American practitioners experience themselves differently, depending on whether they descend from lineages present in the United States since the nineteenth century or those that arrived after 1965, or whether they are PRC-trained physicians of TCM. Some learned through training systems in Taiwan, Hong Kong, or other countries with large ethnic Chinese populations. Temple priests, teachers of *taijiquan* or *gongfu*, and workers in herb shops interact, to a greater or lesser extent, with a European American clientele and in some cases rewrite themselves accordingly. Not only do all these practitioners live at the core of American global capitalism; they witness at a distance the current movement in China that has defined getting rich as glorious. Such a change in the meaning of China contributes to transforming the meanings of Chinese healing in the United States.

Unlike in China, where formal training in state-run schools of traditional medicine may bestow the equivalent of physician identity, in the United States there is no such equivalent. Relatively few second- and third-generation Chinese students go into the study of acupuncture in the United States. Instead, they are more likely to pursue biomedical education and to become physicians who may, in occasional cases, add some acupuncture into their practice. The choice involves questions of social positioning and professional status.

All players in the game are subject to the influences of the larger medical marketplace of the United States. As early as the 1880s and 1890s, Chinese doctors in the United States learned to promote themselves in city business directories and to fabricate credentials as former physicians to the emperor. In our own day, Chinese herb stores in Boston's Chinatown proudly display their "Best of Boston" awards in their entryways. Like the "plastic medicine men" critiqued by Native American scholars (e.g., Jocks 1996: 421), certain Chinese teachers go on the glossy-brochure circuit of New Age workshops, peddling inner balance as a cultural artifact. At the same time, they, too, are part of a living tradition, in which encounters between traditions change meanings for everyone.

Conversion versus Appropriation among European American Practitioners

The Sacralizing of the Self

These versions of Chinese healing among Chinese American practitioners do not begin to exhaust the constituencies engaged in such modalities in the United States or the variations they have generated. The privileging of Chinese modalities and practitioners, it must be remembered, arose out of trends set in motion by European Americans during the 1960s. One such movement involved challenges both to established religious traditions and to the authority of biomedicine, leading to a search for alternative models. European Americans sought out texts and teachers from China, India, and Japan. This move to an imagined East also functioned as a challenge to the version of individualism seen as representing mainstream capitalist society, even as it produced another version of individualism, different primarily in its vision of itself as more humane and radically egalitarian (Prince 1999: 111; see also Riches 2000).

Late twentieth-century white middle-class New Agers sought corroboration of their personalized version of spirituality everywhere they could find it. They looked for it in "a conglomeration of Christian mysticism, Vedic teachings, revolutionary tracts, Madison Avenue pop psychology, pseudo-American-Indian religions, hedonism, and some traditional American values such as individualism, independence, and frontier courage" (Molgaard and Byerly 1981: 153). The search was frequently structured by an ideal of the person as self-reliant and self-determined. The pursuit yielded an eclectic, variegated bricolage—a composite Whitman's sampler in which Walt Whitman himself was one of the grandfathers.

Altar for General Guang Gong among the herbs. Used with permission
from Linda L. Barnes.

Unbeknownst to many of the seekers, they were following a long-standing
American religious trajectory, the exaltation of "Self-spirituality" (Heelas 1996:
2). The core epistemological assumption of this spirituality is that the self
contains the universe. To experience oneself truly is to thus experience the
essence of all spirituality. Indeed, "personal transformation equals salvation"
(Kyle 1995: 137). The distance between this formulation and that of Confucius's
lineage descendant Mencius (Mengzi), who had argued that to know one's own
heart is to know the heart of heaven, is not immediately apparent. Yet the
difference is crucial. Primacy of the autonomous self has little to do with the
Chinese understanding of the self as the center of a nexus of relationships (see

Tu 1986). Rather, it entails the difference between privileging one's own experience as the ultimate guarantor of authenticity, and the task of deepening
the self's authenticity within a constellation of relationships marked by concentric circles of responsibilities and obligations. Still, if any variable functioned to connect the many variations on New Age spirituality, it was this
sacralizing of the self.

Beginning in the 1960s, first hippies and then adherents of the New Age
translated political and social tensions endemic to the white middle class into
the pursuit of alternative meanings in Native American and Asian traditions.
Imagined versions of tribal peoples and of Chinese sages provided symbols for
the rejection of mainstream, middle-class, white society, allowing individuals
to engage in variations on "playing Indian" (Deloria 1998). This rewriting of
the self found expression along a continuum of responses to China and the
Chinese. At one end was a self-transformation that might be designated as
conversion. At the other end, we find full-scale appropriation—the taking over
of another group's practices in ways that may then exclude or marginalize the
original holders of the tradition. Yet, as the two poles of a spectrum, both
represent aspects of a larger phenomenon; both carry elements of their opposite. Neither process is pure.

Modes of Conversion

Conversion never occurs in a vacuum. It takes place at specific historical
moments in particular cultural settings. On occasion, individuals from the
United States convert to Buddhism and in some cases enter Chinese monas-
teries in the United States, shaving their heads and donning Buddhist robes.
They may become lay members of Buddhist communities. In both cases, they
may be de-assimilating from some aspect of American culture with which they
are dissatisfied (see Numrich 1996), reformulating themselves according to
the lifeways of the adopted tradition. The change may prove to be a finite phase
or a redirecting of one's life course.

Conversion occurs in other ways as well. Since the 1970s, the transmission
of certain Chinese healing practices to the United States and to a European
American audience in particular has, in limited respects, paralleled the process
of the dissemination of religious traditions from one culture to another. No
missionaries brought samples of Chinese practices to American soil with the
explicit purpose of disseminating them, but a propaganda campaign mounted
by the PRC government promoted the claims of the Maoist revolution, including the popularizing of traditional medicine. Small numbers of European
Americans responded by going to China—pilgrims who learned to speak and
read Chinese, immersing themselves in Chinese culture for several years. In
some cases, this odyssey involved the study of martial arts and, as a sideline,
of martial-arts medicine to treat injuries arising in one's training. In other

cases, it meant enrolling in programs of traditional medicine, particularly the version of traditional Chinese medicine known as "TCM" sponsored by the PRC.

Personal Transformation and the Politics of Appropriation

Conversion of the type just described is not the only way that European Americans have incorporated Chinese healing practices into their lives. The New Age movement represents multiple approaches to the adoption of new traditions, whether religious and/or healing. Yet the movement as a whole is neither a New Religious Movement (NRM) nor a collection of NRMs (Heelas 1996: 9). Rather, it functions as an umbrella category under which we find some NRMs, along with other practices as apparently unrelated as past life regression, crystal healing, naturopathy, and psychic healing (see Clark 1992). Chinese-based healing practices have often been positioned in the same framework, even as they have contributed concepts and dispositions to the broader field of New Age healing.

During the 1960s and 1970s, when dominant political, economic, and religious institutions came under intense scrutiny and critique, and the very term "religion" became suspect for some, there emerged a countercultural fascination with those aspects of different traditions perceived to be "mystical." The term functioned as code for direct personal access to the divine, bypassing institutional structures and religious authorities. It was popularly assumed that, at the level of mysticism—itself a term of debated meaning and value in religious studies (Schmidt 2003)—all traditions were fundamentally identical, all expressing the same reality. Chinese Daoist and Buddhist traditions were lumped under this heading, as was the divination text the *Yijing*. This process of invention entered the borderlands between conversion and appropriation, sometimes residing more on one side or the other, sometimes sitting awkwardly on the fence. Insofar as the invention was predicated on an assumption of universalism, it coincided with a core sense of entitlement on the part of European Americans to appropriate whatever appealed to them—a sense that overlooked its own roots in political and economic expansionism and domination.

The individuals involved were usually unconscious of the more pernicious dimensions of their actions. Yet insofar as universalism was assumed to override time and space, it allowed the primarily white appropriators to ignore agency and authorship, historical context, and the broader traditions from which they were drawing. The claim that all traditions are alternate versions of the same thing made it possible to overlook real differences and to ignore the specificity of related lifeways and codes of behavior. Selective sampling based on personal taste was the result. In short, it allowed the appropriators to ignore the cultural politics of appropriation (Lutz 1990: 168).

The New Agers lifted up the power of nature as a healing force (Albanese 1990). They excavated the hidden vein of vitalism that had run throughout the history of biomedicine, and they challenged the biomedical focus on the ana-tomical body. They posited, instead, a self comprised of "body, mind, and spirit," buttressing their anthropology with popular books on physics that sug-gested an energetic foundation to all three (see Seem 1987). This triune model was used to argue that all three aspects could become afflicted. Because each represented a variation on energy, the affliction of one could not be entirely separated from the other two. Indeed, a person's physical condition might be read as expressing the state of the other two legs of the tripod. Physical, mental, spiritual, and mystical energy were, ultimately, different spins on a single re-ality, all of them inextricably interwoven. One could therefore read *prana*, élan vital, odic force, orgone energy, or aura as one and the same (English 1983: 31). It was this energetic foundation, and the assumption that *qi* (pronounced "chee," a vital material-psycho-spiritual force) was simply another word for it, that allowed white New Agers to fold Chinese practices into this matrix.

Within this paradigm, a human being experienced illness as "a disturbance in the life force" (English 1983: 31) or as "inhibited soul life" (Bailey 2000: 163). Unless treatment addressed this deepest level, it would produce only superficial results. Indeed, proponents suggested that physical healing might be the least significant version of treatment (Neuenfeldt 1998: 80-81). One repeatedly finds a liquid language employed, in which the goal is to remove obstructions and restore an unimpeded flow of energy.

The bricolage that characterized New Age spirituality also typified the ap-proaches to healing it produced. If one is trying to heal at the level of the spirit, and the spirit is universal, then one can claim the right to cut and paste together all strategies thought to bring about the desired effect. The process is both analogous to and different from what has historically been the case in China, namely, the simultaneous and selective practice of Confucian, Daoist, Bud-dhist, and popular traditions. Although not a result of colonialism pe se, the New Age process paralleled certain aspects of the radical dispossession that characterizes colonial exploitation of other groups' resources. As Karl Neuen-feldt notes in relation to New Age appropriations of the Aboriginal didgeridoo, "By claiming untrammeled access to indigenous knowledge as but an expres-sion of basic humanity, New Age followers in effect demand the right to ap-propriate (and expropriate) what may be restricted (and sometimes sacred/ secret) knowledge and practice" (1998: 75). Indeed, the more secret, the better.

In the case of Chinese healing, the ensuing discourse increasingly spoke in the voice of European American practitioners, on behalf of "American acu-puncture." White practitioners, claiming a place in the world of Chinese heal-ing, did not view themselves as usurping anything. How could they be, if what they were tapping into was universal, and if they loved it? But love, in this case, was "not the opposite of dominance; rather it [was] dominance's anodyne—it

[was] dominance with a human face" (Yi-Fu Tuan in Shanley 1997: 679). In the process, Chinese practitioners were frequently repositioned at the margins of authority—despite their identity as living participants in an ongoing tradition—just as the collective memory of having done so was pushed to the recesses of consciousness and bad conscience, and thereby made to disappear (Lutz 1990: 173). This attitude is illustrated in the comment of one European American acupuncturist, who said that she did not see why it was necessary to speak or read Chinese in order to study or practice Chinese medicine.

Translations into the Material Culture of Healing

The New Age has generated an entire industry of products, ranging from supplies used by acupuncturists and herbalists to patent herbal remedies, martial arts and *taijiquan* classes, and self-help books, tapes, audiocassettes, and videos—not to mention the weekend workshops conducted by their authors both Chinese and non-Chinese—each with corresponding advertisements in practitioner journals, New Age catalogs and newspapers, and the back pages of women's magazines.

The result is a marketplace containing something for everyone. Chinese herbs are a good example. We find packages of dried herbs sold in Chinese herbal stores and food markets; "organic" patent formulas sold in health food stores and, more recently, in the "Wild Harvest" section of local Shaw's Supermarket—often under the general heading of "energy." Pharmaceutical versions are sold in chain stores like CVS, Brookes Pharmacy, and, in some cases, wholesale outlet warehouses. Supermarket tabloids broadcast Vanna White's announcement that she got pregnant as a result of acupuncture, supplemented with Chinese herbs—although she could not remember which ones (Smith 1993: 24). Clairol "Natural Instinct" hair color ads read, "It must be the ginseng—my color looks like it just got a major wake-up call" (Clairol 2002: 2–3).

Both pharmaceutical companies and New Age practitioners stake an open-ended claim to Chinese herbs. The mechanisms of corporate appropriation are located within policies of "global biotechnology, pharmaceutical, and agribusiness corporations and their allies in Northern universities, seed banks, and research centers" (Roht-Arriaza 1998: 255). Pharmaceutical industries routinely assume a right to absorb local knowledge, without sharing the profits with the originators of the information. Such appropriation has contributed to growing disputes over who owns the intellectual property rights related to herbal knowledge (Nason 1997: 247–48). New Age appropriation operates on an analogous assumption, couched in holistic language. Practitioners define plants as a juncture between humans and nature. Arguing that we are all now planetary citizens, they draw on globalization theory, pointing to the internationalizing of ecosystems. David Hoffman writes, "As planetary beings . . . the whole of the world's flora is available to us and rightly so" (2000: 190). Yet the expansionist sense of ownership is not so different, however holistic the formulation.

Few, if any, of the other objects sold in the Chinese herb stores make it to New Age marketplaces. The mud figurines of fishermen, scholars, and martial artists only find their way into the Winterthur catalog for interior decoration. Guanyin is incorporated into the "Motherpeace" theology of *A Woman's Book of Changes*, a feminist rewriting of the *Yijing* in which the appendices correlate individual hexagrams with the Chinese months, zodiac signs, Sabbats, the Hopi Road of Life, the Wiccan calendar, and the tarot (Stein 1997). Books on "the Dao of . . . " have proliferated. Articles about *fengshui* show up in the living arts sections of American newspapers under the heading of interior decorating and occupy an entire British magazine dedicated to the topic and sold in the United States. Mainstream bookstores carry books on teaching oneself the principles of the practice. Nowhere, however, are graves or ghosts discussed. Instead, *fengshui* has been incorporated into the "earth energy tradition"—a theory that the earth has energy lines and constitutes "a self-regulating system," which James Lovelock has dubbed "Gaia" (see Lovelock 1979; MacDonald 1995: 36).

Thus, despite the historical importance in Chinese religious life of a network of relationships that includes ongoing interaction with the dead, this aspect has been the one most marginalized in the whitened, Americanized versions of Chinese healing. As the illustrations from the herbal stores show, the dead continue to figure in people's lives, but their active role in Chinese medicine theory as the bringers of good or of affliction has been stripped away in Americanized practices (see Barnes 1998).

Medicalization

Like the other processes discussed here, the medicalization of Chinese healing practices—the shaping of practice in the light of biomedical influence—has taken different forms, contingent on the commitments of the stakeholders. The participants in each version may pursue what look like similar objectives for what, in reality, amount to quite different reasons. Nevertheless, one can broadly characterize three arenas of medicalization. The first is the medicalizing of acupuncture and herbs effected by the mainland Chinese government in the form of PRC-TCM, the system that has exercised the greatest influence in the United States. The second—which grows out of the first—involves the incorporation of selected Chinese practices into biomedicine in the United States. The third involves the construction of Chinese healing within the "new science" by New Agers and their reactions to the biomedical scientizing of certain practices. In each case, the abridging has obeyed other deeply held worldviews. None is precisely in sync with the others.

The Secularizing of Medicine in China

To contextualize the process by which Chinese medicine has undergone biomedicalization in the United States, it is useful to understand earlier stages as they occurred in China itself. It was, after all, the product of this secularization that entered the United States in the 1970s. As the work of Bridie Andrews shows, this process of medicalization began well before the Communist era. Nineteenth-century Chinese medical literature discussed biomedicine as a standard against which other practices were being measured. Even when it failed to find approval or acceptance in China, it nevertheless continued to serve as a frame of reference. Committed to improving public health, the government of the late Qing dynasty looked for ways to apply Western learning in the service of Chinese medicine. China's defeat in the Sino-Japanese War of 1895 led to calls for "modernization." Traditional academies were transformed into schools that included biomedical faculties. For traditional medicine to retain its status, it became essential that it be included in the curriculum, alongside courses in anatomy (Andrews, in press). Older interpretive and diagnostic strategies, such as *qi*, yin and yang, and *wuxing*, or Five Phase theory—not to mention traditional pulse-taking and theories of demon possession—were rejected as absurd, particularly insofar as they were identified as religious. The government's scientism swept these aspects of Chinese healing under the rug, spurred by the concern that China would be perceived as superstitious and, therefore, ridiculous in the eyes of the world. Reformers wanted in no way to be associated with temple practices, medicine deities, or systems of divination.

The new government in 1913 was even less open to traditional medicine, whose practitioners received no support from the state and, in practice, were stripped of any official significance. Over the century, reformers like warlord governor Yan Xishan, in 1921, promoted the idea that Chinese traditional doctors should incorporate biomedical diagnostic systems in place of pulse diagnosis. Other reformers, like Cao Bingzhang (1877–1956), set out to break down the traditional lineage transmission of medical learning and to develop a standardized system accessible to students of traditional medicine (Andrews, in press).

In addition to the standardization of curriculum, the relationship between the parts of the system also underwent revision. Not only were "superstitious" elements eliminated; the role of acupuncture was rewritten to conceal its historical position as a lower-class practice relative to herbal medicine. Moreover, historically, nine kinds of needles had been used. Although a number of them looked like the acupuncture needles with which we are now familiar, the others resembled small hooks and scalpels and were used for minor surgery involving such practices as bloodletting, cataract removal, and the lancing of boils. Standing in the shadow of an emerging biomedicine, early twentieth-century Chinese medical reformers had a stake in acupuncture not being looked down on as an inferior version of surgery. They rehabilitated the modality, reducing the number of needles to the kind still used (Andrews, in press).

Historically in China, religious healing movements have made the government uneasy, due to the possibility of their overlapping with popular uprisings. (The current controls imposed on the Falun Gong movement illustrate the point.) This general apprehension gained additional currency under a Communist government that represented China's religious traditions—and Confucianism in particular—as so many superstitions responsible for the country's woes. Insofar as Chinese medicine was based on concepts such as yin, yang, and *qi*—concepts intrinsic to Chinese religious thought—it shared other concepts as well, such as illness categories that included affliction by ghosts, with corresponding acupuncture and herbal treatments. With the advent of the barefoot doctor, however, acupuncture's lower status acquired a certain cachet as the "people's medicine," elevating it as a traditional system used in the service of the people.

The principal aim supported by the PRC government was not to model traditional Chinese medical education after biomedicine per se but to rationalize standards of education as had been done in biomedicine. It was this standardized version of Chinese medicine and this form of acupuncture that the United States imported in the 1970s, and that practitioners trained in mainland China subsequently brought into U.S. acupuncture schools. State and national licensing exams exhibit the persisting power of this influence. PRC-TCM serves as the foundation of professional credentialing, even though other schools of practice have also established a presence in the country (Barnes, forthcoming).

The World of the Clinical Trial

Even with these reforms, the U.S. biomedical community had trouble with Chinese medicine almost from the start. In particular, the fundamental paradigm of *qi* eluded an understanding schooled on the anatomical body. Insofar as the twelve major pathways of *qi*—the *jingluo*, or meridians—could not be located through dissection or under a microscope, Western biomedical physicians often assumed they must be figments of the imagination. Yet without that network of *qi*, it made no sense that the insertion of a needle in a person's foot could affect a condition experienced in the head or some other part of the body.

Instead of trying to understand *qi* in terms of theories of the humors—as had sixteenth-century Western observers—or of electricity or magnetism, as had eighteenth- and nineteenth-century doctors, physicians of the twentieth century attempted to interpret acupuncture's effects in terms of the nervous system and of endorphins. Unable to parse the explanation in biomedicalese, they reduced acupuncture to the insertion of needles at painful points, to alleviate pain. Most had no idea that this resolution had long been the West's response to the modality. Physicians concluded that acupuncture ultimately had little to offer. Only the persistence of the grassroots movement resulted in the modality's grounding itself in the United States, although it did so primarily in the yards of the New Age and countercultural communities.

This scenario changed in 1993 when a team led by David Eisenberg published the results of a survey showing that 33.8 percent of Americans used complementary and alternative medicine, paying for many of these services out of pocket. Almost overnight, the biomedical community woke up to the prevalence of these practices, the amount of money being spent, and the popularity of acupuncture among them (Eisenberg et al. 1993). There was only one problem. The *qi* paradigm still made little sense to biomedical researchers or clinicians. Moreover, the analysis of illness in the Chinese interpretive system found few precise correspondences in biomedical diagnostics. What might be classified as a single condition by biomedicine might just as easily be interpreted by the Chinese systems as four or five separate conditions requiring different therapeutic interventions.

Deciding to bypass these apparently irresolvable issues, researchers instead focused on acupuncture's efficacy in the narrowest of terms, using the gold standard of assessment, the randomized, double-blind, controlled clinical trial. Unfortunately, to do so, they had to assume the possibility of a uniform response to what appeared to them to be a uniform complaint, as in the case of lower back pain or high blood pressure. The problem of how to develop a clinical trial model reflective of Chinese interpretive systems has continued to elude solution. In contrast to what happened in the 1970s, however, when biomedical researchers and physicians essentially rejected acupuncture (see Wolpe 1985), there are now practitioners on the staffs of some of the larger hospitals in the United States (generally in pain services). The National Center for Complementary and Alternative Medicine (NCCAM) of the National Institutes of Health (NIH) dedicates a large budget to researching complementary and alternative therapies—acupuncture and Chinese herbs among them.

The effects of time have played a part in these developments. The generation of physicians born in the 1960s and 1970s has grown up in a culture familiar with complementary therapies and Chinese practices. Some came to medical school with the hope of learning and/or developing more integrative models of practice. Defining themselves as holistic physicians on the one hand, for whom the "body, mind, spirit" model is both familiar and acceptable, they also define themselves as scientists who have a stake in developing a literature that substantiates the efficacy of Chinese herbs and acupuncture. Although committed to evidence-based medicine, they do not necessarily assume that acupuncture is a variation on quackery. Indeed, among the various complementary and alternative therapies, surveys of physician attitudes consistently show that acupuncture had the highest rate of physician referral (43 percent) and credibility (Astin et al. 1998). Rather than focusing on the question of whether or not practices like acupuncture work, researchers are turning instead to the question, "What is sufficiently proven by science to recommend its use?" (Lambert 2002: 99).

The End of Science?

Among European American complementary and alternative practitioners, this medicalizing of acupuncture has been met by some with suspicion and by others with enthusiasm. Many of the older white practitioners, who started out in the early 1970s, remember when they functioned as counterculture figures intent on transforming the social order through alternative therapies that treated the individual. They hold different degrees of disenchantment and even hostility toward biomedicine and worry that medicalization will strip modalities like acupuncture down to nothing more than a technological intervention. Their concerns constitute part of a broader cultural critique of technology and its effects, and the suspicion that biomedical science is likely to truncate Chinese practices as these practitioners understand them.

Some of these same practitioners have effected a merger of science and spirituality, inspired by authors of the "new physics"—Fritjof Capra (1975), James Gleick (1987), Danah Zohar (1990)—and their theories of the Dao of physics, chaos theory, and the quantum self, which posit a mystical dimension to science. One can therefore marry it to Eastern religious traditions and, in the words of physicist Gary Zukav (1979), approach "the end of science." Like the "mystical" dimensions of the religious traditions, this aspect of science then becomes part of the larger bricolage.

Adherents of this perspective may be ambivalent about NIH-sponsored studies, insofar as such projects are apt to be reductionist. Nevertheless, they find it exciting that scientific methodology might validate what they have known experientially. Still other practitioners, eager to establish a role in the mainstream medical landscape of the country, fully support the goal of becoming biomedical professionals (Barnes 2003). They argue that only thus will the Americanizing of Chinese practices reach fruition. Not surprisingly, such advocates tend to minimize the less biomedical aspects of Chinese practices—at least publicly.

All three groups have shown considerable resourcefulness in their ability to appropriate the clinical trial process for their own ends. A good example of this has been the use to which they have put the NIH Consensus Statement on Acupuncture, which asserted that acupuncture had been shown to be effective in relation to postoperative and chemotherapy nausea and vomiting, nausea of pregnancy, and postoperative dental pain (National Institutes of Health 1998).[5] The strongest trials were for a single point called Pericardium-6, which was tested for nausea and vomiting. The testing of Pericardium-6 was based on a drug-trial model, involving the application of a needle to exactly the same single point on each patient. As Ted Kaptchuk observed, in commenting on the outcomes:

> No acupuncturist actually uses that single-needle approach to treatment. It's a reductionist version of acupuncture developed only for a replicable random trial. But acupuncturists are using the outcomes to say that acupuncture works, even though that's not what *they* do in practice. It gives them a toehold of legitimacy, from which to build their authority.
>
> The randomized controlled trial [RCT], historically, was used to develop new therapies or eliminate ineffective ones. Ninety-nine percent of the trials were for that purpose. But the RCTs for acupuncture are *not* for that. Instead, they've been used as a way of asserting acupuncture's legitimacy. In reality, no one's going to use the versions of the practice being tested in the trials, because they're not variable enough. The only place they might be used is in the biomedical world.[6]

The acupuncture community, in other words, rather than acquiescing to a reductionist version of practice, is simply making flexible and creative use of it to secure legitimacy. It has been for similar reasons that courses in anatomy and other aspects of biomedicine have been introduced into the curricula of acupuncture schools. In part, this practice reflects an effort to mimic Chinese TCM colleges. It also represents a move to look more like, and be able to interact with, biomedical clinicians. Nevertheless, most practitioners, when speaking within their own circles, are clear that biomedical models have little to do with Chinese healing. Although some practitioners support the use of the RCT model, for many it is a matter of strategy. The commitment to medicalization is therefore rendered suspect. The New England School of Acupuncture (NESA), for example—one of the oldest programs in the United States—continues to offer courses in *fengshui* through its continuing education program, along with courses such as "Qigong: Foundations of Taoist Alchemy" and "Three Spirits and Seven Souls" (NESA 2002).

Conclusion

The four analytical frames discussed in this chapter provide a set of axes along which to interpret the different cases of Chinese healing in the United

States. They point to differences among the categories of users and the interests at stake for each one. They remind us that even when outcomes look similar, they may represent the sum of different reasons and motives, as well as of different cultural locations. They also remind us that the meanings of "religious" in connection with healing are anything but simple. They also bring us back to the original question concerning how it is that certain traditions are able to bridge cultural differences to take root in new soil. How is it that acupuncture is at once the darling of New Agers and of the NCCAM?

In part, we might conclude that it is simply the outcome of intercultural exchange. "We are social creatures," observes Kwame Dawes, "who have consistently shown a propensity to adapt our values, our sense of beauty and art, and our concepts of identity and place according to the cultures and civilizations that we encounter." Such adoptions and exchanges are, he suggests, "arguably inherent in human behavior" (1997: 117–18). Cultures are neither static nor closed; nor are they self-contained. Indeed, with the growing existence of global interchange, it is no longer as clear as it might once have been just what we count as culture (Ziff and Rao 1997: 2). As Mike Featherstone suggests:

> The process of globalization suggests simultaneously two images of culture. The first image entails the extension outwards of a particular culture to its limit, the globe. Heterogenous cultures become incorporated and integrated into a dominant culture which eventually covers the whole world. The second image points to the compression of cultures. Things formerly held apart are now brought into contact and juxtaposition. Cultures pile on top of each other in heaps without obvious organizing principles. (1995: 6)

From this angle, borrowing and appropriation are multidirectional and even natural. Vodou priestesses in New Orleans adopt the image of the Virgin of Guadalupe from Chicano tradition because she wears the pink and blue characteristic of the *lwa*—the guardian force—known as Erzulie. The priestesses see an underlying resonance, only partly visual, and find the adoption an enrichment of their symbolic world. A healer from the Seneca tribe learns acupuncture to become a more effective Seneca healer.[7] Such hybridity has become more the rule than the exception, as groups from around the world encounter each other with unprecedented frequency and, sometimes, intimacy.

The selection process, in many cases, appears to be governed by the perception of some underlying resonance—a poetics of analogy, in which some symbol, some practice, appears to provide an additional resource with which to articulate something intuited, something known, something already believed. The more complex the system being borrowed from, and the more multivalent its symbolic resources, the greater the likelihood that different groups will read their own content into any one of them. Given the very nature of symbols, in some cases multiple groups will pick the same ones and discern different meanings through them. The result, in the case of Chinese healing practices, is a fragmented acculturation, where everything from the spiritual to the technological becomes possible.

In each case, the appropriation is not complete but is, instead, partial and in the image of the selector. Some things seem natural to adopt, and others fall outside the realm of what a person or group can imagine—or at least so people think. One executive I interviewed described herself as having turned to acupuncture for a basic, practical reason. She wanted relief from pain. As she experienced the change of state brought about through treatments, she began to develop an interest in understanding other ways of getting at *qi*—a curiosity that led her to start taking lessons in *taijiquan*. She clearly viewed this second adoption as a change she had never anticipated. Out of such experiences, some people decide to become practitioners themselves. On the other hand, for some, *taiji* falls within an approach to the martial arts located under the heading of exercise and fitness. Each practice can be ready many ways.

This executive's experience illustrates the extent to which all of the United States is coming to speak some version of creole. Nevertheless, "the language of global mass consumer culture is English" (Featherstone 1995: 8). When two traditions interact, each one may find itself forced to identify ways of making sense of the other. The process, however, is not necessarily equitable, particularly when one of the traditions represents a dominant system. While borrowing may be natural, the borrowing does not take place on an even field but in the midst of relationships "saturated by inequality, power and domination" (Renato Rosaldo in Howes 1996: 157). As the preceding examples illustrate, things become all the more complicated when the advocates and receivers of the new tradition represent divergent constituencies. They may be immigrants who do or do not interact directly with the dominant culture and yet who are inescapably surrounded by it. They may be members of the dominant culture who have inherited a legacy of entitlement.

Each of the stakeholders tends to represent its own share of the larger turf as more authoritative, based on its own criteria of legitimacy. For Chinese American practitioners, that legitimacy resides in their own identity as Chinese and in their historical stake in the traditions in question. Few view any of the European American practitioners as having skill levels commensurate with their own. For European American practitioners, in contrast, legitimacy lies in the claim to have developed an "American" practice responsive to the needs of (European) American patients. Biomedical researchers and occasional practitioners locate their authority in the larger domain of biomedicine. Perhaps as much as the New Age types, they view their system as universal, thereby entitling them to excerpt anything they choose, even where the outcome looks little like the system from which it was taken.

The forms taken by different Chinese practices in the United States are invariably located within broader frames governed by multiple structures of social power. Race is one such structure. More recently, the Americanizing of Chinese practices has tended to coincide with their whitening. Because this trend is rarely construed as appropriation, the absence of many Chinese practitioners in assemblies of CAM practitioners goes largely unnoticed. The appropriators operate from deep sincerity even as they assume roles of authority and inhabit more and more of the discursive space related to the practices they have taken on. Indeed, this process may, ultimately, be a substantial piece of what the Americanizing of Chinese medicine comes to mean. Even so, Chinese healing practices, as a system, possess the richness and complexity to coincide with different cultural concerns. This complexity suggests that they will also continue to lend themselves to multiple constructions of the kind described here. However much any single stakeholding group may attempt to assert ultimate authority, I suspect that the practices themselves will continue to elude ownership and will remain contested sites of authority.

NOTES

I thank John Carman, Arthur Kleinman, Ted J. Kaptchuk, and Tu Weiming for their invaluable mentoring over the years. I am also grateful to Susan Sered and Meredith McGuire for their close and constructive readings of this article.

    1. For the purposes of this chapter, I am focusing on the entry of these practices through Chinese immigrants. However, knowledge of acupuncture and moxibustion (the burning of fibers for the leaves of mugwort, or *Artemesia vulgaris*, at strategic acupoints) entered the United States much earlier. Between the 1820s and the 1840s, medical and pharmacological journals in the United States published both original articles and pieces reprinted from European journals on acupuncture, moxa, Chinese herbs, and Chinese medicine in general (Barnes, forthcoming).

    2. Data for this chapter are drawn from fieldwork carried out between 1991 and 2001 through interviews with both Chinese and European American practitioners of some version of acupuncture and/or related modalities. Interviewees were initially selected through listings in the Yellow Pages and then through word of mouth (the method by which clients usually find practitioners). I conducted interviews in practitioners' homes and/or offices, in outside sites such as restaurants, and, on occasion, by telephone. I also sat in on treatment sessions (in the case of one practitioner, once a week for close to two years). I also interviewed nonpractitioners who were in some way involved with the promotion of Chinese healing modalities in the Boston area. The nonpractitioners included academics, store managers, and public officials.

    3. Most spirit money reads that it is a "Hell Bank Note," referring to the yin realm of the dead in the underworld. Possibly due to surrounding Christian influences that may critique funerary practices positioned under the rubric of "Hell," some packets of spirit money now read "Heaven Bank Note."

    4. Although the herbal stores carry no Christian paraphernalia, Chinese churches punctuate the community. As Yon Lee explains it, people may attend a church, have a family altar related to their ancestors, and, on occasion, go to a Bud-

dhist temple. In so doing, they continue a long tradition of drawing on the resources of coexisting traditions. "It is," Lee says, "like taking out insurance. You want to be sure you've covered all the bases."

5. The twelve-member panel also concluded that acupuncture could be effective as an adjunct therapy, an acceptable alternative, or as part of a comprehensive treatment program, for a number of other pain-related conditions for which there was less convincing scientific evidence. These conditions included but were not limited to addiction, stroke rehabilitation, headache, menstrual cramps, tennis elbow, fibromyalgia (general muscle pain), low back pain, carpal tunnel syndrome, and asthma (National Institutes of Health 1998).

6. In conversation with the author. See also Kaptchuk et al. 2000.

7. I am indebted to Tom Csordas for this example.

REFERENCES

Albanese, Catherine L. 1990. *Nature Religion in America: From the Algonkian Indians to the New Age*. Chicago: University of Chicago Press.

Andrews, Bridie J. In press. *The Making of Modern Chinese Medicine*. Cambridge: Cambridge University Press.

Astin, J. A., A. Marie, K. R. Pelletier, E. Hansen, and W. L. Haskell. 1998. A Review of the Incorporation of Complementary and Alternative Medicine by Mainstream Physicians. *Archives of Internal Medicine* 158: 2303–10.

Bailey, Alice. 2000. Esoteric Healing. In *Holistic Revolution: The Essential Behavior*, ed. William Bloom, 163–169. New York: Penguin Press.

Barnes, Linda L. 1998. The Psychologizing of Chinese Healing Practices in the United States. *Culture, Medicine and Psychiatry* 22: 413–43.

———. 2003. The Acupuncture Wars: Acculturation and Professionalization—A View from Massachusetts. *Medical Anthropology Quarterly* 21: 1–41.

———. Forthcoming. *Needles, Herbs, Gods, and Ghost: China, Healing, and the West to 1848*. Cambridge, Mass.: Harvard University Press.

Capra, Fritjof. 1975. *The Tao of Physics: An Exploration of the Parallels between Modern Physics and Eastern Mysticism*. Berkeley: Shambhala.

Clairol. 2002. "Natural Instincts" hair color ad. *Essence*, March 4: 2–3.

Clark, Stephen M. 1992. Myth, Metaphor, and Manifestation: The Negotiation of Belief in a New Age Community. In *Perspectives on the New Age*, ed. James R. Lewis and J. Gordon Melton, 99–104. Albany: State University of New York Press.

Dawes, Kwame. 1997. Re-appropriating Cultural Appropriation. In *Borrowed Power: Essays on Cultural Appropriation*, ed. Bruce Ziff and Pratima V. Rao, 109–21. New Brunswick, N.J.: Rutgers University Press.

Deloria, Philip. 1998. *Playing Indian*. New Haven, Conn.: Yale University Press.

Dubs, Homer H., and Robert S. Smith. 1942. Chinese in Mexico City in 1635. *Far Eastern Quarterly* I(4): 1: 387–89.

Eisenberg, D. M., R. C. Kessler C. Foster, F. E. Norlock, D. R. Calkins, and T. L. Del Banco. 1993. Unconventional Medicine in the United States: Prevalence, Costs, and Patterns of Use. *New England Journal of Medicine* 328: 246–52.

English, June Anne. 1983. Millenialism in the Holistic Health Movement. *Cultural Futures Research* 8 (1): 29–44.

Featherstone, Mike. 1995. *Undoing Culture: Globalization, Postmodernism and Identity.* London: Sage.

Gleick, James. 1987. *Chaos: Making a New Science.* New York: Viking.

Heelas, Paul. 1996. *The New Age Movement: The Celebration of the Self and the Sacralization of Modernity.* Oxford: Blackwell.

Hoffman, David. 2000. The Holistic Herbal. In *Holistic Revolution: The Essential Behavior,* ed. William Bloom, 188–92. New York: Penguin Press.

Howes, David. 1996. Cultural Appropriation and Resistance in the American Southwest: Decommodifying "Indianness." In *Cross-Cultural Consumption: Global Markets, Local Realities,* ed. David Howes, 138–60. London: Routledge.

Jia, Huanguang. 1997. Chinese Medicine in Post-Mao China: Standardization and the Context of Modern Science. Ph.D. diss., University of North Carolina.

Jocks, Christopher. 1996. Spirituality for Sale: Sacred Knowledge in the Consumer Age. *American Indian Quarterly* 20: 415–31.

Kaptchuk, T., P. Goldman, D. Stone, and W. Stason. 2000. Do Medical Devices Have Enhanced Placebo Effects? *Journal of Clinical Epidemiology* 53: 786–92.

Kyle, Richard. 1995. *The New Age Movement in American Culture.* Lanham, Md.: University Press of America.

Lambert, Craig. 2002. The New Ancient Trend in Medicine: Scientific Scrutiny of "Alternative" Therapies. *Harvard Magazine* 104 (4): 46–49, 99–101.

Lovelock, James E. 1979. *Gaia: A New Look at Life on Earth.* Oxford: Oxford University Press.

Lutz, Hartmut. 1990. Cultural Appropriation as a Process of Displacing Peoples and History. *Canadian Journal of Native Studies* 10: 167–82.

MacDonald, Jeffrey L. 1995. Inventing Traditions for the New Age: A Case Study of the Earth Energy Tradition. *Anthropology of Consciousness* 6 (4): 31–45.

Molgaard, Craig, and Elizabeth Byerly. 1981. Applied Ethnoscience in Rural America: New Age Health and Healing. In *Anthropologists at Home in North America,* ed. Donald A. Messerschmidt, 153–66. Cambridge: Cambridge University Press.

Nason, James D. 1997. Native American Intellectual Property Rights: Issues in the Control of Esoteric Knowledge. In *Borrowed Power: Essays on Cultural Appropriation,* ed. Bruce Ziff and Pratima V. Rao, 237–54. New Brunswick, N.J.: Rutgers University Press.

National Institutes of Health. 1998. Consensus Statement on Acupuncture. http://odp .od.nih.gov/consensus/cons/107/107_intro.html.

Neuenfeldt, Karl. 1998. The Quest for a "Magical Island": The Convergence of the Didgeridu, Aboriginal Culture, Healing and Cultural Politics in New Age Discourse. *Social Analysis* 42:73–102.

New England School of Acupuncture. 2002. http://www.nesa.edu/Nes1.htm. Accessed February 27.

Numrich, Paul. 1996. *Old Wisdom in the New World: Americanization in Two Immigrant Theravada Buddhist Temples.* Knoxville: University of Tennessee Press.

Omi, Michael, and Howard Winant. 1986. *Racial Formation in the United States: From the 1960s to the 1980s.* New York: Routledge.

Ong, Aihwa. 1996. Cultural Citizenship as Subject-Making: Immigrants Negotiate Racial and Cultural Boundaries in the United States. *Current Anthropology* 37:737–62.

Prince, Ruth. 1999. Back to the Future: The New Age Movement and Hunter-Gatherers. *Anthropos* 94:107–20.

Riches, David. 2000. The Holistic Person; Or, the Ideology of Egalitarianism. *Journal, Royal Anthropological Institute* 6:669–85.

Roht-Arriaza, Naomi. 1998. Of Seeds and Shamans: The Appropriation of the Scientific and Technical Knowledge of Indigenous and Local Communities. In *Borrowed Power: Essays on Cultural Appropriation,* ed. Bruce Ziff and Pratima V. Rao, 255–87. New Brunswick, N.J.: Rutgers University Press.

Schmidt, Leigh Eric. 2003. The Making of Modern "Mysticism." *Journal of the American Academy of Religion* 71:273–302.

Seem, Mark. 1987. *Bodymind Energetics: Toward a Dynamic Model of Health.* Rochester, Vt.: Thorsons Publishers.

Shanley, Kathryn W. 1997. The Indians America Loves to Love and Read: American Indian Identity and Cultural Appropriation. *American Indian Quarterly* 21:675–702.

Smith, Alan Braham. 1993. Vanna: Acupuncture Helped Me Get Pregnant. *National Enquirer* November 16: 24–25.

Stein, Diane. 1997. *A Woman's I Ching.* Freedom, Calif.: Crossing Press, 1997.

Tu, Wei-Ming. 1986. *Confucian Thought: Selfhood as Creative Transformation.* Albany: State University of New York Press.

Wolpe, Paul Root. 1985. The Maintenance of Professional Authority: Acupuncture and the American Physician. *Social Problems* 32: 410–24.

Ziff, Bruce, and Pratima V. Rao. 1997. Introduction to Cultural Appropriation: A Framework for Analysis. In *Borrowed Power: Essays on Cultural Appropriation,* ed. Bruce Ziff and Pratima V. Rao, 1–29. New Brunswick, N.J.: Rutgers University Press.

Zohar, Danah. 1990. *The Quantum Self: A Revolutionary View of Human Nature and Consciousness Rooted in the New Physics.* London: Bloomsbury.

Zukav, Gary. 1979. *The Dancing Wu Li Masters: An Overview of the New Physics.* New York: Morrow.

20

Rituals of Healing in African American Spiritual Churches

Claude F. Jacobs

Among African Americans there exists a wide variety of religious beliefs regarding health, illness, and healing. These range from mainstream American ideas and practices to traditions that are tied to particular aspects of the African American experience. Much of my research has focused on the latter, especially in Spiritual churches in New Orleans but also in Detroit and elsewhere in the Midwest and South. I have observed and participated in the churches' rituals, formally and informally interviewed leaders and members, and carried out ethnohistorical research. The Spiritual churches arose in the early twentieth century and are characterized by their combination of elaborate rituals, highly aesthetic sanctuaries, intensely emotional services of worship, openness to women ministers, and eclectic belief system. Drawing on Roman Catholicism, Pentecostalism, nineteenth-century Spiritualism, New Thought, and African religious concepts that were incorporated into what is known as Voodoo or hoodoo in the United States, the Spiritual churches have created ritual spaces in which people can combine features of these religions in a variety of ways (Jacobs and Kaslow 1991).

A part of what attracted people to the Spiritual churches in the early days, and continues to do so now, is their reputation for healing and prophecy. According to church members in Louisiana, the Spiritual religion was built on these two gifts of the spirit. Reverend Mother Leafy Anderson, a church leader in New Orleans in the 1920s, claimed that one of her spirit guides was a "great doctor and minister" named Father John, whose power equals that of St. Jude, the "saint of impossible cases." At a 1926 convention of Mother Anderson's association of churches, healing and "message bearing" occurred at almost all the services, which she held two or three times daily, and "Helping One Another" became her own congregation's motto (*Louisiana Weekly*, December 4, 1926; December 11, 1926). Mother Crozier, another early New Orleans church leader, invited everyone to services where she would be "praying for the sick, blind, and lame" and "healing diseases [of] . . . those given up to die by doctors, and pronounced incurable." Her help and advice were available daily for people "in trouble" or concerned about members who had "strayed from the family circle" (*Louisiana Weekly*, September 17, 1927). The most charismatic and mysterious healer in New Orleans in the 1920s was Mother Catherine Seals, who gained wide recognition as a miracle worker among both black and white city residents. The descriptions of her church tell of discarded crutches that lined the walls of the building, and testimonies of followers recount how she restored sight and cured a variety of illnesses. When she died, an editorial in the *Louisiana Weekly* (August 30, 1930) characterized her as having an "uncanny understanding and complete knowledge of human psychology."

Today's leaders of the Spiritual churches are men and women who often are recognized as "prophets," "divine healers," or "spiritual advisers." Prophets are able to "read" or "give messages" to people; divine healers handle assorted illnesses; and spiritual advisers provide counseling on a wide range of matters. Although some ministers put themselves in only one of these categories, others fit in two or all three. Compared with religious leaders who have to learn specific rituals through long periods of apprenticeship, Spiritual ministers tend not use particular ceremonies passed on to them by others in the churches in order to heal or prophesy. What they do and say comes to them while they are "in the spirit."

In my research, Spiritual ministers often told me that they help a large number and wide diversity of people: working-class and professionals, all races, and members of various religions. It is difficult to document the size and characteristics of those who seek assistance, however, since most Spiritual ministers do not keep records and often are reluctant to talk about their activities except in general terms. Furthermore, some ministers like to boast about the people who visit them, which adds to the difficulty of arriving at an accurate assessment of who and how many people are seen. Nevertheless, Spiritual ministers do have private sessions throughout the week with their clients. These individuals are helped in much the same way as are people who participate in regularly scheduled services of worship.

Given the problem of access to private sessions, the lack of records, and the fact that Spiritual ministers report their successes but not their failures, much of my own research has been devoted to describing and analyzing the rituals that occur during public worship. Worship in the Spiritual churches does not have a rigid format. Instead, the leader shapes the service according to his or her abilities and the needs of the congregation. For the most part, the service is composed of the same elements of worship that are found in all evangelical Protestant denominations: prayers, testimonies, musical selections, Scripture reading, preaching, congregational singing, announcements, reports, and collections. Spiritual worship is highly participatory and includes a wide variety of rituals that incorporate objects that in other churches would not be likely to be considered sacred, such as plants, handkerchiefs, pillows, or any number of household items.

Spiritual ministers describe people who look for help in the churches as having "problems," "troubles," or "conditions." These words are used interchangeably to refer to anything physical, psychological, or social that causes an individual to suffer. The general category of problems or conditions includes a number of specific categories: health problems (physical and mental); conflicts between spouses, lovers, or family members; sexual anxiety; and difficulties with the law or in the workplace.

The Spiritual churches reinforce their role in solving people's problems in a variety of ways, reflecting their links to Roman Catholicism, Pentecostalism, nineteenth-century Spiritualism, New Thought, and Voodoo/hoodoo. The same gospel songs typically heard in Pentecostal churches, sung by the choir or the entire congregation, are powerful conveyers of this idea:

> Wait on the Lord.
> Wait on the Lord.
> He will bear your burdens.
> He will share your pain.
> He will solve your problems.
>
> I'm so glad trouble don't last always.
> O, I'm so glad trouble don't last always.
> I'm so glad trouble don't last always.
> O, my Lord!
> O, my Lord!
> What shall I do?
>
> Jesus [is] on the main line, tell him what you want.
> Jesus [is] on the main line, tell him what you want.
> Jesus [is] on the main line, tell him what you want.
> Call him up and tell him right now.
> If you want your body healed, tell him what you want.
> If you want your body healed, tell him what you want.
> If you want your body healed, tell him what you want.
> Call him up and tell him right now.

Identical to what occurs before or during Pentecostal services, Spiritual people offer testimonies. Many of these statements explicitly or implicitly reinforce the idea that God, the source of blessings, fulfills personal needs or desires and thereby resolves problems. Some of the most frequently heard phrases in testimonies include "We come for a blessing," "What you want God's got it," and "It's no secret what God can do. What he's done for others, he'll do the same for you." When people in the churches remind each other that "prayers are the keys of heaven, and faith unlocks the door," they often interpret the phrase to mean that through prayer and faith, one's problems are solved. The leader of the opening devotions at one church that I often attended instructed everyone to repeat each line in the following statement three times:

> Jesus is the light of the world.
> Take him for your partner; make your plans larger.
> He is the answer to all of our problems.

Illness, a major cause of problems, receives attention in the churches in two ways. During almost every service, the sick are remembered through prayers in which God is frequently referred to as "a doctor who never lost a case." In addition, worship often includes a healing ritual not unlike that in Pentecostal churches. At these times, people leave their seats and go to the front of the sanctuary to receive a "laying on of hands," sometimes on especially afflicted parts of the body. Organ music and singing usually overshadow whatever occurs between the minister and worshiper, providing them some privacy. The minister typically gives instructions for things the person should do at home, such as going on a fast, taking ritual baths, lighting candles, or reading particular Bible verses. Finally, the individual is told not to worry and is given the assurance that "everything will be all right."

Prophecy, in the form of readings or messages from the spirit, also occurs during worship. People either go to the front of the church, as in the healing ritual, or merely stand in place. To outsiders, these messages often appear to be based on a minister's knowledge or perception of an individual; they offer practical advice, such as warnings about people, places, and situations to avoid, suggestions about changes in behavior, or recommendations regarding the future. Women are sometimes told to refrain from gossiping so much on the telephone, to stop trusting certain friends, and not to be so anxious about their relationships with men. Young people are reminded to obey parents, and parents to be more understanding of their children. In order to kindle hope and reduce anxiety, messages almost always end the same way healing does. Ministers urge people to "keep on keeping on" and assure them that "everything will be all right," to which the proper reply is "Thank you, kind spirit."

Spiritual people may attempt to resolve a problem by sponsoring or participating in feasts. These events occur throughout the year to honor important Christian saints or other figures recognized by the churches. The most important include St. Joseph, St. Patrick, St. Anthony, St. Michael, the Blessed Mother, the Sacred Heart of Jesus, Queen Esther, and Black Hawk, a spirit guide that the Spiritual churches adopted from American Spiritualism. St. Joseph, as head of the Holy Family, may ensure a full pantry of food, a new home, or harmony between spouses. St. Patrick, St. Michael, and Black Hawk may help repel enemies or resolve legal problems. Although the construction of altars and feasting were a part of Louisiana Voodoo, Spiritual people apparently have incorporated the basic format of today's feasts from a popular Catholic custom of Sicilians in New Orleans, who honor St. Joseph in this fashion.

The causes of problems, according to Spiritual people, may be "natural" or "unnatural." Natural causes are physical, psychological, or social; may produce illnesses such as arthritis, high blood pressure, or diabetes; and may be cured by a variety of therapies. Members consult physicians as needed, purchase patent medicines especially for pain and chronic problems such as sinusitis or arthritis, resort to home or folk remedies, and participate in healing rituals at church.

Unnatural causes of illness refer to sorcery, works of the devil, or "seducing" spirits that are attracted to individuals whose minds are sometimes said to be full of malicious thoughts. Many of these cases are identified by bizarre or inexplicable behavior, including mental derangement, loss of self-control, or inappropriate public acts. Church members' ideas regarding unnatural causes have a variety of sources: Bible passages such as St. Paul's anguish over evil influences on his behavior (Romans 7:15, 18b–19); possession and exorcism in Roman Catholic and Pentecostal churches; Hollywood films such as *The Exorcist;* and Spiritualist seances held to pacify "restless spirits."

In addition to "natural" and "unnatural" causation, many Spiritual people emphasize the "self" as a cause of problems. This derives considerably from the churches' link to New Thought and Spiritualism, whose Declaration of Principles affirms the "moral responsibility of the individual," and the idea that each person "makes his own happiness or unhappiness as he obeys or disobeys Nature's physical and spiritual laws" (National Spiritualist Association of Churches of the United States of America 1953). Advisers in the Spiritual churches who talk about the self as the cause of problems explain that some people have "blocks," or thoughts, that interfere with their daily routines or ability to achieve goals. Such people are said to "stand in their own way" or to "have poisoned minds," both of which limit "progress and prosperity." The importance of the mind and its role in healing is a major point in *The Twelfth Hour Meditator,* a devotional manual prepared by a senior leader of an association of Spiritual churches in New Orleans:

> Know that Thought is supreme, that Ideas rule the world, that no
> man is essentially better than the thoughts he entertains.
>   . . . To improve your circumstances, you must first enlarge your
> consciousness and increase your knowledge. Learn to use your
> powers of Thought and of creative imagination ("the Divine Facul-

ties of the human mind") for the achievement of all worthy desires. Therefore, train your mind to know and use its own powers.

Heal yourself,—and others. Harmful thoughts and emotions are reflected by inharmonious conditions of the physical body. "Mind not only makes sick, it also cures." You can heal yourself and others, when you fully understand why Divine Healing is the result of definite and unfailing laws, and that Healing does not come from without, but from within man.

. . . We affirm health, which is man's divine inheritance. Man's body is his holy temple. Every function of it, every cell of it, is intelligent, and is shaped, ruled, repaired, and controlled by mind. (Griffin 1949: 60–61)

The Spiritual churches' emphasis on the mind is also seen in the selection of themes for the annual meetings of the Association of Universal Truth International Incorporated, Spiritual churches that are headquartered in Detroit. The theme is printed on each year's souvenir program book. In 1997, it was "Building Minds for a New Day"; in 1979, "Let God Do It for You, for He's the Masterpiece of Your Mind"; and in 2002, "Building Minds for the 21st Century." Another example comes from the second edition of the *Catechism of the Metropolitan Spiritual Churches of Christ*, published in the late 1990s. The introduction to the catechism, "Spiritual Mind Treatment," affirms that there is one life and that life is God, that good alone flows to and from the individual, and that this perfect circulation with the infinite rhythm of life leads to harmony and peace. As a part of the conclusion to the passage, the reader is taught to say, "There is no fear. . . no doubt. . . and no uncertainty in my mind. I am letting that life which is perfect control me, and flow through me, right now."

As Spiritual ministers resolve people's problems, they harmonize New Thought and Spiritualism with the Bible and writings of mainline Protestant theologians. A minister who had to help someone who suffered considerable anxiety because of conflicts with other church members based his diagnosis of the problem and subsequent counseling on a verse from Proverbs, which he paraphrased as "So a man thinketh, so it is in him." Another minister told me how he instructed a client who was having marital problems to include in her daily meditations the following revision of a prayer written by Reinhold Niebuhr: "Things that I can change, I will change. Things that I cannot change, I have to change my way of thinking."

This view of the "self" as a cause of problems has influenced Spiritual ministers' ideas concerning the paraphernalia they use (candles, incense, and oils) and the rituals they perform or prescribe (spiritual baths, novenas, and anointings). According to the ministers, such material objects or ceremonies have no intrinsic power but only help to establish belief or faith in the mind of a client or member of their congregation. Spiritual ministers often adopt this perspective on the relationship between the mind and ritual to explain how they deal with people who feel that something has been "done" to them by others through Voodoo or hoodoo. Since many New Orleanians think of the Spiritual churches as perpetuators of the occult, ministers in Louisiana are sometimes sensitive about the subject. Nevertheless, there have been and still are Spiritual ministers who claim to use frogs, beef tongues, and chickens in their rituals in ways that parallel descriptions of Voodoo/hoodoo. Even those who do not use them will occasionally express an interest in their significance. It is important to point out, however, that nearly all the ministers who talk about Voodoo/hoodoo assert that the churches do not teach that a person can be bewitched, but that many problems are "in the mind." In other words, people who believe that they are hoodooed actually are hoodooed, and the work of the Spiritual minister is to change such thoughts.

Discussion

Although it is impossible to assess claims made by Spiritual leaders of the 1920s that they healed physical ailments, and there are no epidemiological studies of the effectiveness of the healing techniques of today's Spiritual leaders, we can examine what happens in the churches in terms of theory from anthropology and religious studies. Is it possible for the Spiritual churches to heal people who turn to them when they have problems? If so, what is healed, and how does it occur? An answer to these questions must begin with a reassessment of the Spiritual religion. Researchers have often described the Spiritual churches as flawed institutions and therefore of limited therapeutic value. One example is Joseph R. Washington (1972: 115), who contends that Spiritual advisers provide poor blacks a "positive-thinking religion" or "peace-of-mind cult" for a price. This characterization becomes even more negative in combination with the view that the limitations placed on blacks by the American social structure account for the "*proclivity* [my italics] of the American Negro to cope by magical means" (Whitten 1962: 322) and with the argument that such magic "produces the illusion that people are masters of their fate, controllers of their environment and not its pawns" (Murphy 1979: 180).

If, however, religious rituals are viewed as deliberately created "sacred time and action" (Paden 1988: 94), then the Spiritual churches' rituals, including healing and prophecy, offer what Mircea Eliade refers to as a sacred mode of attending to the world. The ethos of Spiritual religion and its rituals is dominated by an African American style of expression that Zora Neale Hurston ([1935] 1976:227–28) refers to as asymmetry. In "Characteristics of Negro Expression," she describes asymmetry as the abrupt and unexpected changes seen in African and African American art, music, literature, and dance. In music, for example, one finds frequent changes of key and tempo, so that while there may be rhythm in segments of a composition, the work as a whole appears asymmetrical.

Joel Williamson's comments on blues and ragtime further develop Hurston's discussion of asymmetry:

> [In Negro culture] it was not that one simply moved smoothly from one line to another at an angle where the two were joined. It was as if there were a space between the different lines, leaving them unjoined and seemingly disjunctive. But when the whole pattern was displayed, the audience filled in the spaces and knew that the parts did indeed fit into a broader, never explicitly stated whole. Satisfaction always required a "stretch" by the individual in the audience, a performance by himself complementary to that of the principal. Thus in ragtime the music not only changes direction, it suddenly stops and as suddenly starts up a different line in another key. . . . In black music anything can happen, and it always does. (1984:154)

Although neither Hurston nor Williamson directly applies the notion of asymmetry to religion, their observations are a good fit for the rituals of the Spiritual churches. In this context, asymmetry characterizes the style of Spiritual worship, which draws on the religion's contributing belief systems: Spiritualism, Catholicism, Pentecostalism, Voodoo/hoodoo, and at times mainline Protestantism. What one encounters in the churches' rituals is not a blend of these beliefs but alternations from one orientation to another during the same service, or different orientations at different services.

Worship may begin with a formal, written order of worship, during which everyone focuses attention on the church's main altar as in Catholicism, and then change to the informality and pulpit-centered style of Pentecostalism, during which people sing solos, testify, and pray extemporaneously. While some rituals are typically Christian, such as Holy Communion and baptism, others reflect a Voodoo/hoodoo heritage. Worshipers may attend a feast to request a favor of St. Joseph, a Christian saint, or Black Hawk, an important figure in Spiritualism. A minister can sponsor a novena or hold a seance. Music tempos change from upbeat popular gospel songs to slow, drawn-out hymns. An individual may receive the "laying on of hands" in Pentecostal fashion during healing services or learn adaptations of Spiritualist "mind cure" techniques to solve problems. People hear public sermons that are preached to everyone and get private messages from the spirit realm.

As Spiritual worship unfolds, ministers move from one activity to another, including rituals of healing and prophecy, without explanation of changes in orientation or beliefs. Consequently, there is disjunction but also the sense that a service is a whole entity as a congregation actively participates in it. Similar to the "stretch" required of the listener to black music (Williamson 1984: 154), performances by individuals or groups of people are expected in the Spiritual churches. Worshipers are not supposed to be passive observers of activities led by the choir and ministers. Instead, what transpires is a product of everyone who shares a prayer, song, testimony, or holy dance with the rest of the congregation. In this way, the service moves from one point to another, and depending on the degree of skill and conviction of participants, others become excited and also add to the ecstasy. Spiritual worship, in this way, uses building blocks found in a variety of religious traditions yet incorporates them into ritual performances played out in a characteristically African American expressive style.

REFERENCES

Griffin, O. T. 1949. *The Twelfth Hour Meditator.* N.p.: Watchmen of the Twelfth Hour.

Hurston, Zora Neale. [1935] 1976. Characteristics of Negro Expression. In *Voices from the Harlem Renaissance,* ed. Nathan Irvin Huggins, 224–36. New York: Oxford University Press.

Jacobs, Claude F., and Andrew J. Kaslow. 1991. *The Spiritual Churches of New Orleans: Origins, Beliefs, and Rituals of an African American Religion.* Knoxville: University of Tennessee Press.

Murphy, Robert F. 1979. *An Overture to Social Anthropology.* Englewood Cliffs, N.J.: Prentice-Hall.

National Spiritualist Association of Churches of the United States of America. 1953. *Yearbook.* Milwaukee, Wis.: National Spiritualist Association.

Paden, William. 1988. *Religious Worlds: The Comparative Study of Religion.* Boston: Beacon Press.

Washington, Joseph R., Jr. 1972. *Black Sects and Cults.* Garden City, N.Y.: Doubleday.

Whitten, Norman E., Jr. 1962. Contemporary Patterns of Malign Occultism among Negroes in North Carolina. *Journal of American Folklore* 75: 311–325.

Williamson, Joel. 1984. *New People: Miscegenation and Mulattoes in the United States.* New York: New York University Press.

21

Complementary and Alternative Medicine in America's "Two Buddhisms"

Paul David Numrich

Buddhists in the United States fall into two main camps: ethnic Asians, for whom Buddhism represents the primary religious component of their cultural heritage, and non-Asian converts to Buddhism. These two broad groupings manifest significant differences in their perspectives and practice of complementary and alternative medicine, with important implications for the American health care system.

Literature Review and Research Method

Several types of literature pertain to this study. The first provides background and context for understanding health and healing in contemporary Buddhist America, including Buddhist bioethics, health-related beliefs and practices, and traditional healing systems in Asia (Brun and Schumacher 1987; Numrich 2001; Ratanakul 1999a, 1999b). Second, the fields of immigrant and refugee studies, migration studies, and ethnic studies sometimes touch on health issues among ethnic-Asian Buddhist groups (van Esterik 1992). Third, population-specific health studies and cultural competence materials provide detail on health practices and concerns, although surprisingly little about Buddhism or Buddhist support systems (e.g., temples and religious specialists; Muecke 1983; Canda and Phaobtong 1992; Lipson, Dibble, and Minarik 1996). Fourth, clinical studies have examined the health implications of Buddhist meditation (*Alternative Medicine* 1992; Dane 2000; Koenig, McCullough, and Larson 2001). Finally, innumerable popular books explore health and healing from a Buddhist perspective.

This chapter derives generally from my long-term research on Buddhists in the United States (e.g., Numrich 1996), more specifically from a recent project using informants solicited through my contacts in Buddhist temples and centers located primarily in the Midwest. Following a protocol exempted from human subjects research oversight by two institutional review boards, a research team conducted more than thirty informal, semistructured interviews about the health practices and beliefs of the following Buddhist populations and groups, categorized here according to the two main camps in American Buddhism. These are (1) ethnic Asians: Japanese, including a Buddhist Churches of America temple and a nondenominational temple; Koreans, including a Chogye Seon temple; Tibetans; Vietnamese, including followers of Thich Nhat Hanh; Thais, including all five Chicago area Thai temples; and the Falun Gong, a Chinese new religious movement with Buddhist aspects, and (2) convert Buddhists: Soka Gakkai International; Nichiren Shoshu; Korean Seon; Rinzai Zen; Soto Zen; Thich Nhat Hanh followers; Tibetan Vajrayana; and a nondenominational Buddhist group.

CAM and "Two Buddhisms" Defined

The term "complementary and alternative medicine" (CAM) subsumes a variety of health-related practices falling outside of, or standing in tension with, the conventional biomedical model of health care dominant in the United States and other modernized societies. Although typologies vary, and no standard definition of CAM has yet gained acceptance, observers agree that interest in CAM on the part of both consumers and providers has increased dramatically in the United States in recent years (Eisenberg et al. 1993; *JAMA* and AMA *Archives* special issues, Nov. 1998; Kaptchuk and Eisenberg 2001).

This chapter focuses primarily on selected CAM practices among U.S. Buddhists under the general heading of folk healing (*Folk Remedies among Ethnic Subgroups* 1997), which includes behaviors often identified with popular religion or folk religiosity (Sharot 2001). Two kinds of folk healing will be discussed: (1) herbalism, that is, use of plant-derived medicines that may or may not contain organic curative agents (considered a biologically based therapy in CAM inventories); and (2) appeal to spiritual or supramundane healing forces, that is, engaging in a range of practices purporting to manipulate or propitiate healing forces that operate outside of mechanisms known to modern biomedical science, including incantation, palmistry, astrology, the wearing of protective amulets, and shamanic healing. Such spiritual or supramundane healing forces could be classified under several CAM designations, such as mental and spiritual healing (healing power from the mind or divine sources); nonlocality (unmediated healing at a distance); biofield medicine (use of energy fields in or around the body); and even the placebo response in certain cases (healing effected through a patient's belief in the treatment; Cassileth 1998; *Alternative Medicine* 1992; *What Is CAM?* n.d.). In the concluding section, this chapter will also consider the practice of Buddhist meditation. Meditation refers to mental exercises that focus the mind and may produce physical effects; thus meditation is classified in CAM inventories under mind-body approaches to health.

The "two Buddhisms" theory has attained a degree of consensus in the scholarly study of Buddhism in the United States. American Buddhists fall into two main camps, distinguished by the sociological function fulfilled by Buddhism in each (Numrich 2000). The majority of Buddhists in the United States are ethnic Asians for whom Buddhism plays an integral role in the formation, preservation, and evolution of an ethnic identity rooted in an Old World cultural heritage. These "culture Buddhists" have come to the United States from several Asian countries and represent three large branches within historical Buddhism (Theravada, Mahayana, Vajrayana) plus local variations. Chinese and Japanese Buddhist populations have been in this country for more than a century; the other ethnic Buddhist populations arrived in substantial numbers after the relaxation of U.S. immigration restrictions in the 1960s.

"Convert Buddhists" in the United States were raised in another religious tradition (typically Christianity or Judaism) or were relatively secular and have chosen Buddhism as their preferred spiritual worldview and religious practice. In their case, Buddhism facilitates personal identity modification rather than ethnoreligious identity consolidation. Virtually all branches and schools of Buddhism have a convert following in the United States, the most popular being the various Zen schools of Mahayana Buddhism and the Tibetan lineages of Vajrayana Buddhism. Although the majority of convert Buddhists in the United States are Euro-American baby boomers, a significant number of African Americans and Hispanics can be found in certain circles (notably Soka Gakkai and Nichiren Shoshu, groups originating in Japan). With the recent upsurge in Buddhism's popularity in the dominant culture, many Americans are intrigued and influenced by Buddhist beliefs and practices without considering themselves formal converts.

These two Buddhist camps in America approach CAM from different historical perspectives, personal motivations, and socioreligious contexts. Understandings, practices, and evolutionary trajectories vary both across and within the two camps.

CAM among Culture Buddhists

Folk healing systems are both ancient and widespread in the homelands of Asian American Buddhists. Herbal remedies are common in Thailand, for instance, where Buddhist temples have long served as providers of these and other traditional health services, and Buddhist monks often function as shamanic healers and purveyors of "magical" healing (Tambiah 1984; Brun and Schumacher 1987; Ratanakul 1999a). (Despite the perjorative valence of the word, the term "magic" has been applied to folk practices that attempt to control spiritual or supramundane forces; see Gould and Kolb 1964; Stark 2001.) With the advent of Western biomedicine in recent centuries, these traditional healing systems became "CAM," that is, complementary and alternative to the dominant international medical norm. Asian immigrants to the United States come from cultural contexts in which traditional and modern medical systems are in tension and negotiation (Deepadung 1992; Hui, Tangkanasingh, and Coward 1999).

Informants in the present study reported extensive folk healing practices in the local Japanese, Korean, Tibetan, Vietnamese, Thai, and Chinese communities. However, views differed widely on the religious legitimacy of such practices and their status in local ethnic temples. Several informants made a clear distinction between folk religion and Buddhism per se, characterizing the former as inferior to the Buddha's teachings. Several temples accommodate the folk religious behavior of their members with some ambivalence.

The Thai case illustrates the complex dynamics affecting traditional folk healing practices in ethnic Buddhist temples in the United States. In many Thai temples, herbalism has been transplanted more or less whole from Thailand. Temples in southern states where the climate approximates that of Thailand have planted medicinal herb gardens on temple grounds, whereas temples elsewhere grow plants indoors and import dried herbs via the transnational circuits made regularly by laity and monks. The abbot of a U.S. Thai temple near the Canadian border, who keeps a large pot of medicinal herbs boiling in his temple, makes regular trips into Canada, where customs regulations allow freer importation of plants from Asia and where Chinese herbal stores offer a greater selection than can be found near his own temple.

Most Thai monks in the United States offer advice and ritual services to temple members with health concerns. A monk might discuss the karmic balance of a person's present and previous lifetimes, then prescribe certain ritual or moral acts in order to accumulate merit. Monks also routinely prescribe herbal remedies for particular maladies and chant protective scriptural texts on behalf of laypeople. Specially trained "healer-monks" can sometimes be found in local Thai temples. These monks may be adept at astrology, palmistry, and shamanic healing. In one case recounted to us, a visiting healer-monk healed a local monk's sprained arm by whisking holy water on him (a common Thai Buddhist ritual) and intoning a special incantation.

But traditional folk healing practices may be downplayed or eschewed in some U.S. Thai temples. The lay leaders of one Chicago temple—several of whom are also Western-trained Thai physicians—stopped a newly resident monk from practicing folk medicine because they had established their temple primarily as a repository of *Buddhadharma* (the Buddha's teachings, especially about meditation) and secondarily as a venue for selected aspects of Thai culture. Concern over medical malpractice informed the decision as well. One of the temple's founders, a Thai physician, related the story of a woman with end-stage breast cancer who visited the temple's monks for healing but instead received a lesson on Buddhist doctrines. The woman was so disappointed at the temple's lack of health services found in many temples in Thailand that she began attending a Christian church with a cancer support group, and eventually converted.

We knew of another Chicago Thai temple whose resident monks were said to dispense herbal remedies, yet in our first interview the abbot distanced his temple from all such folk practices, portraying them as inconsistent with the "purified" Buddhism he promotes. He stressed the philosophical and ethical aspects of this purified Buddhism, particularly the importance of meditation in clearing the mind and healing the body. If temple members approach him for an astrological consultation, he will discuss it with them, but he emphasized to us that astrological readings and fortune-telling are irrelevant to purified Buddhists. A subsequent interview with a laywoman, however, suggested that the full range of Thai folk healing practices are present in this temple, notwithstanding the public face of "purified Buddhism." As she noted, many members come to the temple's monks for astrological readings, amulets, and magical rituals, "but the Buddha did not support such things." People who rely on such folk practices should be more "mindful," she said, invoking a technical Buddhist term for cultivating clarity of mind through meditation. In her view they would not need popular supernatural aids if they were more self-confident.

The examples given thus far involve the mainline monastic order in Thai Buddhism, the Mahanikaya, which has thirty-five U.S. temples. "Denominational" and "sectarian" differences can inhibit or circumscribe certain folk healing practices in other U.S. Thai temples. For instance, the Dhammayuttika Nikaya, a reformist monastic movement with twenty-seven U.S. temples, prohibits its monks from functioning as healers, citing ancient scripture. Protective amulets are scripturally acceptable, even though, as one informant told me (while displaying her necklace of amulets), "It is the *dhamma* [Buddha's teaching] that protects, not the amulet." According to another informant, the Dhammakaya revival movement within mainline Mahanikaya (six U.S. centers) also downplays Thai folk healing practices in an attempt to attract upper-class Thais who are disdainful of popular religion. The Dhammakaya monk we interviewed devalued protective chants and similar rituals, stating that the best way to heal the body is by purifying the mind.

Our informants indicated that many Asian Buddhists combine Western biomedicine with folk healing practices, viewing the latter as more complementary than alternative to the Western model. Many privilege the efficacy of

Western biomedical treatments. The abbot of the Thai temple where folk heal-ing practices exist underneath a "purified" Buddhism said that he advises ailing temple members to consult Western physicians first to obtain a physical di-agnosis and prescription. Then he works with the patient's mind. "If the mind is calm, it is easier to follow the doctor's orders," he explained. A Korean physician drew a similar distinction between the physical sphere as the prov-ince of Western medicine and the spiritual sphere as the province of Bud-dhism. In her medical practice she sees only one conflict between the two systems—when a patient uses herbal remedies in combination with Western medicines, running the risk of harmful interaction. She advises patients to inform their Western doctors of their folk herbal supplements, and not to drop the Western treatment altogether. Local Vietnamese followers of Thich Nhat Hanh reject all folk healing practices found in typical Vietnamese temples, relying rather on Buddhist mindfulness to render Western medicine more effective, with fewer negative side effects.

Generational dynamics over time tend to privilege Western biomedicine in Asian Buddhist communities. Among Japanese Americans the Issei ("first" or immigrant) generation brought a strong preference for folk medicine from their homeland, an attitude shared by Nisei (the "second," American-born gen-eration) raised in rural areas in the United States or in Japan (the latter called Kibei). But Nisei raised in American urban settings and the Sansei ("third") generation gravitate toward Western biomedical practices. Pressures to accul-turate impinge on other Asian American Buddhist populations as well, espe-cially among the American-born generations, moving them away from tradi-tional folk medicine and toward Western biomedicine (Muecke 1983; Pang 1989; Nisei informant, personal communication). One Thai informant rued the attitude of members of the "new" generation in her community, as they rely more on the scientific basis of Western medicine than on the traditional basis of folk medicine. She hopes that traditional practices will "spread back" into this generation someday, perhaps as they see Westerners using alternative medical practices and realize, "Hey! We have that already! Our parents' med-icines were useful after all!"

Another important factor further privileges Western biomedicine in ethnic-Asian Buddhist communities in the United States—the significant pres-ence and social prominence of Western-trained health care professionals in the immigrant generation, many of whom entered this country under the oc-cupational preference provisions of recent immigration legislation. Nurses and physicians serve as leaders in their ethnic communities and temples and have a vested interest in upholding the primacy of the Western biomedical model of health care, even if they incorporate some non-Western elements into their own medical practice.

CAM among Convert Buddhists

Folk healing practices are not limited to ethnic-Asian Buddhist communities in the United States but can be found in the convert camp as well. The majority of convert Buddhists in America are middle-class, educated, Euro-American baby boomers. The present study uncovered a variegated popular or folk religiosity among them, including herbalism and appeal to spiritual or supramundane healing forces.

Convert Buddhist herbalism tends to be individualistic and eclectic. Several informants noted that individuals in their group use herbal remedies but not within a communal context. One director of a Rinzai Zen center explained that she takes a laissez-faire attitude toward members' use of herbal remedies. A Soka Gakkai informant related that the organization discussed alternative health and healing practices at length, including yoga, naturopathy, and herbalism. A formal decision was made that such practices are permissible unless they explicitly contradict Soka Gakkai teachings or interfere with core Soka Gakkai practices. Many members practice holistic medicine, we were told, including a variety of Asian herbal treatments. On the other hand, certain practices were expressly forbidden by Soka Gakkai's fourteenth-century founder as marks of a lower order of religiosity, such as soothsaying, palmistry, and astrology.

Given the cultural bifurcation of America's two Buddhisms, convert Buddhists are typically unaware of the folk healing practices found in ethnic temples. Even in temples where "parallel congregations" of ethnic and convert Buddhists coexist, converts tend to limit their involvement to classes on Buddhist meditation and philosophy and rarely participate in the host congregation's ethnoreligion (Numrich 1996). For their part, the ethnic monks and lay leaders typically offer a brand of Buddhism stripped of cultural peculiarities for public consumption by nonethnic visitors. An unanticipated finding of this study was the number of convert informants who expressed great interest in procuring folk healing products and services at ethnic temples.

Generally speaking, it appears that the two folk healing traditions—ethnic-Asian and convert—are fairly discrete and rarely overlap. The leader of one convert meditation group that split off from a local ethnic-Japanese temple put it this way: "Our members don't speak Japanese or go to Japanese herbalists. They're more into New Age cures than traditional ethnic ones." She did not elaborate on the kinds of "New Age" practices they follow, except to mention Reiki therapy, a biofield technique introduced in the United States in the 1930s (ironically from Japan). Tibetan physicians make regular visits to Chicago, attracting a mostly "New Age" clientele, according to the local facilitator. It is unclear whether the services offered are characteristic of the folk healing practices found in the small local Tibetan immigrant community, or whether they have been packaged for Western consumption, a common strategy of Asian Buddhist teachers in the West.

The leader of a Soto Zen center in the Midwest is a nurse with a family history of chronic illness. She has respect for the Western biomedical model but does not like to take too much Western medicine. Members of her center and their relatives seek her advice about alternative practices, including herbalism. She purchases herbal remedies at mainstream health food stores on behalf of elderly people who request them, and she thinks—but is not sure—that ethnic Buddhists make their herbal purchases at Asian groceries. She related a dream cycle in which she saw Native American, Buddhist, and medicinal plant imagery all together. This convinced her that she is an *American* Soto Zen Buddhist, rooted in North American healing traditions rather than Asian. She knows the herbs and vitamins of America, not Asia.

She also described the characteristics of a good Zen teacher. A good teacher reaches deeply into what is happening in an ill person's life. The exchange between teacher and student serves to unpack the depths of the student's existence, awakening awareness and understanding of how illness arises and which "repetitive cycles of suffering need to be softened and released." The notion of the Buddhist teacher as guru, a spiritual guide who employs "skillful means" in shaping the student's life and learning, carries a shamanic quality. For most convert Buddhists, this role is filled by their meditation teacher. Other shamanic figures we encountered practiced the Feldenkreis method of body therapy and Zen therapy. As described by the director of a Rinzai Zen center with certified therapists, Zen therapy is a form of bodywork similar to the Rolfing deep tissue massage method, incorporating principles of energy fields and Buddhist breathing techniques. Zen therapy corrects body alignment and aids energy flow, he told us.

Several convert informants used "energy" language in describing their healing practices. We heard of two members of a Vajrayana meditation group who were critically ill at the same time, one following a liver transplant, the other a terrible accident. Some members of the group performed a Medicine Buddha practice for them, focusing the energy of that enlightened spiritual being on them (Birnbaum 1989). Both recovered in miraculous fashion, we were told. In another case the group did the same for a seriously ill child. One woman in the group reported feeling a "very strong heart connection" with the child, even though she did not know the child personally.

One Zen group reported that it performs a Medicine Buddha meditation once a month, in which they visualize the Buddha and chant Sanskrit and Tibetan verses. Some of its members also perform rituals to Tibetan deities called Taras. When asked if they had any hesitance in crossing lineage boundaries here (as Zen Buddhists performing Vajrayana practices), our informant replied that people easily cross boundaries when they see practical results. She interpreted the Medicine Buddha and the Taras as figures that transcend conceptual forms and connect to the consciousness/spirit/energy within oneself. Through visualization techniques the person melts into the Medicine Buddha, for instance, and then healing energy is absorbed into that person or suffuses the situation at hand. The individual feels a sense of relief as well as connectedness with the other meditators in the group. Later they can tap into the energy of the visualized imagery in other circumstances as well.

Chanting serves a similar purpose for Soka Gakkai and Nichiren Shoshu groups, where repeating the phrase *Nam-Myoho-Renge-Kyo* is the primary ritual act. In times of illness this chant is focused, individually or communally, on a particular concern or body part, thus directing healing energy to the focal point. We heard many cases of healing, such as the woman with relapsed breast cancer who was given seven days to live. A group of Soka Gakkai members chanted for her in the hospital, and she lived another three years. Her non-Buddhist hospital roommate testified that she, too, felt better from the chanting even though she did not understand it. A thirty-year follower of Nichiren Shoshu spoke eloquently of how chanting overcame a family history of mental illness and cancer. This informant also mentioned a woman who began chanting just after being diagnosed with cervical cancer, saying that her chanting has kept her alive for fifteen years.

Most of our convert informants reported that members of their groups combine Western and alternative medical practices in their lives, a finding consistent with other studies of CAM practices in comparable non-Asian populations (Eisenberg et al. 1993; Cassidy 1998). Many in our sample privilege alternative practices over Western medicine. A group of Thich Nhat Hanh followers explained that they all tend to "default" first into alternative therapies, then turn to Western biomedicine if necessary. One rarely uses novocaine during dentist visits, instead practicing mindful pain control. Another did the same for a broken arm until the pain became unbearable, then took Western painkillers. A third uses alternative therapies for chronic arthritis.

CAM in America's Two Buddhisms: Implications for American Health Care

This preliminary research suggests differential CAM profiles in America's two main Buddhist camps, with important implications for the American health care system. This discussion also illuminates larger dynamics at work in Buddhist America.

America's two Buddhisms appear to be following opposite trajectories with regard to folk healing practices. Yang and Ebaugh's (2001: 375) statement about acculturation among Chinese Buddhists can be generalized to other ethnic-Asian Buddhist groups in the United States: "Conscious of their minority status . . . [and seeking to be] accepted as a part of mainstream America, Chinese Buddhists have been Americanizing many aspects of their religion in beliefs, rituals, and organizational structure." As the present study shows, that includes adopting the dominant biomedical model of health care in the United States. Not only does the second generation "wish to forget" the folk medicine of their immigrant parents, evoking Marcus Hansen's ([1937] 1987) classic theory about the loss of Old World culture, but first-generation, Western-trained health care professionals accelerate the acculturation process within the immigrant community. In terms of "segmented assimilation" or "selective acculturation" theories (Portes and Zhou 1993), ethnic-Asian Buddhists seem quite amenable to the dominant American health care model regardless of how much of the rest of American culture they choose to adopt. Access to quality services within the system may be more important to these groups than advocating significant accommodation of traditional ethnic healing practices by the system.

Several leaders in culture Buddhist temples critiqued elements of popular religion, further evidence that ethnic-Asian Buddhist communities are moving away from folk healing practices and toward Western biomedicine. In their critiques, these leaders typically dismissed or reinterpreted folk healing practices through appeal to ancient Buddhist scripture, "purified" Buddhist doctrine, and/or scientific rationalism. Thus it appears that the discourse regarding the parameters of "authentic" Buddhism, which has been playing out in the Asian homelands of Buddhism since at least the late colonial period (Dumoulin and Maraldo 1976; Bechert 1984), is now also playing out in ethnic Buddhist temples in the United States with regard to members' health care beliefs and practices. Whether it is framed in terms of a "great tradition" critique of "little tradition" religiosity (a dichotomy now out of favor in Buddhist anthropology; see Scott 1994) or tension between "elite" and "popular" forms of religion (Sharot 2001), we discovered a clear strain of rationalist reformism within ethnic Buddhist communities that rejects or downplays premodern cosmologies and traditional folk religious practices. This echoes the Buddhist modernism movement in Asia (Bechert 1984).

Unlike culture Buddhists, who have begun to transform their transplanted folk traditions from Asia, convert Buddhists in the United States were introduced to Buddhism either through their own intellectual investigation or by teachers who taught a non-culture-bound and modernist version of Buddhism packaged for Western consumption. The convert healing practices we uncovered may herald the creation of a new form of indigenous American folk religiosity, ironically at the very time that imported Asian folk traditions are waning, and apparently eliciting little critique from convert leaders and teachers. Given the bifurcation of America's two Buddhisms, the twain may never meet in such a way that fusion of convert and culture folk healing traditions could occur. The two groups appear to be moving in opposite directions, culture Buddhists assimilating to mainstream America and its dominant model of health care, convert Buddhists de-assimilating from the mainstream America whose core they occupy, choosing rather to explore both a nonconventional religion (Buddhism) and alternative healing modes. The relationship between Buddhism per se and CAM practices seems less self-conscious among convert Buddhists than among culture Buddhists, the difference no doubt owing to the respective historical contexts in which they stand. The CAM of convert Buddhists is more influenced by non-Buddhist elements in American culture, the CAM of culture Buddhist more by an amalgam of Buddhist and non-Buddhist elements in Asian cultures.

What, then, can we speculate about the future of CAM in Buddhist America? First we must recognize that culture Buddhist groups are more stable over time than convert Buddhist groups. Historically, Buddhism's popularity among the non-Asian populace has been cyclical and individually oriented, so that, despite convert Buddhism's current heyday, there is no guarantee that it will last, perhaps dying out with the baby boomer generation. It remains to be seen whether the next generations will find Buddhism more than an intellectual curiosity. Ethnic-Asian Buddhism, on the other hand, being communally based and intergenerationally anchored, is more likely to survive in the long term. Concerns over whether recent American-born generations of Asian Buddhists will retain their ethnoreligious identity seem overdrawn given the importance of minority ethnic identity and solidarity in a racialized society (Yoo 2000; Kwon, Kim, and Warner 2001; Min and Kim 2002). This means that the trajectory of CAM practices of ethnic-Asian Buddhists will likely have a greater impact on the American health care system than the trajectory of convert Buddhists. With regard to folk healing practices generally, this means less CAM rather than more.

Meditation is a different matter. For the most part, Buddhists in both camps recognize meditation as a core Buddhist practice, whether or not they themselves meditate regularly. Meditation is still not a major component of culture Buddhism, although it is promoted by many clergy and lay leaders, and evidence points to growing interest in some circles. On the other hand, meditation continues to be the hallmark of convert Buddhism, the primary exception being the Soka Gakkai–Nichiren Shoshu wing. Thus both Buddhist camps converge at this point, unlike their divergent trajectories with regard to folk healing practices. The health care system can expect more meditation rather than less in the future. Whether or not convert Buddhism is a passing fad, it has already played a major role in establishing meditation as a CAM practice deserving clinical investigation (*Alternative Medicine* 1992; Koenig, McCullough, and Larson 2001) and institutional investment (e.g., the Mind/Body Medical Institute in Boston and the Center for Mindfulness in Medicine, Health Care, and Society at the University of Massachusetts Medical School). Meditation's perceived general compatibility with mainstream Western biomedicine (insofar as mind-body healing mechanisms lend themselves to testing) also gives meditation more legitimacy with acculturating ethnic Buddhists than many of their traditional folk healing practices.

We can see the outlines of two important contemporary discourses, the outcomes of which will determine the future of CAM in Buddhist America and its impact on the American health care system. One discourse concerns the parameters of what constitutes "authentic" medicine, and specifically whether the biomedical model based on clinical testing will continue its dominance (Relman 1998). The other concerns the parameters of what constitutes "authentic" Buddhism, specifically whether modernist Buddhist critiques will prevail over folk religion. If both Buddhist modernism and the Western biomedical model prevail, their rationalist underpinnings are likely to converge in critiquing certain alternative healing practices construed as being in tension with their respective knowledge systems. Such practices include, in folk terms, incantation, palmistry, astrology, the wearing of protective amulets, shamanic healing, and magic; or, in CAM terminology, mental and spiritual healing, nonlocality, biofield medicine, and the placebo response (at least in certain cases). In this scenario, the two current alternative healing practices in Buddhist America that seem most likely to survive will be herbalism and meditation, due to their approximation of the biomedical model. Of these two, herbalism has less of a chance to have a significant impact on the health care system due to the economic and institutional factors working against it, such as the nonpatentability of botanicals and the dearth of support for research and development in government and pharmaceutical circles (*Alternative Medicine* 1992: 197).

Two larger points can be made here in conclusion. First, the discourse about the parameters of "authentic" religion in the modern period has been replicated in all the major world religions (Kitagawa 1959; Bellah 1970). Thus the modernist critique of folk healing practices is certainly present in other immigrant religious contexts in the United States besides Buddhism. Second, the discourse about the parameters of "authentic" medicine is global as well. Traditional and biomedical systems of healing are everywhere in a state of mutual tension and negotiation. The trajectories proposed here presume the dominance of Western biomedicine in the short term in the United States. This is speculative, to be sure, and even more so in the long term.

NOTE

I thank Dr. George Bond, Ms. Krupa Shah, and Ms. Ann Averbach of Northwestern University's Department of Religion for field research assistance; Mr. Al Hurd of the Park Ridge Center for bibliographic assistance; and Dr. George Bond and Dr. R. Stephen Warner for comments on early drafts of this chapter.

REFERENCES

Alternative Medicine: Expanding Medical Horizons: A Report to the National Institutes of Health on Alternative Medical Systems and Practices in the United States. 1992. Chantilly, Va.: Workshop on Alternative Medicine.

Bechert, H. 1984. Buddhist Revival in East and West. In *The World of Buddhism: Buddhist Monks and Nuns in Society and Culture*, ed. Heinz Bechert and Richard Gombrich, 273–85. New York: Facts on File.

Bellah, R. N. 1970. *Beyond Belief: Essays on Religion in a Post-traditional World*. New York: Harper and Row.

Birnbaum, R. 1989. *The Healing Buddha*. Rev. ed. Boulder, Colo.: Shambhala.

Brun, V., and T. Schumacher. 1987. *Traditional Herbal Medicine in Northern Thailand*. Berkeley and Los Angeles: University of California Press.

Canda, E. R., and T. Phaobtong. 1992. Buddhism as a Support System for Southeast Asian Refugees. *Social Work* 37: 61–67.

Cassidy, C. M. 1998. Chinese Medicine Users in the United States. Part II: Preferred Aspects of Care. *Journal of Alternative and Complementary Medicine* 4: 189–202.

Cassileth, B. R. 1998. *The Alternative Medicine Handbook: The Complete Reference Guide to Alternative and Complementary Therapies*. New York: Norton.

Dane, B. 2000. Thai Women: Meditation as a Way to Cope with AIDS. *Journal of Religion and Health* 39: 5–21.

Deepadung, A. 1992. The Interaction between Thai Traditional and Western Medicine in Thailand. In *Transcultural Dimensions in Medical Ethics*, ed. Edmund Pellegrino, Patricia Mazzarella, and Pietro Corsi, 197–212. Frederick, Md.: University Publishing Group.

Dumoulin, H., and J. C. Maraldo, eds. 1976. *Buddhism in the Modern World*. New York: Macmillan.

Eisenberg, D. M., R. C. Kessler, C. Foster, F. E. Norlock, D. R. Calkins, and T. L. Delbanco. 1993. Unconventional Medicine in the United States: Prevalence, Costs, and Patterns of Use. *New England Journal of Medicine*. 328: 246–252.

Folk Remedies among Ethnic Subgroups. 1997. Report 13 of the Council on Scientific Affairs, American Medical Association.

Gould, J., and W. L. Kolb, eds. 1964. *A Dictionary of the Social Sciences*. New York: Free Press.

Hansen, M. L. [1937] 1987. *The Problem of the Third Generation Immigrant*. Augustana College Library Occasional Paper 16. Rock Island, Ill.: Swenson Swedish Immigration Research Center and Augustana College Library.

Hui, E., S. Tangkanasingh, and H. Coward. 1999. Threats from the Western Biomedical Paradigm: Implications for Chinese Herbology and Traditional Thai Medicine. In *A Cross-Cultural Dialogue on Health Care Ethics*, ed. H. Coward and P. Ratanakul, 226–35. Waterloo, Ontario: Wilfrid Laurier University Press.

Kaptchuk, T. J., and D. M. Eisenberg. 2001. Varieties of Healing. *Annals of Internal Medicine* 135: 189–204.

Kitagawa, J. M., ed. 1959. *Modern Trends in World Religions: Paul Carus Memorial Symposium*. LaSalle, Ill.: Open Court.

Koenig, H. G., M. E. McCullough, and D. B. Larson. 2001. *Handbook of Religion and Health*. New York: Oxford University Press.

Kwon, H., K. C. Kim, and R. S. Warner, eds. 2001. *Korean Americans and Their Religions: Pilgrims and Missionaries from a Different Shore*. University Park: Pennsylvania State University Press.

Lipson, J. G., S. L. Dibble, and P. A. Minarik, eds. 1996. *Culture and Nursing Care: A Pocket Guide*. San Francisco: UCSF Nursing Press.

Min, P. G., and J. H. Kim, eds. 2002. *Religions in Asian America: Building Faith Communities*. Walnut Creek, Calif.: AltaMira Press.

Muecke, M. A. 1983. Caring for Southeast Asian Refugee Patients in the USA. *American Journal of Public Health* 73: 431–38.

Numrich, P. D. 1996. *Old Wisdom in the New World: Americanization in Two Immigrant Theravada Buddhist Temples*. Knoxville: University of Tennessee Press.

———. 2000. How the Swans Came to Lake Michigan: The Social Organization of Buddhist Chicago. *Journal for the Scientific Study of Religion* 39: 189–203.

———. 2001. *The Buddhist Tradition: Religious Beliefs and Healthcare Decisions*. Chicago: Park Ridge Center.

Pang, K. Y. 1989. The Practice of Traditional Korean Medicine in Washington, DC. *Social Science and Medicine* 28: 875–84.

Portes, A., and M. Zhou. 1993. The New Second Generation: Segmented Assimilation and Its Variants among Post-1965 Immigrant Youth. *Annals of the American Academy of Political and Social Sciences* 530: 74–96.

Ratanakul, P. 1999a. Buddhism, Health, Disease, and Thai Culture. In *A Cross-Cultural Dialogue on Health Care Ethics*, ed. H. Coward and P. Ratanakul, 17–33. Waterloo, Ontario: Wilfrid Laurier University Press.

———. 1999b. Buddhist Health Care Ethics. In *A Cross-Cultural Dialogue on Health Care Ethics*, ed. H. Coward and P. Ratanakul, 119–127. Waterloo, Ontario: Wilfrid Laurier University Press.

Relman, A. S. 1998. A Trip to Stonesville: Andrew Weil, the Boom in Alternative Medicine, and the Retreat from Science. *New Republic*, December 14, 28–37.

Scott, D. 1994. *Formations of Ritual: Colonial and Anthropological Discourses on the Sinhala Yaktovil*. Minneapolis: University of Minnesota Press.

Sharot, S. 2001. *A Comparative Sociology of World Religions: Virtuosos, Priests, and Popular Religion*. New York: New York University Press.

Stark, R. 2001. Reconceptualizing Religion, Magic, and Science. *Review of Religious Research* 43: 101–20.

Tambiah, S. J. 1984. *The Buddhist Saints of the Forest and the Cult of Amulets: A Study in Charisma, Hagiography, Sectarianism, and Millennial Buddhism*. Cambridge: Cambridge University Press.

van Esterik, P. 1992. *Taking Refuge: Lao Buddhists in North America*. Tempe, Ariz.: Arizona State University Program for Southeast Asian Studies.

What Is CAM? Classification of Alternative Medicine Practices. N.d. Bethesda, Md.: National Institutes of Health, National Center for Complementary and Alternative Medicine.

Yang, F., and H. R. Ebaugh. 2001. Religion and Ethnicity among New Immigrants: The Impact of Majority/Minority Status in Home and Host Countries. *Journal for the Scientific Study of Religion* 40: 367–78.

Yoo, D. K. 2000. *Growing Up Nisei: Race, Generation, and Culture among Japanese Americans of California, 1924–49.* Urbana: University of Illinois Press.

22

La Mesa del Santo Niño de Atocha and the Conchero Dance Tradition of Mexico-Tenochtitlán: Religious Healing in Urban Mexico and the United States

Inés Hernández-Ávila

La danza protége
La danza cura
La danza alivia
Pero también la danza castiga

[The dance protects
The dance cures
The dance helps
But the dance also punishes]

—Capitana Generala María Teresa
Mejía Martinez

This chapter explores the ways in which the Conchero dance tradition in Mexico City, as well as in many urban areas in the United States, manifests a process of religious healing that is not only collective and individual but also earthcentric yet cosmic. The chapter itself is a story of recovery, by the Concheros themselves, and by the Chicana/o communities with whom they have connected over the last several decades. This story of recovery reveals a ceremonial and

spiritual tradition and belief system that have survived centuries of missionization, effectively blending Catholic and European elements with the original
teachings, demonstrating the creatively dynamic and strategic ways in which
cultures and (indigenous) practices preserve, adapt, and transform. For the
Chicana/o individuals and communities from the United States who have
sought out the Conchero elders and dancers, this story represents a vital healing step toward the retrieval of indigenous ways of knowing and being, a step
that allows for a radical shift in critical perspective, from one that is overwhelmingly Western in its foundation to one that more closely represents Native America. In this sense, the connection to, and participation with, the Conchero community, for many Chicanas/os, helps them to "find their way back
home to what is theirs,"[1] spiritually and culturally, as people of indigenous
descent (which does not necessarily mean a denial or rejection of the other
components of their possible *mestizaje*, or mixed-bloodness). This story is also
one of solidarity and mutual respect between indigenous peoples in Mexico
and the United States. In this sense, it contributes to a reintegration (a remembering and healing of the circle) of indigenous communities in the Americas, in such a way that we are reminded of earlier patterns of migration, cross-
cultural contact, and cooperation.

Since its mythically grounded inception, Mexico City, or México Tenoch-
titlán, has had a centuries-old legacy of sophisticated, urban-centered, socio-
cultural organization, wherein dance played a significant role in the daily and
ceremonial life of the people (see Martí and Kurath 1964; Martí 1961; Quintero
1949; Stone 1975; Mansfield 1953; Kurath 1946: 387–99; Martí 1959: 129–51).
Mexico City today has perhaps the largest urban concentration of people in the
world, and the Chicanas/os who have traveled to Mexico to seek out *danza* are
themselves most often from urban areas. As Chicano poet José Flores Peregrino said many years ago, *"Debajo del 'pa'imiento' hay tierra"* (Underneath the
pavement there is earth); simply put, even in urban areas, it is possible to
center oneself spiritually, to reconnect with the earth and with one's relationship to all of life. The dance tradition allows for a reintegration of the self and
a reintegration of the self in relation to the community and to the cosmos.[2] In
cities throughout the southwestern United States, such as Austin, San Antonio,
Los Angeles, San Juan Bautista, Davis, Las Cruces, and Albuquerque, Danza
Conchera is performed, celebrated, and espoused as a legacy of the Aztec tradition and as an authentic (although reclaimed) Chicana/Chicano spiritual expression of (Mexican) indigenousness.

For those who are familiar with Chicana/o history, it is commonly known
that the Chicano/a sociopolitical cultural movement of the 1960s and 1970s
was vigorously energized by the iconography of the Mexican Revolution of
1910. The revolutionary intellectuals and artists often utilized Aztec iconography to reference their own rupture from the foreign dominance cultivated
by the dictator Porfirio Díaz during his thirty years in power (Torres 1996: 4).

Ultimately, as the revolution became institutionalized, so did the cultural markers. The Mexican nation-state, in need of heroic figures and a compelling past linked to the Americas, invoked a cultural nationalism infused with Aztec iconography, even though Mexico is home to a rich diversity of indigenous cultures. This cultural nationalism continues to employ Aztec references (to a conveniently distant past) while consistently repudiating the actual indigenous populations living in Mexico.

During the late sixties and early seventies, at the height of what has been called the Chicano cultural renaissance, Chicanas/os were drawn to the idea of Aztlan, the mythic Aztec homeland to the north of today's Mexico, and to Mexico-Tenochtitlán (see Ybarra-Frausto 1986: 56–68; Forbes 1973). Chicana/o artists, writers, and musicians in particular found inspiration in certain elements of ancient Aztec thought and culture, such as the warrior aspects of Aztec society, associated with Huitzilipochtli, the Left-Handed Hummingbird, guide to the Mexica-Tenochca on their pilgrimage from Aztlan to Mexico-Tenochtitlán. They were also drawn to the humanistic aspects of Aztec society, associated with Quetzalcoatl, the Plumed Serpent, the Peacemaker, who brought the teachings of poetry, *in xochitl in cuicatl,* as the only way to truth, and the idea of education, *in ixtli in yollotl,* to bring forth the face and heart, as the goal of the good *tlamatinime,* the wise teacher. These teachings represent to Chicanas/os not only what had been denied or ignored but also a way to frame the alternative visionary programs for cultural transformation.

Providing a holistic way of healing through honoring and strengthening the interrelationship between body, mind, heart, will, and spirit, Danza Conchera offers Chicanas/os a way to a spiritual path, corresponding to other indigenous spiritual traditions of the Americas, and a reconnection to the earth as a sacred space, even in an urban setting.

La Danza Conchera and La Mesa del Santo Niño de Atocha

Based in Mexico City and headed by the elder Maria Teresa Mejía Martinez, La Mesa del Santo Niño de Atocha is an established *mesa* of danzantes (dancers) who belong to the Conchero dance community and religious society in central Mexico. The Conchero tradition takes its name from the *concha,* the armadillo-backed stringed instrument that is integral to the ceremonial life of the *concheros.* The *concha* (and the mandolin) is played to accompany the dancer's steps when she or he is dancing, just as it is played, in instrumental refrains or to accompany the *alabanzas* (hymns), during the *velaciones* and the *velorios* (the all-night vigils) associated with this dance tradition. The Conchero community is organized by formal groups known as *mesas* (associations), each one represented by an *estandarte* (banner) that portrays the (often Roman Catholic) image that is the subject of main devotion of the group; the banner also

Capitana Generala María Teresa Mejía Martinez (left) and Capitana de
Sahumador, María Robles (right), in the mid-1950s at the Church of the
Virgin of Los Angeles, in Mexico City. Unknown photographer.

designates the name of the *mesa*, the date of its establishment, and the elder(s)
associated with it, in particular the lineage that demonstrates the legitimacy of
the inherited command of the elder(s).

The members of a *mesa* are ranked hierarchically in a militaristic fashion,
with the highest rank being that of *Capitán General* or *Capitana Generala* (this
hierarchy can be seen as harking back to ancient Mexican practice). María
Teresa Mejía Martinez, during a ceremony held on February 14, 1998, in the
church of Santiago Tlaltelolco in Mexico City, was officially recognized in the
larger Conchero community as a *capitana/generala*, one of the few women at
that rank. As an elder, she is a legitimate *heredera* (heir) of her command,

having been designated by her stepmother, the late Capitana Dolores Ortiz, to carry on the work of this particular *mesa*, which belonged to her father, the late Capitán General Gabriel Osorio.[3]

El Santo Niño de Atocha is a representation of the Holy Child Jesus. From an indigenous perspective, the child figure is also intimately associated with sacred medicines such as peyote and the mushrooms and the Native Sacred Child, the solar deity Tonatiuh as child, Piltzintecuhtli (Wasson 1980: 119–49). The significance of children in precontact indigenous philosophy and iconography explains the appeal of El Santo Niño de Atocha, especially because he is thought to have originated in the Americas, in Plateros, close to Fresnillo, Zacatecas, Mexico. In the early nineteenth century the child figure is said to have become "independent" of the Spanish Virgen de Atocha, who originally held him in her arms. El Niño is then reintroduced to Spain, "where the Child had never been honored separately" (Frankfurter 1988: 38). Yvonne Lange notes, "This is one of those exceptional cases where religious beliefs from the New World have been transplanted to the Old" (1978: 5).

In popular Mexican Catholic iconography, El Niño is pictured sitting on a chair, "wearing a plumed hat, of a style in vogue in Europe in the late seventeenth century, a long gown and cape, sandals on his feet, carrying a shepherd's staff with a basket for flowers in his right hand, and [in his left] a sheaf of wheat . . . a bottle gourd" (Wasson 1980: 141). On the right side of his chest he has a *venera* (a kind of badge) pinned to his cape, "a scallop shell that pilgrims to Santiago de Compostela always carried, to eat and drink from and for alms, and as a symbol of their mission" (141–42). He can be mischievous, disappearing only to reappear with his sandals all muddy and the hem of his gown dirty. Sometimes he loses a shoe; when a small child's shoe is discovered, people often point to it as evidence that El Niño has been near, "searching for those in need" (31). (See image on page 105.)

El Santo Niño de Atocha is the patron of the elder Teresa's *mesa*, as she says, of the *palabra* (consecrated authority) established by her father, Gabriel Osorio; as such, El Niño is the leader, the spiritual guide of her group. The Holy Child of Atocha is well known in the larger Mexican (and Chicana/o) community as well as the protector of travelers, both those who travel by foot, *los caminantes*, and those who drive, *los choferes*, especially the ones who must travel over the most difficult roads. He is also the protector of prisoners, the wounded, and the sick, and he is the doctor for all these ills, just as he protects people from assaults or other forms of violence. It is with considerable appreciation of the significance of El Niñito as spiritual guide, healer, and protector of travelers that I note the appropriateness of the eventual integration of several members of La Mesa del Santo Niño de Atocha into the transnational activities of the White Roots of Peace, whose goal, like the teaching for which it was named, is to extend the Tree of the Great Peace for the shelter of all humanity.

The White Roots of Peace and La Mesa del
Santo Niño de Atocha

For several decades there has been frequent and vibrant transnational movement between *danzantes* in the United States who go down to ceremonies in Mexico City and *danzantes* (and elders) from Mexico City who travel up to visit and teach dance communities in the north. La Mesa del Santo Niño de Atocha's critical role in the promotion of *danza* and indigenous cultural revitalization for Chicanas/os in the United States is due in an important way to the intervention of Native people in the north, specifically the transnational Indian revitalization movement initiated by the Six Nations people in the seventies.

The moment in which the Conchero dance tradition initially impacted the Chicano/Chicana movement community in the United States and influenced the cultural, political, and spiritual expression of Chicana and Chicano cultural workers, writers, artists, and musicians occurred in urban areas such as Fresno and San Juan Bautista, California; Austin and San Antonio, Texas; and Albuquerque and Las Cruces, New Mexico. The *mesa* that extended itself to these urban settings was Andrés Segura's group, Xinachtli, of La Mesa de la Virgen de los Dolores. Members of La Mesa del Santo Niño de Atocha were among the first Concheros to travel into the United States in collaboration with the other participants in White Roots of Peace, a collective of Native people from Canada, the United States, Mexico, and Guatemala. At the time, Segura was still a member of La Mesa del Santo Niño de Atocha. The story of the *mesa's* connection to the White Roots of Peace and the story of the White Roots of Peace itself are important chapters in Native American hemispheric history, which up to now represent a "hidden history" of intentional and concerted manifestations of the spiritual and physical reunification of these indigenous Americas. As Tsewaa (Sun Clan of the Tewa, Tesuque Pueblo), one of the frequent travelers with White Roots of Peace, said, "Recently our Grandfathers' spirit guided us into Mexico and Central America to carry their words and renew these words with our relatives down there" (1975: 3–4). The story of this hemispheric linkage represents one of the building stones of collaboration between Chicanas/os, and Native people from Mexico, Guatemala, the United States, and Canada.

The name White Roots of Peace commemorates a time in the history of the Iroquois Confederacy when the six tribes/nations buried their weapons of war at the first Tree of Peace, promising to leave dissension behind to seek the path of peace. Native people have heard through the oral tradition how we were once all related as original peoples of this hemisphere. Invasion, dispossession, genocide, and ethnocide broke us apart from each other, devastating our communities and shattering the coherence and integrity of our languages, our cultures, our ways of knowing and believing, and our networks for community-building. The members of White Roots of Peace were intent on bringing about a resurgence in Indian pride and a renewal of understanding of the "red road," or the indigenous traditions of this hemisphere. This movement emerged out of indigenous people's need for justice and peace and found its expression in the tribal and individual integrity and dignity of the representatives who consciously undertook the journey. For many Chicanas/Chicanos, the Conchero dancers offered a mirror in which to see themselves connected to the north and the south, a reflection that allowed them to emerge from a categorical *mestizaje* to find their indigenous faces and hearts.

The Healing of the Individual

I want to acknowledge my own intellectual and spiritual location in relation to this chapter. I have been a member of Capitana Generala María Teresa Mejía Martinez's group since 1986, after having first danced with the late Capitán General Andrés Segura's Mesa Xinachtli de la Virgen de los Dolores since 1979. In 1995, I began to engage formally in the documentation and representation of La Mesa del Santo Niño de Atocha, both as an institutionally affiliated scholarly voice of the *mesa* and as a recognized *capitana* of this *mesa* since the year I joined her group. The story of La Mesa del Santo Niño is a part of my life story as well, inasmuch as my own formation as a Chicana/Nez Perce dancer, cultural worker, and intellectual (working within the disciplinary framework of Native American and Chicana/o Studies) has been nurtured and inspired by the Conchero tradition, in particular by my relationship with the elders and members of this *Mesa*, and, of course, by the ancient Mesoamerican cultural heritage from which the Conchero tradition emerges.

Through *danza*, I found a space where my Nez Perce and Mexican Indian lineages could reunite; I was witness to the powerful message of unity between indigenous traditions from the north and the south, and that message reverberated through my body, mind, heart, and spirit. In 1976, when White Roots of Peace came through Texas (San Antonio and Austin), one of the most riveting experiences for me was watching the Concheros dance. The *danzantes* who were traveling with White Roots of Peace were members of La Mesa del Santo Niño de Atocha.[4] I saw the dance as prayer, beauty, harmony, discipline, collective action of the spirit performed in the body, with the feet beating the drum of the earth, and ancient ritual come into present time in a reconnection with the Great Spirit—Mexican indigenousness.

In the dance community in Mexico I was told that *danza* chose me (*me jaló*). It did so powerfully and dramatically, literally saving my life at a time when I was in dire spiritual crisis. On January 21, 1979, my saint's day and

Left to right: Capitán General Andres Segura, Rosa María Escalante, Inés Hernández-Ávila, Olivia Chumacero, and Sylvia Ledesma, in Fresno at a ceremonial gathering in the early 1980s. Photographer, Eduardo Reyes. Used with permission from Inés Hernández-Ávila.

the birthday of my paternal grandmother, my Mamá Inés, I traveled to Austin from Kingsville, Texas, to dance for my life, to defend myself from what was destroying me, to create the space for myself for healing, for consciousness and self-nurturing, for harmony within myself and between myself and all of the Creation. I felt a grandmother's energy enter my body, especially my legs, to help me dance, to help me get started until I could dance on my own. From that day to the present, I have continued to feel and know the healing power of *danza*.

In May 1979, at my first meeting with the elder Andrés Segura, he asked if I would perform the role of the Malinche for his group, a responsibility I accepted and held the entire time I danced with his group, Xinachtli. The role of la Malinche (otherwise known as Malintzin, the young Aztec woman who was Hernán Cortés's interpreter and, depending on whose version, his unwilling or willing mistress) within the Conchero tradition is that of a path opener, an *abrecaminos*, one who goes ahead of the group with her *sahumador* (the clay chalice that holds the sacred fire) burning the *copal*, which cleanses and blesses the way. She and the *alferez* who carries the *estandarte* of the *mesa* are at the front of the group as it proceeds in the *marcha* (march) of the dance.

Her charge is the protection of the group; she must tend the sacred fire in the center of the circle throughout the ceremony. To accept this role was an honor and a challenge, because in *danza*, a person learns by doing, by being alert in a test of consciousness, awareness, and discipline in a traditional setting.

Teachings of la Danza

Decía Cuauhtemoc
con gran decoro
Me quemarán los pies
Pero no entrego el tesoro

[Cuauhtemoc said
with great decorum
They can burn my feet
But I won't surrender the treasure]

In the traditional Conchero *alabanza* "Cuando Nuestra America," (When Our America), where Catholic references predominate, the preceding stanza speaks of the decorum, courage, and dignity of the "young grandfather," Cuauhtemoc, the last *tlatoani*, even as he is being tortured to death. In the Conchero community, the treasure that he refuses to surrender is considered to be much more than material treasure; it is the heart of Conchero philosophy and practice. Some of the more explicit understandings from the Conchero dance tradition that pertain to the concept of religious healing have come to me over the last twenty-four years through the guidance and example of elders such as the late Capitán General Segura, of La Mesa de la Virgen de los Dolores; the late Capitán Emilio Alvarado, of la Mesa de la Virgen de San Juan; the late Capitán General Florencio Osorio, of La Mesa del Cristo Rey de la Montaña; as well as Capitana Josefina García and Capitán Miguel Alvarado, of La Mesa de la Virgen de San Juan, and from La Mesa del Santo Niño de Atocha, Capitán Cruz Hernández-Ibarra, and most especially Capitana Generala María Teresa Mejía Martinez.[5]

The ceremony of *danza* and the life's teachings that emerge through *danza* express ancient understandings that have the power to heal the body, mind, heart, and spirit through the movement of the dance of the cosmos, the dance of life. "*La danza es vida, y la vida es danza*" (Dance is life and life is dance). Tsewaa says, "As I traveled from birth to today, I have come to know the words of yesterday from my grandmother.... She said *dance is life* [italics mine], and a song can bring a spirit back to life when the mind is heavy. She said a greeting to a human person is also a greeting to his spirit" (1975: 3). A *danzante*'s responsibility in life is to know how to move consciously and har-

Left to right: Inés Hernández-Ávila (Capitana); Malinche de la Campana, Irma Cruz Martinez; Capitán Cruz Ibarra Hernández; Capitana Generala María Teresa Mejía Martinez; Conchera de la Izquierda, María Beatriz Madrid de Saavedra, in Davis, California, August 1997. Used with permission from Gricelda Espinosa.

moniously through ordinary and ceremonial time and space, tuning one's own rhythms to the rhythms of the community, the earth, and the universe. This idea of movement corresponds to the Fifth Sun of the Aztec calendar, Nahui Ollin (Four Movement), which was already in progress when the first Europeans arrived.

According to the oral tradition, the task of humanity in this sun is to become conscious, to know how to become men and women of our word (to speak truthfully), to learn how to respect spirit and how to permit spirit to guide consciousness, to know how to understand movement as radical (re)creative transformation. Danza Conchera is a solar tradition, a Sun Dance tradition, manifested not only through the dances that occur during the day but also through the vigils, such as the ceremony for Día de los Muertos, during which marigolds and celosia are used to create an intricately laid-out offering that represents the sun and the illumination that is being given to and received from the *Ánimas*, the ancestor spirits.

Rostas and Droogers state that "the popular use of religion implies a side-stepping of the power hierarchy, in a quest for new sources of power, whether these be spiritual, the desire for self-realization or for a position that gives empowerment" (1993: 10). This "side-stepping" could also be termed a nego-tiation between equals, not so much in a quest for "new sources of power" but as an expression of the continuance of the ancient sources of power, which allow for holistic self-realization through *danza*. Each time the Concheros dance, whether in ceremony or in the dance of life, they negotiate from a place of power and certainty, from the site and centrality of their spiritual connections to their own hierarchies.

José Felix Zavala (1988) notes that the Concheros have three types of hi-erarchies: (1) the human, consisting of the elders in command (the generals and captains), the Malinche, the sargent who regulates the movement of the dancers, the standard-bearer who carries the group's banner, and the foot sol-diers; (2) the semidivine hierarchy, or the spirits of deceased ancestors, elders, and benefactors of the dance, the mediators and guides of the living *danzantes*; and (3) the divine hierarchy, made up of the different saints or sacred beings who are invoked. In this first hierarchy, everyone in the dance community has a place of importance within the ceremony, and the integrity and coherence of the circle are in proportion to the level of self-discipline and collective discipline achieved by the group.

The circle of dance allows each individual to express himself or herself actively and gives each *danzante* the right and responsibility to lead the entire group in a dance, becoming for the moment the one in charge of the ceremony, the one who has the *palabra* (the word, the authority to lead). Within this tradition, the value of everyone's *palabra* and the importance of the generations are affirmed and expressed, such that women, men, elders, and children know they have the opportunity to have their say, through speaking, singing, dancing, or taking on a responsibility for the group; it is the main way that the *mesas* arrive at consensus and manifest a collective consciousness.

The dance tradition offers an exemplary model of social organization to honor both individual autonomy (each dancer chooses the dance he or she is to lead, and each dancer has the right to offer his or her thoughts during the moment for speaking) and collective autonomy (each *mesa* recognizes its own discipline and respects the right of other *mesas* to govern in their own way). The work of the *mesa* is done by consensus, with the elders in charge acting as the heads. Within and between the *mesas*, there is a system of *mutualismo* (mutualism), whereby the members of the group or the members of different groups work cooperatively to ensure that needs are met, whether these are food for the ceremonies or the lending of other forms of their *fuerza* (strength), depending on the circumstances. The *mesas* treat each other with a formal and intricate courtesy and respect, with the implicit recognition of common goals. The tradition is sustained by the *danzantes* through the oral and ritual forms that affirm their original principles, even as they have adapted to a new religion, which they have refashioned over the centuries.

The concept of discipline is crucial because it applies fundamentally to the other name by which the Conchero tradition is known: La Danza de Conquista. From an external perspective, this reference reiterates and celebrates the subjugation and missionization of the Aztecs by the Spaniards. However, while *danza* has ostensibly accommodated to the colonial project, inwardly the tradition has maintained a clarity of purpose that transposes the idea of "conquest" to recall the ancient Aztec concept of conquering the lower self through the sacrifice of the *danza*. Implicit in the earning of a leadership position is the idea that an individual has become a *conquistador* or a *conquistadora de los cuatro vientos*. When an individual becomes known as a "conqueror of the four winds" it is because of his or her example of wisdom, strength, devotion, courage, love, and leadership.

The Ánimas Conquistadoras are those who have crossed over into spirit but who can be called upon for help by those *danzantes* who are still living. These *Ánimas* comprise the second hierarchy described by Zavala, the continuing link with and reverence for the ancestors, the ancient ones and the more recent elders, who are called by name in the permission, or Spirit-Calling songs that formally initiate the ceremonies. The elder Teresa, whom I interviewed in 2002, says, "We venerate them because they save us from all dangers, they are in the grace of the Lord, we continue venerating them so that what they left us will never be forgotten. We will always be with our roots." When Concheros speak in ceremonial settings, they preface their remarks by asking permission "first, of God," then of the images they venerate, and of "the spirits who left us these traditions." For the Concheros, the presence of the spirits provides a protection and a strength for the work to be done, and they, in turn, in a gesture of mutualism, faithfully pray for the *Ánimas* to be "in glory and rest."

According to the elder Teresa, the incense from the *sahumador* is an honoring of our *Ánimas*; we believe that they are with us and they care for us wherever we are." In this second hierarchy individuals from other traditions are respected and seen as members of the extended community that unites the living and the living spirit(s). The elder Teresa has reminded her dancers, on many an occasion, that when times are hard, when a person is faced with arduous tests or challenges or illness, the best thing to do is "to surrender oneself to the spirits," for the spirits will tend to the problems, opening the path, transforming the energy, and otherwise providing the aid or the cure that is necessary. Andrés Segura once said that the leggings which the *danzantes* wear are known as *huesos*, because of the sound they make; he went on to say that these *huesos* are the "bones of the ancestors," the real gold of the culture.

The Ánimas Conquistadoras de los Cuatro Vientos are the link in the hierarchies between the living dance community and the sacred beings that constitute the third hierarchy. The Concheros recognize and mark with ceremony the four corners of the universe and the center, each site having a Catholic and an indigenous signification. The east is the dance for El Señor de Sacromonte (Tlaloc); the South, El Señor de Chalma (Tezcatlipoca); the West, La Virgen de los Remedios (Mayaguel); the North, La Virgen de Guadalupe (Tonantzin), and the center, Señor Santiago Tlatelolco (Xipe Totec). These dances form the Cruz Conchera, the Conchero Cross, which spatially and temporally signifies the cycles of each year. In keeping with the Aztec concept of the male-female duality of the Supreme Being, Ometeotl, two of the four directions, north and west, are associated predominantly with a manifestation of the female principle, and two, east and south, with the male principle. There are other dances throughout the year, including the one associated with the *patrón* or *patrona* of each *mesa*, which is the "intimate" major dance for each group; however, the five that mark the *cruz* are the major ones for all the dance groups.

The Center of the Cross

In July 1979, I danced at Tlatelolco Plaza in Mexico City, at the center dance of the Cruz Conchera. We danced for "El Señor Santiago," St. James, who is called by the Concheros *El Correo de los Cuatro Vientos* (The Runner of the Four Winds). This site, according to the late elder Segura, is the Catholic parallel to the Aztec figure Xipe Totec, the ancient Sacred Being Who Accepts the Sacrifices of the Flesh. During the *marcha en general* (the entrance march), the entire community of dancers (re)established the sacred space of what would be that day's ceremonies, by dancing and singing en masse around the entire perimeter of the plaza, reclaiming the space as an indigenous center and, for that day, *the* center of everything. I could barely contain myself as I observed the profundity of the demonstration, merely eleven years after the 1968 massacre of the students and their allies by the Mexican National Guard in that same space, and having just learned to whom the day was dedicated from the Aztec perspective.

I imagined that for those Mexicans dancing there that day, regardless of their daily politics, there was a conscious recognition of the lives sacrificed eleven years earlier. I wondered how many of them might have had loved ones who were killed that day when thousands of students, professionals, and workers had gathered to protest what they termed the shameful facade the Mexican government was revealing to those who had come to Mexico for the Summer Olympics. In a gesture of faith in collective consciousness, I did not say anything to the dancers from Mexico that day, believing that my remarks under the circumstances would have been superfluous, but I felt in my core that politics and religious ideology were indeed intertwined and interdependent.

I have since discovered a poem published in 1986, written by Roberto

Lopez Moreno, titled "Motivos para la danza" [Motives for the Dance], which confirms my gesture of faith. From the poem, it is not clear that Lopez Moreno is a *danzante*, but his poem is grounded in the Conchero tradition, including the reason for dance, the songs, and an awareness of what Tlatelolco actually represents as the space of the center, and as the moment to offer *danza*/prayer to Xipe Totec. The poet begins, "This morning we are going to talk about Tlatelolco / Let the dance begin," commenting that much time has passed since the day (in 1968) when he recalls "looking at his skin, that he guarded so jealously while the surprise attacks rained from the sky." As he continues to describe his friends, the group of nine who went to the demonstration, some of whom ended up "like frozen birds . . . / smeared onto the indifferent pavement," he urges the "we" he addresses to dance, to destroy everything (bad) with the dance "in order to create light and the new time, to create song." He then merges the Tlatelolco of 1968 with the ancient Tlatelolco, the one of the first age, and suddenly as he employs a line from one of the Conchero *alabanzas*—"*Del cielo bajó*" [From the sky came down], a reference in the *alabanza* to the descent of La Virgen of Guadalupe to bless the people. He chillingly recalls what actually came down, like lightning, from the sky: death to unarmed civilians (Moreno 1986: 14–20)

The poet's reference is not only to 1968; his passage recalls the massacre, in one of the worst attacks by the Spaniards, of unarmed Aztec community people gathered in ceremony. The community of the first epoch is gathered to dance when the soldiers of death appear and sound their footsteps throughout the plaza as people fall to their deaths in the middle of their dance, but within the poem, the community is once again the one engaged in the demonstration of 1968, and that demonstration is a "dance" of life. In response to the horror, Lopez Moreno's next line, "*Que florezca todo*" (May everything flower) is reminiscent of a line from a Conchero *alabanza* and from a song written in the seventies by the Chicano group Servidores del Arbol de la Vida, themselves influenced by the Conchero tradition. Both songs have the line "*Que florezca la luz*" (May the light flower). The poet insists that everything will be rebuilt, will be reborn, will return, with the dance. He challenges everyone to assume responsibility for life and promises to never forget Tlatelolco "from this tumult of earth that rips the skin off." He ends by saying, "Now the dance is finished. . . . Let's dance!" In the context of the Conchero tradition, the poet is releasing his *palabra*, his turn at leading the dance, and reminding us all to continue dancing, because dance is life and life is dance. It is such a congruence of mind, body, heart, and spirit that heals the dancers and the community. The elder Teresa says, "The dance generates a certain energy that is perceived by persons who are near us, and some people with faith are cured."

The elder Teresa offers a message to *danzantes* in the United States. "May their dance be from the heart, may they not do it as a business, or out of licentiousness, or only because they like to dance, may they carry it in their hearts, these are the true roots." The true roots are the treasure of the tradition. The elder Teresa also says in this message, "Keep digging, just because you're over there, don't forget what's ours, our roots, and all of the people who have struggled so that our roots don't die." This is the gold that the Spanish *conquistadores* did not see. These are the healing roots of La Danza de Conquista, la Danza Conchera.

NOTES

Dedicado a la Capitana Generala María Teresa Mejía Martinez y a todo su personal. I wish to acknowledge and express my thanks to University of California, MEXUS (UC Riverside), the Chicana/Latina Research Center (University of California, Davis), and the University of California Davis Committee on Research for the generous support I have received to conduct this research.

1. "Finding one's way back home" is a teaching of the late, beloved Paiute elder Raymond Stone.

2. José Flores Peregrino, poet, musician, and professor from Austin, Texas, said this in conversation more than twenty years ago. He is the head of a Conchero dance group, Xinachtli, in Austin, and his spiritual father is the late elder Andrés Segura.

3. The elder Teresa's former husband, Capitán Pedro Rodriguez, was also designated as one of the inheritors of this command. Capitán Pedro, originally from Axochiapan, Morelos, Mexico, is one of the *danzantes* who traveled with White Roots of Peace. He is still affiliated with La Mesa del Santo Niño de Atocha and continues to work with *danzantes* in California.

4. One of these women, Macuilxochitl, is a respected *maestra* of the dance tradition, having "conquered" many dancers with her powerful energy as a dancer and a teacher. Originally from Axochiapan, Morelos, Mexico, she has been in California for more than twenty years.

5. The other elders who touched my life because I saw them first with White Roots of Peace are the late Capitana María Robles, the late Capitán Ernesto Ortíz, and Capitán Pedro Rodriguez, all from La Mesa del Santo Niño de Atocha.

REFERENCES

Forbes, Jack. 1973. *Aztecas del Norte: The Chicanos of Aztlan.* Greenwich, Conn.: Fawcett.
Frankfurter, Alexander M. 1988. A Gathering of Children: Holy Infants and the Cult of El Santo Nino de Atocha. *El Palacio* 94 (1): 30–39.
Kurath, Gertrude Prokosch. 1946. Los Concheros. *Journal of American Folklore* 59:387–99.
Lange, Yvonne. 1978. Santo Niño de Atocha: A Mexican Cult Is Transplanted to Spain. *El Palacio* 84 (4): 3–7.
Mansfield, Portia. 1953. The Conchero Dancers of Mexico. Ph.D. diss., New York University.

Martí, Samuel. 1959. Danza Precortesiana. *Cuadernos Americanos* 106:129–51.

———. 1961. *Canto, danza y musica precortesianos.* Mexico City: Fondo de Culture Economica.

Martí, Samuel, and Gertrude Prokosch Kurath. 1964. *Dances of Anahuac: The Choreography and Music of Precortesian Dances.* New York: Wennergren Foundation.

Moreno, Roberto Lopez. 1986. *Motivos para la Danza.* Mexico, City: Editorial Factor.

Pinkhorn, Harry. 1993. Marylou Valencia: Danza Azteca. In *Bodies beyond Borders: Dance on the U.S. Mexican Border,* 154–55. Calexico, Calif.: Binational Press.

Quintero, Gregorio Torres. 1949. *Fiestas y Costumbres Aztecas.* Mexico City: Manuel Porrua.

Rostas, Susana, and André Droogers, eds. 1993. *The Popular Use of Popular Religion in Latin America.* Amsterdam: Centro de Estudios y Documentación Latinoamericanos.

Stone, Martha. 1975. *At the Sign of Midnight: The Conchero Dance Cult of Mexico.* Tucson: University of Arizona Press.

Torres, Yolotl Gonzalez. 1996. The Revival of Mexican Religions: The Impact of Nativism. *Numen* 43 (1): 22.

Tsewaa. 1975. Our Spirit Is Free and Our Grandfathers Are Waiting. *Akwesasne Notes,* early spring, 3–4.

Wasson, R. Gordon. 1980. *The Wondrous Mushroom: Mycolatryin Mesoamerica.* New York: McGraw-Hill.

Ybarra-Frausto, Tomás. 1986. El Centro Cultural de la Raza Literary and Performing Arts: Social and Cultural Dimensions. In *Made in Aztlan,* ed. Phillip Brookman and Guillermo Gomez-Pena, 56–68. San Diego: Toltecas in Aztlan, Centro Cultural de la Raza.

Zavala, José Felix. 1988. Los Concheros de Querétaro Tradición Centenaria. Querétaro. [s.n.]

23

Subtle Energies and the American Metaphysical Tradition

Robert Fuller

The impress of secularization has been greater in the field of medicine than in most any other area of modern cultural life. It is for this reason that contemporary fascination with alternative healing systems that postulate the power of "subtle energies" is of particular interest to the cultural historian. Practitioners of Therapeutic Touch, acupuncture, traditional chiropractic, and various other forms of "energy medicine" all espouse belief in healing powers recognized by neither the religious nor the scientific traditions that have historically dominated Western cultural thought. Both orthodox medical science and orthodox theology have typically dismissed these alternative healing systems as irrational cultural aberrations. Yet, strictly speaking, any medical system is rational insofar as its methods of treatment are logically entailed by its fundamental premises about the nature of disease. Those advocating treatments based on the premise of "subtle energies" are thus not necessarily less rational than those engaged in medical science. They are, however, advancing a metaphysical claim concerning the existence of causal forces not recognized by contemporary scientific theory. They are, for this reason, also heirs to a cultural tradition that somehow functions alongside religious and scientific orthodoxy.

Those utilizing these alternative healing systems are, on the whole, well educated and tend to have higher incomes than the general populace (Eisenberg 1993). It would thus appear that those who become involved with alternative healing systems do not do so out of scientific ignorance. Instead, many of those attracted to contemporary "energy medicine" are seeking a more spiritually significant way of viewing the world than either modern science or mainstream religion has afforded them. This is not so surprising when viewed in cross-cultural perspective. Indeed, one of the most important functions of healing rituals throughout world history has been their capacity to induce an existential encounter with a sacred reality. In many societies, healing rituals involve participants in the reenactment of cosmological dramas; the shaman is both healer and a mystagogue, one who mediates between the natural and supernatural realms. In early Christianity healing was thought to be a sign of Jesus' divine nature. For 2,000 years healing has been institutionalized as a function of Christian proclamation and ministry (Clebsch and Jaekle 1975; Kittle 1978). Yet, with the gradual divorce of physical healing from the church's routine activities, there have been few healing practices in Western culture that explicitly foster experiential encounters with a higher spiritual reality.

The persistence of alternative healing systems utilizing "subtle energies" alerts us to the existence of a cultural tradition that for more than 160 years has quietly coexisted with both science and the familiar array of Judeo-Christian denominations (Fuller 1989). The American metaphysical tradition emerged with the introduction of Transcendentalism and Swenborgianism in the 1830s and 1840s. These novel philosophical systems taught American audiences of the role that more-than-physical energies or forces have in determining human well-being. Shortly thereafter, mesmerism, Spiritualism, and Theosophy added new vocabularies for explaining the causative powers of these energies or forces (Fuller 2001: 45–74). Although these systems had their own unique philosophical ancestries, American reading audiences consumed their literature unsystematically and fused their doctrines into a fairly uniform metaphysical tradition. As historian Catherine Albanese has shown, the American metaphysical tradition coalesced around one common theme: belief in the subtle energies of the spirit. In the metaphysical tradition, to be spiritual "is to be sensitive to subtle energies and to respond to them" (1990: 310).

Taken together, these metaphysical systems thrive in cultural territory that exists somewhere between "official" religion and "official" science. Some metaphysical systems are more overtly religious in that they express the desire for mystical connection with a higher spiritual reality. Others are more concerned with expanding the scientific method to include the empirical study of more-than-physical laws and forces. The common aim of metaphysical religion is thus to understand the larger forces that affect human lives in ways that bypass the conceptual categories of either traditional science or traditional religion.

The popularity of contemporary "energy medicine" testifies to how fully the American metaphysical tradition has filtered into the vocabulary with which middle-class Americans interpret their lives. A major cultural function of these alternative healing systems has, in fact, been to provide an initiatory rite whereby these "subtle energies" become experiential realities. The beliefs (doctrines) and practices (rituals) that constitute these healing systems enable persons to establish an interior connection with sacred powers that go well beyond the conceptual worlds of either orthodox science or orthodox religion.

Chiropractic Medicine

Daniel David Palmer (1845–1913) began his career as a grocer and fish peddler in What Cheer, Iowa. Without formal education, Palmer nonetheless read widely and seemed particularly drawn to novel ideas. One of these novel ideas was spiritualism. He also came across a mesmeric healer who tutored him in magnetic healing. Palmer was well on his way to developing his own theory of illness when a janitor by the name of Harvey Lillard stopped by his office. Lillard was deaf. He told Palmer that his deafness had begun when he injured his back seventeen years earlier. Palmer placed Lillard down on the couch and moved his hands up and down Lillard's spine. He felt an unusual lump at one vertebra and applied pressure with his hands. Palmer felt the vertebra move back into place, and suddenly Lillard could hear.

Similar healing successes followed. Palmer reasoned that the vital energy flowing from the brain to the various organs of the body is occasionally blocked by misaligned spinal vertebrae, and he concluded that this blockage was the direct cause of disease. Healing therefore required that misplaced vertebrae be manually forced back into position. He called his new medical philosophy "chiropractic" from the Greek words *cheiro* (hand) and *prakitos* (done or performed). Palmer was not, however, propounding a material or physical theory of disease. On the contrary, his chiropractic philosophy was predicated upon an overtly metaphysical conception of causality. According to Palmer, any truly scientific approach to the human system must begin with the principle that physical life is an expression of a divine reality: "What is that which is present in the living body and absent in the dead? It is not inherent; it is not in the organs which are essential to life. An intelligent force which I saw fit to name Innate, usually known as spirit, creates and continues life when vital organs are in a condition to be acted upon by it. That intelligent life-force uses the material of the universe just in proportion as it is in condition to be utilized" (1910: 35).

Palmer underscored the religious underpinnings of his therapeutic system by explaining that Innate, as it exists within the individual human being, is in fact "a segment of that Intelligence which fills the universe." He wrote, "Innate is a part of the Creator. Innate spirit is a part of Universal Intelligence, individualized and personified" (491). Palmer's monistic cosmology was not unique in and of itself. Indeed, his writings drew heavily upon the mesmerist, Spiritualist, and Theosophical literature with which he was familiar. What was original in Palmer's system was his explication of the physiological routes through which Innate exerts its influence on the human system. Palmer asserted that Innate generates life impulses through the medium of the brain, which in turn transmits them along nerve pathways to their different peripheral endings. Displacements of the vertebrae, called subluxations by Palmer, pinch the flow of the Innate-generated nerve impulses and sever affected bodily organs from the ultimate source of life. As the inside cover of the Palmer School of Chiropractic Medicine's official publication, the *Chiropractor* put it, "We are well when Innate Intelligence has unhindered freedom to act thru the physical brain, nerves and tissues. . . . Diseases are caused by a LACK OF CURRENT OF INNATE MENTAL IMPULSES" (1909, inside front cover).

Palmer's son, B. J. Palmer (1881–1961), expanded upon chiropractic medicine's potential for providing a comprehensive approach to humanity's physical, mental, and spiritual well-being. For more than fifty years he taught chiropractic physicians about the doctrines of Universal Intelligence and Innate. He was convinced that chiropractic medicine had discovered that God resides within each human being in the form of Innate. In one fell swoop chiropractic had brushed conventional religion and conventional medicine aside: "Everything that man could ask or pray for he has within. . . . The Chiropractor removes the obstruction, adjusts the cause, and there are going to be effects" (1911: 27).

Not all of chiropractic's growing legion of physicians were attentive to the Palmers' metaphysical musings. They were acutely aware, for example, that the movement's detractors repeatedly singled out the concept of Innate as an untestable, and hence unscientific, theory. The majority of chiropractic physicians have consequently been eager to relegate the Palmers' writings to dusty archives and have instead concentrated on research into the physical causes of musculoskeletal distress. It is hard to escape the conclusion that chiropractic's public acceptance, professional recognition, and access to insurance industry policies have come in direct proportion to its abandonment of metaphysical interests. The Palmers' innovative spirituality is downplayed, if not wholly ignored, by a majority of the 40,000 chiropractic physicians currently practicing in the United States.

What needs to be underscored, however, is that the ethos of metaphysical discovery is hardly absent from contemporary chiropractic. At least some of the 9 million persons who visit chiropractic physicians each year do so precisely because of chiropractic's openness to Eastern religious concepts concerning the body's subtle energies. As Eugene Linden wrote in a feature on alternative medicine for *Time* magazine, the chiropractic physician he visited for lower back pain considered it just as important to give him "a line of Eastern philosophy" as a spinal adjustment. Linden recounts that "at first I found Christoph's messianic zeal as off-putting as the detached manner of the doctor at my H.M.O. Then Christoph checked my 'energy centers.' . . . Deficiencies in

my sixth (or was it fifth?) 'chakra' notwithstanding, once Christoph had finished his Procrustcan pullings, crackings and pushings, the pain was gone and
I felt 20 lbs. lighter" (1991: 76).

A sizable number of chiropractors share Christoph's metaphysical incli-
nation. For example, G. F. Riekman, a chiropractic physician and former dean
of philosophy at Sherman College of Chiropractic, summarized chiropractic's
distinctive approach to healing for a volume titled *The Holistic Health Handbook*
(1978). According to Riekman, chiropractic is a "New Age philosophy, science,
and art":

> The chiropractic philosophy is based on the deductive principle that
> the Universe is perfectly organized, and that we are all extensions of
> this principle, designed to express life (health) and the universal
> laws. Since vertebral subluxations (spinal-nerve interference) are the
> grossest interference with the expression of life, the practice of chi-
> ropractic is designed to analyze and correct these subluxations, so
> that the organism will be free to evolve and express life to its fullest
> natural potential. (174)

The Holistic Health Movement

The holistic health movement that gathered momentum in the 1970s is
rife with references to the subtle energies of spirit. The basic premise of holistic
approaches to healing is relatively straightforward, and at first glance it appears
to be little more than the rhetoric of a generation of Americans eager to re-
humanize their technological society: "Every human being is a unique, wholistic, interdependent relationship of body, mind, emotions, and spirit" (Belknap, Blau, and Grossman 1975: 18). This is, however, far from a bland truism.
The introduction of the term "spirit" alongside "body," "mind," and "emotions"
takes holistic conceptions of healing well beyond any prevailing model in scientific medicine. It invokes an explicitly metaphysical understanding of the
causal energies affecting human well-being.

Herbert Otto and James Knight edited a volume titled *Dimensions in Wholistic Healing* (1979) that still serves as a helpful introduction to this movement
among healing professionals. Their introduction explains that holistic healing
places "reliance on treatment modalities that foster the self-regenerative and
self-reparative processes of natural healing" (3). Of interest, however, is that
Otto and Knight argue that the resources and powers we draw upon for self-
regeneration are not restricted to those residing within our physical or psychological systems. Rather, "everyone is part of a larger system." Holistic healing
therefore utilizes techniques designed to "open the pathways or flows and

harmonics necessary to unfold the channels of the within the body and the self within the world, the Universe, and God" (10). Thus what began as holistic medicine's rather mild acknowledgment of the body's self-recuperative powers slides imperceptibly into a metaphysical doctrine in which the physical system is seen as receptive to the inflow of "higher" healing energies.

Physician Bernard Siegel was for more than two decades among the best-known spokespersons for holistic healing. Siegel considers it important for cancer patients to read books on meditation and psychic phenomena so that they can learn techniques for tapping into higher healing energies. Describing the "theophysics" he believes will emerge in the near future, Siegel writes, "If you consider God, and you can use this label scientifically as an intelligent, loving light, then that energy is available to all of us. We are part of it, we have a collective unconscious. . . . If you get people to open to this energy, anything can be healed" (1984: 84).

Another excellent example of Americans' tendency to link holistic healing with metaphysical religion is the phenomenon of Therapeutic Touch. Dolores Krieger (1979), a nursing instructor at New York University and a student of Theosophical teachings, developed a healing technique predicated upon the existence of a universal energy underlying all life processes. She believes that Western science does not understand energy in as complete a context as do Eastern religious traditions. She therefore uses the Hindu term *prana* to identify the subtle energy she believes permeates our universe. Krieger explains that *prana* is the metaphysical agent responsible for all life processes and is thus the ultimate power behind every form of healing regardless of the particular rationale or technique a physician might employ. She claims that every living organism is an open system and has continuous access to *prana*. So long as an individual retains contact with this vital energy, he or she remains healthy; illness ensues when some area of the body develops a deficit of *prana*. The act of healing, then, entails the channeling of this energy flow by the healer for the well-being of the sick individual (13).

Recapitulating Mesmer's science of animal magnetism in nearly every detail, Krieger has devised a system of practices for nurses to use in their efforts to "channel" *prana* into patients. She explains that before we can transmit *prana* to a patient, we must first become inwardly receptive to the flow of this spiritual energy into our own system. Healers must learn to purify and open up their own internal chakras. Once opened, these chakras channel *prana* into our human nervous system. Being a healer, then, requires adopting a whole new way of life that will facilitate our becoming receptive to the inflow of metaphysical powers. Instruction in Therapeutic Touch, Krieger says, is an "archetypal journey" that will initiate newcomers into the symbolic realms of human consciousness. It is an "experience in interiority . . . [that] presents you with a rich lode of circumstances through which you can explore and grapple with the farther reaches of the psyche" (77).

New Age Energy Healing

The revival of metaphysical interests during the late twentieth century has generally been called the New Age movement (Hanegraff 1998). Not surprisingly, among the prominent in features of this movement have been a variety of alternative healing systems centered upon the curative role of subtle energies (e.g., shiatsu, kundalini yoga, tai chi, acupuncture). The connection between various forms of "energy healing" and New Age thought is the latter's tendency to promote pantheistic conceptions of God. New Agers typically conceptualize God as a "pure white light" or "divine spirit" rather than the more traditional biblical categories of father or king. New Age philosophies typically advocate an emanationist cosmology. That is, they teach that this pure white light continuously emanates through the physical universe, infusing a vital force into each of the many dimensions or planes of existence. This divine light is understood to enter each person's consciousness through the astral body (aura), from which it is then diffused into the seven interior centers, or chakras, that supply the body with vitality. New Age medicine, then, centers upon opening the chakras to the inflow of pure white light/energy. As one healer explains, "When white light flows harmoniously [from the astral body] into the interior centers (the chakras), our condition becomes healthy and more harmonious. When there is some obstruction in the chakras, blocks are formed, and these blocks prevent energy from flowing freely, and the body is unable to heal itself" (Chocron 4).

One of the best-known contemporary energy healers is Caroline Myss (1996) who reports that in 1983 she suddenly and quite unexpectedly began to channel healing messages from a "presence." This event launched her on a career as a medical intuitive. Her investigations into the body's various energy fields led her to a variety of Theosophical writings, the work of Delores Krieger, and the modern occult classic A Course in Miracles. Myss synthesized her metaphysical perspectives in Anatomy of the Spirit (1996), a book that draws "on the deep, abiding, ancient wisdom of several spiritual traditions—the Hindu chakras, the Christian sacraments, and the Kabbalah's Tree of Life—to present a new view of how body and spirit work together" (7). Myss explains in rich detail how each of the seven chakras is associated with specific emotional and psychological issues in our lives. Because each chakra is also connected with specific bodily organs, emotional and psychological turmoil will inevitably result in physical illness. By helping us gain insight into our "energy anatomy," Myss believes we will have the knowledge needed to further our quest for higher consciousness and spiritual growth.

Many New Age healing systems utilize crystals. Belief in the healing properties of crystals is frequently associated with shamanic traditions, including those of Native Americans. Western interest in the occult powers of crystals, however, dates back to Baron Charles von Reichenbach's studies in the 1840s and 1850s. Reichenbach took up the scientific study of Mesmer's theory of animal magnetism and refined it into his own concept of "odic force." Early in his investigations he noted that crystals seemed to activate this vital force just as effectively as magnets had for Mesmer. His experiments convinced him that quartz crystals had an "exciting power on nerves" and were capable of restoring the flow of odic force throughout the body (1851: 81).

Crystal healing has in recent decades become something of a rite of passage through which many modern Americans have entered into the spiritual path chartered by New Age principles. Enthusiasts claim that because rock crystal is almost entirely devoid of color, it serves as an ideal capacitator and refractor of divine "white light." Crystal healers offer multiple explanations for the therapeutic potency of rock crystals. Healer Korra Deaver, for example, observes that "crystal is able to tap the energies of the universe" (1985: 36). In other contexts she notes that "the healing qualities of the crystal seem to be mainly an amplification of the energies of the one working with the stone" (17). The confusion as to whether these energies are personal or extrapersonal in origin is possibly due only to semantic difficulties in the New Age lexicon. Crystal healers employ a fairly intricate vocabulary—largely of Theosophical and mesmeric parentage—that describes the interpenetration of the various metaphysical bodies we simultaneously inhabit. Crystal healers presuppose that we possess physical, etheric, and astral bodies. The healing power of crystals, then, is due to their ability to bring these bodies into harmony and thereby initiate a flow energy from the etheric and astral planes into the plane of the physical body. Korra Deaver explains: "Crystals act as transformers and harmonizers of energy. Illness in the physical body is a reflection of disruption or disharmony of energies in the etheric bodies, and healing takes place when harmony is restored to the subtler bodies. The crystal acts as a focus of healing energy and healing intent, and thereby produces the appropriate energy" (40).

As crystal healer Katrina Raphael writes, "Crystal healings are designed to allow the recipient to consciously access depths of being previously unavailable, and draw upon personal resources to answer all questions and heal any wound. . . . the person who is receiving the crystal healing has the unique opportunity to contact the very essence of being" (1987: 20). Patients are not alone in being afforded the opportunity to contact the essence of being. Healers, too, find that they have enhanced their capacity to serve as channels of divine energy. Not surprisingly, then, many undertake instruction in crystal healing as a spiritual path in its own right. Thus, Korra Deaver downplays the narrow focus on physical healings and counsels that "even if the breakthrough is only in your own understanding of yourself-as-a-soul, as a Cosmic Being, your efforts will not have been in vain" (1985: 7).

Healing and the American Metaphysical Tradition

This survey of alternative healing systems barely scratches the surface of Americans' keen interest in the healing power of "subtle energies." Practices such as acupuncture, tai chi, yoga, Ayurvedic medicine, shiatsu, and many massage therapies also understand their therapeutic benefits in terms of the presence and causal power of energies not recognized by Western science. According to a handbook of alternative therapies that contains a short introduction to these systems, all are concerned with "healing the whole person and awakening the spirit within." Despite their differences, each utilizes techniques predicated upon what Edward Bauman describes in *The Holistic Health Handbook* as the belief that "we are all affected by the universal Life Energy" (17). Thus, taken together, these alternative healing systems are prime carriers of the American metaphysical tradition. Adherents of these groups have self-consciously committed themselves to a set of beliefs that exist well outside the boundaries of either scientific or religious orthodoxy. They have found scientific positivism too confining. Scientific rationality has failed to sustain their general optimism toward life or to further their quest for a spiritually meaningful life. Biblical religion is quite often even more problematic to them. Most of those attracted to alternative healing systems identify themselves as progressive thinkers and find scriptural religion decidedly "old age." They find themselves, therefore, occupying the spiritual territory in which the metaphysical tradition has flourished.

It is, in fact, tempting to suggest that many of these alternative healing systems attract popular followings less for their therapeutic than for their religious benefits. As the introductory section of *The Holistic Health Handbook* explains, "Perhaps more important than the techniques is the expansion of consciousness they foster" (13). Newcomers to these alternative healing systems go through cognitive and experiential transformations very similar to those that Mircea Eliade describes of participants in the initiation rites of archaic societies. In Eliade's analysis, the function of initiatory rites is to induct newcomers into a worldview that will "involve their entire lives." Such rites must communicate a felt sense of participating in ultimate reality, changing persons' sense of identity to the point where they see themselves as "a being open to the life of the spirit" (1965: 3). Contemporary alternative healing systems perform precisely these functions. They evoke a sense of wonder and mystery, heightening expectation that one is preparing to encounter the primal reality upon which life is ultimately dependent. The entire healing ritual is, furthermore, fraught with death and rebirth symbolism. That is, the therapeutic context inherently suggests that newcomers are hoping to discard a no longer functional identity and discover new insights about themselves and the universe they live in. Finally, the sensations of heat, prickling, and tingling that frequently accompany these healing practices provide dramatic "evidence" of the reality of the subtle energies to which their doctrines attest.

An excellent example of how these alternative healing practices initiate middle-class Americans into metaphysical religion is the case of professional nurses introduced to Therapeutic Touch. Prior to their instruction in Therapeutic Touch, these nurses were professionally trained in the pharmaceutical and technological applications of medical science. After their instruction a remarkable number came to view themselves instead as "channels." Consider, for example, the self-descriptions provided by two of Krieger's students: "A Channel, definitely, for the universal power of wholeness. I am certain it is not 'I' who do it"; and "[I] see myself as . . . a vehicle through which energy can go to the patient in whatever way he or she can use it" (Krieger 1979: 108). Given the fact that Krieger was introduced to metaphysical healing by well-known Spiritualists and Theosophists, the fact that her students now understand themselves as channels or vehicles indicates how quickly "subtle energy healing" can engage Americans' metaphysical imaginations.

As one of Krieger's students claims, "Using Therapeutic Touch has changed and continues to change me . . . [and] requires a certain philosophy, and this change in philosophy permeates one's total existence" (Quinn 1981: 62). The benefits attributed to this change in outlook resemble Abraham Maslow's description of peak experiences: increased independence and self-reliance; the ability to view things in their totality; a more caring (bodhisattva-like) attitude toward others; the sense of being an integral part of the universe; and the abandonment of scientific method as the sole approach to understanding life. Persons trained in nursing science now avidly read books on yoga, Tibetan mysticism, and the relationship between the "new physics" and Eastern religious traditions.

It would seem, therefore, that a good many of our alternative healing systems are far more than purveyors of unorthodox medical treatments. They are also purveyors of a rich spiritual heritage—the American metaphysical tradition. Both the beliefs (doctrines) and practices (rituals) of these healing systems enable middle-class Americans to perceive, and respond to, the subtle energies of spirit.

REFERENCES

Albanese, Catherine. 1999. The Subtle Energies of Spirit: Explorations in Meta-
    physical and New Age Spirituality. Journal of the American Academy of Religion.
    67:305–26.
Bauman, Edward. 1978. Introduction to Holistic Health. In The Holistic Health Hand-
    book, ed Edward Bauman, Armand Brint, Lorin Piper, and Pamela Wright, 17–19.
    Berkeley: And/OR Press.
Belknap, Mary, Robert Blau, and Rosaline Grossman, eds. 1975. Case Studies and

Methods in Humanistic Medicine. New York: Institute for the Study of Humanistic Medicine.

Chiropractor. 1909. Inside front cover.

Clebsch, William, and Charles Jaekle. 1975. *Pastoral Care in Historical Perspective.* New York: Jason Aronson.

Deaver, Korra. 1985. *Rock Crystal: The Magic Stone.* York Beach, Maine: Weiser.

Eisenberg, David, R. C. Kesler, C. Foster, F. E. Norlock, D. R. Calkins, T. L. Delbanco. 1993. Unconventional Medicine in the United States: Prevalence, Costs, and Patterns of Use. *New England Journal of Medicine* 328: 246–52.

Eliade, Mircea. 1965. *Rites and Symbols of Initiation.* New York: Harper and Row.

Fuller, Robert. 1989. *Alternative Medicine and American Religious Life.* New York: Oxford University Press.

———. 2001. *Spiritual, but Not Religious: Understanding Unchurched America.* New York: Oxford University Press.

Hanegraaff, Wouter. 1998. *New Age Religion and Western Culture.* Albany: State University of New York Press.

James, William. [1902] 1963. *The Varieties of Religious Experience.* New York: Collier.

Kittle, Gerhard. 1978. *Theological Dictionary of the New Testament.* Grand Rapids, Mich.: Eerdmans.

Krieger, Delores. 1979. *The Therapeutic Touch.* Englewood Cliffs, N.J.: Prentice-Hall.

Linden, Eugene. 1991. My Excellent Alternative Adventure. *Time,* November 2.

Myss, Caroline. 1996. *Anatomy of the Spirit: The Seven Stages of Power and Healing.* New York: Three Rivers Press.

Otto, Herbert, and James Knight, eds. 1979. *Dimensions in Wholistic Healing.* Chicago: Nelson-Hall.

Palmer, B. J. 1911. *Do Chiropractors Pray?* Davenport, Iowa: Palmer School of Chiropractic.

Palmer, David D. 1910. *The Chiropractor's Adjuster.* Portland Ore.: Portland Printing House.

Quinn, Janet. 1981. Therapeutic Touch: One Nurse's Evolution as a Healer. In *Therapeutic Touch: A Book of Readings,* ed. Marianne Borelli and Patricia Heidt, 58–67. New York: Springer.

Raphael, Katrina. 1987. *Crystal Healing.* New York: Aurora.

Riekman, G. F. 1978. Chiropractic. In *The Holistic Health Handbook,* ed. Edward Bauman, Armand Brint, Lorin Piper, and Pamela Wright, 171–74. Berkeley: And/Or Press.

Siegel, Bernard. 1984. Interview with Bernard Siegel. *ReVision* 7:81–88.

von Reichenbach, Charles. 1851. *Vital Force.* New York: Redfield, Clinton-Hall.

Zinnbauer, Kenneth, Kenneth Pargament, Brenda Cole, Mark Rye, Eric Butler, Timothy Belavich, Kathleen Hipp, Allie Scott, and Jill Kadas. 1997. Religion and Spirituality: Unfuzzying the Fuzzy. *Journal for the Scientific Study of Religion* 36: 549–64.

24

Taking Seriously the Nature
of Religious Healing
in America

Edith Turner

A change has occurred during the last few decades, in America and all Western countries. It is shown in the widespread appearance of different healing methods among the general public, loosely connected with religion or spirituality, or by people becoming alive to a sense of the powers of the earth. This has overtaken our age, and the trend is almost out of the control of the scientists' canon, that is, what hard-line scientists certify to be true, and even out of the range of church teaching in our age. For instance, how might scholars of religion on the one hand or social scientists on the other lay out exactly what is happening when nonempirical healing occurs? Are they able to bring themselves to treat the phenomenon with respect, to take it seriously? I myself have been dramatically healed in San Francisco and have witnessed other healings in my anthropological fieldwork. In this chapter I discuss the San Francisco event, also a curious shamanism episode that had bearings on the primary function of shamanism, healing, and then some of the experiences of a group of healing practitioners who met monthly during the nineties in my house in the city of Charlottesville, Virginia. I have come to see this group as part of a huge unofficial laboratory of spiritual healing across the nation, a laboratory performing "experiments" that, in their multiform ways, are shaking themselves down throughout the population into success or nonsuccess categories, ultimately sorting themselves out into methods that may one day be better understood. The process already seems to be resulting in a markedly improved rapport with the spiritual world.

The first part of this chapter discusses a way to do anthropological field-work and research on religious healing that involves experience. I also show how undertaking studies of religious healing using the anthropology of experience can bring about the loosening of the usual boundaries of social science, and I give examples of this opening-up process. I come from an anthropological tradition of strongly participatory fieldwork among preindustrial people, a tradition of joining in what the people are doing and, in my case, allowing myself to experience what they experience. It can be understood that while carrying out such fieldwork in the sphere of ritual and religion one might indeed get caught in those experiences. Taking advantage of such situations of being "caught," I and a number of other anthropologists doing similar work (given in a list of forty-one first-person experiential accounts cited by Barbara Tedlock 1991: 85 n.17)[1] have developed these serendipitous events into an actual method, looking at them as circumstances to be valued rather than avoided in fieldwork. One realizes that one actually needs to get caught because one may never fully understand a religion unless one experiences it. Subjectivity has the advantage on objectivity here, especially when it concerns religion. The religious studies discipline has been peculiarly averse to being inveigled into the religion of study for fear of losing objectivity. This kind of objectivity appears to presuppose that the religion in question is *not* in fact a religion but is some kind of reaction to difficult conditions of life. This aversion to loss of objectivity is also present in anthropology. Although anthropologists go out and do fieldwork, they still cannot cast aside the skepticism they have been taught in their training and go right into the waters of the religion they are studying. I submit that researchers will not truly be able to *know* the religions they study without such a human and humble plunge. It would involve taking upon themselves, however temporarily, the very contacts with the spirits, the divine, or the good powers that the other group have sensed, however different they may be to their own—while still valuing and admitting the differences; above all, lending themselves to what Victor Turner called the communitas of the group, that sweet feeling of oneness. What one learns is for the sake of the other group, not for oneself or one's own religion or science. The outsider has to give up outsiderhood and listen totally to the others, for the others, inside their own culture, are primary here.

This especially applies to the obscure topic of healing, with its strange sense of something beyond the medical, a sense of power, often felt through the hands. So I start this chapter with experiences that provoke questions, that point the way into the heart of the research material. This method is even akin to the scientific method, the experimental method. From 1984 onward I have been seeking material on healing and shamanism. Experiences of American religious healing also came my way, and I found that these threw light on my fieldwork among indigenous people and vice versa. I will take for the first experience an episode at a time when I was becoming interested in what happens during the laying on of hands, an episode laid in a truly urban setting. It was on November 20, 1996, in San Francisco at the American Anthropological Association annual meetings. In the middle of the night at the Hilton Hotel, when I was in bed trying to sleep, I contracted the most severe giddiness attack, which turned into vomiting. Pam Frese, my colleague and roommate, tenderly gave me assistance, but it was of no avail. All night long the trouble became worse so that I could scarcely lift up my head without the room swimming around. I was going to miss the sessions. All morning I lay there in misery. A little after noon Pam burst into the room. She was excited about something.

"Edie, I met that man called—" She seemed to say, "Daar An."

"Whoozat?"

"Look, I told him you were sick. He put his hands on me—he's just an ordinary white sociologist, he was on the panel on humanism with you yesterday. He said, 'When you go back to Edie, put your hands on *her*, right?' So I came. I don't know what this is all about, but anyway, sit up."

I reared up miserably, and Pam put her hands on my head and shoulders. Then she cried out. "Look at my arms!" Pam was wearing short sleeves, and all along her arms I could see goose bumps pricking up everywhere. "It feels strange!"

At that moment I felt a sensation going up my own back like an extremely strong chill, right up my spine and over the top of my head. These were no ordinary goose bumps. It felt like being turned inside out in one immense bodily shudder. We stared at each other.

I said, "Pam, I feel quite all right!" I gave my head a shake. "I'm not dizzy anymore. I'm fine. Who was that man?" She told me, but I have to be discreet about his name.

I was delighted. Pam said, "Look, you have a rest. I'm going to hear Roy Wagner's paper."

"Wait, I'm coming with you." I put on my clothes, feeling perfectly well, and we went to hear Roy Wagner's paper.

So, it seemed that healing was invading the halls of academe. Until that time it had been my opinion that healers were just using metaphor when they used the term "energy" about their work. After that I had to admit that energy healing was real and that one could feel it.

I began to ponder the implications of the event. It would seem to constitute some kind of datum at the very least, something impinging itself—it seemed purposefully—on our discipline; and I had the feeling it would not be good etiquette to ignore it. It would not even be good anthropology. Worse, it would be rude and ungracious. Subsequently I inquired of other people and did some reading and found I was not alone in having such an experience.

I had thought I had seen through what the New Age was trying to say about energy healing, and here was energy healing. I had felt it: it had set me on my feet. I began to wonder if there were some "ether," some medium, through which healing flows like a jolt of electricity, because that was how I experienced it.

Almost all anthropologists have stories like this or have experienced strange events that cannot be easily explained away. Some anthropologists take a step further to confront the events and try to comprehend them for what they are (for example, Stoller 1989; Goulet 1994; Favret-Saada 1980; and dozens more), not as pathological phenomena and illusions in the mind. It seems that such anthropologists are having to abandon ordinary logic when they see leaks in the paradigms of logic. The leaks may be important.

We all know of the multitudinous varieties of alternative healing, even the great range of New Age tenets behind all these varieties; the terminology of "subtle energy" and "astral bodies," the idea of plants with feelings, and all life as deriving from the mother goddess, and the like; and we know of, and our-selves have used, the supernumerary types of "supplements" available in every health food store, indeed, in regular grocery stores—antioxidants, vitamin E, echinacea, ginko, St. John's wort. The sales are big business. What is the ex-planation of this health "explosion"?

Our enlightened friends among the New Age will give the well-known answers—"Science has let us down. It has led us to unnatural ways of life, and we are afraid that many modern diseases owe their existence to overprocessed foods that satisfy one's greed but make one sick. The environment is polluted, necessitating strong fortification for the body by means of natural, herbal sup-plements. We must live on guard, under discipline, standing together against the rape of the planet"—so the argument seems to run.

There are other trends. Many people feel they have had a previous incar-nation and have therefore agreed to undergo a "past life regression" (that is, a psychic puts them under hypnosis and causes them to remember a previous life). Many try to be sensitive to natural entities, to the seasons, to spirit guides, and the like, and will relate some remarkable experiences. We now have to recognize that *this* is our "Western society," not the small enclave of rationalist scientists, however high the status and power of the enclave. This other ordi-nary society—its ways somewhat hidden and turned toward nature, and not appearing to be a true culture—actually predominates. This is Western society, and historically always has been.

In my fieldwork as a cultural anthropologist in the subfield of ritual and shamanism, I have entered and participated in a number of religious and experiential systems. I am usually very grateful to what is at the heart of these systems. What has happened is that I resonate with every one to a lesser or greater degree, intuiting how they might work, if not actually experiencing them. Apart from two workshops I attended that claimed to be concerned with healing but were run by charlatans, whose proceedings actually caused me to be ill, I have a sympathy with all of them.

In the mideighties I had been reading material on traditional Native American shamanic practices and found that Michael Harner (1980) was an expert on the craft. In 1987 I was planning to spend a year in Alaska to study Iñupiat healing. Their healing was said to be little more than massage and manipulation of aching limbs by gifted healers with some kind of power in their hands. I was given to understand that shamanism had died out in the area. Nevertheless, since shamanism had been the tradition, I took the chance—six weeks before I left for Alaska—to attend a session with Harner, who was teaching the craft of shamanism. His shamanism was a fair rendering of Salish and Lakota practices, fired by his own personal experience when conducting anthropological research among the Jivaro of eastern Ecuador.

I knew that the main function of shamanism worldwide is usually healing. I was learning that once the sensitivities of shamanism are developed in a person, the shaman can use a certain technique for the extraction of harmful spirit forms or energy, and another technique for soul retrieval, both of which are healing procedures that can be activated when the shaman sounds his drum to unite himself with his spirit helper. The first, the extraction of harmful intrusions, starts with drumming and some form of prayer. Then the shaman spiritually explores the sick person's body to find the harmful intrusion, passing his or her hand around the body to feel the pricking or tingling sensation signaling the presence of a bad spiritual object. Shamans used to suck out such objects, but in modern times they draw them out and spiritually throw them out toward open water. With the second technique, soul retrieval, the shaman stays quiet or lies prone and allows his spirit to travel into far places to find the sick and despairing soul. He will then bring it back and spiritually thrust it into the bosom of the ill person.

It appears that familiarity with spirit entities lies behind shamanic healing and many other kinds of religious healing. At the shamans' workshop I came upon that sensitivity in spite of myself. The workshop was held on July 19 in Madison, Virginia, before my trip to Alaska. We participants had been lying on the floor with our eyes closed while Michael Harner, a man with a wonderful sense of humor, steadily beat his drum. We were attempting to go to the "upper world," that is, to first visualize some tree, mountain, ladder, or tall building, ascend it, then abandon the visualization and let whatever was "out there" take over.

The drum sound went before me. I visualized the ancient pile of Salisbury Cathedral in England. I entered the cathedral, with its curious inverted arch high above the crossing, then climbed the spiral staircase to where the steeple began. I found myself looking over the ramparts at this level and saw a rope extending horizontally from the ramparts out toward. In a moment I was across the rope and out on a fluffy cloud facing a monk in a long robe. I was not dreaming or inventing; these things just happened.

"What the dickens?" I thought to myself. "This is all very corny. Churches, clouds, monks?"

"Be quiet," rapped the monk. "It's not for you to criticize. Do as you're told."

I was somewhat impressed. My "visualization" was reprimanding me— or was it a visualization?

"Go on up a bit further," he instructed. There was another floor about three or four feet up. On this level I saw a whole bank of appliances along a wall. The wall was filled with stereos, CD sets, VCRs, dials, and an enormous TV screen in which I saw something dark, very dark red. I peered closer. It looked like a sideways image of some kind of internal organs—unusually dark red ones. They really were internal organs, but they did not look ordinary like the ones in a doctor's picture of human organs. They were elongated, and fatter than human ones. I was quite puzzled, but I heard the drumbeat change, and I was supposed to return. Politely thanking the monk, I returned, across the rope, down the tower, and through the church, and I opened my eyes on the workshop floor. I then told the others in the shaman session what had happened. Nobody could make anything of it.

Later on Wednesday, November 18, of the same year, in the Arctic village of my new research, located beside the Arctic Ocean on the Chukchi Sea, I went to visit the Iñupiat whaling captain Clem Jackson. He was a hunter in his prime. He had just caught a four-foot ringed seal, which was now lying on his kitchen floor. Margie, his wife, told me they were going to skin it, so I came to watch.

Margie, with the aid of the others, managed to turn the seal over. She took her crescent-shaped *ulu* knife and made the first cut into the seal's "parka," that is, into its fleshly envelope, first making a shallow cut into the fat, right down the belly from the neck to the tail, then a cut across the neck making a T. I could see deep white fat inside. Margie began to take off the pelt, marked beautifully all over with small gray rings. She did her cutting from the inside, working underneath on each side of the main cut, pulling it off like a garment. Then she took off the fat, a job in which I was allowed to help.

Now Margie bent over the seal and passed her *ulu* knife in a long line downward, opening up the chest and belly cavity. A great array of organs sprang into view, very dark red, almost black, glistening. I wondered why the internal organs of Arctic animals were so dark in color. I could make out the huge liver lobes, at which I gazed mesmerized: they were dark red. Then appeared an intricate maze of small intestines twelve inches across, dark brick in color; then the broad, hearty tubing of the large intestine ridged like a vacuum cleaner tube. All of it was delicate, set glistening and wet in the body cavity, packed neatly and efficiently and comfortably. I looked and looked.

After that they divided the meat. The work was finished, save for plastic bags and the meat distribution.

A few nights later, lying awake in my bed in my prefab hut, I felt my cheeks alive and burning warm from the cold. I had not felt my cheeks so warm since I used to work on a farm in 1942. I was wondering how I would ever be able to leave this place.

Then I suddenly understood something. What I had seen when Margie opened up the internal organs of the seal on November 18 was what I had seen on the TV screen in my shaman journey four months earlier, on July 19, those dark red internal organs of a strange creature. How could I have foreseen this event? As the memory of the shaman training in Madison flooded back to me—there on my bed in the Arctic village on November 24—I put my hand down toward the bed frame to assure myself that this was real. My hand contacted my heating pad, so it must be real. I was upset. Tears came out from somewhere inside me, seeming to soak down into my deepest consciousness. "What am I to do with this material?" I wondered.

A little later, thinking of the seal's organs, I saw that I had been shown an inside view of a particular object. I had been shown the liver. My father had been a medical doctor, and I had become interested in the functions of the liver. Although I did not know it at the time, my own gall bladder had a tendency to become inflamed with stones that were also upsetting the liver. I remembered how this seal was so healthy. I admired it and longed for similar good health for myself and everybody. I has a sense that the curious lesson I had just been taught had to do with healing. That November in the Arctic I began to try to heal people, myself. By the end of the Arctic research I was convinced that healing and spirituality were indisseverable. I saw that I needed to understand spirituality if I were to understand healing, and I tried to encompass it, to deal with it. The Arctic fieldwork period turned out to be more packed with nonlogical events than any other: the Arctic was indeed a place to learn a different logic.

I concluded that shamans' spirits do go out in quest of their purpose. They can do so if the aspiring shamans are able to disconnect their spirits from the usual dissonances of life. A good steady drumbeat helps to guide the process. Then the soul pays attention to the drum. The attention *releases*; it does not *tie down*. One can go—so one thinks—where one likes on the shaman journey; but it is where the spirit likes, and that is what is so strange. The spirit prefers the journey that is made with the healing of another as its aim. The spirit leads, and it can do so perfectly well. A person's spirit is like an innocent child who has a predisposition to walk and speak and laugh, and who delights in learning. Humans have an endowment, a propensity for shamanism, or prayer, or healing. This is the answer to the sense of strangeness about it. It is the release of the real person, the *iñua*, the soul. Once one has learned, one does not unlearn it.

Core shamanism is being taken up more and more in suburban America. Many modern Americans not directly involved in the practice are curious about the craft and its healing possibilities, and indeed their interest in many branches of healing is growing. Generally, healing practitioners themselves are becoming reflexive and want to discuss their craft with each other if that is possible. In some cases they are warmly disposed to the help of friendly anthropologists in this endeavor. Groups have been formed, such as the Society for the Varieties of Religious Experience, based in Washington, D.C., and especially the unit in Charlottesville, Virginia, called Alternatives.

Alternatives came into being in the late eighties and early nineties. It started with a tiny gathering of five women, fortuitously encountered in the city of Charlottesville, Virginia. Deedee was the moving spirit. She was a tall, powerful elder with a deep experience of an earlier life. She was the wife of a retired diplomat and was now running a women's help and therapy group called Focus. Also present was Priscilla Okugawa, who had been married to a Japanese and practiced shiatsu, that is, acupressure healing. Donna Street was a plumber and carpenter by trade, very commonsensical in her practical life, and she had spirits—"spooks," as she called them—who possessed her when she had a pen in her hand. Then she wrote down words that were nonsense to us, but which she could read back to us in the form of a strange prophecy. She called this "ghostwriting," a gift known among Brazilian spirit groups as "psychography." Edie Newcomb was a blue-eyed old nature mystic to whom the trees showed their throbbing halos of light. I was the fascinated and experiencing anthropologist. We were soon joined by Nancy Lawson, who worked with the elderly at a luxury retirement home and also practiced music therapy with guided visualization—a tiny, neat little woman of indeterminate age possessing beauty of person like a white Oprah. Nancy was a great organizer. Before long she was running a large healers' group in my house—a gathering that met monthly to compare and discuss their different crafts, each healer giving a presentation and performance. A crowd regularly met in my living room. We had run through most of the major healing systems of Charlottesville by the time Nancy had to give up the organizing. However, in the spring of 2002, Deedee Dale revived the group in her own house, and we resumed our meetings with new material.

Alternatives describes itself as a group of inquiring people who explore alternative healing methods: African, Alaskan, north and south Native American, Chinese, and Philippine, as well as nutrition, herbs, vitamins, homeopathy, exercise, laying on of hands, dreams, art therapy, music therapy, rebirthing, chiropractic, personality tests, stress management, and many other alternatives to chemical medicine. The participants themselves are mostly white middle-class people, literate thinking people, wanting to explore and know more about their own craft and those of others. They are mainly women over thirty, with a sprinkling of men.

When the group started in earnest in 1992, I knew that serious research on American New Age and popular medicine was foreign to mainline anthropology, but I knew that the practitioners were people, too, with their own ideas about spirituality. Anthropologists tended to consider such social phenomena "in context" only. That is, they wrote interestingly enough *around* the point that was central to the person concerned but refrained from truly confronting it. They would analyze the conditions promoting such "beliefs" and give possible psychological explanations for the strange phenomena that arose. They would not touch the main point, the experience. Nevertheless, one can see how the principal object of comparative inquiry into healing and religion must eventually be the "spiritual," or what is called "magic," that is, signs of other faculties and powers beyond the casual oddities and differences and circumstances of life. Anthropologists and religious studies scholars have been happy enough to study differences but cannot bring themselves to look at any similarities—because somehow they dread that the phenomena may be real and imply a common human endowment, wiping out, so they think, precious differences and all the richness of cultural variation. Kimberley Patton, who defends the occasions of experience and the common endowment, sees the controversy like this:

> Beyond the rejection of similarity or organizing pattern looms the specter of the now forsaken universal transcendent, the category of the "sacred." Like the slightest trace of arsenic in a punchbowl, any whiff of metaphysic, any attempt to re-couple the divorced religious signifier and its signified, any suggestion that each of the manifold forms of religious experience uniquely reveals a face of reality— "real" reality, not just the clichéd but ever-popular "social construction of reality"—is met with alarm, or far more commonly, derision. (2000: 155–56)

Fearing this specter, mainline anthropologists do not think it appropriate to take seriously what the people themselves say. However, the ordinary public around Charlottesville has been much easier with matters of spirituality. America has been bursting with small healing techniques and "isms" in the New Age style. What did I make of the techniques in Alternatives? Some were of lesser quality; others stood out rather well and were quite interesting. The group included a dowser, Tom Milliren. He was a retired electrical engineer and looked like one. He brought to the crowded meeting divining rods made of coat hanger wire, long and straight, then, at the end, bent downward to make a handle so that the rod becomes a long, inverted L. The bent-down part of the wire is enclosed in a loosely fitting tube to serve as the handle. These rods are finely balanced and can be held straight out, one in each hand; they will stay quietly pointing forward if one is careful but will whirl around uncontrollably at the slightest disturbance. With these one tries to see if the rods are sensing somebody else's orbit of energy, or aura. One stands near the other person, holding out the rods less than a foot away, and the rod arms whirl uncontrollably. That is the close orbit. One retreats a little, and the arms stop whirling. One walks backward from the person to six feet away or more, and the arms whirl again, indicating the location of the outer orbit. The other healers were fascinated with Tom's demonstration, as was I. We stood near him and farther away from him by turns to let him try on us.

For healing, Tom Milliren checks a sick person's energy field by locating gaps in these orbits, especially the close one. If energy shows very close to the person, an inch or two away, there is negative energy present, and the person needs healing. Milliren does this by first praying for permission to heal and for protection, then he raises his left hand to receive energy and lets it flow through his body. With his other hand he makes circles above the person's head until he feels the negative energy building up in the crown. Then he prays again and makes a "whooshing" motion upward with both hands to draw the energy out of the crown. He supports the person to prevent a fall.

With Tom Milliren's divining rods one can go outside and try to spot running water. I did this the day after his presentation and found a place in my front yard where the rods whirled madly, but that was not a place where there should be any running water. Shortly afterward the water bill arrived, and it showed something was wrong. The bill was for $160. When the men from the utility company investigated, they found that the lead-in pipe from the roadside to the house was leaking underground, just at that place. I had to have the pipe replaced. Those rods had spoken the truth.

Toying with the aura idea reminded me of the notion that we can feel the buzz of energy in a person with one's hands. We can try on ourselves. If we put our two hands out, a little apart from one another with the palms facing, then draw them farther away from each other, then nearer—can we feel the difference in the skin? Is there a kind of tingling? I always feel it, and so do many others; also one can try putting one's hand above somebody else's head, a few inches up. One can feel a faint buzz there, too. These are small examples. The same kind of sense is used in various ways by healers who practice Therapeutic Touch and who become aware of the health or distress of someone's energy by a sense in the hands. Also the hand can move around a few inches away from the body, which is a regular form of energy divination. Doing the same with the fingers trembling is another. Many hands-on healers have the sense. This sense of the power of the person as extending beyond the body is echoed by Moreno; Blomkust and Rutzel (2003:4), who said that in a psychosocial picture of the person "the psyche appears as outside the body, the body is surrounded by the psyche and the psyche is surrounded by and interwoven into the social and cultural atoms." Are "psyche" and "human energy field" synonymous? This clearly depends on the context of use, but it seems that they are related.

The theme of energy or the psyche was primary in the presentations of other healers in Alternatives. Karen Johnson was a registered nurse who developed a method of healing called "therapeutic touch," first discovered by Dolores Krieger (1979), an RN and Ph.D. who taught at New York University.

Johnson showed the group how to assess the human energy field that extends several inches outside of the body and to modulate that field to relieve symptoms of physical or emotional pain. At the meeting she gave the other healers an opportunity to experience this for themselves. She would move her hands over the patient's body, about three inches away, slowly, pausing for sensations of change in the energy she felt in the hands. She was looking for loose congestion, heat, thickness, heaviness, or pressure. She might locate local imbalances, such as pins and needles, static, a break in rhythm, or confused vibrations. Really tight congestion or obstruction showed in coldness, blankness, no movement, emptiness, or just leadenness from a long-term deficiency. She would check the entire body. As she worked, she let any surplus energy she mobilized exit through her feet, which she kept loose and easy. She would listen all the time. To heal, she would pray, then clear the congestions, sweeping them away with her hands, letting energy come through her from above and enter her hands as she placed them firmly on the body penetrate deep blockages. The patient would begin to pull gratefully on this good energy, too. It is not the healer's own doing, she said, but comes from its good source. The two, healer and patient, would both have the sense that energy was improved, and would both give a sigh of relief.

Here were two types of energy healing, Milliren's and Johnson's, the one more "electrically" concerned, the other more "bodily." One can recognize the faculty of perception working in both.

As a complement to these, we had four experts on Sino-Japanese medicine: Rosa Schnyer presented the general principles of Chinese medicine, the elements and the yin and yang features; Allan Handelman gave *qigong*, the exercise that cultivates one's inborn energy, or *chi*, and cleanses the body; Julie Taylor gave the story of acupuncture; and Priscilla Okugawa dealt with and demonstrated acupressure, or shiatsu. When performing the *qigong* exercises, I truly felt the threads of energy in the meridians, invisible paths of connection inside the body. These were graphically described by one of my students, Megan Webb, speaking of acupuncture:

> The doctor left me for a while. I closed my eyes and felt relaxed. The needles seemed to start to whirr. Then from the points in my feet, one just below the ball of my foot on the arch and the other in the inside side of the hollow made by my Achilles tendon, I felt a slight building of something rising to the surface from within both of my feet, especially the left. Then I noticed that it felt as if another three, maybe four needles had been placed in my shins. But no one had entered the room. A line of what felt like Christmas tinsel shot up to the inside of my knee and it felt as if two more needles had been placed on my knee.
>
> I felt a little excited, then very, very sad. I was sorry for anyone I

had ever hurt, and found myself breathing with great shuddering breaths. I opened my eyes and found I was just lying on the table. At this point there was a kind of string made of light shooting across the needle points connecting them all, across my body from my hands to my belly to my feet. After a time the sadness and the light flashing passed and I was calmer. A kind of lifting was taking place. Something was lifting up and up out of my body and I felt very light. (personal communication, April 2002)

This description, given much later in the same room, tallies with the presentations on Chinese medicine that our group provided.

Now our group was visited by a man who had had a vivid experience of the human soul, both his own and that of many others, and we came to see how it led to understandings of shamanic healing, African spirit healing, and death experiences. This was Gould Hulse, a commercial artist and accountant from Staten Island who had had a strange death experience and had drawn pictures of it. It came upon him unexpectedly. He had a sudden knowledge that he was lying on the grass of a battlefield. The scene was Shiloh in the Civil War, and he was dying. As he lay there, he realized that he, that is, his soul, naked and small, was being drawn out of his body, and that he was moving up in a kind of big tube to somewhere else. His first picture showed this in simple, graceful, outlined sketches, and in his picture we could see other similar souls moving upward too. (Was there such a flock of souls on September 11 in New York?) In the next picture the tube had flowered out into a wide bowl or kind of chalice where many souls were resting, crowding around the rim. Out of this bowl passed other tubes with souls already in them flying to other destinations. Hulse drew many pictures of this sort, a mass of pictures. The last one showed a final enclosed globe, with one outlet. Hulse's soul was passing through it. Its destination was into a new human baby, the baby that was to become the person who was talking to us and showing us the pictures.

The sense of the soul was echoed by the Arctic Iñupiat healer, Claire, who told me that when laying her hands on a person near death she "saw" the person's soul going far away, "like a boat disappearing into the far distance," and her duty as a healer was to rush after it in the spirit and fetch it back. Now we were dealing with the ineffable, with a visionary world, but it is something that people have truly experienced.

Our deep cogitations about Hulse's experience were later shown to have implications for the healing work of another Alternatives member, Sue Janson, who performed past life regressions. Any individual's soul may have a much longer history than we usually suppose. Sue, in her presentation to the later group, talked about people coming to her with inexplicable discontents, or sadness, or a feeling of something unfinished, bringing anger, which became the source of a growing malady. She would make them quiet down and show them under hypnosis how their memories could reach back to before they were born or even conceived, to a wholly different world, the life their soul lived before this life. Often there was unfinished work to do, and she helped them discover it and live this life in happiness. If one is religious, one wonders why the lives of some really bad people should end without a single chance of realization. Those who reckon there are future lives and past lives somehow grant more hopes to these people, hopes of redemption through the soul's activity in the way the human soul knows best, that is, by going on, persisting, and in some future life adding to instead of subtracting from the intimate and refreshing coactivity of helping humanity along. This is how Sue Janson cured, by setting her patients free from a kind of curse so that they could get on with life and do good. Like my Iñupiat healer friend, she was strongly aware of the existence of the soul. I myself had a faint notion of a possible future life. Donna Street, with her written communication with spirits—"spooks," figures with whom she was friendly—also had some such idea. Also, in my research in Africa I had found something similar, that ancestor spirits did exist, and I helped our Alternatives group to perform one of the African ceremonies in which one takes out an afflicting spirit. One of our group members, Marcia Perkins, asked for this kind of healing. Afterward, Marcia said she was truly healed, though I am sure it was none of my doing.

Confirming the existence of the soul, Justine Owens of the Personality Studies Program at the University of Virginia gave a presentation on near-death experiences (NDEs). She collected about 200 accounts of NDEs from patients at the University of Virginia Hospital. As some know, if a person is clinically dead for a time and is resuscitated, it may happen that the soul finds itself looking down on the body it has left, then finds itself drawn up a tunnel and emerges high above the earth. There the soul may encounter some of its dead relatives. Finally it meets with a being of great light, the same light that is often described by mystics, warm and loving. Classically, this being offers the soul the chance to go back because he or she is still needed on earth. The experience is so beautiful that the person never fears death again. The following description was given by Rick Bradshaw, on November 14, 1992 (personal communication), about the key event in the middle of a near-death experience that he had undergone:

> Then another being entered, "The Being of Light." Each individual uses different words, Buddhists, Christians, and so on. The light of this being was so intense that his light preceded him. I could actually "feel" the light, it was warm, it was love. I felt insignificant and wanted to crawl under the podium, and I wanted to hug him. I was still tense.
> He says, "Do you know where you are?"
> "Yes."

"What is your decision?"

The unused nine-tenths of my brain opened up, and I saw the whole of my life. I recognized the truth. How to react with animals, to other beings. In life we block off, close them off. I was looking back at my life. Was such and such sin? That wasn't so bad. Treating others badly was the worst sin. Love for others was the most important thing, as he loved me. There was instilled a fire within myself to continue to grow, to know, to search.

I said, "I didn't really show others the love I should have." You get what you deserve. I didn't deserve this beauty. I said, "I must return."

He said, "Why? Aren't you happy here?"

I said, "I must give love to those who gave me love."

The NDE is a feature of spirit experience readily accepted by New Agers. In my research, individuals from different cultures have told me stories of the NDE. At that period of my life the stories confirmed the way my thinking was going. However, I also had the sense that attention to this material, because of its association with the New Age, separated me still further from the more scientific anthropologists. It seemed to be a daring act to even speculate on the reality of such phenomena.

The purpose of giving my own modest material here is to go deeper and to search for and sense *the kind of world in which healing takes place.* There exists the everyday world as we all know, practical, and ultimately under the aegis of science and rationality, ranging from road building to dietetics, from PET scans to postage stamps. This system as it is at present defers not only to science but ultimately to the military, the police, the laws of the country, corporations, and employers—a world consisting of absolute pressures laid on the person to obey. This is what Victor Turner called "structure," and what I have called Power I. Meanwhile, around it we build our little lives, with perhaps an armchair at home in front of the TV to hear how the system and its foes impinge on humanity in the form of "The News" or to watch comical critiques of that power—critiques that warm the heart. We do sense our humanity. That humanity has a way of claiming our hearts, threading through the jostling powers of modern life. That humanity is Power II, a mode of being that Victor Turner (1969: 96, 105, 109ff.) termed "communitas," the sphere also of the "liminal," where one enters the limen, the threshold, of spirit things, where one is a whole person. Curiously (apart from those who turn it into dogma), this power is free, well recognized, coming with love of family, love of comradeship, sometimes in the form of sexual love, and full of a palpable healing energy. Its power is that of the structurally weak, power that in spite of all is unconquerable, is able to transmit itself quite irrationally, and ultimately tells the message of the immortal soul to the subconscious. And here miracles occur. Carl Jung had a good idea of it in his collective unconscious.

How do people nowadays regard this sort of material about religious healing and spiritual things? Let us see, for instance, how Catholics regard it. I myself have been a Catholic for forty-four years. How do I personally regard the healings and strange events I have been searching out and experiencing? Taking reincarnation, shamanism, and the presence of ancestor spirits as key issues, they do *not* lie within accepted Catholic teaching. As a Christian I find I have no elbowroom here; I feel the constriction of the developed dogma. I sense this as a fault in the developed dogma. I feel that these controls are a bad thing for the soul, not good, just as foot binding is bad for the feet. But in practice, most Catholics in young and community-minded churches are just as interested in the liberating phenomena as I am and easily relate to the fascinating spirituality revealed in so many of the world's different healing crafts and religious systems. Many Catholics are themselves what one might describe as "New Age." This is so universal that ordinary folks who constitute the Catholic church are likely to be happy with it, perhaps with the exception of male church members in authority positions such as the police or army, or some of the older priests themselves. Broadly speaking, the situation today is that a large number of modern Catholics doubt the value of the developed dogma of the Vatican in the way it is being enforced (see Fox 2000).

Meanwhile, in quite a different spirit, we find within the frame of the original Christianity, Judaism, Islam, and all the religions, multitudinous references to healing, to the immortality of the soul, to prophecy, communication with spirits, and all the shamanic gifts, along with a sense of love past all telling in its joy. Deriving from, indeed rooted instinctively in, this joy, a great many modern religious people are living this love—even unconditional love, living lives of benevolence as found among good Hindus, spiritual Muslims, Buddhists, Jews, and people of all the religions. In the heart of them all is the actual quality and power of spirituality, as they will say. The happiness is there if we cast off selfish desires; unexpected miracles just happen. It is from this spirit, which I call Power II, that religious healing arises, and from this also—where it is effective and genuine—the entire New Age lifestyle arises that I have been discussing.

Let us look at that lifestyle. Such people are universally environmentalist, respectful of nature, often vegetarian in calling, peace loving, and antiwar. Even the Wicca people, belonging to groups based on ancient Celtic religion, later called witchcraft, revere the beneficent earth, help their sisters, and look toward the light. Many New Agers are strongly aware of the body and its "vibrations" or powers, also called "meridians" and "chakras." They sense indwelling spirits and have recently developed their awareness of beneficent space as in feng shui; they also sense the power of herbs. Another related phenomenon is the

Falun Gong, the modern urban Chinese movement with healing as one of its aims, whose members receive a startling visitation, a sacred "wheel" inside them that whirls with light and joy. An anthropology graduate student at the University of Virginia received such an experience in Korea.

Scientists may complain that the whole enterprise is hogwash and that New Agers make the mistake of clinging to holistic medicine and supplements when they should be seeing a doctor. Yet we can see that the two systems might well work together. And, to be fair, we may ask, what damage has the New Age done compared with what nuclear scientists have done to the earth, and compared with the proponents of military deterrence?

So there are alternative attitudes. We do "a little bit know something," as the Dene Zha of Canada put it (see Ridington 1990). We know, just sometimes, there is a power. We know, like the Buddhists, that salvation from suffering and hatred comes through compassion, as it has come down the centuries from the Buddha himself to the laughing Dalai Lama. What are all these holy people keyed into? What is this heaven to which the children belong?

There has always, originally, been a connection of all things with all things. Somehow our biologies grew up in primeval times to know this, as our eyes grew to see light. Lévy-Bruhl ([1910] 1985) described it in his "law of mystical participation." Jung put it well, divining that each individual is deeply connected with every other one, down in regions that we do not much explore. Somehow our actions are imbued with knowledge derived from connectedness, whether we know it or not. Many have experienced the sense of it, especially the sense that Victor Turner and Paul Goodman before him called "communitas," the sense that comes when working as a team with other people, combining to the fullest to succeed in some worthy enterprise. Then we know a distinct joy. Strangely, the New York firemen and those who helped them experienced a time of sweetness and camaraderie that was most unexpected. Sportsmen after a winning point throw themselves on one another, sobbing and laughing. Choirs sing the "Hallelujah Chorus" and experience cold chills. The pilgrims grow quiet beneath the great organ of Chartres when the genius plays, when he sends adrift in dark billows the simple obvious power, the cloud of God. I have heard it. Why do we long for it so?

What most of the anthropologists in Barbara Tedlock's essay (1991) and many others have found is that there *are* strange events. Anthropologists themselves have seen ghosts, seen impossible healings, have been saved in times of danger, seen visions. From this viewpoint positivism is threadbare, leaking, unhealthy, leached, overprocessed, toxic, and not fit to use.

The existence of religious healing must affect the philosophy of religion. I would submit, if we want a real philosophy of religion, we will now need to base it on experience. I say this advisedly; for, as we know from contemporary brain studies, true thinking is and must be allied with the emotions, that is, with the *body*; and the brain acts holistically, like organized light. All parts affect all parts. No true experience can be excised from it. Just lately we have been deliberately unlocking the door that has been kept locked by positivism. If strange phenomena come through, let us look at them. That is not belief; it is not faith. It is merely open-mindedness, open to the possibility of the existence of the soul. Then material on religious healing begins to make its own kind of sense.

As I see it, there is power. We feel it in healing. There *are* spirit figures and forms: some of us have seen them. There is that wide, all-encompassing reservoir in which all things play and communicate, a medium, an ether, if you like. These phenomena do in fact constitute our human element, as we are taking a long time to discover. Let us not suppose that descriptions of quarks and mesons will do for what we are seeing. Curiously, we have to reinstate actual "psyche"-ology as the study of this rediscovered *soul*, with a humanistic anthropology beside it to lay the scenes in their human social settings, to be willing to go all the way with radical empiricism, and to keep to ethnography and away from abstractions. The findings of anthropology confirm that no one system has primacy or the right to impose upon another, because everybody's experience is unique. Nor should any individual or group suffer their own experience to be denied. Above all, religious monopolies and dictatorships have to go.

As for contemporary religious healing in America and its huge jumble of different social levels and types—whether it be healing derived from overseas religions or from local revelations, or involved in the New Age, or found in serious shamanic research, or established like acupuncture with approval of the National Institutes of Health—in this chapter I have led my readers from case to case in anthropological fashion, to stimulate them to look behind the stories to the kind of world in which these events happen, so that they may get a sense from their own point of view of the odd nature of existence.

NOTES

1. Barbara Tedlock in 1991 (69–94) cited the growing number of anthropologists who disobeyed the injunction never to "go native," in other words, they did experience along with their field hosts. She was assessing the changes in anthropology even a decade ago and critiqued past colonialist attitudes that still denigrated natives (82). As of the present decade the scene has again changed considerably, and hundreds of anthropologists are deeply in sympathy with their hosts, refusing deprivation theory and psychology to explain away the religious and healing experiences of others.

REFERENCES

Favret-Saada, Jeanne. 1980. *Deadly Words: Witchcraft in the Bocage.* Cambridge: Cambridge University Press.

Fox, Matthew. 2000. *Original Blessing: A Primer in Creation Spirituality*. New York: Tarcher/Putnam.

Goulet, Jean-Guy. 1994. Ways of Knowing: Towards a Narrative Ethnography of Experiences among the Dene Tha. *Journal of Anthropological Research* 50: 113–139.

Harner, Michael. 1980. *The Way of the Shaman: A Guide to Power and Healing*. San Francisco: Harper and Row.

Hulse, Gould. N.d. Soul and Reincarnation. Presentation to Alternatives, Healers' Group, Charlottesville, VA, 1990. Staten Island, N.Y.

Krieger, Dolores. 1979. *The Therapeutic Touch: How to Use Your Hands to Help or to Heal*. Englewood Cliffs, N.J.: Prentice Hall.

Lévy-Bruhl, Lucien. [1910] 1985. *How Natives Think*. Princeton, N.J.: Princeton University Press.

Morena, Zerka, Leif Dag Blomkuist, and Thomas Rutzel. 2003. *Psychodrama, Surplus Reality and the Art of Healing*. New York: Brunner Routledge.

Patton, Kimberley. 2000. Juggling Torches: Why We Still Need Comparative Religion. In *A Magic Still Dwells: Comparative Religion in the Postmodern Age*, ed. Kimberley C. Patton and Benjamin C. Ray, 153–71. Berkeley: University of California Press.

Ridington, Robin. 1990. *Little Bit Know Something: Stories and Narrative in a Northern Native Community*. Iowa City: University of Iowa Press.

Stoller, Paul. 1989. *The Taste of Ethnographic Things*. Philadelphia: University of Pennsylvania Press.

Tedlock, Barbara. 1991. From Participant Observation to the Observation of Participation: The Emergence of Narrative Ethnography. *Journal of Anthropological Research* 47: 69–94.

Turner, Victor. 1969. *The Ritual Process: Structure and Anti-Structure*. Chicago: Aldine.

PART V

Intersections with Medical and Psychotherapeutic Discourses

25

Dimensions of Islamic Religious Healing in America

Marcia Hermansen

The chapter will consider frameworks and practices of religious healing among Muslims in Chicago, primarily South Asians and Arab immigrants and followers of various American Sufi movements. I will briefly contextualize approaches to illness and wellness from Islamic perspectives and then review some traditional Muslim religious healing practices. My focus, however, will be on aspects of spiritual healing, dream interpretation, and Sufi psychology. My perspective is that of an academic trained in the study of Islam who has lived for extended periods in Muslim societies, in particular Egypt, India, and Pakistan. Due to my personal and academic interest in Sufism, I have been a participant-observer of Western Sufi movements since the 1970s. In Chicago I have been observing an Indian Muslim spiritual healer for about seven years.

In America there are many Muslim communities, varying in their ethnicity, ideological perceptions of Islam, and lifestyles, ranging from "ghettoization" to assimilation to American culture. For some contemporary Muslims, "Islam" is conceived of as a total system, so that "Islamic" medicine or "Islamic" science is not merely a historical subject but constitutes a prescriptive body of knowledge and practice. The ritualized nature of most Islamic religious healing practices is consistent with a concern for purity of the body, the mind, and the surrounding space. For example, advice to troubled persons who might undertake the recitation of specific phrases from the Qur'an includes cautions that the ritual ablution (*wudu*) should be maintained, prayers should be performed regularly, and so on. From this it might be extrapolated that health care institutions and providers in America should try to address Muslim clients' concerns regarding food contents and cleanliness, since the psychological state and potential for healing are often associated with ritual purity.

Islamic religious healing often involves the concept of the charisma or healing power of the revealed word. This positive energy can counteract negative forces arising from other persons through envy or black magic, or from evil entities such as devils or jinns. In addition, the human body and psyche are seen as being made vulnerable by states of impurity or contact or consumption of unlawful substances. Theologically considered, illness for Muslims is not seen as a punishment but can be understood as a test in which suffering, borne patiently, is said to eliminate the effects of sin "as leaves fall from a tree in the autumn," according to a saying of the Prophet.

Engaging the range of approaches to religious healing among Muslims in America raises the problematic of "culture" in contemporary Islamic discourse, where Islamist ideologies reject many cultural elements in favor of legalistic, internationalist definitions of normativity. These legalistic models, however, may marginalize much of the dynamic involved in traditional healing practices. For example, a Dutch researcher on Muslim healing practices in the Netherlands, Cor Hoffer (1992), proposes a distinction between belief in "popular" Islam and "official" Islam, defining official Islam as the teachings propagated by the *ulema* (religious scholars) and *imams* (prayer leaders and officials) of mosques. He characterizes popular belief as local traditions that incorporated pre-Islamic customs. I would argue that this distinction arises from accepting the categories of Islamists (modern Muslim reformers) who are trying to assert their exclusively "correct" version of Islam as normative. In fact, individual Muslims encounter religious healing in a variety of contexts, and Islamic legitimacy may be claimed for any one of these forms, including the "popular" practices.

I therefore agree with the observations of Amy Rowe, commenting on practices of Muslims living in Boston, who noted "the ease with which people bind disparate elements of their experience into a single, unique Islamic approach to health and healing." Among Boston Muslims, "Each of these components—folk or traditional Islamic medicine, textual or Prophetic references and bio-medical resources—are woven together into a total Muslim approach" (Rowe 2001).

Approaches to the blending of religion, culture, and science into a healing synthesis utilized by American Muslims may be broadly categorized according to four themes as follows.

Islamic Norms and Modern Science

Some Muslims adopt Western scientific frameworks while maintaining an Islamic context by establishing "boundaries" so that certain practices—for example, abortion or the use of pork products—would be forbidden in most cases. Magazines and Web sites exist to serve the need to inquire into and establish which are permitted products. For example, a glossy magazine, *Halalpak* (Permissible Pure), published in Madison, Wisconsin, pursues major companies such as Ocean Spray, Domino's Pizza, Kraft, and McDonald's to discover whether any pork products or alcohol derivatives such as vanilla are present in commonly used products.

While many aspects of science are considered by Muslims to be value-free, some dimensions of health care raise ethical issues that may be addressed by Islamic law. A democratization of authority in Islam has empowered "professional Muslims"—engineers and doctors, for example—to join traditional scholars in discussing what is properly Islamic. One of the prominent individuals in this literature is Shahid Athar, a Muslim physician based in Indianapolis, who comments extensively on biomedical and ethical issues. Muslim doctors arc represented in high proportion in the American medical community, and there are several organizations for Pakistani physicians, an Islamic Medical Association, and so on. The Islamic Medical Association, for its part, maintains a Web site (http://www.imana.org) and provides pamphlets on moral and health issues of Muslim clients for distribution to medical facilities and providers.

Recovering a "Prophetic" Medicine

Another approach consists of the recovery of Qur'anic dicta or *hadith* (statements of the Prophet) on health, attempting to develop an Islamic theory and practice of healing out of these. The idea of asserting Islamic frameworks is part of an intellectual project known as the "Islamization of knowledge" that emerged among some Muslims in the 1970s as an attempt to address Western intellectual hegemony. Developing such a framework may be legalistic, in terms of what is recommended, permitted, or forbidden, according to sacred texts and prophetic injunctions; or it may be more broadly philosophical. A baseline Islamic position on healing is the hadith stating that "God is the Healer." In practice, however, modern medicine is usually accepted as being a bounty of God.

One element of the Islamic healing heritage that has received more attention recently is the concept of "prophetic medicine" (*tibb al-nabawi*), the cures and preventive measures recommended by the Prophet and preserved in collections of his sayings. Al-Bukhari (d. 870), compiler of one of the most authoritative collections, included 129 hadith related to medicine and devotes chapters to medicine and to patients. One recommended cure is the consumption of "black seed" (nigella). Products such as oils and capsules incorporating this substance are increasingly being produced for Muslim use. In addition to specific plants and substances, such as honey, preventive measures such as hygiene, cleanliness, and avoidance of excesses are enjoined by this Muslim religious literature.

Some voices among Muslims caution against the attempt to construct an entire system of health care out of the Prophet's traditions. Omar Kasule, the deputy dean of the Faculty of Medicine at International Islamic University in Malaysia, defines Islamic medicine as a system of basic paradigms, concepts, values, and procedures that conform to, or do not contradict, the Qur'an and prophetic traditions. He cautions that these statements establish universal principles that can be defined only in terms of values and ethics, not as specific medical procedures or therapeutic agents:

> *Tibb Nabawi* as reported to us did not cover every conceivable disease at the time of the Prophet, neither can it cover all ailments today or in the future in various parts of the world. This is easy to understand from the context that although the Prophet practiced medicine, his mission was not medicine and he was not a full-time physician. The hadiths of the Prophet should not be looked at as a textbook of medicine. They should be used for the diseases that they dealt with. The proper way to get additional medical knowledge is through research and looking for signs of Allah in the universe. (2002)

Islamization of Indigenous Medical Systems

One example of such a fusion is the Yunani "Greek" medical tradition practiced in Muslim South Asia. Such systems are not necessarily folk or popular, for Yunani medicine is a literate and well-developed system. Although it is not explicitly religious, the expectation is that the healer, called a "hakim," or wise man, will have superior moral and spiritual values that contribute to the cure.

Islamic scholars from an early period had an interest in the spiritual aspects of health, and this was a major area where fusions of healing systems and practices occurred. Muhammad al-Razi (d. 924) composed *Tibb al-Ruhani* (Medicine of the Spirit), and the ethical philosopher Ibn Miskawayh (d. 1010) wrote a work called *Tibb al-Nufus* (Medicines of the Soul). These philosophers drew on the Greek tradition for their concept of person while Islamicizing Asristotle's cosmology into a theistic framework with Islamic terminology. In America, fusion of recent Western psychological understandings of the person and human wellness occurs with selected elements of the Islamic tradition— for example, Sufi concepts of diagnosis and healing through dreams that may be integrated with Freudian or, more often, Jungian theories and techniques. Another instance would be an article in *Halalpak* magazine that discusses anger management in terms of cognitive therapeutic models, as well as statements of the Qur'an and the Prophet enjoining patience in trying circumstances.

Spiritual Healing

Muslim spiritual healers may be Sufi *pirs*, traditional religious scholars, or practitioners of occult arts (*'amils*). Some healers may proffer types of spells such as amulets or prayers. Such practitioners are in some cases believed to have spirits or familiars (*muwakkils*) who do their bidding and to have the ability to remove curses and spells. Mainstream Islamic religious practices such as repeated invocations (*dhikr*) of sacred phrases, reciting the Qur'an, and so on, are also believed to have healing effects. Thus it is difficult to characterize the techniques of spiritual healers as "folk" as opposed to "official," although some of their beliefs and practices may be criticized by contemporary Islamic literalists. A prophetic tradition states that "the evil eye is a reality," while Chapter 113 of the Qur'an mentions the evil of women who blow on knots (cast spells), and the prophet Muhammad recommended certain phrases or litanies to counter this. Therefore, many of these practices have a religious legitimacy, although local traditions certainly embellish them.

Islamic Religious Healing in Theory and Practice

In many contemporary Muslim societies, competing models of healing theory and practice coexist. For example, Muslims in India and Pakistan who experience disease of one sort or another may seek allopathic (Western-style medicine), homeopathic, Yunani (Greek medicine), or various *ruhani* cures (spiritual forms of diagnosis and treatment). These forms of healing may be applied simultaneously, selected on the basis of the type of complaint, or tried successively. Issues involved in the choice would be the resources available to the client, the nature of the complaint, individual beliefs, and social location.

Issues that Westerners might consider under the rubric of relationship problems or family therapy issues might be taken to spiritual healers, as would certain psychological conditions. My impression is that among Muslims living in America, physical ailments are more likely to be treated by Western practitioners, although lingering, nonphysical, or extremely critical cases might be addressed by a spiritual healer.

In South Asian cultures and in the immigrant press and cable TV stations in America, these spiritual healers advertise quite openly. A typical issue of the Urdu newspaper *Pakistan Post*, published in New York (May 23, 2002), carried advertisements for Hakim Miyan Salim, a practitioner of homeopathy and herbal and Greek medicine who specializes in curing back pain, diabetes, and male weakness. He has a toll-free number. Other advertisers claim the ability to solve worldly difficulties and financial and relationship problems, as well as to lift spells cast by enemies and repel the effects of jinns and evil spirits. Immigrants' concerns are reflected in the practitioners' expertise in resolving problems with disobedient and rebellious children, as well as immigration and court cases. While one ad was placed by a dispensary for Yunani medical cures, another offers American-style herbal medicines alongside blackseed oil, an Islamic treatment.

Sufis and certain traditional religious scholars take on similar cases to 'amils but ask much lower fees, and usually the fee is provided voluntarily by the client. This is called giving nazr. A typical nazr given to a pir in Chicago might be twenty-five dollars. The Islamic spiritual healers I am familiar with in Chicago have a multiethnic and multireligious clientele, including American Muslims, Arabs, Bosnians, Sikhs, Christians, and Hindus.

Another type of case handled by Sufis or religious scholars is jinn possession. It is beyond the scope of this chapter to discuss indigenous beliefs about jinns, but basically they are creatures mentioned in the Qur'an believed to be parallel to humans in having volition, except that they are made of fiery substance and normally invisible. In popular folklore they are thought to trouble susceptible individuals, most often females and adolescents.

A related explanation for disturbance, either psychological, in relationship health, or in other aspects of well-being, is the presence of negative influences (atharat) in a certain location. Religious healers may be called upon to divine whether a property should be purchased, whether a location is subject to negative forces, and so on. These forces may arise from evil people or other entities—jinns, ghosts, or devils—in the vicinity. Placing amulets in an affected area may remove the influences. Another source of disturbance or illness in South Asian Muslim culture may be forms of magic (jadu) such as spells (tuna) or black magic (kala ilm).

When South Asian Muslims move into a new home, various religious rituals may be used to purify it from such influences. One is holding a Qur'an khwani, a session in which the entire Qur'an is read by a group sharing thirty small booklets containing sections of the sacred text. In addition, on first entering the new house after purchase, the call to prayer may be given facing the four directions to give notice to negative elements that the occupants are pure Muslims.

Treatments for jinn possession, atharat, and so on might be a stipulated reading, say, 101 repetitions of a specific Qur'anic verse. Even reformist Muslim movements such as the Jamaat Islami consider these forms of religious healing appropriate. The September 2002 issue of their Pakistani magazine for women, Khawatin, contains several articles on this topic, including one subtitled "Jinn Problems and Magical Afflictions Can Be Cured by the Reader in the Privacy of Her Own Home." My point in citing this example is to point out gender-specific interests in religious healing that play on cultural notions of female vulnerability, and to note that Muslim revivalists are not averse to supernatural explanations for certain kinds of afflictions.

Treatments for relationship problems—such as runaway children or spousal abuse—might involve burying a spell in a cemetery. An American cemetery in Chicago has been used for this purpose. A further treatment consists of inscribing Qur'anic verses on plates with saffron, running water on the plates, and then drinking the water over a series of nights.

In addition to specialized spiritual healers, many traditional Muslim scholars from South Asian backgrounds, particularly from Barelvi or Tablighi Jamaat persuasions, may be willing to mediate in healing situations. They may offer advice on disturbances believed to emanate from malevolent forces and so on, since the Prophet is known to have recommended the recitation of the Qur'an for such problems and to have practiced "blowing" on afflicted persons after such recitations.

In religious healing sessions by a South Asian spiritual healer living in Chicago that I have witnessed, the client first expresses his or her concerns. The healer then offers a diagnosis, which may be arrived at by direct intuition or by consulting a *muwakkil* (others cannot see or hear this interaction, although the healer looks into space as if he sees the *muwakkil*). Alternate forms of diagnosis include divinations—for example, using dream symbols, using numerological analysis of the person's name, or having the person randomly point to various diagrams.

Curative practices may include the healer praying for the person. For example, a treatment for infertility involved the healer saying special prayers over a thread and then knotting the thread, which was to be worn constantly by the infertile woman. Knotted in the thread was an amulet (*ta'wiz*), a folded piece of paper with sacred phrases or a magic square. These amulets can be prepared ahead of time and photocopied for mass distribution. Some are targeted to specific uses, and they may be placed in homes, vehicles, or suitcases to protect from theft or accident.

A Palestinian Islamic Religious Healer

Haj Salah is a Muslim religious healer on Chicago's Southwest Side. The *Haj*, a native of Jerusalem, arrived in the United States after 1967. He comes from a family of healers and received some kind of initiation as a child after being given fruits by mysterious figures. After being in the United States for some ten years, he began to see waking visions of spiritual beings who taught him to recite names of God and one special name, which he is not allowed to voluntarily pronounce. However, during the course of certain healing procedures, he involuntarily says this name as if forced, and a healing ensues.

His home is ornately decorated like an orientalist representation of a Middle Eastern home of the 1940s. No empty wall space remains, and intriguing antique objects fill every niche. He spends the night in recitation of the Qur'an and prayer, and he is a *hafiz* (one who knows the Qur'an by heart). He fasts (during the day, Muslim style) for months at a time. The *Haj* prefers to perform healings in the evenings. He uses a particular room of his home and burns incense during the sessions. During the healings he spontaneously says whichever verses of the Qur'an come to his mind. Often these have some semantic connection with the type of illness, for example, the verse of "the opening of the breast" for heart problems.

In one healing performed for a Bosnian couple that had separated, the *Haj* told the wife that her husband had been negatively influenced to leave her by someone else's jealousy. The cure specified that the husband should drink twenty-one times from water in which a certain verse of the Qur'an written on paper had been dipped. This was quite difficult, since the couple was no longer seeing each other, but with the assistance of mutual friends the husband was given the requisite doses. Soon after the twenty-first occasion, he telephoned his wife and reconciled. In telling this story, the Haj recited the verse from the Qur'an "And We made from water every living thing" (21:30).

The *Haj* emphasizes that the healing power is God's, not his. A healer must keep a pure heart, fear God, and keep ultimate death in mind. During a session he mentally implores, "God, you sent me this power, please help me. Heal this person." A verse from the Qur'an may suddenly come to him that he recites. He follows no specific rules or predetermined formulas. Rather, the *Haj* explains that, "You must clear your heart and ask God, no other intermediaries." He does not charge money, but if he is given a payment, he distributes it to the poor.

In discussing the source of a number of the complaints that he treats, the *Haj* explained that black magic seems to spread in certain cultures, and evil is associated with human jealousies and untruthfulness. In the Arab world as in other Mediterranean cultures, there is the idea of envy (*hasad*) that provokes the evil eye, bringing illness or bad luck to others. Some people deliberately practice black arts against others as well. I noted that Sufism was not invoked by this healer in discussing his healing practice and personal religiosity.

Sufi Healing Theory and Practice

One site of fusion between Western psychologies and "Islamicate" dream traditions is the role of dreams in American Sufi movements. Most of the participants in these movements are Euro-Americans, although there are immigrant Muslim and African American Sufis as well. These Sufi movements range from those with universal (perennial) ideas of the unity of all religion, to those whose members strictly follow Islamic shari'a. The former movements often interact with other New Religious Movements or New Age groups in proffering eclectic spiritual practices, including various forms of healing. Membership in American Sufi movements is not extremely large; in a previous paper I estimated that some 25,000 persons belong (Hermansen 1997: 169). I would note, however, their significance in American popular culture, for example, the Sufi dancing movement, the popularity of Rumi's poetry, and so on, being accessible windows for Americans to aspects of Islamic spirituality. Some of these movements place particular emphasis on the role of dreams in spiritual guidance and give significant attention to theories of dream interpretation. One aspect of traditional Sufi practice is said to be submitting one's dreams to the *shaykh* for spiritual analysis and guidance. In the modern, Western context, the process of this traditional mode of spiritual direction is not easily accessible from the traditional texts. Western psychotherapeutic models and practices, however, provide bridges and techniques, in particular those derived from Jungian or Gestalt "dream work."

Pir Vilayat Khan is head of the Sufi Order in the West, a movement brought from India to the West by his father, Inayat Khan, in 1910. He specifically acknowledges the role of Carl Jung's theories of the self and the interpretations of Islamic spirituality articulated in the works of Henry Corbin (d. 1978), a scholar of Islam, in formulating his understanding of spiritual transformation and dreaming (Khan 1991: 48).

A key Corbinian theme, derived from a Jungian reading of Sufi texts, is the idea of active or creative imagination. This is connected to dream work in Sufism by Pir Vilayat Khan. The dreamer who can maintain focus and lucidity is able to work with the symbols of the "World of Images" and participate with awareness in his or her own process of spiritual development. The spiritual master is one facet of the archetype of the self that may appear in dreams or guided meditations in order to bestow guidance.

The Golden Sufi Center, a Western Sufi movement following the British Naqshbandi-Mujaddidi Sufi teacher Irena Tweedie (d. 1999), also incorporates dream work into its practices. Tweedie's successor, Llewellyn Vaughan Lee, based in Inverness, California, offers dream workshops and writes on the topic of dream interpretation. The practices cultivated in ongoing dream groups among this circle include the sharing and collective interpretation of dreams, as well as the cultivation of lucid dreaming. Lucid dreaming, in particular, is understood among some Western Sufi movements as an effective spiritual technique practiced in diverse esoteric paths.

American Sufi dreams and dreamers fall rather strikingly into those influenced more by Jungian theory and those experiencing symbols more familiar within an Islamic Sufi context. Among the more "shari'a-oriented" Western Sufi movements, dreams play a role in the testimonies of followers of Shaykh Nazim, head of the Naqshbandi-Haqqani Sufi order, and feature in the advice of a Mevlevi shaykh to Western aspirants (Algan 1992). The late American Sufi teacher Shaykh Nur (Lex Hixon, d. 1997) of the Helvati-Jerrahi order, discusses several dreams in his biographical notice found in Steven Barboza's *American Jihad: Islam after Malcolm X.* In this case Islamic symbolism of the Prophet dominates.

> One of the other most memorable dreams that I had was on the air-plane coming back from Istanbul after having visited Effendi, my second visit. I dreamt that I was lying on a blanket on a dirt-floored mosque in Arabia, and on the blanket the prophet Muhammad, upon him be peace, was going to lie down for his afternoon nap. He lay down and I took the end of the blanket and folded it over his eyes to shield him from the sun. In Islam, a dream of the rasoolul-lah, upon him be peace, is considered to be the summit of all possi-ble experience, even more magnificent than ·seeing the divine light and disappearing into the divine light. (1994: 199)

The use of dream material on the part of Western Sufi movements con-stitutes an appropriation of the powerful symbolism and depth of an estab-lished tradition that accepts dream material as providing guidance to aspects of the dreamer's being, as well as to external reality. Since modern psycholog-ical theories such as those of Freud and Jung also treat dreams as a means of access to deeper levels of the psyche, a fusion of Western theory and practice with traditional Sufi concepts is possible.

Sufi Psychologies in the West

Another development in "Islamicate" healing practices in America are the range of "Sufi psychologies," sets of practices and frameworks developed pri-marily among Euro-American converts to Islam who are practitioners of Su-fism. These systems tend to view the classical Islamic texts as setting out nor-mative paradigms of the person while they omit the more "cultural" practices found in specific Muslim societies.

Within this typically American "therapeutic" approach to religion, the par-allelism between the Sufi *shaykh* and the Western psychotherapist has been recognized, as has the usurpation of the prerogatives of traditional healers and teachers by the psychologist and psychiatrist in modern Western secular cul-ture (Shafii 1968). American Sufis often choose to contribute to this aspect personally, by being or becoming therapists; institutionally, by sponsoring con-ferences and forming organizations for "Sufi psychology"; and through their writings.

Among American Sufi movements, the various transpersonal approaches engender a number of competing models of levels of consciousness. One may distinguish between psychologies that are directly "inspired" by Sufi spirituality and holistic therapeutic techniques that have their origins outside the Sufi tradition but are used by American Sufi practitioners because they are viewed as consistent with or complementary to Sufi interest in personal transformation and healing. These would include Jungian psychology, the various transpersonal psychologies (e.g., Ken Wilber, Robert Ornstein), and the "soul" psychologies (e.g., James Hillman). All have in common the idea that human beings must find a way to be in touch with and live in harmony and union with some transcendent or transpersonal source of meaning and orientation. Where they locate and how they label this source varies (e.g., how much of it is beyond and how much within the person). The more explicitly spiritual psychologies that see this transpersonal reality as God or the divine are probably the closest parallels to mystical philosophy in various traditional forms of spirituality, including Sufism.

Some traditionalist Sufis in the West, such as those following the ideas of Frithjof Schuon (d. 1998), strongly reject the echoes of modernism in contemporary "scientist" discourse and wish to "retraditionalize" science as a sacred discipline. This traditionalist approach is evident in the works of Seyyed Hossein Nasr, a professor and notable scholar of Islam who is Schuon's spiritual successor in the American branch of the Mariamiyyah Sufi movement.

In addition, each of the two Sufi movements emerging from the Shah Maghsoud Angha line, the International Association of Sufism and the Maktaba Tarigha Oveysiyya, (MTO) Shahmaghsoudi has established its own Sufi Psychology Association. Representatives of these Sufi movements are now teaching in American clinical psychology programs such as the California Institute of Integral Studies and regularly hold academic conferences under the rubric of "Sufi psychology." A journal sponsored by MTO, *Sufism: The Science of the Soul* of the Sufi Psychology Association, features articles addressing Freudian psychoanalysis, clinical studies of the efficacy of Sufi meditation practices, and so on.

I will now review some specific trends within American Sufi psychologies.

Jungian Psychology

Jungian psychology, because it incorporates a spiritual dimension and involves a more compatible approach to dream work, has had a particular following in American Sufi movements. One of Pir Vilayat's leading deputies, the therapist Atum O'Kane, compares the transpersonal and Sufi Order approaches to development, especially on the field of spiritual guidance. These include, according to O'Kane, an expanded vision of the personality as an instrument for manifesting the Universal Self or divine qualities, and the specific practices of the Sufi Order, including meditation, as experienced in breathing practices, the recitation of Islamic litonies and names of God, light practices, creative imagination, and sacred music. Among initiates of the Sufi Order, a special subgroup join the Sufi healing order under Himayat Inayati (1987). Courses in spiritual healing are offered in a number of American cities, including Chicago. Among Sufi healing practices employed are *dhikr* and meditation, using the divine names recited in Arabic to enhance corresponding positive qualities and concentrating on subtle spiritual energy centers of the body (*lata'if*).

Eclectic Work, Bodywork, Dance, Channeling

The Sufi Islamiyat Ruhaniyat Society developed among followers of the American teacher Samuel Lewis (d. 1971). This movement is particularly eclectic in using psychological and therapeutic models, especially humanistic and third wave ones. An important quality of its practice is bodywork, ranging from Sufi dancing (the Dances of Universal Peace) to special spiritual walks and breathing techniques.

The Sufi dance movement was inspired by Samuel Lewis, based on "traditional practices of the Middle East," although in its current form it seems rather more reminiscent of folk dancing or round dancing. Unlike regular folk dances, Sufi dancing incorporates meditation, periods of focusing on sound, vibration, or "attuning" to one's own center or to the moods and symbols evoked in the chants and dances. The leader introduces the chants that accompany the dances, explaining how the symbolism of the movements corresponds to the meaning of the chants, which may come from a variety of the world's religions. Examples are "La illaha illa Allah" from the Islamic "Kalima" (Islamic profession of faith) dance, "Hare Krishna Hare Rama" from Hinduism, "Kyrie Eleison" from Christianity, and "Shema Yisrael" from Judaism.

The dances are taught in several locations in the Chicago area, usually in churches. The participation of immigrant Muslims in such movements is almost nil.

Traditional Islamic Formulations of Levels of the Soul

The leader of one branch of the American Helveti-Jerrahi Sufi Order is an American transpersonal psychologist, Ragip (Robert) Frager, who is head of a degree-granting institute of transpersonal psychology in California. He compares Sufi and Western concepts of person, concluding that "traditional (Western) psychologies address one or two aspects of the soul, not wholistically. Ego psychology deals with the animal soul, outlining the main motivation for existence being that of seeking pleasure and avoiding pain. Behavioral psychology focuses on the conditioned functioning of the vegetable and animal soul. Cognitive psychology deals with the mental functions of the personal soul. Humanistic psychology deals with the activities of the human soul." The closest approach to Sufism, according to Frager, is "transpersonal psychology [which] deals with ego-transcending consciousness of the secret soul and the secret of secret souls" (1999: 5).

This comparison of models or frameworks for transformation is congruent with Ken Wilber's (2000) model of levels of the transpersonal bands of the psyche. The concept of the *nafs* (soul, self, or ego) is central in Islamic concepts of the person. Classical Muslim philosophers and Sufis combined Qur'anic references to "commanding," "blaming," and "contented" levels of the soul (*nafs*) with Hellenistic ideas of rational, animal, and vegetative souls to provide a model of basic human and spiritually advanced development. Translating this into a model of analysis and therapeutic procedure is the work of practitioners such as Frager.

Sufism of Idries and Omar Ali-Shah

The Sufi movements of Idries Shah and Omar Ali-Shah have given some prominence to psychology in their teachings. Idries Shah (d. 1997) was a well-known literary figure who popularized Sufi teaching stories and their potential to impart wisdom and stimulate personal growth. In the United States, his early deputy was Robert Ornstein, a professor of psychology at Stanford University. In the 1960s Ornstein cast Shah's Sufi materials into the idiom of the psychotherapeutic community. His book *The Psychology of Consciousness* (1972) met with an enthusiastic reception, since it coincided with the rising interest in biofeedback and other techniques for shifting moods and awareness. Ornstein has continued to contribute publications in this field over the years and heads the Idries Shah movement in America. There are small circles representing both Shah movements in the Chicago area.

In concluding this section on Sufi psychologies, I note that I have only been able to suggest a rather cursory outline of the frameworks and therapeutic techniques adopted by American Sufi movements. As expected, there is a continuum of practice from the universalist approaches to shari'a-oriented orders. In certain orders stressing the master-*shaykh* interaction, the need for therapeutic models that could be generalized and applied by deputies of the charismatic leader is reduced. In other words, I contend that in larger movements the dispersal of charisma and limiting of personal contact with teachers encourage the construction of systematic models of transformation that can be applied irrespective of the status of the practitioner. This becomes evident once links are maintained through print publications and Internet sites rather than personal contact.

Conclusions

As stated early in this chapter, Muslim approaches to religious healing in America are eclectic and diverse. Recourse to spiritual and religious healing would not be the primary form of seeking treatment for physical disease, and therefore from the perspective of health care deliverers, these Muslim practices are unlikely to conflict with or displace other forms of medical intervention. In his study of the Netherlands, Cor Hoffer estimated that 5 percent of the Muslims there consult traditional healers. Most of his sample group would have been from North Africa, but I would imagine similar statistics for the Chicago immigrant Muslim population, mainly South Asians and Middle Easterners. In the course of my research, I did come across a cease and desist order from the Illinois Department of Professional Regulation against one Muslim religious healer for "practicing medicine without a license." This demonstrates that if religious healers claim to cure physical illnesses, counsel patients to stop taking prescribed medicines, and so on, their role can come into conflict with accepted medical practice.

Sufi healing is not the most common form of Islamic practice among Muslims coming to America, even those from South Asia, where Sufi influences permeate the culture. Many recent Muslim immigrants to the United States have tended to internalize Islamist critiques of folk practices and Sufi ritual as deviant from text-based Islamic rules and doctrines.

In the case of Western hybridized "Sufi psychologies" the reinterpretation or translation, if you will, of Sufi teachings into contemporary psychological discourses may reflect what Dale Eickelman and Jon Anderson (1999) term a "reintellectualization" of Islamic discourse. In their definition "reintellectualization" presents Islamic doctrine and discourse in accessible, vernacular terms even if this contributes to basic reconfigurations of doctrine and practice. While psychological translations from Islamic traditional sources to modern Western systems undertaken by American Sufis could exemplify this trend, it could also be illustrated by the work of immigrant Muslim doctors in bioethics and the scientific rationalization of religious food taboos. This is, in fact, where the two constituencies addressed in this chapter, immigrant Muslims and American Sufis, meet in their efforts to align classical and contemporary bodies of knowledge and practice and apply the results to ever-broadening publics.

REFERENCES

Algan, Refik. 1992. The Dream of the Sleeper: Dream Interpretation and Meaning in Sufism. *Gnosis*, no. 22 51–53.
Barboza, Steven. 1994. *American Jihad: Islam after Malcolm X*. New York: Doubleday.

Eickelman, Dale, and Jon Anderson. 1999. *New Media in the Muslim World: The Emerging Public Sphere.* Bloomington: Indiana University Press.

Ewing, Katherine P. 1990. The Dream of Spiritual Initiation and the Organization of Self-Representations among Pakistani Sufis. *American Ethnologist* 17: 56–74.

Frager, Robert. 1999. *Heart Self and Soul: The Sufi Psychology of Growth Balance and Harmony.* Wheaton, Ill.: Quest Books.

Hermansen, Marcia K. 1997. In the Garden of American Sufi Movements: Hybrids and Perennials. In *New Trends and Developments in the World of Islam,* ed. Peter Clarke, 155–78. London: Luzac Oriental Press.

———. 2001. Dreams and Dreaming in Islam. In *Dreams: A Reader on the Religious, Cultural, and Psychological Dimensions of Dreaming,* ed. Kelly Bulkeley, 73–92. New York: Palgrave.

Hoffer, Cor. 1992. The Practice of Islamic Healing. In *Islam in Dutch Society,* ed. A. Shadid, 40–53. Kampen: Kok Pharos.

Kasule, Omar Hasan. 2002. Prophetic Medicine: Between the *Nass* and Empirical Experience. http://www.iiu.edu.my/medic/islmed/Lecmed; shpro-med98.jul.html. Accessed May 2, 2002.

Khan, Pir Vilayat. 1991. C. G. Jung and Sufism. In *Sufism, Islam and Jungian Psychology,* ed. J. Marvin Spiegelman, 35–53. Scottsdale, Ariz.: New Falcon Publications.

Lewis, Samuel. 1992. *Spiritual Dance and Walk: An Introduction from the Work of Murshid Samuel L. Lewis.* Fairfax, Calif.: Peace Works Center for the Dances of Universal Peace.

McCurdy, David. 2002. A Tradition Whose Time Has Come. *Park Ridge Center Bulletin,* January/February, 2.

O'Kane, Thomas Atum. 1987. Transpersonal Dimensions of Transformation: A Study of the Contributions drawn from the Sufi Order Teachings and Training to the Emerging Field of Transpersonal Psychology. Ph.D. Thesis, Union for Experimenting Colleges and Universities.

Ornstein, Robert. 1972. *The Psychology of Consciousness.* New York: Viking Press.

Rahman, Fazlur. 1987. *Health and Medicine in the Islamic Tradition.* New York: Crossroad.

Rowe, Amy E. 2001. Honey, Hadiths and Health Day: A Spectrum of Healing in the Daily Life of Boston Muslims. http://www.pluralism.org/affiliates/sered/index.php. Accessed June 18, 2003.

Sachedina, Abdulaziz. 1999. Can God Inflict Unrequited Pain on his Creatures? Muslim Perspectives on Health and Suffering. In *Religious Healing and Suffering,* ed. John R. Hinnells and Roy Porter, 65–94. London: Routledge and Kegan Paul.

Shafii, A. 1968. The Pir (Sufi Guide) and the Western Psychotherapist. *R. M. Bucke Memorial Society Newsletter* 3: 9–19.

———. *Freedom from the Self: Sufism, Meditation, and Psychotherapy.* New York: Human Sciences Press.

Spiegelman, J. Marvin. 1991. *Sufism, Islam and Jungian Psychology.* Scottsdale, Ariz.: New Falcon Publications.

Vaughan-Lee, Llewellyn. 1990. *The Lover and the Serpent: Dreamwork within a Sufi Tradition.* Rockport, Mass.: Element.

———. 1991. Dream-Work within a Sufi Tradition. In *Sufism, Islam and Jungian Psy-*

chology, ed. J. Marvin Spiegelman, 131–46. Scottsdale, Ariz.: New Falcon Publications.

Waugh, Earle H. 1999. *The Islamic Tradition: Religious Beliefs and Healthcare Decisions.* Chicago: Park Ridge Center.

Wilber, Ken. 2000. *No Boundary: Eastern and Western Approaches to Personal Growth.* Boulder, Colo.: Shambhala.

Yousif, Ahmad F. 2002. Islamic Medicine and Health Care: Historical and Contemporary Views. *Park Ridge Center Bulletin,* January/February, 4.

26

Health, Faith Traditions, and South Asian Indians in North America

Prakash N. Desai

In the last two decades of the twentieth century, the South Asian Indian presence in the United States and Canada has been felt in all major walks of life. Physicians from India are to be found not only in the major metropolitan area medical centers but also in remote parts of the continent. South Asian engineers abound, particularly in the information technology industry. Newspaper kiosks, doughnut shops, hotels, restaurants, gas stations, and convenience stores have been conspicuous for their brown-skinned proprietors and employees.

History of Indian Immigration to North America

The people from the subcontinent have ventured across the seas and over land for centuries, but in more recent times, that is, during the British colonial occupation from the mid-1800s hundreds to the beginning of the 1900s, Indians were also taken as indentured farm labor to other British colonies, such as South Africa, the West Indies, British Guiana, Fiji, and Mauritius. During the time this commerce was ending, Indians from the Punjab arrived as free men in California and the Pacific Northwest, where they took to farming, first as hired help and later as cultivators themselves. Many of them married women from Mexico who were also migrant farmworkers. These men and their families came to be known as "Mexican Hindus" (Leonard 1997), although a majority of them were of the Sikh faith and the rest were Muslim. This migration came to an abrupt stop with the enactment of restrictive immigration laws in the United States in the 1920s, laws that particularly barred the entry of people from Asia.

Another wave of immigration started around the time of India's independence from the British in the mid-1940s. These immigrants were almost exclusively students in engineering, technology, and medicine, reversing the previous trend of going to England for such training. Following the change in immigration laws in 1965, a third wave, a large-scale immigration of Indians, occurred, first gradually and then exponentially.

Immigration laws that favored family unification permitted relatives of established immigrants to come to the United States in large numbers. Among these relatives were not only brothers, sisters, and their families, who entered the labor market, but also older parents. Unlike the immigrants who had arrived on the strength of their own credentials, their relatives often were educationally less prepared and less likely to meld into the local society. Whereas the earlier immigrants settled in a variety of neighborhoods, the later influx resulted in concentrated residential pockets in all the major metropolitan areas of North America around which developed ethnic markets—the so-called India towns. Adding complexity to a culturally diverse group of immigrants from South Asia, descendants of those who went to the British colonies as indentured labor have of late made their presence felt as people of Indian origin.

According to U.S. Census of 2000, there are approximately 2 million people living in the United States who identify themselves as South Asian Indians (Barnes and Bennett 2002). Not unlike on the subcontinent itself, the Indian immigrants manifest a diversity in their cultural traditions and adhere to a variety of religions (Hindu, Muslim, Sikh, Jain, Christian). Along with their many skills and talents as professionals and entrepreneurs, they bring distinct cultural and religions diversity and polyphony that must find a rightful place in expanding American multiculturalism. This chapter deals with the faith tradition–informed health and healing practices of the Hindus. Most of these considerations are equally applicable to those of the Jain faith, who in some ways are indistinguishable from the Hindus.

In the last twenty years or so, there has emerged a systematic as well as an observational literature on the psychosocial adaptation of these immigrants. A compendium edited by Saran and Eames (1980) was one of the earliest works that focused on a variety of issues, such as ethnic identity, demography, institutional affiliation, and psychological adaptation. Others have studied in some depth issues of affiliation orientation in the lives of these immigrants (Bacon 1996), ethnicity and identity (Lessinger 1995), changing patterns of identity of women (Gupta 1999), and the growth and development of Indian youth (Maira 2002). The work of Karen Isaksen Leonard (1997) is particularly impressive in its account of early Indian immigrants' cultural adaptation, including the evolving pattern of their religious practices.

Religion and Healing In India

The tapestry of Hindu life is woven from many threads of different colors, and there are varied patterns of religious beliefs and practices. As historian Nirad Chaudhari observed, invoking a different metaphor, "It is as if the historic and living Hinduism was an elaborate cadenza to an unplayed composition, on which the Hindus have been improvising variations in near and distant keys without feeling that they are being unorthodox" (1979: 63). For Jawaharlal Nehru (1981: 59), India was like "some ancient palimpsest on which layer upon layer of thought and reverie had been inscribed, and yet no succeeding layer had completely hidden or erased what had been written previously." This diversity makes it difficult to articulate abiding principles or truths; as Martin Marty exclaimed in the introduction to my earlier work, "Where is the canon?" (Desai 1990: xi). On the other hand, there is also substance to the oft-repeated truism: Hinduism is a way of life. The ordinary everyday transactions and the ritual of religious practice are indistinguishable from one another.

As a consequence, strategies adopted by Hindus when seeking help and healing may not appear to a non-Indian to be what is ordinarily understood as religious healing. For an Indian, however, religion typically means more than a connection with a diety or a religious order. Every act is a moral act with a potential to alter the self. A person is not bounded by his or her skin but is a permeable self with different degrees and qualities of affinity with those in the social network (Marriott 1990), all of which determines individual and social response to illness. Restoration of the self is not only a physiological and psychological task but an interpersonal one as well.

Hindu medicine, or *Ayurveda*—meaning the knowledge of life (span)—developed alongside and in tandem with religious thought. The corpus of Ayurvedic literature extends from antiquity to the modern day, although later versions are largely reiterations of older ones. Principal among the early works are the *Carakasamhita*, a compendium (*samhita*) brought together between the first century B.C.E. and first century C.E., and regarded as the oldest, and the *Susrutasamhita*, of the fourth century C.E., the compendium par excellence that deals with surgical procedures. These texts hold that disease interferes with the observance of religious obligation and that a disease-free state is a source of "virtue, wealth and gratification" (*Carakasamhita* I-15). A healthy human body is a prerequisite for the realization of the obligations of life's ethical tasks.

The Ayurvedic theory of pathophysiology is humoral, distinct from the ancient Greek and of which it developed independently. Three of the elements that constitute the body and the universe, namely, wind, fire, and phlegm (water), are visualized as pervading the body through channels and as concentrated in body parts according to the dominant function of that organ. Their balance and smooth, unobstructed flow are essential for health; imbalance, excess or diminution, causes disease. Individuals have particular dispositions in which one or another humor may be dominant, and the balance is also subject to seasonal variation, foods, moods, interpersonal transaction, and physical activity. Of all the principles of Ayurveda, the humoral theory is the most commonly understood among people all over India, and humoral explanations of illnesses are common folk idiom.

The self was also an explicit object of reflection, in both the Vedic texts (Desai and Collins 1986) and the medical texts (Desai 1990). Two sorts of selves were visualized, the first, *ahmakara*, literally the utterance of the word I, that is, self-consciousness, the phenomenal self, or the ego-self, seen as frail, transient, given to dissolution and hence prone to decay; and the second, *atman*, stripped of the psychophysiological functions, became true consciousness, an adamantine core, that moves through the cycle of rebirths from which it is liberated when it achieves nirvana. The ego-self is vulnerable and is prone to fragmentation without appropriate affirmation, approbation, and applause from those in its psychosocial orbit. Pure consciousness is approached through a variety of yogic practices. From a psychosocial perspective, the phenomenal or ego-self is viewed as covetous, a wishing and wanting self, and orients itself through relationships. In a culture that places connectedness in the center of its values, the self is anchored in others (self-objects, in psychoanalytic self-psychology) and turns to them for nurturance, calming, and soothing, for affirmation, and for guiding ambitions. No environments, however attuned to a person, can respond appropriately at all times; the prospect of injury and the consequent additional needs for calming loom large in interpersonal transaction. At such times, operationally a split occurs between an outer and an inner self, or a public and a private self. Action and actor are divorced, and a person achieves an inner distance from situations that feel noxious to his or her well-being. Hence the spiritual ideals of renunciation and detachment.

Contemporary Practice of Medicine In India

The current practice of medicine in India, despite the popularity of the Ayurvedic system, is another matter. Ever since the introduction of biomedicine from the West, commonly referred to in India as allopathy, meaning treatment with agents that have properties contrary to the disease, it has become the dominant practice. Medical practice in the cities and semiurban areas tends mainly to be in a biomedical style (what Fredrick Dunn [1976] calls cosmopolitan medicine); in rural areas, the cheaper and more readily accessible Ayurvedic medicine is the more common practice. However, there is another distinction as well. Consumers distinguish between acute and chronic conditions, such that in urban areas, the Ayurvedic system is patronized for chronic conditions, whereas for acute conditions, even in the villages, biomedicine is popular.[1] Biomedical therapeutic agents are viewed as heavy, with many undesirable side effects, as poisonous (as in antibiotics in the literal sense), and generally as violating the body's natural order.

Hinduism in America

More than a century ago, Swami Vivekananda, the chief acolyte of Swami Ramakrishna and missionary of the Vedanta society, came to the United States to attend the Parliament of World Religions. He brought the message of the wisdom of the East, and in his trail were founded several Vedanta society temples in the major cities of the United States. Madame Blavatsky and the followers of the Theosophist Society also celebrated the Hindu enlightenment. J. Krishnamurty, who later established an ashram on the West Coast, was first introduced to North America by this group of Theosophists. Writers like Ralph Waldo Emerson and poets like T. S. Eliot celebrated the Hindu message in their writings. Since then, a long line of maharishis, swamis, and preachers have established a following in the United States. Most of these messengers from the East had local American audiences in mind, although later they gathered a large following of Indian devotees as well. During the 1950s and 1960s poets like Allen Ginsberg, and later the Beatles, made Indian classical music, the burning of incense, and the chanting of mantras a popular but fringe movement on the continent. Beginning in 1965, the Hare Krishna movement, sponsored by the International Society of Krishna Consciousness (ISKCON), also held sway over many American teenagers, especially white teenagers who had become disenchanted with their own traditions. Over time, Krishna temples have gathered a more traditional Indian devotional fellowship (Eck 1990).

During the last decades of the twentieth century, yoga became a household word in America. Television-sponsored lessons for fitness through yoga, exercise centers, and meditation practices are now widespread. Transcendental Meditation is a trademark. Dr. Herbert Benson's use of biofeedback and meditative techniques for the treatment of diseases like hypertension have become part of mainstream medicine in the United States. More recently the work of Deepak Chopra has captured the popular imagination of many non-Indian Americans. Chopra has attempted to bring together the medical and physiological principles of Ayurveda and the mystical and the psychological from the various schools of yoga, in order to bring the body's energies, senses, and organs in harmony with each other and with nature.

Indians in America

The Indian immigrant community and its first-generation descendants are a relatively affluent minority in North America. Apart from using their resources to purchase lavish suburban homes, flashy cars, and frequent trips to India, members of the community have come together to spend a part of their earnings on building temples. Most urban centers, where Indian communities are often concentrated, boast of several places of worship, some elaborately constructed according to strict rules of temple architecture in the Hindu tradition. These temples are major cultural centers, their construction having anticipated the need for community gatherings. The Indians, given their busy work lives and the traditional American weekend, have adopted the Christian-based custom common in America of Sunday gatherings with special worship ceremonies.

The most immediate organizing principle of Indian social life traditionally has been the caste and kinship network, and not the temple, as tends to be the case in Western contexts. Nor is there a public communal ritual analogous to going to church on Sundays. The adopted tradition of weekend temple gathering does not provide the Indian community with the social organization that a church, parish, or congregation does. At the same time, for the vastly dispersed Indian community in North America, organizing social life around caste or kinship networks is simply not possible, a reality that tends to dilute the social forces of conformity. Caste in America thus loses some of its salience as an organizing principle, no longer serving in the same way as a strict guide to whom one may eat with, to whom one may give a daughter in marriage, or to determining hereditary occupation. Indians have attempted to compensate for this loss through the organization of social and quasi-secular associations, along with building a variety of religious and social organizations within the community. With a few exceptions like the Patels of Gujarat or the Reddys or Kamas of Andhra Pradesh, most successful organizations are constructed along regional lines, the guiding force being language (e.g., Bengali, Gujrati, Marathi, Telegu). Associations that attempt to be pan-Indian have the most difficulty in maintaining a large committed membership. Thus, a consciousness of being from a particular linguistic region of India comes to the fore and serves as an operational substitute for caste consciousness, but with the ever-returning-home Indian community, the reinforcement during such visits continues to keep caste consciousness refreshed.

In dealing with the larger American society, adaptive strategies among Indian immigrants are not uniform. On a path of adaptation, the strategies vary from overidentification, to assimilation (becoming alike), to outright denial of American culture. The most common strategy among those who successfully navigate the narrow straits between culture shock and maladaptation is the Indian ideal of being like a lotus in the midst of mud and water, to have a life in America but to remain internally untouched by it. An outward adaptation in dress, language, idiom, manners, attitude, and sociality masks an inner distance and disinvolvement. The Indian distinction between an inner

Self (*atman*) and an outer self (*ahmkara*) aids in maintaining a semblance of immersion. The other side of this inner-outer split, or a "split level consciousness" (Desai 1982), however, is the difficulty of keeping slurs and slights from affecting the inner world, as often happens at home when one's environment fails to respond appropriately, but more so in an alien land, where there are fewer people to turn to who may uplift one's spirits by their affirming responses. When self-esteem is anchored in others, for example, the eye of a dominant culture, it can be particularly vulnerable to the vagaries of dispositions of important others in the workplace such as teachers, superiors, bosses, and benefactors.

As for their own tradition, the majority compensate for the distance from the land of origin by becoming more aware of and attached to their faith tradition. For a small minority it becomes a passionate attachment, while an even a smaller minority becomes distant and detached from the original tradition (Desai and Coehlo 1980).

Temples and Worship

Hindu temples attract a large attendance on special religious occasions and festivals, but few Indians feel that they are either being unorthodox or, even worse, lapsing from the tradition by not participating in the temple event. The more common practice is to maintain an altar in the home, a space dedicated to house religious icons, and in the absence of readily available genuine icons, photographs of deities. The ritual offering (*puja*), is often compressed into the lighting of a lamp and common folk prayers instead of the more Sanskritic incantations.

A more elaborate ritual practiced in the home is the *havan*, a fire sacrifice.[2] The ritual is an ancient Vedic practice, adapted by the *Arya Samaj*—a path that renewed and rejuvenated Vedic Hinduism—and is a voluntary undertaking on the part of a householder who wishes either to celebrate an occasion like the birth of a child or to pacify adverse forces that might have emerged in the life of the family, such as illness or fission. Some Indian immigrants perform the ritual in their homes, inviting a large circle of friends and acquaintances, and feel united with the benevolent forces of the universe, as the ritual is supposed to accomplish. Those who wish may commission a special ritual conducted in their name at a Hindu temple. There are other variations of the *puja* ceremony, conducted in the home, one of which is a recitation of the story of *Satyanarayana*, about the boons bestowed on those who partake in the ceremony, and the misfortunes incurred by those who shun it. A more individualized practice to appease malevolent forces and restore a person's social and astral balance is the recitation of mantras; repetition of certain hymns, prayers, or multiple names of gods; or donations to the temple or some needy individuals, especially after a recovery from a serious illness, as a way of expressing gratitude to the divine forces.

The rituals marking life-stage transitions (*samskaras*) are celebrated, and for members of the Indian immigrant community they are a way of renewing their familiarity with their own tradition. Rituals for celebrating pregnancy, giving a name to a newborn, tonsure, and the sacred thread ceremony are occasions for family gathering, at home or at a temple.[3] Hindu weddings are elaborate and festive, with families insisting on an authentic Hindu ceremony. It is as if the loss of the immediacy of culture, particularly religion, is compensated for by a celebration that exceeds the usual expectations in India. Even more telling are the rituals at death. Solemn as the occasion is, in modern India the rituals at death are elided and passed over as priestly overelaboration, for the Indian immigrant a desire to be reconnected appears to have been reinforced by distance, and rituals around death are elaborated. As early as the first settlers, the "Mexican Hindus," it was a death that commanded the attention of the immigrants to the religious ritual. In the contemporary Indian immigrant community, the traditions are followed faithfully, with an officiating Hindu priest, incantation from the scriptures, preparation of the body, and cremation, followed by a period of mourning during which the family and friends gather to sing and chant hymns and devotional songs.

Several features distinguish this population not only from the early immigrants in the United States and Canada but also from their counterparts in India. The average income of an Indian living in the United States is estimated to be twice the average income of an American, and a vast number of Indians have college degrees. Their wealth makes it possible for many to travel to India frequently and renew their ties to family and culture, and to build temples and sponsor religious figures coming to the United States and Canada. Indian weekly newspapers, which number over a dozen, have full-page advertisements announcing the visits and receptions of these luminaries of a variety of religious sects in India. Among them are heads of temples or of a particular devotional path, gurus and *babas*, ascetics and astrologers. As the advertisements suggest, some offer spiritual guidance, solace, or religious connectedness, and others astrological predictions about success, prospects of marriage, or health and illness. Thus, unlike, say, the early immigrants to South Africa, Trinidad, and the United States or Guyana and Surinam, who were almost completely cut off from their ancestral lands, recent immigrants have ready access to Indian traditions, through travel and modern information technology. These very assets also permit Indian immigrants to have their children return to India to choose spouses, thus further reinforcing a move toward a more traditional life. All these features of interaction with the homeland—either through visits, sending children to study there, or through the visits of religious leaders to America—tend to reinforce original identification. Most important, the presence of parents in the family who came to this country as older adults has a salient effect in traditionalizing the home.

In health care matters, as in other things, Hindus tend to maintain a flexible "what works best" approach. It is an adaptive response to changing circumstances, making allowances for time and place. As Sripati Chandrasekhar, a noted Indian demographer, observed, "As in all codes of ethics, there is in the Hindu view an admirable and practical dichotomy of the ideal and the permissible. The ideal code of behavior was for the dedicated 'righteous' or saintly minority and the permissible way was for the work-a-day million" (1974: 44). A similar adaptive pattern and practicality was noted by Sheryl Daniels (1983) in calling this response to moral issues a "tool-box approach."

Apart from this practicality, another trait characterizes Hindu response to a developing new reality. Hindus' orientation toward life derives not from religious decree but from relationships and a sense of connectedness. As Pitchumoni and Saran (1980) found in their survey of Indians regarding health concerns, the first response is to receive advice from family and friends, more often than consulting a physician. It is in this context that the high density of physicians in the Indian community makes a decisive difference. More than 32,000 physicians of Indian origin practice biomedicine in the United States, a physician-to-population density in the immigrant population that is almost ten times higher than that for the overall population in the United States. It is more or less a foregone conclusion that Indians in times of a health crisis Indians will call one of the Indian physicians in the network of family or friends before consulting their own physician. Needless to say, given geographic diversity, the Indian community as such does not patronize only physicians of Indian origin. The implication of this tendency to seek advice from family and friends—among whom are physicians practicing biomedicine—is that the system of medicine that this family-friendly physician practices becomes the dominant mode of healing. Ordinary contradictions rarely come in the way of organizing one's conceptual frame of reference. When responding to an emerging crisis what needs to be done most expeditiously comes first, even when the cultural explanation of the crisis is in contradiction to the diagnosis and treatment. These contradictions seldom produce cognitive dissonance. At the same time, humoral explanation of illness, embellished with seasonal and temporal exigencies, continues to be the main frame of reference for a majority of Indians even when they seek treatment from a system that does not include humors in the explanatory system of etiology.

Seeking psychiatric help is a different matter. The stigma attached to mental illness is far more severe than in an American household, and the normal pattern of seeking advice from friends, family, or a psychiatrist known to the family does not obtain. When a school social worker, a family physician, or a non-Indian American psychiatrist finds significant family pathology with cultural overtones and attempts to refer the patient and/or the family to an Indian therapist or psychiatrist, the treatment may suddenly cease. Only when almost all professionals consulted point to a person of Indian origin with impeccable credentials do the patient and the family turn to him or her. The concern of such patients and families is not only the need for anonymity but that fact that the therapist or psychiatrist's ethnicity evokes shame. Here familiarity works the other way: they feel exposed to someone of their own kind, and the likeness acts as a conscience, reinforcing traditional prohibitions and inhibitions.

An illness threatens not only the integrity of an individual but also that of a family and the social network that may have replaced the caste and kinship alliances. In serious physical illness, it is of critical social importance for relatives and friends to call on the sickbed. A seriously ill person's social network gets activated; phone-call chains become the expected routine, and the solidarity of relationships is mobilized. Help seeking follows the native track of the familiar and the intimate, except in the case of emotional illness, where the same considerations of intimacy dictate the pursuit of an unfamiliar path to avoid stigma and shame. There is no strict religious prohibition against suicide, but suicide is rare; an occasional episode stirs the community with anguish.

Food

Like most immigrants, Indian immigrants remain tied to their traditional preferences for foods and cuisine. On the surface it may appear that this preference applies mainly to the spiciness of the food, but there is more to it. Of all the Ayurvedic principles, food and its effects on the body retain the strongest hold on the imagination of the Indian immigrant community. Although immigrants and first-generation Indians who were raised as vegetarians continue to adhere to that diet, not all do so. Often the steadfastness with which the dietetic injunction is preserved is a mark of reinforced religious and caste identification. Even among those whose diet was not vegetarian to begin with or those who adapted to what was most easily available, there is an overwhelming insistence on avoiding eating beef. For the Indian immigrant, the recent medical campaign against eating red meats for prevention of coronary artery disease and colonic cancer seems to justify the religious wisdom.

In the course of everyday family conversation about diet and foods, one commonly encounters invocation of Ayurvedic properties of different foods and their propensity to excite or calm specific humors. Some of this enthusiasm may be passed off as deriving from new scientific evidence, but it also is an assertion of cultural and religious identity. Equally common are dietetic experiments with garlic, lemon juice, carrots, or some herbs and spices such as basil and ginger, which are justified in terms of recent claims of alternative medicine and are a consonant with the belief in original Ayurvedic prescriptions. These propensities are reinforced by older parents in the household and women who have not yet been socialized in the American mainstream due to limited exposure or a compartmentalized worldview between home and work. The most common and universal rekindlers of faith are threats to one's integrity, either physical or psychological. Indians are no exception. Contradictions between scientific orientation and traditional belief melt away. An Indian scientist will most readily wear a particular gemstone prescribed by an astrologer to counter the effects of an adverse astral body in his or her horoscope, in the United States just as in India. A ritual to ward off the malevolence of "evil eye" is practiced in many families, especially with regard to the health of children. Women may "swear off" a particular item from the regular diet, a form of self-imposed suffering or a form of austerity to atone for some transgression committed or to appease gods during unfavorable circumstances, particularly in matters of illness. The practice of observing fasts, such as eating only once a day or avoiding certain foods on a particular day of the week or on a day in the lunar cycle, is common in many families (the Hindu calendar is lunar). Among those more recently converted to nonvegetarian products, the practice of avoiding eating nonvegetarian food on a particular day of the week is a variant of the practice of fasting and is interpreted as a healthful practice. The same holds true for alcohol.

The significance of all forms of intake, and their potential for altering one's disposition, continues to hold sway over the minds of Hindu immigrant families. Religious and common folk rituals are invoked to bear upon the universe around oneself and the family to restore physical and psychological well-being.

Sexuality

In a landscape of adaptation and acculturation, sexuality presents the main challenge for Indians, particularly to the parents of adolescent children. A common stereotype among Indians is that American society is sexually over-permissive. The Hindu belief in a fluid dynamic of the body regards the egress of instinctual drives as subject to excitement and therefore easily heated up. Attempts to contain the egress lay stress on social constraints, that is, externally imposed limits, rather than on limits by internalized prohibitions. The permissiveness of American social surroundings endangers sexual continence, especially that of adolescents. Teenage girls who are learning to be assertive present a heart-wrenching dilemma for their parents. Children who are learning to be American by being less "obedient" and more challenging produce major strife in an Indian family. Some parents, in an attempt to keep adolescent temptations at bay, impose strict rules for socialization, banning dating and other teenage gatherings, sometimes severely restricting the emerging individuality of the children. This dynamic often becomes a source of intergenerational conflict. A few among them pack off their daughters in their early teen-age years to India to live with relatives or at exclusive boarding schools known for their religious orientation.

The perils of easily excitable and egress-prone drives are a cause of marital discord as well. Some husbands and wives monitor their spouse's social inter-actions with others, which sometimes results in distress and marital instability. Another source of shifting marital balances is the emancipating influence of American culture on women. The newfound freedom of movement, expres-sion, and occupation strengthens the resolve of women toward self-assertion. For a good number of them a domestic life without in-laws, the proverbial problem of Indian women, is an opportunity for coming into their own, with the home truly becoming a married woman's own. But this same development that leads to an unfolding of a woman's self, for some men poses a threat to the control they otherwise expected to exercise, and the resulting imbalance from a traditional perspective may lead to discord that is not easily resolved.

There are instances of domestic abuse and violence in marital relation-ships. Whereas a family might seek professional help with regard to intergen-erational conflict, "to straighten out the errant teenager," it is unusual for a couple in the throes of a marital conflict to seek help. More commonly the manifestation of the unhappiness results in a refusal to talk or eat, usually on the part of the wife. More often than not, it is the woman who seeks help when under unbearable duress; a therapist's attempts to involve the husband in a therapeutic dialogue are usually of no avail. Similarly, it is also the woman who observes fasts, forsakes an item of food until peace is restored, makes a ritual visit to a temple or a place of pilgrimage, or has particular mantras or hymns aimed at restoring peace recited on her behalf at a place of worship.

Conclusion

In the last twenty-five years, the Indian community in the United States has grown at a rapid rate, numbering almost 2 million in the 2000 census. This "model minority" includes a large number of professionals, particularly physicians. Their orientation is mainly in terms of relationships, and they ap-proach medical care first through friends and family, except in the case of psychiatric illness. Usually economically successful, highly educated, and with a strong family orientation, the Indian community has experienced social status and respect in North America, especially in the last two to three decades as its size has multiplyied. In the history of Indian diaspora this development is unique, a credit to both the characteristics of the immigrants and the host society.

While the community is diverse, with many regional differences, most Hindus in the United States patronize Western medicine, especially in acute illness. Still, their native assumptive system regarding the body and health and illness derived from the principles of Ayurvedic medicine continues to thrive. This paradox requires an explanation.

On the one hand, the very practical "what-works-best" approach of the community was quick to take to biomedicine, with its promise to accurately diagnose and effectively cure many acute illnesses, especially infectious diseases; being urban and educated or rural and illiterate made little difference in the willingness to adopt biomedicine. Surgical interventions, which had been abandoned by the Ayurvedic practitioners, gave renewed hope with anesthesia, blood transfusions, and sterile techniques. Immunization had an equally positive effect all over India. On the other hand, the task of rendering fragmented, bruised, bewildered selves was taken up by the various forms of guru-ships, traditional means of calming and soothing. Gurus, and other religious personages are the institutional response of Indian society developed over centuries. Whereas gurus are the mainstay when it comes to the need for psychological calming, the turning toward traditional roots is an extraordinarily widespread tendency. The turn to the Ayurvedic idiom of illness that places the person in his or her natural context is a zone of comfort, especially in terms of seasons and food, and herbal remedies which are considered natural, as opposed to synthetic. The distance between action and the actor does not produce dissonance, and a split-level consciousness is in fact a necessary form of adaptation.

Living in North America has not significantly altered traditional ways of dealing with issues of health and illness, although healing preferences need more empirical studies. Of special concern is how long the culture's hold on subsequent generations will last, and how attempts at blurring differences with the host culture will prevail.

NOTES

1. A variant of the Ayurvedic medicine, called *siddha*, is favored in the south of India and is known for its metallic apothecary borrowed from the Greeks. Another system of medicine brought by the colonizers had displaced Ayurveda: the Unani (from Ionian) system patronized by the Mogul rulers of India. With a large Muslim population that favors the Unani system, it also receives government patronage in the form of organized schools and central research institutions today. Homeopathy (treatment with agents that are like the disease, as in desensitization treatment of allergies, an alternate Western tradition) has a significant following also.

2. For an interesting use of the metaphor, as well as the actual ritual, see Susham Bedi's novel *Havan*, translated as *The Fire Sacrifice* (Bedi: 1993), which depicts the life of an Indian immigrant woman and her family, a trajectory marked by ambition and strife.

3. The thread ceremony is a ritual marking the entrance of a boy into the student-celibate stage. He is given a thread to wear across his torso, symbolizing the upper

body garment, and a staff and a bowl, symbolizing his life as a mendicant. The ceremony is observed in the upper three castes, but most consistently among the Brahmins in modern India.

REFERENCES

Bacon, Jean. 1996. *Life Lines: Community, Family, and Assimilation among Asian Indian Immigrants.* New York: Oxford University Press.
Barnes, Jessica, and Claudette E. Bennett. 2002. *The Asian Population: 2000.* Bureau of the Census. Washington, D.C.
Bedi, Susham. 1993. *The Fire Sacrifice.* Trans. David Rubin. Oxford: Heinemann.
Chandrasekhar, Sripati. 1974. *Abortion in a Crowed World: The Problem of Abortion with Special Reference to India.* London: Allen and Unwin.
Chaudhari, Nirad. 1979. *Hinduism.* New York: Oxford University Press.
Daniels, Sheryl. 1983. The Tool-box Approach of the Tamil to the Issues of Moral Responsibility and Human Destiny. In *Karma: An Anthropological Inquiry,* ed. by Charles Keyes and E. Valentine Daniels, 27–62. Berkeley and Los Angeles: University of California Press.
Desai, Prakash. 1990. *Health/Medicine in the Hindu Tradition.* New York: Crossroads.
Desai, Prakash, and George Coehlo. 1980. Indian Immigrants in America: Some Cultural Aspects of Psychological Adaptation. In *The New Ethnics: Asian Indians in the United States,* ed. Parmatma Saran and Edwin Eames, 363–86. New York: Praeger.
Desai, Prakash, and Alfred Collins. 1986. Selfhood in Context: Some Indian Solutions, In *Cultural Transition,* ed. M. White and S. Pollak, 261–90. Boston: Routledge and Kegan Paul.
Dunn, Fredrick. 1976. Traditional Asian Medicine and Cosmopolitan Medicine as Adaptive Systems. In *Asian Medical Systems,* ed. Charles Leslie, 137–58. Berkeley and Los Angeles: University of California Press.
Eck, Diana L. 1990. New Age Hinduism in America. In *Conflicting Images,* ed. Sulochana Raghavan Glazer, and Nathan Glazer, 111–42. Croton-on-Hudson, N.Y.: Riverdale.
Gupta, Sangeeta, ed. 1999. *Emerging Voices: South Asian American Women Redefine Self, Family and Community.* Walnut Creek, Calif.: AltaMira Press.
Leonard, Karen Isaksen. 1997. *The South Asian Americans.* Westport, Conn.: Greenwood Press.
Lessinger, Johanna. 1995. *From the Ganges to the Hudson: Indian Immigrants in New York City.* Boston: Allyn and Bacon.
Maira, Sunaina Marr. 2002. *Desis in the House: Indian American Youth Culture in New York City.* Philadelphia: Temple University Press.
Marriott, McKim. 1990. Constructing an Indian Ethnosociology. In *India through Hindu Categories,* ed. McKim Marriott, 1–39. New Delhi: Sage.
Nehru, Jawaharlal [1946] 1981. *The Discovery of India.* Delhi: Jawaharlal Nehru Memorial Fund.
Pitchumoni, C. S., and Paratma Saran. 1980. Health and Medical care of Indian Im-

migrants in the United States. In *The New Ethnics: Asian Indians in the United States,* ed. Paratma Saran and Edwin Eames, 300–317. New York: Praeger.

Saran, Paratma, and Edwin Eames. 1980. *The New Ethnics: Asian Indians in the United States.* New York: Praeger.

Sharma, Priyavat. 1981. *Carakasamhita.* Varanasi: Chaukhambaha Orientalia.

Shastri, Kalidas. 1974. *Susrutasamhita.* Ahmedabad: Sastu Sahitya Vardhak Karyalaya.

27

Hmong Shamanism: Animist Spiritual Healing in America's Urban Heartland

Phua Xiong, Charles Numrich, Chu Yongyuan Wu, Deu Yang, and Gregory A. Plotnikoff

The Hmong are an ethnic minority with ancient roots in China. Members of this tribal culture have lived in the highlands of Southeast Asia, mainly Laos, since the 1800s. Following their disastrous assistance to the U.S. military during the Vietnam War, the Hmong have made the West, and particularly the United States, their home. There are now more than 100,000 Hmong refugees in the United States, with the highest concentration in Minnesota and Wisconsin. The Hmong have brought with them a rich culture with strong animist religious convictions and active shamanic practices.[1] However, "those Hmong who have come to the United States find themselves suspended between worlds, in a place where religion, language and skills are de-contextualized and where their previous social support system is greatly weakened" (Adler 1995: 1623). Indeed, the contrasts between their new and old homes could not have been sharper or more striking.

As the Hmong make America their home, their practice of traditional healing—Hmong shamanism (*kev ua neeb*)—has been particularly challenged by the multiple forces that accompany acculturation. Such forces include the impact of urban life on a culture that has been rural and agricultural for thousands of years; the difficulty of navigating educational systems for people from a preliterate society; the problems faced when individuals are confronted with health care, social services, and legal systems that have no understanding of Hmong traditional beliefs and cultural attitudes.

Hmong contact with Western health care is often unavoidable. In such encounters, the risks of cultural or religious conflicts and misunderstandings remain high for both patient and physician. The tragic consequences of conflicting views of health, illness, and healing were portrayed in Ann Fadiman's celebrated book, *The Spirit Catches You and You Fall Down* (1997). Since then, inclusion of this book in numerous medical school curricula has fostered appreciation for the cross-cultural dynamics in health care.

Given the suspension between worlds in which Hmong Americans find themselves, it becomes a pressing matter to understand how Hmong religious and healing traditions are decontextualized—or recontextualized—in the United States. Have traditional social supports for healing been weakened or strengthened? Shamans continue to play an important role in interpreting the world and people's personal lives, making it also important to understand how their presence and availability affect patients' choices related to health care.

During the more than twenty-five years since the Hmong began arriving in the United States, Hmong patients have become more familiar with the U.S. health care system. As they develop "new world" diseases, such as diabetes and hypertension, they are perplexed and seek appropriate cures. Increasingly, too, they seek culturally respectful biomedical health care providers and systems. At the same time, the tension between acculturation and traditional beliefs modulates their participation in American biomedicine.

In 1999 a team of researchers began to study the nature and contemporary practice of Hmong shamanism in Minneapolis and St. Paul, Minnesota, to begin to understand (1) some of the ways in which Hmong shamanism has continued to be practiced, including how it has remained the same and how it has changed; and (2) how patients determine the kinds of care they will seek, given the availability of both traditional shamans and biomedical facilities. Members of the team interviewed eleven shamans (five men, six women, ranging in age from thirty-five to eighty-five) and thirty-two Hmong patients (fourteen men, eighteen women, ranging in age from twenty-one to eighty-five).

Body and Souls

Traditionally, the Hmong view life as a continuous circle of birth and rebirth and believe that two worlds—physical and spiritual—exist side by side. Beings in both worlds may interact with one another in various ways. These traditional Hmong views of life and the interconnectedness of things around them are vastly different from many Western views. Hmong believe that humans must live in harmony with their environment because there is spiritual existence to all things. As Conquergood notes: "The Hmong celebrate their humanity not as a discreet and impenetrable part of the natural order, but as part of the circle of life of all creation—caught up in the rotation of the seasons, and deeply connected with the configuration of the mountains, and the reincarnation of life from generation to generation, even from species to species. Life, in its myriad forms, is intimately articulated through souls and spirits" (1989: 45–46). The Hmong believe that a person has a number of souls. Beliefs about the actual number of souls vary. The most common numbers attributed to this belief system are three, nine, and twelve, though some people refer to as many as twenty or even more than thirty souls. Whatever the number, the essence of Hmong spiritual tradition is that the souls and the physical body must function as a single unit to give life and health to the individual. This unit must remain intact and whole for spiritual, mental, and physical health. When this relationship is disjointed or out of balance, illness afflicts the individual. For example, when a soul or souls are lost or taken by other spiritual forces, the physical body reflects this loss by becoming sick. Likewise, when a body part or organ is removed, the body is rendered unwhole. As a result, the soul may lose its ability to find its ancestors in the spirit world after death, or it may be reincarnated into a negative fate. Thus, surgical solutions to medical problems, rather than being seen as curative and lifesaving, may be perceived as a profound force for harm, affecting a person not only in this life but also in many lives to come.

There is, however, a hierarchy of organs that exist in relationship to the souls. Over the last twenty-five years, Hmong people have become more familiar and comfortable with Western medicine and surgery. This aspect of acculturation allows some animist Hmong to agree to appendectomies but refuse nephrectomies, gastrectomies, or the surgical removal of other more important organs, even if the procedure is defined by their physician as lifesaving. This refusal also occurs because Hmong attribute specific significance to certain organs. For example, the liver is the metaphoric center of emotional states and character. Therefore, for some Hmong, accepting a liver transplant may be seen in the same light as accepting death because a new liver means a new personality, a new character. Hmong believe that the organ recipient acquires some characteristics of the organ donor. In addition to the organ, the donor's soul has also been transplanted, leading to harmful spiritual and reincarnation consequences.

Furthermore, Hmong cultural expressions of emotional states can be misinterpreted in the biomedical culture. For example, a Hmong person who is distressed may express that he or she has sickness of the liver (*mob siab*), which may be misinterpreted as an organic liver disease rather than an emotional or psychological state. Another area of possible misinterpretation involves the expression of emotions. For example, an American might say, "I am brokenhearted" (*Kuv tu siab*), whereas a Hmong person will say, "My liver is broken"

(*Kuv lub siab puas tu siab*). In situations like this, an intuitive interpreter who understands the cultural idioms and meanings in both cultures is of great value to the health care provider.

Due to the dynamic interaction of souls, spirits, and people, and the impact of their interactions on health and illness, many Hmong find Western medicine less than adequate in meeting their needs. Having brought a variety of healing practices with them to this country, most Hmong—especially animists—continue to seek traditional healing practices in times of sickness and distress. Among these is the practice of the Hmong spiritual healer (*tu kho mob txiv neeb*), a shaman (*tu txiv neeb*) or spirit teller (*tu saib mob)* who can navigate the spirit world to determine or diagnose the cause of an illness.[2] Many Hmong continue to rely on shamans, trusting their healing skills and abilities to restore health and balance.

The World of the Shamans

Research interviewers Chu Wu and Deu Yang brought with them a clear understanding of Hmong culture and ready access to members of the community. Chu Wu, a conflict resolution and community mediation trainer, had previously done extensive research in Hmong shamanism. Deu Yang, a licenced practical nurse, not only practiced biomedicine but also grew up in a family that practiced shamanism and had assisted her mother-in-law in shaman rituals. Despite all their experience and preparation for this project, however, our interviewers quickly discovered that language would present an unexpected major obstacle in their interviews with shaman practitioners.

Even though the interviewers and interviewees all spoke Hmong, we discovered that we were now dealing with spiritual language used for curing the patient and communicating with good and evil spirits. Words, phrases, and even ideas used in shamanic rituals are understood by shamans and the people around them (the shaman's assistants are usually family members), but a layperson would not necessarily know what was being said. Ritual chants might include words from a variety of other languages (Tibetan, Laotian, Chinese, or even Latin), and it is critical that the shaman not reveal words used to communicate with evil spirits. If one were to use these words carelessly, the power of the spirit could overcome an innocent bystander or harm the shaman and the shaman's family.

In some cases, the shamans we interviewed were protective of the spiritual world and did not readily share the details of their practice. Deu Yang encountered specific difficulties because of her work in biomedicine. Often a shaman may feel that doctors, nurses, and other biomedical caregivers will never understand or accept shamanic practice. Such shamans have no desire to share the private aspects of their spirit life. In other instances, there were problems of timing and accessibility. It became obvious to Chu Wu that he needed to be flexible in his requests for interviews. Even when he approached one of his uncles who is a shaman, he had to determine "the right time to talk. Some days, shamans must struggle with their personal life, because they have to help so many people. When the shaman's own life is uncomfortable, it is not the right time to share." Only by being open to the shamans' availability and sensitive to their needs, was Chu Wu able to build a high level of trust and encourage interviewees to help him understand their shamanic rituals.

Becoming a Shaman

Hmong shamanism (*ua neeb*) combines healing and religion and is a way to health and well-being. Its origins are shrouded in history, but legend clearly identifies its historical significance. The following legend, which is part of Hmong oral tradition, is known by everyone and has no real source other than the combined cultural memory of the Hmong people:

> Shee Yee [*Siv Yis*] was a special healer sent by god to live with the Hmong people in the cave near [a mountain in southwest China]. His mission was to provide medical cures for all the people. He married a Hmong woman . . . [but later] abandoned his people and traveled alone in Mongolia. . . . [An] orphan boy wandered the north for years until he found Shee Yee [who] was moved by the orphan boy's determination to find him. Shee Yee taught the orphan boy everything he knew. The orphan boy returned to his people and taught the elders what he had learned. . . . This created a tradition of shaman, earth medicines, and magic that is still practiced to this day.

The tradition of teaching and transmission now takes the form of being "chosen" (*yuav ua neeb*) to assume the role and responsibilities of a shaman. Being "chosen" is the first step and is generally precipitated by an unusual illness. Men, women, and even children can be "chosen." One interviewee described it as follows:

> I was chosen by Yawm Saub (the creator) to become a healer. . . . When I was twelve years old, I began to experience some body shaking and felt something awaking me. . . . I was very ill and passed away for seven days and seven nights. My family thought I was going to die. They tried everything to help me, until they invited a shaman to look into my illness. Immediately, the shaman informed my family that I [was] chosen to become a shaman. The shaman called my soul and performed the shaman ceremony. During the ceremony, my body was shaking and felt the emotional movement.

Once a person has been "chosen" to be a shaman, "treatment training" is provided almost entirely from the spirit world. Another shaman may provide guidance in determining the external details of the person's practice (i.e., tools needed, altar setup [*teeb thaj neeb*], etc.). "The instructor [*xibfwb*] taught me to prepare the shaman tools and equipment," said one interviewee. "Also, the shaman taught me how to prepare the ceremony and provided a few words of caution." Nevertheless, this other shaman does not provide "training" or "education" in any of the skills needed to be a shaman healer. Such information is provided entirely by the spirits:

> During the seven days and seven nights of my illness, the creator
> already taught me all about the spiritual world. The creator guided
> me through the good and evil worlds. When I awoke, the shaman
> who came to assist me had already connected me to the spiritual
> and physical worlds. I was ready to be a healer. [Then] the instructor
> taught me how to divide the good and evil spirits, and then to sepa-
> rate them apart. Also, the instructor advised me how to follow my
> own path and provide only services I know I am capable of.

In this way, Hmong shamanism differs from many other shamanic traditions as described by popular American authors and promoters of neo-shamanistic practices in the United States, such as Michael Harner (1980). There is no indication that training, education, learning, or attempts to gain the right amount of knowledge to achieve a level of power are part of Hmong shaman traditions. Some shamans specialize in the very illness that afflicted them when they were chosen and will treat only people with similar ailments. Others may be referred to as "generalists" and treat more common spiritual causes of illness. It is also the case that a shaman must first be able to treat his or her own family in order to take on the role of community healer. Our interviews with shamans and patients indicate that the only changes that have occurred in shamanic practices in the United States are physical. For example, certain materials for tools, altars, and so forth are not available; neighbors in urban areas are often disturbed by animals sacrifices and the unusual noises that are part of traditional ritual practices. Appropriate space for rituals is often hard to find:

> The most difficult part is cleaning the house, because most families
> live in rental property. . . . In this country, we are living in a different
> environment. In the past, we were able to bring live animals into
> the house. We used the animals to perform rituals according to the
> tradition. In the beginning of the ceremony, we asked the animal
> permission and halfway through, we connected the animal to the
> spirit. After the spirit was willing to accept the animal, then the fam-
> ily would kill it to offer it to the spirit. Today, in the city we cannot

bring the animal into the home. We [must] kill the animal first and then conduct the healing ceremony after that.

The Role and Practice of the Shaman

The act of being "chosen" requires that the person make a lifelong commitment to being a healer. This includes the responsibility of being open and accessible to the entire community. It often involves certain dietary restrictions and ritual regimens and can be quite dangerous. Unlike physicians, Hmong shamans do not provide a physical diagnosis for the people they help. Rather, they try to determine the "soul status" (*ua neeb saib*) of the person by entering the spirit world to confront the spirit(s) causing the illness. The goal of the shamans' confrontation is not to overcome or defeat the spirits that have taken the soul. Instead, they engage in negotiation (*puaj dab*) for the person's soul. This process might involve offering gifts such as spirit money (*ntawv nyiaj*) and/or the souls of animals in exchange for the soul of the sick person. Negotiation with spirits often requires outsmarting the particular spirit and tricking it into giving up the person's soul. This engagement entails great risk, and stories are told of shamans who have died because the spirits they were negotiating with were too powerful for them and took their souls. The shaman sometimes plays the role of the negotiator, prosecutor, or defender of the victim. As one shaman explained: "We are there to rescue the victim. In order to communicate with the spirit, we have to use their language. Our purpose is to have a good understanding of each other and a mutual respect of one another. Also, we are there to make peace between good and evil." It is clear from our interviews that Hmong shamans are quite specific in their practices, but also see themselves as part of a larger system of healing.

As a community resource, Hmong shamans continue the tradition of providing their services at no charge. In this way, they differ from some other shamanic traditions and from the Western health care system Hmong people face in the United States. When a family approaches a shaman and asks for help for an ill person, the shaman takes several steps to determine if it will be possible to provide assistance. The shaman never charges for his or her services. One of the patient interviewees learned this tradition from a parent who was a shaman: "I know my mother does not accept many gifts from people. One time, I asked her why. She explained it to me that a true healer is sent to save people's lives from the evil. A chosen healer has a high place in heaven and is honest and trustworthy. Shamans are told by their spiritual guides not to cheat vulnerable people or take advantage of people." Shamans themselves also indicated that payment is not a part of their healing tradition: "I am an old healer [in practice for thirty years]. . . . In all my ceremonies, I never asked

Pahoua Vue, a Hmong shaman. Used with permission from Scott Takushi and St. Paul Pioneer Press.

for any price. Whether they gave me any appreciation or not, again, I never asked. I let people decide for themselves. This is a traditional culture that passes down from the other healers and the creator." This is not to say there are no costs involved for the family of the person who is ill. There may be a need to provide an animal for sacrifice. Incense (*xyab*) must be burned, spirit money provided, a temporary altar built, and so on. Also, families may choose to reward the shaman in some way for a successful soul retrieval, although, as just noted, the shaman "let[s] people decide for themselves." This feature of providing care at no charge has continued to be the normal practice even in this highly commodified and commodifying society.

Other changes, however, have occurred in the practice of shamanism in the United States. We asked our interviewees what has changed for them and what difficulties they have encountered. We determined that most of these difficulties involved the physical conditions in which Hmong families live here and the availability of materials native to Southeast Asia and not commonly found here. According to one interviewee, "There are many physical things for me to do, such as battling with a new culture and new illnesses that I could not deal with." Another provided the following account:

> The most difficult thing in this country is that we are not able to perform the rituals like in the past. I could give you some examples. When we arrived in this country, we lived in a rental house or a house was connected to another neighbor. We could not perform a loud ceremony. We could not bring live animals home either. In order to be a successful healing ceremony, you need them to be alive, because you need to present the animal's spirit to the evil spirit. The city ordinance does not allow us to bring a pig or chicken to the city. Today, we go to the animal's farm and throw the cow's horn [*thau kua*] on the ground to appease the animal for offering its life to the cause and then we bring the body home. According to the traditional ritual, we cannot connect the animal's spirit to the human's spirit. We can only connect the spirits when the animal is still alive. Now, the family will bring the body home and perform half of the ceremony. I know some shaman ceremonies have to be redone or are not able to be conducted according to the traditional way. This is very difficult for us to do.

Hmong families may live in crowded neighborhoods, among neighbors who are not friendly to Hmong ritual life, as described in the following comments:

> Here, it is a little hard for those shamans and families who do not have a private home. The ceremonies may take place in a close neighborhood or small house where the chanting and drumming can be very noisy. The neighbors may complain. Also, the family cannot bring the live animals into the city and to the home. The city does not approve of bringing a large animal to a crowded neighborhood. It is not like in Laos, where we are free to conduct the ceremony openly.
>
> When we conducted the ceremony in a crowded neighborhood, people heard the chanting and drumming. They knocked at our door or window to ask us to keep the noise down. Some even called the police.
>
> The neighbors may ask why the family is making so much noise or why the family brings live chickens into their home. Back in Laos, the families were able to bring live pigs or chickens into their house for the ceremony, but here they cannot do it anymore.

Often the traditional shaman tools and materials are unavailable in this country. As one shaman noted, "I don't have all the tools or a permanent place to establish a proper altar." Another commented, "Some of the shaman's tools are not available. I had to create something different and pretend it was a tool for the ceremony." Although these physical obstructions and changes have required changes in shaman practices here, basic use of the ancient traditions within the Twin Cities Hmong community continues. We have even had some contact with young people who either were born here or arrived here as small children and who have been "chosen" to follow the shaman's way.

The World of the Patients

Turning to Shamans, Turning to Physicians

The Hmong community recognizes the need for various types of health care services. Shamanism appears to be widely used—twenty-four of our thirty-two patient interviewees reported using a shaman. But shamanism is often used in conjunction with seeing a physician and only rarely without also seeking biomedical care. This is true regardless of age, gender, length of time in the country, or religious orientation. Two-thirds of the patients interviewed—twenty-two out of thirty-two—reported regularly seeking both shamanic and biomedical treatment but not both. Just two of all thirty-two interviewees used only shamanic care. The other third of the patients reported using either shamanic or biomedical care, but not both.

Shamans and shamanism are not opposed to conventional physician care. All eleven shamans had sought physician care for themselves. Three identified specific instances of collaborating with a physician in patient care. Six of the eleven shamans interviewed specifically indicated that they suggested people seek medical advice for a variety of symptoms. A typical response to our question "Do you ever suggest that a person you are helping go to a medical doctor" was: "It depends on the situation. If I knew the patient's problem was caused by physical harm, I advised him or her to visit the doctors to do an X ray and further examination." However, of all forty-three individuals interviewed, only one identified a physician who had made a referral to a shaman.

Factors Influencing the Choice of Care

In part, the choice to seek shamanic care is based on a person's age and the length of time he or she has been in the United States. The Hmong began arriving in the United States in 1975. Among the twenty-six subjects over the age of thirty, nineteen use both shamans and physicians regularly, four use physicians only, and two use shamans only. In contrast, of the sixteen subjects under the age of thirty, half use both physicians and shamans, and half use only physicians; five use shamans only. Among the twelve persons who have been in the United States for more than twenty years, eleven use both shamans and physicians, while none use physicians only. In contrast, of the nineteen persons who have been in the United States for less than twenty years, eleven use both shamans and physicians and eight use physicians only.

A major factor in the choice of care involves the perceived cause of the illness. For example, all twenty-two patients who turn to both shamans and physicians identified using the shaman for spiritual illnesses (loss of spirit, night fright, unhappiness, stress). They were clear that a shaman's role is to treat the spiritual causes of illness and to retrieve the lost souls of the sick.

A spiritual cause may be indicated by general, nonspecific symptoms such as fatigue, loss of energy, nightmares, bodily weakness, or loneliness. Hmong patients who use both shaman and medical practitioners might view these as problems of a spiritual nature and first seek help from a shaman. If the shaman is able to help them, then they may not feel the need to seek medical help. It may also be the case that the physician is perceived as not having been fully able to address the problem. Both of the following quotations, for example, illustrate the limited nature of the reliance on biomedicine, coinciding with the willingness to work across systems:

> We believe the traditional religion and the medical treatment. If we cannot fully depend on the medical support, we reach out to the traditional healing. Both treatments are good for us. We can depend on either one. They are there to save us.
>
> We need many supports and depend on both. If the person is ill and the doctor cannot diagnose the cause, the person may get worse. We may reach out to the shaman to conduct a ceremony to examine the spiritual causes. We need the shaman ceremony

The small percentage of people who do not seek Western treatment will try a variety of traditional healing practices, including shamanism, herbalism (kws tshuaj), and other home remedies and magic healing (khawv koob). Although the term "magic" is often considered problematic in religious studies, "magic healing" is the only term we have heard as an adequate translation for khawv koob. Fourteen of the thirty-two subjects report using herbal medicines. (This number includes two of the eight subjects who reported only resorting to physicians for their medical care.)

As Hmong have lived in the United States for longer periods of time, they have found themselves suffering from diseases more common in communities of the urban poor in the United States. One interviewee observed the prevalence of diabetes, high blood pressure, cholesterol problems, and cancer. "For the ones listed above," he added, "we never heard of [them] back in our country. We need to understand and know what they are." The very unfamiliarity of some of these conditions generates confusion and attempts to understand the reasons for new afflictions. As another interviewee noted, "I'm not quite sure . . . why these illness[es] occur, but I think it could be that our lifestyle has changed. Because when we lived in Laos, we live by the sun, we had the way of love and close relationships, trust of each other in our communities and through families and relatives. We also walked a lot and our food didn't have a lot of chemicals, and in that way our bodies functioned well, and we didn't have a lot of illness."

Both shaman practitioners and Hmong patients recognize the need for the biomedical treatment of chronic conditions such as dizziness, intestinal problems, diabetes, high blood pressure, ulcers, and the like. They are clear that shamans can only do so much, given that their role is to treat the spiritual causes of illness and retrieve the souls of the sick. Of the two-thirds of our interviewees who have tried both shaman and Western treatments, most have had positive and negative results from both.

Within the Hmong community, reputation and experience determine a healer's effectiveness. This is true for both a shaman and a physician. As noted by one subject, "Every person we go to for help, we have to be aware of their background and have a strong belief in their professional field." The physician's capacity to listen well also influences the perception of his or her effectiveness. When a doctor was not able to help, the subjects generally felt that it was because he or she did not listen well enough or did not understand Hmong cultural background well enough to know what to do. As one commented, "I think the workers and doctors, the way they ask questions and listen to how Hmong explain their illness is very important because the person may have many illness[es] in their body or may be stress[ed] and want to inform a doctor and would like for him or her to listen. Although the doctor may not consider it to be important, but the doctor should try their best to listen to what we are saying and to see what is going on." Religious orientation also affects Hmong heath care choices. Of the eighteen participants who identified themselves as turning only to traditional religion, or "old religion," none used physicians only. Of the seven subjects who identified themselves as Christian, or "new religion," none used shamans only. Many Hmong Christians—particularly those involved in more fundamentalist denominations—may shy away from shaman ceremonies, name-calling ceremonies, and other traditional animist practices because these are seen as going against the beliefs and practices of the "new religion." As one patient interviewee explained:

> Well, our family is converted to Christianity now, and we don't practice shamanism anymore. We still appreciate what the shaman can offer to people. Now, we see doctors when we are sick. We see our doctor and then ask our pastor to pray for us. My family stopped practicing the traditional healing because my husband passed away in Laos. We don't have anyone in the family who knows the ritual ceremony well. My children will not be able to continue the tradi-

tion. The church is a place where my children can go and pray for help.

The one-fourth of our interviewees who seek only Western medical treatment do so specifically for religious reasons. In such cases, they have converted to Christianity and no longer follow the traditional "old" religious practices.

However, it is important to understand that there is a continuum of practices within the Hmong community related to new and old religions. We found, for example, that religious orientation did not affect herbal medicine use. Half of the participants who identified themselves either as following traditional religion only or as Christian reported using herbal medicines. Gender also appeared to affect Hmong health care choices regarding use of medicinal herbs. Eleven of the fourteen subjects who reported using herbs were female. Even some converted Christians continue to use herbal medicine and traditional home remedies such as cupping (*txhuav*), spoon rubbing (*kav*), fright release (*dhaws ceeb*), and other such practices. Christian Hmong who are more liberal may continue to practice some traditions such as name-calling ceremonies, blessing ceremonies, or magic healing. Likewise, while Hmong animists continue to call on the shaman and other traditional healers, they may also call on Christian leaders, pastors, and priests to help them. Some Hmong individuals and families have gone from animism to Christianity back to animism based on health and illness circumstances.

As indicated earlier, our data reveal that issues related to general acculturation clearly affect Hmong health care choices. Conversion to Christianity, access to other health care choices, effects of new or previously unidentified illnesses, and changes in living conditions are all elements that have impacted Hmong people and healing traditions in this country. Nevertheless, it is also clear that a large percentage of Hmong people, whatever their circumstances here, still rely on the traditional and proven methods their ancestors practiced before them.

Practical Guide for Clinicians

Important culturally based diagnoses within the Hmong community include "loss of soul," a devastating condition that might be termed "major depression" but can only be healed by a shaman. Physicians and other health professionals must anticipate the presence of religious and spiritual concerns in Hmong adult and pediatric care. The following questions, developed by Arthur Kleinman (1978: 25b), are currently taught to many medical students:

1. What do you call your sickness? What problems has this caused?
2. What do you think has caused the problem?

3. Why do you think it started when it did?
4. What do you think the sickness does? How does it work?
5. How severe is the illness?
6. What kind of treatment do you think you need?
7. What do you fear most about the sickness?

New questions to consider when serving a Hmong patient include the following:

1. *Do you practice the new ways or the old ways?* This is the equivalent of asking, "Are you Christian or animist?" The answer to this question helps physicians to understand their patient's subjective experience of, and subjective understanding of, ultimate reality. This understanding is important for efficient, effective, and satisfactory care for both parties.

2. *Are you working with any other healers?* The answer to this question helps physicians to comprehend how the patient and/or family wants their religious and/or spiritual beliefs to be seen as resources. This question may help physicians to determine appropriate referrals to chaplains, clergy, or traditional healers for spiritual care.

3. *Are you using any herbs for your condition?* The use of culinary and medicinal herbs for healing is widely practiced in the Hmong community. These herbs are pharmacologically active, albeit mildly so when used appropriately. Research into the indications and contraindications is being conducted by the University of Minnesota Center for Spirituality and Healing and the Bell Museum of Natural History.

4. *What else are you using to help with your condition?* It is common for Hmong elders and heads of households to offer traditional "home remedies" to their family members. (It must be understood that "family" is a very broad term that can include distant relatives who are acknowledged for their abilities in certain types of healing.)

Conclusion

The foremost Hmong traditional healer is the shaman, who is considered an important cultural resource by both Hmong Christians and animists. There is no equivalent health professional in Western biomedicine: the power of the shaman goes beyond the capacities and expertise of physicians. Our focused interviews suggest that Hmong shamanism has become an active form of religious healing in the Twin Cities of Minneapolis and St. Paul. Shamanism appears to be considered effective care by nearly the entire Hmong community. Some Hmong who see physicians continue to rely on shamans for their trusted healing skills and abilities to restore health and balance of the soul and body. Conservative Hmong Christians tend to dismiss these ancient healing practices as contrary to their religious beliefs. However, some Hmong individuals and families have gone from animism to Christianity and back to animism based on health or illness circumstances. A small minority of practicing Hmong Christians use a shaman and always do so in conjunction with a physician.

Hmong religion and healing traditions have not simply been decontextualized; rather, they have been recontextualized. The traditional social support system for healing has not been weakened so much as re-formed. Since the shaman continues to play an important and powerful role in the interpretation of the world and of personal lives, he or she may represent a powerful health care professional for referrals and collaborative care. Hmong cultural attitudes, values, and behaviors influence with whom, when, where, and why a Hmong person will use Western medicine. To provide the most respectful health care, the majority culture will need to further understand the power and importance of Hmong healing traditions such as shamanism. Despite twenty-five years of Hmong acculturation and conversion to Christianity, Hmong shamanism maintains its crucial role in health and healing.

All this suggests that practitioners have an even greater responsibility to listen for what Kleinman Eisenberg, and Good (1978) refer to as the "ethnomedical pathogenesis"—that is, the power of belief to either cause or heal illness. As we continue to serve and interact with the Hmong, we need to remind ourselves constantly about the great dangers that come with stereotyping. One Hmong person's beliefs, values, and practices may differ greatly from those of the Hmong person next to her. Thus, seeking to understand what is most important to each individual and his or her family should be the goal in establishing a healthy relationship.

NOTES

The project was developed and administered by Creative Theatre Unlimited of St. Paul, Minnesota, a nonprofit arts organization with a mission of community building through the arts. Since the early 1980s, Creative Theatre Unlimited has worked with Hmong artists and community leaders to preserve and promote Hmong arts and culture. Funding for this project was provided by the Foundation Fund of UCare Minnesota (the fourth largest HMO in the state), with further support from the University of Minnesota's Center for Spirituality and Healing. Tapes and transcripts of interviews from this project will be stored with the Archives of Creative Theatre Unlimited at the Andersen Library, University of Minnesota, Minneapolis.

Special thanks to our community participants, including the shamans, interviewees, and other participants. Much appreciation also goes to our program consultants: Linda L. Barnes, Director, Boston Healing Landscape Project, Boston University School of Medicine, and Assistant Professor, Boston University School of Medicine; and Paul D. Numrich, Co-Principal Investigator of the Religion, Immigration and

Civil Society in Chicago Project, Visiting Associate Research Professor, Loyola University, Chicago.

1. Animism is the belief that every person, animal, and object has a spiritual element that survives independently and can directly affect the physical world.

2. Other Hmong healing traditions include *Kws tshuaj* (pronounced *"kau chua"*), one who knows about herbal medicine; and *Tu kws khawv koob* (*"du gu ker kong"*), magic healer; a variety of home remedies that most people practice from time to time. See the glossary of Hmong terms. All these practices have remained intact in the transition of Hmong people from Southeast Asia to the United States.

REFERENCES

Adler, S. R. 1995. Refugee Stress and Folk Belief: Hmong Sudden Deaths. *Social Science and Medicine* 40:1623–29.
Conquergood, Dwight. 1989. *I Am a Shaman: A Hmong Life Story with Ethnographic Commentary*. Minneapolis: University of Minnesota Press.
Fadiman, Anne. 1997. *The Spirit Catches You and You Fall Down*. New York: Farrar, Straus and Giroux.
Harner, Michael. 1980. *The Way of the Shaman*. San Francisco: Harper SanFrancisco.
Kleinman, Arthur, Leon Eisenberg, and Byron Good. 1978. Culture, Illness, and Care: Clinical Lessons from Anthropologic and Cross-Cultural Research. *Annals of Internal Medicine* 88:251–58.

28

Spirituality and the Healing of Addictions: A Shamanic Drumming Approach

Michael Winkelman

One area of American medicine in which spirituality is widely considered a vital aspect of healing is in substance abuse rehabilitation (Smith 1994; Green, Fullilove, and Fullilove 1998; Booth and Martin 1998). While mainstream spiritual healing practices are found in Alcoholics Anonymous, a variety of other spiritual practices are also used in substance abuse rehabilitation (e.g., see Winkelman 2001a; Heggenhougen 1997; Jilek 1994). This chapter assesses the role of community drumming and shamanic programs in healing addiction. The putative effectiveness of these practices in treating substance abuse is proposed to derive from the psychobiological dynamics of the altered states of consciousness and other psychophysiological changes they produce. The psychobiological and psychophysiological processes underlying shamanic practices are described to illustrate their potential contributions to the resolution of addiction.

Spirituality and the Healing of Addictions

The epidemiological literature indicates that spiritual engagement provides a protective factor against substance abuse and facilitates recovery (Miller 1998). The vital role of spirituality in substance abuse rehabilitation is widely accepted in the addiction treatment industry (Christopher 1992). Spiritual healing of addiction is primarily provided through Alcoholics Anonymous (AA) and associated organizations such as Narcotics Anonymous. The deeply entrenched role of AA in the addictions treatment industry is reflected in the requirement for attendance at as many as seven meetings a week that many treatment programs have for their clients and in boards of medical examiners' requirement that addicted physicians attend AA.

Nonetheless, the role of spirituality in substance abuse rehabilitation remains controversial. Some object to inclusion of religious or spiritual treatments on the grounds that the effects derive from social mechanisms not requiring a religious orientation. The effectiveness of AA is generally dependent on participants becoming long-term regular members (Project MATCH Research Group 1997). The correlation of virtually all spiritual and religious variables with lower substance abuse and more favorable outcomes in recovery has been repeatedly established, but which aspects facilitate recovery have not been precisely identified (Booth and Martin 1998). The general effects of religious participation on health are indicated by hundreds of epidemiological studies that associate religious participation with lower morbidity and mortality rates (Levin 1994a, 1994b). Levin points outs that questions remain regarding the mechanisms of religion's causal effects, for example, are benefits produced by church attendance, "moral" behaviors, spiritual experiences, contact with a higher power, or a sense of unity with the universe. Correlations of religiosity measures with virtually every health outcome measure suggest that the causal effects of religion on health probably involve a variety mechanisms.

Researchers have attempted to elucidate these pathways and causal mechanisms (see Byrd 1988; Levin 1994a, 1994b; Strawbridge et al. 1997). Religious activities have recognized effects on health through behavioral, psychosocial, and psychodynamic mechanisms (e.g., diet, drugs, activities, relationships, lifestyle). Religion's psychosocial and behavioral pathways include a larger social network and support system, social ties that can provide a network that enables people to cope better with problems, reducing stress, depression, and self-destructive behaviors and providing needed resources. Religion also has psychodynamic effects through beliefs and their consequences for peacefulness and self-confidence that can help reduce stress, anxiety, and conflict, creating emotionally tranquil states. Religion's psychosocial effects provide a sense of belongingness and meaningfulness that may impact health. Religious activities may also induce altered states of consciousness, providing an "alternative high" that meets addicts' needs for altering their consciousness (Heggenhougen 1997; Winkelman 2001a).

Recognition of the important role of spirituality in rehabilitation and the diverse mechanisms through which spirituality may have its positive effects has led to other approaches for inducing these salubrious experiences. One of these developments involves community drumming circles and shamanic drumming activities as adjuncts to conventional rehabilitation programs. This chapter reports on four programs that incorporate community and shamanic drumming activities into rehabilitation programs.[1] These activities have a variety of positive effects that counselors and participants interpret in terms of their spiritual and personal impacts. The apparent effects of these activities are related to psychobiological perspectives derived from studies of shamanism. The shamanic paradigm links shamanic universals to aspects of an evolved human psychology and a "neurotheology" that helps illustrate why spirituality can address the physiological dynamics of addiction.

Contemporary Shamanic Approaches to Addictions Treatment

Contemporary utilizations of shamanic approaches in addictions treatments are found both worldwide (Winkelman 2001a) and in the United States (Winkelman 2003); some of the latter are described briefly here. Mark Seaman provides drumming activities in both adolescent and adult programs at the Caron Foundation in Wernersville, Pennsylvania, a nationally recognized substance abuse treatment center. Seaman also provides similar drumming programs for schools, prisons, and corporations. These programs begin informally, with people picking up percussion instruments as they come in and doing what they want with them. Warm-up exercises allow participants to feel comfortable with the drums and learn how to hit them without hurting their hands. Using coordinated chanting and singing activities, Seaman lays the groundwork for nonverbal communication and coordinated drumming activities. Each participant gets to improvise on the drum "to show how they feel" and produce a feeling of release. Then Seaman introduces a drumming "heartbeat," a pulse rhythm that allows people to "let go," and leading to directed visualization and meditation activities. Seaman makes verbal connections to the Alcoholics Anonymous "higher power" and combines chimes and bells to get people relaxed and focused on internal imagery. He then guides them on a journey into nature to connect with a higher power and achieve forgiveness, acceptance, and surrender. Verbal suggestions encourage release of guilt, healing the damage caused by participants' addictions, and engage processes of "letting go" and accepting change.

Ed Mikenas works in the Lynchburg Day Program in Lynchburg, Virginia, and has provided drumming activities as prevention and recovery resources in after-school programs, for city workers, and in workshops and classes at conferences and at Roanoke College. Mikenas uses drumming to teach people to express themselves and rebuild their emotional health through releasing and integrating their emotions. Mikenas introduces drumming in the context of Afro-Cuban and Brazilian rhythms and the Afro-Caribbean Yoruba-based religions. He emphasizes that this drumming involves an altered state of consciousness and a form of "possession," enabling the participant to possess the spirits. Drumming is what drives the possession; it is not the participants, however, but the spirits who are being possessed by the person. These spirit relationships help people access their unconscious dynamics, connect with a spiritual "higher power," and reestablish connections with their "natural selves" through enhanced community dynamics. Mikenas uses drumming to activate the substance abuse recovery process and reinforce its principles. Participants are allowed to experiment with a variety of percussion instruments. Mikenas helps them learn to play increasingly complex rhythms, beginning with warm-up exercises to coordinate the group and building up to more complex movements and polyrhythmic activities

Myron Eshowsky has a M.A. in counseling and is trained as a shamanic counselor by the Foundation for Shamanic Studies. He has applied shamanic counseling and spiritual perspectives to address clients' psychological, emotional, and spiritual problems (Eshowsky 1993), accepting the nonmaterial spiritual dimensions as real and addressing soul wounding. Shamanic journeying is used to find out information about clients, their power animals, spiritual intrusions, and soul loss. He has worked with clients with significant mental health issues, including sexual abuse, suicidal tendencies, and borderline personality disorders. He also uses drumming groups and shamanic journeying activities for groups of adolescents, particularly at-risk youth and gangs, and has offered his programs through prisons, mental health centers, community-based groups, hospitals, and schools (Eshowsky 1998, 1999). Eshowsky's programs generally engage the group in drumming activities and teach participants to journey on their own, adding storytelling, dancing, divination, and group ceremonies for healing work. He may also journey to obtain information about clients and incorporates information acquired into ritual healings for power animal and soul recovery, and determination of spiritual intrusions and other nonordinary reality effects. His work with adolescents focuses on helping them to find ways to define who they are and their sense of purpose. Ceremony and ritual provide a context to connect with their issues and provide healing and a sense of belonging.

Daniel Smith is a licensed clinical social worker and former director of hospital-based addiction programs who introduced drumming into substance abuse rehabilitation based on his training by the Foundation for Shamanic Studies. He has taught shamanic techniques to other counselors of psychiatric and chemical-dependent clients and at wellness events, conferences, and retreats. Smith, who has worked in a hospital operated by Catholics but has found a way to incorporate shamanic principles in his work, explains, "The key to success is translating the language of core shamanism into client-friendly and supervisor-friendly terms" (2000: 8). Smith creates this bridging of shamanic language with activities such as yoga, breathwork, inner-child issues, music therapy, and mask making. Shamanic healing involves "opening a door, through which it is up to the participant to walk, run, or shut." Smith considers the shamanic approach most appropriate for those with repeated relapse, for clients who understand the dynamics of recovery but cannot achieve sobriety. The shamanic approach helps clients to help themselves but also produces a spiritual awakening and can be used for soul retrieval, depossession and extraction, and power animal recovery, activities that often produce a profound change in addicts' response to life.

Effects of Drumming in Addiction Treatment

Seaman suggests that while drumming is generally presented as a creative activity to allow clients to express themselves, other notable effects include providing a means of nonverbal expression; inducing spiritual experience that is upbeat, fun, and easy; producing "letting-go" and rebirthing experience; allowing people to leave behind the aspects of addiction; and providing visualization activities that allow clients to engage with new possibilities. He told me, "Drumming produces a sense of connectedness and community, integrating body, mind, and spirit." Drumming particularly benefits the intragroup dynamics when they are stressed by conflict, giving the group a sense of community and connectedness, inducing relaxation, and easing tensions through engaging emotions and provoking strong emotional release. Drumming induces an altered state of consciousness, experienced as a rush of energy from the vibrations and energy. Drumming produces a sense of connectedness; a reconnection with the body, self, soul, and higher power; and a sense of connectedness with community.

Mikenas reports many different effects on the participants:

- An altered state of consciousness that entrains the brain and heals emotions. The drum's sound and rhythms are energy that brings up emotional issues. Mikenas adds, "But if you drum long enough, it works as an 'eraser' to remove the effects of trauma. The frequencies of the drums . . . work . . . both sides of your brain; it integrates information.
- Sensorimotor coordination and increased bodily awareness. Drumming coordinates sound and movement that assist in mental, physical, and emotional development processes.
- Communication skills, especially nonverbal. Drumming is a form of communication and "helps you change speaking, feeling, and acting. Drumming helps you address the feelings, the heart, and helps you learn to act from the heart. Drumming also helps you focus and consequently get your needs met. Drumming teaches nurturing, respecting, having fun, participation, and personal relationships."
- Social skills, leadership, and relationship building. Participation in group drumming can enhance the recovery process by instilling lead-

ership and confidence and addressing uncertainty and insecurity. Drumming provides an opportunity to discover personal potentials in a context that requires cooperation and group coordination.
• Personal development and emotional integration. Mikenas suggests that drumming produces a feeling of order: "Drumming helps bring out part of human nature, makes us feel more complete. Drumming gives you pleasurable feelings without having to rely upon addictive substances." Drumming has visceral and emotional effects that make you feel good.

Eshowsky notes the powerful effects of drumming and shamanic journeying in calming teens down, inducing a sense of peacefulness and spiritual experience that allows them to talk about their concerns. He also reports that gang kids have reductions in drug use, drug-related violence, and contact with the criminal justice system that lead to enhanced school participation and performance. Eshowsky (1993, 1998, 1999) reports dramatic results, particularly for people in desperate situations who have not been helped by other counseling modalities. His success includes work with youth in street gangs, in which he helps address despair and powerlessness, using the principles of core shamanism to address soul loss, alienation, disconnectedness, and other consequences of violence, trauma, and abuse.

Daniel Smith sees shamanic work as reintegrating aspects of the self, using soul retrieval and power animal retrieval to redress traumatic assaults that have led individuals to drug abuse. Shamanic journeys provide a regression that gives access to these experiences by providing a context that induces openness and reduces barriers to awareness. Shamanic journeys provide access to entities—ancestors, guides, and allies—that facilitate resolution of these traumas through empowerment. Mask-making and other rituals facilitate the incorporation of helping spirits and changes in personality, creating a new sense of self as a recovering person. Shamanic healing experiences bring people directly into contact with healing spiritual forces. Shamanic work also focuses on the whole body, providing an integration at physical, psychological, social, and spiritual levels. Drumming and dance can provide both cognitive restructuring and physical exercise, as do yoga activities and breathwork, which produce mental-physical bridging. Rituals using symbols of flight (birds, feathers) help prompt visionary experiences and can be used to orient clients to the elementals and directions that provide a sense of calm, inner balance, and connection with a greater power. Rituals produce a connection with the power of the universe and an externalization of one's own knowledge, enhancing clients' sense of empowerment.

In sum, drumming and shamanic activities may enhance recovery from addiction through a variety of psychological, social, and physiological mechanisms. Drumming induces pleasurable experiences and may enhance awareness of preconscious dynamics and repressed emotional trauma; it also can facilitate a reintegration of self, addressing the self-centeredness, isolation, and alienation characteristic of addiction and creating a sense of connectedness with self and others. Drumming activities can provide a secular approach to accessing spiritual experiences; combined with shamanic practices, they provide direct and powerful means of inducing a range of spiritual experiences. Physiological effects of drumming are illustrated in the following psychobiological assessment of shamanism.

Psychobiological Bases of Shamanism

The term "shaman" is widely employed to refer to spiritual, religious, and healing practitioners around the world. Cross-cultural evidence (Winkelman 1992) supports the contention that shamanism is a cross-cultural phenomenon with universal features based in human psychobiology (Winkelman 1997, 2000, 2002).[2] The strikingly similar forms of spiritual healing in hunter-gatherer societies around the world reflect a psychobiological foundation in an evolved psychology. This psychobiological basis helps explain the universals of shamanism, its persistence and modern revivals in neo-shamanism, and its application in contemporary healing practices, including substance abuse treatment.

Although the shamans of hunter-gatherer societies differ in important ways from the contemporary "neo-shamans," they both share characteristics with healers found in cultures around the world. Their similarities include Eliade's (1964) classic characterization of the shaman as someone who enters into "ecstasy" (an altered state of consciousness [ASC]) to interact with the spirit world on behalf of the community. In other papers (1990, 1992) I have suggested the use of the term "shamanistic healer" to refer to these universally distributed practices based in the same biological potentials that gave rise to shamanism. All cultures have institutionalized activities involving the use of ASC in community rituals to interact with the spirits for healing and divination.

These universal features of shamanism reflect brain processes and fundamental structures of consciousness (Winkelman 1997, 2000, 2002). These neurological perspectives on shamanism are based in the functional effects of ASC (Mandell 1980; Winkelman 1992, 2000), community relations (Frecska and Kulscar 1989), and innate modular brain structures that evolved to support specialized human cognition (see Winkelman 2000, 2002). The brain structures that provide foundations for shamanism are involved in the production of integrative physiological, psychological, and social processes. The physiological effects of ASCs involve integrative brain conditions that provide for the functional effects of "ecstasy" and the roles of drumming, chanting, music, dancing, and ritual enactment. The community dynamics produce individual integration into the social group, bonding of social groups, and physiological changes that enhance bonding and healing. Integrative cognitive synthesis is produced by metaphoric re-representation based in the use of specialized knowledge systems of innate modules that use spirits to represent self and others. These metaphoric representations use specialized natural symbolic systems for representation of self and others and manifested in universals of shamanism such as animism, animal spirits, totemism, and soul flight.

ASC, spirits, and community rituals have psychobiological bases that have implications for addictions recovery in (1) the psychological and physiological effects of ASC; (2) the psychodynamic effects of spirit interactions and their self-transformation processes of death and rebirth and soul and power animal recovery; and (3) the community rituals that produce psychological and physiological changes, including elicitation of the body's opioid systems.

ASC: The Integrative Mode of Consciousness

Ecstasy, or ASC, central to shamans' selection, training, and professional practice, is a natural response of the brain and nervous system. ASCs are typically induced through singing, chanting, drumming, and dancing. Other ASC-induction practices include fasting and water restrictions; prolonged periods of sleeplessness; deliberate sleep and dream incubation; austerities such as temperature exposures and painful mutilations of the body; and hallucinogens and other plant medicines. These practices have the same basic overall physiological effects, involving elicitation of the relaxation response and synchronization of brain waves across functional levels of the brain (Winkelman 1992, 2000). Shamanistic practices produce changes in the brains' opioid levels and serotonergic functioning. A variety of shamanic procedures, including drumming, dancing, and group activities, induce release of the body's own opioids (see Prince 1982; Winkelman 1997). These ASCs also enhance the operation of the body's serotonergic system, which is depleted from chronic substance abuse.

Shamanic ASCs involve a mode of consciousness, a natural response of the brain to produce physiological, functional, and psychological integration (Winkelman 2000). The physiological dynamics of ASCs involve activating the autonomic nervous system to the point of exhaustion and collapse; the shaman may appear unconscious but experiences a vivid internal consciousness. This relaxation may also be entered directly through repose and an internal focus of attention. The relaxation response is part of the body's cycles of balance, with adaptive advantages, including stress reduction, growth, and physiological restoration.

The shaman's ASC reflects the integrative mode of consciousness, a normal brain response manifested in synchronized brain wave patterns in the theta (3–6 cycles per second) and slow alpha (6–8 cycles per second) ranges

(Winkelman 2000). The limbic brain system (also referred to as the "emotional brain" and the "paleomammalian brain") produces these slow-wave patterns through serotonin-based linkages between the limbic and lower brain structures. These connections produce strongly coherent and synchronized theta brain wave patterns manifested in ascending slow-wave discharges that synchronize the frontal areas of the brain with coherent slow-wave discharges in the alpha and theta ranges (Mandell 1980; Winkelman 1992, 2000). A primary effect is integrating preverbal information into the personal and language-mediated activities of the frontal cortex.

VISIONARY EXPERIENCE AS PRESENTATIONAL SYMBOLISM. The shamanic ASC is characterized by visual experiences (Noll 1985). These experiences involve an innate capacity, known as "presentational symbolism" (Hunt 1995), that reflects basic structures of the preverbal symbolic mind and depictions of attachments, emotions, and self-processes and interpersonal processes. These experiences can enhance self-awareness, insight, and emotional integration and provide adaptive advantages in analysis, synthesis, and planning. Visions are a natural phenomenon involving release of suppression of the visual cortex and the same brain substrates used in processing of perceptual information. Imagery plays a fundamental role in cognition, providing a basis for integration across domains of experience and different levels of information processing (Winkelman 2000). Mental imagery integrates unconscious psychophysiological information with affective or emotional levels, linking somatic and cognitive experience. Images are a form of psychobiological communication experienced in a preverbal symbol system (Achterberg 1985).

Metaphoric Thought and Self-Representation

Human evolution involved the development of specialized information-processing modules for recognition of animal species (natural history intelligence), self-conceptualization, and mental attributions regarding social "others" ("mind reading"). These specialized forms of knowledge production are combined in fundamental features of shamanism—animism, totemism, and animal spirits—that involve self-representation. The spirit world involves use of innate representation modules for understanding self and social others. Animal allies involve use of natural history intelligence, employing capacities for representing animal species in the formation of personal and social identities. These uses of animal species models to represent the social and self domains provide mechanisms for differentiation and expression of self-identity and social identity, conceptualizing humans through models provided by the natural world.

Shamanism uses the natural history module to incorporate animal spirits as a part of identity and powers. These allies or guardian spirits have psychosocial functions in empowering people in the transition to adulthood, providing powers and strength and guiding the individual in personal and social choices (Swanson 1973). Guardian spirits become aspects of one's personal power and identity. Animals as aspects of self-representation involve "sacred others," the intersection of the spiritual and social worlds in cultural processes. Spirit representations produce a symbolic self and provide for resolution of social contradictions in the development of the self. Spirit beliefs can exemplify norms for the self and for one's psychosocial relations, structuring individual psychodynamics and social behavior. These spirit models for the self provide mechanisms for the management of emotions and attachments. Animal powers and guardians provide alternate forms of self-representation and identity that facilitate social adaptation. Animal spirit concepts of one's self provide control agents for mediating conflict between the different social and personal demands and instinctive selves.

Forms of self-representation are found in the shaman's "soul journey" or "soul flight." The shaman's soul journey reflects innate structures reported cross-culturally and represents self from the "other's" perspective (Hunt 1995), providing self-representations that create forms of self-transcendence. Shamanic identity is also illustrated in the "death and rebirth" experience, a crisis involving illness, suffering, and attacks by spirits, leading to the experience of death and dismemberment. This is followed by a reconstruction with the addition of spirit allies and powers.

Death and rebirth experiences reflect innate processes of self-transformation, a natural response to overwhelming stress and intrapsychic conflicts experienced in symbolic images of bodily destruction. This breakdown of self activates innate drives toward toward psychological integration (Laughlin, McManus, and d'Aquili 1992). These involve aspects of identity change crucial for the recovering addict, providing a change in character and identity that enables addicts to overcome their shortcomings. The concept of animal powers can play a number of roles in healing the addict. Animal powers provide connections with unconscious aspects of the self, contributing to a change of identity. Smith (2000) and Harner and Harner (2001) indicate that soul loss is a significant feature of the dynamics of the chronic recidivist. Soul recovery (cf. Ingerman 1991) reintegrates dissociated aspects of the self alienated by trauma, reconnecting the individual with a broader collectivity.

Community Healing

Shamanic healing traditionally is carried out on behalf of a community, reflecting the fundamental role of the social group in healing. In the case of recovery from addictions, the community provides a therapeutic group that can motivate sobriety and treatment adherence, as well as a social group that reinforces sobriety, spirituality, and changes in identity. The community context also provides social resources for problem solving, resource availability, and social support central to maintaining stability, and reinforcement for a new identity as a recovering addict. Community also plays an important role in psychophysiological transformation and destabilization.

Frecska and Kulcsar (1989; see also Winkelman 1997, 2000) provide evidence that rituals involving community participation elicit the body's opioid system. Community rituals manipulate the opioid-attachment dynamics, eliciting the innate drive for human affiliation and bonding that produces opioid release, which may also be achieved through a variety of ritual activities (Winkelman 1997). The elicitation of the opioid response is achieved by the ritual conditioning of the endocrine system with cultural symbols during early socialization. Manipulation of those symbols in healing rituals evokes the associated physiological responses established through associative learning. The natural release of opioids in human bonding provides mechanisms by which intense involvement in a social group enhances well-being at the physiological level and directly counteracts the biological dynamics that maintain addiction.

ASC, Human Nature, and Addictions Recovery

The universal drive for humans to alter their consciousness reflects the underlying physiology of ASCs and their elicitation by numerous natural means (Mandell 1980; Winkelman 2000). Alcoholics Anonymous (AA) advocates meditation, a change of consciousness, and spiritual awakening as fundamental to maintaining sobriety. McPeake, Kennedy, and Gordon (1991) review the beneficial health effects of ASC and their potential for prevention of relapse. Shamanic ASC and drumming circles provide direct means for changing consciousness and can enhance recovery by inducing consciousness of a power greater than the self. ASCs produce inherently pleasurable experiences, including relaxation, stress reduction, restfulness, and an enhanced sense of well-being; they also can contribute to the sense of surrender considered essential by AA in overcoming addictive behaviors.

The potential effectiveness of ASC procedures for treating substance dependence is suggested in the addiction literature (McPeake, Kennedy, and Gordon 1991; Rioux 1996); in ethnomedical treatments of addiction (Heggenhougen 1997; Jilek 1994); in studies of the effectiveness of meditation in the treatment of addictions (O'Connell and Alexander 1994); and in the practical experience of contemporary shamanic practitioners (Harner and Harner 2001; Eshowsky 1993, 1998, 1999; D. Smith 2000). Substance abuse rehabilitation programs may fail because they do not incorporate the benefits of ASC or provide nondrug methods for achieving ASCs (McPeake, Kennedy, and Gordon 1991).

Traditional indigenous approaches (Winkelman 2001a) to substance abuse treatment incorporate spirituality, natural ASC, and community-bonding and support activities, using culturally congenial processes to facilitate affective release and emotional resolution. Shamanistic practices utilizing plant medicines known as "sacred plants" or "psychointegrators" (Halpern 1996; Winkelman 1996, 2001b) also have had success in treatment of addictions, exemplified in Native American and South American healing traditions using "hallucinogens" (especially peyote and ayahuasca). Shamanic healing techniques can play a role in a holistic addiction counseling that integrates a spiritual perspective with a biopsychosocial approach that focuses on inner realities to produce harmony and wholeness (Rioux 1996).

Shamanic practices have potential effectiveness in addressing contributory psychobiological, psychosocial, and emotional dynamics of drug addiction. Psychological and physiological models of shamanic healing as involving opioid stimulation and serotonergic enhancement (Winkelman 2000) suggest its effectiveness in drug rehabilitation. Shamanic practices elicit natural opioid responses, enhance serotonergic functioning, provide access to repressed emotional dynamics, and enhance social bonding (Winkelman 2000). Shamanic potential for addiction treatment is supported by research on the effectiveness of Transcendental Meditation practices in rehabilitation programs (O'Connell and Alexander 1994). Walton and Levitsky (1994) indicate meditation-induced theta waves address the psychodynamics of addiction from neurological through psychological, cognitive, and personal levels. Meditation enhances serotonin availability, breaking the cycle of dependence and reliance on external substances for a sense of well-being. Meditation can both address the alteration of consciousness sought by addicts and provide a mechanism for rebalancing nervous system dynamics disturbed by long-term drug abuse.

Spirit Relations and Addictions Recovery

A natural drive to transcendence and ASC is thwarted in modern societies by the lack of institutionalized community ASC activities, contributing to dispositions for drug-induced satisfactions. Shamanic approaches may be useful in addressing substance abuse by directly providing ASCs and spiritual experiences. Engagement with spiritual experiences and higher powers appears to facilitate recovery and provide a protective factor against recidivism. The spiritual experience emphasized by the AA approach is more directly achieved by the shamanic practices that directly enter the spirit world than through the Christian religious systems upon which AA was founded. The latter has emphasized a mediatory approach with the supernatural rather than direct entry into the spiritual world, which has been a hallmark of shamanism. Shamanic approaches involve a biopsychosocial approach, the holistic perspective that addiction counseling needs (Rioux 1996). Shamanic ASCs provide direct experiences of the spirit world in power animals and guardian spirits that Rioux proposes be conceptualized as "metaphoric healing energies." Winkelman (2000) shows these power animals represent dynamics of the brain's innate processing, particularly those associated with the paleomammalian (limbic or "emotional") brain. Shamanic practices produce an elevation of unconscious, emotional, affective, and behavioral dynamics, enabling change through providing access to dissociated aspects of identity.

These shamanic and community drumming approaches have some advantages over conventional approaches in integrating ASCs, identity change, and spiritual and community dimensions into substance abuse rehabilitation. In contrast to AA's religious influence and its mediatory approach to the divine, shamanic practices directly induce changes of consciousness and spiritual encounters and experiences. In contrast to the Christian approach of AA, the psychobiologically based approaches of shamanism have the potential to introduce spirituality in a more culture-free and less judgmental framework. Consequently, a shamanic approach to spirituality may be more compatible than AA with the belief systems of some people.

Shamanic and community drumming activities provide direct approaches to address aspects of the Twelve Steps that are not directly evoked in AA meetings. The alteration of consciousness called for in the last of the Twelve Steps is not readily achieved in standard AA meetings. Shamanic practices and drumming provide direct nondrug means of achieving an ASC. The foundation of the AA approach, acceptance of a higher power, is generally based on faith rather than experienced directly. Shamanic practices provide the direct experience of entry into the spiritual world and interactions with a variety of spiritual powers that provide assistance. Shamanic ASCs elicit the paleomammalian brain structures to produce emotional healing by evoking socioemotional and psychodynamic processes, strengthening social identity, and providing the social support that elicits the body's opioid system.

The greater flexibility that a shamanic approach provides is attested to by the adaptations made by Native American groups to incorporating AA and other substance abuse rehabilitation programs into their specific treatment approaches. Aboriginal concepts of spirituality have been incorporated into the treatment programs in Canadian prison systems (e.g., Waldram 1997), enabling shamanic perspectives to play a role in the social and emotional rehabilitation of Native Americans.

Shamanic practices persist because they are based in an evolved psychology of humans, reflecting the operations of innate brain structures and functions (Winkelman 2000, 2002). This neurological foundation of shamanic practice implies its continued applicability to human problems, including substance abuse rehabilitation (Winkelman 2001a, 2003).

NOTES

1. Similar versions of these interviews were published in the *American Journal of Public Health* (Winkelman 2003). This research was partially supported under a NIDA postdoctoral fellowship award to the Arizona Center for Ethnographic Research and Training.

2. This cross-cultural study (Winkelman 1992) revealed common characteristics associated with the healing practitioners of hunter-gatherer and slightly more complex pastoral and agricultural societies. These charismatic leaders who engaged in healing and divination activities on behalf of the entire local community were also believed capable of malevolent magical acts (sorcery). Other characteristics associated with shamans include an ASC experience known as soul journey or soul flight; the use of chanting, music, drumming, and dancing; an initiatory death-and-rebirth experience; therapeutic processes involving soul recovery; diseases caused by the intrusion of objects or attacks by spirits and sorcerers; abilities of divination, diagnosis, and prophecy; animal relations, including control of animal spirits and transformation into animals; and hunting magic.

REFERENCES

Achterberg, J. 1985. *Imagery in Healing, Shamanism in Modern Medicine.* Boston: Shambhala.
Alcoholics Anonymous. 1987. *Twelve Steps and Twelve Traditions.* New York: AA World Services.
Booth, J., and J. E. Martin. 1998. Spiritual and Religious Factors in Substance Use, Dependence, and Recovery. In *Handbook of Religion and Mental Health,* ed. Harold G. Koenig. San Diego: Academic Press.
Byrd, R. 1988. Positive Therapeutic Effects of Intercessory Prayer in Coronary Care Unit Population. *Southern Medical Journal* 81: 826–29.
Christopher, James. 1992. *SOS Sobriety.* Buffalo, N.Y.: Prometheus Books.
Eliade, M. 1964. *Shamanism: Archaic Techniques of Ecstasy.* New York: Pantheon Books.
Eshowsky, M. 1993. Practicing Shamanism in a Community Health Center. *Shamanism* 5 (4): 4–9.
———. 1998. Community Shamanism: Youth, Violence, and Healing. *Shamanism* 11 (1): 3–9.
———. 1999. Behind These Walls Where Spirit Dwells. *Shamanism* 12 (1): 9–15.
Frecska, E., and Z. Kulcsar. 1989. Social Bonding in the Modulation of the Physiology of Ritual Trance. *Ethos* 17: 70–87.
Green, L., M. Fullilove, and R. Fullilove, 1998. Stories of Spiritual Awakening the Nature of Spirituality in Recovery. *Journal of Substance Abuse Treatment* 15: 325–331.
Halpern, John. 1996. The Use of Hallucinogens in the Treatment of Addiction. *Addiction Research* 4: 177–189.
Harner, M. 1990. *The Way of the Shaman.* San Francisco: Harper and Row.
Harner, M., and S. Harner. 2001. Core Practices in the Shamanic Treatment of Illness. *Shamanism* 13 (1 and 2): 19–30.

Heggenhougen, C. 1997. *Reaching New Highs: Alternative Therapies for Drug Addicts.* Northvale N.J.: Jason Aronson.

Hunt, H. 1995. *On the Nature of Consciousness.* New Haven, Conn.: Yale University Press.

Ingerman, S. 1991. *Soul Retrieval.* San Francisco: HarperCollins.

Jilek, W. 1994. Traditional Healing and the Prevention and Treatment of Alcohol and Drug Abuse. *Transcultural Psychiatric Research Review* 31: 219–58.

Laughlin, C. 1997. Body, Brain, and Behavior: The Neuroanthropology of the Body Image. *Anthropology of Consciousness* 8 (2–3): 49–68.

Laughlin, C., J. McManus, and E. d'Aquili. 1992. *Brain, Symbol and Experience toward a Neurophenomenology of Consciousness.* New York: Columbia University Press.

Levin, Jeffrey. 1994a. Investigating the Epidemiological Effects of Religious Experience: Findings, Explanations, and Barriers. In *Religion in Aging and Health: Theoretical Foundations and Methodological Frontiers,* ed. J. Levin. 3–17. Thousand Oaks, Calif.: Sage.

————. 1994b. Religion and Health: Is There an Association, Is It Valid, and Is It Causal? *Social Science and Medicine* 38: 1475–82.

Mandell, A. 1980. Toward a Psychobiology of Transcendence: God in the Brain. In *The Psychobiology of Consciousness,* ed. D. Davidson and R. Davidson, 379–464. New York: Plenum.

McPeake, J. D., B. P. Kennedy, and S. M. Gordon. 1991. Altered States of Consciousness Therapy: A Missing Component in Alcohol and Drug Rehabilitation Treatment. *Journal of Substance Abuse Treatment* 8: 75–82.

Miller, W. R. 1998. Researching the Spiritual Dimensions of Alcohol and Other Drug Problems. *Addiction* 93: 979–90.

Noll, R. 1985. Mental Imagery Cultivation as a Cultural Phenomenon: The Role of Visions in Shamanism. *Current Anthropology* 26:443–451.

O'Connell, D. 1991. The Use of Transcendental Meditation in Relapse Prevention Counseling. *Alcoholism Treatment Quarterly* 8: 53–69.

O'Connell D., and C. Alexander, eds. 1994. *Self-Recovery: Treating Addictions Using Transcendental Meditation and Maharishi Ayur-Veda.* New York: Hayworth Press.

Prince, R. 1982. Shamans and Endorphins. *Ethos* 10:409.

Project MATCH Research Group. 1997. Matching Alcohol Treatments to Client Heterogeneity: Project MATCH Posttreatment Drinking Outcomes. *Journal of Studies on Alcohol* 58:7–29.

Rioux, D. 1996. Shamanic Healing Techniques: Toward Holistic Addiction Counseling. *Alcoholism Treatment Quarterly* 14:59–69.

Smith, D. E. 1994. AA Recovery and Spirituality: An Addiction Medicine Perspective. *Journal of Substance Abuse Treatment* 11: 111–12.

Smith, Daniel. 2000. Shamanism and Addiction: The Mask of Therapeutic Containment, Midwife to Mental Health. *Spirit Talk* 11:8–12.

Strawbridge, W., R. Cohen, S. Shema, and G. Kaplan. 1997. Frequent Attendance at Religious Services and Mortality over 28 Years. *American Journal of Public Health* 87:957–61.

Swanson, G. 1973. The Search for a Guardian Spirit: The Process of Empowerment in Simpler Societies. *Ethnology* 12:359–78.

Waldram, J. 1997. *The Way of the Pipe: Aboriginal Spirituality and Symbolic Healing in Canadian Prisons.* Peterborough, Ont.: Broadview Press.

Walton, K., and D. Levitsky. 1994. A Neuroendocrine Mechanism for the Reduction of Drug Use and Addictions by Transcendental Meditation. *Alcoholism Treatment Quarterly* 11:89–117.

Winkelman, M. 1990. Shaman and Other "Magico-religious" Healers: A Cross-cultural Study of Their Origins, Nature and Social Transformations. *Ethos* 18:308–52.

———. 1992. *Shamans, Priests and Witches. A Cross-Cultural study of Magico-Religious Practitioners.* Anthropological Research Papers 44. Tempe: Arizona State University.

———. 1997. Altered States of Consciousness and Religious Behavior. In *Anthropology of Religion: A Handbook of Method and Theory*, ed. S. Glazier, 393–428. Westport, Conn.: Greenwood Press.

———. 2000. *Shamanism: The Neural Ecology of Consciousness and Healing.* Westport, Conn.: Bergin and Garvey.

———. 2001a. Alternative and Complementary Medicine Approaches to Substance Abuse: A Shamanic Perspective. *International Journal of Drug Policy* 12:337–51.

———. 2001b. Psychointegrators: Multidisciplinary Perspectives on the Therapeutic Effects of Hallucinogens. *Complementary Health Practice Review* 6:219–37.

———.2002. Shamanism as Neurotheology and Evolutionary Psychology. *American Behavioral Scientist* 45:1875–87.

———. 2003. Complementary Therapy for Addiction: "Drumming Out Drugs." *American Journal of Public Health.* 93(4):647–65.

Winkelman, M. and W. Andritzky, eds. 1996. *Sacred Plants, Consciousness and Healing: Yearbook of Cross-Cultural Medicine and Psychotherapy.* Vol. 6. Berlin: Verlag und Vertrieb.

29

The Healing Genes

Kaja Finkler

At one time it was believed that traditional healing would disappear in light of the great success of biomedicine, especially since religion and religious healing are usually juxtaposed as mutually antagonistic to science and biomedicine.[1] Biomedicine, which became wedded to the scientific enterprise in the late nineteenth century, is viewed as removed from mysticism, determinism, or belief in fate, and, unlike religion and religious healing, it separates the material and mystical worlds. Owing to these postulated differences between science, medicine, and religion, some scholars have suggested that modern humans differ from "primitive" peoples, who adhere to the religious worldview, precisely because modern humans have power to control the natural and social world. For instance, Anthony Giddens emphasizes that in the high modernity of today, "fate and destiny have no formal part to play" but operate by "human control of the natural and social worlds" (1991: 109). The world of "future events is open to be shaped by human intervention [and is] regulated by risk assessment" (109). The modern outlook stands opposed to preordained determinism and is opposed to fatalism, which refutes modernity.

Giddens's assertions are reminiscent of earlier scholars' beliefs that religion was an illusion that would disappear, once scientific knowledge revealed the "errors" of religious beliefs. However, recent articles published by Eisenberg and colleagues (1993, 1998), studies by scholars (Barnes, Plotnikoff, Fox, and Pendleton, 2000; Csordas 1994; McGuire 1988), and reports in the mass media[2] attest to the fallacy of the assumption that religion and religious healing in which it is embedded have disappeared in the modern or postmodern worlds.[3] In fact, Barnes and her co-authors (2000) report that more than thirty medical schools have introduced courses on the relationship between spirituality and medicine. Barnes (2003) also reviews an extensive literature explaining the relationship between biomedicine and spirituality, notwithstanding the numerous barriers to this relationship. Moreover, investigations such as the Mantra Study (Krucoff et al. 2001) presuppose that religious beliefs influence treatment outcomes, and National Public Radio (2002) recently reported on a number of doctors who use spirituality in their work with mental health patients.

In this chapter, my concern is with the religious underpinnings of what is ostensibly a purely scientific enterprise, specifically the Human Genome Project (HGP) and the new genetics that form part of contemporary biomedicine. I will suggest that ideologies of the HGP, which utilizes the most advanced technology of the times, are sustained by Jewish and Christian religious ideas. Although it may appear that contemporary scientific ideas are far removed from religious beliefs, closer scrutiny reveals that Western religious notions undergird the HGP. I begin with a brief overview of modern society's shift to the secularization of medicine and then turn to the new genetics, which became an integral part of biomedicine. I will discuss the cultural nature of biomedicine and the religious nature of the new genetics, suggesting that it is being regarded as the Book of Life and the Holy Grail by some HGP scientists. In this context, I will also present a brief summary of the theological concerns with the new genetics.

Science, Medicine, and Secularization

The scientific revolution of the seventeenth century and the Enlightenment of the eighteenth century championed human rationality and freedom from religious authority, promoting a new consciousness that led to the secularization of society by removing the "domination of religious institutions and symbols" (Berger 1969: 107). Concurrently, the new consciousness led to the loss of a sense of certainty that previously had been sought and achieved by religious beliefs in an ordered and determined cosmos ruled by God or, as in antiquity, by Fortuna[4] and fate. In a more contemporary reading, Langdon Gilkey defines fate as "blind forces of nature, of genetic inheritance, of disease and uncontrolled scarcity, of social structure and tradition, of local or family custom and, most important, of the inner psyche—all those forces that shape human existence in directions antithetical to or destructive of conscious human goals and purposes" (1968: 66–67).

Contemporary biomedicine was spawned in nineteenth-century Western Europe and the United States and became committed to scientific practices, especially following the Flexner report of 1910.[5] One of the aims of the Flexner report was to establish biomedicine as a standardized and acultural, objective system of knowledge, following the scientific laboratory model. Yet an extensive literature demonstrates how biomedicine and the scientific enterprise alike are socially, culturally, and historically molded. In recent times, we have come to acknowledge that biomedical knowledge, like any medical system, is a cultural system (Hahn and Kleinman 1983; Finkler 2001; Lock and Gordon 1988; Martin 1997) and that biomedicine, like science itself, is not an acultural form but one that has emerged during a particular historical moment in the social formation of Western society (Fujimura 1996; Haraway 1991; Hess 1997; Latour and Woolgar 1979). Like all other knowledge systems, biomedicine reflects the themes of the society and culture of which it forms a part, while concurrently imposing these themes on cultural conceptualizations.

Similarly, genetic knowledge is culturally coded. According to Peter Bowler, "Without denying the important factual consequences that have flowed from the development of genetics, the history of the field will show that the new science was invented to serve human purposes—it did not grow automatically as a consequence of factual observations" (1989: 12). Thus "theories are invented rather than discovered" (13). From Bowler's vantage point, genetic models are constructed to "reflect the values of the social groups whose interests are best served by the promotion of these particular models" (17). Examples abound: with the emphasis on genetic etiology of disease, extrasomatic factors can be easily ignored, including a personal biography, or what I call "life's lesions" (Finkler 1994). Joan Fujimura also makes a compelling case for how genetic knowledge becomes constructed when she demonstrates that, in the late 1980s, the view of cancer changed from a "set of heterogeneous diseases marked by the common property of uncontrolled cell growth to a disease of human genes" (1996: 1). This change was brought about not by new discoveries or epistemic advances but by negotiated social processes and networks of relations in the laboratory (Latour 1987).

The Human Genome Project

The Human Genome Project stands at the vanguard of the new genetics. It was conceived in the late 1980s and formally instituted in October 1990, with the optimistic goal of identifying, mapping, and sequencing all human genes to make them accessible for biological study, and to unlock the secrets of all diseases. The HGP promotes a biochemical causal model of human affliction. It has cataloged 3,000 to 4,000 single gene-linked diseases. The goal is to identify multiple gene-linked diseases, or polygenic disorders (Cranor 1994: 125; Hubbard and Wald 1997). The project's proponents anticipate that if all the genes involved in a disease are identified remedies can be found to correct the faulty genes. According to the Web site of the National Human

Genome Research Institute, "Our genes orchestrate the development of a single-celled egg into a fully formed adult. Genes influence not only what we look like but also what diseases we may eventually get." The HGP also promises to usher in an era of molecular medicine, with precise new approaches to the diagnosis, treatment, and prevention of disease.[6]

If the premise of the HGP is correct—with the mapping of the entire genome, cures will eventually be found for all diseases—it will have a profound impact on biomedicine. Medicine will move from being a reactive to a preventive practice because there will be a "cure" for each defective gene even before its effects become manifest. Great benefits to industry are foreseen because the pharmaceutical industry will be able to develop a large therapeutic repertoire to attack fundamental aspects of human disease (Hood 1992: 158).[7] Theoretically at least, the HGP is regarded as a panacea for all ills.[8] As such, it also promises people control over their own fate. It anticipates that if people seek testing, they will be able to control diseases they will eventually develop. By doing so, it will become possible for people to plan their lives to the point of opting to bear only healthy children with predetermined characteristics, following a genetic engineering model (Silver 1999).

The new genetics, which refers to knowledge and procedures based on DNA technology developed by the HGP, is thus beginning to constitute a pivotal part of biomedicine. It tends to attribute disease etiology to genetic inheritance, and it is foreseen that treatment will be targeted to an individual's genetic makeup (Jonsen 1996) inherited from one's family. Patients may in actuality be asymptomatic but will be treated for diseases that are predicted to occur in the future (Finkler 2000; Jonsen 1996). Moreover, the new genetics tends to redraw the boundaries between healthy and unhealthy people. Potentially all people will be regarded as unhealthy, possible carriers of malfunctioning genes or genetically predisposed to a multitude of diseases. The new genetics could reveal asymptomatic conditions that may remain forever asymptomatic, or it could disclose susceptibilities or risks for developing common diseases such as breast cancer or diabetes. In the last analysis, people will become, what I call elsewhere "perpetual patients," who will be constantly threatened by some genetic condition (Finkler 2000) or by their predisposition to it.

Religious Dimensions of the Human Genome Project

As I noted earlier, some scholars have suggested that modern humans are very different from our "primitive" forebears. Gilkey, however, concludes his incisive work by stating, "Today, as throughout history, mankind lives in terms of 'myths'—the 'religious' myth that man has been set in the center of things by a sovereign divine will, or the 'scientific' myth that scientific man can sovereignly determine his own destiny and freely alter the march of historical events to suit his chosen moral purposes. Today, as in the past, intelligence requires that we ponder critically the empirical validity of these myths" (1968: 76). Generally speaking, contemporary humans may indeed have different sensibilities from their forebears, but Gilkey and others (Douglas and Wildavsky 1982) are correct to insist that contemporary humans are not so different from humans of the past at least in one respect: their belief in predestination and fate.

According to Geertz (1973: 92), "genes lay a template for human existence" in much the same way as religion does. But the human genome as presented by its proponents is not just a simile for religion; rather, religious ideas undergird conceptions of the genome. This assertion is reinforced by HGP proponents' many claims that the human genome is the Book of Life and the Holy Grail. Such formulations promote a perspective permeated by predestination. Popular critiques commonly refer to scientists working on the genome as "playing God," since knowledge of the genome will permit humans to manipulate their own destinies.

One could, of course, argue that the images drawn from the Book of Life or the Holy Grail are just that—images in words, mere metaphors. But words reflect, as much as create, realities. As Fox Keller asserts correctly, "Words have a power to impinge on the world that is unquestionably real" (2000: 138). She continues, "The power of words derives from a relation to things that is always and of necessity, mediated by language-speaking actors" (139). The comparison between the Book of Life and the Holy Grail in relation to the human genome discloses the reality its proponents maintain. I will return to this point shortly.

Francis Collins, head of the HGP, stated that he sees no conflict between religion and genetics and that uncovering the genome is a "religious experience" (1999). He also wrote, "If healing is something which Jesus Christ in his short time on this earth spent so much time on, it is something that those who would follow him should also consider especially important. Such is the theological justification for the Human Genome Project" (Collins 1997: 95). Collins observes that "understanding the genes that play a predictive role in diseases . . . will facilitate the development of new treatments. It is part of our mandate as Christians to pursue such medical advances, attempting to emulate Christ in his healing role" (1997: 96).

In her original analysis of the history of the genetic code, Lily Kay notes that "scriptural representations of the genome as the Book of Life have come to signify a kind of divine intervention" (2001: 297). The Book of Life first appears in Jewish Scripture (Psalms 69:29), which says that those who lack merit should be "blotted out of the book of the living." The idea is developed further in the New Year's (Rosh Hashanah) Talmudic tractate (16a), which states, "Everything is decided on New Year's day, and the judgment is sealed on the Day of Atonement." There is a suggestion here that human beings' good and evil deeds are recorded in the Book of Life. Likewise, in Christian teaching, there is a suggestion that one's destiny is written into the Book of Life (Jeremias 1910: 795).

Various scientists, including Gilbert (1992) and Kevles (1992), refer to the Holy Grail when discussing the genome (Nelkin 1996). The grail pertains to Christ's cup, always ephemeral, that contained the blood from his wounds. The quest for the Holy Grail possesses numerous significations, including a search for spiritual enlightenment (Weston 1965; Ross and Ross 1919; Waite 1961). By merely viewing the grail, one took communion, a ritual partaking of life everlasting. But most commonly it refers to "the idea of the quest for the secret of life" (Ross and Ross 1919: 386). The grail also "became the emblem of moral purity or of triumphant faith" (386). Gruenwald (1997) believes that the Holy Grail is a search for transcendence, a struggle between good and evil, and a quest for meaning that is especially relevant in modern times, when humans are confronted with the "crisis of credibility" because of a loss of "certainty of our [religious] conviction" (Holm 1994: 26). I suggest that the scientific search for the Holy Grail reveals its quest for a certainty that it lacks—for the secret of life and for a kind of immortality, which one's inherited genes provide.

The HGP has led some (often its critics) to think that some humans believe they can replace God. The God metaphor occurs in reference to what the genome can and cannot accomplish. For example, critics of the HGP express the concern that knowledge of the human genome and the presumed therapies it will yield is regarded as a form of humans "playing God." Blake argues that knowledge of the genome promises a blissful future without diseases, in much the same way as do the Hebrew scriptures:

> The blessing of God in the Hebrew Scriptures is the promise of a state of blessedness in the future that is worked out by human persons in the context of creation of the world. . . . The promised blessing of the HGP, the promise of genetic health is also placed in the future. A biblical theology of blessing expands the understanding of well-being from the physical, genetic health suggested by the HGP to a broader sense of well-being that looks beyond unrelated individuals to community and society, beyond physical health to relational vitality. (1997: 16)

But Blake also warns against the peril of genetic determinism that can slide just as easily into racism and eugenics. He calls attention to the dangers of "playing God," especially if the scientific community is isolated from the rest of society.

The metaphor of "playing God" is examined by others as well (Verhey 1997; Feinberg 1997), who, contrary to Blake, maintain that if genetics can achieve therapy or at least diagnosis, it should be celebrated (Verhey 1997: 70).

Theologian John Feinberg even claims that since all humans have sinned and therefore must face death, then "if there is something that genetic technology could do to address that problem, then that use of this technology would be acceptable. In effect, we would be using this technology to fight sin and its consequences" (1997: 187). In this manner, humans may "play God" in healing, to satisfy God and also eliminate original sin.

Arguably, these formulations reflect contradictory notions of God's work. For example, Blake's reflections mirror Jewish notions of God as providing blessings. In contrast, the majority of Christian theologians embrace notions of redemption from sin by means of HGP's potential for alleviating disease, seen as the consequence of original sin. Some would even take the notion of genetics not simply as "data to be accounted for, but in some cases as theories which tell the theologian something about how God is ordering life in the world, and even in some cases something about God" (Gustafson 1994: 14). In short, God reveals himself in the knowledge of genetics, suggesting the overconfident notion that humans can actually know God, if only they knew genetics.

Contemporary Christian theologians endeavor to reconcile modern genetics with religious concepts, including the notion of God, free will, and determinism. For example, Hefner (1968) observes that those in search of God's truths can find it also through biological theories. Hefner recognizes that "theologians as varied as Augustine, Calvin, Schleiermacher, and H. R. Niebuhr have interpreted the Christian faith as a kind of determinism, focusing upon God's determinants as the foundation of man's existence" (20). Hefner extends the notion of determinism in yet another direction, suggesting "the human being is created by God to be a co-creator in the creation that God has brought into being" and that the "conditioning matrix that has produced the human being—the evolutionary process—is God's process of bringing into being a creature who represents the creation's zone of a new stage of freedom" (1993: 32).

In sum, according to Hefner, human freedom is determined by genetics. In his words, "I mean that freedom is one of nature's ways of creating new conditions under which the genes and their programs must exist" (1993: 99). The freedom that human beings are given by their genetic heritage leads them to become cocreators. We must search, he argues, for our free will in the human genome: that is, human beings are genetically determined to have free will. Thus, theologians such as Hefner and others believe that predestination and free will are built into our genetic makeup. Insofar as Christian anthropology asserts the inherent free will of human beings, Hefner has assigned it a genetic basis.

It is not my intention here to debate these arguments that ultimately reflect a genetic reductionism, although I hasten to add that other theologians regard the creator/cocreator hypothesis as controversial (Howell 1999). Rather, I raise this theological proposition to suggest that the ideology of genetic inheritance, which presumes to reflect an objective reality, in this case is informed by the assumption of a Christian religious reality. Hefner states clearly "that the desire and ability to alter our genes is very much grounded in our genes" (1994: 26). Eaves and Gross, too, claim that genetics "constitutes a model system for the interaction between science and theology" (1992: 264), rather than genetics determining theology. Eaves, a biologist, regards the double helix as having "very strong parallels to how revelatory events function in theology" (1989: 196). He states, "In the category of biological realities, which may provide the raw material for theological construction, we may cite three: namely *givenness, connectedness,* and *openness.* To a greater or lesser extent, the DNA encodes part of the moral and spiritual history of our race" (206). Genes reveal a divine presence (Nunez 2000:111). Eaves and Gross assert that "genetic research influences the kinds of theological models that are most congruent with reality and the kinds of metaphors that are most productive in historical transformation" (1992: 267).

Many scientists and physicians may deny that they hold a religious perspective, at least in relation to their work (Pollack 2000), asserting instead the differences between science, scientific medicine, religion, and religious healing. Nevertheless, I wish to stand on its head the argument proposed by these theologians and biologists who seek a synthesis between religion and science. I suggest that Jewish and Christian worldviews provide the "raw material" for the belief in genetic determinism as exemplified by the HGP.[9] As Dorothy Nelkin (1996) has observed, the HGP is enveloped in a religious perspective of determinism.

First, if we accept that genetic inheritance foretells our future state of health and determines our being, paradoxically, we return directly to the idea of predestination.[10] The concept of predestination refers to a belief that God predetermines or foreordains whatsoever comes to pass, especially good and evil (A. S. Martin 1919). In Cole's words, "It is humbling, then, to regard our genome and recognize how much it determines who we are" (1994: 20). The notion that humans are determined beings comes into bold relief in Gilbert's assertion that we must acknowledge that we are "determined, in a certain sense, by a finite collection of information that is knowable. . . . It is the closing of an intellectual frontier, with which we will have to come to terms" (1992: 96).

Interestingly, in keeping with the view that genetic inheritance shapes a notion of predestination, paradoxically it may also promote a sense of control, in the modern mind, over one's fate. This contradiction exists in science, as noted by Gilkey, as well as in modern humans' experience of predestination: science gives "a sense of control over the determining fates through intentional activity; that is, rational activity directed at chosen ends" (Gilkey 1968: 66).

Science paradoxically encourages humans to seek knowledge freely and to explore nature and human behavior, while concurrently understanding them as "totally determined beings" (67).

Gilkey's theoretical paradox can be seen in how people experience related aspects of their lives. For example, in my research, people have indicated that the knowledge that, due to their genetic inheritance, they will be afflicted by a disease gives them a sense of control and the ability to act. To hold such contradictory conceptualizations is arguably a modern sensibility. This assertion comes into bold relief in numerous narratives by adoptees seeking their birth mothers, as well as by individuals with a family history of breast cancer (Finkler 2000).

Conclusion

Freud (1961) claimed that science would subvert religion. Yet religion flourishes in contemporary America even though, ironically, many theologians' recognize that the power of humans to shape their "own future is concentrated in the biological sciences" (Hefner 1968: 6). If we accept the notion that scientific knowledge, including medical knowledge, is embedded in Western cultural values,[11] then we need not be surprised that the belief in genetic inheritance echoes a religious ideology, especially the notion of predestination. To the extent that religious sensibilities in American society have been naturalized by their very pervasiveness,[12] religious ideology can unreflectively and seamlessly slide into different domains of American consciousness. For this reason scientists tend not to recognize that the ideology of genetic determinism is embedded in, and infused with, religious constructs.

Many healing systems the world over formed part of a religious tradition. For a healing practice to be undergirded by religious beliefs, it need not necessarily be identified by some special symbols that flash "religion." While in some instances, religious and biomedical healing exhibit certain similarities (Finkler 1994), we tend to emphasize their differences. Yet religious ideologies can be expressed in the guise of scientific beliefs because science is not an acultural system. It is produced by actors who come out of certain religious traditions, in much the same way as gender biases are embedded in both religious systems and biomedical ideologies (E. Martin 1997; Phillips 1997), or, for that matter, as Max Weber (1958) proposed that Calvinism lay at the roots of the development of capitalism.

The philosopher Ian Hacking has gone even further, suggesting that the exclusionary nature of science and its search for unity may reflect the monism of the Jewish and Christian tradition of the One over the many. For instance, Hacking suggests that the search for unified principles in the cosmos, as exemplified in Einstein's search to unite all phenomena, "in some minds is rooted in a religious conception of the world and how God must have made it" (1996:46). Hacking's observes that "Einstein's cultural roots in Judaism were deep" (47).

Whether the ideology of genetic inheritance is religious or secular—and arguably we can regard it as both—what we must guard against are the consequences of unquestionably accepting the genetic determinism shaped by notions of predestination. Ironically, these very notions give individuals a modicum of a sense of control because they know what the future holds for them— a predestined genetic disease (Finkler 2000). In true American fashion, people believe that they can control their future by avoiding other risk factors that may be considered related to that disease. Yet these perceptions carry other dangers. If disease is viewed as genetically inherited and the individual as being predisposed to disease owing to his or her family medical history, society and the medical world can comfortably ignore actual precipitating causes of most diseases, including environmental factors and other extra-somatic risks (Hubbard and Wald 1997; Mckeown 1985). Moreover, as I noted earlier, the attribution of disease to genetic inheritance permits biomedicine to take no notice of a person's conditions of existence, or life's lesions, that may contribute directly to his or her health state.

In the final analysis, religious healing is embedded in systems of beliefs rooted in certainty and unwavering faith, whereas scientific beliefs *ought* to be questioned and tentative. Genetic inheritance is uncertain because it occurs by random chance, notwithstanding that the advocates of HGP are certain that genetics will explain all known human diseases. In actuality we have little, if any, control over genetically inherited diseases. The control humans do have is to eschew the production of environmental causes that tend to induce genetic mutations. What is interesting about the HGP is that it promotes a notion of healing through genetic manipulation that may have its roots as much in science as it does in religion, which some contemporary Western humans may consider a "primitive" mode of thought. The contradiction is compelling.

NOTES

I wish to thank Linda Barnes and Susan Sered for their fine comments on an earlier draft of this chaper.

1. See, for example, Johnson (1998), who summarizes in the popular press the disputes and accommodations between religion and science.

2. See, for example, the survey reported by Sheler (2002).

3. As I have argued elsewhere (Finkler 1994), religious healing stands in a symbiotic relationship with biomedicine. The more biomedicine fails to heal, as in cases of chronic illness, the more alternative healing, systems, including religious healing, flourish the world over.

4. The ancient Roman goddess of fortune.

5. For a discussion of the Flexner report see Starr 1982.

6. The National Human Genome Research Institute 1998. See also the special issue of *Time*, January 11, 1999, which heralds the future of medicine as resting in genetics and genetic engineering.

7. At the time of the inception of the HGP in 1988, it had a budget of $27.9 million; this progressively increased until, in 1998, the program's budget grew to $302.6 million. See National Human Genome Research Institute 1998. Collins (1999) similarly reported on the alliance between the HGP and the pharmaceutical industry.

8. See, for example, the program on *Sixty Minutes II*, an interview with Francis Collins, who foresees the HGP as being able to heal all diseases in the future.

9. This is especially prevalent in evolutionary psychology, which claims that "we are survival machines, robot vehicles blindly programmed to preserve the selfish molecules known as genes." Dawkins quoted by Yancey (1998).

10. It is important to stress that there are numerous interpretations of predestination in Christian theology. John Calvin, for example, defined it as "the eternal decree by God, by which he determined with himself whatever he wished to happen with regard to every person" (quoted by McIntire 1987: 429).

11. For an extensive bibliography that explores this assertion further, see Finkler 2000. One of the earliest proponents of this view was Fleck ([1935] 1979).

12. For a survey on the role of religion in contemporary American life, see Sheler (2002).

REFERENCES

Barnes, Linda. 2003. Issues of Spirituality and Religion in Health Care. In *Cross-Cultural Medicine*, ed. JudyAnn Bigby. 237–67. American College of Physicians-American Society of Internal Medicine.

Barnes, Linda, Greg Plotnikoff, Ken Fox, and Sara Pendleton. 2000. Religious Traditions, Spirituality and Pediatrics: Intersecting Worlds of Healing: A Review. *Journal of the Ambulatory Pediatric Association* 106:899–908.

Berger, Peter. 1967. *The Sacred Canopy*. New York: Doubleday.

Blake, Deborah. 1997. The Human Genome Project: Blessing or Betrayal? *CTNS Bulletin* 17:10–18

Bowler, Peter J. 1989. *The Mendelian Revolution*. Baltimore: Johns Hopkins University Press.

Cole, David. 1994. Genetic Predestination? *Dialog* 33:17–22.

Collins, Francis. 1997. The Human Genome Project. In *Genetic Ethics* ed. John Kilner, Rebecca Pentz, and Frank Young, 95–103. Grand Rapids, Mich.: Eerdmans,

———. 1999a. Designer Genes: The Ethical and Social Implications of Genetic Research. Keynote address, James. M. Johnson Scholars Issues Forum, University of North Carolina, Chapel Hill.

———.1999b. Genetics and Faith. Lecture presented to Christian Physicians Association of North Carolina, University of North Carolina, Chapel Hill.

Cranor, Carl F. 1994. *Are Genes Us? The Social Consequences of the New Genetics*. New Brunswick, N.J.: Rutgers University Press.

Csordas, Thomas. 1994. *The Sacred Self.* Berkeley and Los Angeles: University of California Press.

Douglas, Mary, and Aron Wildavsky. 1982. Risk and Culture. Berkeley: University of California Press. 1970/1992. *Natural Symbols.* New York: Vintage Books.

Eaves, Lindon. 1989. Spirit, Method, and Content in Science and Religion: The Theological Perspective of a Geneticist. *Zygon* 24:185–215.

Eaves, Lindon, and Lora Gross. 1992. Exploring the Concept of Spirit as a Model for the God-World Relationship in the Age of Genetics. *Zygon* 27: 261–85.

Eisenberg, David, R. Davis, S. Ettner, S. Appel, S. Wilkey, and M. Van Rompay. 1998. Trends in Alternative Medicine Use in the United States, 1990–1997: Results of a Follow-Up National Survey. *Journal of the American Medical Association* 280: 1569–75.

Eisenberg, David, R. Kessler, C. Foster, F. Norlock, D. Calkins, and T. Delbanco. 1993. Unconventional Medicine in the United States. *New England Journal of Medicine* 28:246–83.

Feinberg, John. 1997. A Theological Basis for Genetic Intervention. In *Genetic Ethics,* ed. John Kilner, Rebecca Pentz, and Frank Young, 183–92. Grand Rapids, Mich.: Eerdmans.

Finkler, Kaja. 1994. Sacred and Biomedical Healing Compared. *Medical Anthropological Quarterly* 8:179–97

———. 2000. *Experiencing the New Genetics: Family and Kinship on the Medical Frontier.* Philadelphia: University of Pennsylvania Press

———. 2001. The Kin in the Gene. *Current Anthropology* 42:235–63.

Fleck, Ludwick. 1935. Genesis and Development of Scientific Fact. Chicago:University of Chicago Press.

Fox Keller, Evelyn. 2000. *The Century of the Gene.* Cambridge, Mass.: Harvard University Press.

Freud, Sigmund. 1961. *The Future of an Illusion.* New York: Norton.

Fujimura, Joan. 1996. *Crafting Science.* Cambridge, Mass.: Harvard University Press.

Geertz, Clifford. 1973. *The Interpretation of Cultures.* New York: Basic Books.

Giddens, Anthony. 1991. *Modernity and Self-Identity.* Stanford, Calif.: Stanford University Press.

Gilbert, Walter. 1992. A Vision of the Grail. In *The Code of Codes,* ed. Daniel Kevles and Leroy Hood, 83–97. Cambridge, Mass.: Harvard University Press.

Gilkey, Langdon. 1968. Evolutionary Science and the Dilemma of Freedom and Determinism. In *Changing Man,* ed. Kyle Haselden and Philip Hefner, 63–76. Garden City, N.Y.: Doubleday.

Gruenwald, Oskar. 1997. The Quest for Transcendence. *Journal of Interdisciplinary Studies* 9:155–72.

Gufstafson, James. 1994. Where Theologians and Genetecists Meet. *Dialog.* 33:7–16.

Hacking, Ian. 1996. The Disunities of the Sciences. In The Disunity of Science: Boundaries, Context, and Power, ed. Peter Lewis Galison and David Stump. Stanford, Calif.: Standford University Press.

Hahn, Robert and Arthur Kleinman. 1983. Biomedical Practice and Anthropological Theory: Frameworks and Directions. *Annual Review of Anthropology* 12:305–33.

Haraway, Donna. 1991. *Simians, Cyborgs, and Women.* New York: Routledge.

Hefner, Philip. 1968. Introduction. In *Changing Man,* ed. Kyle Haselden and Philip Hefner, 1–31. Garden City, N.Y.: Doubleday.

———. 1993. *The Human Factor.* Minneapolis: Fortress Press.

———. 1994. Determinism, Freedom, and Moral Failure. *Dialog* 33: 23–29.

Hess, David. 1997. *Science Studies.* New York: New York University Press.

Holm, Randall. 1994. In Search of a Holy Grail: The Religious Quest for Certitude. *Eastern Journal of Practical Theology* 8: 26–41.

Hood, Leroy. 1992. Biology and Medicine in the Twenty-first Century. In *The Code of Codes,* ed. Daniel J. Kevles and Leroy Hood, 136–63. Cambridge, Mass.: Harvard University Press.

Howell, Nancy. 1999. Co-creation, Co-redemption and Genetics. *American Journal of Theology and Philosophy* 20: 147–63.

Hubbard, Ruth, and Elijah Wald. 1997. *Exploding the Gene Myth.* Boston: Beacon Press.

Jeremias, Alfred. 1910. Book of Life. In *Encyclopaedia of Religon and Ethics,* ed. James Hastings, 792–95. New York: Scribner's.

Johnson, George. 1998. Science and Religion Cross Their Line in the Sand. *New York Times (Week in Review),* Sunday, July 12: 1–20.

Johnson, Thomas. 1987. Premenstrual Syndrome as a Western Culture-Specific Disorder. *Culture, Medicine, and Psychiatry* 11: 337–56.

Jonsen, Albert R. 1996. The Impact of Mapping the Human Genome on the Patient-Physician Relationship. In *The Human Genome Project and the Future of Health Care.* ed. Thomas H. Murray, Mark A. Rothsteing, and Robert F. Murray Jr., 1–20. Bloomington: Indiana University Press.

Kay, Lily. 2001. *Who Wrote the Book of Life?* Stanford, Calif.: Stanford University Press.

Kevles, Daniel. 1992. Out of Eugenics: The Historical Politics of the Human Genome. In *The Code of Codes,* ed. Daniel Kevles and Leroy Hood, 3–36. Cambridge, Mass.: Harvard University Press.

Krucoff, Mitchell, et al. 2001. Integrative Noetic Therapies as Adjuncts to Percutaneous Intervention during Unstable Coronary Syndromes: Monitoring and Actualization of Noetic Training (MANTRA) Feasibility Pilot. *American Heart Journal* 142: 760–67.

Latour, Bruno. 1987. *Science in Action.* Cambridge, Mass.: Harvard University Press.

Latour, Bruno, and S. Woolgar. 1979. *Laboratory Life: The Social Construction of Scientific Facts.* Beverly Hills, Calif.: Sage.

Lock, Margaret, and Debrah Gordon. 1988. *Biomedicine Examined.* Dordrecht: Kluwer Academic Publishers.

Martin, A. S. 1919. Predestination. In *Encyclopaedia of Religion and Ethics,* ed. James Hastings, 225–35. New York: Scribner's.

Martin, Emily. 1987. *The Woman in the Body.* Boston: Beacon Press.

———. 1997. The Egg and the Sperm. In *Situated Lives,* ed. L. Lamphere, H. Ragone, and P. Zavella, 85–98. New York: Routledge.

McGuire, Meredith. 1988. *Ritual Healing in Suburban America.* New Brunswick, N.J.: Rutgers University Press.

McIntire, C. T. 1987. Free Will and Predestination: Christian Concepts. In *The Ency-clopedia of Religion*, ed. Mircea Eliade, 5:427–29. New York: Macmillan.

Mckeown, Thomas. 1985. *The Role of Medicine: Dream, Mirage, or Nemesis*. Princeton, N.J.: Princeton University Press.

National Human Genome Research Institute. 1998. http://www.ornl.gov/hgmis/faq/faqs1.html 4/20.

National Public Radio. 2002. Weekend Edition, February 23.

Nelkin, Dorothy. 1992. The Social Power of Genetic Information. In *The Code of Codes*, ed. Daniel J. Kevles and Leroy Hood, 177–90. Cambridge, Mass.: Harvard University Press.

———. 1996. Genetics, God, and Sacred DNA. *Society*, May/June, 22–25.

Nunez, Theodore. 2000. Review of Holmes Rolston: *Genes, Genesis and God. Environmental Ethics* 22: 111–12.

Osherson, Samuel, and Lorna Amara Singham. 1981. The Machine Metaphor in Medicine. In *Social Contexts of Health, Illness and Patient Care*, ed. Elliot G. Mishler et al., 218–49. London: Cambridge University Press.

Phillips, Susan. 1997. Problem-Based Learning in Medicine: New Curriculum, Old Stereotypes. *Social Science and Medicine* 45: 497–99.

Pollack, Robert. 2000. *The Faith of Biology and the Biology of Faith*. New York: Columbia University Press.

Ritenbaugh, Cheryl. 1982. Obesity as a Culture-Bound Syndrome. *Culture, Medicine and Psychiatry* 6: 347–61.

Rodin, M. 1992. The Social Construction of Premenstrual Syndrome. *Social Science and Medicine* 35: 49–56.

Ross, J.M.E., and Margaret Ross. 1919. Grail, The Holy. In *Encyclopaedia of Religion and Ethics*, ed. by James Hastings, 386–89. New York: Scribner's.

Silver, Lee. 1999. How Reprogenetics Will Transform the American Family. *Hofstra Law Review* 27: 649–58.

Starr, Paul. 1982. *The Social Transformation of American Medicine*. New York: Basic Books.

Time Magazine. 1999. The Future of Medicine, January 11.

Verhey, Allen. 1997. Playing God. In *Genetic Ethics*. ed. John Kilner, Rebecca Pentz, and Frank Young, 60–74. Grand Rapids, Mich.: Eerdmans.

Waite, Arthur. 1961. *The Holy Grail*. New Hyde Park, N.Y.: University Books.

Weber, Max. 1958. *The Protestant Ethic and the Spirit of Capitalism*. Trans. Talcott Parsons. New York: Scribner's.

Weston, Jessie. 1965. *The Quest for the Holy Grail*. New York: Haskell House.

Yanagisako, Sylvia, and Jane Collier. 1990. "The Mode of Reproduction in Anthropology." In *Therapeutic Perspectives on Sexual Difference*, ed. Deborah L. Rhode, 131–44. New Haven, Conn.: Yale University Press.

Yancy, P. 1998. The Unmoral Prophets. *Christianity Today*, October 5: 76–79.

PART VI

Conclusion

30

Religion and Healing: The Four Expectations

Martin E. Marty

Religious approaches to healing and physical well-being can present physicians, nurses, medical researchers, and other health care professionals with a veritable maze. The claims of flamboyant and well-publicized "faith healers" can puzzle, even put off those who stand as observers. At the same time, we know that millions of educated and serious people in our scientific age do connect the faith dimension of their lives with their search for healing. What help is available for sorting out the various claims such people make, the expectations they have?

For ages and until recently most healers acted through religious means. Even quite recently, most people looked to religious resources for aids to healing. But it is also true that in recent centuries some of the ties between religion and healing have come to be jeopardized, tested, broken, and even spurned. The rise of scientific medicine in the age we call *modern* progressively called the old religious approaches into question. Many people in faith communities thereupon compensated by becoming suspicious of the very medicine on which most of them relied in times of crisis. It seemed as if the scene was being divided between "medical materialists," who made no room for faith, and "faith healers," who paid at best grudging respect to medicine and scientific research.

Caught between these were less easily categorized people desiring to be well: patients with diseases or disabilities, and sufferers who sought help. For them, neither medical materialism nor faith healing alone sufficed to account for reality or provided sufficient resources for healing. So many have called the old divisions into question that we might begin to speak of ours as a *postmodern* situation. Theorists, scientists, practitioners, and patients, on one side, have come to be more open to the voices of faith and the spiritual searches for well-being. Meanwhile, on the other side, theologians, religious philosophers, pastors, and ordinary believers, discerning such openness, have grown friendlier to science. They have become hopeful that their own inquiries and proposals will have a bearing on the search for healing.

Today, outlooks on life that we might call "merely" or "utterly" secular no longer have a simple monopoly (if they ever did) in the quest for well-being. Spiritual understandings of well-being have become at once both more tentative and more promising.

No one should portray the new situation as one of easy concord or relieved tensions between the two general approaches, and in fact the public would be ill served by an absence of conflict. Theoreticians, scientists, practitioners, and patients, if they are reflective, remain probing, skeptical, full of doubt, and inimical to credulity. On the other hand, theologians, philosophers, pastors or rabbis, and believers, if faithful to their promptings and traditions as they voice their expectations about wholeness, may call for some suspensions of disbelief to permit the opening of fresh conversation.

These representatives of religious fields seek not so much assent to their often conflicting findings and proposals as respectability for their inquiries. They are devising larger frameworks that will give thoughts about healing, efforts to heal, and interpretations of the healing process as much range and scope as possible.

Just as no single entity exists as "modern medicine," so no single element connects all things in a zone marked "religion and health." People in faith communities seek guides to help them comprehend the signals about healing that they get from their physicians, from mass media, and from literature designed for the nonspecialist. In turn, both patients and professionals in medical fields, in order to make sense of the world of religion, are looking for maps of its zones. More and more of them are aware of theological contributions to medical *ethics,* and interest in religious *interpretations* of medical worlds and healing processes is now also growing.

Two recent surveys surprised researchers in locating more than 250 published studies of religious factors in epidemiology. The authors recognized that "epidemiologists are largely resistant to the development of any 'epidemiology of religion' as an interdisciplinary enterprise" (Levin and Vanderpool 1987; Levin and Schiller 1987). But they propose that scholars would do well to posit one or more "epistemic relationships" (ways of addressing theories of knowledge) that would serve at least as starting points for future explorations.

Levin and Schiller (1987) first note and then complain that most empirical research has simply and naively measured only institutional religion, asking who belongs to and attends church or synagogue. But physicians who hear the voices of their patients or are alert to their culture know that understandings of faith and healing do not simply follow the lines of denominational membership. People also send out other signals to indicate what they mean when they practice religion or when they voice faith-filled hopes.

What follows in broad outline are four classifications ("ideal types," as sociologist Max Weber would call them), designed to show what North Americans from broadly conceived religious clusterings expect when they speak of healing. These are by no means mutually exclusive denominational camps. Many individuals can be "plural belongers," and some draw on one class for one set of needs and on another for a different set.

These four fundamental outlooks do, however, represent distinct expectations. The people at ease in one of these four classifications differ as much from those in the others as medical researchers differ from shamans, herbalists, and witch doctors, or as much as chiropractors or acupuncturists differ from neurosurgeons. The categories can help physicians know what to look for and listen for as they observe what patients or health seekers are drawing upon, claiming, or hoping for. They may also help religionists to discern some boundaries and to pursue their own further inquiries. Clergy, theologians, and ethicists will have their own comments to contribute.

The categories offered here reflect my own observations of the religious world in the past four decades. They may suggest a matrix for research in medical and theological schools or for comparison by health seekers and religious searchers alike. While intending to be faithful to complex sources, I have generally used nontechnical language. This does not mean that I "talk down" to experts in nonreligious fields, to people not professionally occupied with theological vocabularies. Instead, I wish to "talk across" the borders of communities and disciplines to intelligent people who, when they in turn talk across similar boundaries, also have to engage in acts of translation.

I have assigned to the four clusters names that are not and never will be names of sects or schools of thought. They are coinages designed to obscure any traces to sectarian impulses and institutions or to conventional scholastic outlooks. Other mapmakers and explorers may fill in details, redraw lines, or add other labels.

Overlaps and spaces between the four approaches exist. Here my metaphor of mapmaking has proved inadequate. In cartography, boundaries are boundaries and designate something precise. Still, we recall from primitive maps that when pioneer cartographers came to draw the edges of the charts, they would fill in the unexplored regions with pictures of fanciful dragons and sea monsters. These represented the spheres where their ignorance left them stranded. Large zones are inevitably open for the figurative cavortings and snarlings of such beasts here. In these early postmodern days we are as blighted by ignorance as we are tantalized by prospects of new knowledge, therapy, and experience.

It must be stated that mapmakers' jobs are not those of travel agents: they are not in the recommending business and maybe not even in the warning business. Nor can they be compared to priests who commend a particular way or apologists who defend one religious system as true. The very designation of approaches that are finally mutually contradictory suggests that they cannot all be true in the normal sense of that term.

In summary, I offer the four categories as an attempt to answer this question: *What precisely do people have in mind when they express the hope or make the claim that their faith has something to do with the understandings of illness and health and the processes of healing?* Here are the categories.

"I Am the Master of My Fate": Autogenesis

In medicine "autogenesis" means "produced within the organism." So in general matters biological as well as humanistic, the autogenous is self-produced, self-generated. In religion, the autogenetic therefore would represent a purely naturalistic and humanistic religion. Such religion is not likely to show up in the almanacs and yearbooks, yet all scholars recognize it. Such a worldview contains no reference to God or gods, to supernatural or supra-human forces that act upon a person. When the autogenetic type combines religion with healing, the result is strenuous human impulses and endeavors toward the possible achievement of well-being.

Why should we allow the designation of this approach as religious, when in our culture religion has ordinarily been associated with God or gods? For one thing, many people who employ it insist that they are also religious, and their voices should be heard. For another, these citizens strive for something that in so many respects resembles that which conventionally religious people pursue. We can best understand them as being at least quasi-religious.

This sort of humanistic religion has even achieved a measure of official recognition. The United States Supreme Court had to take up this question in *United States v. Seeger* in 1965–66, when a conscientious objector to military service received exemption. The young man was recognized by the Court as religious, which he claimed to be, but he explicitly did not believe in a supreme being. The plaintiff cited a definition by the Reverend John Haynes Holmes, one that the Court found convincing: religion is "the consciousness of some power manifest in nature which helps man in the ordering of his life in harmony with its demands. . . . [It] is the supreme expression of human nature; it is man thinking his highest, feeling his deepest, and living his best."

In 1961, in *Torcaso v. Watkins,* justice Hugo Black footnoted a ruling that also allowed for religions that lacked reference to a supreme being by pointing out that "among religions in this country which do not teach what would generally be considered a belief in the existence of God are Buddhism, Taoism,

Ethical Culture, Secular Humanism and others" (to which I might add, most notably, much of denominational Unitarian Universalism).

Adherents of such religion in the formal sense of the term may be proportionately few in the United States. In fifty years of inquiring about belief, the Gallup poll has never found more than 6 to 10 percent of its sample disbelieving in "God or a universal spirit" (*Gallup Report* 1985: 50). In this relatively small cohort, naturalistic religion must share partnership with many thousands of people who are formally atheistic or agnostic, who refuse to designate themselves as religious and thus are beyond the scope of this chapter.

Autogenetically religious people, however, tend to be articulate. They often find company with citizens for whom belief in God or a universal spirit is vague, thin, almost unable to be summoned, or on occasion violently rejected. Yet from the times of ancient religious naturalism and Stoicism down to the present, there have been significant calls for people to "tough it out" when in pain, to "seek self-transcendence" in times of misfortune. Those who hold such religious outlooks claim to have resources for promoting well-being. They profess no deity, but the mythical figure behind all these endeavors is Prometheus, who stole fire from the gods and generated humanism. The philosophical patron is Protagoras, for whom the human "is the measure of all things."

"I am the master of my fate." The autogenetic approach does not call those who hold it to be critical of medical materialism. Indeed, this view begins with materialist notions of the human body as a merely biological entity. Technically, such a type is reductionist, meaning that religion expresses "nothing but" this or that biological need under unnecessarily confusing and never helpful theological terms.

Having begun naturalistically and materialistically, however, religious humanists are not necessarily content to be passive in the face of threats to health. Many develop interests in the interaction of mind and body. They are quite eager to talk of the psychosomatic connection. They contend that attitudes of mind may well have influence on the condition of the body, but this "mind" is also part *of* natural processes. No outside unseen power or force impinges or need impinge upon it. The best-known recent figure to give visibility to such an approach is Norman Cousins. In *Anatomy of an Illness* (1979) and subsequent work, Cousins relies on philosophy and humor more than on any suprahuman *or* supernatural reference in order to begin his inquiries or to effect his therapies. Some of the more conventionally religious people find a kinship with Cousins and his kind.

Many articulators of Promethean views discipline their inquiries about health in relation to elaborate systems of symbols. Here they match perfectly the classic definition of religion proposed by anthropologist Clifford Geertz. Religion is "(1) a system of symbols which acts to (2) establish powerful, pervasive, and long-lasting moods and motivations in men by (3) formulating conceptions of a general order of existence and (4) clothing these conceptions with such an aura of factuality that (5) the moods and motivations seem uniquely realistic" (1973: 90).

Those who use the autogenetic framework often seek out the company of the like-minded. They may ritualize the search for health, as in certain Unitarian Universalist orders of worship. They are often uncommonly interested in the ethics and promotion of preventive medicine for themselves and others. However, if they cannot often be found in a denomination or sect, this is natural, for they accent autonomy or self-determination and may choose to "go it alone."

The alert physician or medical researcher will often find resources in this outlook on which to draw. Stoic heroism can have health-giving power, and defiance of the fates can help a patient summon strength. We currently lack studies that set out to measure the impact of what (to use Clifton Brown's phrase) the "religiocification" of humanism does in pursuit of health (1971: 18). We need to measure what separates it from ordinary naturalism or what in it might be more productive of well-being than is humanist religion of sorts that do not focus on healing.

It may seem inefficient to call "religious" such a hard-to-define and fragile minority outlook. Yet medical professionals, of all people, are ready to deal with the exceptional. In any canvass of all the options in the West today, it is clear that the autogenetic approach not only fills out the "left" end of the spectrum but may well become an ever more self-consciously expressed faith. One may have to listen more closely to comprehend it as religious, but in the sense given to it by the Reverend John Haynes Holmes and in the definitions of many others, so it is.

"I Am in Tune with the Infinite": Synergism

In medicine synergism represents the "cooperative action of discrete agencies (as drugs or muscles) such that the total effect is greater than the sum of the two or more effects taken independently." Similarly, synergism in religion implies the cooperation of human and superhuman activity. In the present context we do not associate the synergistic with a personal God, a God humans can address, though in traditional disputes over theological synergism in the West such a connection was constant. Instead, synergism (syn "with" + ergon, "work") here evokes the energies of a person "working together with" forces, agencies, or powers beyond the visible and beyond that which is immediately empirically verifiable. Thus it is not content with medical materialism as a beginning point.

The people representing this approach occupy a more prominent place in opinion polls than do religious humanists. The Gallup Report says that "while the vast majority of Americans [94 to 98 percent] believe in some unifying and

organizing power behind the universe, far fewer (66 percent) believe in a personal God who watches over and judges people . . . [a God] to whom man is
answerable" (1985: 50).

Many millions of Americans could locate themselves religiously in this
spiritual sector. They wish to cooperate with their religious resources in order
to produce better health and well-being. In a typical half year of American book
publishing, for instance, hundreds of what came to be called "New Age titles"
on health and well-being appeared (see Tuller 1987; Lenz et al. 1987). Whereas
descriptions of miracles or faith healing occupy only a couple of pages in extensive modern surveys, for example, in *The Healing Arts* (Kaptchuk and
Croucher 1987), "imaging," "breathing," meditation, herbalism, and hypnosis
are but a few of the many technique for being in tune with the infinite.

Advocates of synergy find its force to be somehow inherent in the universe,
in nature, and then in "supernature" of some sort. Its power is somehow
accessible to humans, though not in the form of a personal God. Disease and
disability are described as disruptions of the positive elements in this working
agency. What people believe and think, how they organize life, what regimens
they pursue, how they ritualize response—all these make up what the public
has come to know as "holistic" therapies.

Some of these conceptions draw on contemporary versions of Western
Enlightenment religion. As such, they recall reference to "nature's God," a god
who needs no revelation in scripture or in a particular history. This power or
force or energy is simply available in the structure of things. These synergistic
approaches, however, may also draw upon ancient, Eastern, or occult religions
and ways.

One North American advocate, Richard B. Miles, aptly summarized the
worldview of the synergistic, holistic types as

> a point of view about the Universe, about human life in the Uni-
> verse, and about how one finds this extra something in life. . . . The
> basic assumption . . . views the Universe as a friendly and supportive
> place. . . . Harmony and resonance are the result of vibrations which
> enjoy one another. Within the assumption of a friendly Universe . . .
> [the] creative intention, emerging from within the individual, leads
> each person to . . . stand in communion with a benevolent Universe;
> seek a personal knowledge of the inner vision and spirit of the
> Higher Self (God within) through creative intuition and imagina-
> tion. (quoted in Wimber 1987: 274)

Some contemporary physicians and biological researchers may themselves
practice holism as a complement or supplement to "scientific medicine." Or
they encounter holistic practices (though never under that name) in the circles
of people they might regard as "primitives"; in urban America, Vodou, shamanism, and the practice of magic still survive as methods for obtaining heal-

ing. One glance at the advertising section of the back of popular magazines shows the vogue of the synergistic approach.

Medical professionals will more likely observe the synergistic type among those within middle-class cultures who want to be "in tune with the infinite." It is a popular notion among educated people who have access to holistic texts and to the centers where holistic medicines proliferate. Whenever one comes across best-selling books or sold-out workshops devoted to healing that do not draw on the support of God-inspired faith healers, the chances are that they will advocate synergism and will speak the language of "spiritual forces."

The synergistic type, normally cooperative with scientific medicine, sees itself in a "yin and yang" relation to medicine. Or its partisans recognize this approach as one that may lessen the need for medical intervention in the first place. Rarely is it an out-and-out rival, for it regards itself as scientific and sees medicine, properly practiced, as an enhancement of what is in nature or in the natural force, the "work" of the universe.

Recall that some aspects of this approach may be found among adherents of another. We recognize that a synergistic approach is also possible in, and sometimes integral to, more explicitly theistic Western religions, though it does not exhaust their possibilities. For example, three of the major new religions of nineteenth-century America—Mormanism, Adventism, and Christian Science—have synergistic features. A Christian Scientist "cooperates" with principles inherent in the metaphysical order yet still prays to God in pursuit of "science and health." A Mormon cooperates with influences of moral good that inhere in the process of "growing into Godhood" yet still prays to God as a responsive external agent. The Adventist runs effective modern hospitals and prays orthodoxly to the God of Christian faith but still advocates strenuous bodily disciplines in order to produce good health synergistically. God enters the picture in all these cases. However, as believers in this God, the members of these three groups finally belong with theists in the next class.

It is possible for an epidemiologist to measure longevity among devotees of these faiths and assess whether their disciplines and beliefs are effective in the communities that profess and practice them. The medical materialist in the laboratory, of course, would not attribute health that is credited through these means to the supernature professed in these religions. Instead, the materialist would credit the salutary practices themselves, practices that could be identical with those of nonbelievers who on other than faithful grounds practiced vegetarianism or calisthenics and avoided nicotine, caffeine, and alcohol.

In dealing with practitioners of religious or quasi-religious holistic health systems, the physicians who listen will almost immediately recognize the advocacy of synergy. They may even find reasons to endorse synergistic practices without assenting to the metaphysical context on which each draws. When a synergistic understanding competes with conventional medicine, patients may be deferential. They may be reluctant to start an argument and may not bring up the "alternative medicine" they practice. Thus one may undergo radiation or chemotherapy in the daylight of the clinic and then moonlight in a circle where people "image" the disease, find mythological frameworks for addressing it, and rely on powers inherent in the infinite universe in efforts to transcend the illness and induce the cancer to go into remission. Physicians may find little reason to intervene against such practices unless participation in them leads to a patient's neglect or repudiation of prescribed medical practices. Autogenetic approaches, on the other hand, need not represent such competitions or challenges.

The task of measuring the effects of synergetic practices poses problems for science. It is easy, as already noted, to measure longevity and the state of health among advocates of nontheistic holistic approaches. But how would one measure and credit or discredit the agency of the unseen, invisible forces? How would one go beyond recognizing that people motivated in certain ways to undertake certain health-giving practices have experienced good health through the equivalent of a "miracle"? Achievers of these miracles work with the forces in the universe and the properly synergetic disciplines that bring people into proper contact with them. How can that be measured? There is room for sophistication in studying the claims of this company.

"God Experiences with Me": Empathy

Concurrent with the move from the force-filled synergistic approach to the empathic type is a move to belief in the divine agent. This agent, God, experiences with humans—"empathy" is from the Greek *empatheia: en* (in) + *pathos* (suffering). At this point along the spectrum, then, distinctive theism emerges. Some scholars would even want to reserve the term *religious* for just this point. Thus theologian Julian Hartt: "We ought to say that a man is not really religious unless he feels that some power is bearing down on him, unless, that is, he believes he must do something about divine powers who have done something about him" (quoted in Gustafson 1975: 97).

It is not likely that such a stringent approach to language will win out in the Supreme Court, in encyclopedias of religion, among many world religions, or increasingly in popular culture. But it is true that in the face of this third class one grows confident that people are speaking of religious healing in more explicit and historically recognizable terms. Here researchers and physicians locate many millions of believers within at least Judaism, Islam, Catholicism, Orthodoxy, and Protestantism, people who worship a God and pray to this God. They somehow connect this God with nature and with the physical condition of humans, but they ordinarily resist reference to "miraculous healing" as a suspension of the "laws of nature." They may even make a theological point against such notions of miracles as being contrary to their understanding of faith.

For an example of this rejection we turn to a noted Islamic scholar, Fazlur Rahman, who points to an instance where Muhammad showed some anxiety over the fact that miracles were no vouchsafed to him. But the Qur'an finds God almost chiding the Prophet, and Rahman summarizes: "Although, therefore, God has the power to create miracles, there shall be henceforth no miracles because they are out-of-date. The Qur'an is, of course, talking of 'supranatural' miracles but still upholds other 'natural' or 'historical' miracles" (Rahman 1987: 35).

Those whom we associate with empathic versions of theism tend to use "wholistic" approaches (I use this spelling simply to differentiate from "holistic"). They ordinarily resist narrowing the concept of wholeness and health to the absence of infirmity or disease. They thus provide fewer subjects for epidemiological research than do synergetic or "miraculous" types. Such believers concentrate instead on the larger human ecology, the search for well-being that comes with life in social systems and circumstances which reduce suffering and are devoted to justice. But for present purposes we must focus on the narrower interests, addressing health as an alternative to infirmity and disease and not as part of a social system.

A second mark of the adherents of this view: they tend to have accommodated their religious outlooks to modern scientific viewpoints. To some scientists who cannot conceive of development within orthodoxy—thus seeing all religion as "fundamentalistic"—this may look like compromise instead of developed faith. But the believers themselves work with more dynamic concepts of God and process. Indeed, in their liberal and modernist stages—rare in Islam and Eastern Orthodoxy—but even in more moderate versions, they have worked to anticipate and advance scientific progress.

For such believers, the historic warfare of science with theology recalls old, unhappy, unproductive encounters that must now be transcended. They may be critical of the impersonal disposition of health care or of unjust medical systems and eager to complement technical medicine with insights drawn from their traditions and faith communities. But they readily commend themselves to the care of those who advocate and practice the most advanced scientific medical techniques.

Some would ask: Does this mean that they believe in God but not in miracles or in supernatural intervention? Does it mean, therefore, that they have a limited view of God as one who is all-powerful but who, astoundingly, does not have the potency to effect miracles of cure? Does it mean that they commend themselves to God's care and then, in effect, turn Deist and see God as having no living encounter with what concerns them?

Not as they tell it. If one listens for the testimonies of those who advocate responsibility to God and empathy with God, one will hear them delighting when unexpected reversals of the progress of a disease occur. These believers welcome cures that are not immediately explicable in conventional medical terms. They may even use language redolent of the concept of miracle in their sacramental and prayerful activities. Yet they would not be measured by these uncharacteristic expectations and do not hold God to account because "miracles" do not occur.

Philosophically, ever since the time of Immanuel Kant (d. 1804), such believers live on "this" side of a great divide in worldviews associated with his name, even though they may not know it or refer to it. Kant contended that one could know only objects of experience, phenomena (for example, the effect of radiation on cancer cells). Noumena, elements that lie beyond experience, cannot be known because no one can confirm or deny them. Post-Kantian religion, therefore, assigns the source of what others call miraculous healings to the realm of the noumena. These cannot be "checked out," just as the mind and will of God cannot be measured or known empirically. To be able to speak assuredly of a miracle rather than of something merely exceptional and inexplicable, one would have to know the mind and will of God.

Before Kantian philosophy, however, there had long been anticipations of this view in Western theologies that professed belief in a *deus absconditus*, a hidden God. One can even go back to the Book of Job and the Psalms in the Bible for such witness. This God could be known through the revelation regarded by a believing community as authentic—as in the Qur'an, the Hebrew Scriptures, the New Testament. Believers did not assuredly connect this God's works with a reading of particular signs, like cancer remission or the healing of arthritis, as being certifiably a miraculous expression of the will of God. Similarly, the withholding of cure would not be seen as a sign of God's displeasure, of God's arbitrary or mysterious refusal to engage in positive, particular intervention on behalf of a prayerful and responsible ill person.

A popular book brought to wide public awareness one version of Jewish thought about the empathic view of God: Rabbi Harold Kushner's *When Bad Things Happen to Good People* (1981). Although formal theologians often treated the book condescendingly, Kushner did speak out of a context that many of them employ. For them God is the ground of order and of innovation. Biologist Edmund W. Sinnott posed the issue of order: "One of the attributes of God is the Principle of Organization." Hence medical knowledge is possible. And philosopher Alfred North Whitehead spoke to the issue of innovation: "Apart from the intervention of God, there could be nothing new in the world, and no order in the world" (quoted in Rolston 1987: 317).

Such empathic theism, then, departs radically from godless autogenetic views and from force-filled synergetic approaches, which see transformations (toward illness, toward cure) as being innate or inherent in mysteriously conceived nature. But this third type of faith also rejects those theisms that it sees concentrating on an apparently tyrannical, arbitrarily predestining deity who kills or cures. At this point, religions like Islam may appear to deviate in part from the empathic approach, yet Islam's lack of interest in contemporary miracles keeps it from being in the fourth category of our study.

Those who concentrate on the sympathetic or empathic view of God in biblical traditions often stress the accounts of the God who would persuade, cajole, and revisit a people, as God has normally been seen doing in biblical Israel. In Whitehead's phrase, this dimension of divine experience reveals God as "the fellow-sufferer who understands." All such theisms which begin with the love and care of God have to deal with or temporarily bracket a corollary issue. That is, how to deal with "the dark side of God," with pain and suffering and evil, and with the question whether these are caused or permitted by God or are beyond the power of God. This is not the place to take up the theologians' task, which means to address the antinomies or deal with the paradoxes of religions. I am dealing only with their direct bearing on the voice of illness and the expectations of healing.

I have spoken of this as an empathic approach, in the spirit of philosopher Charles Hartshorne, who said that God is a "sympathetic spectator who in some real sense shares in the sufferings he beholds," a God who "derives whatever value possible" from sufferings and, I would add, presumably shares in whatever leads to their transcendence (quoted in Rolston 1987: 319).

Citation of names like Whitehead and Hartshorne may lead some to suspect that empathic views are confined to a formal school called "process theism." However, it would be misleading to restrict them to that philosophy. The strand of piety runs deep in the Bible, in many Jewish and Christian forms of therapy and devotion, and wherever God as "sufferer with" (as opposed to God as "agent of suffering and miraculous cure") receives first attention. Most who worship a mysterious but empathic God do not follow the theme to one logical consequence, its witness to a "finite God." Those who are classically orthodox leave more to the mysterious side of the hidden God than do such philosophers.

Worshipers and sufferers who hold empathic views of God readily acknowledge that in biblical times people held worldviews in which both the arbitrary character of God and the miraculous "signs and wonders" of healing *were* daily occurrences. As part of their therapy, therefore, they tend to retell the stories of that ancient world as they reinterpret them, as they witness to the reality of faith even though such interruptions of the natural order with the divine order are not expected or accounted for.

The more extravagant theistic faith healers in our time are most critical of religious believers of the empathic type because they do not expect, account for, or claim miraculous cures. Those who do not look for ordinary "supernaturalistic" miracles respond by saying that they have not less faith but a different kind of faith; not no theism but a different interpretation of theism. Therefore, in their turn, they charge that those who seek faith healing are vulnerable to charlantary, exploitation, or inappropriate theologies that do not do any sort of justice to the mysterious ways of God. Empathic theists seem less impassioned, desperate, or exuberant than do people at a faith-healing revival. But they bid the critics to observe them when they are engrossed or exulting in the many ventures in the laboratory, the clinic, the university, the legislature. These they conceive as arenas of divine activity where agencies of healing can develop.

Through the centuries people holding these forms of theistic traditions have overcome heritages of mistrust and have encouraged scientific medicine. They have built hospitals and promoted research. Muslims promoted medicine, not miracles, yet believed in God as healer. They did not all seek shrines. Not all Catholics went for healing to Lourdes or Campostello. Jews did not all go to the Pool of Siloam. They built universities and laboratories. But they also kept coming together to worship God, to ask for divine participation in their life—and they still do. They see illness and health as something that affects their larger community of faith, not just one individual. They engage in intercessory prayer, commending members of the community and others to divine care.

In the world I am calling postmodern, where science and faith meet again, many in these traditions are more ready than in the recent past to bring the healing dimensions of their faith to the fore. They allow their faith dimensions to come forward in the search for care and cure. Physicians know their hospital chaplains. They see ministers in these traditions distributing sacraments with healing intent, their priests using anointing oils. Medical professionals may know that some of their churches have encouraged the development of "orders" (like the Episcopal Order of St. Luke) that deal specifically with healing, or that they schedule special healing-oriented services of worship. They overhear unaffiliated believers who share this outlook expressing the idea that the ill are to be sustained by a God whose character it is to "suffer with" or share the experience of healing.

Believers within this empathic context commend themselves and their fellows to the God whose love they believe to be stronger than death. From such faith they get courage to cope with tribulation and often triumph. They believe that answers to intercessory prayers will help sufferers to deal better with their setbacks and to interpret what is going on in their bodies, whether in time of sickness or health. Such believers do not expect any divinely instigated interruption of what they perceive to be "laws of nature." They bring some presuppositions not restricted to those of medical materialism, and they feel rapport if the physician is respectful of the sets of meanings that patients bring. They want to be assured that it is appropriate to speak of religious faith in clinical settings.

Can these approaches to religion and healing be measured? Can their effects be tested by epidemiologists and students of human ecology? The instruments for doing so are difficult to conceive. Such believers would be the first to say that empirical methods cannot touch or measure the divine point of reference, the God who shares empathy with humans.

After their centuries-long encounter with modern science, leaders in these communities have become more stringent and skeptical in interpreting signs. Thus at Lourdes, the most frequently visited Christian shrine, attended by 9 million each year, the appointed Catholic authorities declare fewer than *one* healing per year to be certifiably and unexplainably a "miraculous" cure of "so-called 'organic' diseases" (Kaptchuk and Croucher 1987: 101–2). Scientists working on simply secular premises would not be likely to find many evidences with such a narrow base!

The empathists must be measured by a wholistic standard, not by the number of miracles wrought. The survival of healing and indeed the fresh accent on it in this scientifically informed community of believers are signals to the medical community of the resilience of faith. They are signs that faith has a bearing on attempts to provide care and cure. In the late twentieth century, such broad approaches characterize millions in great religious bodies. Yet they are often overlooked or seen as "less religious" than those who claim supernaturalistic cures. At times members of the medical community may dismiss the role of faith for empathic theists, or even make the mistake of lumping them with those who claim that legs were miraculously lengthened by inches or that cancer cells were suddenly transformed to healthy ones—all a result of faith healing.

"God Worked a Miracle in Me": Monergism

The term "monergism" does not come, as do the terms for the other three types, from words with analogues in biology and medicine but from theology itself. This is appropriate, for this approach is single-mindedly theological and theocentric. It ascribes all agency to a God who may withhold physical healing or may impart it to those who follow prescriptions such as praying for cures. This name comes from an early Protestant controversy in which the party of monergists, over against *theological* synergists, allowed no integral role for human cooperation in "rebirth," in becoming right with God. Monergism left God as the sovereign agent.

In extreme forms, monergists are most familiarly and sometimes exhaustively connected with the highly visible and flamboyant "faith healers," but they are by no means confined to such extravagant expressions. Millions of very serious, often highly educated, sometimes scientifically informed people adhere to the monergistic view that a personal and all-powerful God who created and established the laws of nature can and will directly interrupt the regularity of such laws to effect miracles when it pleases his mysterious will to do so.

Some of these believers work out elaborate syntheses, which in effect return to a pre-Kantian mind-set. That is, the noumenal is for them accessible, and they speak with confidence of its effects in the natural world. Faith and fact simply match. Others may compartmentalize their lives, dwelling intellectually within a scientific worldview that they are often adept at relativizing. On one hand, as people of faith they can be believers in a supramundane order of being, which, they must say, only apparently conflicts with the presuppositions and effects of science. They ask: If "signs and wonders" were present in ancient (for example, biblical) times, on what grounds should one determine that they have ceased now? To consider that miracles have thus ceased, they say, is to express weak faith, half faith, wrong faith, or lack of faith.

The fixed center of all monergistic systems is that, whatever else happens through the use of medicine and the agencies of human care, God's response to disciplines and prayer for healing can be the direct, miraculous, personal, and particular intervention in acts of healing. They may include healings of so-called organic diseases that cannot be explained except by divine reference.

The trend among articulators recently has been away from the terms "miracle healing," "supernatural healing," "psychic healing," and "faith healing." Miracle healing, we are told, can occur under the agency of Satan and demons. Supernatural healing is not always synonymous with divine healing: demons can act, too. Psychic healing includes the occult. Faith healing sounds too synergistic, too reliant on the participation or achievement of humans. That leaves the preferred "divine healing, . . . the direct intervention of the one and only true God, the living and *personal* God" (Baxter, quoted in Wimber 1987: 6–7).

This monergistic tradition has survived and even prospered in the modern world, where some fundamentalisms grow concurrently with technological development. Often the same people use and welcome both fundamentalist faith and technology. By no means do all monergists join with the suspicious or antimedical faith healers in shunning hospitals. They may with true enthusiasm support scientific research and its applications, while adhering to a metaphysic and faith that includes the prospect of divine disruption of regularity and process.

The monergist type prospers in contemporary charismatic and Pentecostal movements, millions strong, and in the folk piety inside some of the more formal religious institutions. Its advocates are critical of those who claim open and frank faith in God but then resist supernaturalistic accountings of healing, seeing them as covert or halfhearted secularists. A follower within the divine-healing movement points out that one way to be faithless is to "find it difficult to accept super-natural intervention, especially physical healing, in the material universe" (Wimber 1987: 8).

Thus at Lourdes and wherever the pious claim direct healing phenomena, scientifically minded religious authorities tend to be embarrassed. They try to dampen fervor or minimize the claims; they even formally examine claims and usually dismiss them. Monergism is also a part of orthodoxy within some traditions. Leaders in these contexts refer to "signs and wonders" more economically and modestly than do those who call themselves divine healers.

Monergism as a metaphysical proposition need not limit humane sympathy or empathy and may even energize them; monergistic believers are as capable as others of crying or shouting in anger at a deity when a terrible disease takes a beloved child, when visions of the agony of mass starvation or plague confront them, or when they suffer pain. They simply relegate to the realm of mystery any final accounting of why God withholds healing and comfort when God does so, or they may at times blame their own apparent lack of sufficient faith. In either case they reserve the right to assign credit to the same God when they perceive signs and wonders happening.

Claims of faith healing today are so extravagant that they get much, though rarely good, press. The scientific community writes them off as belonging in religious analogues to the *National Enquirer* and not the modern university or clinic. They sometimes catch the eye of wan believers, some of whom wonder if there might not just be something to such healing, when the unexplained occurs in the context of prayer for healing. Yet the monergistic type is prevalent in so many locations and forms that those who do not share its worldview are finding it ever more urgent to try to gain insight into it.

Social scientists, being post-Kantian sorts, find difficult if not impossible the task of setting up instruments for measuring the effects claimed by monergists. Almost by definition, it is finally impossible to engage in scientific inquiry on this subject because satisfying answers to the questions monergists ask would have to give an accounting verifiably connectable with the ways and works of God, and God is not available for empirical verification. At the same time, it should be possible to engage in more careful examination of faith healing in communities than we have seen to date; certainly, much attention has been given to exposing the manifest frauds at their margins.

Do people who belong to communities that share this metaphysic and faith and who pursue practices congruent with them live longer and in better health than do others? Do they have fewer and shorter hospital stays? Why do not physicians and medical researchers get to measure a leg before and after the Pentecostal prayer that releases God to act to lengthen it? Why are so many verifications of a nebulous, unattributable character? How does one draw lines between "the unexplained" and what the community regards as "miraculous"?

Furthermore, could the marginalized faith-healing communities have insights into the obsolescence of some scientific paradigms that the synergists now so regularly employ? If so, why are the synergists so often regarded as being more respectable than the monergists? Are cultural biases or unquestioned theological or antitheological presuppositions present in the different kinds of regard shown the two? These questions simply indicate the wide compass in which further inquiries would occur.

One may well despair of efforts by scientists to measure and assess the effects of monergistic divine healing, since scientific measures cannot accept the rules of the game of such faith communities. And yet frustration on that front does not remove claims of divine healing as a legitimate subject of humanistic, social, scientific, and laboratory analysis.

Monergistic faith is believed by many to be a factor in their well-being. It sustains millions in community and motivates their participation also in the clinical world. It challenges and complicates isolated scientific medicine. As such it may seem to be at once a threat to science and a way of putting questions that could help elicit fresh inquiries.

Conclusion

That religion has a bearing on the larger contexts of wholeness and well-being is coming to be an established point. In narrower contexts where wholeness is dealt with as the absence of infirmity, disability, or disease, it is much more problematic. It is not likely that the problem focused this way can be capably addressed, unless the public and the professionals have better instruments for knowing what the expectations of various sorts of believers are. Discriminating among the types can also have a bearing on the delivery of care. It can permit more intelligent understandings of the various personal and communal meanings that serve either to complicate or to promote health in today's world.

We are early postmoderns, primitives in a new period of understandings. It may be that the wisdom and practice of one or another or all of these types, and the communities through which they live, can be of help to scientists, whether these would be measurers or healers. Taking these types, or better, these people, seriously might help us buy some time until more appropriate understandings begin to appear. Although the logic of empirical science in the laboratory may not have changed much in recent decades, the models for interpreting that work have.

Some inherited hostile attitudes of science to every dimension of faith in respect to care and cure derive from what may once have been necessary safeguards against religious intrusions into medical fields. The scientist stood guard at the door to protect human freedom. Today the religious person may as readily be there to protect human dignity. Therefore, some of the hostile attitudes of the past may be seen as increasingly limited and obsolete. They may grow increasingly unfruitful. It would be as unscientific to overlook the insights of faith communities as it may be faithless to fear the effects of science in the healing communities.

REFERENCES

Brown, Clifton T. 1971. Black Religion—1968. In *The Black Church in America,* ed. Hart M. Nelsen, Raytha L. Yokley, and Anne K. Nelsen. New York: Basic Books.

Cousins, Norman. 1979. *Anatomy of an Illness as Perceived by the Patient.* New York: Norton.

Gallup Report. 1985. Religion in America, 50 Years: 1935–1985. No. 236 (May): 1–57.

Geertz, Clifford. 1973. *The Interpretation of Cultures: Selected Essays.* New York: Basic Books.

Gustafson, James M. 1975. *The Contributions of Theology to Medical Ethics.* Milwaukee Wis.: Marquette, University, Department of Theology.

Kaptchuk, Ted, and Michael Croucher. 1987. *The Healing Arts: Exploring the Medical Ways of the World.* New York: Summit.

Lenz, Robin, et al., comps., 1987. A Sampling of New Age Titles. *Publishers Weekly* 232 (Sept. 25): 37–55.

Levin, Jeffrey S., and Preston L. Schiller. 1987. Is There a Religious Factor in Health? *Journal of Religion and Health* 26: 9–36.

Levin, Jeffrey S., and Harold Y. Vanderpool. 1987. Is Frequent Religious Attendance *Really* Conducive to Better Health? Toward an Epidemiology of Religion. *Social Science and Medicine* 24: 589–600.

Rahman, Fazlur. 1987. *Health and Medicine in the Islamic Tradition: Change and Identity.* New York: Crossroad.

Rolston, Holmes, III. 1987. *Science and Religion: A Critical Survey.* Philadelphia: Temple University Press.

Tuller, David. 1987. New Age: An Old Subject Surges in the '80s. *Publishers Weekly,* September 25, 29–35.

Wimber, John, with Kevin Springer. 1987. *Power Healing.* New York: Harper and Row.

31

Afterword:
A Physician's Reflections

Harold G. Koenig

Religious Healing in America examines the many kinds of healing practices that exist in this culturally, ethnically, and religiously diverse nation. The description of healing here has cast a wide net, including much more than just physical healing but also healing in relationships with others, healing in relationship with one's own self, healing in one's relationship with God, and healing on the community or cultural level as well. This broad definition goes beyond the traditional focus of healing in biomedicine, beyond physical organs and physical diseases to the whole human person. The focus of biomedicine on the physical alone and the neglect of other parts of the person have left many improving physically but finding themselves wounded emotionally, relationally, and spiritually. The resurgence of interest in many forms of religious healing testifies to this failure of allopathic medicine to heal, despite its increasing capacity to cure.

The healing of the whole person requires a multidisciplinary and multicultural approach that is sensitive to the individual's history of experience and the history of the community in which that person is formed. Biomedicine by itself cannot address all these different aspects of the person. Specialists in other areas are needed, and there is plenty of room for religious healing. It is where the expertise of biomedicine leaves off that the role of religious healing begins, especially in a populace where 95 percent believe in God, nearly 70 percent are members of faith communities, and weekly religious attendance is over 40 percent (Gallup 2002).

Understanding and respecting the unique contributions of allopathic medicine and religious healing systems each supporting the work of the other in true integration is what holds the greatest hope for the wholeness and healing of persons. Research is showing that complete dependence on one or the other does not achieve the health benefits that an integrated approach achieves (Koenig, McCullough, and Larson 2001). Christian Scientists, Pentecostals, or members of other groups who rely entirely on religious healing practices do not achieve the same degree of health as those who also utilize traditional medicine (Simpson 1989; Wilson 1965; Spence, Danielson, and Kaunitz 1984). Similarly, persons who rely entirely on biomedicine and their own personal resources have been shown to suffer more depression and lower quality of life, whether or not physical health is improving (Koenig, Pargament, and Nielsen 1998).

According to physician Ralph Snyderman, dean and chancellor of Duke University Medical Center, a new field called "integrative medicine" will be the medicine of the future (Snyderman and Weil 2002). Snyderman acknowledges, "We must admit that our current delivery system as a whole is no longer able to deliver the best of care to most people. In fact, it may collapse totally because of its inability to provide what the public, the profession, and the purchasers want and need" (396). His solution is integrative medicine, which he describes as follows:

> We believe that the health care system must be reconfigured to re-
> store the primacy of caring and the patient-physician relationship,
> to promote health and healing as well as treatment of disease, and to
> take account of the insufficiency of science and technology alone to
> shape the ideal practice of medicine. The new design must also in-
> corporate compassion, promote the active engagement of patients in
> their care, and be open to what are now termed complementary and
> alternative approaches to improve health and well-being. . . . In addi-
> tion to providing the best conventional care, integrated medicine fo-
> cuses on preventive maintenance and health by paying attention to
> all relative components of lifestyle, including diet, exercise, stress
> management, and emotional well-being. It insists on patients being
> active participants in their health-care as well as on physicians view-
> ing patients as whole persons-minds, community members, and
> spiritual beings, as well as physical bodies. (396)

He further emphasizes that medical education and practice must "use the best in scientifically based medical therapies whenever appropriate but provide compassion, pay close attention to our patients' spiritual and emotional needs, and suggest appropriate complementary and alternative approaches when they improve conventional medicine" (397). Snyderman, a major figure and trend leader in allopathic biomedicine, twice underscores the importance of the spiritual aspects of care. "The integrative medicine of today," he predicts, "will simply be the medicine of the new century" (396).

Integration and mainstream adoption, however, require understanding of and appreciation for the contributions and limitations of each healing system. The chapters in this book provide a wealth of information and insight into religious healing systems that allopathic physicians would benefit from knowing about. Likewise, understanding and respect for the wonders of modern biomedicine and recognition of their own limits by practitioners of religious healing systems are also necessary. Mutual understanding and support in the end will benefit not only the person who needs healing but the healer as well.

REFERENCES

Gallup, G. 2002. The Religiosity Cycle. *Gallup Tuesday Briefing*, June 2. http://www .gallup.com/poll/tb/religValue/20020604.asp.

Koenig, H. G., M. McCullough, and D. B. Larson. 2001. *Handbook of Religion and Health.* New York: Oxford University Press.

Koenig, H. G., K. I. Pargament, and J. Nielsen. 1998. Religious Coping and Health Outcomes in Medically Ill Hospitalized Older Adults. *Journal of Nervous and Mental Disorders* 186: 513–21.

Simpson, W. F. 1989. Comparative Longevity in a College Cohort of Christian Scientists. *Journal of the American Medical Association* 262:1657–58.

Snyderman R., and A. T. Weil. 2002. Integrative Medicine: Bringing Medicine Back to Its Roots. *Archives of Internal Medicine* 162: 395–97.

Spence, C., T. S. Danielson, and W. M. Kaunitz. 1984. The Faith Assembly: A Study of Perinatal and Maternal Mortality. *Indiana Medicine*, 77(3): 180–83.

Wilson, G. E. 1965. Christian Science and Longevity. *Journal of Forensic Science* 1: 43–60.

Index

Italicized page numbers refer to illustrations and tables.

Shweder, Richard, 13, 24n1
Siegel, Bernard, 380
Siegel, Hanna Tiferet, 236–37, 240, 247–48
Sikhs, 423–24
silence, 93, 191, 212, 259–60
Simpson, O. J., 189
Sinnott, Edmund W., 497
Sisters of St. Joseph of Carondelet, 196–97, 202
slavery, 184, 188–90, 283, 285
Smith, Daniel, 458, 460
Smith, Linda Tuhiwai, 156n2
Snyderman, Ralph, 506
Social Gospel, 5
social justice, 93, 99, 201
social networks, 84, 425
"social service culture," 200
Society for the Varieties of Religious Experience, 394
sociology of medicine, 35–36
"sodomizing," 184, 187, 193n4
Soka Gakkai, 344–45, 349, 351, 353
Sokoll, Marjorie, 243
Somalis, 159–64, 169–70, 171n1, 201
Sontag, Susan, 45
soul journey, 457–58, 460, 464, 468n2
soul loss, 160, 451, 460
soul retrieval, 391, 393, 398, 403, 449, 459
South Asian Indian immigrants, 423–37
   America, life in, 427–34
      food, 432–33
      sexuality, 433–34
      temples and worship, 429–32
   America, religion and healing in, 427
   immigration, history of, 423–24
   India, religion and healing in, 425–27
      contemporary practice of, 426–27
South Asian Muslims, 407, 410–13, 420
Southern Pentecostalism, 133–34
space of sickness, 31, 35–40
Spanish Harlem (New York City), 129–30
speaking in tongues, 6, 132–33
Speer, Robert E., 132
spells, 3

Spirit Catches You and You Fall Down, The (Fadiman), 440
spirit guides, 333, 336–37, 363, 390, 445, 460
Spiritism, 123–24, 129
spirit money, 313, 328n3, 445–46
spirits, 14, 169, 175, 177, 179–80, 183, 367–70, 444–45
spiritual advisors, 104, 334, 337
Spiritual churches. See African American Spiritual churches
spiritual feminists, 73, 77, 83, 249
spiritual healing. See healing
Spiritual Healing Project, 49–57
Spiritualism
   African American Spiritual churches and, 333, 335, 337–38, 340
   American metaphysical tradition and, 376–77, 384
   biomedicine and, 22
   Latino/a Pentecostalism and, 123–24, 129
   Wicca and, 65
spirituality, 9–10
   anthropological view of, 393–94, 401
   in Chicano/a communities, 206, 214
   "end of science" and, 324
   in Hmong communities, 441
   in home birth movement, 71–72, 75, 79–84
   in Islamic religious healing, 415, 417
   in Japanese communities, 220–21
   in Jewish healing movement, 234–36, 243
   in New Age movement, 314–16, 318
   in substance abuse rehabilitation, 455–56
"Spirituality and Aging in the Japanese Experience," 217–26, 226n2
spirituality and religion, 9, 73, 75, 77–85, 85n2, 201
Spiritual Midwifery, 78
Spivak, Gayatri, 76, 78–79
spoon rubbing, 451
spousal abuse, 413
Starhawk, 258
Starr, Paul, 39